Believing in Opera

Tom Sutcliffe

faber and faber

First published in 1996
by Faber and Faber Limited
3 Queen Square London wc1n 3au

Typeset by Faber and Faber Ltd
Printed in England by Clays Ltd, St Ives plc

© Tom Sutcliffe, 1996

Tom Sutcliffe is hereby identified as author of this
work in accordance with Section 77 of the Copyright,
Designs and Patents Act 1988

A CIP record for this book
is available from the British Library

isbn 0–571–17809–x

10 9 8 7 6 5 4 3 2

Believing in Opera

For Meredith,
with love and gratitude,
and in memory of Tim, Lindsay and Dale

Contents

Acknowledgments ix

Foreword by Matthew A. Epstein xiii

1 Believing in opera 1

2 Peter Brook and theatrical opera 17

3 Theory of interpretation 37

4 A repertoire of classics 53

5 The design matrix 79

6 Patrice Chéreau: revolutionary classicism 99

7 Ruth Berghaus: Marx, feminism and the absurd 125

8 David Alden: expressionist shock 165

9 Peter Sellars: Americanizing everything 195

10 Richard Jones: burlesque profundities 227

11 Graham Vick: neo-realism and emotion 261

12 Albery, Pimlott, Cairns: British expressionism 291

13 A line of renewal: from Hall to Pountney 317

14 Brian McMaster's eclectic imports 355

15 Frankfurt and after: from Neuenfels to Decker 377

16 21st-century opera: going for a song 413

Appendix: *Bühnenreform* (Theatre Reform)
by Alfred Roller 427

Postscript 433

Index 437

Acknowledgments

I could never have experienced so much opera, had I not worked for the *Guardian* at a time when its editors were prepared to give readers a broad diet of extended reviews, including coverage from the USA, Australia and Europe. Music and opera reviews of length are rare these days. The music review seems to be a dying form. But twenty years ago, even ten, there was real interest. I owe thanks to Peter Preston, Alan Rusbridger and various arts editors, above all Michael McNay who helped me join the staff of the paper in 1973. He was succeeded by Stuart Wavell, Tim Radford and Patrick Ensor, all of whom tolerated me as their deputy – letting me write reviews and features while they were hands on editing the next day's edition. Their successors – Roger Alton, Helen Oldfield, Jocelyn Targett, Ian Mayes and Claire Armitstead – variously encouraged or tolerated my operatic vocation. My most supportive patron at the *Guardian* was the features editor of the 1980s, Richard Gott, who paid a high price for not publishing his confessions ('I was guest of the KGB . . .') long before he was outed with disproportionate sensationalism in the *Spectator*.

Another boon was being asked to write a column on opera for *Vogue* by Beatrix Miller in 1975, prompted by Kensington Davison: various *Vogue* features editors, notably Drusilla Beyfus, helped me, but it was Bea's patronage that counted most – as I realized when I was nuclear-Wintoured in 1987. A most encouraging patron has been Antony Bye at *The Musical Times*, who published a number of longer pieces which were invaluable preparation. Writing a regular column about British opera performances for Patrick Smith, the wise and supportive editor of *Opera News* in New York, has helped sharpen my perspective. Some of this material was first tried out on patrons of the Glimmerglass Opera Festival, thanks to a generous invitation from Paul Kellogg to speak there during a relaxed week's holiday in a house on the lake. A commission from Thomas Voigt to supply a report on new and interesting British directors and designers for the 1994 *Opern Welt* yearbook was further preparation.

Lufthansa generously assisted me in 1993 and 1994 with free flights to Germany to see productions in Stuttgart, Munich and Frankfurt. I had previously visited Frankfurt at the suggestion of my friend Pamela Rosenberg during the last years of Michael Gielen's far-sighted regime there as music director (she was his Girl Friday). My Lufthansa-supported visits reinforced those memories, by enabling me to view excellent videos of Berghaus's and other work in the Frankfurt archives. Sadly, since no public release arrangement has been negotiated with the singers and instrumentalists concerned, those quality videos (including a full recording of the Berghaus *Ring*) are not generally available. They are fascinating historical documents, especially now that Berghaus herself and Axel Manthey her designer are no longer with us.

The biggest financial assistance for this project, without which it could not have been completed, came from the Leverhulme Trust in 1991, when I got a Leverhulme Fellowship, thanks to which I spent six months away from the *Guardian* for research.

The first above many whom I must thank for encouragement, support and advice over the years is my wife Meredith Oakes. She certainly deserves T. S. Eliot's 1922 tribute to Pound in *The Waste Land*, '*il miglior fabbro*', for she is the better critic. This book is dedicated to her, not least because her judgment has so often reinforced (and sometimes softened) mine. It is also dedicated to the memory of three extraordinary friends and influences on me: my elderly cousin Tim Swayne, who dropped me in the deep end of the operatic pool by taking me aged 18 to Bayreuth and Salzburg; the great film and theatre director – and critic – Lindsay Anderson whose warm and acerbic judgments on my views and reviews over the years transformed my critical perspective and style; and finally the generous and always affectionate Dale Harris, whose radical firmness of view, commitment and vast experience of the performing arts helped establish my taste and secure my confidence. I must also thank Neil Belton of Century Hutchinson (now of Granta Books), whose original commission in 1988 launched this whole ambitious project, though in the event he was not to be its publisher, and Michael Durnin, my editor at Faber, who picked up the project when Neil could not carry it through and presided over its crucial last restructuring.

All the following in various ways have helped me think more

clearly about the art of opera in the theatre: the late Kevin O'Mahoney, the late Frank Granville Barker, the late Katharine Wilkinson, the late Wolf Rosenberg, Pamela Rosenberg, Anthony Arblaster, Bettina Munzer, Tim Coleman, Patrick Smith, Bayan Northcott, Bill Alban, Suzanne Graham-Dixon, Jacques and Nelly Lasserre, Paul Sheren, Miguel Romero, Professor Emrys Jones, Professor Malcolm Griffiths, Edgar and Charlotte de Bresson, Maggie Sedwards, James Hogan, Christopher Fettes, Christian Hoening, Irene Hoening, Shelagh Nelson, Antje von Graevenitz, Michael Musgrave, Jean-Marie Amartin, Brian McMaster, Mark Jones, Nicholas Payne, Helen O'Neill, Peter Jonas, Elijah Moshinsky, Graham Vick, David Fielding, Antony McDonald, Tom Cairns, Paul Daniel, Richard Jones, Keith and Emma Warner, Tim Hopkins, Patrick O'Connor, Michael Kennedy and Jeremy Isaacs.

Foreword

Prima le parole, dopo la musica
Prima la musica, dopo le parole (*Capriccio*, Richard Strauss)

In this book Tom Sutcliffe focuses attention on a subject that is long overdue for treatment in such a concentrated and specific fashion: opera as *not only* musical and vocal performance, *but also* poetry, theatre, acting, movement, dance, design and lighting – that is, opera as an all-encompassing art-form, opera in its home the theatre, which is what in fact opera-houses all are. Often, indeed usually, the primary critical response to operatic performance is devoted to musical qualities. This book therefore rights a wrong that has long required remedy.

As a youngster, I arrived in London in 1964 to see performances at the Royal Opera House, Covent Garden, of *Madam Butterfly* designed by Sophie Fedorovich and *Otello* (with McCracken, Gobbi and Carlyle conducted by Edward Downes) designed by Georges Wakhevitch. Both were famous decorative productions – the *Butterfly* was revived for the last time in 1993 by Nicholas Payne, after years in store and rejection of a newer production. In the 30 years since my first visit, Covent Garden has changed to the point where it can present a firmly 'interventionist' *Ring* directed by Richard Jones and designed by Nigel Lowery. It has recently seen productions by Luc Bondy, Harry Kupfer, Peter Sellars, and Tim Albery. In the mid-1960s its major theatrical input came from Luchino Visconti and Franco Zeffirelli, and later from Peter Hall, John Copley, Götz Friedrich, Elijah Moshinsky, and John Cox – and there were still, in the days when Georg Solti was musical director, productions in the repertoire originally created by Peter Brook and Tyrone Guthrie.

Opera as theatre is an art-form that has deep roots in 20th-century British culture. From the pre-war days of the Sadler's Wells Opera and the Carl Ebert regime at Glyndebourne Festival

Opera, British audiences and critics have had the opportunity to see operatic work which was distinguished not only musically but also visually and conceptually. However, an ongoing critical conservatism has always made it very difficult for operatic interpretation to move forward as it has been able to do on the European continent. Sutcliffe's analysis in the first part of the book of the circumstances of Peter Brook's brief time working at Covent Garden in the late 1940s and early 1950s is most telling. We in the USA are even more conservative in our view of opera as interpretative theatre, and are still mired at least a decade behind the British scene.

Tom Sutcliffe's extraordinary experience of and interest in the interpretation of opera make him uniquely qualified to bring this vital subject to the fore. He found his vocation as critic and observer of European opera over the last 30 years, and it has been a passionate vocation. He has watched the development of the British operatic scene through the administrations of such crucial leaders as Brian McMaster at Welsh National Opera, Lord Harewood and later Mark Elder, David Pountney and Peter Jonas at English National Opera, Nicholas Payne, first at WNO, then at Opera North, and now at Covent Garden, and Moran Caplat, Brian Dickie and Anthony Whitworth-Jones at Glyndebourne. All these men contributed greatly to the development of opera as theatre in the UK, and in all cases there have been great successes and disastrous failures. Tom Sutcliffe has, I think, understood very well the influences on the British scene – especially from Middle Europe – and his chapters on Ruth Berghaus, Patrice Chéreau, Hans Neuenfels, Herbert Wernicke and Willy Decker are particularly telling and important. As the great musicians of the Royal Opera, Covent Garden (including Rankl, Kempe, Kubelik, Solti, Davis and Haitink), have succeeded each other as music directors over the last 50 years, this most international of British opera companies has slowly but surely changed from a bastion of opera as costume pageant to a showcase for opera as drama and theatre. I can applaud this development, and recognize Tom Sutcliffe's perhaps insufficiently acknowledged effect on this process as a critic who has helped change public and aesthetic opinion. British opera, despite the unending financial difficulties and crises it constantly faces, has worldwide repute and influence. With this book, especially in his formulation of theory to accompany his monumental descriptions of practice, Tom Sutcliffe puts the theatrical and interpretative side of opera in the clearest possible perspective as cultural history. No other book has ever attempted to provide such a clear record of a controversial movement in theatrical and operatic history.

Believing in Opera will long continue to be of interest to opera-goers and all those concerned with the performing arts, as well as to actors, singers and students, stage and opera designers, colleges and universities, indeed to everybody involved in the vast subject of *Theaterwissenschaft* – so well furnished with material in the German-speaking world, so little regarded in the Anglo-Saxon.

Matthew A. Epstein
New York, March 1996

1 Believing in opera

Richard Jones's 1993 Netherlands Opera staging (at the Musiektheater, Amsterdam) of *Der Fliegende Holländer* designed by Nigel Lowery: Kathryn Harries as Senta with chorus of spinning women and mysterious picture on the floor. Photograph © Hans van den Bogaard.

In theatre and in opera we can and should apply moral standards, but there is no rulebook defining the right approach to performance and interpretation. Opera is not a sport. The purpose of performing opera is to bring the work to life, to make its meaning tell, to help the audience believe in the truth and vitality of its message. Every serious attempt to perform an opera adds to the richness and depth of that process.

Aficionados of the interpretative and performing arts know that what happens in front of their eyes and before their ears matters profoundly – because of what it means. That process of mattering is the reception into the mind by a member of the audience of the sense intended or perceived, not invariably the same thing. When we in the audience are engaged and pleased, we feel that our experience is mattering. The performance rings true for us, and that truth has implications which resonate. This is the crux of modern controversies about theatrical and operatic interpretation and the obligation to composer or playwright. We may associate works we know with all sorts of elements. We may think that the music of *The Ring* 'is locked in time in the middle of the last century: it has a gravitas, a dignity, a spaciousness that does not accord with paper-bags, pistols, syringes, Mexican Waves and so forth', as the broadcaster John Amis wrote in his column in the *Tablet*. We may believe like the composer and critic Robin Holloway that the music of Wagner's dramas requires the flowing woollen and skin costumes German chieftains wore a thousand years ago. But those are *our* associations, connected with *our* knowledge of the gothic revival or of the deeper past or of grand opera in the time of Queen Victoria; they are not inherent in the works themselves, articulating stories to stir emotions and provoke mirth and grief.

I have never found satisfaction in a performance from knowing that it is being done as it should be, from seeing decorum observed – as if theatre were like the splendid courtly rituals of the Sun King at Versailles. It is true that the codification of a performing art such as classical ballet, where great skill and physical presence and preparation count for so much, can lead enthusiasts to devote their attention to the mere fact of the satisfying of outward forms, the accomplishment of the appearance. Equally, the technology of mechanical reproduction which has become so sophisticated at the end of the 20th century encourages a fetishistic devotion to the superficial actuality, not the idea it exists to serve.

I remember that when I was a child and playing with my friends we used to say, 'It's all right; it's only make-believe.' But it wasn't all right, because what was most frightening was not what happened, but what we thought it meant – what it ended up meaning in that so much richer, more potent world inside our heads. I used to frighten myself in all sorts of ways, imagining what might be, what probably was if only I knew. When I started going to the theatre, around the age of four (because the theatre was just a street away), I found the world of the ballet completely fascinating – not because of the rules of movement that governed what happened on stage, but because of the unspoken sentiments and passions, the defiance of the everyday, that it represented. Perhaps the verbal repartee of boulevard entertainment would have been too adult. But ballet suited the young and innocent imagination perfectly. There was no need to translate what was implied, to put in other terms the distant imaginative horizons revealed to me in these works – so wonderfully alternative to life, bicycles, shopping, ration points, the cleaning lady Mrs Fosbrook, Goofy our chow, the stony Southsea beach, the old lady next door who taught me to play patience. Going to theatre was like going abroad, whether it was ballet with Alicia Markova and Anton Dolin, or *Song of Norway*, or *Carmen*, or Ivor Novello's *Perchance to Dream*. Nobody ever had to explain to me about reality and imagination, about the relationship between what was happening in front of me on the stage and what I was lapping up inside my head and storing for future nourishment. In many ways the live theatre was much more fulfilling than the cinema, because the realization was less oppressive, less constraining. The cinema did it all for one. In the theatre it was up to me. I can remember the shock of discovering that not everybody regarded the theatre – and what happened on stage – as important. I think it was my father who later maintained the concept, 'It doesn't matter; it's only a play' – in the same way that fiction, borrowed from the library, didn't matter because it was only a story.

But the point of the theatre is, after all, what happens in the minds of the audience, what they/we believe. The purpose of the performers is to make believe, and the believing that goes with operatic performances is affected by a wider array of elements than in the case of any other art-form. In an ideal operatic performance, the singers will be able to realize their vocal lines with a wealth of colour and technical vocal facility, and will be singing in the language they share with the audience to which the listeners can immediately and subtly react. The context of the story will be indicated in various ways by the setting and the clothes that the characters and chorus are wearing. The music will profitably distort how time affects the tale. In opera the music – when it is running – cannot be stopped, but how it flows is crucial to how we react to it.

Music as it so irresistibly floods over us results in firm emotional conviction. And the flow of the music into our minds and memories has all sorts of subliminal surreptitious flickerings. It is precisely when time is – in a sense – thus suspended by our own digestion that the work in our imagination as audience may be at its most fruitful. The purpose of performance is, after all, invariably what happens inside the minds of the individuals experiencing and receiving the performance. Many things in opera can astonish one: the sound of a voice on a particular note, a glance, the lighting on stage, a passage of orchestral music so familiar but suddenly so infinitely beautiful. This book is not a compendium of all those delightful lost moments. But it is focused – with determination and sufficient clarity – on the issue of theatrical interpretation, the vital context of everything else in the experience which qualifies and fertilizes the whole meaning. It is the circumstantial theatricality of an operatic performance that governs the business of believing what it is all about. The process of believing is very complicated in opera. One may be profoundly influenced and affected by the music. Opera is *prima facie* music. But what one believes and how one is led to believe it is a consequence of the staging, with its physical images and designs, its sense of a period or none, its manipulation of time. Believing precedes feeling, and believing (or the suspension of disbelief, the acceptance of convenient conventions – such as that plump Pavarotti is in fact a young peasant, with romantic dreams, named Nemorino) is the purpose of everything that is done. Believing is the basis of effective interpretation.

There is a tendency to get stuck on the surface of the performing arts, to assume that what you see or hear is what you get. But, as with all creativity, what is interesting is not what is obvious, but what the obvious leads to, ambiguous subtleties approximating to what we feel to be truth. If, as a Redemptorist Father reassuringly reminded me, certainty is the enemy of faith, then beyond doubt the point of theatre and opera is starting hares – not catching them. In this book I attempt to provide a monument to those theatrical realizations of operas that made me think, that took me further on my journey with the work, that perhaps sometimes made me accept as worth attention an opera I had previously written off as uninteresting. Books about opera generally talk about the story and the music as if that just about adds it all up. But I have come to see – over the last 35 years – that, as with the Christian creeds, so with music and story in opera, the statement is not the end but the beginning of understanding.

There is a clear difference in dynamic between the most elevated and sophisticated forms of musical and spoken theatre. Opera has a non-linear, non-argumentative, non-logical character – which is intensely demanding if audiences give it proper attention. The combination of music and text is innately suggestive, like lateral thinking. Textual understanding is not the priority. Reading and understanding text unmodulated in performance by the nuances of vocal and musical qualification (as happens increasingly in opera-houses because of surtitles) may detract from and *obscure* other aspects of the imaginative stimuli being offered the opera audience to edit and assimilate.

Audiences always love surtitles, because being able to read what is being sung (which may be hard to make out even when you understand the language of the singing) makes us feel gratifyingly in control. We live in a strongly verbal culture, and understanding the verbal side of opera can make us smugly confident we know what's going on. Yet, while enabling an audience to follow a cold text closely, surtitles often hinder spectators from observing and responding to the detailed acting, the reactions by other characters to the singer in full flood, the meaning of movement – the whole context. Singing words audibly is never easy, and it is not good for the future health of opera if surtitles make performance in translation less viable. New and young singers need to learn to communicate musically in their home tongue. In their apprenticeship they need to experience what it actually feels like to achieve direct poetic and dramatic communication with the audience using a shared primary language. There is a huge difference between singing your own language and being understood, and singing another language and not being understood – or being partially understood. Young singers need to grow into truthful actors rather than just reproduce the effects of acting. If you are talking to somebody you usually look at them to understand what they mean, but nowadays opera audiences can spend much of their time reading surtitles above the performance – eyes buried in printed text. That is not theatre.

A lot of meaning in a performance is conveyed obliquely through the attitude of characters to each other and to what they are themselves singing (their musical and textual material). Is Leporello proud of what his Catalogue aria is outlining about his master's seductions in *Don Giovanni*, or amused, or shocked? Is it a friendly warning to Elvira, or an aggression against all women not far from rape? A performer might convey a whole range of ideas, and Elvira's reaction will build her characterization in turn. But to follow such details requires the audience to attend continuously to faces and movements, stage pictures and atmosphere. In effect, surtitles encourage audiences to refer back to and draw on their generalized memory of the work they are hearing (more than they are seeing) rather than respond to the specific performance of the moment.

Some may question if that matters. It is true that one of the good things about listening to opera on record or on radio is the bonus of hearing the finest casts singing in the original language with a direct translation of what they sing available to hand: just as Handel's Italian operas in 18th-century London were followed exactly in an auditorium well-lit throughout the performance, if one were not too busy quizzing one's neighbours. The concept of surtitles in the opera-house is not unprecedented, and it is better for an audience to understand some of the language they are hearing than none. But it is dispiriting, when one visits Paris (the capital of operatic snobbery as manifested in a commitment to 'original language' that has coincided with and helped cause the disappearance of the tradition of native French opera) to hear, for example, Tchaikovsky's *Eugene Onegin* sung in unstylish, impersonal, internationalized Russian by a cast containing not a single native Russian speaker. You do not have to understand Russian to recognize the detailed nuances of, say, Sergei Leiferkus's superb delivery of the text through his singing – and to know when that kind of artistry is not happening.

Opera is and always will be two things, and can be approached with equal validity from either end. It is music harnessed to dramatic purpose, music in which the composer becomes a playwright – with the assistance, usually, of a librettist (or poet, as Verdi would say). The music is the means whereby the drama is realized, and, though listeners following opera in terms of just music and words are missing out on theatre, there is no denying that what they are enjoying is opera. They experience opera rather as one may read a play on the page, peopling the stage in their mind's eye with more or less detail according to their own imaginative fire.

Equally, and this is my major concern here, opera is *theatre plus* music of the highest expressive quality, without which one would not perceive the insides of the characters or sometimes their situation. Every great operatic composer has felt himself to be the servant of theatre, and most (by no means just Wagner) have seen themselves as servants with vital revolutionary programmes of theatrical improvement to put into effect. Dissatisfied with the operatic theatre they inherited, they have wanted to create something more powerful and real, better able to convey their compelling metaphysical burden. Handel's detailed stage directions reveal how important theatrical realization was to him, and the same can equally be said of Gluck, or Berg. Opera composers are propagandists, in a sense, whose propaganda is so persuasive because their music of genius performs as a surreptitious and subversive theatrical fifth column.

The mixed or dirty (that is, impure) musico-theatrical character of the operatic art is, incidentally, what makes it resistant to television. It is almost impossible to present staged opera truthfully on television, for much that is vital in the actual theatrical experience gets omitted. The television director's editing suppresses a great deal in terms of lighting, atmosphere, incident and reaction that the audience in an opera-house is accustomed to absorb effortlessly or subliminally. This *gesamt* character may also suggest that modern opera production style is not just a temporary fad, is in fact more fundamental than merely a question of style or aesthetic – which may be legitimate matters of personal taste. Because it is not linear like spoken drama, opera readily suggests a surrealistic kind of collage on stage. Hofmannsthal's *Ariadne auf Naxos* is a prophetic work. Its staging invites cinematic sleight of hand.

As we approach the 21st century, we cannot disinvent the cinema. Opera is an art-form very like cinema where we find often heroic narratives with varieties of information edited together for particular conclusions. What in poetry would be figures of speech, rhythm and rhyme, in the cinema (and in opera) have all sorts of visual and musical equivalents. Narrative and context are explored through a variety of atmospheric and verbal means.

Cinema audiences find it easy to understand what is being expressed and communicated by so many non-verbal means with a jumble of images carefully balanced by editing. To a large extent the narrative process in film is defined through a sequence of reaction shots: one face after another keeps us close to the idea of events interpreted from different points of view. Presenting opera on stage also frequently demands and receives a kind of collage of different physical and visual elements, as well as the theatrical equivalent of montage. In live opera we the audience have to do the editing ourselves as we go along – though the skilled stage director sets up channels (especially at crucial passages) that should irresistibly command attention.

The variety of ingredients in opera and their inter-relation are just as complex and rich as cinema. It is not helpful that conservative critics and progressive theorists have defined the styles of (for example) Ruth Berghaus and Patrice Chéreau as 'deconstructionist' or 'post-modern'. The term post-modern is only a commercial tag, a marketing aid for a certain fashion – above all in architecture. If Berghaus and Chéreau are 'post-modern', what is modern in opera – perhaps the New Bayreuth of Wieland and Wolfgang, Wagner drained of context and politically dangerous associations? In architecture, especially, Modernism had an agenda. But post-modernism is a games-playing assembly of historical references without any agenda except a commitment to decoration. In some sense, if post-modernism implies the association of disparate decorative details, none of structural significance, opera could be said to be an essentially post-modern art-form. The conventions of singing, and certainly the display aspect that is the glory of the vocal art, are seldom of direct narrative consequence. A piling-up of narrative irrelevances in displays of physical grandeur has always been part of the operatic tradition. Opera composers have always understood why they needed to involve so many artistic elements in pursuing their metaphysical purpose; and equally audiences (especially the flamboyant rich) have always wanted to deny the moral seriousness of their 'entertainment'.

The term deconstructionist implies a negative, wilful under-mining of the natural narrative process. But so-called deconstruc-tionist productions, like the famous Patrice Chéreau *Ring* at Bayreuth (1976–80), have not aimed to undermine the emotional and intellectual power or the metaphysical substance of the works they were examining and presenting, or to mis-apply irony in superficial games-playing. What is disparagingly called decon-structionist is only a sincere attempt to bring into play all the foot-notes and sub-text that the intelligent reader with leisure might eventually come to perceive.

For the theatre can always do the impossible, even if some of its audience find that experience too stretching. Every production is in a sense a living edition of the work concerned. The issue is just that some editors (producers) are better than others: some are per-verse, some are stimulating, some miss the point. Critical judg-ment is certainly easier to apply once one has granted a serious moral purpose to composers. The objective test is the truthfulness of an opera's theme, what it says about 'virtue' – and how far its staging reflects that. The theatre, let us never forget, is not a game; the laws of the theatre are laid down by the lord of misrule. Many theorizers throughout theatrical history have tried to codify rules for the theatre, but rules are alien to the theatre and never last. Think of how Jakob Lenz, forerunner of Georg Büchner, disposed of the unities in his remarkably modern comedy *The New Menoza*. Remember the jokes in *Les enfants du Paradis* about Shakespeare and the French taste for classical decorum. In recent years there has been some attempt by period performance purists to erect as tablets of stone the evident or presumed wishes of the composer about staging, or the principles that may have governed the theatre and opera of his time. But changed circumstances invariably require different solutions.

What does one (in the audience) come to believe? In opera, for instance, where the more regular and sophisticated one may be the more one knows what to expect, an important question is, can one retain the possibility of being surprised? Most certainly, if I myself lost that excitement of uncertainty, I would see no point in going to the opera. Every good performance, every good bit of a bad performance, opens up one's mind to discoveries and percep-tions that then sink back into one's fertile but ruminating mem-ory of the work – a memory that is in itself an anticipation of a never to be completed or fulfilled possibility. One is a traveller, a pilgrim, who goes on in hope, but who knows there will never be a definitive arrival.

This is a book about performance and interpretation. But it is not about those standard essentials which are common to most performances. The operatic novice might want to focus on those. But what matters with opera, like all performance arts, is never the obvious or routine but those subtle distinctions which interpretative artists of real talent bring to their work. It is those incidentals that characterize individual performances and give them their potency, often built from tiny elements which the composer or playwright no doubt anticipated arising from performance. By their nature such elements are discoveries, insertions, happy accidents, the real life and blood.

But, equally, this book is not an objective series of descriptions concerning what performers on particular occasions thought *they* were doing. Rather, it is a report from the battle-front (so to speak) in my own mind – where the war was being fought out by the performers (to whom I am so eternally grateful) wrestling with their narratives and coming up with various kinds of suggestiveness. What I report on here is the reflection of performances that mattered to me, the impression they made inside my head. Those shadows cast, those paths beaten out through the undergrowth, are what performance is for. What has mattered, looking back at my extensive experience since I started taking opera more seriously, is the excitement, the revelation, the suddenly enhanced view of what had previously seemed a frustratingly truculent and impervious kind of artistic work: the effect on my thoughts and feelings as a member of the audience. My aim here is to mediate the process of interpretation. That intermediary role I regard as the essence of criticism.

Contextualizing is the heart of interpretation in the theatre. Verdi commented to Giulio Ricordi on how Patti's Gilda sang her reply (*'Io l'amo'* [I love him]) to Rigoletto's question whether she still loves the philandering Duke of Mantua in that extraordinary scene outside Sparafucile's inn by the Mincio: 'I cannot,' wrote Verdi, 'describe the sublime effect of those words as she sang them.' The point is the sublime effect, and where it happened – inside Verdi's head. Everybody can imagine a comparable situation by analogy from their own experience of remarkable artists, and understand why Verdi – a man of the theatre to his fingertips – wanted to tell Ricordi about it. But the real message of Verdi's remark is not precisely what Patti did or did not do. What matters was what it led to inside Verdi's head – recognizing the reality of the emotion depicted, and its implications, the time-stopping thoughts of what might stem from that statement, and (above all of course for Verdi the dramatist) the starting of a time-bomb of irony which ticks ever more ominously and desperately throughout the rest of the opera until its final despairing tragic cathartic cadence. Patti probably *did* nothing. The simplest statement is often in the theatre the most potent. Whatever she did then, she had earned the right to do by what she had already done in the earlier stages of her interpretation – not least in '*Caro nome*'.

I have as a critic often sided with unconventional and novel theatrical interpretations. But just as I know those worthwhile interventionist directors have not been merely shocking for egotistical reasons, so I have not found their work thrilling and provoking just because of the supposed perversity of my taste. The more I have looked into the history of operatic and theatrical interpretation, the more clear it has become to me that our century's revolutions in the cinema and in the theatre are closely related, that the language of film has irreversibly changed the terms of theatrical performance. The cinema is enormously manipulative in its games with imagery: film is all about association and the mysterious logic of sequential editing. The modern theatre has equally been freed in its new-found imaginative range to abandon literalism, to play with time and space, even to conjure with incoherence. Certain kinds of tangential raving in the theatre may be the only way to bring people to a closer view of the truth. Human beings do not just understand by means of logic. Thinking via theatrical experience is usually crabwise or lateral.

Those who believe in only one (straightforward, logical, naturalistic) way of presenting opera and theatre need to recognize that the condemnations by the conservative taste of associative, non-naturalistic interpretation is nothing new. The problems were defined almost a century ago. In operatic history controversies about interpretation go back to Gustav Mahler and Alfred Roller at the Vienna Opera.

But I start half a century later with the Peter Brook experience at Covent Garden after the Second World War. That famous episode is fascinatingly but insufficiently documented in the critical articles of the time – with far too little solid descriptive account of what Brook's work consisted in. Brook was premature in what he wanted to do with opera. Others took up the baton and carried it forward, as I describe. But before proceeding to the work of individual producers, it is as well to consider (for a few chapters) the theoretical basis behind the kind of operatic stagings that I think worth discussing. Theory matters. So I discuss what interpretation implies, what the classic repertoire has become, how adjustment and transposition and loans within the different European operatic cultures have provided an engine for innovation in a highly fashion-conscious and continuously self-reforming art-form. I also take account of the team work that establishes the design matrix underpinning so much of the best innovative work of recent years. With some principles established or suggested I turn to the major interpretative talents in opera over the last 20 years. Much of the description that follows is of stagings that have been seen by conservative critics as the worst demonstrations of producers' or directors' licence – which is precisely what I most warm to. I seldom waste description on work I have not liked. Patrice Chéreau transformed my thinking about how opera could meaningfully be staged. The two American geniuses of opera, David Alden and Peter Sellars, in various ways have affected British operatic thinking. Their political motivation and theatrical skills have set high and new standards. Richard Jones is the most original and acute of native British producers, with his disciple Tim Hopkins. Graham Vick, the other indisputably major British operatic producer, with what seem to me his soulmates Stephen Lawless and Matthew Richardson, represents the best of sensitive, stylized, neo-realist work. The panorama of this book is not exhaustive nor are the influences and links presented as some kind of network. Theatre and opera are ephemeral arts and when it comes to copying good ideas we are looking at a complete melting pot. The historic 1980s Frankfurt regime of Michael Gielen was vitally important in European theatrical history – especially its most characteristic talent, Ruth Berghaus, whose *Trojans*, *Parsifal* and *Ring* established her as a crucial innovator: the Wagner productions achieved in collaboration with an extraordinary designer, the late Axel Manthey. Manthey and Berghaus died within a few months of each other in, respectively, late 1995 and early 1996. Gielen and his dramaturg Klaus Zehelein's regime also supported a number of notorious young Turks: Hans Neuenfels, Alfred Kirchner and Christof Nel, for example. The most talented offspring of that era today are Herbert Wernicke and Willy Decker, the present leading German producers. Germany with its 86 opera companies has the best chance to be an engine-room of innovative opera interpretation. The influences go backwards and forwards. The work of Walter Felsenstein and his disciples was also the forerunner of the 1980s pioneering by the Welsh National and English National operas – though the big names often came from elsewhere: like Lucian Pintilie, Rudolf Noelte, and Peter Stein whom Brian McMaster imported to suggest new possibilities in what had been an unadventurous Cardiff company. The aftermath of Brook's work at Covent Garden, eventually, was the serious work by Peter Hall and Elijah Moshinsky at Covent Garden and Glyndebourne. And the best of Jonathan Miller and David Freeman were harbingers of the English National Opera's so-called Power House regime – presided over (as host to the producers concerned) by David Pountney. The support for Nicholas Hytner at ENO was matched by the interest Nicholas Payne, at Opera North, showed in Steven Pimlott, Tim Albery and Tom Cairns. There's an awful lot of good work to remember. But the liveliness of the directorial scene does not guarantee that opera has in any real sense now got a future. What indications are there of the way ahead – lit by Janáček or Britten or Philip Glass, or by a wholesale revisiting of the experience of 18th-century *opera seria*?

Performance is seldom written about fully enough. The records (and reviews) of productions 50 or 75 years ago were never detailed enough to feed the imagination accurately. When critics are satisfied they feel no great need to do more than approve: negative reviews are seldom profound. As a critic of opera from the late 1960s, I tried to distil my reactions at the time. Without those first judgments and descriptions (however much adapted here) there would have been sparse basic material for this whole exercise. The more closely one looks at what is condemned as *produceritis*, the more doubtful one becomes about any systematic or sweeping condemnation of non-naturalistic or non-narrative approaches. Performers need to express their responsibility with an unfettered imagination, though innovation naturally does not always equal excellence. The modern way is not always best. Bad eccentricity is the worst thing of all. But produceritis has often thrilled my imagination. Anyway, what exactly is the nature of the unwritten contract between interpreters and creators (composer and librettist)? Is there perhaps a good reason that we can welcome productions with unprecedented relocations and surrealism that certainly would not have been anticipated by the original creators or performers? We need to examine not only the history of opera, but also the cause and effect of Modernism, and how the 20th-century omnivorous appetite for culture feeds a spiritual and metaphysical concern which the decline of conventional religious observance has left often unsatisfied.

Nobody has spent a whole book on operatic productions before. And but for the long reviews of the relevant performance that I straightaway published, I probably could not have remembered that work in any detail. Part of our response to classics in performance, when they are on the way to becoming familiar, is that we reserve a memory panel in our minds to which we add further details on each fresh exposure to the work in question. That is our own concept of the work, with its foggy bits, its ready emotions, its affectionate nostalgic moments that are overlaid with our own autobiographies. This book reports on what I thought good, what I saw, and how it affected me inwardly in my understanding. My aim has always been to further the process of understanding and interpretation. Interpretation, the mounting of the operas on stage, is the truest criticism they can receive – the best, the only way of extending their lives effectively.

The purpose of performance is not so that the original creator of the work can be admired or worshipped, though we may well feel like doing that. The aim is to breathe life into old bones. Only thus can these gems of human imagination have consequence. Fostering that meaning is the real responsibility of performers. Any theory of decorum and duty owed to the original composer and librettist is pointless. The purpose is to make the truth tell. The place where truth tells, and where 'believing' occurs, is inside the individual minds of the audience.

2 Peter Brook and theatrical opera

Peter Brook's 1949 staging (at Covent Garden) of *Salome* designed by Salvador Dali: Ljuba Welitsch as Salome with Herod seated and Herodias in the background. Photograph © Roger Wood

The pre-history of modern operatic production in Britain is, noto-riously, what happened to Peter Brook in the late 1940s at Covent Garden. Almost at the same time in the aftermath of the Second World War, Walter Felsenstein from 1947 and Berthold Brecht from 1949 were transforming the scene in East Berlin. Brook's contemporary Giorgio Strehler was launching (in 1947 too) his interpretative career in Milan. In Britain the period also saw the beginning both of the experiment with subsidized arts (including opera) and of the English operatic revival – thanks to the new and extraordinarily accomplished operas of Benjamin Britten. *Peter Grimes*, *Albert Herring* and *The Rape of Lucretia* had a musical confidence and dramaturgical originality more sophisticated than any operas written in English since Purcell's *Dido and Aeneas* (1689) or Gay and Pepusch's *Beggar's Opera* (1728). All this oper-atic innovation in London predated the reopening of the Bayreuth Festival (delayed until 1951) where Wagner's grandsons, the brothers Wieland and Wolfgang, were to establish a new aesthetic of light and shade and abstract shapes, freed of any too politically specific architectural context and cleansed of nationalistic associ-ations. Bayreuth had actually been modernizing in theatrical terms since the 1920s. But its ethos had remained conservative, the festival in no sense the pace-setter that Wieland's New Bayreuth became. For a thoughtful operatic public over a period of perhaps 25 years – until Patrice Chéreau's 1976 centenary *Ring* made its revolutionary mark – Wieland's aesthetic seemed the most fruitful path into the heart and mind of Wagner's works. And not just Wagner's. New Bayreuth was not applied to Mozart, or the then neglected, undiscovered or misrepresented operas of Monteverdi, Handel, or Gluck. But the monumental neo-classical aesthetic Wieland adopted for *The Ring* and *Parsifal* influenced the staging of other philosophical works in the operatic pantheon.

Brook, aged 23 and with no former experience of opera, was given the opportunity by David Webster (manager of Covent Garden opera, newly created in 1946 and endowed with proper government subsidy for the first time ever) to mount *Boris Godunov* and *Salome* at the Royal Opera House. Brook had

Georges Wakhevich to design *Boris* (in 1948), and Salvador Dali for *Salome* (1949), and their unconventional design solutions contributed to the controversy surrounding him – though Wakhevich's *Boris* was defended in the *New Statesman* by Desmond Shawe-Taylor. The outcry united the Covent Garden public and the music-critics, who as usual were theatrically conservative, against Brook. Similar indignant alliances have sprung up in the face of adventurous policies in Bayreuth, Frankfurt or (confronted with Peter Jonas's change of mode there) Munich. The issue of interpretation which became so dangerous in the Weimar Republic and Nazi Germany, especially in connection with the works of Wagner, continues to have political echoes. But the newspaper and magazine cuttings reveal a remarkable similarity – almost word for word – between all the complaints voiced about Brook's controversial operatic work in the late 1940s and the tirades against David Alden's productions at the Coliseum in the 1980s or against Richard Jones's new *Ring* production at Covent Garden in 1995. In the course of the last decade and a half, the conservative voice in the British musical press has employed much the same vocabulary, based on the same concepts, when criticizing ground-breaking innovative productions at the English National Opera and elsewhere. Produceritis has in fact turned out to be an extremely infectious disease, and one much longer established in the operatic bloodstream than some of the violent objectors to modern production styles seem to realize.

The need for something radical in the opera-house was acutely defined by Alfred Roller, Mahler's associate at the Vienna Opera and the original designer of Strauss's *Rosenkavalier* and *Frau ohne Schatten*, when in 1909/10 he called, in an article headed *Bühnenreform* (see Appendix, p. 427), for a kind of theatrical experience 'where what happens on stage frankly signifies, rather than being, or pretending to be'. The recognition that operas generally (and not just those by Wagner) may embody submerged religious, political and philosophical agendas within their simple musically fleshed-out narratives – and that such agendas should be positively indicated in the staging, rather than remain an arcane pursuit for the thoughtful – is not everywhere accepted. Those who wish to avert their gaze from the often challenging content of operas, or pretend that they should not be allowed to become more than a culinary and often vulgar diversion, must be reminded that the history of opera in Western culture coincides with the history of modern post-classical theatre. The ancient Greek and Roman theatres seem to have had no opera as such, no distinction between musical speech and song. Music is simply a continuously available weapon of great power in the dramatic theatre. It is a profoundly significant fact that Shakespeare and Monteverdi, at the dawn of the modern theatrical age, were contemporaries. Shakespeare's theatre and Monteverdi's opera in their own ways deal with themes that society needs to face. Performance brings them home in each succeeding age.

Ernest Newman when he reviewed Brook's 1949 *Salome* used the word 'inanity'. He wrote: 'One absurdity followed fast on the heels of another; space fails me to deal with all of them.' Even the young Peter Heyworth, resonating from the pages of the Oxford undergraduate magazine *Isis*, said 'Mr Brook may think what he achieved is, at any rate, good theatre . . . but it is exceedingly bad opera.' Critics of opera were, then as now, predominantly orientated towards music. The rules of theatre, whatever they might be (and music-critics inevitably had severely limited experience of theatre), were something different.

The burden of all the complaints was the now so familiar *canard* that Brook had failed to carry out the composer's and librettist's (or playwright's) 'instructions'. Stage directions, which reflect the theatrical conventions of their time, were held to be a more significant contractual obligation than the exercise of imaginative responsibility. Significantly, *Boris* was attacked by Newman for being 'like a film'. It was certainly true that Wakhevich was primarily a film designer. That was why he had been engaged. In *Salome* there was the additional difficulty that European stars had been experimentally prevailed upon to sing in English translation. The new Covent Garden after the war had adopted a vernacular policy. On top of that was a furious Herodias, complaining of the unpractical weight of the towering head-dress she had to bear. And Karl Rankl the conductor dug his heels in, refusing to take a curtain-call – since he and Brook were not speaking to each other. *Salome* was the culmination of Brook's struggle against unfriendly odds and unsympathetic conservative criticism. Looking back in 1993 on the episode he admitted that it was the sheer chance of the new institution being run by an enthusiastic amateur, David Webster, that had led to his employment there – just as similarly in Stratford the gentleman amateur Barrie Jackson had opened the doors to all sorts of daring possibilities at the Shakespeare Memorial Theatre.

'Webster was a dear generous man, but a pure amateur,' according to Brook:

> Nowadays it couldn't happen. But he was really open. No professional, very likely, would have dared engage me then. The music director Rankl by contrast was a closed professional, and not the class of great conductor that for instance Mitropoulos was, who could be relaxed at the end of a disastrous rehearsal and say 'Tomorrow, it will be fine'. Naturally Webster was fighting for survival from the first day. What I believed in was very little supported, even at Board level. I was pushed out because what I was attempting was an exploration in a direction which was clearly not understood.

Rankl joined forces in opposition with the young chorus master, Douglas Robinson. Brook faced an entire permanent staff opposed to what he wanted to do, though he had been engaged as director of productions with a free hand to rearrange working practices, achieve longer rehearsals and hire more flexible staff. The Royal Opera House was not an institution established like a German house, with almost civil service status and conditions, but it did have regular staff, some of whom were as effectively established in post as the old bureaucratic retainers of Munich or Stuttgart, and far harder for a new regime to sack. A new German Intendant has the right to sack anybody he chooses at the start of his regime. At Covent Garden, however, radical change was impossible. Dali's *Salome* designs were sabotaged, according to Brook, by a wardrobe mistress 'who had been there 30 years'. On the Board of Covent Garden, Edward Dent was sympathetic to him, but also close to the Covent Garden old-timers. Brook observed covetously that in the ballet far more novelty was allowed. His only mentor was Tyrone Guthrie who was 'a practical, total and important influence' both in his Shakespeare stagings and in due course in his Covent Garden *Peter Grimes*. Brook, engaged to work full-time at the opera-house, followed Guthrie's *Grimes* rehearsals constantly. Guthrie was the only artistically worthwhile theatrical craftsman around. Brook found Guthrie's *Traviata* impressive too with the 'beauty and lightness of all the movements of the chorus, who just adored working with him'. Foreign guest producers at Covent Garden, including experienced German producers, were 'abysmal', according to Brook.

The principle of Guthrie's work which Brook followed too was that 'theatre must be alive at every instant'. Guthrie disinterred what he thought was buried in the work and transformed it, without any special concern for continuity. What mattered was energy. At Covent Garden Brook also directed *The Marriage of Figaro*, and a revival of *Bohème* using the sets and costumes from the original pre-First World War Royal Opera House performances. He did this with almost no rehearsal and it gave him enormous pleasure because it worked so well. But he was relieved to get away from Covent Garden because he 'didn't believe there was a long-term transformation possible'. The storms of public protest were not just directed against Brook. But the unconventional production aesthetic of *Salome* focused the resentment and took much of the blame for the general discontent.

Brook formed his own view of what was important. In fact there had not been much of an established London staging tradition for *Boris* and *Salome* for him to offend, and none at all (of course) for his premiere production of Arthur Bliss's *The Olympians* in 1949. *Boris* had been famously done by Feodor Chaliapin a number of times from 1913 on, most recently at Covent Garden in 1928; Chaliapin's acting ability had of course made its mark. What precipitated the storm now was the mere fact that Brook boldly proclaimed an agenda, stating he wanted to make a radical improvement to opera as theatre. This offended the established view that production deserved a secondary inferior place in the operatic endeavour. It is hard today, with little sympathetic criticism on record, to know exactly what Brook did on stage that was so offensive.

Brook had become artistic director at the opera because of the success of his Stratford *Romeo and Juliet*. But the Covent Garden public and the critics were not ready for his challenge. Photographs of Wakhevich's set, which provided the backdrop for revivals and restagings of *Boris* over 30 years, reveal nothing remotely as shocking as recent so-called deconstructionist stagings – just a non-naturalistic arrangement of the space, and various levels decked with a few significant motifs: a number of focal places around the stage with rhetorical potency for characters to stand up and deliver.

Brook was allowed to reply to the critics of his *Salome* in the *Observer* on December 4, 1949, and described in some detail what he was about. Dali had been chosen because:

> his natural style had both what one might call the erotic degeneracy of Strauss and the imagery of Wilde . . . We conceived *Salome* as a sort of

triptych. We made the set symmetrical, with a focal point, a stone slab – 'Perhaps an altar once' – old, crumbling, buried in the rock far downstage in the acoustic heart of Covent Garden. From the very back of the stage sweeps Salome's entrance. (Traditionally she comes from the side. We bring her from the centre. Scandalous? Or better theatre?) Away from this slab wind the narrow steps into the well. When Jokanaan comes out he stands on the slab, and when Salome lies in erotic frenzy on the stage she lies across it. When she dances it is as though the whole drum of the set is a vast cistern, under which Jokanaan is imprisoned. When Jokanaan is killed deep underground, the stone bleeds. It is out of it that the head is offered to Salome. It is on this slab, with fatal logic, that Salome is crushed to death.

The centre platform is reserved for the protagonists. It is raised to make it better for sound and to help the voices to carry over the impossibly loud orchestra. It is, also, as small as possible, because we wanted to discourage the singers from movement. We wanted them to take up stylized positions in built-up costumes and express the drama with their most impressive instruments, their voices. We aimed at cramping the dance. No singer is supposed to be a dancer; the more the dance could be *carried* by the orchestra and *indicated* by the singer, the less the embarrassment and the greater the illusion.

The effect? Terrifying words? Why? Why should we be afraid of fantasy and imagination, even in an opera-house? When the curtain rises strange vulture-like wings beat slowly under the moon; a giant peacock's tail, opening with the opening of the dance, suggests the decadent luxury of Herod's kingdom. A handful of such visual touches over the 96 minutes of the opera are designed to lift the audience into the strange Wilde–Strauss world, and to point the essential stages of the tragedy.

In the restraint sought by Brook for Salome's actual dance, he was following Strauss's own suggestion. But good intentions are not enough. A public has to be convinced. Performers must also be won over and made effective. The public often needs to be educated for new challenges and opportunities. New theatre conventions are not necessarily or immediately plain and understandable.

Brook's controversial attempt to convert Covent Garden to 'good theatre' should be seen in the context of a much wider movement in opera. This movement started at least 50 years earlier in Vienna where Mahler and Roller collaborated famously and controversially. The process then continued in the late 1920s at

Klemperer's Kroll Theatre in Berlin. But equally there was a drive in many corners of the world during the 20th century to make opera make sense in terms of communication between the characters on stage. An art which, since the time of the castrati two centuries earlier, had been dominated by singers was being asked to make the dramatic realism and truthfulness of its themes and ideas articulate and coherent. *Verismo*, the opera of Puccini and Mascagni where singers still dominated, had led the way in a sense – by preparing the public to expect a kind of cinematic naturalism, however prone to the prevailing musical convention. But the rise of cinema transformed the terms of trade for the theatre: for spectacle and the illusion of 'realism' in the theatre could no longer compete with the cinema. Inevitably the meaning of the theatrical illusion came to take precedence over merely seeming realistic. In any case by the late 1940s new operas which were vehicles for singers were not regularly appearing and entering popular affection. The value of the different elements in the operatic equation was being reassessed. Theatrical truth, meaning and intention were becoming the new standards all around the operatic world. That was the crucial aspect of 'realistic Music Theatre' (the often repeated phrase of Walter Felsenstein, director of Berlin's Komische Oper, and the post-war guru of opera as theatre). 'I don't like Beckmesserish demarcations. Theatre is a complete world,' are Felsenstein's words, quoted in Götz Friedrich's 1967 Henschelverlag book on the director. At Covent Garden Brook had put all his energies into establishing the operatic imagery and acting as truthful, realistic and coherent, so that – as in the straight theatre – the members of the ensemble would really fit together and support each other within a single credible psychological framework.

Brook was not, in fact, to see Felsenstein's work until some time after he had been virtually forced to leave Covent Garden. In London newspapers had reacted with farcical hysteria to the news that the Government was purchasing the freehold of the Royal Opera House; Brook, the press suggested, was to be Stalinist dictator of the place. In 1951, in a genuinely Stalinist Berlin, Brook was astonished and excited by Felsenstein's *Bartered Bride*, which, as he put it, 'used socialist realism to the hilt' (it won the Stalin Prize – Felsenstein himself was very far from supporting that aspect of the regime). With black, white and grey Bohemian settings of total naturalism, and rehearsed in detail for six months, it was performed, Brook said, 'as you would play a play of Tolstoy'. Clearly any comparable overturning of the existing aesthetic at Covent Garden was doomed to failure before it began. A convincing demonstration of Brook's objectives, a fair example of his vision, would have required far more pains and patience than a 'young genius' of 23 could command in either the company or the audience. Covent Garden's between-the-wars style, dominated by Sir Thomas Beecham, always set musical values above everything else, with visiting star singers and conductors, and little of the ensemble commitment and design experiments which progressive German opera-houses were then displaying.

Arnold Haskell, in his 1938 Pelican classic, *Ballet*, defined the essential difference between opera and ballet as the fact that 'opera continually offends through the figures of the singers: mountainous women dying of consumption, ugly women assuming the roles of *femmes fatales*, fat head-waiterish tenors aping ardent young lovers. A part of Chaliapin's greatness was the truth he brought to opera.' The leading music-critics of the post-war decade were not interested in theatrical values, even when (as in the case of Philip Hope-Wallace) they were theatre critics as well.

Not every Covent Garden performance suffered from the tendency of opera to separate out into those basic elements which, with everything in balance, should combine seamlessly: singing, symphonic continuity in the conducting, spaces that support the unbuttoning of narrative and the projection of inner emotion, evocatively expressive costumes, a sense of credible life that is sometimes romantic and colourful. But the storm Brook created was phenomenal. The audience was truly furious about the *Salome*. The Board had known (as the minutes of its November 11, 1949 meeting recorded) that the engagement of Brook represented the adoption of a 'definite policy of being more adventurous than previous managements . . . Such a policy was bound to involve risks, and could not be criticized even if a single production was a failure.' It was admitted by Webster that Rankl had stopped speaking to Brook in the final stages of rehearsal, but Webster sanguinely acknowledged the conductor's conservatism: 'Dr Rankl mistrusted any style of production other than the traditional style to which he was accustomed.' A *Salome* that Hope-Wallace described as being set in 'a French cabaret in the dark with spiders let down from the roof and a lot of silly and irrelevant bogy-boo' was bound to offend Rankl, though Hope-Wallace contended that this Brook staging was far less bad than Guthrie's *Carmen* at the Wells. But then Webster and Dent at the Board meeting on November 5, 1947 had concurred that Brook 'had a musical mind and a first-class musical approach'. Finally, on December 14, 1949 the Board recorded the view that some productions 'had been over-elaborate, and that it was better, if anything, to under-produce rather than over-produce opera.'

The battle for reform then was lost. Brook, categorized as dangerously experimental, was sent packing. Apart from productions at the New York Met of *Faust* and *Eugene Onegin* in 1953 and 1957, he abandoned opera altogether until his miniature 1981 and 1992 Paris experiments with *Carmen* and *Pelléas*. In both cases the Bouffes du Nord promoted the performances under special titles to distinguish them from 'the real thing', operatically speaking. It was a tragedy for British opera that Brook was chased away, as the psychological subtlety of these far later experiments showed. In 1992 *Impressions of Pelléas* was a concentrated (more than expurgated) version of Debussy's opera with piano duo accompaniment, seamlessly reconstituted by Marius Constant, the composer who earlier created *The Tragedy of Carmen* for Brook in 1981. The reference for Brook's *Pelléas* was Proust: 'In that closed bourgeois, end-of-the-century beginning-of-the-century world, which Freud blew open, revealing everywhere this enormous activity going on hidden under respectable surfaces,' Brook said, 'Proust discovered that if you entered into that with an extreme almost abnormal sensibility, you could penetrate . . . Proust is Bergman and beyond.' Maeterlinck, author of the Debussy 1892 text, provided a symbolic drama, simplifying everything, creating characters without 'apparent density' in a kind of privileged limbo. But whereas, as Brook sees it, 'Music normally simplifies,' here it was 'as hypersensitive, complex, sexually *étrange*, volcanic, passionate, violent yet idealistic and intuitive as Proust - or as a character from Proust.' For Brook Debussy's work takes place nowhere, with characters from no country in no time in no place. Yet the composer brought almost naked his understanding of human psychology and his extraordinary Proustian anatomical dissection of finest shades. Debussy's intuitions, his appreciation of silence, his sense of oriental values as opposed to mere oriental decoration, transformed the symbolism of Maeterlinck's words, ideas and images into something deeper. The metaphysics of the opera with its 'truth' theme is

27

the enigma of other people's feelings, the elusive certainty which is that act of faith called love.

Music has always featured in Brook's plays at the Bouffes. 'One goes,' as he has explained, 'from one style to another without thinking style itself is the end of the road. It's just another way to capture that same feeling of truth with different nets. I suppose I've always moved between opera and cinema and theatre. Not that I'm very fascinated by the forms, but the forms are nets through which different things can be caught. Opera led me in the end to a total impasse, because it seemed to me, that conditions were impossible. The conditions of performance militated against what the musical language could express.'

Carmen needed radical surgery from Marius Constant to fit Brook's requirements. But Debussy's opera reduced almost imperceptibly to a single span of 100 minutes and salon-style piano accompaniment. It was like looking at the work through binoculars. What interested was in sharp focus. The full expanse of misty orchestral landscape was barely missed since Debussy's pianism was, after all, orchestral. Chloe Obolensky's designs were simple and suggestive of the *fin de siècle*: a square carpet between two rectangles of water at the front, the acting space marked by a lit pair of flickering oil lamps. At the back on the right was the Bechstein and its pianist with another oil lamp: opposite a Japanese vase of blue and white hydrangeas. (Another Bechstein was off stage.) Vast Japanese screens masked the wing-space, various easy chairs and a chaise longue were dotted about, spread with plain fine fabrics. At the centre was an emblematic goldfish bowl and a pile of volumes, one of which the little boy Yniold started reading. Yniold was pivot of the whole performance: Brook achieved a typical mastery with the youngest and most innocent talent on show.

The characters entered, gathered round the piano, like friends after dinner. Mélisande – oriental in kimono – went to the front, sat on the ground. Everything seemed perfectly natural. Though the period presented was Debussy's the events seemed to be happening now rather than in a Ruritanian never-never land. The opera's theme being completely modern, the designs enabled Brook to be both in and outside period. The point was the unwavering truthfulness of the passions and ambivalent feelings on stage, exposed in close-up. Geneviève started to read out the letter from Golaud describing his encounter with the mysterious

Mélisande (scene 2 of the original). Then she broke off as Brook showed a flashback of the meeting of Golaud and Mélisande in the forest (on the front carpet). Mélisande, orientally inscrutable, no longer seemed like a neurotic feminist waiting to break away, as she does in many productions: the exotic alienation between these accidental lovers made effortless sense.

Debussy followed Maeterlinck's structure of a long series of scenes in different locations affecting the characters' relationships. Using a single location, Brook marked out the scenes with lights or with small actions. Yniold spread hydrangeas ahead of Mélisande, or turned out the oil lamps. The walls glowed with the ripple reflections of the water. Golaud slept tossing and turning on the chaise longue. The curve of jealousy and anger was followed with voyeuristic intimacy - every phrase and hint in the music answered in the conviction of the characters' behaviour. It was all too close-up for faking. Like a Japanese flower arrangement every detail, every move and gesture carried its own relevance. Scenes like the cave with the sleeping beggars, the sheep changing pasture, the climb to the peak of the castle were excised. But there were no jagged edges or awkward transitions. The strange dreamlike quality of the authentic Pelléas performance was there. Brook suggested Mélisande's long hair, Japanese theatre-style. What was meant mattered more than the precise physical description. Mélisande's ring was thrown wildly in the air, lost in the little dip of water, but it could easily have been found there. The text was crystal clear. Brook's straightforward pure approach made the performance indelible.

If one reads today how Stanislavsky applied the principles of the Moscow Art Theatre to *Eugene Onegin* in the 1920s in his Moscow opera studio production, it is obvious that Brook, Tyrone Guthrie, George Devine and other so-called 'drama producers' (in a surreptitiously derogative phrase used by Dennis Arundell about theatre directors working in opera) were all pursuing something very like Stanislavsky's objective in stagings at Sadler's Wells, Covent Garden, and the Met in the 1940s and 1950s. At the same time in East Berlin from 1947, Walter Felsenstein too was moulding his Komische Oper company to a similar purpose. The search for a truthful and believable theatricality in the opera-house was an inevitable agenda, about which toilers in the operatic vineyard had long been concerned. Opera was not taken seriously in theatrical terms during the first half of the 20th century. Complaints by those out of sympathy with conventions tolerated by opera enthusiasts always focused on appearances. International opera-stars often looked wrong for their roles. Sets were imaginatively poverty-stricken and decoratively irrelevant. Costumes showed a fake couturier grandeur.

Stanislavsky's operatic work, however, was virtually unknown outside a special circle in Russia – until the American publication of a mass of reminiscence about his operatic work in 1975. It would be inaccurate to attribute direct influence, though there is no doubt of the overlapping agendas. The Russian revolution produced a diaspora of genius, most famously in the ballet. Fedor Komisarjevsky, who until 1919 had run his own theatre in Moscow presenting straight plays and opera, brought his talent as a director to London for a time. When he recognized that London found him too controversial, he moved on to the US where he managed to stage not only plays but opera as well. Komis, as he was known, was son of a Russian tenor who was a teacher of Stanislavsky; Komis's sister was the first Nina in *The Seagull*. With Guthrie and Michel Saint-Denis, Komisarjevsky helped create the directorial and interpretative tradition in British theatre that later gave rise to the Royal Court Theatre, Royal Shakespeare Company, and National Theatre. Komis with Guthrie and Saint-Denis were pioneers of the director's role in theatrical interpretation which the abandonment of actor-management had necessitated. The successful young stars of London theatre in the 1930s (John Gielgud, Ralph Richardson, Laurence Olivier) were not drawn to become Victorian-style hierarchical actor-managers. Yet the real reason for the emphasis on ensemble theatre in the 20th century was not just that it was a more democratic era – some of the time, in some places. It was the change of focus in theatrical performance, away from the star alone to the whole social environment – all expressed with a new kind of emotional accuracy that needed a director to ensure all those qualities that a recorded medium like the cinema had to achieve, such as consistency and continuity and coherence. And once the director's role was established, it meant a focus of initiative with powerful expressive possibilities within the terms of current theatrical practice. Call it produceritis, if it offended. But when there was no longer a style of the age, a convenient bundle of conventions, which all could follow almost unconsciously, there had to be an outsider, an observer, as adviser and editor. Hence directors' theatre – and opera.

The development of Britten's own English Opera Group – after it became clear that John Christie at Glyndebourne was not the right sort of patron for him – drew on this same theatrical source. Basil Coleman, who directed important Britten premieres in the 1950s, many Sadler's Wells productions, and an admired *Billy Budd* for BBC TV in 1966, had worked as an actor with Guthrie. For instance Coleman had understudied Alec Guinness as Hamlet in October 1938. It is fascinating how in a way Guthrie's modern-dress staging of *Hamlet* anticipated operatic developments decades later: many of its elements were shared by the aesthetic of the Elder–Pountney regime at the English National Opera in the 1980s. Kenneth Tynan, looking back on a fabled era, in 1953 wrote of the Guthrie *Hamlet* that 'the costumes, deliberately startling, included lounge suits, flannels, trilbies and (for the graveyard scene) a seaman's jersey and gumboots'. That might be *Peter Grimes* territory. Indeed, Jon Vickers's performance of Grimes was created in New York with Tyrone Guthrie as producer – a fact which possibly helps explain Britten's rejection of Vickers's psychologically remarkable, robustly masculine interpretation. For Guthrie became an Aldeburgh unperson while staging Britten's *Beggar's Opera* in 1948, thanks to his criticism of Peter Pears's Macheath as being like 'Stainer's *Crucifixion* on skates at Scunthorpe'; the role, Guthrie told Britten, 'needed a real man'.

What Brook attempted at Covent Garden was symptomatic. It belonged with work elsewhere, even if that was not properly recognized at the time. In Britain, the ensemble principle was pioneered at Sadler's Wells and the Old Vic under the artistic direction of Lilian Baylis. When the Old Vic and the Wells became separate institutions, the latter the home of opera, most of the regular opera producers were theatrically undistinguished specialists, though the Wells management recruited producers from the legitimate theatre who often had been actors. The pioneers who created the Wells tradition were a mixture of musical academics, like Edward Dent and Dennis Arundell, and theatre people. Opera producer and theatre producer were not then distinct professions or careers. In 1940 Tyrone Guthrie staged *The Marriage of Figaro* at the Wells and followed it with *Fledermaus, Traviata, Bohème, Carmen, Falstaff, The Barber of Seville* over the next decade, as well as doing *Peter Grimes* and *Traviata* at Covent Garden, both of which works he also directed at the Met in New York after making his US operatic debut there with *Carmen* in 1952. George Devine between 1951 and 1955 (before he was absorbed completely with managing the Royal Court Theatre) produced *Don Carlos*, *Eugene Onegin*, Sutermeister's *Romeo and Juliet*, Lennox Berkeley's *Nelson* and *Die Zauberflöte* for Sadler's Wells Opera. Norman Tucker at the Wells recruited Michel Saint-Denis for *Oedipus Rex* in 1960, and then in 1962 brought Glen Byam Shaw (whose dissident triumvirate with Devine and Saint-Denis had fallen famously foul of the Old Vic trustees in the 1940s) on to the Sadler's Wells establishment. There were other theatrical talents too: Basil Coleman, Guthrie's protégé at the time of the Britten *Beggar's Opera*, staged *Samson and Dalila*, *Luisa Miller*, *Don Pasquale*, *The Pearl Fishers*, *A Village Romeo and Juliet*, *Murder in the Cathedral*, *La belle Hélène*, *Peter Grimes*, *Die Entfuhrung aus dem Serail*. Peter Hall directed *The Moon and Sixpence* in 1957.

On the whole, what the theatre knows as 'production values' could not reasonably have been expected from, say, the young Welsh National Opera company in the 1950s or 1960s. Even in WNO's 1975 *Otello*, staged by Michael Geliot, theatrical standards in Cardiff were amateurish. The introduction by the Arts Council of crusaders Brian McMaster and Nicholas Payne into the management of WNO in 1976 was a vitally necessary move. By contrast, Glyndebourne, where from 1934 critics and public prompted by John Christie felt they were getting what opera was really all about, was from its early decades right up to the 1960s the preserve of a tiny roster of foreign producers. It was difficult for native theatrical talents to emerge, whether in design or direction. When Sean Kenny made a name for himself as a designer in the 1960s, he did it not in opera but by working on musicals. Yet Sadler's Wells and Covent Garden, though not Glyndebourne before 1970, continued periodically to try to engage directors from the legitimate theatre with the intention of achieving something more theatrical and believable. Opera producers who showed real creative initiative were, almost invariably, not opera specialists but new arrivals in the art-form. Thus Peter Hall brought to Georg Solti's Covent Garden fresh ideas and courage to try and achieve something much more challenging and complicated. Importing Luchino Visconti and Franco Zeffirelli at Covent Garden (the latter also at Glyndebourne) was an acknowledgment of need and a recognition that, with Maria Callas's emergence, opera in Italy had had a resurrection reinvigorating the staging and dramatic credibility, something worth tapping into. Visconti's international-standard *Don Carlos* at Covent Garden was momentous, stylishly distinguished in every department, and lasted through three decades as a jewel of the Royal Opera's repertoire.

John Tooley was continuing a recent tradition at Covent Garden when he commissioned the *Ring* production for the 1976 centenary celebrations from Götz Friedrich and Josef Svoboda – though there was a frisson because of the Marxist political regime in East Germany where Friedrich, a Felsenstein disciple, had originated. The Czech team of Svoboda and Vaclav Kaslik had staged *Pelléas et Mélisande* at Covent Garden, and would have done *Nabucco* had not their idea of setting it in a concentration camp been rejected by the Royal Opera House board. Colin Davis's collaborator as joint artistic director at Covent Garden, taking over from Georg Solti in 1971, was originally to have been Peter Hall. And Hall's stagings of *Moses and Aaron, Eugene Onegin,* Tippett's *Knot Garden* and *Tristan und Isolde* promised fruitful teamwork. The approach to Friedrich was an attempt to fill in for the gap left by Hall, when he did not take up this appointment. Lord Harewood at Sadler's Wells engaged the Felsenstein disciple Joachim Herz to produce *Salome* at the Coliseum in 1975 and *Fidelio* in 1980. The example of Carl Ebert and Günther Rennert at Glyndebourne seemed to demonstrate the benefit of bringing foreign masters into British opera. Yet, by 1976, when McMaster took over the Welsh company, there was a distinct British home-grown line of specialist opera producers well established – though McMaster, who had seen a lot of European opera stagings while working for EMI, consciously rejected them.

It was McMaster at the Coliseum (before going to Cardiff) who persuaded Lord Harewood to employ Joachim Herz and his designer Rudolf Heinrich for *Salome*, when both John Dexter (Harewood's first choice) and Ingmar Bergman were not available. McMaster and Harewood sought something special to fit Josephine Barstow into the title role of a work which formerly the Wells would never have tackled. McMaster, once he was his own boss at the WNO, was unprecedentedly open to innovation. British theatre and opera never knew such an influx of foreign talent, in a way anticipating the Thatcherite economic policy of inviting massive foreign capital investment, though the standard complaint in conservative circles was that the new ways of staging opera and exploring for hidden meanings were Marxist. For a time Cardiff's company gained a considerable European reputation.

Without that demonstration of confidence and adventure, the history of opera production in Britain at the end of the 20th century would have been totally different. Many of the previously unknown producers McMaster took on in the 1980s were untried in opera and engaged by him on the grounds of their theatre work which he had seen. Lucian Pintilie he hired after seeing *The Wild Duck* in Paris, and Andrei Serban after *The Cherry Orchard* in New York. Göran Järvefelt was based in Gelsenkirchen, and McMaster (looking for somebody to stage a new *Zauberflöte* in 1978) was in the audience alongside John Tooley when Järvefelt's staging was new there. Tooley disliked the staging, so McMaster bought it for Cardiff. He brought a wide range of theatre directors from different and remote cultures to tackle opera. He took very big risks.

Felsenstein and his methods were famous. One of the most influential London seasons ever given by a foreign theatre company was the visit of Brecht's Berliner Ensemble, neighbour to Felsenstein's Komische Oper. But Felsenstein himself was never engaged to produce in Britain, being thought an ideologue – though never a political supporter of the East German regime. In Charles Osborne's *Opera 66* (Alan Ross), an article about Felsenstein's Leipzig colloquium on 'realistisch Musiktheater' is preceded by an attack by Frank Granville Barker on Rolf Liebermann's remark to a Hamburg Contemporary Music Theatre forum in 1964, that opera is a form of total theatre in which the 'first prerequisite is the work of producers and designers.' Liebermann, Barker suggested, should have known better – since he was a composer. Barker claimed that modern interpretation was nothing more than a change at the top, directorial whim instead of prima-donnas' wilfulness. But Liebermann's momentous Paris Opéra term (which was the death of the French singing tradition, since the company devoted to opera in French was disbanded) gave opportunities to Patrice Chéreau and Peter Stein, brought in Jorg Lavelli and Giorgio Strehler as guests – all without reducing the presence of star voices in cast lists. This successfully renewed the theatrical tradition at the Palais Garnier. The *Marriage of Figaro* directed by Strehler there was highly influential. According to the American director Peter Sellars, that production changed his entire view of what theatre (and opera) could do.

Liebermann also launched – 44 years after the composer died – Friedrich Cerha's completion of Alban Berg's *Lulu*, the quintessential 20th-century opera, based on Wedekind's plays, and both a theatrical and an advanced musical masterpiece. *Lulu*, dating from 50 years after *Parsifal*, is like the rare flowering of a cactus which even 60 years later shows no signs of repeating the miracle. In Schoenberg's view the harmonic flux of Wagnerian language necessitated the Modernist revolution, but *Lulu*, however extraordinary its music and gripping its ideas, is a dead end. Certainly it perfectly represents the Modernist agenda – thematically, in the way it shows the relationship of the sexes, and technically, in its extreme complexity of musical inventiveness combined with a healthy lyricism for the singers. No doubt *Lulu*, for which Berg made no compromises in his musical language and arcane and complicated compositional method, is the exception that proves the rule. The melodies of *Lulu* have nothing to do with Puccini's language, or Prokofiev's, or Janáček's, or Britten's. Yet the drama is minutely expressed and explored, with deep emotional impact. *Lulu*, finally hallowed by performance at Glyndebourne in the 1996 summer festival, remains a one-off, a distinct species, a unique answer to a special problem, and not a pattern for any composer to imitate. All masterpieces are no doubt unique. Yet the one-off inimitable phenomenon typifies the modern operatic quandary, for a theatrical art-form which has always been fuelled by imitation. A critical issue for opera at the start of the 21st century is the renewal of the repertoire, the creation of new works with popular following. Few composers (outside the field of rock music) have in the latter part of the 20th century seemed able to provide new songs for singers, let alone opera. The maintenance of an interested and committed audience has depended on the imagination of directors and designers who between them have been bringing a limited pantheon of masterpieces to life over and over again. How long can that go on?

3 Theory of interpretation

David Alden's 1991 English National Opera staging (at the London Coliseum) of *Oedipus Rex* designed by Nigel Lowery: Philip Langridge as Oedipus with his guilt-branding sign. Photograph © Douglas Jeffery.

What I am saying about interpretation in the theatre, about how operas are being staged now, involves the recognition that both opera and classical music have become – in a sense – museum arts. At the dawn of the 21st century there is no point in pretending that contemporary attempts to create new operas are anything more than an annexe to what has become a permanent classic repertoire, a pantheon of presumed 'masterpieces'. The 20th century, the age of anxiety as Auden and Bernstein have justifiably dubbed it, is obsessed with the past, and has lost the certainty of a common contemporary musical language. Opera enthusiasts live in the past not in the present: there is no consensus about how to write operas today, no steady active line of productivity including successes and failures, no generally accepted musical style with lyrical effect and expressive declamatory function. In the past such linguistic security did exist (however much talented artists wanted to change and develop the expressive possibilities) and there was very little insecurity among composers about how their operas would be interpreted – no problematical distinction between the work they were creating and the style of presentation on stage which it would receive. People working in theatres and opera-houses knew where they stood in relation to present taste: the novelty they sought to exploit was within recognized parameters.

How is the judgment of history exercised? With performed works, that judgment has always taken effect through public response to the events or works, to the entertainment and provocation they offer, the vitality in the philosophical agenda of their creators and performers. With Handel and *opera seria* composers of the age of Metastasio there is no doubt opera expressed the civilized ideals of the age of enlightened despotism, a sense that rulers should not be swayed by personal lusts and affections, and should be capable above all of clemency. But did the opera-going public share that agenda? For them these works were perhaps primarily about comic emotions and a – for some onlookers – comic display of vocal and physical vanity by singers who often were freaks of nature. Quite quickly the whirligig of fashion submerged monuments of genius. In our fraught and insecure century some of those lost masterworks have been disinterred to marvellous acclaim. Detective work by academic music historians (even a humane critic like Wilfrid Mellers in *Man and His Music*) usually depends on score-reading and a musical equivalent of literary criticism. Yet the only ultimate testbed of viability is theatrical performance – done by particular talents. Institutions that specialize in unknown operas (the Wexford Festival and the lamented Camden Festival, London) have often demonstrated that historical neglect was justified. Despite successful revivals of Monteverdi, Cavalli and Handel, the causes of Carlo Pallavicino, Giovanni Bononcini, Alessandro Scarlatti and Johann Hasse (to name a handful of once famous successful opera composers) remain dubious – though even very obscure names in 18th-century opera are now being performed successfully and revealing their often surprisingly superior attractions: names like Nicolò Jommelli whose *Armida abbandonata* has been recorded by Christoph Rousset, and Carl Heinrich Graun whose *Cleopatra e Cesare* turns out (under the baton of René Jacobs) to be a lavish vocal delight. The issue of the relationship between text and music in an operatic age dominated by a librettist (Metastasio) suggests an aesthetic from which the late 20th century is infinitely remote.

Taste changes. History (whether political, social or cultural) is made up from the viewpoint of the present – often in order to discuss the present, more than the past. Today's rating of quality in the historical operatic pantheon is an expression of current taste about what the purpose of opera should be today. By comparison with the operatically pioneering and prolific 17th and 18th centuries, the 20th century may have a high success rate with new operas that are important and genuinely original. But the audience eagerly awaiting new works – which used to be crucial in the repertoire – has vanished.

Staging is the test. In live staged operatic performances musical worth is matched with dramaturgical purpose. What is this dramaturgical process? Dramaturgy is a term borrowed from the German theatre world in recent years. The word with its overtones of 'turgid' especially provokes those who maintain opera does not need so much thinking out loud. But thorough dramaturgical preparation has been central to the 20th-century revolution in theatrical staging – whether the critical process has been carried through by the producer/stage director, or by assistants entitled 'dramaturg'. The dramaturgical process is like presidential speech-writing – with a committee of people deciding on a line. That fact helps confirm the political, philosophical and public thrust of opera. The dramaturg (according to Brecht) prepares the work for performance in a thorough, academic and non-judgmental way, acknowledging every detail before the process of interpretation by director and designer begins: dramaturgy is a resource, objectively assembling what is going to become a subjective version. In most German opera and theatre companies dramaturgs prepare the programme notes; at Bayreuth and many other opera-houses these for many years have included highly complex, original or reprinted, critical and exegetical essays. Such publications reflect the serious intentions in the process of interpretation. Sometimes – as at Frankfurt during Michael Gielen's regime from 1977 to 1987, with Klaus Zehelein as Chef-dramaturg – a dramaturgical department is effectively editing the work in progress of the designers and producers as they develop the commissioned interpretation, assessing it, guiding it, responding to the team's ideas, proposing new approaches.

Interpretation has become the central critical issue. It is no accident that a period of experimental staging, where the aim of many productions is clearly to bring an old classic into new relevance to the contemporary audience, has coincided with a time when the issue of authenticity in methods and manners of musical performance should have assumed great prominence. In classical music there has grown up – since the early 19th century and the development of both the symphony orchestra and the maestro – a tradition of fidelity to the musical notation of scores. The performers of classical music are trained in the 'realization' of the composer's notated score. 'Interpretation' of notes allows for the personality and charisma of the performers: for individual shadings, variations of tempo within quite narrow parameters, characteristic timbre and attack, distinctive strategies in using a work's rhetorical structure – the continuity and cumulative consequence of the articulate mosaic that forms a work of music. Music, the composer's notes on paper, may seem to endorse the notion of a prescriptive performance tradition. But in reality performance, though now technically preservable or recordable, is just as fragile, temporary and vital a phenomenon as ever. Today the cultural wish to have history rescue the present is balanced by a strong conviction that opera needs reconstruction and rejuvenation through performance and interpretation. The scores are codes created by the composer for a specific time in history, but their meaning in the sounds, colours and words of an actual performance is indubitably of the present day.

The controversies about interpretation and authenticity in opera have their parallels elsewhere – in politics, of course, but also in religion. Opera productions are sometimes judged as naively and unimaginatively by supposed enthusiasts as the more inventive or progressive theological glosses have been judged by strictly orthodox or traditionalist Christian believers. In religious teaching contextualization has always been a crucial element. Pope Pius XII, no progressive, insisted in his 1943 encyclical *Divino afflante spiritu* that the Bible be studied in the context of the historical circumstances of its composition – intending to exclude misapplication in the circumstances of today of texts ripped from original context. Superficially such a ruling in opera would seem to imply 'historically authentic' staging. But the issue arises, what is the purpose of interpretation? What is the truth that is being pursued? Biblical scholarship, whether Protestant or Catholic led, has been a guaranteed escape route from Jehovah's Witness-style literalism about the 'Word of God'. The result of Pope Pius's ruling was that biblical texts were clearly and unquestionably to be regarded as contemporaneous exercises in the criticism of ideas. New Testament narratives about Jesus were to be understood as imaginative literary creations whose status as fact Christian scholars could reasonably debate. Thus Pius XII prepared the ground for the Second Vatican Council, when modern biblical criticism was brought into focused relationship with the 'signs of the times' – a greater understanding of the needs of the modern world. By applying literary and historical criticism to the stories that embodied Christian tradition, a theology developed that could vitalize the faith stories in the context of contemporary life.

Modern interpretations of opera provoke the same range of prejudices, anxieties and taboos as progressive biblical and theological scholarship – and for similar reasons. The campaign against innovation at Bayreuth after the 1976 unveiling of Chéreau's centenary *Ring* was as ferocious as the fulminations by the late Archbishop Lefebvre and his Catholic fundamentalist followers at Écône, who were against changes in Roman Catholic liturgy and theology endorsed by the Second Vatican Council, and claimed the new ways were not authentically Catholic but diabolically modernist, as condemned by earlier popes. Opera, like religion,

often deals in veiled archetypes and mythology. Even when operatic stories seem specifically the stuff of everyday life, familiarity
lends them universal resonances. With theological controversies, a
latent Christian consciousness in the secular mind is linked to a
conservative tendency and love of decorum: similarly with opera
the public has an automatic feeling that conventional, naive narrative must be the anchor of flighty theatrical fancy. Religious dis-
putes may filter down from bishops and scholars into public
consciousness; non-church-goers are instinctive conservatives for
whom Christianity is essentially about miraculous events – the
physical resurrection, the virgin pregnancy and birth, the physical
ascension – even though such tests of belief are not rational.
Learning to use and interpret or translate fables may indeed be the
first cultural experience in a child's life, but fundamentalism
remains in the popular mind somehow more 'authentic'. The sci-
entifically impossible, reinforcing subconscious ethnic memories,
is usually felt appropriate territory for religious expression. The
non-praying public thinks the truly religious should buy the
package of incredible simplicities. Tradition seems easy to grasp.

Equally, in opera the improbable character of some (many?)
operatic stories is what the ordinary non-opera-going public asso-
ciates with an arcane and inaccessible art. As with madness and
eccentricity, before psychoanalysis explained causes and proposed
cures, the ordinary public liked to categorize. Most debates about
'producer's licence' range people for whom operas made for performance exist to be explored, adapted, exploited and intensified,
against others who want interpretation simply to reproduce the
historical circumstances and means of the work's original performance. Those who, like me, would allow a wide discretion to present-day performers point out that performance is impermanent,
that it leaves unsullied the notes of music or text encoding the creator's concept.

To write for performance is to require interpretation. The creator of works for performance signs an open-ended contract with
future performers; their creative collaboration may need to be free
of debts to the past. Creative renewal in present-day interpretation is a fine homage to dead artists, who counted on the goodwill
of future users. Performance implies adaptation, 'wear and tear'.
Controversies about interpretation are usually about taste. Is the
performers' sense of decorum appropriate?

To understand why operatic production is so controversial, one

43

must acknowledge how political or philosophical commitment and the passions of religion lie very close to the roots of verbal creativity. A complaint against interpreters today is their wilful neglect of the 'composer's wishes'. This implies a theory of 'delegation', whereby interpreters are implicitly delegated to carry out a composer's or librettist's instructions. Such constraints would be thought absurd in the legitimate theatre where radical adaptation of original texts has been common, from Garrick to Brecht – though the disapproving reaction of the Samuel Beckett estate to Deborah Warner's *Footfalls* staging in 1994 was perhaps a sign of a conflict between authenticity and vitality in the legitimate theatre (a hint that theatre itself may be joining opera in the cultural mausoleum).

Interpretation is how we understand, how we put things in terms to which we can relate. Interpretation is the digestion of our civilization's diverting and stimulating cultural resources, ravishing the visual sense and mobilizing minds and imaginations. But there are important differences in kind between the response of an audience to a performance and the reaction of an individual to a picture, poem or novel. Making sense by looking and reading is of course interpretation, which may sometimes be highly eccentric and subjective. But interpretation via performance is a secondary mediation between creator and public – which may cause misapprehension as well as inspiration. Performance is a kind of 'translation', as in Quince's 'Bless thee, Bottom! thou art translated' in *A Midsummer Night's Dream*, though the word misleads by implying a polarity between simple right and wrong.

Interpretation is an act for the present context: criticism in action. It requires a critical stance towards the work being performed, a stance which naturally will be affected by fashion or modishness. Those unpersuaded often claim they have been seeing a misrepresentation. This is a process very different from literary criticism – the interpretation of written fiction. Chief characters of famous novels and plays can exist in the popular imagination, but the reader always interprets autonomously in reading. Ideas are private. Novels are only publicly performed when adapted for stage or screen. Words, sculpture and painted image are unaffected by various forms of interpretation – though reactions to Salman Rushdie's *Satanic Verses* suggested other dangers.

Performance is public. That is why some operatic interpretations can be accused of blasphemy. Emotions like hatred and distress are common in opera-going. Vitriolic passions get aroused. The act of operatic interpretation is potentially blasphemous for people with rigid notions about their favourite works: part of the opera-house audience is bent on worship.

Nelson Goodman in *Languages of Art* (The Bobbs-Merrill Company, 1968) explored the issue of the authenticity of art-works (whether made in one or more stages by the artist and collaborators, or requiring performance and a social context). He used the term 'autographic' to describe art-works where 'the distinction between the original and forgery of it is significant; or better, if and only if even the most exact duplication of it does not thereby count as genuine'. A poem, though, is immune to faking. It exists in a form completed by the artist and therefore not requiring further intervention between the art-work and the user or appreciator. But nothing special attaches to the medium of the poem, the language of which it is an ideal partial exemplar, which distinguishes it (and all literary art-forms) from art-objects whose uniqueness and finite character makes them candidates for the cultural reliquary or museum. Non-autographic art-works, Goodman called 'allographic', a distinction taken up by Jonathan Miller in *Subsequent Performances* (Faber and Faber, 1986) and embroidered with biological terminology. Goodman added 'an art seems to be allographic just insofar as it is amenable to notation' – which ignored the processes of oral culture and tradition. The artist as hero and god seems less promethean if he has not done it all alone. There is no reference to opera in Goodman's subject index.

Performance is enacted and public: its politics and everyday life are of course imaginary – it is representation not documentary. What it represents and how that becomes telling and significant are the real issues in interpretation. Opera is the most complex of the theatrical performing arts. Plays and operas have to be interpreted to come alive. But though legitimate theatre has controversies about meaning and direction, it is comparatively straightforward and natural-seeming. There have been storms around Peter Brook's work: his famous 1970 staging of *A Midsummer Night's Dream* and 1962 *King Lear*. Yet interpreting a play text in the theatre is almost a linear process, compared to opera which has various streams of meaning and material – which can need to be laterally related to each other in performance. Opera, theatre plus music, is essentially surrealistic – with far more imponderables than the legitimate theatre.

People interested in 'authentic' or 'period' performance of opera face the same conundrum that anti-modernists had to face in the Catholic Church. To apply a knowledge of historical performance practice to old scores is a fine and useful scholarly process with practical implications. But the circumstances of performance today, the needs of the contemporary world, are enormously changed from those facing the initial performers in the past. The aim of performance cannot be merely documentary – to reproduce history, to relive the past. It has to be to understand and exploit the product of the original creator's imagination in the circumstances of today. Experiences on the way to the present context cannot be forgotten, for the present is the product of the past – however much some traditionalists and authenticists wish the study of the past could provide an escape from the responsibilities of the present. Opera is not just a language to be 'translated' in theatrical terms. Its code-form (readily reproduced and disseminated) is as unaffected by use and interpretation as computer software. But the process of transferring notated and written material into performance, the need for an intermediary, has thrown up dangerous fallacies about notation and recording (for which ever more capable technology now exists), and the concept of the definitive or ideal once-for-all-time interpretation.

The fallacy about words or notation is to imagine that the notated code-form *is* the work – that it should have the unique status that a painting has and be regarded as autographic. In music and opera, notation and text are only a map with a route to performance. The fallacy of recordings is the idea that a performance, whose sound (and to an extent visualization) can be fixed mechanically and retrievably, *is* the work – that one could have a finished product that is, effectively, *it*. With works created for performance, the creator anticipates repeated and variable realization of the seed-concept that he or she has provided. There is the expectation of growth into (and fulfilment as) a series of performances in a range of different contexts at different times. Both these fallacies relate to a third – that there could be a definitive or perfect performance, that the last word in a stage-work's representation could ever be said, an error which stems from a wrong sense of the author's intention and the nature of notation.

One can discuss a play text as a kind of literature and an opera as a kind of music. But performance is collaborative and practical and presented for an audience. Opera as a musical phenomenon seems, like music, to concern fixed parameters of performance. Musical recordings, endlessly repeatable, support the notion of a 'correct' performance as the one traditionally established or familiar. 'Interpretation' aims at the re-creation of a 'correct' or 'authentic' simulacrum. The revival of interest in historic performance styles (both musical and theatrical) can reinforce this idea. And modern recording technology (not to mention the recording companies' promotion departments) invites the implicitly definitive or 'perfect' performance: manufacturers naturally purvey only the best!

Modern stagings of opera are as unpopular as modern art with some people. The 20th is the first century in which the new has come to seem alien, just because it is new. In opera performance, the last 20 years have seen a different vision applied to familiar material. Some critics believe that what have been called 'deconstructionist' methods are a fad. Actually, so-called 'deconstructionist' productions generally reflect a fuller, more inquisitive and receptive engagement with the elements of works. It is true that Jacques Derrida's games with words, the convenient elision of his obscure thoughts and criticisms with the ineluctable ambivalence in every verbal attempt to control meaning, seem easily adaptable to opera and music where meaning and value depend only partially on a literary dramatic argument. For Derrida speech should be the ideal medium of philosophy, not writing: for speech is closer to the consciousness, more transparent to the thinker's thoughts than writing. Socrates was authentic, Plato dependent and interpretative (for writing misrepresents, and Plato uses writing to attack the inferiority of memory transmuted into writing compared with what is recalled in the mind without transformation). True meanings are always modulated by context. The performance is more true than the notation. The operatic or musical score is an inferior order of statement. Could Derrida believe in the notion of ideal performance? Would it need to be controlled by the original creator, the writer, or could performance ever displace extemporization? That must be a fruitlessly speculative question. Derrida's kind of deconstruction, in which writing is finally restored to a greater significance than speech, scarcely applies to the theatre or opera. We can never be sure what the signified is in the theatre, a world of multiple signifiers. 'Deconstructionist' productions are simply called that because they seem to take the original narrative coherence apart and displace the

47

material into surprising and novel contexts, flouting decorum, breaking the naturalistic rules in surrealist fashion. This is not a new theatrical departure, though the justification for it may be fresh. Licence has always been the tool of court-jester and clown, and of the slave in the victorious Roman general's triumph chariot whispering 'Remember that you are mortal'. In ancient Greek dramatic festivals, comedies by Aristophanes had a carnival and dislocating purpose. Rules of decorum that inhibit the tragic imagination, with the comic left unfettered, are an untenable kind of neo-classical theory. Theatre is about disturbing as well as pleasing. Its primary rule is 'anything goes' which can work on the imagination and be tolerated by the public. Theatre, including opera, is a social escape valve for politics and philosophy. The trouble with well-intentioned European subsidy of opera and other arts today is that it can make them the preserve of the privileged, prone to respectability and auto-censorship.

Free will, which in performance means interpretative responsibility, is as necessary to the arts as to life. The author of a work intended for performance invites performers to collaborate. He suggests the path to the work. He may even imagine a preferred outcome. But the inescapable fact about performing arts is that the creator depends on others to finish his creation anew each time it is performed. This is a dynamic relationship. It is also a fertile statement about how culture relates to the human condition. To put it theologically, in the performing arts the original creative artist is like God making the world because of his love and welcome for the other. But if that creation were bound, it could not be a response to love. Speaking eschatologically, only in the final analysis is it possible to force a distinction between the use and abuse of creative freedom. Life means unfettered creation. The creator of a work for performance, whether composer, playwright, librettist or choreographer, knows that vitality requires the risks of creative licence. Performance is living art.

Opera created for the laboratory of performance, for constant re-evaluation, cannot be fixed in interpretation. Every opera can be interpreted many different ways. An essentially experimental collaboration demands compromises between the range of disciplines involved. Performances are frequently frustrating, seldom consummate in every department. But there are many compensations – musical, theatrical, ideological, visual. Opera has traditionally seen rivalries rather than willing committed collaboration. In

Handel's day there were the singers, leading castrati and prima-donnas, with their vanities – a tradition that survives: Callas versus Tebaldi, Scotto versus Ricciarelli, the well advertised (but mythical) estrangement of Pavarotti and Domingo. There is the wounded *amour propre* of conductors too: sticking to the primacy of music, and in some cases leading the pack of reactionaries against the 'usurpation' of 'producers' opera'. Sometimes vocal stars connive at this resistance to 'interpretation'. The audience has its say too. Lucian Pintilie's staging of *Carmen* in 1983 produced a huge postbag to the Welsh National Opera, as did Ruth Berghaus's *Don Giovanni* (also for WNO). Steven Pimlott's unconventional staging of *Don Giovanni* for the little British touring company Opera 80 met equally strong condemnation from part of its regular audience. When the conductor Michael Gielen was in charge of the opera at the Frankfurt Opera, premieres of productions by Hans Neuenfels, Berghaus, Christof Nel and Alfred Kirchner met catcalls and boos. Similar rows re-echo through the 20th-century history of opera in performance. Gustav Mahler and his designer Alfred Roller faced the problem in the Vienna of their day. Wieland Wagner in the 1950s was held by many to have desecrated Bayreuth with his productions of *Parsifal* and, especially, *Die Meistersinger von Nürnberg*. Walter Felsenstein, founder and leading producer of the East Berlin Komische Oper, called Wieland a gifted amateur. Wieland emphasized scenic simplicity and exploited lighting for atmosphere and scene changes, with remarkably impressive standards of acting. His singers attended scrupulously to acting and gesture and had a remarkably sophisticated identification with their roles.

This kind of commitment – as associated with Lee Strasberg's New York method acting school – was new in opera. Similarly Wieland's abstract designs and symbolism broke with the story-book naturalism that was usually the prevailing theatrical convention at Bayreuth. Cosima Wagner during 20 years as festival director at Bayreuth never allowed the *Parsifal* production to be altered. The opera was only released for stage performance outside Bayreuth when it came out of copyright in 1913 – though the New York Metropolitan Opera had already jumped the gun.

Patrice Chéreau's centenary Bayreuth production of *The Ring* in 1976 was widely scorned in the serious press. Twenty-five years earlier the modernist enemy had been Wieland. Now Wieland, who had died prematurely in 1966, was 'the tradition'. The purity and abstraction of his stagings – free from the supposed political agenda of Chéreau, Götz Friedrich, and others influenced by Brecht and Felsenstein – was the golden age. Thanks to Chéreau's *Ring* and other modern stagings, the Met in 1989 went in for a *Ring* staging that 'followed Wagner's stage directions', with trees, a real horse for Brünnhilde, and winged helmets. Ricordi's detailed notes about the staging of the 1881 revision of *Simone Boccanegra* were used for an experiment at the Florence Teatro Communale in 1988. All stage movements scrupulously adhered to Ricordi's record; sets were equally authentic. The result suggested the fallacies in this kind of authenticity.

Pintilie in Cardiff presented *Carmen* as a popular entertainment being toured to a central American guerilla encampment: a round of applause from all on stage greeted the toreador's song – like some old chestnut or favourite hit (as it is for today's public). The audience were invited to see *Carmen* as both an historic cultural artefact and a meaningful contemporary tale. But hundreds of correspondents complained to the company that it wasn't *Carmen* – implying they could tell a real *Carmen* if they saw one. Why change loved and familiar relics?

For the critic, a crucial test of a performance is whether it mobilizes the various drives in the work, whether it is really a window on that living, changing, breathing organism – what is essential in the composer's and librettist's creative impulse. In opera as in legitimate spoken theatre, it is sometimes a mistake, when considering the meaning of a scene, to regard all the words uttered as meant. The fascination and theatrical power of opera lie in the qualification of words by music, and – then – the further qualification of both by the subtle expressive power and acting of the opera-singer. The mixture of conventions is a rich framework for anatomizing human relations.

To hold such a high view of performance and interpretation, regardless of the financial and physical resources that opera needs, is in principle perfectly rational. The elements of opera are not everyday. People do not sing their thoughts and intimate conversations, nor do they fluently project them into passionately coherent musical structures. Wagner's *total art-work* is a minefield of pretension bristling with subliminal interpretative possibilities. The ideal of the definitive interpretation mostly comes from academics and critics whose ideas are fixed and static owing, perhaps, to a formative experience combined with extensive study of – and familiarity with – the text or score. Music lovers hooked on particular recordings also like the idea – victims of the recording industry's claims. Though a concept of an ideal performance may exist (or have existed) inside the composer's mind, that should not govern interpretation; for in the performing arts work cannot be definitive – in opera especially, involving as it does so many different disciplines and imponderables, musical, scenic, verbal, structural, historical, philosophical. The notion of definitive performance is always unhealthy and may destroy interpretative vitality. Performers are engaged on an unending pilgrimage towards the ideal interpretation. But as with every practical aspect of human existence, utopia has to remain a dream.

Opera performances do demand extremely devoted concentration and commitment, precisely because they are not ritualized (however scrupulously rehearsed and repeated) but inspirational. A common old misapprehension, since cinematic effects became so artful, has been to suppose that physically complicated or romantic scenarios invited or expected technical facilities 'unrealizable' in a convincing fashion on the theatrical stage. Operas are often located in an impossible physical situation, their best performers frequently unromantic to behold – which cinema and television have taught the public to find unacceptable. The opera enthusiast disenchanted with staged opera can declare his own perfect interpretation to exist in pristine state in his imagination. Is not the reality of performance always 'unsatisfactory', with singers too fat and unlovely, storms and battles (and imaginary worlds like Valhalla) too much for theatre technology to create naturalistically? Was not Wagner a film director manqué? Does not the epic or psychological realization of today 'distort'? The truth is that the most exquisitely memorable and successful operatic interpretations possess almost intangible and subtle qualities – that their combination of visual, verbal, aural and humane elements are memorable for a mixture of ideas and feelings that relate intimately to the passions that matter most to us in our own lives. The strange reflection of life that opera presents is not so much outside us, as easily taken into our own experience.

Opera can be enjoyed in many dimensions. But to challenge the superiority, despite inevitable risks, of full-scale performance is like preferring Shakespeare on the page because no actors can do full justice to his poetry, characters and situations. Life in the performing arts should be about trying and failing. The notion of the definitive version is only a convenient fiction, an always unattainable standard for performing artists and audiences to dream about – reinforced by the myth of definitive recorded interpretations. Listeners love their favourite versions which have cost good money, and been selected with discernment. Easy to lose the proper distinction between performance and the work itself, that ideal concept to which the creative imagination of the artist was leading. Paradoxically, what is in its combination of elements a very artificial art-form relates more closely than any other art to the realities of feeling, concern and commitment in our normal lives. The dreams that opera offers are strangely intimate – and that is the secret appeal of the art.

4 A repertoire of classics

Peter Stein's 1986 Welsh National Opera staging (at the New Theatre, Cardiff) of *Otello* designed by Lucio Fanti and Moidele Bickel: Jeffrey Lawton as Otello having an epileptic fit in act 3, and Donald Maxwell as Iago. Photograph © Clive Barda.

The focus of this book is firmly on what have seemed to me the most interesting, engaging and often innovative interpretations of fully staged opera during the period from the mid-1970s to the present day. Because I do not mention conductors and singers much, it does not mean I regard the musical and vocal aspects of performance as a side show. Beyond argument the quality of music in an opera is what governs whether it has gained or can acquire classic status, whether it possesses a spirit to challenge interpreters. The greatest operas have music that is as sublime in effect as any pure (non-operatic) music in the canon, even though the structure of operatic music is seldom classically symphonic. Since Wagner it is axiomatic that great opera is great music. The lack of new operas of real musical accomplishment in the last 25 years is a universal failure by composers.

There is no challenge to the received opinion that music has primacy in opera. Even though my burden here is completely theatrical, music was the essential factor, with pride of place, in every staging I describe and explain. Music is where opera gets its persuasive and expressive power. Writers discussing opera in performance almost invariably concentrate on musical and vocal criteria. The history of opera is usually seen as the history of operatic composers and singers, with very occasional acknowledgment of librettists. Few books about opera and music go into technical details about performances and the history of presentation – the cost of promoting opera in the past or the level of profit achieved by impresarios. John Rosselli's *The Opera Industry in Italy from Cimarosa to Verdi* (Cambridge University Press, 1984) and his subsequent *Singers of Italian Opera* (CUP, 1992), are important pioneering exceptions.

In opera the process of theatrical interpretation starts from a musical response, for music is the *fons et origo* of opera, the reason for and means of the composer's creativity. Provided a performance involves singers of real sensitivity and expressive ability, with a conductor who makes the text audible and vital, who can mould the musical sequence and dramatic pace, it is up to the imagination of the audience to 'amend' (the word Shakespeare's

Theseus used in *A Midsummer Night's Dream*) a production's conventionality or lack of dramatic credibility or threadbare visual quality.

Mirella Freni's visit to Covent Garden at the age of 53 in 1988 to portray the youthful Tatyana in the umpteenth revival of Peter Hall's then almost 20-year-old staging of *Eugene Onegin* was magical and fascinating – simply by virtue of the vocal technique and musical art of a veteran performer with still astonishingly fresh gifts. Opera in performance always involves compromises. Almost never is everything right. Maybe Freni could not have taken a comfortable or convincing place in a more believable, naturalistic or even deconstructionist production. In its own way her performance was overwhelmingly persuasive. Design and production are crucial for the theatrical vitality of opera interpretation in our time. But it would be ridiculous to scorn a live performance with Freni's commitment, authenticity and high vocal artistry. Regular opera-goers are used to performances redeemed by the confidence and skill of a principal performer.

Opera productions have never mattered very much to critics in the past. Performance has always been taken for granted. Opera in the theatre is still a matter of conventions blending the sophisticated and the banal, a poor cousin to the legitimate (non-musical) theatre in terms of purely theatrical impact, though a rich cousin in terms of lavishness of scale. The stage was a recognized forum for singing – for the personal charisma of vocal stars. But opera critics were, and still are, usually music-critics, for whom opera is above all about musical expertise – and staging must always be problematical compared with the unchanging musical definition. Operatic performances were singer-led, hence the defective theatricality had to be unremediable. That was just how opera was.

Why has opera production grown up, and acquired such importance and controversy in the course of the 20th century? One explanation is the lack of a continuing and constant series of new entries to the repertoire. Another is the way Modernism has affected the creation of serious music, limiting the supply of new operas compared to the fertile output of 19th-century opera composers. Another is the changed status of contemporary art. The altered musical language of serious composers has broken the ongoing relationship between great singers and respected composers. There is no longer an operatic constituency eager for new work, or a shared language of music and drama in which composers can readily flourish and acquire fluency. Culture implies a contract between creators, interpreters, and an appreciative public. In opera, both practitioners and audience are now at sea. Retrenchment in the repertoire during the 20th century has left great singers scared even of established modern classics. Since the late 1970s it is the actual productions that have had the novelty value and grabbed the headlines. Singing no longer predominates.

The development of the long-playing record and video recording have changed the terms of trade too, preserving performances partially, and satisfying a public taste that is also scared of modernist adventure. There may even have been a decline in vocal standards, with faster, more stressful careers for singers in the aeroplane age. Recordings may have made the public more critical of the average achievement. The naturalism of the cinema has no doubt altered the way the public suspends disbelief, and made fat sopranos and static artificial styles of operatic acting unacceptable. Since the Second World War the role of the producer has continued to enlarge. (Producer is what in Britain used to be called stage manager. Producers take overall artistic control and develop the acting and stage movement, performing the task of the 'director' in non-musical theatre. In the United States the title is stage director; producer means impresario, manager or administrator. In France the term is *metteur en scène;* Germans use the French word *Regisseur* – though *Regie* meaning direction, and *Inszenierung* meaning production are more usual.)

Wieland Wagner's New Bayreuth – reinterpreting Wagner's operas and stripping them of any possible Nazi associations – led towards a more general recognition that staged performance required contextualization and could not be dictated for all time by composers in their stage directions. Design and acting in opera as elsewhere in the theatre must always be the unfettered imaginative responsibility of the interpreters. Our new seriousness about staging has not made opera performances less pleasurable or entertaining. Opera still exploits the art of song in dramatic context. The orchestra role is still lyrical accompaniment that can paint the physical and psychological circumstances of the characters. The other side of the equation – involving musicians, staging and lighting technicians, scene painters, wigmakers, dressmakers, and many others – is always theatrical impact and vitality. The difference these days is the recognition that it may all also be an intellectual and philosophical adventure. While opera records are to be enjoyed on a purely musical level, opera in the theatre is always the pursuit of meaning in a broader sense than the purely literary. How the audience apprehends the singers' words is only part of their response.

Yet musical qualification of text is the crux, in opera as in song. Understanding the libretto as just words without music is oblique and off-centre. Theatre is about communication between people on stage, subtly modulated in its dramatic and social meaning, and in its implications, by acting and stage context. But in the theatre words do not simply mean what they say. An opera text has both the ambiguity it would naturally possess in the legitimate theatre, and also the additional complication that, when text is sung, the music carrying the singer also itself modulates the meaning and the intention. Music is what makes opera matter, by both characterization and the audience's response. Music contextualizes the events and words, lends perspective and dynamic to the process. Music is the engine.

This is why the agenda of minimalist composers like Gavin Bryars, Michael Nyman, Philip Glass and John Adams, who in the 1980s successfully broke the taboo against lyrical outpouring and catchiness in so-called serious music, is so unfortunate for opera, where the whole tradition – from Monteverdi and the earliest recitative operas – was to use music to sharpen and heighten the reception of text. Minimalists provide what sounds attractive, accessible and welcome – for an audience that broadly rejects Modernism and prefers traditional tunefulness. But the melodies which the minimalists 'reconstruct' are never dramatically pointed enough.

The new technology of surtitles has certainly made opera more accessible. It also has confirmed the internationalization of the art, dubiously detaching sophisticated dramas from the language culture where they originated. Internationalization, which goes with a snobbish rejection of vernacular adaptation and naturalization of foreign operas, is another late trend that helps explain the disappearance of new operatic works in the popular repertoire. In the 19th century, new nation states were wanting to create their own national operatic culture. They no longer try. Yet a language-based art-form like opera cannot really be international, however non-national music may be. The music is the source of the misapprehension. Since music is the crucial factor in opera, the delusion has grown that the verbal language of an opera is somehow less central – whereas really it is the vital cultural anchor.

Modernism was an international phenomenon, transcending boundaries, needing a world constituency to obtain sufficient followers, depending on generalized and utopian ruling-class assumptions or a global village mentality. History shows that viable new operas must be national and local. Even a specialized mass audience, as opera has, is rooted in a specific language culture – however much the media, dominated by American cinema and English-language publications, may imply that fashion and culture are internationally homogenized. What built the original repertoire was not internationalization, though the colonization of Europe by Italian *opera seria* in the 18th century may provide a useful lesson about the future of opera in the 21st century.

The best operatic interpretations today are all founded on dramaturgical insight and exploit the sophisticated facilities of the modern stage. Some argue that operas from earlier ages do not need interventionist interpretations. The composer putting notes on paper has always been thinking of theatrical realization. Live performance is the *raison d'être* of opera, the crucible where it earns the status of *Gesamtkunstwerk*, becoming what it is meant to be.

Performance is difficult to pin down in words. Essentially ephemeral, it is aimed at an audience's subjective response. Styles of performance go out of fashion as easily as clothes. One forgets performances. One retains piecemeal impressions of the works being performed, rather than specific interpretations. Few can evoke in detail how performances years earlier made their effect. Video recordings help reinforce fragile memories of long past performances, but videos are not a reliable guide to what happened on stage. Lighting and atmosphere are often vastly altered for tele-recording. The television director interposes himself and his taste and attention, selecting what the audience at home will actually see. Videos narrow the attention range of the viewer to a small part of the stage, concentrate on the small action, neglect reactions, edit out most of the imaginative stimuli that would have been working in the opera-house. In the live experience eye and mind take in and respond to everything, creating a far profounder, more intriguing happening in the realm of the imagination. The live audience edits for itself, discovers its own emotional, metaphorical and philosophical overlaps and connections.

Academic opera studies stick to notes on the page, which make drama and literature departments feel ill-equipped to enter into argument. But what may be most significant and meaningful in a performance is not obvious in musical notation – or in text. It is hard or impossible to read the combination of drama and music on the page with a kind of literary critical sense. Operatic meaning is like a volatile oil, released to full apprehension only in the fraught, turbulent, risk-laden process of live theatrical realization, where misconceptions are rife.

Yet of all theatrical arts, opera most needs to be discussed in terms of its live realization without which analyses of meaning and method are often faulty. What on the page precisely did Mozart and Da Ponte mean by *Così fan tutte* (that sublime exercise in marital psychotherapy)? The emotional intentions and attitudes of the characters remain mysterious until plumbed in performance. Even then the outcome and truth about the relationships should be ambiguous. Do the lovers revert to their first choices for spouse, or accept that their infidelity has revealed the real destiny of their feelings? Theatrical truth is provisional, not absolute. Mozart's 'comedy' has a potentially tragic aroma, more subtly uncomfortable and painful than any other theatrical experiment in flirtatious liaison. *Così*, like the nature of human passion (love, commitment, emotional security) which is its topic, changes in the event, can only be diagnosed in performance, its ambivalence impenetrable. Mozart caught the quicksilver fickleness of human emotions in a Shakespearian way. Everybody has mixed feelings about the other people they know and love. For the century after Mozart's death, the emotional truthfulness of *Così* was held to be shockingly scandalous rather than painful and accurate. Its ambiguities and truth-telling did not appeal to a Victorian moral sensibility.

There has now been a sufficient body of operatic productions in the Anglo-Saxon and European operatic worlds to earn recognition for opera as *of* the theatre – rather than just needing to be *in* a theatre for performance of its unsatisfactory mixture of genres. The histories of opera and legitimate theatre since Shakespeare and Monteverdi overlap. Originally of course the music of opera was only there to serve the poetry (very much, no doubt, as in the classical world of Greece and Rome). But the opulence of the experience, the presence of the music (as in London theatre of the mid-1890s), reduced the operatic agenda to mere entertainment, instead of being what the ancient world had always known as a forum of society's profoundest dreams and fears. The single constant in all the controversies about opera production of the last two decades has been the producer's wish to relate the works being staged to contemporary circumstances and passions. And no music-critic has yet followed Jan Kott with an opera book called *Monteverdi Our Contemporary*.

When all art was contemporary, when people and their tastes were firmly rooted in their own time, there was no need for a kind of meta-criticism to help people consume the great works of the past, or performers adapt to the present-day works which originally had different functions and resonances. Interpretation as a contemporary account, a current truth, is the central issue in all the rows about 'correctness' in the presentation of opera. This problem of different messages, different meanings, is not confined to opera. Great classics in all branches of the arts are repeatedly being repackaged for a consumerist world that is increasingly and neurotically self-obsessed. In all the performing arts, but especially in opera, the diet is heavily made up of old masterpieces: more and more people, thanks to recordings, television and an increasing number of live performances, enjoy and learn from operas that were originally the preserve of the few. What in the straight theatre used to be called 'revival' is in opera the norm. Performers of text-based performing arts (directors and designers conceptualizing the presentation) almost always defamiliarize the familiar, if their audiences are to experience the freshness and inspiration that familiarity obscures.

Taking a rational view of interpretation from a utilitarian point of view, there are no clear boundaries or narrow perimeters in the theatre governing how a piece should be performed. Audiences and performers do not distinguish properly between the work and its interpretations. Controversies about staging spring from muddling up the opera on the page – as completed (more or less) by composer and librettist, sometimes the same person – and its interpretation, as realized and qualified in all sorts of ways in the opera-house.

The spread of approaches detailed in this book, which is a critical mirror of past performance, shows this to be true. It would be surprising if the range of works in the operatic pantheon (or repertoire library), a remarkable corpus of classic works, could be staged truthfully without exploring all the resources of theatre and the current imagination. What factors have governed changes of style and method in the dramaturgy and composition of the works we care about? How do we know which operas are worthwhile? What are the limits of 'interpretation'? Are there any boundaries beyond which interpreters should not go? Why do public and critics sometimes feel that updating, dislocation and so-called 'deconstruction' have destroyed or handicapped the classic works they think they know so well? Can a modern theory of operatic performance contend with a fundamentalist-type challenge to the truth and authenticity of modern interpretation – the way criticisms of modern theological understandings are made by religious fundamentalists?

In 1967 Pierre Boulez, avant-garde composer and conductor, told the readers of *Der Spiegel*, 'Sprengt di Opern Häuser in die Luft!' (Blow up the opera-houses!): actually, theatres and opera-houses burn down of their own accord readily enough, unprompted by intellectuals, even these days. But Boulez's injunction is still remembered, and his reasons. In the twilight of the 20th century, opera-houses, their repertoires, and their audiences remain just as obsolete as they were when Boulez pronounced. Opera seems like a flatulent 19th-century escapist taste for luxury. It is easily criticized as overblown, unintellectual, lacking in modern artistic sensibility or relevance, thoroughly alien to 'the music of the future' (Wagner's utopian concept).

In fact, for Boulez, Wagner was never anti-modern. It was not inconsistent for him to conduct *Parsifal* at Bayreuth in 1966, in the purified classic staging by Wieland Wagner that was the essence of the New (post-1951) Bayreuth aesthetic. Boulez's contemporary Stockhausen shortly embarked on an operatic project of megalomaniac proportions – an autobiographical seven-day sequence of operas, still unfinished. Opera still *is not* a contemporary art. Its survival *is* rooted in nostalgia. We who believe in opera wonder if it will still be being performed at the end of the 21st century. The typical art of the 20th century is the cinema: opera was of the 19th century.

In 1990 when the English National Opera programmed a '20 +' season of works written in the 20th century ('plus Mozart' for a little commercial insurance), there was much institutional self-congratulation – though the 'modern' opera repertoire to be tackled at the London Coliseum included Puccini's *Tosca* as well as Berg's *Wozzeck*. The season was not specially unpopular. Average attendances (during an economic recession) dropped from 76 per cent to 72 per cent.

Before the First World War, opera impresarios built their programmes predominantly on works that were novelties for audiences. Dusty revivals of operas popular 100 or even 50 years earlier, except a few perennial classics, were the exception. Today most brand new opera shocks or bores. Despite the appeal of the 'new simplicity' of Philip Glass, John Adams and John Corigliano – who in the 1980s were launching opera premieres to instant, comparative popularity – the repertoire continues to be recycled, not renewed or replaced. An opera critic sees the same few works repeated over and over, in different interpretations. That is very unlike the diet of theatre and film critics.

Until the invention of recording technology, opera did not exist outside the opera-house, though there were vocal scores sold and used by amateurs with orchestral reductions for one or two pianos. The natural state of opera is as a community witness. With its profound celebratory character, presenting social crises through dramatic music, opera originated in the Italian attempt to revive or re-create something like the great religious festivals which saw the birth of classical Greek theatre. Music in the theatre is as old as the theatre. Music to accompany religious rites, intensifying the meaning of words, has always been part of human experience. Away from church ritual there has always been lyrical song. The aristocratic founding operatic experiments in Florence and Mantua between 1590 and 1610 were a conscious 'neo-classical revival', seeking the style and technique that belonged to the poetic tragedies of Aeschylus, Sophocles and Euripides. The potent words of that lost classical theatre, the core of a 'classical education' for generations, carried implications of chanting and music – even if no notation then seemed detectable. Song and dance had been integral parts of those neo-religious ancient Greek festivals – blended as in the rituals of the Catholic Church. Opera somehow seems to be, but is not, more recent than the spoken theatre of the Renaissance.

The first operas in Florence by Caccini, Monteverdi and Peri at the turn of the 17th century were cousins of the spoken drama being created in Spain, Italy, France, Germany and England around the same time. The poet, the librettist, came first in most of the experiments – though the 20th-century rediscoverers of these works, looking backwards through history beyond the melodic feasts of Mozart and Handel, and often belonging in a different language culture from Italian, cannot perceive the relative supremacy of the words. Umberto Eco made a medieval intellectual thriller about the disappearance in the Dark Ages of what

Aristotle had written on comedy. But perhaps comedy, at the heart of existence as Dante implied, needed Aristotle's thoughts less than tragedy. The Western Church maintained a long tradition of interpretative preaching, sometimes with overt dramatization of the faith stories. Secular theatre in the Renaissance, whether popular or courtly, reflected everyday life at various levels of society. The new taste for theatre was whetted by current political and religious topics, a thoroughly contemporary agenda – entertainment as art.

Opera, though a neo-classical experiment, was a different form, new in method and potential. Opera like spoken drama drew vitality and popularity from novelty value – in its unprecedented mixture of means, and in its new words, new music, new dynamic of performance. Spoken words, though of their era, were less subject to changing tastes than music: they could be published and read on the page by readers not yet given to novels. Many playwrights rapidly entered a classic pantheon: Shakespeare, Tirso, Racine, Molière, Goldoni, Sheridan, Goethe, Schiller, Ibsen, Strindberg, Wedekind, Chekhov, Brecht, Horvath. The modern and experimental Büchner was an exception proving the rule, awaiting rediscovery decades after his early demise, inviting the dramatic skill of Alban Berg.

But opera until the 19th century was a different story. No composer survived the chill of fashion before Gluck's *Orfeo ed Euridice* (1762). Mozart's *Idomeneo* was forgotten after his death. He was excoriated for *Così fan tutte*. Opera was written for the present, using the latest musical language, without much sense of a future artistic destiny. Its geniuses had to prepare their own theoretical platform. Sometimes their musical language was ready to hand, but also, from earliest times, opera was dominated by 'idealism'. Almost every great opera composer proved to have a reform agenda - overt or implicit. The neo-classical aesthetic-cum-religious revivalism of Monteverdi and his pioneering contemporaries gave way to other philosophies of decorum. Propagandists (often composers) claimed to be restoring what had been distorted or mislaid in the present condition of the operatic art. Monteverdi, with *Orfeo*, *The Return of Ulysses* and *The Coronation of Poppea*, discovered a new artistic objective, creating and exploiting unprecedented vocal conventions of declamation with expressive orchestral interludes all based on an imaginary historical model. Opera still invites reform. The most creative operatic minds today approach the task with a self-conscious agenda of innovation. Operatic fashion through history may be a desire for novelty, new formulas displacing old. Many composers admit to a reform agenda.

Handel attempted to follow fashion in opera and give his public what they seemed to want – operating almost commercially and running into financial disaster. He may seem an exception, fulfilling his profoundest operatic potential in oratorios. But the oratorio itself, as transformed by Handel, is part of the reform tendency. Cheap-to-mount Covent Garden concerts with operatic structure, the oratorios' moral and improving character (more improving than magic or semi-historical fables) were commercially viable and popular because of their serious mythological worlds. Sententiousness was to the taste of the age. The operatic chorus, as exploited by the creators of 19th-century operatic epics, owed more to Handel's oratorios than to experiment on the operatic stage as such – where a chorus could be a problematic extra extravagance.

In classical Greek theatre the chorus formed a social context – representing the populace, celebrating and expressing the popular will. In opera the chorus often fulfils a political role, registers a political landscape. But though the polyphonic madrigal had a representative purpose in the experiments of Marenzio and Cavalieri (the *Intermedii* for the wedding of Ferdinando de' Medici and Isabella of Lorraine in Florence in 1589), the central expressive tool for opera has always been the solo melodic line revealing heroic character in dramatic action – even when solos interrupt and delay the resolution.

In opera the reform instinct appeared with Monteverdi, and recurred with Metastasio (the librettist), Handel, Gluck, Mozart, Beethoven, Weber, Bellini, Verdi, Wagner, Smetana, Puccini, Janáček, Richard Strauss, Berg. Today we have reached the end of the line. No composer is renewing the repertoire. Thanks to the lack of a serious lyrical capacity in avant-garde musical language, every modern opera must be a revolutionary creative initiative from the ground up. There are no 'givens' in today's serious music, and comparatively few successes, though the consciousness of distant cultural horizons, of a challenge to be scaled, is old. Opera composers, the theoreticians of reform, always know more about the art than their audience does. Just as there are no rules of decorum, so the origin of opera composers' language is undetectable.

Theoretical baggage did not apply purely to composition. Music has always been only one element in an artistic experience that needs to be live to be palpable. The elements of performance, the singing above all, have always been crucial. The specific voices, instruments, scene, lighting, and sense of reality or magic reverie have always made radical differences to the audience's receptiveness. It is nothing new, either, for aspects of operatic performance to be controversial. In the 17th century epic sea battles and castrati caused riots and drew pointed comment.

The great castrato stars, the first masters of *bel canto*, were perceived, not surprisingly, as lacking naturalness: to Gluck the expressive theatre of Garrick was an antidote. A century later, when Wagner's preference for representational scenery in his mythical narratives seemed inescapably indicative, Adolphe Appia and Edward Gordon Craig proposed a new theoretical way. For Cherubini a neo-classical revivalism was the keynote to performance of his operas in Napoleonic France. *Verismo* composers were pioneers of cinematic realism. Weill counted on satirical expressionism. In the USA, even the would-be sincere acting of the Method filtered into opera. As a rule production methods and style have been as prone to fashion as music itself: the new work and its presentation were seen as elements in an aesthetically coherent continuum.

The repertoire of operatic achievement has steadily expanded, even though it has often been preserved in libraries only haphazardly. The pantheon of operatic masterpieces is crowded. Gluck, Mozart, Beethoven, even Weber, certainly above all Wagner, Puccini and Berg all produced works that – despite their seemingly inevitable quality now – were responses to reforming agenda. As well as concepts of structural and aesthetic form there was a sense of ideological purpose. Even Puccini, greatest of all operatic entertainers whose masterpieces remain popular hits a century later, had an ideological sub-text.

Gluck wanted to establish new emotional realism, a credible sense of tragedy. His *Orfeo ed Euridice* was a proclaimed 'Reform' opera. At the prompting of his new librettist, Calzabigi, Gluck was in revolt against Metastasio after 20 years loyal service to the Italian poet, the most famous and influential librettist ever. Gluck promoted 'beautiful simplicity' and dramatic aptness. The castrato's desire to show off was firmly in second place once Gluck's new priority had been established – tragic credibility with the audience. His programme of reform continued for the rest of a long operatic career in which what mattered above all was genuine sentiment: *opera seria*, the form Metastasio controlled and dominated, was about to be transformed.

Mozart continued this revolution, but advancing towards comic ambivalence and social conflict. With his treatment of the female psyche, Mozart was opera's founding feminist, making propaganda for true sexual equality. No doubt an alteration of the image of womanhood in opera was inevitable once the female soprano voice took centre stage. Beethoven's *Fidelio* moved into openly revolutionary territory. Verdi and Wagner without politics would be inconceivable. Shakespeare's frequent theme of a ruler's responsibility to the ruled had its most thorough exploration in the masterworks of 19th-century Italian and German opera, boosted by the dramatic power of music. The true nature of the 'social contract' was never far from Wagner's mind.

The history of European music since Mozart is the history of a growing operatic ascendancy. Opera has never been seen as pure music (purity being freedom from pollution by the verbal), but it became with Wagner and later Berg the primary forum for musical innovation. This reflected its power with the public, its ability to engage with humanistic ideas through narrative qualified by music which could stir all classes and conditions. A successful opera composer does not have to be a great composer, but most composers of distinction have embraced the challenge of opera which became, simply, the most *progressive* musical form, and for long remained the medium where musical achievement seemed most complex and avant garde. When Schoenberg concluded the art of composition needed a revolution in method, he was driven by the apparently unsurpassable harmonic idiom and formal accomplishments of Wagner in *The Ring* and *Parsifal*.

But Schoenberg's theories of tonal equality and note rows turned opera into a problem form – an art associated with the harmonic excesses of florid romanticism. Thereafter in the 20th century a medium which had emphasized novelty, and pursued a reform agenda, was bypassed by innovators, and, because the revolution destroyed the musical language itself, opera became an artistic backwater. The most important quality of dodecaphony was its abandonment of rhetorical line and poetic analogy, its reinstatement of polyphony as a prevailing technical device. Both factors are intrinsically unoperatic. Musical qualification of an understandable sentence is awkward to achieve in the various personal musical languages found now. Definition of character is equally elusive. Yet opera still retains the advantage over spoken drama of presenting conflict and debate simultaneously and rapidly. Meanwhile popular operatic taste has stubbornly resisted the change in musical language, preferring the simple diatonic diction of romanticism. The repertoire has stopped growing and atrophied, become old-fashioned, outdated. Until the 20th century and the internationalism of culture reflected in new technology and Modernism, there was never any question that opera would stand up – if at all – in the language of the people where it was performed, its host nation. The French never succumbed to the prevailing European fashion for Italian-language opera during the 18th century. But though there had been episodes of vernacular opera around Europe since the 17th century it was the identification of *opera seria* with the *ancien régime* that turned the attention of the 19th-century middle classes – the theatrical and operatic patrons in lands stirring with a new sense of nationalism – to opera in their own tongue. The importation of Handel and his Italian operas was a craze in early Hanoverian England, a country presided over by imported German-speaking monarchs, and the exception that proved the rule. In fact it was Handel's English oratorios which really defined his role in English and European culture: his Italian operas were entirely forgotten. Italian was seen as the language of *opera seria* right up to the early classical era of Haydn, but Mozart allowed and expected his *Figaro* to be put into German when it was to be performed in German-speaking lands. The two most unpredictable monuments of 20th-century opera, the works of Janáček and Britten, are wholly based in their respective language cultures reflecting new operatic circumstances in Britain and Bohemia, the founding of a corpus of local opera, with sufficient naturalized and vernacular work. Yet they sit alongside opera in the predominant 'imperial' language – in Prague there was a German opera-house.

The public has continued to prefer familiar music with accessible rhetoric and stirring poetry. Neo-classicism and other old recipes in the 1960s made way for the self-conscious authentic or historicist movement - the early music business. The historical operatic repertoire began to open up. To Gluck were added first Handel and then Monteverdi and Cavalli, with Hasse, Rameau, Lully, Cimarosa close behind, as well as neglected works by composers who had never vanished into obscurity. The operatic perspective since 1914 has changed very substantially. At the start of the 20th century, most operas came from Italy, France and Germany. In France and England before the television age, opera was an expensive taste – metropolitan fare not too often encountered in the provinces. After Auber's genius faded, the operettas of Offenbach in France drew a wider audience and created an appetite (later to be satisfied by Lecocq, Messager and Audran) that lasted a hundred years, but has now withered because of internationalization and Liebermann's sacking of the French salaried establishment of singers at the Palais Garnier. In England the taste for simple ballad operas established by Gay survived into the early Victorian era – revived by the librettist of Weber's *Oberon*, J. R. Planché, with his *Olympic Revels* for Madame Vestris – and had an autumnal glow with Balfe's *Bohemian Girl*. Grand opera was always eclectic, found occasionally on the circuit of touring theatres that were the core of the theatrical industry. Gilbert & Sullivan's Savoy operettas, so skilful, witty and popular (earning their creators great riches), remained utterly *sui generis* – succeeded, though not replaced, by West End and Broadway musicals.

In Italy, partly because music and musicians served the tide of resurgent nationalism fervently, opera after the Napoleonic upheavals continued as a demotic art – though one consequence of national unification was a determined rebellion by the new bourgeois MPs in the all Italian parliament against the continuation of operatic subsidies inherited from the former despotic kingdoms and duchies of the peninsula. Yet the famous scene in Visconti's classic film *Senso* (1954), where the Fenice opera-house in Venice witnesses a demonstration against Austrian rule, accurately illustrates the link between opera and Italian nationalism. Verdi, whose name spelt a nationalist statement – Vittorio Emmanuele, Rè d'Italia – was MP for his home region of San Donnino in the newly formed all-Italian parliament at Turin from 1861 to 1865, though his political influence was more effectively mobilized through his controversial and often censored choice of opera plots. In the time of Verdi, and even beyond the age of *Verismo*, opera in Italy was promoted by impresarios as a risky if sometimes profitable business: both Verdi and Puccini were kept on retainers by the publisher Ricordi for some years before their success generated much income. Italian opera depended less on aristocratic or royal largesse to secure seasons and provide commissions for new work and new productions – though even in Italy this rare illusion of financial viability was really a complex web of royal or municipal subsidy, upper-class patronage and ticket-sales. In Italy the opera-house, like the medieval cathedral and parish-church, remained for most of the 19th century a centre of social life and business activity, a marriage bureau and gambling hive, more than a space for spiritual stimulation and diversion. You could and often would go to the opera-house without entering the auditorium. Ever since the first operas made their appearance in the 1590s and 1600s as antiquarian experiments at the Florentine court, composition and performance depended as much on wealthy sponsorship or state subvention as on entrepreneurial impresarios and ticket-sales.

France was close behind Italy in developing a native operatic repertoire, thanks to that successful Italian migrant, Lully. But from the age of the Roi Soleil on, French opera was predominantly an act of state – which in the age of François Mitterrand's Bastille it remained. What started as a flashy divertissement for the royal court was never a common taste – except as *opérette*. After the revolution it was a hobby for the Jockey Club, and a social opportunity for the professional bourgeoisie. A genuinely national school of French opera did not achieve universal recognition until the successes of Gounod's *Faust* and Bizet's *Carmen* 150 years after Rameau made French opera a patriotic phenomenon. The shape and scale of the 19th-century Paris Opéra (the Palais Garnier), its limited capacity in the stalls, its comparative intimacy, was indicative. Garnier, an outsider, won Napoleon III's competition with a design reflecting the *gloire* of the Deuxième Empire – though his theatre, with its pivotal position on Haussmann's new Paris street-plan, was not opened until 1875 and the Third Republic.

Opera in France remains a political issue, which explains the power exercised by trade union *syndicats* at the Paris Opéra with their long-established work agreements, and the vast extent of French taxpayers' generosity to the opera. When Rolf Liebermann was imported by President Pompidou in 1971 to reform standards, the dominant factor was international prestige: the Paris Opéra, which had worked mainly in French, was supposed to compete with Covent Garden and Vienna. The scandals and extravagances of the saga of Mitterrand's creation of the Bastille opera continued a long French tradition. The Opéra Bastille, an opera-theatre dedicated in theory to opera for the workers (on the site of the notorious *ancien régime* prison), was a bizarre monument for the bicentenary of the French Revolution. It was typically wrong-headed to offer the task of running it first to an elitist career musician (Daniel Barenboim) with no commitment to vernacular opera or egalitarian theatre, and then to a master-manipulator from the ephemeral world of haute couture (Pierre Bergé) with small sympathy for popular taste. Mitterrand spent £300 million on the 'most German opera-house ever constructed'. The building is flawed in its acoustics and unfinished, its Salle Modulable (adaptable space) a concrete shell. Ticket prices are too dear for artisans from the poor suburbs nearby for whom a vernacular Volksoper-style repertoire might have been attractive. The Bastille does not use its extravagant stage technology to run as a repertoire house. It remains a challenging conundrum for its director, Hugues Gall – a professional at last, capable of addressing the problem of its vast frigid auditorium.

In Germany, where the Holy Roman Empire left many capital cities and aristocratic or episcopal fiefs, operatic culture was since the 17th century, when Schütz learnt from Monteverdi, always widespread. Opera was not as popular during the 19th century as in Italy, but most royal and ducal courts enjoyed opera-houses. Richard Wagner hoped perfectly reasonably for patronage from mad Ludwig II of Bavaria. The classics of German *Singspiel* (Weber, Marschner, Nicolai continuing the tradition established in the 18th century by Hiller and later taken up by Mozart) were popular and allied to an unpretentious and unsophisticated operetta taste that by the *fin de siècle* was provided with Leo Fall's *Dollarprinzessin* and *Die geschiedene Frau* (blight of young Anton von Webern's life, making his way as a repertoire conductor). In Iberia good theatres flourished in Lisbon, Barcelona, Oporto and Madrid and there was a tradition of *zarzuela*. In the USA, as the 19th century wore on, there were operatic audiences in New York and San Francisco and touring.

But opera was by nature rare and uncommon, compared to the theatrical culture of boulevard or music-hall. Opera did not yet have to face the competition of cinema and television, nor could an operatic impresario of the naughty 1890s have foreseen the way serious composers began to turn their backs on the public from the First World War on, with modern art becoming more arcane as the technology of mass reproduction and dissemination grew ever more sophisticated in the democratic modern age.

71

Schoenberg's reform of musical language was extremely disruptive. Since character and narrative were traditionally in opera both focused through memorable melody, unmelodious music was bound to forfeit the audience. Schoenberg's new kind of opera, with different structure and tempo, in practice alienated audiences from composers and poisoned the well of lyrical expressiveness. The subject matter of new operas grew recherché too. In opera, characters depend on melodic lines to become alive, which means a diatonic system of home keys and modulations, or some equivalent process of resolution. Instead, new opera has tended to a neurotic abandoned free-style that matched psychologically fraught situations, tales of despair and disaster, but served comic or everyday social events poorly. Stories in 20th-century operas have seemed as alienating and unappetizing as their music. Other more amiable modern traditions remained unexplored. A public faced with the brutalities of 20th-century life reflected in modern art preferred to escape to the remoter past.

A vocal line could not efficiently communicate to ordinary listeners, or even relate to language, if it was too jaggedly instrumental in lay-out. Opera-singers stuck to the familiar and undemanding, concentrating on *Verismo* war-horses or Mozart and Rossini. The opera diet came to be dominated by unquestionable and recognized masterpieces. But if the raw material of new opera has been in short supply, there has been a vast extension in accessibility, familiarity and popularity for opera – previously caviare to the general. The opera enthusiast used to need pianistic skill (at best in competent duet) to realize scores unheard in the local opera-house rep. The 20th century has been the age of recorded music, cinema, television, radio. Puccini's success as operatic composer, melodist and orchestrator, was more widely appreciated right up to the present time than any previous opera composer's. Think of World Cup Football and *'Nessun dorma'*. No wonder Puccini's pre-eminence seems everlasting despite attacks on him by Professor Joseph Kerman and W. H. Auden.

Technology has made the 20th century an era of international art tourism, of browsing through all ages and civilizations, of cultural self-consciousness and promiscuous consumerism. The past is a contemporary resource, and a burden for present-day creators. Communication has standardized the cultural diet. The pantheon of artistic achievement is no longer remote and arcane, but open for all. Everybody, according to Andy Warhol, could be a star for 15 minutes. Art is now for all. An age of frenzied socio-logical and scientific change has needed to feel its roots and foundations wherever it could. Some 20th-century operas are growing popular as the public gradually comes to terms with the language of modern music. Janáček (whose women are as much social victims as Britten's men) and Prokofiev (whose Slav operatic taste for fairy-tale fantasy is less magical and escapist than Rimsky's, more ideologically insecure and intriguing) no longer frighten the mass audience, though they are still emotionally and intellectually challenging. Public taste adjusts.

What may seem the distracting manipulation of imagery and references in modern operatic productions is no more 'difficult' to 'read' than the associations and 'montage' juxtapositions of television and poster advertising campaigns. The musical language of the 20th century is wonderfully varied. A lot of it may not be as singer-friendly as Bellini and Donizetti once were. But recordings of folk-singing (as the taste for 'world music' has demonstrated) prove there really is not just one uniformly convenient expressive vocal language. Historical awareness has raised questions about the idea of progress in performing techniques and instrumental technologies, as well as in the rules of composition. If different styles of singing are appropriate for the realization of different periods of song, assumptions about operatic aesthetics are equally unsettled. What is a beautiful sound in one age may not beguile the next. Experiment has its place. The search for 'period authenticity' and the search for contemporary meaning in familiar operatic works are related. Though the last 25 years have seen almost no accretions to the familiar repertoire, the 20th-century operatic pantheon is crowded with great names: Puccini, Debussy, Ravel, Richard Strauss, Janáček, Berg, Britten, Weill, Prokofiev, Shostakovich, Stravinsky, Poulenc, Gershwin, Bartók, Schoenberg, as well as lesser talents including Pfitzner, Busoni, Samuel Barber, Falla, Roberto Gerhard, Tippett, Menotti, Henze, Goehr, Nicholas Maw, Oliver Knussen, Schreker, Copland, Hindemith, Dallapiccola, Berio, Birtwistle, Bernstein, Zimmermann, Maxwell Davies, Carlisle Floyd, John Adams, Nigel Osborne, Richard Rodney Bennett, Judith Weir, Stockhausen, Gerald Barry, Wolfgang Rihm – nobody as fertile as Verdi, but many composers who have created a distinctive and original handful of operas.

The revolution in theatrical interpretation of recent decades has shown what a rich stimulus to the imagination opera can be. In the

English-speaking world opera has never been more popular. In the USA, there are few full-time opera companies outside New York's two (the Met and City Opera), but extended seasons in Houston, Los Angeles, San Francisco, Chicago and Seattle. Opera America, the umbrella for all the opera companies, lists 30 opera seasons each year. An Opera America survey has shown that in the USA attendance at its companies rose 35 per cent between 1982 and 1992. About 22 million saw opera on television or videotape or heard it on the radio. In Britain there are now six permanent companies, and various small-scale touring affairs. Australia has operas in Sydney, Melbourne and Adelaide, Canada in Toronto and Vancouver. Opera is far better subsidized in Germany (with its 86 companies), in France and in Italy – though the future for the latter is uncertain. Yet the transformation in the opera worlds of the USA, Britain, Canada and Australia is the biggest change of modern times – symbolized by the familiar image of Jörn Utzon's Sydney Opera House (an architectural monument and definitely not an ideal opera theatre).

The English-speaking world has only a small native internationally recognized operatic repertoire, nothing like Shakespeare. But for English-speaking audiences opera is newsworthy: producers' licence as controversial as any current artistic question. The demand for talented singers, the range of permanent jobs, the chance for freelance careers, all have enormously increased. This is a breakthrough. For the English-speaking public, in spite of various early 18th-century efforts at vernacular forms, opera remained the imported 'exotic and irrational entertainment' of Dr Johnson's notorious phrase. This popularization in the USA and Great Britain has come about gradually. Sometimes stars from Italian opera have caught the English-speaking public's imagination. Caruso, with his talent as a cartoonist, was followed by Tauber, Gigli and Björling into the spotlight of a predominantly Anglo-American recording industry. Pavarotti and Domingo have exploited television chat-shows to become as famous as film-stars.

In the English-speaking world opera has become popular without a native repertoire to help – as in France, Germany or Italy – thanks to the enthusiasm of a few advocates, putting classic operatic masterpieces into English and selling them cheap for the benefit of ordinary folk. Lilian Baylis at the Old Vic and Sadler's Wells could not have done it with just Vaughan Williams's *Hugh the Drover* and *The Poisoned Kiss*, or Delius's *Village Romeo and*

Juliet. Unlike Czechoslovakia, where a fully fledged operatic tradition grew up in the mid-19th century, England had almost no distinguished native opera. Puccini's *La fanciulla del West* was premiered in New York, but as unlikely to start a native American tradition as Weber's *Oberon* was to do the same for England. Since opening in 1883, up to the present time, the Met had commissioned and premiered many works, and tried to give a chance to American works. But of the 26 tackled, few became (like Puccini's *La fanciulla del West* and *Il trittico*) regular repertoire pieces. It was the genius of Britten grafted on to Henry Purcell that made the crucial difference. A genuine and distinguished native English tradition after 1945 became a reality. English translation of classics helped a composer with an absolutely individual style and a highly unusual political and philosophical agenda to create a characteristically English diction for opera. Michael Tippett's *Midsummer Marriage* expanded this new native repertoire with terpsichorean abandon. Britten's *Peter Grimes* gained instant recognition as a new dawn, a fundamental change in English-speaking operatic life, though Britten's individual agenda of socio-political themes, with their narrow specialized personal vision, did not at once seem universal. Tippett's *Midsummer Marriage* was treated even more patronizingly and dismissively by cognoscenti than *Gloriana* and *Billy Budd* had been. It took different productions, different stage images, to show what these works could be: a Brechtian *Grimes* (at Covent Garden staged by Elijah Moshinsky), a post-modern *Midsummer Marriage* (Tim Albery's debut as an opera producer in Leeds), a domesticated, de-classicized *King Priam* (from Nicholas Hytner for Kent Opera). New operas in the past arrived complete with a visual image as well as a musical style. Alfred Roller's designs for the original Max Reinhardt staging of *Der Rosenkavalier* were a standard that subsequent designers felt obliged to imitate. Strauss's publisher, Fürstner, only licensed the work for opera-house performance with Roller's designs. There was no separation between the work and its theatrical realization. A similar perception (with nothing like that restriction by the publisher) applied to Britten too. The English Opera Group continued the line laid down in Aldeburgh at the composer's own festival: *Albert Herring*'s local Suffolk types had to be patronizable comic cameos. But after Britten's death in 1976 the limitations of this 'vernacular' approach became plain. The operas' vitality was being masked by rules about performance. Elements unconsciously buried by the composer merited investigation.

The new approaches to opera staging in Britain did not come from jaded palates. There had not been enough local opera for that. English-language versions to suit and involve the English public, with superbly designed and executed productions, naturalized the art-form. Television and simultaneous translation on screen made a once inaccessible and elitist world of international productions available in that limited way. The liberation of British producers from a rigid commitment to narrative simplicity and old-fashioned naturalism was pioneered by various hands – not always very skilled or intelligent or imaginative. Tastes changed through the 1970s. The achievements of Patrice Chéreau and Giorgio Strehler, stylish but questioning, set an example. The innovative theatricality of Felsenstein's disciples at the Komische Oper in East Berlin, Götz Friedrich, Joachim Herz and Harry Kupfer, was seen at Covent Garden, the ENO and WNO. Soon British producers were following suit. In summer 1987 at the tail-end of conductor Michael Gielen's artistic regime in Frankfurt (under the co-leadership of Gielen's chief dramaturg Klaus Zehelein), many British designers made pilgrimages to that technologically sophisticated opera-house with its huge revolving stage to check out original work by Ruth Berghaus, Hans Neuenfels, Herbert Wernicke and Alfred Kirchner. Peter Brook, whose Covent Garden opera productions in the 1940s were so fiercely resisted, did not return to conventional opera. But Peter Stein from the Berlin Schaubühne was wooed back, despite his unfortunate Paris *Rheingold* experience, with the invitation to direct *Otello* at WNO. Design started to be recognized as the crucial interpretative element in the new operatic dispensation.

In the 20th century the repertoire has expanded haltingly, and formed a fascinating challenge to interpreters. The newly theatrical priority does not undermine the primacy of singing but tests the quality of familiar masterworks. The 20th century has found a new kind of operatic sophistication in live performance. In the 1890s operatic controversies were about composition or singing technique, and opera-house programmes consisted of new or recent works. There were classics in the repertoire: Gluck's *Orfeo ed Euridice*, Mozart's *Figaro* and *Don Giovanni*, Bellini's *Norma*, Weber's *Freischütz*, Rossini's *Barber*, Donizetti's *Don Pasquale*. What stirred audiences and critics were new or comparatively new works (Bizet's *Carmen*, Gounod's *Faust*, Massenet's *Werther*,

Wagner's *Lohengrin*) and new voices (Adelina Patti, Emma Albani, Minnie Hauk, Nellie Melba, Jean and Edouard de Reszke, Milka Ternina, Victor Maurel, Francesco Tamagno, Lilli Lehmann, Emmy Destinn, Luisa Tetrazzini). Questions of interpretation were on the agenda: that was why Richard Wagner conceived his Bayreuth festival-theatre. He had written at length about reforming performance practice, and his works were on a special scale of seriousness. Bernard Shaw's *Perfect Wagnerite*, which recognized the political thinking in *The Ring*, eventually was to be the foundation of Patrice Chéreau's centenary staging at Bayreuth in 1976. Changes at the famous Wagner festival in the years after the composer's death led to new approaches in other operatic centres. *Gesamtkunstwerk* implied equal status for all elements of the operatic experience: design, acting, lighting, choreography, the evocation of social and historical context. Within a few years of the *Ring* premiere, Gustav Mahler and his designer Alfred Roller were stirring up the public of the Vienna Hofoper with productions of *Tristan und Isolde* and *Don Giovanni* that broke convention and set new standards of theatricality. The challenge of interpretation was seen again.

The modern movement in art was partly a return to primitive roots, to technical essentials. Partly it was the assertion that Modernism demanded total novelty, should owe no debts, that art was facing a novel situation. It was posing the issue of interpretation in a new way. The tradition did not contain enough within itself to relate to contemporary circumstances. The autonomy of performance has become an increasing fact of life in the 20th century. It was also a new environment (which the general public found suspicious) where the emotion-free objective patterning of *neue Sachlichkeit* was as legitimate an artistic expression as narrative-laden representation, laced with sentiment and emotion. But opera composers continue to be bewildered by the artistic retrenchments and specializations of Modernism. A composer with a profound individual musical language is needed to speak effectively to today's opera audiences.

5 The design matrix

Steven Pimlott's 1992 Netherlands Opera staging (at the Musiektheater, Amsterdam) of *Samson and Dalila* designed by Tom Cairns: the Philistines' cultural superiority inside the epic-scale temple of Baal.
Photograph © Jaap Pieper.

In the days when the content of the acting and how the actors behaved on stage were settled through conventions understood by both performers and audience, the musical director or conductor often took charge of the staging. In Baroque opera, for example, gestures of a singer's hand towards the eye or the heart were at once recognized by audiences as indicative of the falsehood of a statement being uttered, or of the romantic devotion felt by the singer to the person about whom he or she was singing (something like the mimed language of classical ballet or Japanese Kabuki or Noh theatre). Later the theatrical performance was 'directed' by the 'stage manager', a job-title now applied to the person in charge of scenery, front curtains, props and getting everybody on and off stage during the show. These days, however, even if the designs are in principle decorative and aesthetic rather than conceptual, there has to be a producer with a genuine sense of artistic commitment to pull all the elements of a theatrical realization of opera into proper coherence and focus. For all sorts of reasons, not least financial, audiences have grown very accustomed during the 20th century to filling in with their imaginations for missing naturalistic details – even when the purpose of a setting is to pretend to be mimicking reality or nature. Painted scenery in the 19th century exploited the rules of perspective to make a stage set seem like a picture through which the suitably costumed performers could move (but not move very much) convincingly. Early cinema, like early portrait photos, also used painted backdrops. But once that artificiality became unacceptable, because more sophisticated cameras made location shooting possible, the principles proposed by Adolphe Appia and Edward Gordon Craig prevailed – that the stage space should be arranged (with steps and epic platforms) in a way that allowed and heightened the effective and expressive movement of groups of characters and choruses. The visual language of the scenery – even when the staging was not conceptual and exploring the submerged ideas in the story or relating the original context to entirely different circumstances with their own potent resonances – combined hints of reality with all sorts of other details and, in effect, statements of a more overtly declaratory sort.

Conservative polemicists complaining about *produceritis* (the intrusive creative interventions of interesting and imaginative producers, viewed as a kind of disease) are inclined to look back to a golden age of operatic simplicity when theatrical production was innocent of sub-text. In reality the naturalism and uncluttered narrative of 19th-century opera stagings in fact relied on conventions, and was only an appearance of naturalism within the limited technical circumstances of the wood and canvas available. It was up to the audience to understand the hints of lifelikeness in painted scenery and standardized positioning on stage. Something similar no doubt happens today when those who can appreciate it see the work of Peter Sellars, or Patrice Chéreau, or Richard Jones. The theatre (including opera) is not primarily about what is natural or historic, but about what is understood – what can convey truth and meaning, what can genuinely sway heart and mind. Verdi, as is well documented, was obsessed with the precise detail of how his operas were staged – not least with every aspect of the casting. There was never any question in his mind about the importance of the theatrical side of a performance. Nowadays that buck stops with the producer, for practical not egotistical reasons. That is not because of the complexity of the expressive stagings of various directorial geniuses. It is the nature of the discipline.

The producer (or stage director) is usually the strategist of the production. But in a complex collaboration such as opera interpretation – involving input at various times over many months from many different sources, and aiming to mobilize skills (and not just the cast's abilities) in a variety of fields – it may not always be the producer who has the best ideas. It is just his or her responsibility to decide the outcome, to edit, to select, to receive what the design and lighting team and dramaturgs and conductor and singer-actors can offer (not that all these potential sources will necessarily be in play).

Conductors do from time to time feel entitled to interfere with the stage direction, believing that the power of the music (central to the operatic experience, as everybody agrees) gives them precedence. At the Bregenz Festival in summer 1991, Pinchas Steinberg conducted Richard Jones's new staging of Tchaikovsky's *Mazeppa* and rebelled against what had been developed – even though he had apparently been uninterested in the production during planning meetings. At the premiere Steinberg neglected his orchestra, and turned to face into the auditorium – advertising his disapproval especially during the execution scene, which was done by a tram. Jones had his victims stretched on the ground with their necks over the rails as the tram moved towards the footlights. David Alden at ENO in 1984 did it with chainsaws below stage, but suffered no remonstrations from the conductor. In Cardiff in the mid-1980s Richard Armstrong fell out with the producer of *Rigoletto*, Lucian Pintilie, because the scene where the Duke learns about the abduction of Gilda from his courtiers was staged in a gym as an exuberant semi-comic work-out. In practical terms the hierarchy governing operatic performance must have the producer or stage director at its head, while the conductor is in charge of the tactical execution of performances where the singers do the most vulnerable hard work, taking the main responsibility for focus and impact themselves.

What actually happens when a new production is being created? Producers are not walking around with their ideas fully developed, ready to present them to some opera management. Tendering for the opportunity to mount a production might seem like good economic and artistic sense to an opera company, though it would not necessarily save money. Producers naturally dream, have plans and preferences. Like poets and playwrights they have bottom drawers filled with projects, shadowy wishes and ambitions. They get to see operas they like or which attract them, and when they don't like the stagings they see they may find their negative reaction suggestive and useful. Most opera ventures deal with established works, which usually have recognized performance traditions, so the material under consideration is in the public domain. Moreover, very few operas indeed have not been recorded. The age of the CD brings more and more remote works (especially *opera seria*) within easy reach. Musical familiarization is far simpler to acquire today than it would have been when the works were newly composed – or than it is when creating a premiere staging of a brand new opera.

Not many producers working under normal operatic conditions in big opera-houses are extensively consulted by managements about casting. In a number of German companies, for instance, star singers are retained on regular salaries and because of their contracts expect to get the best roles. Houses like Munich and Cologne and Hamburg and Stuttgart from time to time boast artists in their companies who would be regarded as very special guests in London and Paris. Few opera managements would force a producer to work with talents he positively disliked, and occasionally a producer who has been engaged before casting is complete (a rare occurrence) will be expected to vet the distribution of roles,and able to suggest serious alternatives. Peter Sellars's highly individual style does not function with just any opera-singers. He has a roster of fine vocalists who can act, a personal troupe of regulars, and David Freeman's Opera Factory is also mostly a personal company. Casting never happens in a vacuum: for many opera companies it is a profoundly financial exercise, with precise consequences in terms of ticket-sales which will affect the budgeting. At the box office the choice of a particular artist can balance out the comparative unpopularity of a particular work.

Inevitably there will often be something tentative about the early planning stages of an operatic venture. In some opera companies there may be what amounts to a production team already on the staff – or at least an inclination towards certain talents. But the fascination of being an impresario is still that it means the creation of an entire special team for a limited and specific number of performances. Managements are naturally aware more or less of precisely what they are buying. They wish to achieve a balanced match between the vocal talents and the theatrical profile of the event. Design and casting provide about 60 per cent of the necessary preconditions for success. But the central issue is the collaboration between producer and designer, where there are various models of how best to work.

One way is for the producer to give a vague description of what he thinks about the opera and its imagery to a designer in order to see what this seed can grow into. He will want to avoid being too specific, so as not to choke off the imaginative fancies to which the designer (sometimes most profitably) may be drawn. The designer may come up with a solution that is absolutely unacceptable to the producer, or may pick up the drift of what the producer was imagining and flesh it out. Best of all is for the designer to pick up the ball and run with it, moving into dramaturgical areas not previously glimpsed by the producer but welcome to him. Opera is above all collaborative.

This sort of preparation and planning is effectively dramaturgical – putting together a critical understanding of the music and text and stage directions with ideas about what kind of stage-world will be the physical context of the performances. Design is often perceived by critics and public as a superficial element, a matter of the aesthetic style of costumes and set which designer and producer have opted for as a whim. But design can confirm the public's expectations – and continue the established performing tradition.

In the last 20 years operatic and theatrical design have come to be considered substance rather than just style. Of course, until the invention of video recording, design was the main surviving relic of past performances – except for a few written descriptions of voices and acting by, for example, Burney and other 18th-century European travellers or handbooks of singing which attempted to define the artistic ambitions of their day. Theatre museums have props and costumes. Early photos show how some artists looked. Drawings and paintings give an idea of the stage picture. The prevailing design aesthetic was to look appealing or noble or just pretty. Opera had to be (in a sense) fun, meaning fashionionably *à la mode*. The classical allusions of Baroque opera to feathered headdresses and armour were succeeded by the supposedly more authentic historicist approach of the 19th century. That in turn gave way to the studiedly naturalistic, then to either rhetorical simplicity or frilly fantasy (Oliver Messel). Designers adapt to and set fashions. The ancestors of modern design, Appia and Craig, rejected unnecessary detail and freed up the stage space from naturalistic associations in order to concentrate attention physically on the characters on stage. The aim was to universalize via an epic forum-style architecture. Richard Peduzzi, designer of the Chéreau *Ring*, got his monumental sense of scale from Craig, adding a fantastic elaboration of naturalism underpinned by symbolic implications. His method since his *Ring* has often involved allusions to the orders of classical architecture. In the history of stage design in the 20th century, the idea of depending on an artist or painter to provide something (in sets and costumes) characteristic of his or her own artistic personality has been one way forward. An interior for an Oscar Wilde comedy designed by Rex Whistler was clearly more Whistler than Wilde. David Hockney's version of Hogarth for Stravinsky's *Rake's Progress* at Glyndebourne was very Hockney.

Designers of opera productions fall into two broad categories: those making interpretative work, with proper dramaturgical foundations, whose designs encapsulate the concept and philosophical message of the production; and those who are using history or current fashion merely to provide a pleasing and realistic (or approximately realistic) environment. An early reaction against pictorial naturalism in the 20th century took the path of evoking alternative artistic worlds, giving various movements their theatrical spin-off. In the 1920s and 1930s, certain famous painters (Picasso, De Chirico) painted ballet and opera backdrops and devoted themselves to designing whole stage environments. There was also a kind of utilitarian reductionism of an increasingly puritan flavour pursued by the heirs of Motley (a name wielded in the London theatre from the 1930s on by three powerfully artistic sisters). This school was readily open to influences from Central Europe (Poland, Czechoslovakia). So the cluttered set, its details filled in for the sake of ever more minute truthfulness to life, gave way to sparsely filled sets with only the minimum of actual props and elements – or perhaps no props, just lights and vague spaces. There was not a lot of detail in the set Jocelyn Herbert made for Harrison Birtwistle's *Mask of Orpheus* (staged by David Freeman, 1985). At the Royal Court Theatre and elsewhere, the modern style of uncluttered set design pioneered from the 1930s on by Motley meant that, if doors and windows were needed, they would be physically there, but not just for their own sake, to fill in naturalistically. Simplicity and lightness were Jocelyn Herbert's hallmarks; Ralph Koltai also rejected laboured naturalistic detail, and combined open space and minimal details with machinery for changes of level and location – providing the performers with a context of mechanical aids which seldom combined to form any sort of credible or organic visual statement. Alison Chitty, to some extent the artistic heir of both Herbert and Koltai, lacks Herbert's delicacy of touch but is attracted to Koltai-type machinery. British and Czech modern design have their Bauhaus-type brutalists who consider function before any imaginatively stimulating imagery. Another type of constructivism (the influential Stefanos Lazaridis, who started out as a provider of glitz in the manner of his fellow Greek Georgiadis, and ended as an often severe conceptualist) assembles mechanically adjustable environments, very precise about how the director will physically manoeuvre the performers around the space, but masks them with an aesthetic overlay of period elements. Designers like Koltai, Timothy O'Brien and Lazaridis are all fully engaged in the dramaturgical exegesis. In the 1980s, the odd architect moved into opera. Hans Dieter Schaal for instance created the enormous revolving Carthage set for Ruth Berghaus's Frankfurt production of *The Trojans*.

Some graphic artists of note, painters, caricaturists, have been employed as opera designers just because their personal style of work has a cachet and is distinctive, popular, attractive or amusing. Many will consider the best designs always to be by painters and artists who are aesthetically worthwhile in their own right, and capable of making a personal statement. Artists who take to designing are usually far more widely famous than professional designers and therefore can do what they artistically want without argument. You do not ask a Picasso for a back-cloth and complain about the result.

Over the last 20 years David Hockney has been one of the most successful painters to create a succession of opera and ballet designs – in the line of famous decors by Cocteau and Picasso, commissioned by Diaghilev. Hockney belongs with Osbert Lancaster, Gerald Scarfe, Maurice Sendak in a world of recognizably personal designs where the artist has been able to make a statement through the work if he feels so inclined. Parts of Scarfe's ENO *Orpheus in the Underworld*, for instance, were played in front of hoardings decorated with huge Scarfe caricatures of Victorian gents, red-faced, pot-bellied, top-hatted, eyes narrow, tongues curling in lascivious anticipation – a sort of criticism of the Offenbach's original audience (and through them implicitly of their heirs today). That made it too easy to get out of the target area. Scarfe also included Margaret Thatcher in the role of Public Opinion, complete with a brood of predictably tame ministers in her vast Victorian bustle: a cosy contemporary satirical touch that bordered on the affectionate. No doubt it is complicated, sustaining an excoriating manner in the *Sunday Times*. Scarfe's Mrs Thatcher, supposedly promoting Victorian virtues, really was endorsing Victorian vices: poverty and inequality. But she did not fit the theme of the humour very well. Generally Scarfe's ideas were a superficial gloss on Offenbach's pointed political and social satire. But Michael Frayn's lame 1995 reworking for ENO of *La belle Hélène* as *La belle Vivette* proved again how tricky it can be finding current British equivalents to the well-focused subversive jibes that helped make Offenbach the popular giant of musical theatre which he became. David Pountney's *Orpheus* production was heavily pantomime. Scarfe's caricature of Thatcher was less genuinely oppositional than decorative. Offenbach wrote for his own time. His works resonate because of their music and because of their immortal themes, but not always for the close-up details.

The vein of humour in *Orpheus in the Underworld* runs into *Fawlty Towers*, but the circumstances of Offenbach's carefully judged stories make the wit more consequential.

Hockney the designer has demonstrated both advantages and limitations, especially as collaborator with a producer. Despite its visual distinction, his work lacks much genuine interpretative or critical energy. His sets and costumes have been stylish and fun – good at conveying conventional narrative too. He joked effectively in *Le rossignol* and Ravel's *L'enfant et les sortilèges* (the Covent Garden double-bill taken from the Met's *Parade*, staged by John Dexter). Poulenc's *Les mammelles de Tirésias* and *L'enfant* revealed his 'French touch'. Imitation is the sincerest form of flattery, as well as being normal theatrical convention. Hockney has never been frightened of mimicry. But, like some other distinguished painters turning to theatre design work, he has remained personal and original.

He needed spaciousness to allow for the manipulative and revealing lighting of the flats that make up his sets. His *Zauberflöte* was extravagantly expanded by the Scala Milan: the entire Glyndebourne production was shipped to Milan and erected in the Scala's huge scene shop for stage staff to copy – the actual designs were touring the world at the time in the exhibition *Hockney Paints the Stage*. John Cox, discreet producer of that *Zauberflöte*, has pointed out how the audience is not supposed to imagine a whole world off stage, or over the mountains – as some sets and productions can successfully and potently evoke. With Hockney the artist's imagination stayed within the frame – what Hockney, in this sense very much an easel painter, wanted to say ended with the frame. He left many more options open for the producer than designers usually do. The sets looked better when rebuilt as blown-up for Milan because the Scala's lighting rig, set up for ballet, had the old-fashioned battens and floats for stage lighting that suit two-dimensional sets. Hockney preferred examining his sets under working striplights that were absolutely even in the illumination they threw: at the Scala his *Rake* and *Zauberflöte* looked their best because the lighting battens could be coloured to make the painted flats and drops glow, and there was enough space between the cloths to throw light on them and enhance the perspective he had painted in illusionistically. From the point of view of technical practicality, Hockney achieved quick changes from scene to scene by having one three-dimensional stage picture inset within another.

Hockney designed his *Zauberflöte* in New York, working from Cox's written instructions rather than creative discussion, and put many experimental ideas on to the model stage, before finalizing his solutions. Cox, when rehearsing at La Scala, had to stand in for a singer and found that the surroundings gave the performers no sense of being in a three-dimensional world when they were on the set. In Georgian theatre that lack of illusion for the performer would have been normal. But today's singers are used to a more supportive physical world around them. Still, *Die Zauberflöte* has a long tradition of whimsical pantomime-style treatment. It was created to be diverting and popular, whatever secret agenda Mozart harboured supporting the Masons, that secret society of 'undesirable' subversives, bourgeois progressives and intellectuals. Hockney fastened on some serious themes, contrasting high life and low life, prince and worker, standard in Mozartian drama. The performance traditions of *Die Zauberflöte* are either teutonically sober or lightweight. Many of the popular Christmas pantomimes that are common in British theatre are just as close to fairy-stories containing quests for enlightenment.

Cox felt that Hockney's *Rake* and *Zauberflöte* sets were both short of tension points, where a dramatic communication could be physically telling. The spaces did not help the singers, who melted into the environment rather than standing out from it. Like his paintings, Hockney's sets were flat (though a certain lack of dynamic purpose in the stage action was Cox's own fault). Hockney invariably saw his operas as childlike fantasies not real life. When creating *Tristan und Isolde* for Los Angeles and Florence, he used a huge model box (1:10 ratio to the stage area, a real privilege) which had a lighting rig whose miniature lamps could be focused accurately. This allowed crucial experiments with lighting changes. Hockney's *Tristan* had surfaces at right angles to the lights, which made a particular kind of polychrome glow – though the scenes depicted were storybook, romantic, and un-neurotic. Hockney had no real statement to make about the work. The toytown touch of Hockney's *Ubu Roi* at the Royal Court had ignored the roughness and violent anarchism of Jarry's play, defusing what was intended to shock. Fun cannot be a sufficient dimension of a designer's work. Many operas demand a painful suggestiveness, rather than the resolution of problems. The theatrical imagination needs to be subversive in illustrating. Designs that announce they are pretty have not asked the right questions.

Problem-solving, sorting things out, may very well be the worst designer's vice. If Hockney had strong producers, he might create truly dynamic spaces.

Hockney's paintings toy with the moment, pretend to eschew the vitality of movement. Their aesthetic world fits in with his design concepts. As a draftsman he is strikingly original and recognizable. Yet his work in the theatre is seldom radical. Designs for Glyndebourne and the Met have been uninquisitive. Hockney's art is domesticated and playful, too conscious of its convenience and comfort. His agenda is to relate to tradition. He serves and serves up tradition in his legitimate games with the past, though history is just as much about the present (as the pre-Raphaelites and Gothic Revival showed). To focus on narrative in art it helps to take a historical perspective. Hockney's work is inside the theatrical tradition with its strong formal sense, colourfulnesss, and easy accessibility. He calls himself an illustrator and relishes a certain hedonistic simplicity. His stage designs, evocative and entertaining as they are, though seldom provoking and thoughtful, could even be his most effective and characteristic achievement.

The limitation in his approach was shown up by Timothy O'Brien's ideas for Elijah Moshinsky's Covent Garden staging of *Rake's Progress*, which was almost contemporaneous with the famous Hockney at Glyndebourne. Hockney entertainingly deployed his cross-hatched Hogarth imitations, with a flat sequence of naive witty narrative pictures. By playing just one neo-classical game of Hogarthian reproduction, Hockney's 'solution' ignored the structural complexity of Stravinsky's eclectic mixture of musical citations and influences, the historical consciousness of composer and librettists, W. H. Auden and Chester Kallman. Moshinsky and O'Brien, witty, atmospheric, and broadly theatrical in a Brechtian way, brilliantly expanded on the submerged profundities though by no means revolutionary beside German teams like Ruth Berghaus and Axel Manthey. O'Brien's designs did not disturb the essential narrative structure with additional symbolism or references.

At Glyndebourne, Osbert Lancaster did five operas from 1953 to 1970: *The Rake's Progress, Falstaff, L'italiana in Algeri, The Touchstone* (both these by Rossini) and finally Nicholas Maw's *The Rising of the Moon*. The Lancaster aesthetic was a sort of affectionately cosy self-congratulatory whimsy. Of course, few design professionals can offer the stylishness and aesthetic coherence of a

Hockney, Scarfe or Lancaster. Few sets really show up as visually beautiful. Beauty on stage is revelation not imitation. The Glyndebourne excursions into Maurice Sendak's pop-up children's book world of sophisticated adult whimsy for Oliver Knussen's *Where the Wild Things Are* and *Higglety Pigglety Pop!* (where Sendak was librettist) were a special case. It was an open question who was illustrating whom in this collaboration. Sendak was just as theatrical as illustrative in these works, as in his designs for other operas (which he had not written himself) like the Ravel–Falla double bill, *L'enfant et les sortilèges* and *L'heure espagnole*, and Prokofiev's *Love for Three Oranges*. The latter got a surprisingly similar treatment in many ways from the Brothers Quay collaborating with Richard Jones for Opera North. As with his book illustrations, Sendak delighted in completing his fantasy in three dimensions, and evoking the charm of fairy-story and pantomime. Richard Hudson's sets for Sondheim's *Into the Woods* were evocative in very much the same way as Sendak, though Hudson also gave Jones as director an opportunity for real theatrical invention.

The liberation of design in the last two decades of opera production has enfranchized a great range of different individual designers. Few trained designers specialize exclusively in opera, with its imaginative opportunities and enticing budgets. The widescale breaking of conventions started in the Czech theatre at the time of the Sezession and around the First World War. Joseph Urban, designer of the Ziegfeld Follies and for the Met, was born in Vienna, but Czech. Alfred Roller (Mahler's 'chief scenic artist' at the Hofoper) was born near Brno. The continuance today of the Prague Biennale, devoted to theatre design, indicates how seriously Czech theatre has contributed to the renewal and extension of the ephemeral art of 'decors'. Josef Svoboda has been a seminal figure, designer of Götz Friedrich's Covent Garden *Ring* though of little other work in Britain. Svoboda had the technical facility and grasp of stage engineering to realize the theoretical ideals of Craig and Appia (working with light and shade) in a more adventurous way than Wieland Wagner ever did. Svoboda benefited from the commitment to subsidy of the post-war Czechoslovak communist governments, and created almost a design factory. His craft was apolitical and his kind of theatre was considered free of political content. Svoboda devised the extraordinary swivelling platform of Friedrich's first *Ring* production, a device that created a memorable and fundamental poetic image for Erda, rising from below stage like the Freudian subconscious, but also for the sense of power and its misuse which underpins the entire Wagner tetralogy. Felsenstein's frequent designer, Rudolf Heinrich, with whom Herbert Wernicke (for one) was apprenticed, is another crucial name. All the important producers of European opera in the last 20 years have collaborated with serious designers: Ezio Frigerio (with Strehler), Richard Peduzzi (with Chéreau), Axel Manthey (with Berghaus). In Britain Timothy O'Brien, John Bury, Stefanos Lazaridis, David Fielding, Richard Hudson, Tom Cairns, Antony McDonald, Nigel Lowery, the Brothers Quay, Charles Edwards, Lez Brotherston, Ian MacNeil, Stewart Laing have all played important roles in the theatrical liberation of opera.

The old vernacular design tradition in Britain had always been essentially decorative and entertaining, striving to be handsome, cute or nostalgic. In the music and opera of the 20th century (as in the theatre) nostalgia has always been popular. Some traditionalists have no alternative to the vernacular tradition: *Carmen* in mantillas, *Figaro* in powdered wigs, familiar styles readily grasped. Puccini's operas seem to demand predictable environments, though *La bohème* has been successfully updated, and was 'deconstructed' in Stuttgart by the visually distinguished Ulsterborn designer and now producer Tom Cairns. Student poverty is not restricted to Paris in the 1830s, the period of Murger's *Scènes* on which the libretto is based. Even a conventional designer may mix periods, or avoid too specific a sense of period, or present the narrative in an abstract setting that neverthless goes through all the expected motions. A solidly grounded tradition is an unavoidable factor for any production team. The traditional solution is commonplace. But opera has, through music, the ability to express positively so much more about the interior life of characters than film. The context of operatic characters needs to imply that inner drama – which music usually etches more deeply than the libretto.

In his Stuttgart *Bohème* Cairns (frequent collaborator with Antony McDonald on many Tim Albery and Ian Spink productions) took giant picture frames as his design theme, with stage flats that looked like incomplete canvases leaning against Bohemian studio walls. Cairns also updated to the present day this first staging of a central repertoire work which he directed as well as designed. Traditionally *Bohème* easily falls into the cute and picturesque. But to get an ideal focus on the dreams and delusions of its love affairs may not be best achieved with solid sets.

The specialist theatre designers have been far more influential than any visiting famous painter and cartoonist on this corner of aesthetic history. The profession – with the exception of real design artists like Chéreau's invariable colleague Peduzzi (a professor at the Ecôle des Beaux-arts in Paris) – is suggestible and responds to tricks and effects to be observed all around. It is a living tradition. Designers are tempted by insubstantial gestures like updating. They may adopt a new frame for a work with no proper dramaturgical underpinning. A visit to a training course, or (say) to the Linbury Prize for Stage Design competition entries, quickly shows how rare originality is. In the ephemeral world of theatre almost nothing is new.

The most adventurous British designing recently has resulted not from painterly work, but from solid research collaborations and amalgamation of a mosaic of design inputs from architecture, painting, and furniture – recent and ancient. Lazaridis does not draw much while preparing his ideas – but realizes them in a model box with busy assistants. Design should be a dynamic engagement with the dramatic process. In opera the designer needs to have fathomed the subliminal implications of the plots, gone beyond the simple formula of narrative. Opera is an associative art-form, mobilizing a range of different and not at all obvious aspects of a story, uncovering latent themes.

A word like latent, when authenticity is high on the agenda especially of musicians and therefore becoming an increasing factor in opera, opens a can of worms. What is latent? Would not any such explanation be a purely subjective opinion? Can what the composer never dreamt of be latent? Interesting performances today do not come from giving people what they expect, nor reproducing what already exists. Audiences may feel a production of *Carmen* in a central American rubbish dump outside a barracks (MASH-style) is not authentic. But is *Carmen* the rose between the singer's teeth, the glossy black hair, the passionate breasts heaving? Or is it the obsessiveness of the doomed enchantress Tarot-card player in Peter Brook's vision?

When rehearsals start, the producer must have the whole process of interpretation mapped in his mind. There is little time for further strategic discovery in the production. The set is being built or ready. The cast cannot be altered, except by *force majeure*. The skill is conceiving how the singers will work, knowing what they are like as personalities – and then being able to persuade them to do convincingly what is necessary, on stage and in relationship with the rest of the cast, realizing the matrix imagined by the producer and invested in the designs. Inevitably, design and casting will have been fixed well before rehearsals began, and will be beyond adjustment. The rehearsals can be one week or eight: Peter Stein cautions that for a long rehearsal period a producer needs to be capable of filling the time usefully. There can be too much time. The major objective of the producer is psychological. His authority and persuasiveness must give the cast confidence to fulfil their mission. He prepares them intellectually, spiritually, and by enabling them to perform in a particular style or manner of behaviour. Blocking movements, the energy needed in manoeuvres and gestures, the dynamic relationship between movement and the stage space: those are where compromises happen, needing sensitivity to the efforts of the performers, an eye for effect. In practice the real skill is managing, enabling performers to do with conviction and intent what they must (which rehearsals have proved appropriate) – and follow a line of truth and clarity in their action and acting.

Each production in a sense creates its own theatrical language, whose conventions count on the audience's acceptance and susceptibility. That is why original or oddball modern productions seem unconvincing on television, where there is no audience support and little sympathy for the conventions. Another factor in live performance is the theatre space itself and the alertness of the audience. Audiences are not interchangeable, though the sharing of critically successful productions between opera companies assumes they are. In practice an audience in Amsterdam is governed by a different cultural climate from that at the Coliseum. Similar, if smaller, variations can be expected on a British company tour of venues round the country. Audience receptivity may be created and manipulated by an intelligent committed management using advance promotion and dramaturgical aids in the programme literature.

No production team or management can ignore the *genius loci*. The rehearsal process is predicated on the actual theatre and locality where a premiere takes place. A production may need to work in different places, but often will not. Co-productions work best if they are artistically homogenized, suitable for different international casts whose members will bring their own portable interpretations – and where the social, intellectual and spiritual expectations of the audience are shared (Geneva and New York, for instance). This is 'lowest common denominator' opera – which needs the simultaneous text translation of surtitles. The language the singers sing may even be the audience's, though hard to hear because of imbalance between orchestra and voice, or poor opera-house acoustic, or singers' incompetence.

The casting of opera is crucial, the theatrical raw material of the staging, defining the sounds to realize the composer's dream. Yet in practice casting is usually dictated by musical considerations. The very specific technical and emotional demands of operatic music make casting far more constrained than in the straight theatre. For that reason – and because the success of the music is so basic and so potent in performance regardless of the staging – operatic casting usually starts with getting the voices right, and only then tries to suit the producer's wishes and questions of appropriate characterization. Opera casting, with big international companies, can be fixed years in advance and singers can change. It can also be readjusted right up to the premiere and beyond (for sickness or vocal decline or double-booking by agents, or financial wheeler-dealing between companies – like football transfers).

If opera can make its stories ridiculous on stage, that is because vocal technique has often been more important than theatrical credibility. It is up to what conventions are acceptable. Shaw wrote in 1923: 'I must also admit that my favourite way of enjoying a performance of *The Ring* is to sit at the back of a box, comfortable on two chairs, feet up, and listen without looking. The truth is, a man whose imagination cannot serve him better than the most costly devices of the imitative scenepainter, should not go to the theatre, and as a matter of fact does not. In planning his Bayreuth theatre, Wagner was elaborating what he had better have scrapped altogether.' Shaw's advocacy for the 'theatre of the mind' reflects its era, newly escaped from the conventions of Victorian literalism. Shakespeare's plays were no longer being cut and forced into some naturalistic mould. Reinhardt, Appia and Granville Barker (Shaw in rare chauvinistic vein cites the latter) had invented a sort of rostrum theatre of rhetorical statement and reactive relationships. The new principle of theatrical reality placed enormous emphasis on text rather than physical context. Literary historians revealed that in Shakespeare's day nobody felt a need to reinforce the slight pretence to reality. Recognized conventions left naturalism to the spectators' imagination.

Operatic circumstances today include having to be filmed for video and competing with other areas of public performance where the principals generally must look credible. Looks cannot be disregarded. Television imposes its own conventions, though the extended episodes of opera resist sound-bite fragmentation. Making dramatic sense in live performance does not require the trappings of superficial romanticism, however much ballet (for instance) may be about physical actions and appearances. Looks and the look of the event mean much in an art like ballet, where aesthetic judgments are forever being applied. But live theatre need not be anything like as lovely as cinematic close-ups. In opera, appearance is another area of interpretative compromise.

The subject of casting and voice types as categorized for the convenience of German, Italian and (to some extent) French opera planners is complicated. In English there are no equivalents for many definitions of the voices (*Fach* is the German for range or type) attached to roles in the current German repertoire. Rigid views on the range and timbre required for particular roles do not correspond to today's fragmented repertoire and variety of operatic enterprises. Opera embraces a variety of modes – from traditional grand opera right down to touring piano-accompanied performance in a drawing-room or garden tent. What this variety of operatic performance demonstrates is that there are more ways of making operas work than their composers could ever have imagined. Musical artistry thrives on adapting performance to available talent. Many fine soloists have made a virtue of what some 'experts' find defects. So opera can endure very straitened circumstances with total conviction.

Johann Strauss's perfect operetta, *Die Fledermaus*, for instance, is a very demanding score with two difficult soprano roles and a character tenor needing top calibre artists. But Herbert Wernicke's production in Basel used three professional singers; the rest were straight actors. The orchestration was totally adapted for a band of only nine instruments (the same scale of operation as City of Birmingham Touring Opera's *Falstaff*, *La bohème* and *Die Zauberflöte* staged by Graham Vick and craftily re-orchestrated by Jonathan Dove). Wernicke's set for his own production (as he invariably provides) was a red-plush carpeted circular staircase running from below stage up into the flies: an image communicating social distinctions brilliantly, as well as providing a physical environment profoundly and dangerously suggestive of intoxication. The grand staircase in the romantic operetta and opera tradition evokes various memories and implications. Here the small orchestra was seated on stage in the well of the staircase. The most remarkable effect of using actors, however, was to reinvigorate the roles of Falke, the arranger of Prince Orlovsky's entertainment, and of prison governor Frank. When vocal values predominate, characterization is often unsubtle. Different types of singer and actor help in various ways to fit operas meant for grand theatres into reduced circumstances. Success depends on the personality of the performers and a proper response to the new context. Opera-singing is not so unlike ordinary acting.

If design and casting are 60 per cent of opera production, the other 40 per cent is vital – namely, what happens on stage in the theatre in front of a specific audience with a particular response to the theatrical language and culture of the event. The design advertises what the basic assumptions of a scene will be, suggesting how the characters regard themselves. Design is the substance of the production, though it is the often unspoken (and unsung) communication between individuals caught in the flow of the drama, advertising their thoughts and feelings, that creates the vitality of the stage – mobilizing the passions of opera's emotional dialogues, ensembles, asides and soliloquies.

Just as there is a hierarchy of truths in the objective analysis of the content and intent of an opera, so there is a hierarchy of significance in what is said and done. And productions need to be very clear what matters most. In the Chéreau *Ring* at Bayreuth, for instance, one of the most notable operatic stagings of the last quarter-century, the delivery of Alberich's curse was advertised with a devastatingly bright circle of white top-lighting from the flies bearing directly down on top of the character, almost burning an incandescent hole in the stage floor. In his curse Alberich rejects love, and in that denial of human feeling is enabled to seize and possess the power of the Rhinegold. In every opera staging of worth there will be a similar series of critical moments, of revelatory turning-points (just as Aristotle described in his *Poetics* on tragedy) when the audience moves into different gear: not always a question of lighting. Understanding and responding to such moments, which the composer has usually enshrined in the music, is what gives a production its sense.

The new significance of design is not universal. The 20th century is an age not just of change but of uncomfortable coexistence between different artistic approaches and styles. When there is no single line in fashion, anything goes. The language of the new intrusive breed of designers could be called post-modern, using the space to evoke ideas about the images they are wielding. Theatre is subject to cyclical fashions, and very imitative. The unfashionable quickly becomes the latest thing – if it succeeds. White box sets give way to black box sets. Choruses all wear little, peasant-black, skirts with hats and cripple boots, men in trilbies. The superficial aspects of design, the fashionable solutions, easily descend to self-parody – but parody is a basic theatrical mode. Shorthand solutions serve their purpose.

The issue is not what style of decor is used, but how the decor works or speaks. There are so many starting points. Elijah Moshinsky's BBC television Shakespeare productions exploited memories of famous paintings. Michael Yeargan, who has become Moshinsky's usual designer, has picked up on his appetite for pictorialism. Many designers start from the familiar work or place or style. Jonathan Miller's Little Italy *Rigoletto* at ENO was courtesy of Edward Hopper. If something in the theatre succeeds it will be copied. When the American John Conklin added post-modern bits and pieces to his admired decor for John Corigliano's new sentimental comedy *The Ghosts of Versailles* at the Met, they were actually just decorative (a clock-face, floating furniture, a miniature Montgolfier balloon, all originating in superficial aspects of the characters and narrative). The set for *Ghosts of Versailles* made fun of the work's premise and did not provide much of a fertile basis for understanding. The secret of good design is always a firm dramaturgical foundation.

6 Patrice Chéreau: revolutionary classicism

Patrice Chéreau's 1976 centenary staging (at the Bayreuth Festival) of *Götterdämmerung* designed by Richard Peduzzi and Jacques Schmidt: Manfred Jung as Siegfried, Gwynneth Jones as Brünnhilde, Karl Ridderbusch as Hagen in the furious oath-swearing of act 2 before assembled vassals. Photograph © Siegfried Lauterwasser.

If Wagner had died at the same age as Mozart, he might have been a victim of the 1848 counter-revolutions from which he was forced to flee, and his oeuvre would not even have reached *Lohengrin*. If he had lived as long as Edward Gordon Craig, he would have experienced the beginnings of the Modernist aesthetic revolution which his musical innovations helped precipitate. He might also have encountered the growing distaste for the kind of gothic revival illusionistic theatre that his operas' complicated stage directions suggested. Wagner was a great theoretician of the theatre, whose circumstances did not provide quite the right theatrical workshop – Bayreuth was a huge financial gamble.

As the 19th century gave way to the 20th, arguments raged among experimental artists outside the operatic world over what would be the 'correct' or authentic way of staging Greek classical drama or Shakespeare. Some of the most interesting and experimental theatre reformers were talented artists like the popular portraitist Sir Hubert von Herkomer, famous for naturalistic story-telling paintings: Herkomer's experiments also included primitive cinema. The variety of approaches is fascinatingly documented in John Stokes's *Resistible Theatres* (Paul Elek Books, 1972). Craig and Adolphe Appia were the most famous, most specialized names. Both saw contemporary styles of operatic staging as unhelpful to works like Wagner's – despite the scenic principles suggested in the composer's stage directions. Mahler and Roller in Vienna, their art based more in practice than in theory, had a similar agenda.

For Appia and Craig, Wagner like Shakespeare was not simply a story-teller. Stories and the theatre process were a world of significant parables that needed freeing from specific localities and eras – to be universalized. Both rejected realism or what we would now call naturalism, the idea that theatre should imitate life as cinema often pretends to. (Or used to pretend to. It is remarkable how the cinema in a mere century has gone through what seems like the entire life-cycle of an art-form, from experiment to classical status to decadence to decline.) Craig, for example, later bitterly criticized the post-revolutionary Russian tradition of theatrical realism, which was applied to operatic classics by Stanislavsky who earlier worked with Chekhov. Like the Moscow Arts Theatre, Craig sought to make performance as truthful as could be, but he wanted the stories to point to the spiritual. The trappings of Wagnerian naturalism in the opera-house he thought inappropriate and irrelevant. The point of Wagner's epic marathons in music-theatre was not nordic revivalism. Appia and Craig wanted to recreate something close to the ancient Greek communal neo-religious festival. The audience's imagination at Bayreuth should be freed from beards and shields and flowing robes. With the context purified, people would be closer to perceiving history and morality properly, the bigger questions to which Wagner's stories and music were a grand gateway. This dreaming by Craig and Appia of an authentic world theatre was an early symptom of Modernism's recourse to and colonization of the culture of all other races and eras. Civilized man became a universal tourist and collector. An international aesthetic concept of world culture typified 20th-century consciousness. The convenience of instant translation in live performance provided by surtitles belongs very clearly with a process of cultural tourism. Like all tourism there is a certain delusion about the way the tourist is supposed to be able really to consume and digest the cultural diet provided. In reality it is as difficult for anybody to 'use' an alien culture as it is for a Frenchman who speaks no English to grasp the greatness of Shakespeare.

Appia and Craig's designs, so expressive on the page, foresaw an additional subtlety in performance on top of their more pure imagery. They wanted piled-up steps and restrained classical columns arrayed in tiers to encourage a dynamic of movement. Singers and actors were to be athletes, capable of expressing with their bodies, of being positively, meaningfully choreographed. When Wieland Wagner with New Bayreuth after 1951 demonstrated how this expressiveness could develop, further seams of implication and meaning were plainly there to be mined – such as the historical associations of particular costumes, and the symbolism implicit in dislocated or surrealist environments. Such jarrings and cross-editings were already commonplace in the montage of artistically conscious films, with their multiple blended solecisms. There had also been collages and vulgarities in the theatre of Jarry (*Ubu Roi*). But Appia's aesthetic purity had limitations. What would it mean for Wieland to cast a black singer in the role of Venus? A richer mix ought to suit the pretensions of *Gesamtkunstwerk*.

Craig and Appia might be alarmed at the 'deconstructionist' revolution in theatrical interpretation to which their purifications led. But the operatic theatre of Patrice Chéreau and Ruth Berghaus descends from the assumption behind Craig and Appia's theories. A composer like Wagner would not know what was best for the staging of his work. Theatre performance was a creative art, and performance required primary responsibility. Just as the art of the past is now contemporary and available, so artistic theory is tested in the present day. Modern operatic performances contain mixtures of surrealism, dislocation, and epic portentousness. The search for meaning and the best way of expressing it is the engine of theatrical innovation in opera.

Bayreuth's centenary *Ring* production in 1976 was the moment when this revolution suddenly became palpable. Wolfgang Wagner had followed up the innovation of Götz Friedrich producing *Tannhäuser* in 1972 by inviting Patrice Chéreau to collaborate with the French composer and conductor Pierre Boulez. Wolfgang had considered Peter Brook, who still rejected mainstream opera. Peter Stein, the leading theatre director in West Germany, had proved uncooperative with the Bayreuth ways of working. Chéreau, on the Left in French cultural politics, was a disciple of the Italian Giorgio Strehler from the Piccola Scala in Milan. Strehler's mainhouse Scala productions in the 1970s (*Simon Boccanegra* and *Macbeth*) pressed beyond the decorative naturalism of the Visconti school that dominated, in a refreshing but essentially conservative vein, the post-war tradition of opera staging. Visconti's work was the context for Maria Callas's sublime yet tragic career. The sharp conviction of Callas's acting, with its passionate cinematic naturalism, was another vital element in the development of modern opera staging – because it proclaimed an inescapable theatrical seriousness.

Strehler's productions were characterized by an elegance of design, speed of movement and theatricality of effect that did not, however, distort the basic realism of the stage events. Strehler was a man of taste, with idiosyncratic stylistic quirks – such as a predilection for dim, almost non-existent stage lighting. His *Boccanegra*, for instance, opened in complete darkness: what one saw was a conspiratorial dance of lanterns. Above all Strehler's method was to concentrate on the acting and characterization of his singing actors. Visconti, a leading film director in the Italian neo-realist school, did not try to match the poetic vision of *La terra trema* in the opera-house, but borrowed the romance and self-conscious style of traditional opera for his highly theatrical films. A sensuous opulence in his style seemed in the 1950s to consort well with the *bel canto* operatic repertoire that interested him. Both Visconti and Zeffirelli tolerated the conventionality and conservatism of the operatic performers with whom they worked in post-war Italy, accepting, too, the limitations of the existing operatic performing tradition.

Strehler had his own theatre (the Piccola Scala) with links to the French innovators at the Théâtre Nationale Populaire (TNP), and to Brecht and Felsenstein. He followed the same method of scrupulous and extensive rehearsal to achieve valid, credible theatrical interpretation in theatre or in opera. There was no significant difference of expectation or objective between both kinds of theatre. His almost invariable designers were the husband and wife team of Ezio Frigerio and Franca Squarciapino, always creating subtle, beautiful and historically sensitive stage pictures. Chéreau's designer has been Richard Peduzzi, sometimes in association with Jacques Schmidt for the costumes. Whether a Strehler *Ring* at Bayreuth, had it come about, would have risked as much as Chéreau is doubtful. Strehler in his opera productions has been less inclined to conscious anachronism, to political and historical reference. His stagings (marvellously achieved in his best years) were linear and consistent, proceeding organically from within the work.

Chéreau at Bayreuth had little time to prepare. His only experience of opera when he started rehearsals for *The Ring* had been *Les contes d'Hoffmann* for the Paris Opéra at the Palais Garnier, and *L'italiana in Algeri* for the Spoleto Festival. He accepted the discursive quality of Wagner's epic, and used the opportunities that allowed for the expression of big ideas. He was daring, and was regarded (to start with) as a scandalous, or blasphemous desecrator. Wieland's and Wolfgang's abstract stylization had been equally controversial in their day. But Chéreau's 'deconstructionist', supposedly Marxist *Ring* signalled a new phase in operatic performance.

Chéreau's bicentenary Bayreuth *Ring* from 1976 to 1980 also drew its confidence if not its manner from the work of the East

Berlin theatrical establishment (Brecht's Berliner Ensemble and Felsenstein's Komische Oper). Chéreau's aesthetic was closer to Strehler. His visual taste was quite different from the Felsenstein tradition – as any comparison between Chéreau's Bayreuth *Ring* and Götz Friedrich's Covent Garden *Ring*, with sets by Svoboda and costumes by Ingrid Rosell, soon revealed. Svoboda's swivelling, heaving, piston-operated platform was ingenious and original, but the Rosell costumes were typical of the Komische school: Wotan in a pseudo-Elizabethan collar like Snow White's stepmother in the Disney cartoon; Fricka looking like Gloriana. Because of the sheer quantity of German operatic productions, German designers have an established theatre language to work in, a recognized stylistic shorthand. A certain shiny theatricality with leather-look fabrics and bald wigs amounted to a recognizable manner. Friedrich was still employing it in his 1990 *Elektra* at Covent Garden. Chéreau formed his character in a series of famous and distinctively sombre-looking productions for the TNP, so well-photographed as to merit publication in souvenir book form. *The Ring* confirmed Chéreau's fame in France. Peduzzi, his invariable designer, came up with a sequence of shadowy architectural environments. The spaces spoke by themselves in an unmistakable visual style. With little operatic work in France, compared with Germany, there was not an established manner to react against. Chéreau could please his own taste for *The Ring* once he had established with Peduzzi and Schmidt an eclectic but politically alert approach.

For the English visitor (and critic) Chéreau's blend of influences was initially bewildering. Wagner performance in England had just about by the 1970s absorbed the novelty of Wieland's Bayreuth. But the dense philosophical and political dialectic in Theodor Adorno's writing had scarcely penetrated the myopic insularity of British thought and theatre: in polite circles a rule of no politics at the dinner table prevailed. Adorno's *In Search of Wagner*, originally written in 1937–8 in London and New York, was first published in English in a translation by Rodney Livingstone in 1981. Adorno, Marxist culture-critic and philosopher, was the most famous of the so-called Frankfurt school. Appropriately, Klaus Zehelein, who was Michael Gielen's chief dramaturg during his time as opera and general music director at the Frankfurt Opera from 1977 to 1987, was himself a student and disciple of Adorno. Shaw's *Perfect Wagnerite* view of what he saw as

The Ring's socialistic mythology was less controversial and a lot more penetrable than Adorno's thoughts on Wagner. But to take Wagner's revolutionary politics seriously at all in the staging of his operas was not welcome in Britain where the operas were still seen as tarnished by Hitler's affection for them and the open admiration for the Nazi party of the composer's daughter-in-law Winifred. Nietzsche remains a name suspect to a British sensibility.

After the war the British, including those critics writing about music and opera, tended to regard revolutionary socialism as unsympathetically as fascism. Britain resembled Wieland's Bayreuth, in that Wagner was tolerable only if politically (and metaphysically) cleansed. Many of Wagner's political writings were seen as an embarrassment – despite Shaw's advocacy of the composer. Politics was alien to opera, and since metaphysical discussion easily led to politics, it was widely felt that too many ideas and too much cleverness were wrong for opera. British writing on *The Ring* has been largely free of semiotics and structuralist analysis: Robert Donnington's *Wagner's Ring and its Symbols* explained Wagner's adapted mythology in terms of original Norse myths and heroes (pre-Christian German folk-religion) with Jungian psychology as a vital filter. One would identify with the ideas of *The Ring* through the heroic dilemmas of the central characters – such as the profound emotion Wotan expresses about Brünnhilde. The tetralogy was read in terms of personal salvation not social or political or moral analysis.

This agenda lingers. The 1989 Otto Schenk *Ring* at the New York Met, conducted by James Levine, attempted to re-create Wagner's original theatrical conception as the most convincing way of presenting the work – with characters as 'real Nordic gods', to quote Deutsche Grammophon's promotional literature, 'not as allegories for capitalism, communism, consumerism or any other ism'. Levine held that, 'There may only be two ways of putting *The Ring* on stage successfully: either thoroughly representationally, trying to represent Wagner's own stage pictures as perceptively as possible; or thoroughly abstractly, as Wieland Wagner did at Bayreuth in the 1950s and 60s.' On the one hand were unspecific cloudy images made with light, on the other were very specific Norse-myth picture-book designs. Real Nordic gods were no doubt like the real beings representing qualities in Monteverdi's *Return of Ulysses* (Human frailty, Fortune, Love, Time) or the real Pluto in *Orfeo*, or Diana and Jove in Cavalli's *La*

Calisto. Separating the real and the representational in theatre is always revealing.

The initial 1976 reaction from British critics to the Chéreau *Ring* is worth revisiting. The production was later virtually canonized at the conclusion of its five years at Bayreuth. Although Wieland's famous 1951 *Parsifal* remained current in the Bayreuth repertoire for over twenty years, under Wolfgang's management *Ring* productions usually ran for five years followed by a blank year at the festival without a *Ring*. The Peter Hall staging, new in 1983, lasted only four years. The shadow of Chéreau's hallowed effort encouraged Hall to present an uncomplicated narrative that characterized the tetralogy as a naive fable. With Hall, Solti made his belated Bayreuth debut – changing Wagner's orchestral pit cover which normally guarantees superb balance between orchestra and voices at Bayreuth, and comparative lack of strain for singers. After an almost disastrous reception for the Hall/Solti experiment, Hall did not return to rework his approach in subsequent seasons. Since the festival requires the launch of a complete *Ring* in barely a single week, revision is inescapable.

The Chéreau *Ring* was certainly the shock of the new. He was credited by a number of critics with a mere juvenile desire to outrage. 'Had we all come to the wrong opera?' Edward Greenfield asked in the *Guardian*, describing Chéreau's work as a 'shock-at-all-costs production', and accusing it of undermining the epic quality of *The Ring*. 'That this box of tricks, reminiscent of Satie and his trendy friends of the twenties, should be presented as the centenary production at the Wagnerian shrine is of course a scandal, and it was roundly booed at the end. Those who affect to find its naughtiness important or significant can only be suffering from the most jaded of palates . . . Seen once, the production has fun in it, even wit, but I can think of nothing that so closely compares with drawing a moustache on the Mona Lisa.' The sentiment of Greenfield's reports was 'Don't trust the French', as in Britten's *Billy Budd*. He recorded with enraged accuracy many of the details of Chéreau's imagery, but would make no sense of it all – like a missionary refusing to be corrupted in a brothel. *Die Walküre* had something in its favour: 'for years I have been longing to see horses on stage in this opera, [but] those provided by M. Chéreau are merely roundsman's nags placidly delivering heroes' bodies instead of milk.' Might it have been better with Arab steeds?

In *Siegfried*, 'The mercy was that the costumes . . . were effectively timeless, not identifiably Victorian at all, and that made a fair difference to the sense of involvement in an epic.' After *Götterdämmerung* the conclusion was: 'So many of the new ideas bore no relation to what the music was plainly telling you. It was bad enough having Hagen in crumpled lounge suit like a Soviet commissar carrying his spear around all the time . . . but the suspicion grew to certainty that Mr Chéreau could never even have heard the music before putting forward his dotty ideas, a child playing with an expensive *Ring* paintbox.'

The *Times* critic, the late William Mann, was in contrast remarkably perceptive. He attributed the booing partly to German chauvinism and nostalgia, but mainly to unthinking conservatism provoked by the 'parody and sarcasm' that were part of Chéreau's approach. The booers were especially aggravated by the fact that Chéreau's staging made 'so many illuminating, often unkindly truthful points about *The Ring* . . . His work has proved his theatrical flair and expertise.' Chéreau's fundamental premise was that the significance of the mythical subject-matter of *The Ring* was timeless, multifarious and ever-changing and 'that myths are, by their traditionally accretive nature, full of inconsistencies'. Mann understood and responded to Chéreau's language of gesture – the eloquence of action as well as acting – and had no difficulty disentangling the levels of meaning simultaneously invoked by the singer/actors' naturalistic behaviour in a highly self-conscious design context. The theatrical impact fascinated him, even though he had never seen Chéreau's theatre work before.

The standing of the centenary *Ring* was by no means unanimously recognized, even after the generally favourable response of critics to Chéreau's 1977 revival with its revision of some scenes and careful re-working throughout. Andrew Porter of the *New Yorker*, by far the most powerful critic in the USA in the 1970s and 1980s, did not go to Bayreuth to check out Chéreau's production at all between 1976 and 1980 – though he did give a view of its television version by Brian Large, after witnessing the Peter Hall *Ring* staging at Bayreuth. The English Channel is a language barrier. English theatre has seldom had much contact with France, Germany, or elsewhere in Europe apart from a few special individual cases like Michel Saint-Denis, Max Reinhardt and Fedor Komisarjevsky. Spoken theatre is tightly hemmed in behind language barriers. Chauvinism thrives on ill-informed comparisons.

Look, said Bernard Shaw in his 1923 preface to *The Perfect Wagnerite*, how the English attribute to Herr Reinhardt the successful innovations in approach and theatrical design style actually accomplished by Harley Granville Barker and William Poel. However, thanks to its music, opera of course knows no such immutable frontiers.

Chéreau has done much remarkable work in the spoken theatre. His staging for the TNP of Marivaux's strange play about human nature, *La dispute*, was seen on the Lyttelton stage at the National Theatre in 1976. The style of acting he seeks is always direct, forceful and proud – with enormous vitality and rhetorical expressiveness in the timing and physique of movement. He edits the action and disposition of characters on stage with great scrupulousness and cinematic concentration for the expressive rhetorical effectiveness that carefully organized change can provide. Of course movement and action are part of the actor's weaponry, but how often in old-fashioned opera productions do the characters seem to be waiting for something to happen, the lack of vitality in their reactions suggesting a kind of suspended animation? Sometimes they will imitate a naturalistic manner of activity. But Chéreau – especially in his *opera seria*-style staging of Mozart's *Lucio Silla* – timed the entrances and exits and encounters to achieve maximum attention and consequence. And often movements were launched into with a kind of rapt speed that demanded attention and a certain kind of understanding from the audience.

Chéreau has also chosen to work almost invariably with one designer, Richard Peduzzi, which has given a very clear character to his work. Peduzzi's sets often have an imposing architectural quality, usually with post-modern reference to the classical orders. Chéreau and Luc Bondy, whose *Marriage of Figaro* for Salzburg in 1995 was a wonderfully experimental and challenging homage to Giorgio Strehler, the master of both directors, have been the brightest star directors in French theatre over the last twenty years. As boss of the Théâtre des Amandiers at Nanterre (in the north-west of Paris) Chéreau devoted himself to the plays of the late Bernard-Marie Koltès, whose works of statement employed the elliptical style and elusive situations of Pinter and Beckett. But familiarity with Chéreau's theatre-work was not (and is not) necessary to grasp the importance of his five or six opera productions. He is not the only theatre director to have achieved a great deal in opera with a comparatively small corpus of work. The same would apply to Reinhardt, Stanislavsky, Brook, Peter Stein – and certainly Bondy.

Almost twenty years after those late July days when I was in the audience at Bayreuth for the Chéreau *Ring*, the overwhelming sense that I had then of witnessing a theatrical revelation and revolution has not been diminished by many subsequent extraordinary experiences in the theatre and opera-house. Why was it so astonishing? Was it politically motivated? Chéreau is unquestionably a man of the Left in terms of French cultural politics, but to see his work simply as following a political agenda is to misrepresent it. With hindsight, after viewing the *Rings* of Ruth Berghaus, Herbert Wernicke and Richard Jones, the demonstrative philosophizing of Chéreau's staging (in some visual details and in its evocation of Wagner's own era and rejection of abstracted mythology) was less important than the romantic projection of the human relationships in the story. The language of the acting and gestures Chéreau obtained was naturalistic, not balletic and surrealistic like Berghaus at Frankfurt.

The Peduzzi sets and Schmidt costumes were only part of the magic – though Peduzzi created many epic spaces often loaded with interpretative implications, to which Manfred Voss's marvellous subtle lighting added special sense and realism. Schmidt provided clothes from specific different eras that combined to suggest timelessness. At least as important was the vitality and naturalistic energy in the way the cast and even the chorus moved on stage, the sense of psychological realism. There was the feeling of a theatre production, and the acting had a logic and continuity about it that seemed unprecedented. If it could be done with Wagner it could be done with anything in the opera-house. Opera-going does not generally provide that kind of acting, in that kind of expressive atmospheric context – filled with significance and epic moment. Callas, if one watches the video of her middle act of *Tosca*, had fantastic dramatic fervour. But she commanded the stage in all her scenes like the star she was, and the aesthetic of the productions she was in had none of the Chéreau *Ring*'s mixed visual and theatrical elements – in meaning, in design, in use of the stage space.

Audiences were not used to such fertile imaginations. Whether the performers were responding speedily to action or dialogue, or whether they were gesturing in a theatrically expressive way, everything they did on stage was recognizably on a human scale.

Not only was there none of the usual pomposity of conventional Wagner productions, with their ponderous sense of some unstoppable established ritual, but the narrative process was reinforced by the usually natural behaviour of everybody on stage – even when Chéreau asked for something totally strange, like Erda in *Siegfried* rolling wormlike across the stage in a sleeping bag. I wrote (in the *Guardian*): 'The violence that suddenly explodes on stage thus seems to contradict the conventional view of *The Ring* as a series of cosmic dilemmas presented in ritual style. Chéreau's *Ring* isn't an escape from reality into some fabled world where nostalgic nobility finds profound expression; it's our own dirty little corner.'

What I saw was not just a conceptual proposition in the shape of a series of pictures with (for Bayreuth and Wagner then) bizarrely unusual clothes and alien environments. The designs and lighting were beyond question enormously atmospheric and beautiful. Brian Large's television version tends inevitably to get so close to the performances of the principals that Chéreau's command of the timing and perspective of the action is simply invisible. It was exhilarating to watch the theatrical concept develop among Peduzzi's evocative spaces. All those individual switches of attention which a live audience makes are impossible with an edited television version. The human eye and brain are much more resourceful than the camera. In the Festspielhaus one was constantly relating the central action to the surroundings: atmosphere and design were not, as they are on television, periodically sensed – but continuous. The richness of Chéreau's staging gripped one's concentration, the dramatic process had huge vitality. There was never any question whether the behaviour of the characters made sense.

There was also the audience reaction. Fanatical French Wagnerites and neo-fascist Bavarians united in screaming abuse after the performances. A Wagner protection society had been formed during the winter after the 1976 premiere, and it distributed leaflets before the next summer's performances pointing out where Chéreau had gone wrong. By July 1977 books were already on sale attacking the centenary *Ring*. It was impossible not to be involved in these reactions. The audience watching and listening at the 1977 festival were part of a debate which Chéreau's staging had provoked. To decide whether his production was an appropriate response to the problem of staging the work, one had to marshall one's reading, not just about the meaning of the work in history but about the function of performing it at Bayreuth then.

Chéreau ensured that none of the events of his *Ring* were merely routine illustrations of familiar narrative elements. That was why it was so telling (and proof of the power of his work) when protesters all around the auditorium united in roaring out '*Genug!*' ('enough'), at the foul violence of Hagen's assassination of Siegfried. This *Ring* was, though it was not appreciated immediately, a story-telling romanticization: emotional, deeply credible. Characterizations rang true, however ugly and out of tune some of the singing was.

The Ring is a problem for advocates of vernacular (that is, traditionally naturalistic) stagings. There is no doubt what images Wagner was imagining for the theatre. But those images belong in history. For Siegfried to wear a tuxedo may by the 1990s have become unremarkable, having been seen a few times – by those who see everything. Fashions and innovations, the latest thing, always wear out fastest. But horned helmets and cloaks and tunics are also unremarkable, hackneyed, unoriginal, traditional. *The Ring* is not only about the feelings of its characters: its epic theatre is a consequential social conflict.

Chéreau did not placard the stage in an obvious way. He introduced a range of references. *Rheingold* presented the gods as privileged members of a pseudo-18th-century *ancien régime*. Wotan was an old pantomime pirate in a brocade waistcoat. His women were fashionable ladies of the 1870s and 1880s. Only Alberich and the Nibelungs looked in period and in class, with black or dark grey dust-coats standard for workers and foreman in factories for 50 years and more after the *Ring*'s first performance. The Rhinemaidens were Toulouse-Lautrec whores from Montmartre. The stage directions talk about the Rhine at the start of *Das Rheingold* and of sportful Rhinemaidens. Peduzzi set a primitive hydro-electric dam across the stage, with the gold in its bowels. Dry ice rushed through locks and over pistons. The Rhinemaidens toyed with Alberich. His head was up one of their skirts. Love, when he rejected it and empowered himself to steal the gold, was blatantly erotic. The symbolism of water generating power was clearer than in a fairy-tale staging.

Theatrical interpretation is cumulative in effect. One did not concentrate on each detail, nor was one's reception obscured by its fiercest and most dramatic moments. Relaying the succession of images in Chéreau's *Ring* no longer has the fetishistic, anachronistic, or iconoclastic delight it once possessed. One can get an impression in the Philips video of the production. One cannot imagine, because one lacks the context of audience and the original theatre space, the impact of the violence and sexuality. Hagen, presented by Chéreau as a bullying Weimar political heavy, was the huge Karl Ridderbusch. Killing Siegfried in the third act of *Götterdämmerung*, he bounded like a bear across the stage, snatched up his spear, rammed it with incredible phlegmatic delight and brutality into Siegfried's back – plunging the weapon repeatedly into the twisting body on the ground. That was what caused the cries of '*Genug!*' There had been a similar if less furious audience interruption when Hunding killed Siegmund in the middle act of *Die Walküre*. Again Chéreau offered a kind of sadistic revenge, culminating in a vicious stab through Siegmund's genitals (Siegmund paying in his sexual organs for the delight he had experienced from stealing Hunding's wife Sieglinde, his own sister). And when Wotan in *Rheingold* stole the ring of power from Alberich, he jabbed his spear through the Nibelung's hand, literally making the sparks fly from the factory-metal stage floor. Froh and Donner had a fierce struggle with Wotan to force him to release the ring to the Giants. Waltraute wrestled with Brünnhilde in *Götterdämmerung* for the ring that, she hoped, could save the 'war-father' in Valhalla. Siegfried disguised as Günther in the first act of *Götterdämmerung* had to fight Brünnhilde to get back the ring he entrusted to her care for her protection. Every victim who lost the cursed ring by force uttered a terrible scream as they released it – almost as if they were being raped. These actions are all required by the opera text. But their manner of realization was crucial and distinctive – and memorable.

All such frighteningly selfish echoes and admonitions (the currency of our violent century) were matched with a very strange lighting effect. When Alberich cursed the future possessors of the ring, he was picked out by Chéreau with a brilliantly ferocious circus-style spotlight. After Alberich had left, the light that had shone on him continued to burn a hole in the stage – as if the curse were already working. Froh and Donner examined this phenomenon cautiously, almost humourously, careful not to be scorched. When Siegmund at the *Todesverkündigung* rejected Brünnhilde's summons to Valhalla, after she had wrapped him in a shroud, he similarly was spotlit in violent white light which contrasted strikingly with the atmospheric twilight of the scene's wonderful eye-stretching evening light. After Siegfried's death, his body was spotlit the same way, isolated between the orchestra-pit and a black front-cloth. Here were lighting effects as punctuation and underlining: much more interesting as interpretation than the follow-spots of conventional stagings which concentrate on the legibility of the singer's face – not by any means necessarily the most telling feature. Chéreau's lighting punctuated the story, and created a precise sense of time passing – with subtle fluctuations of light and shade.

The disjunct periods of the costumes and the diverse assortment of locations caused difficulties for some critics and members of the audience. Chéreau's Valhalla, or rather his second thoughts on Valhalla after rejecting the Matterhorn as an image, was a neo-classical mausoleum (Wahnfried the main architectural reference). Brünnhilde's rock was based on the disturbing picture *The Isle of the Dead* by the Basel painter, Arnold Boecklin. Hunding was like Orson Welles playing a Victorian factory owner, and Siegfried was James Cagney innocently involved in a Mafia-run casino. Frock coats and dinner jackets have cultural associations (1930s cinema) that imaginary costumes for Norse gods lack. At the start of *Rheingold* the gods wore taffeta robes like 18th-century coronation costumes and seemed to be camping out on the steps of their neo-classical or post-modern palazzo. Loge appeared as a carpet-bagging Mr Fix-it in a tailcoat, just like the Abbé Liszt but with a hump on his back.

Thoughtful opera producers like Chéreau know that meaning is ambiguous. The motivation of the characters was not always crystal clear. Siegfried overwhelmed with guilt after subduing Brünnhilde (while disguised as Günther) was understandable but odd. One truly inspirational touch was the long expressive winding-sheet with which Brünnhilde wrapped Siegmund during her annoucement of his invitation to Valhalla. In the first act of *Walküre*, where Wagner asks for a shaft of moonlight to break in on the sibling lovers, Peduzzi had the entire back wall of the factory-courtyard set split and slide aside to reveal a bright moon casting romantic shadows. Television cannot reproduce the impression made in the theatre by that physical movement of the set. At the end of the act the whole back-wall vanished. The pair were simply making love in the forest: highly romantic.

Chéreau handled chorus and extras with a truly cinematic feel for the entire stage space. The retainers watching as Matti Salminen's sombre Hunding consumed his meal in the eerie courtyard of *Walküre* act 1 needed only slight adaptation to become the sinister gang of thugs surrounding Siegmund when Hunding killed him. The layout of that devastating sad denouement was striking and impressive. The clearing for the fight was in front of what looked like real trees and low bushes – shadowy cover for ugly cut-throats and muggers. Wotan used his spear to disarm Siegmund, flipping the hero's sword into the bushes, while Brünnhilde comforted Sieglinde at the front of the stage; later Wotan moved, sorrowing, to cradle the dead Siegmund.

The whole of the taut middle act of *Götterdämmerung*, with the summoning of the vassals converted into a breathtaking rally of all levels of Weimar-era German society, was irresistibly gripping. Siegfried did not make his exit at the usual point, as if his protestations about Brünnhilde had satisfied all, but stayed around rather hang-dog until the more ominous music began, then slunk off with a worried look. Chéreau always had a quick eye for detail. The drinking of blood-brotherhood ignored the pompous rhythm suggested in the music. Günther drank with a quick, neurotic gesture. Siegfried delayed until the words of the oath were all concluded. Chéreau's images often operated on different levels of meaning. Wotan, looking like a 19th-century conjurer in a velvet dressing-gown, explained his problems to Brünnhilde dressed in traditional Valkyrie rig, with spear and helmet. When Wotan removed the black cloth concealing his missing eye, and marshalled all the details of fate as he saw them, in conversation with his reflection in a full-length cheval mirror while a pendulum-like ball swung beside him, his conventional blasted eye-socket was as apparent as his conventional spear of judgment and power. The stage picture for the conclusion of *Götterdämmerung*, a Victorian factory or dock whose owners had just been involved in a desperate personal disaster which was attracting dour crowds of detached observers milling about, culminated in a totally realistic and emotionally stirring funeral pyre. Actual flames burned, for which the Bayreuth fire service had to lay on extra hands – Wagner's theatre being largely of wood. The action gave the narrative – restrained, sincere, simple. The conceptual control, the acting, the strength and stylishness of the designs, made this among the most telling and momentous interpretations in many years' opera-going.

The unexpected coup of Chéreau's *Ring* did not lead him to

switch career and, like Jean-Pierre Ponnelle, become a production-line opera man. The choice might have been made; offers
flowed in. After *The Ring* Chéreau was a hot property. But like
Stein, he always demanded extended rehearsals and special facilities that were difficult for opera companies to accommodate.
While *The Ring* was still in the Bayreuth repertoire he tackled the
completed three-act version of Berg's *Lulu* in 1979. Not until five
years after that did he try opera again – Mozart's adolescent *Lucio
Silla* at the Piccola Scala, Milan, the Monnaie in Brussels, and at his
own Théâtre des Amandiers at Nanterre. He was invited back to
Bayreuth for *Tristan und Isolde*, but gave up the project. He was
also in Barenboim's abortive plans for the Bastille. Eventually he
was tempted to the Châtelet Theatre season in 1992 for *Wozzeck*,
and to Salzburg for *Don Giovanni* in 1994 – though the latter
proved an exercise in style and stylishness, with Peduzzi's setting
reminiscent of *Lucio Silla*, and the central role done as a very
mature roué by Ferrucio Furlanetto: strangely void of moral context and metaphysical consequence.

Chéreau's production of Berg's *Lulu* (the premiere of the opera
as posthumously completed by Friedrich Cerha) was an extraordinary undertaking. Here was the unveiling of an opera that was
already a recognized cult object – one of the most intricately
wrought compositions and unusual themes in the 20th-century
repertoire. Its source, Frank Wedekind's plays, is a major landmark of 20th-century drama. It had Boulez conducting. Chéreau's
own status had been reinforced by the recognition for his
Bayreuth *Ring*, continuing in the festival repertoire. The opera
was fairly familiar as a torso. Its first two acts were often followed
by a performance of the last two Symphonic Pieces. Berg at the
time of his death had almost completed the opera, bar the orchestration and some composition for the final act. Though Berg was
writing in the mid 1930s, Wedekind's turn of the century era was
usually regarded as appropriate for the style of the designs (by
Rudolf Noelte in Frankfurt in 1970 for instance). But Chéreau
held that in 1979 the pre-First World War period could only be
approached through a haze of nostalgia which would hinder a
proper understanding of Berg's and Wedekind's work.

Peduzzi designed a series of grandiose, epic, malachite and marble interiors for Chéreau. The work was presented at the Palais
Garnier in very high style, furnished and clothed as if for the rich
fashionable industrial family of Visconti's film *The Damned*. *Lulu*

is not precisely a political statement about fascism. Yet its central issue is freedom and enslavement, and the extent to which people are able to choose such conditions. The most gripping and thrilling musical moment in the work is Lulu's phrase '*O Freiheit*', after her escape from prison and hospital, with palpable sense of release, an exhilarating cry in her highest register. Chéreau saw the character of Lulu from a post-Genet angle. For each of her men she was a different creature, but she always remained herself, independent, untrammelled by those disparate views of her held by others. Peduzzi's sets and Schmidt's costumes, as in *The Ring*, had a monumental, impressively coherent feel. They formed a telling expressive foil for the action. There was Dr Schön's luxury mansion after the wedding, but also – as site for Lulu's murder by Jack the Ripper – an eerie demi-mondaine public lavatory under the baleful glare of a full-moon shining above a vast flight of stone stairs. The social symbolism and monumental impressivenss of the stairs, very operatic both there and at Dr Schön's, was obvious. The painter's portrait of Lulu, with more than a little resemblancc to Garbo's Queen Christina, grew larger each time it appeared, ending as a sort of heroic saint's altar-piece, hoisted aloft on a pulley in the public toilet where the lesbian Countess Geschwitz made the ultimate sacrificial gesture for her beloved Lulu – offering herself to the Ripper as substitute.

Chéreau never fails with his theatrical timing and performance rhythm. He understands the extent to which rhetoric and delay combined with the actors' expressive movement can enliven a scene and its meaning. There was a sardonic gallows humour throughout this piece. Yet Chéreau – without being dogmatic – held to the seriousness of Berg's vision of an authentic, unimprisonable, savage animal character for Lulu herself. There were no jokes. Instead the audience gained a terrible sense of fate and impending doom, overwhelmingly powerful emotions. As with *The Ring*, the acting was unwaveringly intense. The producer's most vital function is to settle the confidence of the cast in realizing his ideas. The impact of the acting in *Lulu* was even greater than in *The Ring*. Chéreau's *Lulu* world was prophetic, anticipating the socially cruel life of the 1980s – like the early 1930s which Peduzzi's Pabst-like designs evoked with such graphic virtuosity. Chéreau's images did not carry a weighty burden. This was not the crude theatrical world of *The Ring*, but a kind of sophisticated psychological torture – though death had, as in *The Ring*, a shocking immediacy.

I only saw Chéreau's *Contes d'Hoffmann* at the Paris Opéra at the end of 1979 – nearly four years after he launched it. The Peduzzi designs obviously looked forward to aspects of *The Ring*. It too presented cast-iron Doric columns at the base of the ware-house or dock building, on one side, with a cream-coloured neo-classical Belgravia mansion on the other. Deep upstage, behind the architectural features that formed the imposing bulk of the set, a river front of little houses was visible in distant perspective. Crowds of curious workers wandered among the arches of the dock-warehouse on the left side of the set. The bourgeoisie flooded out of the mansion dominating the centre of the stage, to witness the sequence of colourful episodes in Hoffmann's search for inspiration. The style of the acting here was less rigidly con-trolled than in *Lulu*, less securely period. *Hoffmann*, being about disappointment and the shattering of dreams, did not require the violence and shock of the *Ring*'s deaths. At the end, a nicely timed coup, all the scenery went into the flies leaving the naked space of the Opéra stage area. Characters exited at the back – through the theatre wall.

Once again, it was the appearance of the production and the rhythm and atmosphere of the performances that gripped atten-tion. Daringly, and awkward for the keepers to control, a big black shire horse carried Dr Miracle's coach on to the set. The prologue and epilogue with Stella (the actress Hoffmann pursues) took place in front of a gauze painted to resemble the Palais Garnier's permanent front drop-cloth. The aims and significance of the pro-duction were elevated. This was high art. For Chéreau putting an opera on stage was a creative as much as a recreative exercise. He brings a necessary arrogance to the job. The original work was not a hallowed relic, for him, however much respect it deserved, but fodder for his creativity. Producers in the text-based world of British theatre are usually in the business of tidying up the action. Chéreau in *Hoffmann* seemed content to leave loose ends, bun-dles of eclectic allusions, games with the theatrical convention. He displayed an enormously inventive and imaginative energy.

Hoffmann was an unfinished monument by Offenbach, whose performance always requires re-editing. Chéreau arranged the tales so that the poet lost his shadow ('sold his soul') in the first act to the machinations of Giulietta, was deceived by the mechan-ical doll Olympia in the second, and failed to inspire and preserve the profound performer Antonia in the third, thus concluding with the work's strongest music. Prologue and epilogue were done in front of the Garnier's front drop, thus distinguishing between the presentation of the poet's stories and of his actual situation. Hoffmann wearing a white suit seemed to represent the modern artist playboy. The design was Offenbach's period. Chéreau has usually preferred the period of actual composition to the supposed time of the narrative. Chéreau's Hoffmann had his creativity broken, obsessed with the imaginative burden of a past from which he could not get free (the quandary of the 20th-century artist). One of the most striking images was Chéreau's conception of Spalanzani, creator of the living doll Olympia. Spalanzani propelled himself round the stage on a mechanical chair, crazy as Dr Strangelove. Olympia was, almost throughout, a genuine automaton – apart from a brief substitution by the singer for her long, funny aria, which was staged with winning theatrical sleight of hand. *Hoffmann*, like *Lulu*, was a rare instance of the Paris Opéra achieving something significant, and no doubt the difficulty of mobilizing such a traditional operatic institution was one reason for Chéreau's reluctance to return to the scene of his triumphs.

Does Chéreau, with only a small number of opera productions to his name, deserve to be so high in my pantheon of opera producers? Considering the works he has chosen to stage, he could scarcely have repeated himself or got stale. His *Ring* was historically of profound significance and at first suffered vilification precisely because of its positive qualities. Chéreau has never wavered in his artistic vision, nor in the resolution with which he has set out to create art in the theatre. His work represents an uncompromising visual taste and dramatic understanding, with a typically Gallic seriousness about what many Anglo-Saxons might regard as ephemeral. The French are serious about clothes and food, and enthusiastically absorb cultural theories like structuralism and semiotics. Chéreau's vision can be explained in intellectual terms. Yet in fact he is an instinctive theatrical interpreter with a strongly emotional and in many ways romantic response to the subjects he tackles. Typical that he has devoted himself so seriously to the plays of Koltès, with their heightened operatic, almost arioso language. Chéreau is also a creative film-maker. In opera his productions have very lively acting and a studied visual context. In many ways he is less brilliantly, and vulgarly, theatrical than Strehler, who in effect is his guru. French taste pivots between the extravagant southern and the cerebral northern. Chéreau's next opera, *Lucio Silla*, demonstrated almost puritanical severity and control.

Mozart wrote *Lucio Silla* at the age of 16 for Milan, where Chéreau's staging was first seen. *Opera seria* is very distant from the post-19th-century operatic world – but not far from the world of French classical theatre: Racine's neo-classical tragedies influenced the great Baroque librettist Metastasio. Chéreau was attracted to the task of giving theatrical vitality to *opera seria*, a form that tends to be regarded as closer to the circumstances of a vocal concert or unstaged oratorio. (Romantic opera actually represents a marriage of oratorio and *opera seria* with chorus added to the heroic soloist in stories that breach the classical unities of place and time.) In *Lucio Silla* lengthy recitatives resolve the action of the drama and are interrupted by marathon pyrotechnical arias that combine psychological exploration with bravura musical display. Mozart's youthful, very original score is profoundly perceptive about characterization in its melodic dimension.

Chéreau brought brilliant dramatic insight to Mozart's sophisticated articulation of the recitatives (with some judicious pruning). As usual with Peduzzi and Chéreau, the designs were essentially interpretative. The colour scheme was black and grey, lighting occasionally warming the set to sandstone. The great scene where Cecilio encounters Giunia at the tomb of Marius gave Peduzzi the idea for a predominant structure running straight across the back of the set in the form of a kind of memorial wall representative of all the classical architectural orders. In appearance stone-like, this monumental structure almost the width and more than the height of the proscenium dominated the space – not a wall so much as an architectural bas-relief pierced with recesses, some capped with the outlines of classical capitals. Other subsidiary wall structures would slide out of the set at right-angles, the whole thing like a museum display. As parts of wall came forward or slid back, expressive shadows from top-lighting cut across the stage defining the scene changes and evoking the epic scale of this Edward Gordon Craig-like design project. The prevailing impression was of dignity and restraint. Yet this object into which characters from time to time vanished had constant fascination for the audience, providing a sequence of new dimensions. A wall used as a machine, both defining the context and suggesting entrances, exits and a sense of rooms or compartments in life, was a device Peduzzi also exploited in Luc Bondy's remarkable *Winter's Tale* staging at Nanterre. This was not a normal theatrical effect, not looking like something, imitating as naturalistic theatre scenery does. It was a statement about the hierarchical society depicted in the opera, about the decorum that ruled it, and about the classical and Augustan era when the opera was composed and the historical era of the story. It matched the musical and dramatic form of Mozart's opera, which in turn reflected the manners of the Enlightenment. Schmidt's severe costumes in sombre black velvet, the men in black coats or cloaks, tricorn hats and wigs, the women in black dresses, were contemporaneous with Mozart's work (as usual with Chéreau), suggesting mourning and puritanism. In haute couture, black is the smartest simplest colour, never out of fashion. The story was typical of *opera seria* – a virtuous autocratic ruler looks for a secure marriage. Lucio Silla, the Roman dictator Sulla, wants to marry Giunia, wife of Cecilio, a proscribed senator presumed dead. The missing husband returns secretly to Rome to combine with the patrician Cinna (himself in love with Lucio Silla's sister Celia). They conspire against the dictator. Like Pasha Selim, Silla hesitates to insist on the marriage with Giunia. Like Sesto in *Clemenza*, Cecilio tackles the planned assassination of the ruler alone and fails. Silla, unable to achieve Giunia's hand without consent, resigns from public life and leaves the stage to the lovers. The anguish of private emotion and public duty was a theme always fascinating for Mozart, closely related to the issue of woman's right to choose.

Chéreau tackled the opera because, he said, he sought the restraints of the form and wished to escape from the psychological naturalism he had needed in Wagner. Formalized choreography governed the rare chorus eruptions. Confrontations between characters took a rhetorical style. The recitatives were intensively worked. Suspense and passion made the dialogues genuine and perfectly led into the extension of aria form. The detailed character relationships were fully rounded and expressive. The vitality of the acting and the naturalistic swiftness of physical movement were very unlike the statuesque static way most producers approach *opera seria*. People entered and left the stage with an urgency about communication, always tugging at each other's elbows as if engaged in intimate impassioned debate, sometimes literally falling to the ground in their distress. Giunia even collapsed flat on her back at one point, starting her next entry supine.

At another she launched into her aria dragging herself along on her knees. Typical of Chéreau's approach was the way Cecilio seemed about to depart into the wings after his lengthy, passionate recitative dialogue with Giunia, when she just touched his hand. Instead of making his exit, he burst into song, each aria piling on the agony, but apparently swelling naturally from the developing energy of the scene. Mannered, but highly effective. Cinna and Cecilio, the two conspirators, originally castrati, were here done as usual in travesty by sopranos – Chéreau's approach helped create a metaphor of masculine commitment.

The fact that Chéreau's involvement with opera has been so extremely sparing perhaps fed the anticipation of his new *Wozzeck* staging at the Châtelet in Paris (1992). Despite the success of the 1976 Bayreuth *Ring*, *Lulu* (1979) in Paris and *Lucio Silla* (in 1983), Chéreau never specialized in opera but stuck to theatre and the film. In *Wozzeck*, his first opera for nine years, it was thrilling to find again, as hallmarks of his direction, the uncompromising faithfulness and clarity in the reactions and communication between characters that one expects only in the most serious theatrical performances. This really was like a consummate performance in non-musical theatre, opera fully and compellingly realized as theatre.

There was no question of making allowances for singers' acting. Yet Chéreau's cast, vocally superb, was constantly supported in their singing by the logic and coherence of the stage action. Chéreau freed them to unpack the emotional agenda of Berg's still rebarbative atonal music without pretentiousness or misjudged effect. There was classical severity and restraint about Chéreau's *Wozzeck*, nothing extraneous, stage design, clothes, music, movement, chorus, extras all working organically together. The expressionism of the 1920s when Berg was composing the opera has often (as at ENO in David Pountney's staging) been used as a design code. Chéreau brought a fresh eye to Berg's work. Even absurdly comic characters like the Captain, Doctor, and Idiot had the dignity of their human reality restored, neither just demonstrating a producer's concept nor placing the opera in inverted commas as a self-conscious homage to Expressionism.

The set designs by Peduzzi were immaculate. This was not culinary theatre, to be looked at for its own sake. Peduzzi's silently moving, assembling and dis-assembling, single-colour boxes with sometimes steep Germanic roofs, sometimes a mere skeleton outline of walls, evoked both the period small-town location of Büchner's original 1830s play and the abstract 1920s forms and colours of Paul Klee (contemporary with the work's composition). Nor did Moidele Bickel's costumes, simple and clean-cut, labour to be historical. Chéreau again showed himself a true disciple of Strehler, in the acting style he encouraged and the extremely evocative lighting scheme by Dominique Bruguière, at times impenetrably sombre, making one really stretch one's eyes.

There were no intervals, and none of the clumsiness of anecdotal set-changes. Barenboim, conducting, started the music with the house-lights still up. At the end – as Marie's child, abandoned, went towards the bridge over the orchestra-pit for his exit – the house-lights came up again. The story belonged in the audience's reality. Chéreau staged the conversation between the frenetic Captain and Wozzeck using a pair of sharp follow-spots. The house-lights gradually faded and tragic gloom descended. The Captain (Graham Clark, penetrating as usual) entered from the auditorium, crossing over the orchestra-pit on a bridge which later from time to time was used to suspend characters, symbolically as it were, above the music. Clark's Captain was a remarkable creation, with hands like a fish's flippers and an infuriatingly pompous way of leaning back on his heels, jovially hectoring, button-holing Wozzeck with nightmarish attentiveness. The complex choreography of their encounter, the Captain catching and holding Wozzeck exactly the way Chéreau staged the encounters (around the arias) in *Lucio Silla*, was later matched by the subtle physical direction of the second scene with Andrès and Wozzeck's doing their ablution duties, swabbing the floor with huge brooms. When Wozzeck talked about the ground moving mysteriously under them, Chéreau had the pair stumble against each other as if stung. Wozzeck conjured the idea out of the stage floor, tracing an outline - while the light changed suddenly, glowing warmly on the back wall of the set, an early hint of Wozzeck's fatal derangement.

Chéreau created a memorable sexually overt mating ritual for Marie and the drum-major, a fierce hunt that was hidden abruptly as a blackout curtain discreetly closed the stage. Similar 'editing' with a dropped curtain to hide the scene or achieve an instant cut was used all the time by Chéreau for his *Ring*. Another tour de force was the encounter of the Captain with the Doctor – in manic Spike Milligan style, always in a hurry, chopping and changing his direction, and absurdly pointing his finger the way he was going.

To evoke the idea of the pond beside which Wozzeck murdered Marie, Chéreau dropped a Japanese-style cloth from the flies which was then bubbled up and down by a funnel of air – a storming swirl of water seemed to be mixing with ominous clouds of mist in the deepest twilight. The same kind of stage effect later swallowed up Wozzeck, while searching for the knife he had used. The first scene with Marie and her child was presented in a triangular front-stage space isolated by lifting the edge of the blackout drape. Marie read the devastating Bible sentences, flipping over the pages seeking for comfort, while the child held up a lighted candle. Another impressive touch was the single light-bulb glowing way upstage throughout the penultimate musical interlude after Wozzeck's death – a light of hope apt for extinction by the devastating final scene of the child playing hobby-horse with the same very wide broom that had been Wozzeck's tool, symbol of an inescapable future, destined for the bottom social caste. There was animal desperation about Waltraud Meier's more extreme notes, uttered with magnificent disregard for safety, as a beautiful poignant Marie, her scenes easy and natural, the final innocent misery completely free of artifice. Chéreau's selfless, unaffected, normal Wozzeck was all the more moving because of Franz Grundheber's essential decency, a good fellow (*'ein guter Mensch,'* as the Captain says) fated to disaster.

As always with Chéreau, all the mass of detail fostered a firm sense of theatrical reality. Chéreau's vision of the tragic circumstances was totally persuasive. The severity of his imagination and the scrupulousness of his control of the dramatic process in *Wozzeck* confirmed his pre-eminence in the world of opera. Peduzzi too is a unique talent and a marvellously individual disciple of Craig. The success of Chéreau's *Ring* marked the acceptance into the mainstream of a modern approach to operatic interpretation. Chéreau's individual signature, his classic assurance and taste, have guaranteed a very high standard of accomplishment, and re-established a theatrical seriousness in the presentation of opera that used to be rare indeed.

7 Ruth Berghaus:
Marx, feminism and the absurd

Ruth Berghaus's 1985 staging (for the Frankfurt Opera) of *Das Rheingold*
designed by Axel Manthey: Heinz Hagenau's Fafner carries off June Card's
Freia; Gail Gilmore's Fricka with handbag and platform shoes protests;
Manfred Schenk's Fasolt and Bruce Martin's Wotan take stock.
Photograph © Mara Eggert.

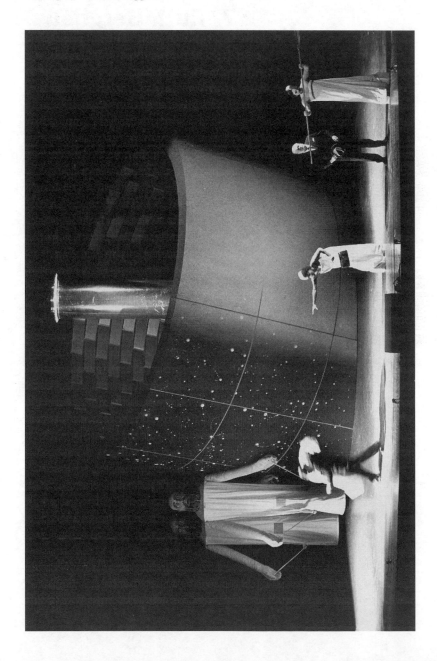

The most important interpretative artist engaged by the conductor Michael Gielen during his era as music director at Frankfurt – the decade from 1977 – was beyond question Ruth Berghaus, who died in January 1996. Berghaus in 1964 had choreographed the battles in *Coriolanus* for the Berliner Ensemble having ten years earlier married Paul Dessau – the composer who was most closely and productively associated with Brecht as librettist and playwright, after Kurt Weill and apart from Hanns Eisler. Berghaus's operatic initiation was as producer of Dessau's operas. Eventually it was Berghaus and the designer of her Frankfurt *Parsifal*, Axel Manthey, with whom Gielen and his Chef-dramaturg, Klaus Zehelein, collaborated on the new Frankfurt *Ring* which was given complete in three cycles in summer 1987 during the last months of the Gielen regime, and never revived. Berghaus's *Ring* was a memorable, utterly distinctive version, the most original approach since Chéreau at Bayreuth – and of historic importance. But, though it was unaffected physically by the catastrophic Frankfurt Opera fire on November 12, 1987 (four and a half months after Gielen's departure), planned further cycles were cancelled because of the closure of the opera-house for rebuilding, and negotiations with Gary Bertini's new regime to loan it for appearances elsewhere in Germany came to nothing.

Before her production of *Don Giovanni* for WNO in October 1984, Berghaus (an exact contemporary of Gielen's, born in 1927) was virtually unknown in Great Britain – except as a fabled and eccentric phenomenon on the German operatic scene. She had run the Berliner Ensemble for six years in the 1970s, and her black and white *Barber of Seville* staging with flown-in back-cloths at the East Berlin Staatsoper in 1968 had remained in the repertoire there for many years. Her Munich production of the same opera in 1974 was famously controversial – on an acting space that depicted a naked female torso, with a bosom as the balcony. Berghaus was definitely unsympathetic to the emotionalism and manipulative populist theatricality that Felsenstein sometimes encouraged at the East Berlin Komische Oper, where a kind of moving psychological realism close to the work of Strehler and Peter Brook was the staple. Berghaus's starting point in opera was Brecht's conviction that the purpose of performance was to make people think rather than make them feel: to avoid any identification with what the audience were seeing, but instead pursue an objective exposition of the ideas. Brecht had never considered that his ideas about dialectical theatre would be applicable in opera, but Berghaus showed that they could be. Her approach was analytical rather than psychological. It was not necessary, she said, to show emotions for the audience to experience them in their reaction to how the scene was performed, as directed by her. For Berghaus, surrealism became a vital asset of dialectical theatre. Her manner was provocative for good discernible reasons, and also because her artistic career began as a dancer and choreographer, where the relationship of given language to representation was never problematical. She liked using a language of gestures that audiences could often find obscure: but that obscurantism was stimulating and could free the audience's imagination. She had studied dance with a famous Weimar era dancer, Gret Palucca, who brought her and other pupils to *Mother Courage* in the late 1940s. In opera she pursued Brecht's idea of '*erzählerische Arrangement*' – that the disposition of the stage both in scenery and in the blocking of the characters' movements should be indicative of the story to be presented, while avoiding the unnecessary repetitiousness of conventional opera, where the music suggested actions (often) which then would be physically imitated or filled in. Equally, what had been already said did not need repeating in terms of some matching (expressive) physical demonstration or movement.

Her first production for Gielen in Frankfurt was *Die Zauberflöte* in May 1980, followed by *Die Entführung aus dem Serail* in December 1981. In March 1982 she tackled Janáček's *Makropoulos Affair*, then *Parsifal* in November 1982, and *The Trojans* in December 1983. The Berghaus/Zehelein *Ring* started with *Rheingold* in December 1985, adding *Die Walküre* in May 1986, *Siegfried* in November 1986, and *Götterdämmerung* in March 1987. This large body of productions of classics by Berghaus provided a real signature for the Gielen regime. In *Zauberflöte*, as in the WNO *Giovanni*, her designer was Marie-Luise Strandt. In *Entführung* Strandt did the costumes, but Berghaus designed the set herself in collaboration with Max von Vequel-Westernach (Gielen's Frankfurt technical director). He later executed the amazing Carthage cityscape designs of architect Hans Dieter Schaal for Berghaus's *Trojans*, the fullest use to date of the great Frankfurt revolve. Her *Makropoulos* had sets by Erich Wonder and costumes by Nina Ritter. For her Wagner stagings, the designer was the remarkable Axel Manthey, whose purity and simplicity of concept had a rare organic unity.

Berghaus's work was unprecedented. She cut right away from naturalism – not just in the settings and costumes she used, but in the actions and gestures. Her freedom as an interpreter originated in her professional dance background. Modern dance is a long way from the pictorial and decorative narrative conventions of Bournonville and Petipa. When dancers convey meaning today they can draw on a very wide range of elements. A Berghaus opera production was not an updated or relocated account of the opera plot, for example – though some of its elements might be indelibly stamped with a particular period. It was not about period. To a large extent it took the narrative as read. A major force in her work was the conviction that story-telling was not a superficial process but had to involve articulation of the sub-text. A Berghaus staging was about the creation of a fertile expressive environment for themes and philosophies buried deep in the fabric of the opera – sometimes consciously by the composer and librettist, sometimes surviving from the narrative source of the story, sometimes reflecting the composer's era, or the age when the story was composed, or the period of the story, sometimes because the metaphysical dimension that caught Berghaus's imagination was modern, and specially apt and relevant. These Berghaus environments had an autonomous flavour with elements even of humour. She used movement (by the chorus and by individuals) but rarely extended to dance. She picked up and quoted visual motifs from contemporary German art. She never wasted. Whatever occurred was meant and had meaning. She wove a rich dense web of references that were rooted in an exhaustive dramaturgical foundation.

My reaction to her *Don Giovanni* for WNO was initially negative. Like most of an opera audience I had expectations about the work, and was quite at sea with Berghaus's method, her complex presentation of footnotes and inessentials. Berghaus's neglect of narrative decorum was frustrating. But what looks like a footnote can seem central once the audience is tuned to the right wavelength. Berghaus invited us to see Giovanni himself as a metaphysical catalyst of sexuality: the ultimate penetration and orgasm occurs when he dives voluntarily into that underworld of burning sexuality for which he is destined. Not knowing Berghaus's work, I came to her *Don* hoping to get a lecture on Christian salvation by Tirso de Molina, with perhaps a peppery spoonful of Hayek on personal responsibility. Tirso's brilliant religious play *El condenado por desconfiado* (Damned for Despair), staged with great theatrical lucidity by Stephen Daldry at the Gate Theatre, London, in 1991, has reinforced my conviction that Mozart's opera needs its theological skeleton to show through on stage, the moral ghost in the machine. People are always uncomfortable with the metaphors of eternal life and damnation. Tirso knew how alluring vice is, especially in a stage villain-hero. Because the Don is serious about sex, the coinage of love, he is both universal and sympathetic. Tirso's play and Mozart's opera show that those who find the Don most threatening are men to whom the women owe obligations, the men who 'own' the women: the theme, as in *Così*, is that women cannot be trusted not to give themselves. Few productions of *Giovanni* make clear that the work shares *Così*'s moral ambivalence – that all men are subconsciously sympathetic to and at one with the seducer.

My sense of *Don Giovanni* was still in thrall to Peter Hall's fine romantic Glyndebourne production showing Giovanni as a disciple of the fallen angel, who tragically refuses to repent and so misses out on paradise. Instead, Berghaus presented the creative force incarnate, Eros, libido, the Bacchic impulse that fertilizes and gives future life. It is always disastrous to limit operatic meaning. *Don Giovanni* is a mystery about human life, aspiration and reality. Does the stone guest stop the Don in his tracks? Is the phoenix of libido reborn in the fires of hell? Do we leave *Don Giovanni* convinced we should sin no more? Or do we gain a more truthful sense of sin and human motivation, based in Mozart's extraordinary amalgam of the tragic and comic? Dent's *Mozart's Operas* and the Robbins Landon and Mitchell *Mozart Companion* debate Mozart's use of the term *dramma giocosa* for his opera, because most music critics want to define exactly what Mozart intended. But the ambivalence of feeling and conclusion in Mozart's operas is theatrically vital. We reduce these works, and we pervert good theatrical productions of them, by squeezing them into straightforward statements of 'real meaning'.

Berghaus offered essentially a behaviourist interpretation, bending all her efforts to present the Don as irresistible, unchained libido. For once one did not doubt that the catalogue of sexual conquest was genuine, whereas Da Ponte's scenario never actually shows the Don successful in seduction. Scarcely any of the dialogues or ensembles were staged in a way that suggested real communication between the participants: they were usually fully occupied outlining some passing fancy of Berghaus's about their character in isolation. This avoided a risk, objectionable to Marxist theory, of sentimental identification with the events shown. Berghaus's staging gave the implications of everything cerebrally without allowing any revisionist indulgence in the actual experience: behaviourism puts a particular gloss on responsibility. Berghaus did not blame the Don, who was after all the mere victim of a concept. Having grasped the stone visitor's hand, during the last supper, he let it go and returned to his seat again. When he finally dived through the trap in the mound to hell, it both satisfied the tiresome needs of the plot and was a personal choice. Da Ponte's morality was too bourgeois to be worth defending, but *Don Giovanni* with no moral is severely reduced.

To outline all the perverse and sometimes illuminating details of Berghaus's intricate and frustrating production, as with all her stagings, will take many words. The Don (William Shimell) wore leather trousers and coloured shirts, which often were ripped from his back to reveal the slim figure beneath. Ottavio's popstar silver lurex suit suggested Elvis-like egotism. He later became a Saint Sebastian pierced with arrows for *'Dalla sua pace'*. *'Il mio tesoro'* coincided with a pretty snowstorm, suggesting his inner emotional turmoil and frigidity. Berghaus's presentation of Ottavio had more facets than anybody has ever suggested, for the role is usually bland and unexplored. Both the Don and Leporello at different times sat with their feet in a basin, holding a teapot from which they poured fluid on to their feet. A case of cold feet? Shimell as the Don was not allowed to get to the flesh and blood of the role. Berghaus made the climate seem wintry, so that her *Giovanni* world cooled off as the Don's departure grew closer.

Four years later this staging was revived by Ceri Sherlock, Berghaus's WNO assistant when she created it. Meanwhile, I had seen six of her best productions in Frankfurt and come to terms with her theatrical language. What she wanted to achieve was more familiar to the company – though the revival had a substantially new and young cast. Berghaus challenged the conventional equation of sex, politics and religion that always puts women down. Her central point was that for Mozart's women the Don was more liberator than exploiter. While most productions of *Don Giovanni* idolize the Don at the expense of the other characters, even though he has none of the big singing numbers, Berghaus's Don was desired as much as desiring. He was the basis for the wish-fulfilment and imaginative projection in the dreams of his women. Berghaus's staging freed the females in the story from permanent victim status. Moreover the production was fun, as much as it was provocative. Like Chéreau's Bayreuth *Ring*, which had at first struck some critics as eccentric or misjudged, this *Giovanni* on revival had acquired classic inevitability.

For the first act the stage floor looked like the nobbly surface of a human brain – the subconscious – into which different swords were stuck, bending and swaying with phallic pendulousness. If not exposed brain matter, then it was dried mudflats stuck with acupuncturing swords, which symbolized the Cross and then the penis. The message was the same when the women stroked the organ of the Don's aggression, as when Elvira tried to domesticate him by putting a red sock on his right foot. Anna was just as hooked on the Don as Elvira, or for that matter Zerlina, who saw her future in red high-heels rather than brown sensible shoes. Berghaus's *Don Giovanni* presented service as a personal rather then a class commitment. In a sense all the women were in competition with Leporello, who enjoyed his menial role - even trimming the Don's toenails. The costumes (like Leporello's flung-on Pierrot coat) aimed to suggest rather than define. That has always been Berghaus's method, colourful as the Don's silky shirts, brilliantly allusive. The washing of feet suggested the Last Supper – or Mary Magdalen, evoking service and spirituality. Distorted religious imagery was there in plenty.

The second act set suggested a volcano that had erupted through the brain matter, with a flimsy pavilion on top of the mound for the Commendatore's tomb, his domain. When the Don finally disappeared into this mound, his clenched fist salute was both Marxist and a mark of George Bernard Shaw's triumphant life-force. Because the production had promoted the equal seriousness, but very different motivation, of all the characters, the true context of the Don's conclusion was clear. This was an inevitable consummation – fate not punishment. Rather than sentimentality, Berghaus offered a human cross-section with clear, funny and conflicting intentions. The stage was literally packed with events, with a mass of comic detail. Mozart's ideas were dangerously liberated, rather than pinned down.

Audiences may not grasp such a full interpretative landscape all at once. It was not Berghaus's aim that everything should be at once consciously apprehended. Her best stagings shared the abundance and imaginative extravagance of the natural world. An account of what they contained must recognize that their elements were meant to work within a performance perspective. Questions a thoughtful audience will ask are: where is meaning invested? what acts are loaded? But just as a great musical interpretation by a pianist, violinist, or singer, or a remarkable piece of dancing, is more than just what happens, so in Berghaus's most stimulating productions the whole is more than the sum of its parts, when analysed and separated out.

In December 1981 Berghaus created her production of *Die Entführung aus dem Serail* in Frankfurt. Gielen in 1987 called it her 'most radical' staging. It was her second Mozart there, after *Zauberflöte* designed by Marie-Luise Strandt (not reckoned as a success by the company). For *Entführung* Berghaus had Dorothea Glatt-Behr as dramaturg: Strandt was confined to providing costumes. The radicalism was in the mixture of elements, the freedom from any period naturalism, the evocation of various ideological shadows in the material, and the contemporary nature of Berghaus's theatrical argument – projected with such details as Blonde's trilby hat and reading of the *Financial Times*, or the feather-winged 'angel' observing the escape attempt. Berghaus here, as often, balanced the earnestness of her intellectual commitment with many light touches, trapdoor jokes, sight gags. At the very end, instead of going into the sunset of 'happy ever after', the lovers were left as if stuck in a maze unable to escape (from each other?). This brought echoes of Selim's last remark to Constanze, that he hoped she would never have cause to regret rejecting his suit (*'nie bereuen möchten, mein Herz ausgeschlagen zu haben'*). The lovers wandered among the bad-tempered and now thoroughly hostile Janissaries: a touch of European *noblesse oblige* lost in the Third World.

Mozart's *Entführung* is much more than a diversion about reunited lovers. The surprising humanity of his Pasha Selim is not sung but spoken: a unique phenomenon in opera. Constanze's rejection in her aria (*'Martern aller Arten'*) of Selim's threat to force her complaisance, to rape her, is not just an astoundingly demanding vocal line, but involves a kind of miniature orchestral concertante as well. Sir Thomas Beecham in his brusque male chauvinistic way put this down as a structural mistake by Mozart: 'The unhappy Pasha has either to sit or stand listening to her, while she and the orchestra amuse themselves with something like seven minutes of music . . . I have taken it upon myself to solve the problem of this absurd bug-a-boo by transferring the air to the beginning of the second scene of Act III' (where the heroine is in prison with Belmonte). Beecham was (unsurprisingly) blind to the dramatic consequence of this feminist blitzkrieg, which leaves the Pasha powerless, certain that his siege of Constanze's feelings is hopeless.

For Berghaus this central aria became a crucifixion (as many Constanzes know it to be vocally). Berghaus had Constanze sit motionless through that extended and expressive orchestral introduction to '*Martern aller Arten*'. Then she removed the marriage head-dress Selim had given her and ripped off her white dress, revealing beneath it a red frock (the colour of martyrdom – and of whores, the first feminists). She crossed herself while singing. Berghaus's Pasha was pictured throughout as a genuine though frustrated devotee of Constanze. In appearance (until after the attempted escape) he looked the image of the enlightened 18th-century European gentleman. This Pasha had absorbed the lessons of European Enlightenment, Berghaus suggested, but what good did it do him?

Later, in case there were any doubt what Constanze's act amounted to by way of self-sacrifice for her narcissistic fiancé Belmonte and for Selim, she nearly fainted when (back in her white dress again) she was at last reunited with Belmonte. She was shown having to be supported by Pedrillo and Belmonte, like a Deposition of Christ from the Cross. Constanze's redemptive fidelity was an enlightening pattern for all, though Berghaus's Belmonte was discouragingly egocentric and probably blind to what had happened. The fate of female operatic heroines is more often to be didactic than happy ever after. Opera has established woman as hero more firmly and proudly than spoken theatre, actively working for sexual equality. It is very important that the first operatic heroes were male castrati singing soprano. In the world of 17th- and 18th-century opera, incomplete men pioneered the public acceptance of a high voice as a heroic vehicle riding out the musical conflict. The diva can dominate the stage in her redemptive sacrificing vein, her voice riding the orchestra far more tellingly than the female speaking voice dominates debate.

The design concept, Berghaus's own, for Frankfurt's *Entführung* was very simple – a white cage standing above the stage floor and capable at critical dramatic moments of being tilted from side to side and forward. *Entführung* as much as *Così* is the demonstration of a psycho-social experiment: the Pasha's estate was an isolated, experimental environment to test certain theoretical propositions – of which the most fascinating implied by Mozart was the Pasha's superior humanity, his recognition of the rights of woman not to be forced to love (whether in the sexual or emotional sense). True love requires freedom, and Mozart's mature operas were a sustained assault on the idea that men may choose, but women may not. For Mozart the freedom of the heart was the essential freedom on which all others depended. He saw that it implied sexual equality. Berghaus in Frankfurt linked this perception to the Christian notion of redemption through love. Without freedom love, whether of God or of anything or anyone else, was worthless. Mozart's seraglio, Berghaus showed, invited everybody to abandon the unliberated old world of sexual and social hierarchies.

Various doors and trapdoors hidden in the walls of her set's white box-structure were capable of opening into the wings or the back of the stage. The set was fronted, at the start, with a wire net bearing various creatures and plants, a snake, an orchid, a branch of figs, strung across its squares. A wire stretched taut diagonally across the set suggested the neurotic tensions between the central characters, later serving as a guide rope when the box was tilted – for example when Belmonte sang '*Konstanze! dich wieder zu sehen*'. Belmonte delivered his first number ('*Hier soll ich dich*') as an 18th-century concert aria, in powdered wig and period jacket beside a harpsichord. He bowed to accept applause, the lights went down, the harpsichord was removed at the back of the box, and when the lights came up again he was no longer in 18th-century wig and coat but wearing leather 16th-century-style jerkin and hose, his appearance for the rest of the opera: an Elizabethan-style romantic adventurer. This aspect of *Entführung*, as Marivaux-like experiment about the reality of love, Berghaus saw as far more significant than the taste for things Turkish, the jokes about foreigners – no doubt very popular when the opera was new just one century after the defeat of the Turks at the gates of Vienna by the Polish king, John Sobieski.

Once Belmonte arrived on the Pasha's territory, having concluded his soulful song about Constanze, Berghaus used a typical comedy style for the more-or-less modern-Arab-dress Osmin, ever outwitted by the hero, who stole his crescent-shaped knife and teased him with mock fighting. It was just right (for Mozart's era and for today) to give Belmonte a sort of European cultural superiority complex. We discovered Pedrillo on a prayer-mat doing press-ups during Osmin's second-scene aria. Regularly Berghaus suggested characteristic European disrespect for muslim culture. When the Pasha made his entry in his smart 18th-century European clothes, brusquely kicking a slave out of his path, the chorus that welcomed him was a joke crowd from an Arab tourist advertisement. Then, at '*Immer noch traurig*', Selim fetched Constanze a white chair to sit on and Berghaus presented his subservience to her in a series of tellingly choreographed movements. He had his face against the earth in despair, then kneeled to her. She started to cut off lumps of her hair with scissors. He rushed about the back of the set in agitation. She, still seated, spread her limbs at '*Töte mich, Selim!*'. She held his hands, he held her hair, gave her a white rope. After she left, Pedrillo interrupted, poking his head up through the trapdoor much used by Osmin and himself. Belmonte came up too, his sword naked. Selim absent-mindedly made him sheath it. Osmin popped up through the trap to find Pedrillo with the intruder, and the '*Marsch, marsch, marsch*' trio of their farcical battle, concluding the first act, was replete with lunatic silliness.

Blonde's scene with Osmin played up comically the idea that he liked her to treat him rough. Once again Berghaus emphasized European 'advantages'. Blonde could read the *Financial Times*, but Osmin could not read at all. Their sexual struggles were carried through with much comic business: Blonde, left standing on one foot, fell over. Constanze, sung by the black US soprano Faye Robinson, entered (for '*Traurigkeit*') in her white southern belle's dress wearing a white nuptial head-dress, as if sleepwalking: a shaft of white light led her across to the chair of privilege provided by Selim on which she stood to sing, holding on to the diagonal taut wire, sliding slowly along it as the whole set tilted. At the end her head rested on the wire, her arms flopped over it. Blonde, who had sat on the floor throughout, straightened her up. They sat together on the ground, Blonde in green dress (a holy colour for Muslims) with red sash, knees up, feet touching, hands held.

Selim rushed in greatly excited. Blonde left, whispering 'Courage!' Selim flew over to Constanze, arms spread like a bird, tried to catch her: '*Morgen, musst du mich lieben.*' She squatted centre-stage: he bounced on the balls of his feet, suggesting joy at the anticipation of her surrender, sat by her on the floor, legs spread out. She raised a knee, put her hands together round it. He jumped to his feet threatening to strike her, kicked at the chair, threw it around. Before the coloratura in her aria began she crossed herself, took off her muslin cap, removed her dress to reveal a scarlet dress beneath. He, on the floor, crawled towards her touching the ground with his forehead as if his legs were powerless, started to kiss her white dress, spread out on the ground like a skin, trying unsuccessfully to approach her as she sang her aria, then lay spread-eagled on the floor in despair – his threats vain. She, having been standing, at the end lay down in a similar position opposite him, her arms outstretched as on a cross, their feet touching (yin and yang) in a symbolic representation of achieved sexual equality – as in a tomb. He spoke to her, struggled to rise, went desperately to the back door, came back to her, stepped on the dress, knelt by her, kissed her mouth. The lights fell.

Next we saw Blonde picking up the chair and the dress, which she cradled like a baby. Pedrillo came to her, kissed her wrists and hands, cuddled her thighs, lifted her up, threw her in the air, got on top of her; she escaped, he caught her foot. She said, 'Ozzzzmin', indicating a fat tummy with her arms. She sang her aria, climbing up and hanging out from the side of the frame. Pedrillo, preparing to get Osmin out of the way, drugged the wine and threw the drug bottle over the back wall of the set. Osmin popped up like a jack in a box through the trap, nervous about the alcohol. One of the bottles was tied to a string, movable like a ball in a game with a cat. Inebriated finally, Osmin fell down flat on the ground – out cold. In the subsequent reunion quartet of the two pairs of European lovers, all the complicated emotions, accusations and doubts – a trial run for Mozart of the same phenomenon in *Così fan tutte* – were staged with great and subtle intricacy, a piece of deeply psychological narrative investigation.

Berghaus's first two acts outlined her thesis about the role of Constanze. The final act represented an ambiguous outcome, leaving open several possible meanings while tragi-comic in tone. The walls of the white box disappeared, leaving a black box (of night) for the abduction itself – with much innocent vaudeville: red lights for stop, green lights for go, a dumb servant, a rude sailor mis-handling the ladder, angry Arab tribespeople in black djellabahs, and so on. Belmonte's demanding aria was staged as if the singer were finding his way through a maze – which is how many tenors sound in it. Pedrillo's serenade was almost in the dark. The omi-nous comedy of Osmin's discovery of the ladder with a feathery winged angel in attendance was delicious. When the Janissaries came in after preventing the abduction, they seemed more like a Swat squad on a picnic than Moorish seraglio guards. Constanze and Belmonte did their prison duet half buried in the stage trap-door. Selim when he delivered his merciful judgment appeared in traditional arab garb, would not listen to the thanks and perfidi-ous protests, moved quickly on to the forestage. All did not end well. Berghaus concluded with questionmarks. Her *Entführung* was clear, provocative, funny, and very musical: a marvellous vehi-cle of interpretation.

My second taste of her strong operatic meat was not in fact *Ent-führung*, which I only saw in the closing weeks of the Gielen regime in Frankfurt in 1987, but *Parsifal*, with Axel Manthey as designer and Zehelein as dramaturg. Like *Entführung*, *Parsifal* was created with Gielen as conductor. During his time as music director, Gielen conducted only 23 of the 49 new productions – leaving chances for such musical assistants as Michael Luig, Peter Hirsch, and Michael Boder. Gielen's Mozart conducting was del-icately inflected, scrupulously clean and lyrical, intimate, airy and full of subtlety, a natural un-selfconscious partner for Berghaus's modern communication skills. Similar buoyancy and relaxed expressiveness, a sort of passionate delicacy in Gielen's musical interpretation, also defined the quality of Berghaus's *Parsifal*, *Ring* and *Trojans*. These epics, freshly explored (and in the case of *The Trojans* sung in a new German translation by Lida Winiewicz and Anneliese Felsenstein), were the core repertoire achievement of the Gielen years.

Manthey, Berghaus and Zehelein created a completely unpre-dictable *Parsifal* world – though in character with Hans Neuen-fels's famously controversial Frankfurt *Aida* of January 1981. Manthey was like neither Peduzzi, Chéreau's designer, nor Wieland Wagner. Frankfurt's *Parsifal* was not post-modern but not abstract either. There was a slight echo of Wieland in the spi-der's-web-like markings on the wall behind Klingsor. Wieland's famous Klingsor image in his long-lasting Bayreuth staging, an araneiform head at the centre of a web, was naive and obvious by comparison with Manthey's approach, which had neither natural nor architectural elements, neither trees nor columns. Wieland's concern in 1951 was to de-Nazify *Parsifal*. The abstract round-table rituals managed to be unspecific about sexuality and the metaphysics of a test and quest opera that excludes half the human race. Naturally, *Parsifal* is often seen as a predominantly musical phenomenon whose theme of disruption and healing is perfectly suited to musical expression, but scarcely stands close or deep dramatic analysis. Berghaus and Zehelein were never going to obscure what Adorno called the 'master caste' aspect of *Parsifal*, with superior potency restored by the hero's renunciation, for Zehelein was a student of Adorno.

Among the Berghaus/Manthey elements was a jovial, rugged, curly-haired, mechanic-like Parsifal in bright red dungarees and shirt, a schoolmaster Gurnemanz in a tight-fitting long frock coat and dark glasses with a long white stick in his hand, an Amfortas wrapped like a mummy in a bloody sheet with a paper crown on his head, a red arrow-like spear that became the male symbol when Parsifal held it up at the appropriate angle in the closing moments standing inside a glowing neon-red circle (Manthey's image for the Grail), knights in full length coats carrying brief cases like city workers, Kundry in black or white feathers, a red swimming-cap and elbow length gloves in yellow (for left hand) and blue, and Klingsor in a white dinner suit. Manthey stuck predominantly to the primary colours – most notably with the line of flower maidens in presentday clothes.

Usually audiences identify with the knights' order, feeling it represents high aspirations, that its neo-Christian rituals are about something crucial in the cosmic Manichaean struggle. Wagner borrowed enough Christian imagery to bolster the boy-scout sexual purity that the opera appears to endorse. Berghaus brought a jaundiced feminist eye to all of this. Her staging was a positive critique, at odds with the traditional view of its themes. The audience were forced to think about the Grail-knights in an essentially unsympathetic way, as an unhealthy clique (a Wahnfried clique, Adorno called them).

At the top of the front cloth (and programme) was the outline of a naked woman on her side, then a huge arrow pointing to the right, and below three blobs of red, yellow and blue. When the cloth rose, Berghaus presented 'professor' Gurnemanz with the four squires asleep in front of a vast blackboard with an open book stuck to it. The squires with bald heads were in Hitler Youth-style shorts, shirts, ties, and dark grey raincoats, their eyes made up with strange racoonlike black. This last detail was shared by all associated with the Grail. In the blackboard were metal rungs which the squires used later to attempt to climb their steps to Parnassus. It was schooltime! with Gurnemanz as tutor in Nietzschean studies. Kundry appeared at the top of the steel structure crossing the set, waiting her turn to descend. Amfortas on his reluctant way to the lakeside treatment centre surrounded by exhausted 'knights' and 'squires' was handled with none of the usual care and respect. If necessary they dragooned him with rabbit punches. When he found Gawain had gone AWOL '*ohn' Urlaub*', Gurnemanz took out a notebook and wrote his name down for future punishment. Gurnemanz on singing '*wundervoller heiliger Speer!*' crossed out the right-hand page of the book with a large white X. Berghaus never neglected the details: two of the squires who were helping Amfortas returned with their towels and sat down to put on socks and boots. The sense of fatigue and degeneration was tangible: one of the squires (sung by women) crawled on hands and knees very slowly across the stage; there was a lot of creeping and crawling, as the students positioned themselves to assault blackboard and book. At '*Um mitleid wissend*' the swan killed by Parsifal appeared in a painted abstract triptych of a red arrow going into a bird's neck, which opened up behind and above the sloping triangular blackboard structure just as Parsifal clambered on to the set over the top of the blackboard, trampling on the open 'rulebook', then sitting all over it as he descended towards stage level. It was while sitting on the book that Parsifal broke his bow in pieces: a comical intruder from another class (in both senses). His sudden violence towards Kundry at the mention of his mother was equally impromptu. His bluff mystification at the nature of the proceedings and his naive interest were a fair comment on the pretension of the opera itself: no easy nut to crack. The transformation had a strange dignity – Parsifal adopted a sort of foetal position and the stage started to revolve, using the vast Frankfurt facility.

The cavelike Grail-hall, revealed as the great gong sounded, contained plainly absurd and degenerate rituals. The knights were not processing but *in situ* already, watching for Amfortas to do the communion on a ledge above. Agonizing, trying to leave, he was propped back up again. The knights seemed terminal too. Gurne-manz eventually took Amfortas his ritual red coat. The knights held up their briefcases instead of receiving communion. For the exposition of the Grail, a great circular glowing red neon tube, all faced towards it and opened their greatcoats – as if they were dirty old men 'flashing' in a public park or basking for a moment in ultra-violet light. Not at all the decorous behaviour usually asso-ciated with the rituals of *Parsifal*. From the cave-roof a great ici-cle pointed down towards the centre of the glowing red tube. Many of the knights had black masks over their eyes like 3-D spectacles. Communion by warm glow made them weave around in drunken ecstasy or high aesthetic pleasure. One brother dropped dead, unnoticed by his brethren. It was a sect as unhealthy as Waco.

The middle act opened with Klingsor summoning Kundry on a spear-shaped ledge below a spider-web wall. Later the magic cas-tle and gardens were presented as an upended closed book, down whose spine Klingsor's magic spear, taken from Amfortas, pointed. Klingsor was a fallen angel, his eyes still, like the squires' eyes, lined with black. As he summoned Kundry the spear up above flashed neon red. His relationship with Kundry was sug-gestively realized. She climbed up the platform to him. He opened his coat and spread it out for her. She laid her head on his stom-ach, sleepy. Later when she tried to climb on top of him, he pushed her away, greatly agitated – for of course he is self-castrated. Kundry took up the coat, stroked its inside at '*Ach, jammer, jam-mer*', and put it on – Klingsor showing its yellow inside for it was his Grail-knight's cloak. With Parsifal's entrance imminent, Kling-sor started a kind of shadow-boxing and mimed fencing. Parsifal approached without seeing him. Then the revolve changed the scene to the enchanted garden presided over by a book-cover with decorative squiggles all over it. Parsifal's attempted seduction by the flowermaidens in red, yellow and blue was genuinely sensual as they painted round his erogenous zones. Credible sensuality is rare in Wagner performance. Like a Busby Berkeley troupe, they lined up in S formation, lying back, arms spread like flowers. All fell flat when Kundry, in a cool white robe, took over the tempta-tion, stationary, from just under the edge of the book. Berghaus manoeuvred this crucial scene with great care and delicacy. Parsi-fal came to Kundry, knelt behind her, took her hand, rubbed it over his temple, kissed it. She started to undo his shirt. He held her hands. She pushed him back, and he lay flat on his back, rubbed his eyes, covered his face, rocked back and forth from side to side. Her dress was covered in signs like the book-cover. The gestures between them had almost religious symbolism. She fought his resistance, grew more intense. There was some of the admonitory pointing with fingers, up and down, that Berghaus often used to suggest significance. Kundry even had Parsifal in a kind of half-nelson. When she summoned Klingsor to deliver the final blow, the stage (the lighting showing it in silhouette) revolved till the arrow pointed straight forward at Parsifal at the centre. Parsifal took down the arrow, dragged it off stage, as Klingsor collapsed down the spine of the book.

The triangular shapes in Manthey's designs were all spear heads, including the strange blackboard. Gurnemanz's hut against a tri-angular hillside in the third act continued that reference, with fewer incidentals, and general restraint. The book of the first act was open in the middle of the stage: Parsifal, having planted his spear nearby, looked at the book first mystified, then with dawn-ing recognition, then lay all over it, and felt its edges. The expected rituals (Kundry and the water; Gurnemanz and the holy oil) were fulfilled. The Good Friday spell was indicated by Kundry and Parsifal pulling off the stage covering to reveal the sloping trian-gle covered in twirling broken lines in primary colours: Manthey's woodland abstract. Transformation to the looming, ominously cave-like Grail-hall had the stage revolving again, this time anti-clockwise. The knights were in a dreadful condition, collapsing, dropping dead, shuffling around. Amfortas's reference to '*meinen Sünden*' (my sins) almost caused a riot. The denouement was quick, when it finally came: with Amfortas cured and collapsed on the floor, Parsifal was crowned with Amfortas's paper crown and almost hidden in the over-large red coat he was wearing. Kundry kissed Amfortas's forehead as he lay on the ground. The 'commu-nion' had Parsifal standing in the glowing red circle, a dove in his hand, the spear pointing up and out – forming the male symbol, an O with an arrow pointing out of it. Parsifal stood, more and more crumpled by the weight of responsibility: the ritual, with the knights opening their coats and flashing, was entirely devoid of nobility.

Parsifal never makes simple sense, even in a conventional stag-ing. Its almost buddhist message of sexual renunciation, strange but necessary for Wagner, is as Adorno believed suspect politically and philosophically. The Grail knights may be exonerated as a late version of Sarastro's enlightened masonic monks. Nothing in this fairytale with a clean ending tallies with real life or politics. Berghaus and Manthey did not answer the questions. But the images with which they presented those questions removed the opera from its dubious spiritual sanctuary.

The Trojans and The Ring staged by Berghaus were the two grandest ventures of Gielen's era at Frankfurt. Trojans made remarkable and unprecedented use of the stage facilities of the new Frankfurt opera-house, rebuilt after the war and opened in December 1951. An architect, Hans Dieter Schaal, who had never made theatre designs before, covered the entire vast revolving stage with a single neo-brutalist cityscape set for the Carthage of the second part of Berlioz's epic. Frankfurt's total stage area is nine times larger than the normally visible stage space immediately behind the proscenium in most theatres; the diameter of its revolve (125 feet) is three times the width of the proscenium (43 feet). That is what a revolve should be if it is to create the effect of scenery or people passing across the stage rather than merely turning round on it. Schaal's extravagant concept could not have toured to theatres less generously provided with stage space. After the Frankfurt fire this Trojans production, though not burnt, became unrevivable. Bertini, Gielen's successor, never intended to bring it back, though Berghaus's Ring had been scheduled for revival in late 1988 with Gielen conducting. Trojans was the more specific to this opera-house, but when the stage was rebuilt both of these revolutionary, technically demanding productions had become remote. Original singers were no longer on contract; Catarina Ligendza (Berghaus's Brünnhilde) had retired. Berghaus's Parsifal was scheduled for the 1992/3 season, but with Walter Raffeiner, the original Parsifal, out of the running and technical glitches on the rebuilt stage, the revival was cancelled.

The vision for The Trojans realized by Berghaus and her design team in 1983 was monumental. Schaal's maquette of Carthage was shown at the Queen Elizabeth Hall foyer as part of the London International Festival of Opera exhibition of Mara Eggert's Frankfurt production photographs in 1988. Without a volumetric drawing of the Frankfurt opera-house, the model did not easily convey what a huge area of stage space the Carthage set covered. Throughout the Carthage scenes (acts 3 to 5) the entire space of the stage revolve carried a vast raked architectural structure, a collection of buildings and spaces that, as it periodically turned, presented a variety of views and locations to the audience. The stage-masking that normally covered wings and flies was removed. Here was an an entire city, Dido's newly founded model realm, within the black concrete shell of the stage walls, like a controlled experiment or museum exhibit. Never has an opera-house set provided such a coherent sense of location, physically propelling a music-drama seamlessly, beautifully, tellingly, without set changes, or the artificiality of curtains, or any other laboursome theatrical ways of indicating different places. Berghaus could achieve almost cinematic dissolves. Berlioz's stage directions suggest gardens, a forest, a hall of greenery, the sea shore. The scenario includes operatic numbers and orchestral interludes, and can seem clumsy or dramatically stilted in pace and timing. It is on an experimental and almost too ambitious theatrical scale. But Berghaus's straightforward laying-out of the narrative and Gielen's astute conducting got the proportions right. Frankfurt's *Trojans* was never inflated. The pyrotechnics in this monumental stage architecture lent a grandeur that suited the work ideally.

Revolving stages were invented to move quickly between two or three ready-assembled sets, with the front curtains drawn, or at least the lights down. Berghaus's scene changes were open, showing the set revolving from one suburb to another with the full depth and extent of the stage set continuously visible. The built scenery covering the revolve, some of it as far back as 125 feet from the proscenium, showed various walled spaces with doorways and steps, and a great open space at floor level. Most memorably it contained a huge sweeping ramp rising to 20 feet above the stage floor which, after turning full circle for the seashore scene of Aeneas's final abandonment, became columns and vertiginous catwalks like a harbour. From the highest point of this light-dappled salt-breeze construction Hylas, the Phrygian sailor, delivered his sweetly lyrical effusion full of nostalgia for another country and culture from which the Trojans were forever exiled. The cost of constructing this set was higher than any other during Gielen's decade.

Production is not just design. Berghaus's need for such a space was not merely hubristic. The scale was romantic, but the purpose went beyond the ambition to evoke the metaphysical context that Chéreau and Strehler know as being 'lord of the smoke' (or dry ice). The visual metaphor of Schaal's stage design and the imaginative context it provided for Berghaus's gestural language and choreographic action were powerful reinforcement for Berlioz's epic purpose. Berlioz's opera and Vergil's *Aeneid* on which it is based are almost two millennia apart. But their theme is as relevant and arresting today, at 'the end of history', as ever – describing the death of one world and the search for a new, revolutionary ideal. Berlioz distilled the few sharply focused, dramatically etched relationships he needed. But large ideas need space. Tim Albery, whose *Trojans* for Opera North, WNO, and Scottish Opera was far more economical, complained: 'We can't get away from that predominant image of post-war British theatre – that the stage is a room, and that that room is the world.' Perhaps a stage can feel like the world outside without a massive revolve. Berghaus's Carthage was no indulgent mix of nature poetry and travelogue prettiness. It was a statement about urban life and leadership and privilege and social order, no doubt glancing at the improbable and fraught East German state. Hans Dieter Schaal's imagery and scale of perspective were not house-trained. The scale of the thing was highly suggestive and serious. Frankfurt's revolving stage gave the broad modern theatrical pageantry a positively cinematic quality ideal for the structure of *The Trojans*, both in narrative and in music. Schaal created another modern world under construction, not just a different room – hinting at the experimental idealism of an immediate socialist past. Berghaus's millennialist sympathies showed in the constructivist set details and the colour-coded costumes designed by Nina Ritter – a modern uniform of black and white stripes for the native Carthaginians with trilbies for the men, and yellow and black squiggles for the Trojans who also had cloth masks over part of their faces. Her chorus movements were hierarchical and socially indicative rather than individually expressive. The movement of the revolve embodied the metaphysics to which the production aspired. Surprisingly, when Berghaus with Manthey as designer turned to *The Ring*, they scarcely exploited the facility.

The two-act opening section of *The Trojans*, The Fall of Troy, was, in total contrast (and not surprisingly), a keep-it-simple sequence of boxed-in scenes. Inside Troy was an enclosed stockade, filled with crowds of rejoicing Trojans (unconscious irony) expecting the end of the war. The black soprano Gail Gilmore, gloriously intense as Cassandra, delivered her anguished warnings at the front, musing among symbolic models of temples, the wooden horse, and other statuary. Hector's ghostly visitation to Aeneas was on the same set, with the bottom of the stockade broken open and a bed centre-stage. Hector's shade and other ghosts were represented by stuffed dummies strapped to the backs of black-clad Noh-theatre-style stage-hands: an eerie credible nightmare. Carthage was to be the happy dream. Ritter suggested an inanimate, inescapable burden, carrying a desperate message.

The chorus of Trojan women, awaiting destruction after Cassandra's call to commit suicide rather than become slaves, gathered in a narrow upper room with sloping floor, ceiling and walls with, behind them, a camera-like focus on a brightly lit seashore horizon from which the Greek soldiers emerged. The women's arms reached up towards Cassandra standing on a catwalk above, indicating in a profoundly moving way the historical moment of unavoidable fate. Cassandra, taking her life, covered herself with a coffin lid (an image from other Berghaus stagings), her rigid frame stretched on the ground. Earlier she helped the Trojan women tear off their wigs – flowing like the hair of William Blake saints – and descend between floor joists at the back of the room. Ritter's Greek shields bore the threatening outline of an opalescent skeleton.

Carthage offered many visions. There was the farmworkers' chorus, with hooked knives threatening Dido on her seat, a royal sacrificial victim to guarantee fruitfulness; later, after her self-immolation, the population went back to their daily round with a spring in their step. There was the Royal Hunt and Storm, with apparent bundles of grass (in fact a large movement group) piled against a cliff suddenly acquiring a life of their own – shaking, shuddering and parting to make way for young lovers and for the royal pair, climbing over and through them in a highly erotic way. This reflected Berghaus's dance background typically. Dido's procession to her grave, walking from the harbour up steep steps to the catwalks, became an extended farewell to what she had created for her people. She went through the bulk of the set, eventually reaching the boat with its standing oars which was to be her funeral pyre. The revolve irrevocably, slowly returned to its original alignment.

After the Wagnerian celebrations of the 1970s, and the centenary of *The Ring*, there was a decent pause in the launching of new productions. Bayreuth carried on regardless – even if the shadows of Chéreau and Boulez hung heavily over Hall and Solti, Kupfer and Barenboim, and Kirchner and Levine. Gielen marked his final months with three complete cycles of the Berghaus *Ring*. It had been built chronologically – unified enough aesthetically to make its impression even with months between each part. The Frankfurt management took video recordings under an agreement with the unions to record productions to help staff producers staging revivals: the German repertoire system involves widely spaced performance of productions, sometimes months apart, when the singers (and stand-ins) have difficulty reproducing what was originally intended. Videotapes of the Gielen stagings survived the fire. With *The Ring*, improved cameras in fixed positions halfway back in the stalls had infra-red facilities for dimly lit scenes, providing excellent quality (a great help to the flagging critical memory). Occasionally they home in on the action, but without the constant editing and changing camera angles of television opera, usually re-lit for television, to the detriment of the videos of the Chéreau *Ring*. The Gielen era productions were also superbly caught by the still photographer Mara Eggert. A small souvenir book of the Berghaus *Ring* by Eggert coincided with the completed cycles. No other *Ring* world has ever looked quite like this – a boldly glossed autonomous view, its emphases unadulterated by nostalgia.

A few days before her production of *Götterdämmerung* opened, Berghaus gave a radio interview to declare, 'We must take the boredom out of opera.' People were used to reading a book with one eye cocked on the television, one ear clamped to a headphone. They were hungry for information. Berghaus was doing the theatrical equivalent of lateral thinking. Her *Ring* was rich with subversive expressive allusion, not all fitting the straightforward narrative. She did not arrive for rehearsal with all solutions planned. Elements of meaning hung loose. If her staging of footnotes and sub-text was discursive or not instantly relevant, she knew people in the era of rock videos were supposedly used to creative mix-ups.

She was not flippant about *The Ring*. However much humour she used, however little of the pompous high seriousness of teutonic opera was there, the approach was intensely precise and defined. What was subversive was her refusal to close off and sort out possible meanings. Many theatre directors want to define their view as if demonstrating a theorem. Berghaus's productions did not seek justification or point to something apart from themselves.

This style stirred up those unsettled by her dynamism, irreverence and independence – who were usually those for whom operas had a sacrosanct style and existence on the page, governing how they should be staged. But Berghaus did not want the arguments and moral quandaries of *The Ring* to be safely transposed to a romantic context or to the naive domestic politics of recent German history: she wanted to provide just enough of a readable environment to enable the characters to be understood in their attitudes and actions. In this version of Wagner's theatre world they were what they sang and did, just as Beckett's characters in *Happy Days* or *Waiting for Godot* are defined by their text, live in their words – and can live in the oddity and perceptiveness and accuracy of what they say because their environment is not naturalistic, is limited and specific. The purity of Berghaus and Manthey's images and actions fitted very profitably into this aesthetic of the theatre of the absurd.

Axel Manthey, her *Ring* designer, made the stage a kind of kinetic art-form. Manthey's settings originated in simple outlines on the page, but then became extremely assured, solid images and structures. *Rheingold* covered the introductory ground at, for Wagner, a rapid pace. The opening tableau underlined the mechanical, 'given' aspects of the story. The Rhinemaidens, who belonged in a toyshop-window, floated above the stage in front of a dark cloth like Christmas decorations, glossy and glowing, one higher than the other two. Alberich was a silver-haired workman in woolly arm-warmers, baggy dungarees, and boots, with orangey-red make-up round his eyes. Entering from the left, he was bent double with the effort of lifting his feet with both hands at the knee for each step he made. Soon he was having to struggle through the solid folds of a curtain portrayed as fixed while half-drawn to the side of the stage, a toy landscape, and the Rhinemaidens, communicating through clear and evocative sign language, began to revolve as if on a ferris-wheel – swinging gracefully from side to side. At the top of the set a simple white curling line indicated the surface of the Rhine and gradually moved from right to left. The Rhinemaidens wore tight cocktail gowns that rested like toys on solid red plinths, which showed below their dresses and lit up at moments of alarm. Berghaus always liked jokey alarm signals. The Rhinegold was a huge golden ball moving down the folds of the curtain, and hailed by the Rhinemaidens. Alberich shaded his eyes, blinded by the dazzle, cupped his ear in his hands to listen, did a little test run for stealing the gold. When he snatched it, the red bases of the Rhinemaidens' dresses flashed red on and off in vain alarm.

Berghaus could have been implying that the moral conundrums of Wagner's tetralogy were childish games-playing. The debt to the Giants and the myth of Freia's energy-giving golden apples were absurd accounts of the abuse of privilege, the politics of the playground, rather than metaphysical analogies. Was Wotan, perhaps, engaged in a mistaken exercise in Reaganomics, without which the tragic events would not have occurred? There is a comic side to Wagner's version of 'man's first disobedience', placing the blame squarely on the creator.

Rheingold had many light and comic touches. The Rhinemaidens' come-on was in a similar vein to their pointing with their fingers at their temples (indicating a screw loose somewhere), or their fingers held up straight in warning to command attention (something other characters did too). At times a Rhinemaiden would use one finger to count off a number of points on the fingers of the other hand. In the second scene Berghaus's approach to Wotan and Fricka was distinctly deflationary. Absurd rather than tragic figures, they and the other gods were wrapped in huge white bathsheets up to their armpits. Instead of shoes they had to walk on boxes or plinths strapped to their feet – a step up creating a telling image of tottering authority. Then there was Fricka's large silver lamé handbag containing her lipstick, which conveniently suggested the bourgeois moral values she would proclaim in act 2 of *Die Walküre*. Few Wagnerian singers have delivered ringing phrases while simultaneously reddening their lips. Wotan of course had lost an eye. Manthey's design for his head-gear was a crown covering one eye. Masking an eye with a hand was one Berghaus way of suggesting a character's inadequate vision. Fricka had half-mask head-gear that matched Wotan's. Wotan and Fricka were discovered asleep in front of the spindle-shaped shining golden Valhalla tower (symbol of industrial might) against a wall of stars mapped out in squares like a segment of the heavens.

One innocent attraction of *The Ring* is how designers create supernatural elements like dragon, giants and woodbird. Here Fasolt and Fafner were trade-union officials in dark grey suits, white shirts and soft hats; accompanying them, but walking behind them, was a pair of 18-foot high carnival giants with medieval honest artisan features – arms operated by puppet sticks.

Freia had the same glossy make-up as the Rhinemaidens, and a garland of green leaves round her middle. Berghaus pitted the dignity of organized labour against the vulnerable impracticality of the god class – images that were hints. The text was always audible and pointed, the debates held with intensity.

Loge, the gods' spectacled negotiator, was marked out from them because his wrap-around bathsheet up to his armpits was black with spangled lining like an Indian robe, and his skin was red all over. He wore trousers like the workers and did not have the uncomfortable privilege of walking on plinths or boxes tied to his feet. Loge, a Marxist intellectual, owed loyalty to no particular class and, as Alberich found, was not trustworthy. Loge envied the god's box-shoes status. When Freia was thrown to the ground during the negotiations over her future, he stood on her boxes testing them out. His movements were the most naturalistic of all, and he suffered a lot of aggravation from Fricka and others.

Some scene changes used the revolve simply. At the end of the opening scene on the bed of the Rhine, Berghaus had an upward-pointing neon arrow climb the side of the proscenium to mark the return to the upper world of the gods. For the descent to Nibelheim, the mines of Alberich, the arrow pointed down. Manthey's concept of Nibelheim was a red wall with lots of black cave mouths that, at the Nibelungs' entry, filled with shield-shaped pictures of Munch-like screaming children's faces. There was gold dust everywhere. Alberich reclined on top of a factory cupboard. Mime was in baggy trousers and gold gloves, with red make-up round his eyes. Alberich coveted Wotan's box-shoes, put them on top of his safe cupboard. Wotan carried not only his assegai-like spear, but also a painting or shield of a sad tired face: these detached face placards were one consequence of Freia's removal by the Giants. Another was the gods' lack of strength to continue wearing their pretentious plinth-shoes. Back outside Valhalla after Wotan's and Loge's seizure of the ring, Alberich's curse exploited one of Berghaus's most firmly indicated gestures – a left hand pointing to the right with fingers spread. The direction of the complex changes of mood and attitude in the denouement, as Fasolt was murdered and the gods saw their way clear to Wotan's sunny future, was typically thorough and convincing. However apparently odd the circumstances, the behaviour registered by Berghaus in the acting was convincingly developed. Freia for instance went to examine Fasolt's corpse, touched his lips, and Loge pronounced an epitaph over the dead giant. The procession to enter Valhalla had all the gods back on their built-up shoes climbing a flight of absurdly tall steps, risky with such footwear. The Rhinemaidens peeped round the edge of the set to see what their stolen gold had bought. It was always fascinating to observe how much detail Berghaus injected into the seemingly straightforward.

Her anti-romantic, anti-heroic approach to *The Ring* continued with *Die Walküre*. Wagnerian tradition has taken Wotan and Siegmund, not to mention Siegfried, at their own grand reckoning. Berghaus's presentation of the story, mixing the absurd and the tragic, looked with naive simplicity at the reality behind the official images. Wagner's stories, unlike Mozart's, can seem unambiguous and lacking in irony. What you read is what you get. But there are, as Berghaus demonstrated, unanswerable questions in Wagner's apparently straightforward moral fable. Berghaus, unlike Chéreau, avoided subjective identification with the heroes. *Walküre* continued the light, entertaining style – with touches of whimsy. It changes the audience's reading of the events if a character, while singing, ticks off the points on the fingers of one hand (or in Siegmund's case, on one occasion, both). Berghaus offered a joyful mimetic simplicity that spoke directly, without intellectualizing. Her detail was always purposeful. Complexity was in the overall interpretation, freed from being lamely chronological. The Wotan of *Walküre* had already become in his heart the Wanderer of *Siegfried*.

Siegmund when first seen wore a green velvet jumpsuit. Sieglinde was in a full-length red velvet ballgown with an awkwardly long train. Their sibling status was unmistakable, indicated by the way they kept staring at each other with a hand held up covering an eye – a gesture evoking the half-helmet that was Wotan's crown in *Rheingold*. Siegmund climbed into Hunding's hut through the roof and down the trunk of the old ash-tree that penetrated it, using the great sword-haft sticking out halfway down as a foothold. The hut was made of three triangular panels; it had a glowing gas-log hearth at the front of the stage. Brother and sister moved as if in terror of reality. Siegmund, cheerful, plump, curly-haired, cowered against the wall. Hunding turned up in golden medieval full armour. For the song to spring, when the moon broke in on the sibling lovers and the door was opened, the whole of the hut rose into the flies – leaving the tall phallic totem-pole-like tree-trunk at the centre surrounded by a speckled cyclorama. A leaf broke from the trunk and loopily dipped toward the ground. A branch lowered from the flies. The lovers had all the *Liebensraum* they needed.

In act 2, Brünnhilde was discovered astride Wotan, dressed in what must have been the Wanderer's old raincoat and black shoes, not the box-plinths of *Rheingold* – abdication was clearly in mind. She had borrowed his trilby and spear and was riding him along the triangular ramp with its abstract mountainscape associations: a playful affectionate relationship. When Fricka entered on the warpath in defence of bourgeois marital morality, she was carrying a bentwood ballroom chair before her that came poking round the edge of the set like ewe's horns. She was reduced to beating her fists on the ground in frustration, and stood like a diver threatening to throw herself from the mountainside ramp. When at last she had won her point, she stripped Wotan of his escapist mac and trilby, and hung his boots of office with their built-up box bases round his neck.

The second scene, with Siegmund and Sieglinde stretched out under the ramp in 'another part of the mountain', was a mirror image of this, thanks to the revolve. Brünnhilde in helmet, chain-mail and carrying her protective wing-shield, stood on the ramp above Siegmund to summon him to join the other heroes in Valhalla: the chair, unoccupied, dominated one end of the ramp. He threatened to put his sword into Sieglinde, centre-stage immediately below Brünnhilde. The denouement, the fight between Siegmund and Hunding, again used the revolve – and showed both scenes simultaneously, the edge between the two sets running up the centre of the stage like a chasm between them, from which dark recess Wotan sombrely emerged after the death of Siegmund.

The Ride of the Valkyries, through the modelled folds of another *trompe l'oeil* red curtain, a favourite Manthey image, was an assembly of zombie-like young men, naked except for diminutive briefs – who were arranged on a display hillock like a lot of trussed chickens, breasts up. The Valkyries in helmets, full-length war-skirts and silver-lamé tunics, manipulated their male quarry down a slippery slope, and then laid them out and polished them up on a circular stepped platform, heads flat to the floor, rib-cages stretching upwards, legs together, prepared for the dissection class or oven. Brünnhilde tied the broken bits of the sword Nothung on to Sieglinde like a back-pack, using torn remnants of her red velvet ballgown. For Wotan's sad farewell to Brünnhilde the circular rostrum revolved to hide the steps and heroes. Brünnhilde was enthroned on a kitchen chair on top of what looked like a cone. Real flames sprang up. Even Wotan could not get past the heat, but lay distraught on the slope below.

Though Wagnerites take *The Ring* very seriously, Wagner's epic can seem more like soap-opera than political statement, a tale of human types that runs to comedy as much as to tragedy, and with an ambivalent conclusion. Tone and structure, hugely inflated in comparison with, say, *Don Giovanni*, are on a similarly passionate roller-coaster about the triumph and defeat of the will. The second act of *Giovanni* seems to be repeating the first act which ends with the Don escaping the fate planned for him by Anna, Elvira and Ottavio. The second two operas of the Wagner tetralogy repeat the first two, in following Wotan's dream of a saving hero. The difference is the character of Siegfried, a permanent comic rebuke to those who wish to regard *The Ring* as a Nietzschean paradigm. Just as Wotan's moral status is undermined by the comedy of *Rheingold*, so Siegfried's cannot survive the cruel comic spotlight of the opera that bears his name. Siegfried is an innocent child of nature, a Wordsworthian naif, but Wagner makes him a child of *human* nature in a state of arrested development, and one who – unlike Wagner's other innocent fool, Parsifal – does not earn enlightenment. Siegfried is not the solution – he is the problem. Humanity is a bad pupil. Like Wedekind but unlike Brecht, Wagner has no solution to this – which helps explain why a Marxist reading of *The Ring* ends in sentimentality. Nietzsche was right to say Wagner was indelibly Christian, not post-Christian as the composer liked to imagine.

Berghaus's *Ring* led towards this plainly post-*Parsifal* view. Her *Siegfried*, the best achieved of all her *Ring* operas, was simpler and sharper than her *Walküre* and *Rheingold*. The predominant idea behind Manthey's foursquare locations for this third *Ring* opera (the third act ending up where *Die Walküre* concluded) was of birth through the circular mouths of Mime's and Fafner's caves into a brave new featureless world, an empty green landscape. Siegfried was a slow-witted schoolboy in ill-fitting white shorts, shirt, cotton jacket, knee-length socks and black boots: Mime was a laboratory assistant in a white coat. On one side of Mime's cave was a fire and forge, on the other a desk for Siegfried's lessons with a red duvet beside the desk (boarding education, of course). The tramp-Wanderer was an unwelcome intruder into Mime's little kingdom. During the quiz, a wonderfully comic encounter, he went through the contents of the entire cave searching for Nothung, which was secreted in a glass display case near the fire, and then left his shoes behind. In many productions Siegfried suddenly and improbably turns out to be an apt pupil of the dwarf smith, well up to forging Nothung while simultaneously singing at the top of his voice. Part of opera's magic power! Berghaus had him treat the hammering like a heavy metal comic act. After shattering the two pieces of the sword, with a Brechtian flourish he stuffed them inside the desk and took out the finished product, fixing it in the vice on the edge of the desk. When he brought Nothung down with tremendous force to shatter the desk-anvil in half, the cave-mouth and back of the set split apart too – the circle becoming a keyhole.

The act 2 meeting of the Wanderer and the dispossessed Alberich was memorably staged. Licht-Alberich and Schwarz-Alberich (other names for this matched pair of anti-heroes, two sides of a single Manichaean coin) squatted together at the front of the stage, anxiously leaning back in tandem, glancing sideways in nervous anticipation of Fafner, to all intents and purposes 'waiting for Godot'. The production's most brilliant coup followed the death of Fafner, who was represented both by an ominous red-smeared mouth-and-nose deathmask that emerged wormlike from the cave mouth itself into which Siegfried climbed bodily, and also by the figure of the giant crawling out with Nothung stuck in his breast. Fafner was once again, as in *Rheingold*, a red-faced trade-union commissar in charcoal grey suit and trilby. Registering Siegfried's victory, the grimacing deathmask turned on its side.

Dying, Fafner enumerated some warning points for Siegfried, counting them off on his fingers holding one hand high. Siegfried marked off his fingers too, but not from understanding. The deathmask retracted into the black recess of the cave-mouth. The woodbird flitted on stage, in the shape of a curly-haired choirboy clad in dungarees carrying a black-feathered shield like a bird-wing. He nicked Fafner's trilby and tried it on for size, then handed it to Siegfried and delivered his message about what there was to find inside the cave. Siegfried went through the circular cavemouth into the depths.

In a flash, Mime and Alberich dashed on from either side, the former in grey greatcoat and trilby, the latter in dark fur-coat and slouch hat, a pair of disreputable market traders. The woodbird boy squatted by Fafner's corpse, hidden behind his wing-shield, overhearing all. Wrangling broke out between the two Beckettian tramps, with a parade of spiv-like gestures, hats primly re-positioned, dust (of the other party) brushed off the sleeves of coats. When the row hotted up too much, the woodbird ran off. Siegfried returned sporting the tarnhelm. The woodbird put his hand up as if in class, finger extended high, and gave Siegfried his next vital message about Mime and the dwarf's intentions. This is always a very funny episode, one of Wagner's best jokes, with Mime giving voice to his real meaning instead of the diplomatic falsehoods he thinks he's saying. Berghaus turned it into a tour de force of balletic frenzy. Mime hopped on and off Siegfried's red duvet which the hero cuddled like a teddy-bear and got into quite a tangle with the poor woodbird whom he almost knocked out. Mime's carefully prepared poison drink was crazily shaken about in a blue cocktail shaker. Siegfried chucked the tarnhelm and ring casually on to the duvet where the woodbird fielded them just in time.

After Mime had been disposed of, a red plush curtain closed the cavemouth. Siegfried tipped the bodies of Mime and Fafner over the edge outside the cave. The woodbird filled in the rest of Siegfried's instructions, and started to push the hero upstage towards the cave mouth. The curtains there drew back and, all of a sudden, instead of a cave it had become the entrance to the world beyond. Bird and hero passed through the mouth together, born to the next stage of the drama. Berghaus re-established the meaning behind the opera's familiar symbols. Rather than treat the established tradition as fetishistic, she evoked the truths within. From the death of Fafner to the conclusion of the act is a shortish span. Berghaus made it a rich web of meaning and wit. It was Gielen's idea to adhere to Wagner's stipulation of a boy soprano for the Woodbird. Berghaus and Zehelein realized the advantage of incarnating the woodbird on stage as a figure like Cupid in Monteverdi's *Coronation of Poppea*, linking to the idea of Siegfried's dependence. Not until his innocent encounter with Brünnhilde was he ever thrown back on his own inadequate human resources. Equally Manthey's unusual set encapsulated the true meaning of the fiery encounter with Fafner. Just as Nothung was re-forged in Mime's schoolroom, so Siegfried was tempered in Fafner's cavemouth. Perhaps Siegfried has more in common with that other Victorian masterpiece, *Alice in Wonderland*, than we think. It is also about awakening from the subconscious, which is in itself the hallmark of modern operatic staging. As Berghaus had it, Fafner, Erda and Brünnhilde were dragged from slumber to advance Siegfried's comical cause.

For the Wanderer's consultation with Erda in act 3, she wore a blue 1950s ballgown, and stood in a pit leaning against a model of the globe lit up with little lights. Memories of their 'old flame' relationship were revived, and suggestions of the Wanderer's terminal weakness. There were tricks too. Encountering Siegfried, the Wanderer picked his pocket in a trice and got out the tarnhelm. Later Brünnhilde, wakened by a kiss, revived like a light being switched on, in a state of traumatic shock. Far better imagined by Berghaus than the usual Bottom–Titania exchange, this was not a marriage made in heaven. Catarina Ligendza's Brünnhilde (recalling that she was the young hero's aunt) managed to carry herself off very much as Siegfried's senior, suggesting trouble ahead – as turned out.

Berghaus had a simple scheme. The revolve was barely used. The sets were elementary and rigorous, costumes ripe with implications but unrelated to period or context outside this stage world. Her actual direction of the acting was very rich. Until the meeting with Brünnhilde, usually one of the most unconvincing and ritualized love scenes in theatre history, the events were unflagging.

Unlike the other *Ring* operas, *Götterdämmerung* is a working-out, not a new start. It is, as the scene with the Norns confirms, the fulfilment of an inescapable process. The Gibichungs' hall may seem a new location, but the link between Hagen and Alberich underscores the continuity. Manthey brought back some familiar elements such as Brünnhilde's breastlike mountaintop from *Siegfried* and *Walküre*. The Rhinemaidens, though not suspended as in *Rheingold*, had the same glossy look, the same mixture of green make-up and red lips, red shoes, red stockings. Waltraute returned from *Walküre*, and Brünnhilde played nostalgically with her helmet and spear. Alberich, first lord of the ring, returned both for Hagen's watch and for the scene where the Rhinemaidens ask Siegfried to restore the gold ring to them.

The Norns were swamped up to their armpits, like Winnie in Beckett's *Happy Days*, in vast white crinolines with galactic petticoats underneath, and entered under a curtain of Loge-like flames stretching across the proscenium anticipating '*Das Ende*'. Instead of breaking their rope, they seemed to be concerned that it was their curtain (of respectability) which was wearing out; they wielded their needles ineffectually. Lovers of equine theatre were pleased to find Grane, Brünnhilde's usually absent steed, on stage – though immobile and lying on her side. Adorno joked that Grane's fate, forced to carry Brünnhilde into the flames of the funeral pyre, was a case of gratuitous cruelty to animals. The stuffed horse lay there during the denouement. When Siegfried concluded his Rhine journey at the Gibichungs' Hall, Grane was there behind him as the boat bearing them nosed its way through the central doorway. The trilby was back as a symbol of dishonesty. Even Brünnhilde put one on guiltily while plotting Siegfried's death with Hagen and Günther at the end of act 2. The chorus of vassals wore trilbies over their black balaclavas, above a uniform of smart grey trousers, black padded arms and copper breastplates. Their women moved like mannequins or Stepford wives, lips and eyes wide in brainless surprise under copper headdresses. Gutrune, her manner similar, picked hairs off the black suit into which Siegfried changed after he had drunk the magic potion and sworn blood-brotherhood.

As in *Walküre* the Frankfurt revolve was simply used, the set divided up by a pair of monumental walls coming to a point that represented the Rhine, covered with aqueous dappled green reflections. On one side of the wall was the Gibichungs' Hall, a white space decorated with a fresco of an elegant hand on the wall to the right of the central door, seven chairs, a glass exhibition case containing Wotan and Fricka's half-head crowns, and a seaside-view telescope on a stand through which Gutrune vainly tried to see the way ahead. On the other side of the wall was Brünnhilde's mountaintop mound, which became the site of Siegfried's murder by Hagen, and then later the funeral pyre bursting into real flames. The wall went up into the flies for the final conflagration. The revolve turned, the flames on the mound burned high. And, as the ritual concluded, the wall returned to its place, with Gutrune sitting and searching through the telescope – a telling hint of unresolved questions.

The most striking sequence of all was the death of Siegfried. When he sat up to sing his last touching lines the stage was empty. Then after he died the vassals, back on the scene, suddenly fell to the ground beside him – reviving a few bars later and kicking his corpse down the slope. Both Siegfried and Hagen became like the walking dead during the final manoeuvres as Brünnhilde prepared to put the opera to rest. An image to take away was the Nancy

Reagan-like Gutrune, keeping up appearances with smiles and quick little gestures. Using recognizable codes of behaviour and a modern aesthetic, Berghaus picked a confident path between moral awareness and theatrical exuberance. Gielen's interpretation and conducting, similar to Boulez but with greater delicacy and musical emotion, matched Berghaus's witty fresh lyrical exuberance perfectly.

Berghaus's achievement with *The Ring* was widely recognized. After Gielen left Frankfurt, she was in much demand. I saw her world premiere production of Wolfgang von Schweinitz's three-hour-long *Patmos* at the Munich Biennale (Hans Werner Henze's modern opera festival) in 1990, her *Ariane et Barbe Bleu* at the Paris Châtelet theatre in 1991, her *Rise and Fall of the City of Mahagonny* in Stuttgart in 1992, and her *Rosenkavalier* in Frankfurt in 1993. But never was there the focus and conviction about the ideas that distinguished her superb Frankfurt work.

Patmos filled the whole of the large Congress Hall of the Deutsches Museum with a massive architectural set by Hans Dieter Schaal (designer of her Frankfurt *Trojans*) that looked like an industrial ruin and container gantries. Berghaus had a big chorus, eight dancers, and a cast of seventeen for this theatrical realization of the Apocalypse, epic theatre in the tradition of Max Reinhardt, but done in modern style. The music blended medieval rhythms and organum-like repetitions with contemporary polyphony suggesting Bach via Webern and Stravinsky, musical post-modernism, singable and catchy yet without tunes. By contrast Berghaus's intricate stage action was visionary, sober and jubilant, with not a hint of end-of-the-world hype or coarse theatrical tricks in Marie-Luise Strandt's costumes and props – mostly referring to particular nightmares of German nationalism.

The style ranged widely. Characteristically for Berghaus, the pair of singers simultaneously taking the role of John (heroic tenor and bass) wore macintoshes and trilbies and seemed more like journalists than evangelists. The admonitory men's quartet sported Prussian officers' uniforms; the main chorus wore student uniforms, and ended in haloes and white robes. Two Angel trios and the New Angel and Old Angel (female soloists) had halo-like wings and nun-style head-dresses. X, the Bach Passion-style Christ figure, had a white fencing mask and protective costume, his rapier lit up at its tip: a reminder that one joy of Berghaus stagings is their refusal to be relentlessly serious. For the long letters to the churches at the start of Revelations (Schweinitz used all the biblical words) the quartet of officers brought out typewriters. The Christian symbolism was not heavy or pious: the dance group were eventually on point for the last beautifully restrained battles with the dragon and the scarlet woman. Sweeping choric actions underlined the text, highlighting special messages with eye-catching gestures and visionary faints. X, or Christus, climbed into the control cabin of the gantry or sat in a passport-photo machine emitting resurrection-like flashes. The great gong and percussion in the orchestra thundered out for the earthquakes. A wisp of dry ice erupted from the fifteen cattle-pens at the centre of the stage. With lighting changes and simple expressive movements Berghaus gradually worked up to her heavenly Jerusalem, conveying the message with strange dignity, never just illustrating the story. Her staging was hypnotic, contemporary, spiritually provocative and never churchy.

Feminism was Berghaus's prevailing theme in Paul Dukas's *Ariane et Barbe-Bleue* in Paris. Unlike Strauss's *Ariadne*, Ariane would never submit to Dionysus - and unlike Bartók's Judith she walked free after saving Bluebeard from his rampaging peasants. Berghaus's formidable Ariane in a Struwelpeter wig and Indian trouser-suit was unimpressed with the jewels discovered by the Nurse behind locked doors. Her aim was to get as quickly as possible to the seventh forbidden door so that she could disobey Bluebeard's injunction – 'the primal duty when an order is menacing and unexplained,' as she said. The set, once more by Hans Dieter Schaal, was strikingly lit all in white. It suggested Parisian roof-tops and chimneys rising dramatically to the rear, odd windows and skylights. The succession of jewels that tumbled out of chimneys and erupted from windows touched by the Nurse were actually female dancers (costumed by Marie-Luise Strandt) with amethyst and emerald in their make-up, moving crablike on their bottoms over sloping roofs, legs pointing like the glittering reflections of cut stones. Ariane ripped the lid off a women's world, using balletic movement.

Bluebeard never had a chance. The wives in the second act were much attached to his Onassis-style motor-launch, which was on its side, surrealistically washed up on the roof at the right of the stage. As voices off-stage uttered warnings, Ariane entered holding an umbilical cord, a bright red rope, perhaps the much needed guidance that the audience needed for Berghaus's minotaur-like labyrinth of meaning. It was not the story as Maeterlinck and Dukas imagined it. The peasants were threatening male figures in black jump-suits. The nurse was in a trilby, legwarmers, Doc Martens and miniskirt. It was not a ruritanian Duke's castle, and there was no feudal village. Berghaus subtly and believably humanized the wives: their strange wigs and make-up at the start resembled the jewel dancers. But Dukas's atmospherics were too fragile for such robust intervention. Berghaus's witty world of modern wealth and social power did not go with the music's diluted post-Wagnerian mixture. Dukas's fairytale dreamlike opera was stretched out of shape by all the shouting from Paris rooftops.

Not a single boo greeted the premiere of Berghaus's new Stuttgart staging of *The Rise and Fall of the City of Mahagonny*, with Zehelein (joint director of the Stuttgart Opera with Gielen's former Frankfurt assistant Pamela Rosenberg) as dramaturg. But *Mahagonny*'s satire should make opera-goers uncomfortable, even if they can wriggle out of the target zone. Why else did Weill employ chorale material and Bach Passion-like counterpoint, except to intimate communal morality? Berghaus had the advantage of having been married to Brecht's other composer, Paul Dessau. The notorious falling-out of Brecht and Weill, which was precipitated substantially by *Mahagonny*, became after their deaths a debate over whether this political parable was operatic or for the theatre. Berghaus's production was cool and objective, but her '*alte sachlichkeit*' lacked fire. The outrage at capitalist corruption, which stirred Nazi demonstrations in 1930, seemed artificial. The collapse of communism had shaken Berghaus's conviction. She was too respectful for the old firm's period piece, and her style-conscious staging had few jokes and little energy.

Brecht's surreal and ironical story-line about a tropical gold-rush boomtown flooded with deceit and delusion shares in first-world arrogance. But the images of designers Hans-Joachim Schlieker (sets) and Marie-Luise Strandt (costumes and requisites) were smart rather than sleazy, more like the shiny black and white of Kupfer stagings than the vulgar pop Americanism Brecht imagined. A soap-opera aesthetic might have been more apt. Berghaus ironed out the irony by adopting a fashionably uniform style. Satire should establish, or take as read, the norm from which it departs. Berghaus's theatre language, jarring for Wagner, Mozart, and Janáček, was too buttoned down for Brecht's louche tastelessness and never found an alternative to downmarket imitation yankee. Graham Vick at the 1990 Maggio Musicale in Florence (see p. 273) and Declan Donnellan at Wexford in 1985 (though sadly not at ENO in 1995) responded more imaginatively, with respectively extravagant and economical styles.

Schlieker's opening set was a massive companion-way on an ocean liner. The steps were pulled up into the ceiling once the Mahagonny population had descended, leaving a stage-wide hall (floor marked for deck tennis) with looming opaque windows and a recess at the end containing a mobile platform and a throne in a dust-cover. Under the dust-cover was an electric chair for Jimmy's execution. The theme was rearranging the seats on the *Titanic*. Begbick, Fatty and Trinity Moses, who appeared on the upper steps in yellow Mao-suits, rolled jerkily down over and over after sharing a Beckettian dialogue. There was no truck and no silent film titles announced the scenes. Brecht's captions were spoken, sometimes chorally, always emphatically. Later the trio adopted Pierrot rig and white tailsuits, respectively. Gestures towards the text included plastic potted palms and a car seat. The stage was surrounded with xeroxes of Jimmy's face. The girls, sloping down the companionway in a half-hearted Busby Berkeley routine, introduced the Alabama Song. For people who thought Otto Dix too fierce, this sanitized decadence might have sufficed – gold frocks compensating for an absence of golden hearted whores. The quartet of Klondike pioneers in fur coats also launched themselves down the steps with theatrical flourish. The later story developments were handled very respectably. The motto of the production might have been Jack's line *'Das ist die ewige Kunst'* (That's what I call eternal art). A white grand piano was lowered from the flies for the interrupted recital. The lumberjacks were soon dressed in velvet evening suits. Once the hurricane had bypassed Mahagonny, Jack in tails ate himself politely to death, miming the munching of forkfuls proffered by dinner-suited gents. Two ballerinas teetered across the stage with gauze circles attached to their hands and bizarre hairstyles, like ghosts from Stephen Sondheim's *Follies* spiriting away the dead Jack and Joe.

The final decline and fall degenerated into a bizarre wedding procession headed by Bankbook Billy and a subdued Jenny in fake tiara; the backs of xerox mugshots from the opening scene were turned over to reveal a selection of Brecht's assorted slogans: ominous but scarcely terminal. Berghaus's staging took a pro-Weill, anti-Brecht approach that matched Stuttgart's strongly operatic casting and the sombre weight of the conducting. The major aim seemed to have been to register the score in operatic splendour with robust singing.

Berghaus's treatment of *Der Rosenkavalier* was also a case of style over content. Like Puccini operas, this Strauss can seem cut and dried for interpreters. For decades all versions acknowledged the tradition of the original 1911 Roller designs. With its Cherubino-like central role (for a principal-boy mezzo) Strauss and Hofmannsthal's loaded conundrum of sentiment and artifice looked proof against deconstruction, shamelessly celebrating class privilege in a *Dynasty*-like fable of love at the top, where hero in travesty and innocent heroine twine fates and voices at equal high pitch. Frankfurt provided a fresh classy cast, with Deborah Polaski as a questioning ambivalent Feldmarschallin, Ildiko Komlosi's confident Octavian, and Pia-Marie Nilsson's pious uptight Sophie. Berghaus substituted self-conscious consumerist 'culture' for rococo decorative excess. Her ideology did not connect to Hofmannsthal's comedy and satire – the romantic humanism of Octavian's initiation. Like her Stuttgart *Mahagonny*, the not revealing enough choreography came first. Also the stuffing was knocked out of Ochs (a firm but prosaic Daniel Lewis Williams). Here was not the larger than life, vulgar egoist, but a bearded fat man in a fashionable white suit, in the third act sunk in mystified passivity – victim of a charmless feminist reading. Heinz Oswald's costumes (especially the 'clients' and tradespeople in the first act) were Karl Lagerfeld out of *commedia dell'arte*. Erich Wonder's monumental sets made the first act a glowing ante-room of translucent polychrome glass tiles – like a jewel-box. The middle act and its presentation of the (genuinely silver) Rose was in a spectacular library with a central turret staircase crowded with volumes, and towering lit-up stacks that swayed and circled on the edge of the revolve. Faninal's upwardly mobile ambitions were reflected in 'culture' pinned down on the page. A dagger fight with Ochs brought on a stretcher trolley and hospital drips. The last comic act was at the bottom of a vast tunnel staircase, going straight downstage to an underworld den or nightclub: majestic squalor like the fascist grandeur of Peduzzi's set for the Ripper scene in Chéreau's Paris *Lulu*. Hired underclass thugs in masks made *Cabaret*-type appearances. The bed where Ochs vainly tried the seduction was on a mobile hydraulic arm wobbling nervously over the orchestra-pit:

an aesthetic statement, luxury with admonitory hints. Instead of a black boy servant, the Marschallin had a dancer moving on his knees, his face a black mask.

Imagery and ideas were far less startling than Berghaus's best work in the 1980s. Her *Rosenkavalier* suggested lack of sympathy with Hofmannsthal's comedy: an ideological problem. The energy in her *Ring*, *Entführung* and *Trojans* came from the way she incorporated the philosophy and narrative motivation of Mozart, Wagner and Berlioz into her version of the history of the present day. That needed imagination, energy, daring – readiness to think again. Unlike Chéreau, she did a great deal of operatic work, not always with good results. The confidence behind her objective, thought-provoking and strikingly unusual methods meant that even when the results were questionable there was plenty worth studying. Berghaus, who was 68 when she died, was in the 1980s the most original and challenging interpreter in the world of European opera.

8 David Alden: expressionist shock

David Alden's 1994 staging (for the Bavarian State Opera, Munich) of *Tannhäuser* designed by Roni Toren and Buki Shiff: Landgrave and fetishistic minstrel knights in the valley before the Wartburg – Jan-Hendrik Rootering as Landgrave Hermann, James Anderson as Heinrich der Schreiber, Günter Nöcker as Biterolf, René Kollo as Tannhäuser, Gerhard Auer as Reinmar von Zweter, Claes H. Ahnsjö as Walter von der Vogelweide, Bernd Weikl as Wolfram von Echenbach. Photograph © Anne Kirchbach.

Only a few opera producers from the United States have real individual signatures. American companies mostly do not offer artistic autonomy to the more innovative and adventurous directorial talents, and those newcomers who want to work rather than dream can easily perceive the terms of their trade. Pleasing patrons is the name of the game, which makes for caution all round. Perhaps not too many American artists are drawn to a performing art where their taste is likely to be fettered and where there is little chance of serious profit. In France and Germany film directors try their hands at opera, but Steven Spielberg and Oliver Stone have yet to venture in. The American way of paying for opera – how Europe did it too, before the 20th century – is over-dependent on the whim of princes. Money aristocrats provide patronage for most US opera companies. Managements spend a great deal of their time fund-raising. Nowhere in the world can an opera company survive (let alone make money) on the take from ticket prices. In the USA, where the role of subsidy has always been severely limited and is likely to reduce further, experiment is discouraged. There is little sense, in the normal run of American productions, of opera's social or political relevance, or of the idea that opera focuses on the individual in society. US opera is home-grown, conventional and increasingly (encouragingly) popular, but seldom subversive or challenging. It is the preserve of self-made institutions like Pavarotti (the television network star), or the Three Tenors, or Beverly Sills, the light coloratura soprano who, as boss of New York City Opera, ended the company's long-standing and eclectic language policy of performing sometimes in English, sometimes in the original language. Surtitles became the norm and opera in English disappeared in what was surely a threatening development for the future of opera and singing in the USA. At the Met, where a special kind of simultaneous translating was finally adopted in the 1995–6 season, the usual plump 'international' diet has tended to make Covent Garden look radical, even before the more adventurous Royal Opera policy of the mid-1990s. On the other hand, the tyranny of the market and popular taste (at the opposite extreme from the tyranny of subsidized artistic whim) probably accounts for the rise of minimalism as an operatic style. The attempt to please has been restored as a respectable aim for American composers. That may be very healthy.

US patrons, many also art collectors, are sympathetic to the new and modern. The late John Dexter's work at the Met was generally welcomed as innovative, whether or not successful, and did not alienate the audience. American composers are having greater popular success with new operas than composers anywhere else, though the musical languages forged by Philip Glass, John Adams, Dominick Argento, Carlisle Floyd and John Corigliano suggest an unambitious and limited future for opera. Glass, who graduated from the avant garde to the hugely popular, thanks in part to the acceptability of modern dance and painting in New York and the generous appetite for the new there, became in the 1980s the most prolific composer of new operas anywhere in the world. He is a major figure in the modern movement, even if his operatic material is musically thin, repetitive and comparatively characterless. Not for the first time in the 20th century composers have rejected complexity and variety, as Carl Orff's blandly anonymous *Antigone* did in 1949. Glass is not trying to make things too easy for the audience though. His early philosophical operas demoted the importance of the text, in a sense, by using words that would be inaccessible to the audience, and would therefore take on whatever meaning he wanted, working like a mantra. Adams's *Nixon in China* and his later *Death of Klinghoffer*, as staged by Peter Sellars, toured many of the cities that regard themselves as operatically world class. The premiere of Corigliano's *Ghosts of Versailles* was a popular hit with Met audiences in December 1991. In Britain Michael Nyman followed the fashion with *The Man who Mistook his Wife for a Hat* and other efforts. Minimalism is modern and popular – at least in music. There has been an appetite for less angst, and less meaning, for which modern dance showed the way, using physical energy to bring a message of buoyancy and joy to audiences – without painful arguments or narrative to disturb. The world of dance, under the scrutiny of the *New Yorker*'s critic Arlene Croce, developed a language of abstract actions and eccentric (often imaginative and expressive) designs. Expression came to be recognized as not just, or even, telling a tale. Activity was its own artistic reward. Robert Wilson, the leading stylistic trend-setter in the avant-garde world of dance and music, staged Glass's *Einstein on the Beach*, and launched a whole genre of minimalist opera whose godparents were the dance traditions of Merce Cunningham, Alwyn Nikolais and Twyla Tharp. American patrons have enjoyed acknowledging artistic innovators. The hand-jiving gesture language that Peter Sellars has incorporated into his kind of operatic acting, a memory of his puppet-theatre apprenticeship as well as a borrowing from Indonesian theatre, shows a relationship with the modern language of American dance – a popular association.

Significantly, the passed-over English opera producers who used to dominate Covent Garden and the Coliseum in the 1970s, like Colin Graham and John Copley, have found a real welcome on the American opera circuit and its Australian extension, after being displaced from ENO and the Royal Opera. There was also a liking in the USA for more conventional highly machined talents like the late Jean-Pierre Ponnelle (whom Christopher Alden, David Alden's less original twin brother, assisted for four years). But that did not mean Christopher Alden needed to leave the USA to develop his career or his name for innovation. He found a berth as director of production at the Long Beach Opera outside Los Angeles. Some US and Canadian producers have made a successful transition to Europe, apart from David and Christopher Alden and Peter Sellars: Frank Corsaro, Francesca Zambello and Robert Carsen have probably been the most celebrated exports, though neither Zambello nor Corsaro has been notably original. Corsaro's commitment to theatricality and colour in his work at New York City Opera, when it still performed regularly in English and had a commitment to the less privileged, was a crucial formative influence on the Alden twins. Corsaro's British opportunities came from his collaboration with the children's books author Maurice Sendak and the young English composer Oliver Knussen; the results, at Glyndebourne, were entertaining and stylish, thanks to the way Sendak applied his highly idiosyncratic visual imagination. Carsen, who served his apprenticeship in England, may seem closer to the innovative names on the European scene; his approach to Bellini's *La straniera* for Wexford in 1987 was darkly stormy and romantic with fervent but vital acting and singing from its young stars. He has made a mark in Geneva (with, for instance, Boito's *Mefistofele*, starring Samuel Ramey) and in Antwerp with a Puccini cycle. His *Cendrillon* for WNO and *Midsummer Night's Dream* for ENO (originally seen in Aix) were lively and practical – the former even evocatively atmospheric. Zambello is efficient as she showed with a decent *Benvenuto Cellini* in Geneva and with her *Khovanshchina* at the Coliseum. Her vulgarized and brash *Billy Budd* (in Britten's original four-act structure) transferred from Geneva to Covent Garden in 1995. But both Zambello and Carsen have played safe, scarcely attempting to refine the acting or explore the ideas of the works in any depth, and sticking to an aesthetic almost as unchallenging as the staid product of, say, Bliss Hebert and designer Allen Charles Klein.

Peter Sellars and David Alden are great infuriators. It is not hard to predict which audiences and critics will not like their productions in Britain. But their passionate detractors are matched by supporters and advocates. In fact, these two Americans have few qualities in common. The Alden twins are eight years older than Sellars. Their careers have followed more conventional paths – they have both worked for a wide range of different opera companies. Sellars from his prodigious time at Harvard onwards has manufactured his own special opportunities, and exploited his notoriety as a genius. (This was recognized in 1983 when, at 26, he won a \$136,000 Genius Award from the MacArthur Foundation.) Sellars has managed to create special festival-like conditions for his productions. He needs or prefers familiar collaborators. He evidently likes to work with artists and singers he knows, who have become a sort of operatic repertory company for him.

Meanwhile David Alden (born 1949) operated at ENO within the constraints of company casting policy. Alden and Sellars have shared the modern conviction that staging operas means forging a design context, a physical location which can say something about the significance of the event and force the audience to engage critically with the material. This has made for provocative productions, relevant to the audience's cultural assumptions. What was shown on stage had to be telling and was pared down to focus on the potent interpretative core. Yet Sellars and Alden have not shared a visual taste. Sellars's usual designers are American – Alden in Britain has worked with British or British-trained designers, perhaps in that way helping anchor his work in the culture and country where he lives and which has enthusiastically adopted him and his work. A producer's visual taste is the major factor in the interest and individuality of his work. Both Alden and Sellars direct acting so that every movement on stage is owned and intended, grounded in character. Both think theatrically. Their language may be different but both are as controversial in the USA as in Britain. These certainly are two of the most distinguished and distinctive innovators of the 1980s and 1990s in the English-speaking operatic world.

Alden used to be identified strongly with a particular seam of work at ENO; his most important operatic statements of the last decade have probably all been in Britain. He was a talisman for the ENO regime of David Pountney, Mark Elder and Peter Jonas. Bringing Alden to the Coliseum was an act of conviction and artistic commitment by Pountney and Elder. The link came about as follows. Pountney, in 1976 when he was still Scottish Opera's youthful director of productions, was engaged to stage Carlisle Floyd's *Bilby's Doll* for Houston Grand Opera. He arrived a month before his own rehearsals were due to start, and found Alden working on *Don Giovanni* there with the young Michael Devlin in the title role. So he lined himself up in the spare time to be Alden's assistant. Alden has not been without work in his home country: he can look back on about ten major productions there since 1980, including *Turn of the Screw* in Santa Fe, *Wozzeck* in Los Angeles, *La Calisto* in New York and Conrad Susa's *Transformations* at the Spoleto Festival in Charleston. These have been one-off events. He has not built an audience for his work in the USA as he has in London. Recognition of Alden's stature has come through his work in Britain and, to an extent, in Israel. ENO audiences rose enthusiastically to the challenge he set them, but his engagements required total and unwavering support from Jonas, Elder and Pountney. Lord Harewood was very hard to persuade, and the decision to give the new *Masked Ball* production to Alden required an hour's fight at Board level. The Board wanted Nicholas Hytner to do the job.

Alden was already 30 when he began to attract attention in Britain. *Mazeppa*, the Tchaikovsky rarity which got a cut-price ENO production at the Coliseum under the NorWest Holst scheme, was the major breakthrough – its chainsaw execution below-stage was immediately notorious and became a symbol of ENO's brave new production world. It was perhaps easier for the audience to be receptive to Alden's approach because *Mazeppa*, though it had an enticing romantic score by Tchaikovsky, was not part of the familiar repertoire. Jonathan Miller's updating and relocation of *Rigoletto* in Mafia-dominated Little Italy, New York, had become an established popular ENO hit. But Miller's *Rigoletto* did not dwell much on the violence and cruelty which are the mark of the New York Mafia world. This was a deodorized Mafia, superficial mimicry. The Duke (or 'Duke' as the boss was called, pronounced 'Dook') was more comfortable and familiar even than Robert de Niro made Al Capone in the film of *The Untouchables* – where the quest against evil was punctuated by gory assassinations. Verdi's dramatic universe incorporated poisoning, stabbing, suffocation, betrayal. But his expressive power was applied to exposing the damage in his hero-victims' souls. *Mazeppa* was different: it contained barbarism along with its politics and morality, and it could not be staged honestly without confronting that barbarism.

Alden's production at the Coliseum was greeted rather as Edward Bond's *Saved* had been when new at the Royal Court Theatre in 1965. People would admit such things happened, but could not accept that they deserved to be put on stage uncompromisingly. A century ago Tchaikovsky conceived *Mazeppa* as a nationalistic exercise about a Ukrainian hero who led a revolt against Peter the Great's newly westernized Russian state – drawing on Pushkin's poem, *Poltava*. Tchaikovsky paralleled Mazeppa's selfish political ambitions with his wilful passion for his god-daughter, many years his junior, whom he carried off against the wishes of his old friend, her father. Mazeppa tortured and executed the father and his followers, and his Cossack revolt was pursued to its disastrous conclusion with arrant brutality. It was not a pretty tale. At the end the girl, Maria, was out of her mind and Mazeppa's plan for Ukrainian independence was totally shattered. Credible violence and cruelty were the essential elements in Alden's theatrical language for *Mazeppa* – though including such gory detail proved extremely controversial and Alden's later ENO and WNO work has continued to cause surprise and sometimes offence.

Staging violence, or rather suggesting such extreme barbarity and brutality, was not unprecedented in the opera-house. The killing of Siegfried in Chéreau's centenary *Ring* at Bayreuth was carried out with shocking ferocity. *The Ring* and a few other Wagner operas demand the presentation of convincing violence on stage: the wounding of Tristan by Melot, the murder of Fasolt by Fafner, the killing of Siegmund, Mime, and Fafner. But few operas are as underpinned by a culture of political violence as *Mazeppa*. Audiences have to be persuaded to take violence seriously – just as they need to be persuaded about the love they are being shown.

Peter Hall in his halcyon operatic days used to bewail the tendency of opera audiences to overlook the pain and emotional disturbance underlying a perennially popular opera like *The Marriage of Figaro*.

Alden made the violence of his *Mazeppa* believable by relocating the story to the time of the 20th-century Great Dictators (Hitler and Stalin). Conventionally it would have been staged as a *Boris Godunov*-style costume drama with colourful heavy robes and processions and muddled masses pressing around the stage. The updating provided a frame of reference in which design and choreographed movement could be combined to authenticate ritualized thoughtless political violence. Alden anyway seems to need to draw on the audience's memory of the Nazi holocaust, to establish a continuum of political violence and systemic cruelty. Such associations challenge the audience to identify morally because the more recent experience of evil is always taken more seriously than cruelty softened by history. Operas from the past have rarely been given a social interpretation: they have been seen as a romantic anecdotal interplay of larger-than-life characters, and loved for the reassuring voluptuousness of their music. It is shocking and provocative to remind audiences of the political reality submerged behind music.

There was a link between the boos that in December 1984 greeted Alden's *Mazeppa* staging with its modern instruments of torture – electric drills, chainsaws, bludgeoning hose-pipes, electric shocks – and the jeers that Götz Friedrich's *Tannhäuser* received in July 1972 in Bayreuth when his pilgrims' chorus raised their clenched fists in a 'workers' salute to the audience. Friedrich's frisson of Marxism in a former shrine of fascism (whose passing some, including Winifred Wagner, still regretted) was a more localized and opportunistic gesture than Alden's wish to bind into the fabric of the first British staging of *Mazeppa* the recognition that the Cossack at the core of the story was a monster, and that Tchaikovsky's opera was a dangerous parable of political reality in the 20th century. It was still eight years before the break-up of the Soviet Union and 'ethnic cleansing' in Bosnia. Friedrich's gesture was not seriously proposing a Marxist cause in Bayreuth, though Chéreau's *Ring* in 1976 was to be regarded by some critics as overtly Marxist in inspiration. Friedrich was not personally interested in politics in East Germany nor in arguing about political developments there. The creation of the Felsenstein school of operatic interpretation at the Komische Oper, Berlin, was a form of tokenism. Felsenstein always lived in a flat in West Berlin, and Friedrich 'defected' to the West at the first opportunity. Opera under Stalinism was a nostalgic, humane, liberal form of escapism – even though not intended for the bourgeois.

To assert that violence is necessary in a staging of a 19th-century romantic tale, to reconcile audience and performers to its use, is not easy or automatic. The representation of violence, sex and nudity on stage has never been married to the physical singing convention of opera. It is controversial, questionable and difficult. But when violence in cinema fiction and television newsreel reports is routine and exaggerated in detail, the creative artist cannot simply blank out that area – as French classical theatre scrupulously did for reasons of decorum. This is not an Augustan age. No such decorum governs general behaviour, and there is little genuine privacy. Alden broke the established operatic decorum in various ways. The combination of a specific design language (notably provided at ENO by his frequent designer David Fielding) with the precise, detailed and truthful direction of individual characters, and energetic chorus work, allowed his epic operatic landscapes to deal in horrors. Alden plainly and convincingly (for many in his audience) told the truth in his productions – both about the people in the drama and about the politics touching their lives. The harping on images and actions from the recent history of political violence, Nazi or Stalinist, was challenging but reasonable. The history of the century demonstrates that.

In *Mazeppa* it was also an advantage that the chorus had to carry their scores – that they had not had to learn their parts under the special circumstances of the NorWest Holst series of disposable economic productions of rare operas (which had been launched the previous season with Nicholas Hytner's *Rienzi*). Alden turned this apparent handicap to advantage. Because the chorus carried their music they had to be more static than usual, and the image of Stalinist conformism was emphasized when some of the chorus were stationed in the upper stage boxes wearing hats and coats like Soviet apparatchiks at a May Day parade. This image of the chorus became a powerful symbol of political disengagement and toadying conformism, passively endorsing Mazeppa's personality cult. Fielding emphasized that, with a carefully placed photograph-portrait of the Hetman leaning against the proscenium in front of the main curtain.

In the first scene the chorus were seated in rows holding their music and facing across the stage from left to right – the masses separated both politically and physically from the elite, watching discussions. Fielding's set was a white-walled utility barrack-room lit from above by naked lightbulbs not far beyond head height, with swing doors at the corners and in the middle of each side. Striplights round the top of the walls cast a repellent, unthe-atrical glow. Fielding was determined to prevent any sense of the pleasant illusion of entertainment that conventional theatre light-ing can encourage. Old wooden doors from demolition dumps were used to enclose or isolate smaller spaces and focus on more intimate moments. During those rapid rearrangements the strip-lights were lit. In front of this brutal environment, Maria (a glow-ing star performance from young Janice Cairns) sang of her infatuation with the middle-aged Mazeppa. Malcolm Donnelly as Mazeppa, with grey suit and neat clipped moustache, was able to emerge spotless from the torture chamber below-stage where he had just witnessed a chainsaw decapitation. When Maria's father, Kochubei, a tight-suited patriarch with cropped silver hair and spectacles, refused Mazeppa's request for her hand, the Hetman simply ordered his Cossacks to take what he wanted. Their com-pelling peasant abandon had earlier been enthusiastically sug-gested in a Gopak choreographed by Ian Spink. Men in macintoshes and trilbies danced fiercely with androgynous youths, an eerily sexual contemporary demonstration that had nothing to do with the implied 1930s period of the staging, but a lot to do with contemporary choreography. The hint of alien mores reminded the audience that the Russian empire was not just Orthodox Christian, but on the borderline with Islam. Maria's abduction by Mazeppa's men was staged by Alden with a memo-rable image of disjunction. The ENO chorus, holding their books, fled helter-skelter from their now overturned ranks of chairs.

Alden continued as he started. The torture, violence and depri-vation caused by Mazeppa's tribalism continued in the later acts as the pace of the opera stilled to an agonized and obsessive fatalism. If the production gloried in its images of blood and violence, the unrelenting cruelty of civil war among Balkan-style partisans, it needed to emphasize the contrast between Mazeppa's impeccable Mr Clean image (enhanced by the genuineness of his romantic attachment to Maria, at least until the denouement), his neat grey suit, white shirt and clipped moustache, and the consequences of his policy. Alden had to show the sharp edge of Mazeppa's blunt morality. There was no flinching from the graphic cruelty that separated romantic image from brutal reality. Following that sombre storyline, Alden achieved a cinematic focus for such scenes as Liubov, Kochubei's wife (superbly characterized by Felicity Palmer), persuading her daughter to intervene with her lover on behalf of her father – the rush to save him being, of course, sickeningly too late. When an operatic ensemble is drawn so purposefully together, the sum of the parts is definitely greater than the whole.

In the final scene Mazeppa, the now elderly Cossack boss who had reduced his entire world to mayhem, felt the slight stirrings of conscience confronted with his desperate beloved Maria. Should not he do something to help the crazed refugee she had become, as to gain her he had torn the whole community apart? Orlik, his hatchet-man, asked: 'Is she dearer than the head upon your shoulders?' Mazeppa, with a shrug, sighed 'Let's go' – abandoning her, walking off safe and free. Alden's Tchaikovskyan *Apocalypse Now* offered no retributive justice to reassert the optimistic bourgeois view of humanity.

Over two years later Alden and Fielding collaborated again on an ENO production (Fielding having since designed *Xerxes* for Nicholas Hytner, opening two months after *Mazeppa*). In Verdi's *Simon Boccanegra*, the tragic tribalism was not unlike *Mazeppa*, but the emphasis, as usual in Verdi, was on the conflict between private morality and public duty – as expressed in the renascent relationship of Simon and his long-lost daughter. Music prepared the ground perfectly for cathartic recognitions and reversals such as Aristotle described in the *Poetics*. In *Boccanegra* the daughter was not just physically lost, but (having been brought up by Simon's old enemy, the father of his dead beloved) spiritually cut off – like Debby in John Ford's *The Searchers*. Alden presented the continuum between mother and daughter inescapably: the corpse that was tipped out of Maria's coffin was Janice Cairns who then acted the daughter, Amelia (or Maria).

The conspiratorial prologue immediately established Alden's non-naturalistic approach, with its blend of black modern plebeian clothes, leather jackets, overcoats, men in floppy hats, women with heads covered in black shawls. Dark red and black contrasted, on the distorted walls of the set, with a crescent moon in shadowy cloud on the white wall, an ordinary pannelled door on the right, a shadow running across the floor, the sense of crowds penned in. Alden suggested syndicalism, organized labour, an election illicitly and mysteriously fixed. It is Fiesco's dread that Simon will win the vote so cunningly manipulated by Piero. This seemed far more understandable when removed from a history-book colourful 14th-century Genoa. Strehler's famous, beautiful Scala production staged the prologue in pitch black, with shafts of light stabbing through to focus on particular faces. Alden responded to the political undertow with equal but different theatrical rigour. This wasn't, strictly, updating – the substitution of one period for another. It was freeing from any specific time, a design language evoking various periods. Gabriele Adorno, the tenor hero with whom Simon's daughter is in love and who threatens her father, was seen first in 18th-century waistcoat, boots and cravat, later in bits of medieval armour. Maria was in a billowing medieval robe. Boccanegra became a medieval symbol himself, wrapped eventually in an Italian tag on a long piece of material that had stretched across the front of the stage during the great Council-chamber scene where Paolo was forced to anathematize himself for abusing his closeness to Boccanegra, and where the Doge himself outfaced the squabbling tribes of Guelphs and Ghibellines. Swords had been sown across the back of the stage like ears of corn. The seaboard of the first act was evoked with huge rocks on a white floor, in front of a small inner stage dominated by a stormy sky. A coffin leant against one of the rocks on the left, beneath a protruding carving of a saint. The vastness of the Coliseum stage was well used for the cool, sad reserve of the scene before the mutual recognition of father and daughter. Some critics' obsession with decorum and conventional pictures prevented them noticing how scrupulously Alden had managed the energy flowing in relationships on stage, how he had built the actions and reactions of living theatre. The great movements were carried off to match the grandeur of the music, in an epic realization.

There were many of the familiar Fielding elements on the set: ordinary wooden kitchen chairs, cheap pinewood platforms, door and window openings flush with blank flats around the back of the stage. The sleepless Doge, about to be poisoned, wore a candlewick dressing-gown and sat on a gothic seat supported on adjustable television-set legs. Economical to obtain, this also went with Fielding's telling mixture of ancient and modern, with Fiesco in an old carpenter's grey cotton overall coat. Most unusual of the 'props' of the production was a giant 'iron' hand suspended above the Council chamber scene and Boccanegra on his throne in medieval robes of office. When the masses invaded the set, this hand was rudely lowered to the ground and broken up – a telling climax to the effective crowd movement and sword fights between patricians in ancient robes and plebeians in leather jackets. Alden put together for *Simon Boccanegra* a different scenario from that he had deployed in *Mazeppa*, though also severely economical. But his determination to break with the conventional decorum and rhythm of Verdi detracted for some from his command of the tragic scale. However well regarded the music and singing, little credit was given for the way the direction enabled the musical qualities to make their mark. Alden has been sensitive to the needs of music in all his operatic work.

Alden's next Verdi, *A Masked Ball*, was just as daring and individual. The underpinning central concept was Gustavus's self-dramatization, his inadequacy for the role of monarch and his romantic sense of doom. During the overture Arthur Davies as Gustavus (a charming elegant Edward VIII kind of figure given to wearing fashionable casuals from Next, or amusing disguises) came out through the red plush curtains behind the massive ornate neo-classical gold picture-frame – large as the proscenium opening – that in Fielding's design was placed leaning within the proscenium space. He glared longingly, desperately, at the audience, an introspective Hamlet figure, obsessed with fate and death and time running out. Then he leant a giant hourglass against the picture-frame. On the left on the forestage, there was a spotlit deathmask against a rising hillock covered in skulls. At curtain up Oscar, Gustavus's chain-smoking conspiratorial intimate in a red wig, goatee beard, trilby and specs (a travesty role brilliantly sung by Lesley Garrett), was swinging a chandelier at floor level like a pendulum and dancing with it with angel-of-death wings fixed to her/his shoulders. The king's servants were modish, camp scene-shifters in swishy black silk robes. When the courtiers and the conspirators (Verdi's two distinct choruses) emerged on stage into a corner-space with two huge blank walls above high classical skirtings, they were a motley crew of smart modern Swedish gents and officers in Stalinist uniforms. The aesthete king was far removed in tone from his puritanical court, where everybody swigged alcohol in typical Scandinavian desperation.

Verdi's opera on the 1792 assassination of that theatre-obsessed (and homosexual) Swedish king, Gustavus III, was originally censored by the Neapolitan authorities, sensitive about the shooting of a monarch. Verdi eventually relocated the opera in Boston a century earlier. Today stagings often revert to Sweden. Gustavus is facing a conspiracy of would-be assassins, enraged by his extravagance and eccentricity. He is fixated on Amelia, wife of his prime minister Anckarstroem. She is in love with him too – though neither of them, nor the husband, is aware of these feelings. She turns to a palm-reader to help kill the emotion, and is told to obtain a herb that must be picked under a gallows at midnight. The king, overhearing the assignation, meets her and shares a moment of blissful musical romance. Anckarstroem arrives – prompting Amelia to hide behind a veil – and warns that the king is about to be ambushed by assassins. The king swaps clothes with the minister and escapes. But soon the conspirators insist on unmasking the lady, and Anckarstroem, betrayed, joins the conspiracy and draws the lot to exterminate Gustavus.

Alden's designer, as for *Mazeppa* and *Boccanegra*, was again Fielding. The look of the production was arresting, clear and touched with grandeur. Fielding used simple colours, defined adaptable and tellingly dramatic spaces, and provided a sequence of memorable images. Most striking was the ballroom of the final scene, dominated by a huge horseman of the Apocalypse. The production was lit with fastidious expressiveness by Wolfgang Göbbel from the Berlin Schaubühne, a frequent collaborator of Peter Stein and Luc Bondy. *A Masked Ball* looked much more finished than *Boccanegra* – whose slight air of extemporization was an unintended consequence of budget and schedule difficulties. But *Boccanegra*'s sketchiness grew to be liked. The second scene was a suburban seance on a wet afternoon. Gustavus (disguised as a sailor) played pranks and had his palm read. From there on Fielding's designs became increasingly disturbed and manic. Linda Finnie as Madame Arvidson was a type like Madame Sosostris in Tippett's *Midsummer Marriage*. She seemed to go into a genuine trance, with a mysterious response, stripping down to her petticoat (as Janice Cairns's Amelia did too) at the emotional revelations. Her 'cave' was an expressionistic room with a collapsing iron bedstead and a metal lamp angled crazily and horizontally. Every chorus entrance was preceded by a flurry of snowflakes. The door was from Doctor Caligari's Cabinet. A provoking, energized, intensely expressive surrealism was balanced

against Alden's teasing-out of the disparate threads in the complicated story, where Verdi often presents three or four different
points of view about what is actually happening, simultaneously
on stage. That would have been beyond an old-fashioned period
costume staging of *Masked Ball*. Everything was related to the
drama, nothing was extraneous or inexplicable, if one thought
about it.

The great scene at the foot of the scaffold, with its famous ironical chorus of scoffing and chortling conspirators, started out as a
continuation of the seance. Janice Cairns as a strong, healthy-
voiced Amelia sang out her terrors while a great blood-red square
stage-flat teetered above her, hanging from the flies. The herb she
was seeking grew like bamboo out of a mound of skulls. The floor
and backdrop were an ominous midnight blue, brightening and
lightening after Gustavus's arrival when the couple shared their
emotion in a *Tristan und Isolde*-like world of love beneath a vast
pock-marked moon at the back of the stage, which then surrealistically turned into a clock-face, its hands performing a lunatic
dance around the eleventh hour.

Neither Arthur Davies as Gustavus nor Cairns's Amelia could
quite match the climactic thrill of their great duet, but the staging
expressed a lot of what the voices could not. The conspirators,
with their black coach also surprisingly bringing Madame Arvidson in a silver-lamé ballgown, performed with a studied ferocity
that dangerously matched the morbid wit of the music.
Anckarstroem's row with Amelia, back home, continued the
seance idea. The ironies in the drama were acutely registered. As
always with Alden, there was great physical tension between characters on stage. Amelia unknowingly drew the lots, for
Anckarstroem and the other chief conspirators, out of a huge urn
that Anckarstroem had exhumed from below the floorboards –
like a guilty secret. He then shovelled out spadefuls of black earth,
preparing the grave into which – in the last moments of the opera
– the mortally wounded Gustavus slipped. The dancing at the ball
was left entirely to the music to describe. The chorus wore white
masks and stylish grisaille party clothes. Amelia added colour in
her yellow elegant gown. The scene where Anckarstroem
extracted details of Gustavus's disguise from Oscar, with its
implicit web of betrayals, was beautifully sorted out. The three
chief conspirators were in Cambridge blue tail-suits and red
gloves. Gustavus had a red heart and ribbon on his left breast. The

actual assassination was stage-managed to perfection, almost choreographed – both Oscar and the silk-clad attendants sported black angel wings. Anckarstroem, more in line with history than with Verdi, was dragged into the crowd, to be tortured, and hustled off to execution despite the king's forgiveness. The idea was that assassination was the king's greatest performance, his immortal moment.

Alden's highly charged, grippingly emotional account was seen through the central character of Gustavus and packed full of expressive and effectively theatrical ideas. The Alden principle at work here once again was that operas were not simple costume dramas where characters just happened to sing rather than speak, but psycho-historical mysteries whose resonances and implications (submerged in music) invited daringly imaginative amplification and experimental synthesis – so that they merged with the imagery and philosophy of life and art today. Though Alden was said to be going against the composer's intentions, no composer would choose to be buried in a museum rather than dominate current theatrical life.

Alden worked with (for him) a new designer, Nigel Lowery, on Stravinsky's *Oedipus Rex* and Bartók's *Bluebeard's Castle* for ENO in 1991, and the economical acting style and expressionist movement were also a new departure for him. Lowery's designs were brilliantly simple – a single triangular room, adaptable, lit with extreme care by Richard Riddell, and offset with some back- and front-cloths. The change of tone suggested that Alden's postmodern symbols were always consciously investigative. Like Colin Davis's Stravinsky, Alden's was perhaps more emotional than the composer would have liked, but true to the Greek origins of the story and an object lesson in Aristotelian catharsis. Lowery's colourful strip-cartoon approach freed the responses to the drama and emotions. *Bluebeard*, however, was less hyped up than its stagings usually are, and did not compete with the refulgent orchestral score. It examined the central dramatic conundrum without offering a solution to what is more poem than play.

Alden used actors, off stage and amplified for Stravinsky's Narrator (James Griffiths), and on stage (Paola Dionisotti) for his reworking of bits from other poems by Bartók's librettist Bela Balazs. This was effectively atmospheric. Dionisotti in the Bartók, wearing a shiny red suit, caught Sally Burgess's skirt as the libretto suggested to try and stop her entering the 'castle'. The links in the double bill were slight: Alden's Jocasta, in beehive hairstyle and silver lamé, sported a fur coat which was passed on to Judith. The doorway on the right of the set was re-used in *Bluebeard*. The huge left-hand door was cut into the place where, in *Oedipus*, a panic-stricken silhouette, arms raised, had been seen. The hands seemed to be disappearing into the door.

The Stravinsky/Cocteau opera, usually treated as more oratorio than opera, was presented by Alden as all done by numbers. To underline that, numbers were placarded on everybody's backs. The set contained a tape-recorder (symbol of truth-will-out). Each statement was preceded by the character who delivered it tripping over a rising threshold on the left. Events stumbled along, as it were. The audience was allowed to happen on the truth. The drama was sharply focused, with striking images. Tiresias's mask made Richard Van Allan look as doll-like or automaton-like as he sounded. False teeth in lurid pink and pearly white on a shifting drop-in cloth and an eye in a fish-tank displayed a mechanical obsessiveness that in no way spoiled the impact of Philip Langridge's gory appearance as the blinded Oedipus, but the blood was restrained considering Alden was the man who brought chainsaws to the Coliseum.

In *Bluebeard* there was even less assertive imagery. The drama and its repetitions were gone through with very precise direction of the central pair and a minimum of props: a large key, a pair of doors, a vomitory void at the back from which the other wives eventually crawled and into which garments (and illusions) disappeared. The swords of the Duke's armoury stuck up through the floor. A meat-hook (or was it a damaged sprinkler system?) hung from the ceiling. But there were no exaggerated mimes of threats or overdone suggestions of violence. Judith retreated through the right-hand door, after the left one opened. As she scrawled each number on floor or panel, the stage each time became a new room thanks to a play of coloured light. There was a front-cloth with translucent red blobs. The overall lighting was red-shift. Alden's *Oedipus* was about the vanity of ignorance and the unfairness of life. His *Bluebeard* presented the central creative relationship of our world as man and woman held in a vice of uncertain knowledge gradually explored, power and affection constantly exchanged. Alden raised questions more than he answered them. He let the opera he was staging exploit suitably Freudian dream images and visual puns without forcing matters or being too subjective.

That was certainly true of his *Elektra* for the Welsh National Opera, where he returned to collaboration with David Fielding – though Fielding worked under the pseudonym Paul Bond (conscious of his move to be director/designer). Paul Bond was a pun on Ball's Pond – Fielding's 'school' of design had become known as the Ball's Pond Road school, an area in London where a number of young designers including Fielding lived.

Alden's unflinching approach to violence and cruelty made him a perfect candidate for *Elektra* with its excessive orchestral means, its quality almost of a *Psycho*-like over-heating – in anticipation of axe revenge. Hofmannsthal's text has its characters engage in lacerating monologues and dialogues – pioneering modernism that turns this central Sophoclean sequel about the House of Atreus into a moral debate of great contemporary significance. Is revenge barbarous or necessary? The Christian sentiment – 'Vengeance is mine saith the Lord, I will repay' – has never stopped the kind of blood that Elektra wants. There are some things, as the 20th century found, that cannot wait.

Presenting violence on stage is always risky. It can become anecdotal mannerism. The faked decadence of Götz Friedrich's sadomachistic black theatrical leather in his Covent Garden *Elektra* was routine and thoughtless. What impressed about Alden's Cardiff *Elektra* was its simplicity, restraint and imaginative precision. Alden applied his familiar imagery carefully and very effectively. A naked light bulb glowed on and off with tyrannical whimsy. A cracked shiny black floor on the right of the set yawned into a dangerous gulf at the murderous climax. A dirty bloodstained tiled wall with a single shower fitting at its centre (the opening image) rose and fell like a portcullis, defining the dramatic structure and admitting the audience to the deeper manias of Agamemnon's palace. Side-walls shifted nightmarishly as horrid relics were exhumed from below a stage which was basically black and bare, apart from a single door at the back round whose frame the light inside the palace glared balefully yellow – and then, after Orest's duty was done, turned an almost solid red. (The imaginative brilliance of Göbbel's lighting was crucial.) At the front, where the shiny black floor sloped sharply up to the left, a lurid indelible bloodstain just beneath the shower-tap recalled the cause of the tragedy: the murder of Agamemnon, whose horribly decayed poster-photo Elektra dragged up from the entrance sloping down below-stage at the front. The stain also evoked Murder itself – the moral issue. To emphasize the sacrificial aspect, a revoltingly butchered oxhead was dragged on stage by one of Klytamnestra's servants, and licked and drooled over – a reference to Salome with Jochanaan's head. When Aegisth was finally despatched by Orest, he was crushed to death by the great door ripped from its hinges; his body lay covered by it, one arm over the edge. Elektra, revenge-sated, strangled herself during her ecstatic dance with the electric light cord — whose erratic earlier flashes suggested memory of the original crime.

Cleansing the blood-baths was beyond the lumpen Teutonic maids whom Alden showed attempting to scrub that spreading stain at the start. They were brutalized but banal, like concentration camp warders, and the problem existed for innocent and guilty alike. The most distinctive aspect of Alden's staging was the way Klytamnestra and Elektra, mother and daughter, expressed the bond of emotion in their relationship – however coloured it was by deeds to come as well as deeds past. There was a certain mutual dignity in all these sufferers. The baroque triumphal exuberance with which Klytamnestra's Confidant and Trainbearer injected their queen with heroin was no different in quality from the way Elektra herself welcomed Aegisth with a zanily flaunted standard-lamp (symbol of domestic ease) on his way to perdition. Alden responded to the comic undertones of Aegisth's arrival as sardonically portrayed in Strauss's music here. Aegisth turned that into a comic sexual prop, Absurdism brought to the rescue of Expressionism: typical of Alden to mix comic and terrifying.

Alden's was a production shot through with perception and served with remarkably committed acting and singing by an international and local WNO cast. Quite apart from Alden's command of theatrical energy and ability to achieve performances that maintained remarkable precision, once again the most compelling and fertile questions were left just surfacing in the audience's mind. Alden's scalding star performances included Janet Hardy's robust Elektra, like an Olympic shot-putter but touching and believable, risking all, voice imperious as an axe; Felicity Palmer's fascinating blood-curdling Klytamnestra; and Jeffrey Lawton's relaxed, comically irrepressible Aegisth. The way Alden suddenly evaporated the tension at Aegisth's entrance was real theatrical genius.

The opera Alden has staged most frequently in his career is Berg's *Wozzeck*. The Lyric Opera of Chicago, originally committed to presenting the Chéreau staging first seen in June 1992 at the

Paris Châtelet Theatre, decided to engage Alden for yet another *Wozzeck*, when the cost of the Chéreau proved too great. The Alden opera stagings I have described in detail are all high romantic or early modern works. The British critical onslaught on him continued unabated for longer than a decade. Certain critics are excessively irritated by the details: Max Loppert's 1987 *Financial Times* review of *Boccanegra* talked of 'familiar theatre doodles' and found that 'the bare light-bulb, the lonely wooden chair, the mix and match of unrelated clothing styles (chain-mail, greatcoats, Bisto kid suits, medieval robes) and the dislocated stage management all have an overpowering air of *déjà vu* ... the world of *Monty Python* comes dangerously close. Like a precocious adolescent, Mr Alden has gone mad on Surrealism.' Many critics (but not his ENO audience) seemed incapable of looking behind the conscious indecorousness of the productions, the rejection of specific period, the desire to free the stage picture from the weight of extended naturalistic and dramatically irrelevant filling-in, and see the detailed and terrifying focus on the moral experience of the characters. Alden has always taken his lead from the vocal predominance that marks out all the central characters in operatic narrative, and has found a way to balance their musical refulgence with a theatrical language capable of mobilizing both the tension of communication and the range of varying emotional registers.

The enmity of conservative critics did undermine the confidence of the ENO management. The solution, for Alden's *Ariodante* in April 1993, was to find an entirely new designer – Ian MacNeil, who had created the set for Stephen Daldry's stylized National Theatre production of *An Inspector Calls*. Alden's Handel production was geared to the dreamlike inner worlds of the characters suggested by their arias. The recitatives of a Baroque opera are normally where important incident or movement occurs in the story. But in *Ariodante* the remarkable arias and even a few duets are the focus of action. Unlike *Alcina* and *Orlando*, also based on Ariosto, both plot and text are entirely concerned with states of mind, a psychological exploration. Alden left behind most of his familiar references to totalitarianism and prison camps. MacNeil encouraged him to think of a quite different theatrical world – crumbling Baroque plasterwork, a suspended painted Baroque-style ceiling, shiny black floor and transparent or tinted perspex panels (in place of gauzes to isolate the forestage). At the back of the set the wall opened on to a small picture-frame inner-stage where the subconscious nightmares of Ginevra were shown being acted out when her world fell apart (her father, the King of Scotland, was sexually abusing her – though not too graphically – and the dead Ariodante was returning to haunt her). *Ariodante* required a strong choreographic dimension, having originally involved Marie Sallé's dance company – in the vain attempt to stir interest in Handel's first Covent Garden season and operatic farewell after which he turned to oratorio. Act 2's typically Handelian ballet of good and bad dreams was later added to *Alcina*.

The substitution of Louis Quinze for Alden's more severe plain wooden chair did find favour. The devious Polinesso, a strong characterization by countertenor Christopher Robson in spangled great-coat and lank long hair, shared his intrigue with the audience (against Ariodante and Ginevra's passion) from a gilt padded chair set at the very front of the stage. Ginevra's nightmarish imaginings after she was disgraced by the scheming of Polinesso were played out in dance and mime on the recessed inner stage. But the Alden signature was unchanged. MacNeil's costumes even had a Germanic tinge – especially the modern operatic version of 18th-century great-coats and boots. Ginevra wore a fluffy wedding frock and veil (Dalinda's disguise to fool Ariodante into thinking Ginevra was unfaithful with Polinesso). Ariodante's brother Lurcanio, who wound up the story by discovering Polinesso's plot and preventing Ariodante's suicide, was in 16th-century costume (like Belmonte in Berghaus's Frankfurt *Entführung*, combining a pre-Enlightenment sense of honour with the era of Ariosto). The combat in the last act to defend Ginevra's name was fought in Renaissance armour. The chorus of extras, whether valets, shepherdesses or ladies in waiting, wore smart Baroque-flavour costumes and wigs.

MacNeil's use of hanging perspex sheets to start with was clumsy. But after the dressing-room formalities of the opening scene Alden achieved a real memorability. The moonlit ruined scene of the second act, where Ariodante was gulled into doubting his fiancée's honour, was actually set on top of the painted ceiling of the first act, the reverse – as it were – of powder-blue skies and an idealized existence. This strange hill of a set amounted to a depressing, disturbing peak of moonlit anxiety, beautifully mysterious and shadowy. Ariodante, literally on a 'high' to start with, then awkwardly descended, sliding off the top to terrible misery and decline. The visual images were very striking. Alden's close intense direction supported the central characters without deconstructing an opera which is anyway completely unbuttoned and frank in emotional motivation. In particular Ann Murray's delivery of the great ten-minute aria '*Scherza infida*' (with poignant bassoon obbligato) was a tour de force, full of vocal risk in changes of colour and attitude, an epic *cri de coeur*. Amanda Roocroft as Ginevra brought piercing sensitive alarm to her usual sprightly joyousness, duetting gorgeously with Murray. These two, at the romantic centre, were matched by Nicholas McGegan's stylish, confident conducting.

Alden's first Wagner production, *Tannhäuser* for the Bavarian State Opera, Munich, in summer 1994, got the predictable dose of first-night booing. The audience adored Zubin Mehta's conducting and the singing. It was the launch of the opera festival – whose focus was no longer on the traditional Mozart and Strauss productions of the Everding/Sawallisch years but exclusively on Peter Jonas's new wave. The hiring of Alden, Richard Jones and Tom Cairns as producers had sharply divided an audience which might have recognized itself being guyed by the second act courtiers of the Wartburg song contest below the bold slogan 'Germania Nostra' inscribed in 'stone' at the back of the set.

Alden and his Israeli design team of Roni Toren (sets) and Buki Shiff (costumes) had their tongues gently in their cheeks. Yet this was not at all a coarsely political production, smart with obvious fascist consciousness. Neither did it take a simple line on Venusberg and decadence. The elegant and stylish women with their lacquered hairstyles at Venus's court, including a whore in a red-light doorway halfway up a black backdrop on top of a classical frieze, were easily recognizable later among the guests on the Wartburg, as if at Hedda Goering's salon in pre-war Berlin – the hairstyles were the give-away. One was wearing a leopardskin, gripping its tail as if it were a whip. There were also various perverse knights from Venus's kingdom. Tannhäuser's competitors for the song contest were not unlike Spielbergian adventurers – one in 1920s aeronaut's rig. Sexual liberation in the 20th century has made a wide range of sado-masochistic fetish imagery available to mainstream theatre and opera, providing a very specific sort of stylization (closely akin to the French writer Genet and the Japanese Mishima). Love and violence are carried far into the realm of brothel-fantasy, and away from any genuine kind of social action, thus heightening the hero's loneliness and angst.

Court functionaries in white tailcoats and trousers were always rearranging the chairs (though it was not obviously the *Titanic*). Tannhäuser's offence was to tell all in song – plenty of other guilty people around had memory lapses.

For Alden *Tannhäuser*, anticipating both *Meistersinger* and *Parsifal*, was a convenient metaphor for the moral crisis of the present day, a crisis advertised by Kierkegaard and Nietzsche when Wagner was composing and revising his opera – and further defined in recent German history. Instead of the Deus ex machina of Enlightenment operas, Wagner dealt with Tannhäuser's unredeemable guilt by having the saintly prayerful Elizabeth die for him – she had already stopped him being murdered for his blasphemous Venusberg syndrome by assembled outraged knights. At the end the chorus of pilgrims to Rome, liberated from their burdens of post-nuclear pumice-stone rocks, brought forward not Elizabeth's body but the now leafy dead sprig in a glass relic-case, which the Pope had told Tannhäuser would have to sprout before he could be saved.

Alden undermined the resolution of Wagner's pilgrim hymn in its final rescension, implying that was not a real solution: Wolfram von Eschenbach walked mournfully upstage, unconvinced. 'Our Germany', so central to the European cultural heritage, was a long way from absolution. Roni Toren's sets combined a nuclear-blasted landscape with dislocated classical details. A huge leaning pillar on the right of the stage made its statement against a blasted back wall which revealed various stages of damage as the opera proceeded. On the Wartburg, the back of the set rose to form a grand platform on which the knights and ladies paraded (including the strange crowd seen in dreamlike slow motion during the Venusberg overture). Pat Collins's lighting and Vivienne Newport's drugged choreography made the stage watchable and often beautiful. Typical Alden touches included incidentals like the odd naked lightbulb, a suitcase for Tannhäuser's poems, and many overturned chairs. Not at all a private language. Alden's approach was easily accessible for the Bavarian public, and the production became a sort of cult. The rather-right-wing young conductor Christian Thielemann finally decided it was not an interpretation he could associate with.

Alden's direction of the final act was unusual and memorable, with Wolfram, Elizabeth and Tannhäuser (at the end of the world, as it were) picking their way over a balustrade on its side – which ran from a jagged hole at the centre of the back wall right to the front of the stage. Here René Kollo in the title role, who had been stressed by his earlier music, told the story ringingly of his failed pilgrimage to Rome. Waltraud Meier was slinkily ravishing as Venus, vamping excessively in the tradition of *Sunset Boulevard.* Nadine Secunde's large-scale and spiritual Elizabeth was a potent intercessor.

After a gap of three years, during which British commentators published various obituaries of Alden's interventionist approach to theatrical interpretation, he returned to the Coliseum, scene of his many controversial splendours. The opera was *Tristan und Isolde*, and initially he was teamed with Charles Edwards as designer, who had combined with David Fielding (under the pseudonym Paul Bond) on Alden's WNO *Elektra* in Cardiff. Edwards planned a more intimate and psychological production than emerged with Ian MacNeil's evocative ruined 19th-century operahouse proscenium as the central item. Edwards's original idea had been to have just one interior room set for the whole opera, with somewhere – on a wall – a picture of the sea for the first act, and a mirror for the second. The room would have changed subtly to reflect the stage of the confessional process in which the opera engages (*Tristan und Isolde* is all about states of mind). As usual in mature Wagner, the memory of the characters is constantly being exercised, and the history of which they know themselves part rehearsed – as if there were no other way for them to define where they now found themselves. The suggestion that the stage we saw was the world of the characters' imagination would have created – as Edwards planned – a terrifying intimacy.

Alden's production as it emerged was perhaps the most successful in his career in Britain to date, and owed much to the visionary beauty of MacNeil's sets and costumes – even if Mac-Neil's theatrical instincts were not quite dramaturgically consistent with Alden's. There was a tension between a sometimes crude filling-in and a more self-consciously aesthetic concept of the space. The predominant idea was that the greater reality in this opera is the interior reality of the characters, not the anecdotal detail of the narrative – which anyway only impinges briefly, for a few minutes' musical duration, in a span of hours. Alden saw that to present the events in a naturalistic stage context would undermine the metaphysical imaginative dimension that runs parallel (and interwoven with) the narrative. As so often in Wagner the debate of romance between the central characters (a 19th-century equivalent to the narrator's commentary in a medieval courtly love epic) is the greater intimacy, a truer reality than mere physical events. The characters place themselves by sharing a poetic vision. Their duet after a few moments of premature climax, just as they recognize their entry into each other's lives, evokes a kind of poetic entanglement far from sexual love-making. In this opera it is in their minds that they commit adultery. So it was crucial for Alden that Tristan and Isolde consent to their drug-induced passion in a conspiratorial way – with a terrible inward shared grin (after consuming the magic potion) at the prospect of their burgeoning relationship, though Alden kept them always far apart on the stage, emphasizing that they almost never meet physically. The great love is an imaginative exercise – with full musical projection to make it more telling.

The subject of the opera is what its central characters (not just Tristan and Isolde, but also Brangäne, Kurwenal, King Marke, and even Melot) are thinking. The references in MacNeil's designs to theatrical illusion, using an old proscenium arch filled in with a wall as the central element for the first two acts, was profoundly suggestive of the notion that the 'events' in the opera are secondary to the characters' feelings and memories. We seemed to be witnessing the mutual construction of an epic romantic novel, to which all could make a contribution. But also, the characters' repeated examination and relating of each other's stories, their sense of 'history' and their own history – and of the mythology into which it turns as they experience it – was a theatrical process which legitimated Alden's exercise of directorial prerogative.

In a powerful sense, which was partly a consequence of the large-scale but slightly immobile and inflexible artists playing the two lovers, this romantic novel-like quality was emphasized by and reflected in Alden's conception of the roles of Brangäne and Kurwenal – roles taken with extraordinary vitality and fluency by Susan Parry and Jonathan Summers (the latter a veteran of Alden's ENO Verdi productions). Both responded strikingly to the Alden method. The opera's narrative and the moral problems of the story were viewed through the prism of Brangäne's eyes. She became here almost a Jane Austen figure, fearful of her own worst thoughts, of the richness and danger in her romantic imagination. She showed us her worried, agonized gaze contemplating the consequences of her interventions in the events: a narrative controller, but out of imaginative control of what was happening. Alden had Kurwenal and Brangäne stand in for their lord and lady in typical operatic displacement – like the proxy pairing of Despina and Alfonso in *Così* or the low-life doubling of Papageno and Papagena for Tamino and Pamina in *Die Zauberflöte*. The mirror of a highly reflexive narrative showed more of the game.

Despite the difficulty of managing the somewhat clumsy and, in the case of George Gray's burly Tristan, unsatisfactorily acted central roles, Alden's staging had a marvellous expressive beauty about it and his direction of character was very fine. Elizabeth Connell's rage as Isolde at the indignity of her fate, being married off to King Marke, was extremely fierce and bitter. The sweetness into which she was transformed by the 'wrong' magic potion was all the more striking. Mark Elder, his conducting as successful as Alden's producing, allowed the musicians real expressive discretion, never pushing the pace, unfolding the story and its terrible moral pains with a majestic and fulfilling detachment. The staging seldom conveyed any narrative naturalism. But the elements were there for the audience's imagination to work on. Kurwenal with wild long hair and a kilt was a highly evocative figure when he first appeared in the shadows in a stage box-like recess to the left of the angled proscenium at the centre of the set.

For the first act the curtain rose very slowly to reveal no ship but a dark stage across which, at an angle and at the centre of the space, stood a ruined theatre proscenium. The opening looked bricked up with a modern doorway cut into the brickwork on the right. Recesses on either side could have held statues or been part of the auditorium design, but were also accessible from behind the proscenium. The one on the left (which could also be approached by a ladder from the front of the stage next to where the figures of Isolde and Brangäne were seated on and among luggage) was also half bricked up. The sense of travel was clearly registered, with Isolde and Brangäne sitting as it were in the hold, beside their trunks. The keynote of the opening act was the furious indignation of Isolde, her emphatic and desperate resentment of what was happening to her, and the horror of Brangäne at what her imagination told her this rage would precipitate. The sound of the young sailor backstage was very sweet. Kurwenal's first appearance in the recess on the left, his face caught in the shadowy lighting by Wolfgang Göbbel, was ominous and still. Brangäne's body was constantly in tortuous distortion as she agonized about her duties and her thoughts, and was subjected by Isolde to furious dictatorial treatment.

The wall in the proscenium rose to reveal a horizon, with, in contrast to the previous romantic gloom, very bright orange light on a blank back-cloth, the male figures of the sailors, a wheel and helmsman, providing a touch of naturalism against a lurid sky. The chorus at various points of the act threatened to move out of this proscenium zone. As usual with Alden these expressive chorus movements were brilliantly manoeuvred. The overwhelming power of Isolde's character was constantly underlined in her style of behaviour; Brangäne at one point waltzed with Isolde a little way to calm her. The pointing of the encounter with Tristan, Isolde taking a veil and wrapping it over her head, he offering his sword and breast to her to remove his life, was memorable. The timing of such actions as Brangäne's remembering where the potion was, and what it could do, and her presentation of the drink itself in a bowl on a flowing classical side-table at the centre, were managed to fine poetic effect. The terrible toothy smiles of Tristan and Isolde into the audience as the potion took effect were horribly suggestive.

Alden has always directed the central performances in his best productions with scrupulous care. Perhaps not every move in the middle act of this *Tristan* made perfect sense. The scene showed the proscenium swivelled the opposite way on a different axis, its right side now far nearer the front. At one point Isolde made her way into the right recess, stepping though a hidden door rather awkwardly. As always the lovers were kept apart, and there was no lying down in reverie. The proscenium was open part of the time, the flames of Brangäne's warning fire burning through a hole on the stage. The torch that was doused as a signal was a blazing sword. The proscenium glowed gold. At the start the two women were sitting on the edge of the stage at the front. The wall in the proscenium gave a sense of intimacy to the debate. When it rose again, at a crucial point, it seemed to reveal a vast inner room of the imagination in a shimmering palace of romance, with hidden doors in its back wall and a surface like reflecting water. Brangäne kept watch by a door at the distant back of the set. The sense that this was a realm of the romantic imagination registered with great aesthetic beauty. Alden had Isolde repeat the image of the potion being drunk. Tristan, for a time, was symbolically in a black blindfold. The side of the proscenium glowed gold with warm red at centre-stage. In the visionary inner room the back wall rose slowly out of the set, and the scene was ready for the painful denouement. All the important text was delivered downstage. The reactions of Melot and Kurwenal and Tristan were exactly choreographed by Alden at the heart of the false proscenium. Isolde remained on the extreme left, a helpless element in the tragedy. The virtual suicide of Tristan on Melot's spear satisfied the sense of guilt. As with Peter Hall's old Royal Opera production, the arrival of the hunt (and the indignant betrayal by Melot) had been rapid events in a few moments, followed by very extended and painful poetic debate, especially from the serenely mellifluous Gwynne Howell as Marke. The dead stags dumped on stage reminded one that what was at issue was not the quality of what Tristan and Isolde had or had not done, but the betrayal in their hearts of Marke and their duty.

The last act defined with extraordinary poignancy the focal point of the tragedy, Tristan mad yet movingly conscious of abandonment. Alden made it a Beckettian endgame on an empty stage – with a glowing distant yellow horizon at the back. The shepherd, in dark glasses, maintained his watch by the prompt box, staring blindly into the auditorium. Kurwenal dreamt on the floor at the back. The wounded Tristan slept upright on a chair at the centre – cutting the outline of a Henry Moore statue. Kurwenal paced the stage as if caged, felt its vastness, implied the lost hopelessness of the situation. Almost it was a dance of frustration and anticipation. The lighting changed, flowing across the undecorated blank set like clouds: its registers more emotional than if there were scenery to illuminate. The lookout and Tristan's fevered reaction seemed more hopeless and deluded than usual. Isolde, arriving too late from her boat, stepped on stage at front right, more in Tristan's imagination than in fulfilment: as he fell down and died, spreadeagled at the centre, his heart was exposed (literally, in the rose-coloured wound under MacNeil's tramplike costume for him). The arrivals from the other world emerged like spirits at the rear horizon and sank back below that horizon as their role was fulfilled. Kurwenal committed suicide on one of the soldier's spears, as Tristan had on Melot's weapon – the later imitating the earlier. A row of soldiers with huge reflecting shields climbed up on to the stage at the rear, a dramatic vision, then sank back. Isolde faded out towards the horizon. The simplicity and aptness of the images emphasized the text and cut away unnecessary literalism. The focus on the strikingly managed performances was clear and sharp. Alden concentrated on the balance between subjective and objective, the sense of simultaneous memories and development of parallel worlds mixing inconveniently and tragically. This was poetry more than narrative reality, though the events of the narrative all occurred as required. It was a much more filled out and interventionist approach than the famous Wieland Wagner staging at Bayreuth had been, with its modern abstract-sculpture iconography. Alden put an unfailing emphasis on the passions of the five central characters, and by challenging their motives exposed the poetic reality of Wagner's most potent metaphysical morality.

In a variety of assignments Alden has provided meaningfulness and a fresh perspective. His work has a particular rhythm and character, encouraging intensity and commitment, but with a highly individual aesthetic. He has always had to make compromises, because of severe budgetary constraints. His aesthetic is certainly more Europeanized than Peter Sellars's. Sellars makes a point of drawing on a local parochial American ambience. Alden is close to the style of Herbert Wernicke, Patrice Chéreau and Hans Neuenfels – closest to, but better than, the last. He is German-influenced in his style, no doubt. His art is most potent in the mobilization and motivation of the performers. Nothing seems to limit the adventurous and uncompromising range of his imagination.

9 Peter Sellars: Americanizing everything

Peter Sellars's 1990 staging (for Glyndebourne Festival Opera) of
Die Zauberflöte designed by Adrianne Lobel and Dunya Ramicova: James
Maddalena's Papageno and Kurt Streit's Tamino baffled at the service station
by the Three Ladies, quasi-Andrews sisters (Denise Hector, Fiona Kimm,
Annegeer Stumphius). Photograph © Guy Gravett.

Peter Sellars (born 1957) has used quite different means from David Alden to achieve the dislocation or defamiliarization that will draw an audience's response. He has also managed to find support in the United States for the greater part of the work that has built his reputation. He leads the opera bratpack in the USA, such as it is, and has stolen the headlines ever since he first emerged. Alden rarely engages in debate: he prefers his work to speak for itself. Audiences at Sellars's productions tend to be greeted with a cyclo-styled preface or hand-out to explain the theory justifying what they are about to see and to prime their reaction. Sellars with his eye-catching punk hair-style uses publicity as Jonathan Miller does in an unending impish charm-offensive. He is a natural media star, with a complex engaging intellect, whose reputation preceded him to Britain in the columns of *Vogue*. The way he exploits his image is like a Hollywood film director but that style explains how he can work in a climate largely hostile to his method and message. He can choose singers and actors sympathetic to his predominant role (off stage) in all his productions, but again that is necessary to preserve the purity and effectiveness of his language. He is a highly intelligent original – experimental yet inclusive, rather than dictatorial. Though his work never lacks clarity, he would say that his aim is not to sort things out but to open them up – to ask questions more than to propose answers. His rejection of translated opera may seem like an example of pointless Sellars obfuscation, but reflects his instinct that opera should be a challenge to the audience, that the contents of the event should not be easily embraced, and that an audience reading the production should be prompted by many other elements than just the opera's text.

The style of his productions has its origin in the puppet theatre with which he was stage-struck as a child, and where he managed to work from an early age. He started directing as a student at Harvard. His sympathy for the exotic, for foreign inspirations like oriental puppet theatre, is characteristically American. He likes a hyperactive nervous physical style in his performers, but also incorporates a gesture language from Indonesian theatre – what has been called hand-jiving. This eclecticism relates to the collectors' mania that has decorated rich American residences. 'Hopefully we're re-creating culture from what's left over in a form that might speak again,' was how he put it when he was doing Messiaen's *Saint François d'Assise*. Borrowing, acquiring and transposing are usual imperial processes. The variety of theatrical expression is naturally eclectic and impure – when adaptation becomes interpretation, or re-creation slides into invention. The borrowings of cultural imperialism are infective: victim and victor often reverse roles. Even his distaste for opera in English translation, his preference for the arcane challenge of original-language performance, reflects a New World view of culture as loaned rather than owned. In the 1989 Pepsico SummerFare programme he wrote: 'I rather enjoy the sensation of being surrounded by the detritus of New York in the 1980s and being constantly reminded and astonished that [Da Ponte's] text, like [Mozart's] music, represents the 1780s.' The audience must get its information by osmosis, though he accepts surtitles. Of course the language of opera is more than words, and much can be understood without understanding the text – indeed in the English-speaking world audiences are very accustomed to the text (in the composer's original language) being opaque. Sellars has scoffed at the poor quality of ENO's English translations, saying they are always inferior to the original. But just because it is not a famous lyricist like Lorenz Hart fitting Da Ponte to English, that does not mean the attempt should not be made.

His early ventures (according to his account) included a *Rapunzel* accompanied by Beethoven's Op. 31 no. 2 piano sonata and 40 or more high-school productions, from Chekhov one-act plays to *L'histoire du soldat*. Stravinsky, the conversation books as well as the music, was his presiding deity. At 18 he went to Paris for a year before Harvard. He saw Strehler's *Marriage of Figaro* and Chéreau's *Les contes d'Hoffmann*: the former being 'the most perfect opera experience, almost, that I have ever had,' the latter being his first encounter with operatic work 'that critical of its source'. He joined a puppetry delegation to Moscow where he acquired a taste for Russian theatre. At Harvard, an academic star, he was allowed Special Concentration – a customized course, doing what he pleased. At 21, the central image of his *King Lear* was a collapsing Lincoln convertible. Losing his lead actor he took the title role himself, hiding cribsheets all round the set. He staged the *Ring* for puppets. His Handel *Orlando* at Cape Canaveral with the third act on Mars won the approval of Andrew Porter, *New Yorker* music-critic at the time. Sellars has been a loner. He dubbed the British new wave of producers 'these clear-eyed bright young men who are getting old'. The Pountney approach was 'basically writing theses rather than directing productions'. But a producer who sets *Giulio Cesare* at the Cairo Hilton and glosses its ancient Roman story with an overlay of modern presidential press conferences, political advisers and 1980s American imperialism, is engaging in political protest and scarcely non-analytical. In 1985 at 27 he briefly became director of the embryonic American National Theater at the Kennedy Center, Washington. In typical style he transposed Sophocles's *Ajax* (1986) to a post-Vietnam War context with black US army generals, turning it into the tale of an embittered General Rambo who had gone off his head.

Invariably, Sellars's interpretative principle has been to repatriate European classical art-works to his native homeland, recasting them in the street clothes and tone of California or the East Coast. Sellars stagings refer to the US of Ivy League intellectualism or to the brutal 'melting-pot' of drug-crazed slums. He has toured his more famous productions to Europe, though he is less fashionable, and more challenging and interpretative, than Robert Wilson, another admired US cultural ambassador. At Glyndebourne Sellars's world premiere staging of *The Electrification of the Soviet Union* and his idiosyncratic interpretation of *Die Zauberflöte* were both revolutionary, but fitted into the revised eclectic policy of a management seeking special guests. *Die Zauberflöte*, with vast blown-up colour shots of Los Angeles as backdrop, omitted the dialogue – when the production had its first run of performances.

After failing to gain acceptance in Washington, he switched fully to opera. Non-musical theatre he declared moribund, 'battered and painted into a corner where it IS television. It'll starve in its corner and finally be airlifted out in a few years.' Sellars described opera as his country of exile where he was regrouping his forces. Opera was the only sufficiently theatrical form to work in, with its significant scale of gesture and its centrality to the culture (as he saw it). His Harvard thesis was about the experimental Soviet producer Meyerhold's concept of musical realism. Meyerhold was the antithesis of Stanislavsky. In the 1920s, when Stalin closed his theatre down, Meyerhold was employed (generously, in spite of their mutual enmity) by Stanislavsky. After Stanislavsky's death Stalin had Meyerhold shot. Sellars fantasizes that his ideal theatre today would be as dangerous politically as that. In Africa and the Philippines, he points out, theatre has been central to people's notion of their identity and their struggle for rights.

In Sellars's theory opera unites Stanislavsky's notion of psychological realism and Meyerhold's concept of abstract design – the latter described by Sellars as a 'choreographic bio-mechanical approach to art through action'. With emotional truth and freedom of expressive gesture as the twin poles of 20th-century art, Sellars holds it as crucial that opera should combine Brechtian alienation with a deeply emotional (and music-induced) identification with the characters' human feelings. 'Because people are singing you can't possibly confuse it with naturalism,' he says, but the audience must make a positive emotional identification. He also finds it politically interesting that opera's technical complexity necessitates both special audience concentration and a model capacity for human collaboration by all those involved in the performance backstage. Opera is a refined type of cooperation, a matrix of a functioning society.

In his first contact with British opera Sellars was not just the producer or stage director of Nigel Osborne's Glyndebourne Touring Opera commission, *The Electrification of the Soviet Union*, but the originator of the whole October 1987 project using Craig Raine's strikingly frank and fresh ballads and lyrical songs about lost dreams of youth. Sellars's theatrical style for the production was even more impressive than the strong text and music. It used harshly edited confrontations, and unnatural-seeming gestures, exploiting the fact that the convention of opera is unnatural, that conversations and thoughts are not in real life sung out loud. Sellars drew confidence and freedom of manoeuvre from his rejection of any real attention to naturalism and attempted various expressive effects (inevitably not persuading all his audience). The performers really worked their bodies on stage. The manner they were employing was pioneered by German and Polish producers, by the 'expressionism' of Yuri Lyubimov from Moscow or the Romanians Liviu Ciulei and Lucian Pintilie who had worked at the Welsh National Opera, and especially by the angst-filled choreography of Pina Bausch.

The most distinctive element in Sellars's controversial staging was George Tsypin's mobile two-level set. Other Sellars productions have employed a doll's-house approach: his Amsterdam *Pelléas* was on three levels; his Glyndebourne *Die Zauberflöte* had Sarastro's priests and the zone of the Trials in a subterranean crypt. On first view, the *Electrification* set presented a large flat wall across the stage, containing a door and three windows with blinds. When this wall had vanished, the Frestln's sitting-room appeared on an upper level – a frilly Victorian room on a wagon on rails stretching across the stage. If the top of the set was masked by the partially raised front flat, the stage below showed a whitewashed rough plaster wall that both suggested and helped to shape various rooms. This remarkable hinged screen-like wall (operated by invisible stage-hands) contained a stove, another door, and various little windows. It had a life of its own, one moment encircling and swallowing Serezha Spectorsky on his bed, the next disgorging a new collection of actors in an entirely different configuration. The contortions of the wall kept up the sense of insecurity, suggesting the birthpangs of revolution, a mysterious new world folding and unfolding. Sellars, as usual, was sparing with the nudity and violence, though there was enough of the former to cause the popular ENO baritone, Alan Opie, as Serezha, to bow out of the central role a month before opening night, handing over to the more slender Omar Ebrahim. Anna Steiger as the prostitute Sashka stripped to the buff in dim lighting as part of her love/sex scene with Serezha. As for Nigel Osborne's music, the 'struggle to crack open the egg of modernism that one was born in', as the composer described his development, produced a radical switch of style – a much stronger interest in song-form. Almost romantic melodies descending from Debussy, Ravel, Mussorgsky or Stravinsky were blended with the more familiar repertoire of Osborne sound effects. There were even some tuneful vocally rewarding songs that admitted a distant relationship to past composers.

Long and short scenes succeeded each other with cinematic fluency. The central character, Serezha, was a young writer, a kind of Doppelgänger for Leonid Pasternak himself, who also appeared in the opera (which was mainly based on Pasternak's autobiographical sketch about his youth, *The Last Summer*). Other characters included Serezha's sister Natasha, her ominous friend Lemokh who was 'a student of the proletariat', and the Frestlns, a Jewish family to whose son, Harry, Serezha was tutor. At the Frestlns, a put-upon governess called Anna secretly mouthed anti-semitic curses on her mistress. Serezha wanted her, but round the corner was a welcoming tart, Sashka, to whom Serezha readily resorted. Her drunken husband staggered in making terrible puns. In a steamy scene between the two, narrative coherence seemed not to be the point. The opera aimed to evoke feelings and impressions, like an album of antique photographs.

With a new work it is hard to distinguish between the producer's contribution and the composer's and librettist's. Sellars has been less interventionist than Bob Wilson. The style here was scrupulously consistent, with slow movement, ponderous delivery of text. Nothing was inserted that did not support what Osborne and Raine provided. What made for controversy was the dreamlike, hypnotic rhythm of events and actions, achieved by careful cinematic editing, and rejecting all conventional operatic notions of 'realism'.

Sellars's taste for the ominously intangible perhaps explained 'why *Electrification* arrived as such a strange creature from Mars on the British theatre scene. It was all about internal life, a sense of questioning every element in one's life, a larger historical moment enveloping all these tiny little details,' he said: it was a blatant case of what semioticians would call auteurism. Sellars did not admit that his was a private vision. His commitment to new operas suggests he sees interpretation as a secondary-level art. He works choreographically to liberate the performers and open up a whole extra range of interpretative nuance. When Susan Larson, tackling Cleopatra's florid arias in *Giulio Cesare*, wanted to be left unencumbered with stage business to make life easier, Sellars insisted on loading her with much detailed complex action and gestures. Florid, demanding coloratura, he considered, needed a matching contortion to make singing easier (on the principle that if you want something done, ask a busy person). Replying to criticisms of his frequent collaborator, the conductor Craig Smith, for letting the music drag, Sellars said: 'I like things to go either too fast or too slow.' The productions like their producer engage in coat-trailing.

A similar emphasis on choreography and expressive movement was a feature of Sellars's direction of the two John Adams works, *Nixon in China* and *The Death of Klinghoffer*. In both works, as in *Electrification*, he was the creator – in the sense that he fixed the shape the work took; composer and librettist answered to him in the collaboration. Sellars's American vernacular acting married effectively both with the dance language of the original Chinese ballet (copied from a documentary record of the Nixons' banquet with the Chinese rulers) and with Mark Morris's spell-binding new choreography. Sellars originally staged *Nixon in China* in Houston, then took it to Amsterdam for the Holland Festival (Edo de Waart conducted). The opera worked on the idea of the 'real' humanity behind the public images of the leaders in question: Chou, Mao, Chiang Ch'ing, Kissinger, and Pat and Richard Nixon. Its heart was acts 2 and 3, when the historic rapprochement between the USA and the People's Republic was being digested (literally and with many emotional burps) by the prime participants. The politics lent Adams a borrowed significance. The pensive tone was standard operatic stuff from Monteverdi's Seneca in *Coronation of Poppea* onwards. Most sung lines were arpeggios floating above a nervously excited musical texture without much structural coherence. The music was often alert, but also strangely passive and inconsequential. Modified minimalism needs far clearer structures to become properly effective as a dramatic language.

Sellars's production was not eccentric, and far more conventional than the expressionism of *Electrification*. It suggested the cultural superiority and maturity of the Chinese – their exotic and delicate aesthetic tradition symbolized by a lilac back-cloth of twisting treetrunks. A bureaucratic glaze seemed to dominate both Chinese and Americans. Nixon's Spirit of 1976 Boeing landed on stage, lowered from the flies. This was opera as newsreel, or joking about newsreels – and it connected with the *cinéma vérité* mix of Jean-Luc Godard's films, in one of which Sellars once collaborated as a performer. Set-piece scenes revealed a sure touch for the toasts and talk with Mao.

The piece was at its most engaging in Pat Nixon's ironical sightseeing trip and Chiang Ch'ing's revolutionary ballet, *Red Detachment of Women*, in which the American visitors were wittily and involuntarily swept up. The apparently unruffled narrative surface suddenly lurched about like a seismograph. What was truth and what was fiction? What was really happening on stage? Were these just states of mind? An imaginative dimension continued through the simply staged monologues and discussions of the final scene, with its revolutionary ballet swinging along regardless in the background – behind the six beds of the leaders. Only music could make such a piece last, and Adams was not original enough, though Alice Goodman's text was strong – as were Sellars's team of singing actors led by James Maddalena and Sanford Sylvan.

The issue in John Adams's *Death of Klinghoffer*, which Sellars called 'a meditation', was the morality of political terrorism and how terrorism and politics relate in the media. Terrorism, politics by other means, breaks the rules of democratic fairness. A century ago terrorists were anarchists targeting hereditary rulers, but democracy has made everybody a target. Terrorism and total war are similar forms of breakdown. *Klinghoffer*'s story was more fall-out from the Balfour declaration, and its solution of the Jewish question by ignoring the Palestinian question. The hijack of the (now wrecked) Achille Lauro cruise ship was a Palestine Liberation Front demonstration in which Leon Klinghoffer was killed, his body thrown overboard.

To call the Muslim religion Hagarism is to recall the biblical dispossession of Ismael, Abraham's firstborn by his concubine Hagar. Hagar and Ismael were two danced characters in Adams's opera. Sellars was reminding the audience that though Jews and Arabs continue to claim difference above all from each other, Islamic law is not far from Levitical proscriptions. The message was very unpopular in New York. In Sellars's energetic staging Palestinians, Jews or whatever all wore a uniform style of pastel-shaded contemporary casual garb: slacks and shirts, skirts and blouses, designed by Dunya Ramicova. The pastel colours changed subtly to be more solid as the work advanced. Sellars and the powerful librettist Goodman declared their work with justification to be religious – which her sharp-edged lines of painful poetry, one of the longest and most political opera texts since Metastasio, certainly were. Allah and Jahweh are the one God but the different faith communities scarcely share a common humanity, which would remedy the tragic issues of *Klinghoffer*. That was the central message of Sellars's staging. Goodman's libretto disinterred coolly, dispassionately, without too much manipulation, the imagined feelings of the leading players in the *Achille Lauro* drama.

It was significant that this opera came from an almost all-American team, for in the American myth of Eden-plus-democracy terrorism is the greatest blasphemy. The USA is designed as a rational state and system of peace into which new immigrants elect. Yet its founding required dispossession of the native population. Was an opera where a character called 'Rambo' says

'America is one big Jew' un-American? US critics, with their homeland poised between umpire and empire, knew Sellars, Goodman and Adams were rejecting that national myth.

Klinghoffer aimed to purge the American conscience. Adams's emotionally charged tonal language was persuasively passionate. In the prologue, played using a mobile circular sitting-room on wheels, good musical jokes recycled Tchaikovsky and Wagner; later echoes evoked Britten and Tippett. Without any obvious tunes, but harmonically robust, the drama and commentaries achieved pacey theatrical intensity, using recitative and arioso as impersonal as Cavalli. This opera–oratorio was not documentary like *Nixon in China*. Its accessible music, with few repetitive minimalist ticks, supported its serious burden quite free of the neurosis of Schoenbergian modernism.

George Tsypin's monumental set was an epic four-floor steel contraption that suggested both the cruise ship's gangways and steps and the rigid ideological frame controlling the characters: the extravagance of the structure, which put it beyond presentation in Britain even though Glyndebourne shared the commission, reflected the clout of Gerard Mortier, Belgian director of the Brussels Opera who commissioned it. At floor level there were clear spaces where Mark Morris's company could expressively dance out the story. Sellars and Tsypin also used video close-up, with the singers of various arias on stage projected and magnified on banks of screens dropped into the set showing cast of face and lip movements. Opera is an art without close-ups. A sub-theme was what television makes of such events.

The atmosphere was subtly adjusted by sensitive lighting and white or black cloths at the edge of the stage-frame, which ran up or were lowered like Vienna blinds. The speed of dancers' and singers' movements was part of the style: singers often have to function choreographically in Sellars productions. Morris's dance language combined the American vernacular of great movie musicals with Twyla Tharp, intensifying and reconstructing natural everyday gestures, walking, leaning, running, turning, hands moving in tiny spasms or held aloft and extended, couples suddenly, crazily pirouetting – energy mixed with relaxation. Sellars did the same in the central performances. The double act of Sanford Sylvan singing and Keith Sabado 'dancing' Klinghoffer came to a moving climax for the 'dying fall' descent of the body into the sea. In turn dancer and singer pulled each other on a shroud-like sailcloth over the floor, suggesting movingly the balletic image of a floating corpse, lost but never forgotten.

In Sellars's Salzburg Festival and Opéra Bastille staging of Messiaen's *Saint François d'Assise* the cultural references might have seemed alien, but were in fact strictly applied to the meaning of the text. A frieze of television sets hanging round the proscenium arch was unusual ('like a giant illuminated Rohan MS', Sellars explained) and so was the piling up of television sets to form architectural features – a convent doorway, a Calvary group of crosses, the saint's death-bed and tomb. It was blatantly ironic for St Francis to preach the simple life against this array of consumer symbols. But how better could Sellars bring in elements from the real world? What registered via the television screens as truthful documentary pictures of blood, flowing water, living flowers in the wind, birds, a suffering young saint mortifying his flesh, also made a strong contrast with the usually artificial forum of the opera stage. Watching the video screens periodically, from time to time the imagery changed. These extraneous images, purporting to be 'real life', were a flickering, modern accompaniment.

Sellars condensed and polished his Messiaen staging after its birth in the Salzburg Felsenreitschule. The Opéra Bastille, an ultra-modern theatre on an epic scale, a would-be cathedral of opera today, underscored Sellars's imagery perfectly – and suited Messiaen's approachable contemporary musical language. The right of the stage was filled with massive wooden ribs and platforms like a church or barn or ship, which filled up with the chorus from time to time; on the left was a steeply raked wood-floor hillside and at the front an island made with wooden planks and another rectangular platform right above the orchestra pit. This was a space for Sellars to conjure with. On the forestage an army of tuned percussion instruments was laid out – including on the left the *ondes martenot*. The back of the set was filled with an enormous screen of multicoloured neon lighting tubes which on cue fulfilled Messiaen's wish for coloured lights to match his music. The most striking element of the production was a winged angel in red (Sara Rudner) whose gesture towards the palm of her hand registered the idea of stigmata.

Apart from some hyperactive hand-jiving by the chorus – familiar Sellars action, raised left arms in salute, jubilation expressed in manual gesture language – and the ecstatic hieratic movements of Dawn Upshaw's ravishingly pure-toned Angel, this was a simple, positive staging without pretension or obscurantism. Most impressive were the uplifting conclusions of the fifth tableau (the Angel Musician) and seventh tableau (the Stigmata) with José Van Dam's impressively cantatory and declaiming Saint as the central focus, spotlit on the hillside. The quantity of incident was well judged to support such powerfully descriptive music. There was no swamping with diversionary business.

Messiaen was never a man of the theatre. His sense of timing as a composer reflected his work as a church organist – who suited himself after services when the aptly named 'voluntary' was finished. *Saint François* was about the glimpses of paradise a saintly life afforded – if only we noticed – and how music opened a door on mystical revelations like St Francis's in a different timescale and imaginative universe. Messiaen was ambitious to put such things on stage. His musical language and words were typically sentimental and naive. Fanfaring Hollywood hallelujahs mixed with birdsong and tuned percussion. Life has never been as simple as art. The musical vision had humility and a clarity that Sellars rightly did not touch. The music achieved visionary intensity; the best scenes were deeply moving. Sellars's staging reflected and emphasized Messiaen's religious message.

There has always been an important difference in principle between Sellars tackling a new contemporary opera and Sellars interpreting classics. Few producers, in any case, have in recent decades set their mark so firmly on a succession of new works in the opera-house. The Adams and Osborne operas did not count on the frisson of stylistic decorum being breached, though inevitably their modernisms were not universally palatable. The Messiaen production, with its use of television screens, was criticized for departing from the 'naturalism' that the *maître* had originally insisted on for the opera's first Palais Garnier staging. But Sellars could not be called perverse in his search for a visual and gestural language to accompany Messiaen's highly coloured music, nor for his adherence to a patent and simple narrative style with naturalistic acting. Despite some expressive contortions and mannerisms in his production style, Sellars has always mainly sought acting of almost cinematic realism.

His staging of *Giulio Cesare in Egitto*, Handel's ravishing, highly accomplished Italian opera for the fashionable rich theatregoers of 18th-century Hanoverian London, was not dressed by Sellars in Baroque wigs and ostrich feathers – or even togas and tunics. Sellars's encyclical at the premiere told the audience that he detested updating as 'cheap and gimmicky'. Nevertheless he turned Handel's Italian Baroque at one level into an opera about an American president visiting a Middle Eastern political hot-spot, with echoes of Vietnam, the Lebanon, Iranian hostages, and JFK's 'affair' with Marilyn Monroe. There were inviting parallels to be drawn between Julius Caesar's imperialism (distorted by Baroque opera cliché) and the American imperialist scandals and irresponsibilities of the post-war decades. Handel's beautiful, sad and comic work, with some of the most memorable tunes ever to have graced the operatic stage, took place in the wreckage of the Cairo Hilton. Arias became press conference statements. Aides became secret service sleuths. The head of Pompey the Great was lifted from a hatbox, while the music with all its daring demands on the vocal skills and mellifluousness of the singers poured forth, regardless of conscious anachronism.

The first scene took place beside a hotel pool-side. On the left of Elaine Spatz-Rabinowitz's set was the Isis Bar, balcony above. On the right the walls were blasted like Beirut in the 1980s, with shattered glass and floors of burnt-out hotel bedrooms rising into the flies. At the back was a coarse cheap 'Egyptian' fresco. Caesar, preceded by his frenetic security man Curio equipped with an electronic bomb sniffer, was a Kennedy-style president upholding Pax Americana at an impromptu press conference with micro-phone stand and tooth-white smiles for the cameras. Sellars gave a new context to an old tale. In George Bernard Shaw's fantasy on the story (*Caesar and Cleopatra*, 1898), the character of Julius Caesar was a bit of a self-portrait, heavy with aphorisms, a Roman general bubbling with Fabian philosophy and wit – but clad in toga with period props. Updating, though inevitable with Sellars, was less important than the focus on the expressive embroidery of arias and duets. Conventionally, Baroque operas are supposed to be nothing but *bel canto* singing. They are complex mosaics with the arias as articulate cameos. Handel's lyrical imagination was one of the most sublime manifestations of the singer's art. But his works have often been called undramatic. Until the interpretative revolution of recent years all stage action in Handel operas always stopped for the beautiful vocal fireworks and their deadeningly predictable 'da capo' form – requiring a closing repeat of each song's opening section (the A-B-A form).

Sellars applied an invariable rule. The more florid and vocally demanding an aria, the more physically abandoned and intricately discursive was the action he required the singer simultaneously to undertake. The piling on of detail not only released a more impassioned singing style but converted it from a laid-on bravura display into a psychologically painful revelation of character. Handel's dramatic subtlety and serious intent were properly mobilized in the theatre when the performers turned their bodies into expressive instruments, with hand movements, facial subtlety and physical deportment revealing exactly the feelings and intentions that drew from them such remarkable, musically able lines. Singers might claim they had a difficult enough task merely getting the right notes out sufficiently beautifully. But Sellars with his own company had proved that complex and technically demanding music were best served by piling on the agony; truly liberated expression comes from making the singers do more and more intricate things. This had commonly been the most characteristic Sellars trademark. The emotional contrasts of the music were organic to the structure.

All too easily the jokes in Handel's operas become camp, the magic vulgar. Sellars's modern setting in *Giulio Cesare* had lots of incidental humour. Ptolemy in PVC windcheater and brightly striped T-shirt, a self-portrait of the producer perhaps, seemed like a temperamental young tennis star, vain, insecure, immature, almost pathetic in Drew Minter's cub-like boisterous performance. Sextus (excitingly done by Lorraine Hunt) became a hysterical urban guerilla blasted by the sight of 'his' father Pompey's bloody head – produced from the hatbox by James Maddalena's straightman Achillas. In his aria about a serpent's venom, Sextus gave himself a fix with a 'snake' from the flower-bed, in fact a hosepipe in which he then got impossibly tangled up. A mix of farce and tragedy was basic to Handel. Cleopatra's wonderful lament ('Piangerò' – one of Handel's greatest) was sung by Susan Larson in a denim jumpsuit, blindfolded, before a vastly overblown Egyptian front-cloth that very gradually rose as she sang – revealing the foreshore where Caesar (the firm American countertenor Jeffrey Gall) had been shipwrecked. Everybody knew Caesar and Cleopatra were saved in the end: but Sellars had such imagination and effective control of pace and mood that the downturn in fortune registered with total conviction. 'Piangerò' could stand for universal despair, moulded with resilience, instead of just being a pretty and opportunistic song. Cleopatra and Caesar's entanglement seemed genuine (on his part at least), and

Cleopatra no longer seemed the night-club tart that most stagings have made her. Sellars lent dignity to all this remarkable line-up of worthwhile parts.

Operas are not just zany extravagant ways of telling history. Any composer with the theatrical instinct to succeed in opera has quickly recognized the power for propaganda it represents, promoting moral, political and sometimes religious ideas and philosophies under the sugared guise of entertainment. The agenda may be hidden. The trick is to reveal the truth of feeling and belief within the music, words and situations. But the study of history and politics is less about facts than about the interpretation of facts, and that is what has made Sellars's stagings so thought-provoking. Present-day East Coast America being Sellars's native environment, that was where his images originated. Julius Caesar's Egyptian sojourn, infatuated with Queen Cleopatra and nearly destroyed by her incompetence, gave Handel and his librettist Nicola Haym in 1724 a perfect mix of naive and complex sex and politics. Love with its power-games and manipulations tickled the theatrical appetite of Handel's day as much as it has obsessed today's soap-opera audience. The polarity between art and nature that was so clear to the 18th century may be barely comprehensible to today's audiences. An era when the powerful routinely covered up their entire physical frame with wigs, gloves, pock-mark patches and heavy make-up would not be easy to read. What exactly should we make of the fact that in *opera seria* heroic male roles were sung by castrated men with, often, fully developed breasts – and sometimes even by women? Surely the sophisticated element in Handel's audience, presented with the heavy irony and high emotions of *Giulio Cesare in Egitto*, could distinguish between Baroque appearance and reality. It was an age of game-playing and role-playing, when what actually counted were power and money, and when social custom permitted, indeed encouraged, decorum and disguise as a perfectly adequate means of class mobility. The power struggle between Cleopatra and Ptolemy has always in literature and drama been perceived as a mainly comic, unequal beauty contest overshadowed by the waxing might of the Roman imperium. In Handel's day the story rang bells because the intruding Romans represented great family dynastic interests contemptuous of the alien royal traditions with which they were tangling: just how many people saw them as Handel's Hanoverian patrons? So *Giulio Cesare* was not just a delicately comic romance. It was also a satire on the abuse of power and the serendipitous insecurity of the political process. As in Monteverdi's *Coronation of Poppea*, the chief protagonists played for the highest stakes. But Handel's Caesar was also endowed by history (and geography) with detachment. Caesar was a *deus ex machina* present from the start of the opera who enjoyed his risky involvement in events right up to his final departure. Unlike Aeneas's dalliance with Dido, Caesar and Cleopatra were never deluded into thinking their 'love' was more than an imaginary and delicious diversion – the ultimate *Brief Encounter*.

Sellars did not need to feel shy about adopting Handel. The music remained seductive as ever. In any case, unlike many old-fashioned opera productions which were just visual window-dressing behind the singers, Sellars articulated the story believably with his personal company of singers who could act, and used a setting that explained the politics in the action. But though the composer's view of human relations and politics was sophisticated and witty, the remarkable thing was how uncomfortable the comedy and intrigue became. The countertenor Jeffrey Gall, a first-class actor, was an ideal tool for Sellars's political portrait. The contrast between Haym's formal Italian text and Gall's modern American gestures, whether 'playing' with Susan Larson's naughty but nicely touching Cleopatra or handling public appearances, was delicious – though humour and emotion would have told more with text in the audience's vernacular. Gall mixed registers with virile attack, using an extreme range of colour in his singing, and polished decorations and flourishes. Drew Minter's singing as a chubby-chasing Ptolemy was also subtle and adaptable. Both men were vocally and physically daring, opposite Mary Westbrook-Geha's formidably large Cornelia, in Thatcher-like royal blue two-piece. Cheryl Cobb's Nirena (Cleopatra's eunuch feminized by Sellars) was impressively passionate. Even Craig Smith, ponderous maestro, finally found an unobtrusively relaxed style to explore all corners of this exhilarating operatic epic, just five minutes short of five hours – almost as long as *Götterdämmerung*, and never tiring.

In Sellars's stagings of classics by Handel, Mozart and Debussy, updating and transferring the story more or less to his native America created a vital energy in defamiliarizing and surprising his audience. He turned *Tannhäuser* at the Lyric, Chicago, into the sex scandal of a telly evangelist lured to Venusberg sleaze. At the

Pepsico SummerFare festival his much travelled Mozart/Da Ponte trilogy, which he personally recorded in Vienna thanks to a $5 million television budget, offered *Figaro* as chauffeur to Count Alma-viva, an egomaniac plutocrat inhabiting a Trump Tower duplex or triplex 52 floors above Fifth Avenue in the Manhattan clouds. *Così fan tutte* was played out at 'Despina's Diner' on Cape Cod with her odd-job-man and frustrated admirer Alfonso as a Vietnam veteran. *Don Giovanni* became a black drug-baron, violent, raunchy, unscrupulous, quick on the draw in every sense, on the dope-crazed mean streets of colourful upper East Side Spanish Harlem (or perhaps the Bronx).

Sets and costumes are not superficial trappings. Sellars's updat-ings of the Mozart/Da Ponte operas required imposition of or mixture with unexpected scenarios. Each work was differenced (to use the heraldic term), though Sellars was true to the spirit of the originals. He regarded it as essential to play Mozart's three greatest comedies in present-day American street clothes, overlaid with the popular images and circumstances, the current habits and mores of American society. *Figaro*, *Giovanni* and *Così* com-manded attention not as art history detritus – exercises in re-cre-ating a vanished society – but as vital modern theatre. What mattered was not what they told us about Mozart or his era, but how they articulated present-day questions of sex, politics and personal morality. Mozart originally wrote very modern operas. *Giovanni* may have been a mythical old story, but the notoriety of Casanova had made it newly relevant. Beaumarchais's *Figaro* was seen as a scandalous attack on decent society, and banned by the court of Joseph II. *Così*, an account of wife-swapping and related emotional traumas drawn (Sellars maintained) from Mozart's own life, had, thanks to Victorian respectability, for a long time in the 19th century virtually lapsed from the repertoire.

In 1989 Sellars's approach made the three dramas seem as if written yesterday. The notes and Italian words remained of their time. Everything else was up-to-date: the stories, the way charac-ters behaved towards each other, the props, gestures, body lan-guage. Rather than having to identify with people in fancy costume playing historical games, the audience confronted the pressing social tragedies of our day. Sexual language, especially, will date faster than anything. Sexuality is about familiarity: few people know about dressing (let alone undressing) in Mozartian clothes. Sellars's Mozart made the sexuality authentic, was physically graphic and natural. This effect was most telling and surprising in *The Marriage of Figaro* when Cherubino stripped off to reveal ice hockey plastic protective padding (he/she was an adolescent yearning for real masculinity and maturity). The scene where the Countess and Susanna dress 'him' in a flimsy pink blouse was genuinely sexy. Subsequent intimacies between Cherubino and the Countess, interrupted by the Count just before the cupboard incident, were torrid. Sellars had been building and polishing his Mozart/Da Ponte cycle stagings since 1985, with some major crucial cast-changes in the final year before the video recording. Story-lines were scrupulously re-imagined to conform to new locations, complete with synopses in the programme. Bartolo had accepted a professorship 'perhaps at the Italian department of Columbia'; Cherubino was an AWOL teenager; Figaro was the chauffeur; Don Curzio had a 'pay or play' attitude, the Count 'a severe Ed Meese-type memory lapse'. The wedding included yuppy go-go dancers. The last act took place on 'a high ledge not intended for human beings' according to the unusual synopsis with which Sellars prepared his audience.

The opening act of *Figaro*, in a narrow airless laundry-room dominated by a sofa-bed with fridge, washing-machine, drier, double steel sink, wall-phone, soap-powders, bleaches, ironing-board, steps, cardboard boxes, was brilliantly directed. Not only the props in Adrianne Lobel's sets were specific. The characterization had virtuoso accuracy too. This gangling youth who made straight for a box of juice in the fridge (Susan Larson) was almost a properly male Cherubino. Basilio, a young man in a bomber jacket covered in zips with a ghastly leering wink, inflated the joke about translation to the present day still further. The comedy around the old chair, revamped by using a collapsible sofa-bed, was mint fresh. The chorus rounded up by Figaro to announce the wedding was a motley crew of postman, cook, butcher, doctor, secretary, commissionaire – anybody with a spare moment up the Trump Tower. Some rich people in New York prefer to live in hotels. None of the dangerous emotions of the act 2 estrangement of Count and Countess was missed. The Count was so worked up he could not spot Susanna on the floor by the bed. And for the problem of how Cherubino would jump from the 52nd floor, there was a terrace one floor down.

Sellars revised his productions scrupulously, when touring them round the world over a period of years. In 1989 the big innovation in the last act was that, instead of blacking out what was going on inside the grand reception area behind the vertiginous ledge, Sellars revealed all, producing an enormously detailed subtext that reflected and responded to the sequence of arias and aimed to uncover genuine anguish in the characters. The Count was shown going off for a quickie with a go-go girl. The plot thickened before the audience's eyes, including an evocation of the phantasms in Basilio's song, filled with self-loathing, about careful disguise.

Sellars risked upstaging the crucial reconciliation, and, with the music becalmed, the whole edifice of the staging began to crumble. Rashly he and Craig Smith the conductor added to the usual music. The lovely E flat serenade adagio was used as an interlude between acts 1 and 2, upstaging '*Porgi amor*'. The singing was often underpowered. But Sellars is always suspicious of easily smoothed over musical reconciliations: his *Così* ended with everybody on stage in a turmoil of permanent motion, unable to relate happily to anybody else. Not just marriage, but life itself, seemed virtually out of the question.

Don Giovanni as designed by George Tsypin took place on a mean Manhattan street scene with graffiti, boarded-up shops, roadworks, an aluminium-shuttered church, the detritus of human desperation and destruction. Anna was being raped near tenement steps by a black man (Eugene Perry in 1989 was the Don, with his twin brother Herbert Perry as Leporello). The Commendatore was a Mafia godfather in a heavy black coat. Ottavio was a local cop. Paramedics, quick on the scene, attempted to revive the Commendatore. Only at the end did the audience learn why Anna was entangled with the Don – when she confessed to Ottavio she was a junkie by injecting herself with heroin as she sang '*Non mi dir*'. Ottavio wept tears of painful devastated betrayal. This substituted scenario was intensely disturbing – though such artifice works far better on stage than on video. Elvira's first entry, looking nervously behind her as she approached the tenement where all the characters seemed to either live or congregate, was followed by a wild scavenge through her tote bag for a kitchen-knife with which to murder Giovanni. When the Don bribed Leporello back into his service the deal involved generous snorts of cocaine. Masetto, a tall black niceguy, was mugged by a gang of hoodlums. The last supper Leporello provided for his master, with music from a huge ghetto-blaster, was a big Mac with all the relishes. But comedy turned into a kind of drug-crazed nightmare when the statue seemed to emerge from the floor behind the glass-door of the tenement. The whole set jerked and started to come apart, as if hit by an earthquake. The Don was finally dragged to damnation in the sewers by a small, pure, innocent little girl who came from behind the church shutters to take his hand: irresistibly emotional and perhaps sentimental, but actually true to the metaphysical purpose of Tirso which Mozart and da Ponte carried forward. Sellars, despite his specific New York settings, has always been ready to add surrealism to his basic neo-realism. He is also a 'believer' – that essential qualification for directing *Don Giovanni*.

The first half of *Così* was set up like a television soap, buddies and broads socializing at the local diner. This won joyful laughs from Sellars fans as the production paraded the familiar trappings of the red-neck, blue-collar lifestyle – a bit like the television series *Roseanne*. Such repellent jollity was only there to be knocked down in the second half, which was the more painful because more specific and truthful. David Freeman's Opera Factory version was similar in touch, and as entertaining and successful. But Freeman played on the *Così* conventions where Sellars cut right through them to a new level of intensity, going all the way with the opera's nihilistic logic. How could anybody ever think it was just a frilly amoral comedy? The desperation that overwhelmed Sellars's Ferrando and had always afflicted his Alfonso was tragic and disturbing. The singing quality was not the point: Sellars's singers could act. Frank Kelley and James Maddalena, Ferrando and Guglielmo in *Così*, were also his Basilio and Count in Figaro. Sanford Sylvan was Alfonso and Figaro. Sue Ellen Kuzma was Despina and Marcellina. The sexy Cherubino (Susan Larson) was also Fiordiligi. This was all company work. The best sung Mozart in 1989 was *Don Giovanni* with the Perry twins as Don and manservant marvellously exploiting their physical similarity. Even compared to Ruth Berghaus's disparate provocative images, Sellars exposed new depths of human pain in what have too often been considered lightly familiar masterpieces.

It was a risk entrusting *Die Zauberflöte*, a Glyndebourne core repertoire work, to an iconoclast like Sellars just before the Mozart bicentenary. Glyndebourne must please. But it was worth it. The publicity primed everybody to cheer or jeer as Sellars blended Mozart's evergreen parable with the contemporary

American scene. Sellars said he was freeing the work from being a mystical problem piece. Other productions he had seen never showed how frightening and scary it all was – under what duress the characters were operating. Any laughter should come as an 'incredible relief in the confused power struggle'. A novelty was Sellars's unusual (and money-saving) doubling of some roles – repaying the carte blanche he was given in the casting. He even toyed with the idea of using an English text by Alice Goodman, librettist of *Nixon in China*. He took a crisp fresh perspective, thoughtful, lucid, emotion-filled, precisely musical, joyous – and above all entertaining.

Sellars quickly found enough culture-shock to sound the reveille for traditional Glyndebourne audiences. Instead of druids or children's picture-book fantasy, his *Zauberflöte* was played out against backdrops that were garishly colourful photographic projections of Los Angeles streets, freeways and seaside. Much of the action took place on an upper stage, in front of and between pictures of roadscapes, a beach, a park, a petrol station, a cliff-face. Mostly, until the concluding dawn, it was sunset or dusk. Six feet below, at normal stage level, was a kind of grey low-vaulted crypt – a subterranean world inhabited by Sarastro's cult followers, slaves to punk fashion. This was the scene of the initiation trials and encounters of the second act. The keynote of Sellars's production was unfussy simplicity, all the way to the final scene. After the platform structure had carried the Queen, ladies and Monostatos away upstage into irrelevancy, hiding them behind a huge dropped-in photograph of dawn in LA, the chorus flooded forward, relaxed and easy, filling the space: society reunited and healed in an act of faith and celebration.

The acting style was almost all didactic, straightforward and televisual, evenly accompanied by Lothar Zagrosek with confidently projected singing. Sellars's background in puppet theatre was a crucial factor – suiting his naive approach to the narrative (condensed as a result of cutting the spoken dialogue and relying for energy on the musical structure). The sharp lighting changes, instant scene switches and silhouette effects also related to puppets and television. Sellars of course added his typical hand movements and gesture language relating to Indian and Indonesian theatre, or Japanese Noh and Kabuki. Everything inessential was excluded which meant, notably, all but three words (*Ein, zwei, drei*) of Schikaneder's spoken dialogue. Without dialogue, Sellars was free to stage the heart of the story without the scenes sinking inescapably into a comic never-land. And he did not have to work at updating, inventing ways of making his new context jell with the text. The tone was simply contemporary – Sarastro a bespectacled Hindu-cum-Buddhist West Coast cult guru, neatly bearded in grey Nehru coat and yellow shawl, a flower painted on his forehead. There were almost no props, except the flute and Papageno's bells, a few manhole covers between the upper and lower worlds (or inner and outer, to be Jungian), a briefcase and revolver for police officer Monostatos, a dagger for the Queen and Pamina, a set of steps for the Speaker and a ladder for Sarastro.

Tamino was first seen wearing jeans and white T-shirt, doped out of his head at a spaghetti junction (nicely suggesting the 'dragon' of modern civilization). The three ladies (acting like the popular 1940s singing trio, the Andrews sisters) wore black dresses, long black gloves, pearls and black pillbox hats. The Queen was striking in aquamarine silk two-piece with fierce black handbag. Pamina was in a plain scarlet dress. Papageno sported an ostrich-feather bird-suit, red lipstick and speckled tights – a joker from the beach culture. Monostatos wore a plain-clothesman's suit. ('You know me – I'm on the case', read his red neon supertitle.) The three boys on skate-boards slipped in and out of lurid T-shirts and Bermuda shorts. The old woman, or Papagena to be, was a terminal Parkinson's disease patient with drip-feed and wheelchair – an image revived by Sellars for his Amsterdam *Pelléas*.

The text was not translated but, from time to time, Sellars provided explanatory (sometimes exact) surtitles across the front of the upper stage in bright red neon ticker-tape-style micro-signs. Scene changes were announced. Nobody could possibly have failed to follow what happened, and what was meant by what happened – the purpose of Mozart's sublimely provocative entertainment with its irresistible musical sugaring. The themes were marriage-breakdown (Sarastro and the Queen), reconciliation (Tamino and Pamina), and wholeness (Papageno and Papagena). When Papageno got his big mouth locked up, it was true that we hadn't heard him tell a lie. Sellars, not a man for half-measures, did without all the spoken text – but then, as we have seen, he also omitted the usually comic 'dragon' at the start, or found a new theatrical way of filling in for the dragon. Next scene at a petrol station, Tamino squatted on a TV set slurping a can of Bud. In the second act Papageno kissed the terminal case in the wheelchair.

The emotionalism was tested to destruction by the six little Papagenos and Papagenas in yolk-yellow chick-suits. But Sellars's best recommendation is the way he can mix references and levels of intensity and meaning.

Papageno's sense of abandonment and loss was painfully plumbed. It was not just an idiot game, danger free. This vitally prepared for Sellars's most brilliant stroke: the scene for the armed men (done by Alastair Miles and Howard Haskin, singers of the Speaker and Monostatos) and the subsequent trials of fire and water which became, instead of an awkward-to-credit embarrassment with tacky theatrical effects, the pivot of the entire work. Sellars had Ai-Lan Zhu lead Kurt Streit slowly across the crypt, in silhouette, both singers stark naked. The central issue of man and wife was firmly and tellingly established in a most touching, unprurient way. This absence of innuendo had been prepared for serenely with a simple gesture by the Queen of the Night during her appeal to Tamino. She rested one black-gloved hand lightly on his tummy, drew it down slowly over the front of his jeans to rest on his thigh. Not sexy, but significantly sexual. With Sellars every movement counts.

That was true too of Sellars's collaboration with Simon Rattle and the Rotterdam Philharmonic on *Pelléas et Mélisande* at the 1993 Holland Festival, a Netherlands Opera production. Here, however, was an atypical, high-profile event more in line with Sellars's Chicago *Tannhäuser*. He was not the star attraction. The cast was not his familiar company but a top-flight British line-up including Elise Ross, then Rattle's wife, as Mélisande. Sellars demystified Debussy, relocating the story (apparently) on the United States seaboard. Instead of misty dreamlike romanticism, in Sellars's altered scenario Prince Golaud was a sort of rich exile, protected by security guards, or maybe local police, who were shown keeping undesirables off the property. The sheep that Yniold hears going back to their pens, in the scene before Golaud's killing of Pelléas, became instead the three sleeping beggars from the 'grotto' getting arrested – the 'shepherd' converted into a senior cop among many.

Instead of a series of different scenes with particular and distinctive flavour in various parts of a medieval castle, Sellars used a single set, thus leaving the music to flow uninterrupted in a seamless stream. This was a kind of steady-state *Pelléas*, the separate scenes not shaped apart as there were no scene changes for the later composed entractes to accompany. Each act was run together into a continuum, taking place in and around a cutaway concrete doll's house, like a sort of strip cartoon. Johannes Schaaf's *Fledermaus*, also at the Amsterdam Musiektheater, had used a similar doll's house set for the opening act at the Eisensteins.

The designer George Tsypin provided for Sellars a set suspended on three levels that presented four clinical rooms with light-panel ceilings, of which the central one had internal stairs. On the right, high up, there was a narrow concrete balcony in front of a window that glowed red for jealousy and displayed the silhouette of the listening Golaud (Willard White) – while Philip Langridge's middle-aged Pelléas played none-too-innocently with Mélisande's modestly sweeping gold locks. The neo-brutalism of the decor included stepping rungs in the concrete wall up to the balcony and a huge disused sewage pipe sloping down from the right of the proscenium towards the 'beach' and water's edge on the left. Pelléas and Yniold descended it at full tilt. The pond, well and seashore were all suggested with blue strips of neon. The sea-pools below the 'house' were evoked with a multi-coloured mass of neon, glowing and twinkling like sunsets, re-using a lighting effect from Sellars's Messiaen staging.

It all looked very like a hospital wing, and also quite like Lavelli's Paris Opéra staging – apart from the black housemaids and nurses. In the top left room, with a view of the ocean, Arkel was in his electric wheelchair. Pelléas's father (a new non-singing role referred to in the text, but introduced here on stage by Sellars for the first time) lay collapsed on a hospital bed in the room below, drips attached. The middle room acquired an adjustable bed for Golaud when he also was ill, and at the end for Mélisande. After the interval Pelléas's father and other patients got better. At the start of the opera Golaud was contemplating Russian roulette by the sewage pipe; at the end he offered his wrists to two cops, confessing to the murder of Pelléas, as they snapped handcuffs on: an open and shut case. Each act ended with the safety curtain down. In one scene, Golaud and Pelléas explored in front of the curtain with a torch.

There were problems of scale in this miniaturized approach, and in Sellars's invented sub-text – which included Felicity Palmer's Geneviève in pink cardigan, trousers and pearls sitting reading a book beside the sickbed of Pelléas's father. Sellars, unusually, seemed determined to leave nothing to the imagination, explaining everything in soap-opera style. Every possible detail was being played out in a next-door room to the one where the audience was supposed to be following the actual scene and action from the Debussy/Maeterlinck opera. The precise direction was very clear: carefully considered details such as how Golaud dismissed, with a wave of his hand, the security man who had come to investigate whether he had a problem. Everything was organized to point up the intensity of feeling within the characters – Willard White's powerful Golaud, especially, was utterly believable. The production, though updated and translated to America, was conventional and straightforwardly naturalistic with no expressive choreography, no hand-jiving. Sellars seemed to be making a point of doing without some of those tricks that had become a personal signature, but that also required the goodwill and technique of familiars to be properly done. Once the scenario had been put across, the single set grew uninteresting. Debussy's opera almost requires scene changes for its particular *tinto*. Sellars was awkward with the growth of emotion between these none-too-young lovers. His Mélisande, not at all exotic, was more like an impassive Mia Farrow in a range of jumpsuits.

Sellars certainly made palpable an opera that was all about states of mind. So much concrete detail reduced the poetry of the piece, made it into a rather sordid 'yellow press' romance, in which sex (far from being imagined by the characters) was probably taking place just off stage. Debussy is not only mists and moping. But Sellars's typical, almost routine Americanization of *Pelléas* did not discover special revelations. You gotta have a gimmick if you're going to stay ahead – to quote Stephen Sondheim's classic line in the musical *Gypsy*. But, perhaps, for Sellars it needed to be a new gimmick.

In late 1995 Sellars staged *Mathis der Maler* at Covent Garden as a 'life-as-art' documentary account of crucifixion in our time. Hindemith's opera used the artist Grünewald's Lutheran conversion, and the turmoil of Germany at the time, as a way of looking at the artist in a Germany facing 20th-century fascism and intolerance. Sellars's docu-drama of urban guerillas in modern Los Angeles showed fascist police, poison gas. Rioting groups of poor Americans and immigrants battled against the privileged 'moral majority' forming up beside Newt Gingrich. This was the latest version of Sellars's characteristic theatrical scenario. The seven tableaux of Hindemith's opera were presented on a single set without a hint of Grünewald. George Tsypin's design was an overt artistic statement rather than a place: instead of naturalism Tsypin provided a platform that was a pseudo-constructivist evocation of a flimsy wooden artist's easel with broken glass office blocks where there might be a canvas.

Sellars refused to have a copy of Grünewald's great Isenheim altarpiece dominating the set – with its image of Christ's flesh on the Cross covered with thousands of little wounds and even a few actual thorns still sticking in, after the mocking and beating. For Sellars the altarpiece was a tacky idea. He provided instead the Passion of present-day American people, illustrating the emotions he hoped the audience would share through the expressive miming of a small movement group. Instead of Hindemith's history Sellars offered his personal statement about the struggle between life and art.

That is a crucial theme of *Mathis der Maler*. But Sellars's solution seemed to be degenerating into routine, his style bordering on mannerism. He will not turn to the entertaining eclecticism natural to theatre, but transposes narratives to the modern USA so that audiences will not in an escapist way leave the theme in history: he wants 'reality' in his sense (though anything on stage is as much a metaphor as it is in the more apparently 'realistic' medium of film) to stare us in the face.

There can no doubt be too much complexity in the theatrical imagery of a Berghaus or Richard Jones. But this neglect of history was not benign. Where Hindemith's plan allowed the enemy a chance to explain himself, Sellars insisted on a singular, loaded historical view that was easier to brush aside, if one did not buy the politics. Hindemith's questions about the Reformation and Weimar require human intimacy and the historical context to be in the foreground of this (in a sense) *Meistersinger*.

Stig Andersen's Cardinal Albrecht von Brandenburg wore a grey suit throughout. When the text spoke of Reformation matters, one saw only a stagey version of Sellars's modern USA. This focused the morality, but imprisoned the audience in a one-eyed vision – a scenario that, however, happened to be closely related to both *Klinghoffer* and his recent (and more successful) John Adams collaboration about present-day issues: *I was looking at the ceiling and then I saw the sky*. There was something rather puritanical about Sellars seating the chorus, uncostumed, in the stalls circle near and on either side of the proscenium. On stage, meanwhile, violent extras expressed Sellars's own scenario, some indulging in expressive arm and hand wiggles, others gunning each other down, while the central drift of the text continued to pour our from characters in conflict and argument, sharing obscure emotions about things unseen. His treatment of the chorus was a sure sign that something was wrong with Sellars's approach. One could equally well refuse to stage the chorus of *Boris Godunov*, for convenience and to be tidy, and perhaps more naturalistic than the convention of a stage crowd allows. Sellars never wants to make things easy for the audience. But he should have faced this problem honestly. Surtitles ran across the set in red, up the reflective glass above the easel structure – as well as being in silver-grey on the usual board below the proscenium arch. But the opera would have worked better in English. Hindemith's tableaux were forced into a single inflexible unchanging mould. *Mathis* is not just about pain. Yet Sellars showed the paintings as bloodstained sheets, like abstract Expressionist masterpieces. There are other ways of focusing a theme.

Sellars was in need of a rethink. Even for those who respond readily to the principles behind his aesthetic of reinterpretation, it was beginning to seem that not every opera could benefit from his invariable Americanizing. Perhaps the historical German Reformation was particularly hard to accommodate to Sellars's universal matrix of a modern United States. The Reformation's mixture of ideological shift and economic transformation looms implicitly over *Mathis der Maler*, like Matthias Grünewald's painting of suffering that Paul Hindemith felt inseparable from his drama. When Sellars on his return to Glyndebourne for Handel's oratorio *Theodora*, in May 1996, simply employed a neutral set, a plain white box dominated by giant old cracked and broken 'glass' bottles, it seemed as if he had himself seen the limitations of being too specific in a way that an audience was more likely to resist than accept. In *Mathis* he had edited out the historical consciousness of Hindemith's opera which the composer intended to advance. But here was the 'new wine in old bottles' aspect of Handel's work boldly on stage – in case Sellars ever felt like forgetting it.

Locations in stage productions are always imaginary, always just themselves – a stage set – in mundane physical fact. The nature of the contract is that audiences can be in many places with many thoughts at one and the same time. The set of *Theodora* was perhaps, on first impression, a modern museum lecture theatre ready for an address with a smart black podium and designer chairs – in the United States of America (of course). The five bottles were decorative, though no doubt as worth studying in themselves as any unusual phenomenon. What was Sellars meaning by them? In the re-setting of the stage for different scenes they were moved by stage-hands with great care, as if they were as delicate as egg-shells. In one sense they symbolized human souls: there are five named characters in Handel's oratorio. Suffering souls on the brink of destruction – that which was likely not to be preserved, or would soon be transformed – these pale, coloured (probably in reality plastic) bottles gave the atmosphere a tone of reserve and delicacy, almost of prayerfulness. And the frequent use of the word prayer in Thomas Morell's text was the defining motif in Sellars's production. Many of the arias were effectively prayers, extended cries to eternity, a summoning through potent vocal expression of an individual's intercessionary concern. The inner power of prayer mobilized the strength of moral truth with a burning intensity and thoughtfulness before our eyes and ears. Mere performance turned into something more real than ordinary mundane life outside the theatre.

The chorus arrived in twos and threes in highly colourful clothes, orange and red T-shirts (designer, Dunya Ramicova). Ordinary people. Then there was a television crew – a cameraman, a microphone baffle. Eventually Sellars added the sort of security figures to which the modern age is accustomed, even in 'great democracies'. The President arrived with two uniformed armed guards in state-of-the-art helmets, carrying lethal weapons. Four soldiers ran in parade order across the front of the stage. The rentacrowd mob was disproportionately enthusiastic in their wel-come for Valens's statement. The ruler later had a comic heart attack during his aria and had to receive aid from a team of med-ical auxiliaries. There was much waving around of cans of Bud or Coca-Cola. Superficially, it seemed as if *Theodora* would be a re-run of Sellars's famous *Giulio Cesare in Egitto*.

But the dramatic structure of *Theodora*, with its formal cho-ruses, is less amenable to directorial intervention in some ways than Handel's operas. *Theodora* proved to be an extraordinary return to top form by Sellars. He used just as much as he wanted of the inevitable and anticipated Americanization in order to free himself to concentrate on the expressive and defining elements of his inter-pretation. The problem (or advantage) in bringing an oratorio to life as drama was the articulation and realization of the choruses of 'Romans' and 'Christians' (different varieties of Americans – read human beings – as Sellars showed them here). Both choruses used Sellars's familiar gesture language more fully than in any of his productions. The Romans were colourfully dressed and, in their cups, slobbish. The Christians were pure, almost demure, in blacks, whites and greys – some in surplice-like angel robes. Calm and collected. The gestures used by both choruses related best to an almost charismatic undertow in the Christians' music: the language of their hand and arm movements tellingly blended the style of the baroque stage and the familiar exuberant arm-waving of happy-clappy saved-again evangelical Christians today.

With a neutral environment designed by his frequent collaborator George Tsypin, Sellars could economize severely on his usual literalism. Instead of transposing location in a possibly banal or gimmicky way, he could insist on a vaguer imaginative prompting of his audience – suggesting the interior lives of characters, their concerns, their sense of dramatic crisis. That, after all, is at the heart of every oratorio. The gestures helped to release the emotions being experienced by the characters and communicate them to the audience. Sellars showed the Christians grasping perfectly that this was indeed their time of trial in the religious sense – the test which they would pray to be spared in the 'Our Father'. He intricately devised for his choruses a whole individual choreography of similar gestures, almost as if he were challenging memories of Mark Morris's contributions to theatre. But this physical inventiveness and hyperactivity in fact individualized the chorus, lent them personality – so that, though they sang their lines communally, they were taking responsibility for themselves. Soloists, when present, usually sang along with the chorus – sharing that ideal. Their gestures in solos and duets were even more telling. Healing hands were held against foreheads. A movement of the arm and hand carried power with it, reinforcing the sense in which an arch of Handel's melody has a metaphysical trajectory.

The story centres on the rejection of a political policy by members of the ruling community. Didymus does not believe that religious conformity can or should be imposed. Theodora is shown stripping off her jewelry and all signs of wealth and rank, and converting to a form of puritanical, conscientious Christianity. Handel's original audience, who were not specially sympathetic to his theme, were the wealthy merchant class of London in the 1750s –

not unlike the Glyndebourne audience now witnessing and responding so enthusiastically to Sellars's interpretation. The coolness and precision with which he showed the extermination of the heroine Theodora and the soldier Didymus, who had chosen to die with her, reflected the almost universal acceptance by Americans today of the appropriateness of capital punishment. On stage at Glyndebourne there was a demonstration of exactly how Americans execute their guilty parties. The performance seemed like science turned to an art, and the power of Handel's terminal duet accompanying it was extremely painful to experience. Sellars made his point – and for most of his audience it was devastatingly credible.

Theodora, as oratorio, was written by Handel to form a popular learning experience. Sellars's direction made it all add up with inescapable potency. The point of his approach, as always, was not the Americanizing, it was what we (the audience) understood by it. We were not Americans, mostly, at Glyndebourne. But we grasped and felt the argument. Sellars's economical approach made his purpose more immediately effective: when, for example, the prison cell where Theodora was sleeping and where Didymus visited her was defined simply by a square of yellow light. There were often great shadows on the back of the set, suggesting the scale of heroism. The lighting was not just effective, but essentially expressive. Time passed. The narrative grew into an intimate epic. Sellars is a master of theatrical language, which nobody could fail to perceive. But not just because of the simplicity of means. Where his real power lies is in the physical freedom of expression with which he can endow his performers – a freedom that makes heroism natural and not studied, that enables great claims to be humbly stated.

The potency was of course not just attributable to Sellars's imagination and scrupulous control of the staged event. Handel's score is astonishingly direct and imaginative, the product of the mature genius. William Christie conducting gave all the impulse required and supported the cast ideally. The image of a President Clinton clone presented by Frode Olsen as the 'Roman governor' Valens was highly accessible – a suitably releasing and witty element to balance the tragic tension that was never far below the surface. Richard Croft as Didymus's colleague, the other uniformed guard-cum-soldier, was wonderfully ambivalent in his response to the events.

But at the centre of the performance were three singers of

extraordinary quality, who gave themselves uncompromisingly to Sellars's purpose: the countertenor David Daniels as Didymus, the soprano Dawn Upshaw in the title role, and – most overwhelming of all – the mezzo Lorraine Hunt as Irene, dressed in a simply flowing dark dress. Hunt is a veteran Sellars performer who has never inhabited a supporting role with such fervour and commitment, and who served as the intermediary of the whole experience, almost as if she were a figure from one of the Bach Passions. Her use of gestures was completely assimilated to the still calmness of her passionate utterance. She was totally free physically in what she did, able to sweep the ground with her frame, illustrate her musical line in movement, and yet seem completely, powerfully contained.

Sellars was not just bouncing back from a difficult period in his career. He was showing audiences and critics, many of whom did indeed need persuading, precisely what he was (and had always been) about in his very personal and beautiful method of working on the opera stage – a technique both physical and spiritual. The lesson was inescapable. Most of the Glyndebourne audience for *Theodora* found that it was not difficult to believe, if they just let themselves.

10 Richard Jones: burlesque profundities

Richard Jones's 1994 staging (for the Bavarian State Opera, Munich) of *Giulio Cesare in Egitto* designed by Nigel Lowery: the huntsman tracks his prey – Marcello Lippi's Achilla and Christopher Robson's Tolomeo set up in frozen aggression by Ann Murray's Cesare (centre). Photograph © Wilfried Hösl

Comic genius and a manic intensity are unusual qualities for an opera producer. Even a normal sense of humour is not the predominant characteristic expected from the breed. In operatic comedy it is the acting of the star performers that generally matters, not the concept of the production. And most operas that producers want to tackle to establish reputations are romantic tragedies. For all sorts of reasons opera – even comic opera – is usually no laughing matter: the length, the cost, the complexity of the arrangements on stage. The excesses of opera have often been pilloried as comic by outsiders, which is perhaps why many practitioners strive not to be inadvertently funny in their work, or indeed funny at all. There are dangers in being funny – not least that public and critics may not appreciate comic inventiveness. Opera is serious, and requires effort. If people saw the funny side of all the labour and pretension, they might never stop laughing.

Richard Jones (born 1953) is almost unique in his generation of British opera producers in that he makes jokes on stage, frequently and shamelessly. Jones has no qualms about breaching decorum. He knows the interpretative power that comes from going almost too far. Peter Sellars often inserts jokes too. But people are uncomfortable laughing at Sellars productions in case they laugh at what is specifically *not* meant to be funny. Also Sellars lectures his audience in advance too much, sharpening their intellectual responses with propaganda – whereas Jones believes if the audience cannot warm to what he is doing and be reasonably sympathetic, it is pointless to argue or prompt them. Tim Albery's *Chérubin* for the Royal Opera revealed a strong and unsuspected sense of humour – but Albery got many of the laughs from his designer Antony McDonald. In Germany Ruth Berghaus, Herbert Wernicke and Willy Decker have cracked jokes, but with Berghaus they could be treacherous, intellectual traps, and that took the fun out of them.

Jones is a brilliant director of comedy and farce in the legitimate theatre. His stagings of *Too Clever By Half*, *A Flea in her Ear* and *La bête* were among the most memorably theatrical and witty shows in London for decades. Jones has worked in theatre and opera with a number of designers, all of them visually acute and individualistic. He encourages them to be astonishing. For his Feydeau he had the Brothers Quay, who are, more usually, experimental film-makers. His first opera, *The Rake's Progress*, for the small-scale touring company, Opera 80, early in 1986, with Nigel Prabhavalkar as designer, had a taut and simple post-modern collage of quick-change scenes very well directed and paced – and a memorably sardonic and potent interpretation of Nick Shadow from the young Steven Page.

Another early foray into opera by Jones was Ambroise Thomas's rare *Mignon* at Wexford in 1986. He warmed to its world of sophisticated French comedy and the strong poetic dimension of Barbier and Carré's libretto based on the characters in Goethe's *Wilhelm Meister*. He also warmed to the conflagration in the second act. Richard Hudson's settings included an evocative Palladian front-cloth of the Italian land *'wo die citronen blühn'* (where the lemon trees bloom). A variety of drop-cloths and hinged panels closed off other scenes with galleries on either side, and footlights at the front evoked the theatre world of the mid-19th century. These theatrical games were a lot more exuberant than Hudson's usual style. Philine's dressing-room was a range of cupboards sliding from the wings to cut the stage in half. All through, Jones injected the sort of frank theatricality into the performance that had distinguished Trevor Nunn's *Nicholas Nickleby* – tricks like suddenly playing curtain-calls upstage to create the illusion of the whole theatre building having been switched round back to front. Philip Doghan's Laerte was gloriously extravagant in manner, appropriate for the actor-manager who partnered Philine – Mignon's rival in Wilhelm's affections. Jones achieved in the acting an infectious ease, fluidity and liberal imaginativeness. The cast exercised on top of the dressing-room cupboards. Frederick eavesdropped from up there and suddenly leapt down to confront Wilhelm – as if it were Bergman's *Smiles of a Summer Night*. (Another hugely unusual and imaginative Jones production in the West End was the clever Stephen Sondheim musical *Into the Woods*.) All this unbridled panache reached its climax at the second curtain, when the stage was in ruins after the catastrophic fire following Philine's performance of *A Midsummer Night's Dream*, with shipwrecked dropcloths aslant the set and exhausted, smutty, smoke-blackened ballerinas lying around in heaps. Jones, a good jazz pianist in his own right, is a devotee of everything about the ballet – its incidentally comic as much as its poetic qualities.

Rigoletto a year later, also for Opera 80, had Clare Mitchell as designer, and confirmed Jones's skills and imagination – though the Opera 80 budget was inevitably rather constraining. Nobody has approached the irony and metaphysical content of the tale with such clarity, such an ideal match of music and dramatic characterization – blending humour, pathos, sentiment and bile, exposing how Verdi's conception turned the material into an overtly Christian parable. Verdi was not content with Victor Hugo's coarse malcontented jester, whose daughter was really a passive victim: he wanted to emphasize the Shakespearian dimension even further, the irony and tragedy. The opera hints at a blackness in the hunchback jester's soul, and Gilda, who sacrifices herself for a worthless love, is a kind of Christian icon. Lucian Pintilie for WNO in Cardiff expressed the moral idea, but not the theological overtones. Verdi was by no means a conventional Christian or supporter of the Church, but faith in the human spirit was a constant and vital factor in his beliefs. Jones's staging left no doubt that Gilda acted in full knowledge of the Duke's infidelity and Sparafucile's murder contract on his life. She was shown squinting through the keyhole of a free-standing door at the front of the stage, and later – before she walked in and was stabbed – begging heaven's forgiveness for the 'sinners'. The design underlined the Christian theme by having a Florentine-style image of the Virgin Mary dominate the set, painted over a pair of double doors at the upper level. The set provided a Renaissance background (with palatial hall and stairs to the right of the Virgin and a panelled wall to the left), but the costumes belonged to the mid-19th century when Verdi was composing the opera. Monterone emerged to deliver his curse through the double doors on to the catwalk at the back, which cut across the painted virgin like the arms of a crucifix. The walkway was approached by a mobile staircase that was sometimes whirled around with Rigoletto helplessly marooned on it, at other times used to form a telling tableau – as when Rigoletto found himself almost crucified at the heart of a cross-shaped grouping. The front of the set was closed with an arras curtain above which hand-puppets outlined the story at the start and reprised it later. Following parallel narratives is something Jones likes. A blindfolded angel figure was an element in the ducal celebration of the opening scene – an illustration of the Christian 'justification' theme. The other courtiers, highly stylized in their behaviour, adopted bird masks or bland businessmen's faces on blank placards with eye-holes that they held in front of their heads. The narrative was presented scrupulously, focusing on the central trio of relationships, with a youthful lightweight Duke, a convincingly acted hunchback, a sonorous Sparafucile as devilish fatal tempter. The role of the latter as a diabolical figure summoned up by Rigoletto's will was suggested when Rigoletto said, 'Demonio,' as the professional cut-throat appeared. The hunchback was not the hand of divine retribution. It was the sin of pride to see himself as such, and Gilda's gift of life to the Duke was a demonstration of the doctrine of grace. Perhaps Verdi did not conceive the opera to be pointed like that: equally, he might have agreed that Jones was only emphasizing what evidently propelled the pathos and tragedy.

Jones's *Macbeth* for Scottish Opera-Go-Round in February 1987 was his first production with Nigel Lowery (born 1960) who became his preferred designer and was later his collaborator on *The Ring* at Covent Garden. Conservatives complain about the pair's appetite for theatrical tricks, their liking for virtuoso over-elaboration and hyper-activity on stage. Genius in the theatre as elsewhere is always going to be controversial. Jones and Lowery have distinctive gifts. To criticize their extravagantly imaginative inventiveness is to miss the point that this kind of excess is precisely where their special quality lies.

Verdi was adamant that theatrical considerations should be foremost in the presentation of his *Macbeth*. The chorus of witches was as important an element as Macbeth and Lady Macbeth: the latter should sound 'rough, hollow, stifled', even 'devilish'. Jones inevitably reverted to the Shakespeare model of just three witches rather than the full-scale chorus of the early Verdi opera – since Scottish Opera-Go-Round was a small company using just piano accompaniment. That strengthened the focus of the drama. The key to Jones's success with the piece was his ability to match what can seem like incongruities of tone in the music with an equivalent theatrical intensity that was never po-faced. Some of the production's most potent moments exploited a macabre humour: Jones working on the small scale switched with skill and confidence between a sometimes agonized expressionism and a well-observed social wit. Banquo's ghost, when required to appear at the head of the banquet table, materialized as an unwelcome dish under a meat cover on a plate. Lady M had plonked a huge salver with a meat cover there. Macbeth lifted the lid to start serving and instead of cold cuts there was a comic cut – the bearded Banquo, not the roast. The effect was chilling. Danny Kaye did the same trick in *The Court Jester* in 1955. It may be risky to joke at such a time, yet terror and hysteria are never far apart. So many ghostly appearances in opera have been accidentally risible that it was worth trying, if not positively wise, to meet the problem head on. Lowery's set was an extremely simple ochre box with doors and flats that got moved around to isolate segments of the stage – such as the room where Duncan, here depicted as a blindfolded child king, was murdered. The furniture was a set of three pairs of chairs of varying heights. Duncan was greeted and at once placed on the most elevated high chair. The table, in two sections, was much lower at one end than at the other, which was useful when it was required to be a ramped rostrum. Some of the flats were pierced with windows or recesses (for Dunsinane woods and the line of Banquo's royal heirs). Changes of scene happened at the speed of lightning – often covered with music that Verdi had intended for dancing or chorus entries. Jones skilfully pursued the ideas of the production in numerous little details: the staging was intricately embroidered. The expressiveness expanded the audience's imagination, the way they saw such familiar material. The singers used Andrew Porter's English translation, with many restored Shakespeare resonances.

Jones produced a smart, stylish *Manon* for the students of the Royal Northern College of Music, which was later taken into the Opera North repertoire. Tidy economical designs by Richard Hudson were painted in rag-rolled grey-green. One of those steeply raked neo-classical room sets Hudson likes led the eye to a deep perspective backstage, an inner room or architectural view complete with model churches and mansions; the corniced side walls with bold ledges and adjustable openings allowed speedy entrances. A little cut-out coach swept across the front of the opening Amiens inn scene to general delight – clever toy demonstrations are always popular on stage. A *trompe-l'oeil* of a green apple and serpent by the back window of the lovers' Paris house hinted at the sinful subtext of the Abbé Prévost novel on which the opera was based. The Cours-la-Reine was signalled with a large model rhino and half-skeleton male and female human models suspended from the flies. The gaming-house had stylized tables leaning precipitously forward; it opened with a flurry of panto-style luminous gloves and sleeves plucking and twitching in ultraviolet light. Stylized social mannerisms are a typical Jones phenomenon. Hudson's period costumes provided some fresh operatic glamour. Chorus were in uniform blacks and greys. Principals, apart from the sombre ecclesiastical lover Des Grieux, wore bright colours. Jones's quick-witted stage action was theatrical and modish, neatly focusing the narrative without being decoratively naturalistic. The chorus manoeuvred geometrically around the stage, movements with clockwork precision – aptly since the composer Massenet was obsessive about punctuality. Geoffrey Dolton's Lescaut and Helen Field's Manon pirouetted and flitted around with great vitality, their gestures expressive and eccentric. Dolton's horrid winning smile in the opening scene, fancying his cousin as much as did Robert Poulton's Bretigny, was memorable. Patrick Power's Des Grieux played the straight man, stolidly impassioned, studiedly uncomfortable: a human version of Manon's lamented *'petite table'* with cabriole legs. Colin Smith's lighting edited the events sharply, sometimes using spots at the footlights to cast imposingly expressive shadows on the back wall. Jones worked at the start to play up Manon's *'faiblesse'* or inconstancy as if she were almost schizoid. Field became more persuasive as she relaxed. Dolton was a heroic young blade as Lescaut. The trio of kept women enjoyed their moments but, like the chorus, they were depersonalized in this Jones interpretation. Though still individual in style the production was almost too neat and contained for emotional development. Jones loosened up the acting with the idiosyncratic movement he got from the cast and often bizarre physical gestures and positions. But, unlike his *Three Oranges*, or *Too Clever by Half*, or *Rheingold*, this *Manon* was in many ways an exercise in style. In earlier productions Jones did not always deploy perfectly the suggestiveness and quirky range of ideas that have since become so provocative and characteristic of his work.

Jones's deliciously inventive staging of Prokofiev's fairy-tale opera *The Love for Three Oranges*, created for Opera North (1988) and staged subsequently by ENO, was his first big hit production created expressly for a full-scale company and proper operahouse – opera with all the trimmings. It became as popular and familiar to audiences as Jonathan Miller's *Mikado*. At ENO revivals, one had the sense that many of the audience had seen it already, and were anticipating each *coup de théâtre*. The real and infectious relish of the singers in their work made this very Russ-

ian, ornate, Fabergé-egg-like, scrupulously self-conscious entertainment irrepressibly joyous. This was the opera that included an
element of audience participation for the first time in a Jones production – though that sort of break in normal decorum is typical
of his character as a producer. Scratch cards were handed out
before curtain-up with appropriately scented patches: on a signal
from the stage the audience were supposed to scratch a special area
of the card and sniff for smells that would be appropriate to what
was happening. They were warned to expect the signals at unan-
nounced points in the performance, which was a nice gimmick for
getting audiences alert and into the spirit of things. Donald
Maxwell with etched eccentric vocal delivery was one of various
singers who got to make a meal out of Leander's creepy walk and
his attenuated arthritic artificial rubber hands, an accessory also
provided for the King of Clubs. Jones had an acrobat double for
Truffaldino, who tumbled hysterically across the stage before the
singer himself, presented as a camp, fat Billy Bunter, waddled on.
ENO's regular 'heavy' through the 1980s, the exceedingly tall
Richard Angas on extra built-up boots, was a natural for Creonta's
bloodthirsty cook. For the famous March (the most persuasive
and familiar musical number in Prokofiev's score) the chorus
paraded in insect-like gas masks. Farfarello by his farting propelled the obsessive Prince on his adventuresome grand tour,
under the curse of the ill-willed Fata Morgana. The spiteful,
chimp-like Smeraldina helped a crocodile suit to swallow one of
the chorus males got up in *'Allo, 'Allo*-style black berets, mous-
taches and spectacles. Tim Hopkins, Richard Jones's assistant and
disciple, who is a major directorial talent in his own right, directed
the later ENO revival – and himself acted as compère introducing
the aroma-cards, with their implicit olfactory decadence.

Mazeppa for the Bregenz Festival (and also later Amsterdam)
was Jones's first operatic venture on the European mainland – and
not typical of his timing and usually wicked virtuoso mixture of
acting styles. It was in Russian with a mostly Russian, non-Eng-
lish-speaking cast, and had the uncomfortable handicap of a conductor (Pinchas Steinberg) antipathetic to Jones's kind of
interventionist production. When Jones wanted to introduce a
flock of birds as an element in the first scene and at the end, Steinberg threatened to abandon the job. He also condemned the execution scene as 'not tasteful'. Jones had not tackled a 'serious'
dramatic opera since *Macbeth*. The designers, as with *Flea in her*

Ear and *Love for Three Oranges*, were the Brothers Quay whose set was spectacularly evocative, with two compelling side-walls decorated with slavonic-looking symbols. The set with doors at both sides and a balcony on the right, curled up and then down from a narrow apron stage at the front – a sloping hillside stretching to the furthest reaches of the stage and ending in a memorable landscape-like back-cloth. The doors were in peasant-cottage shape and style, windows bizarrely distorted. The front-cloth was the ominously enlarged image of a bald man. In the opening scene Maria, who chooses to marry Mazeppa against her father's wishes and ultimately goes insane when she learns of his execution by Mazeppa, appeared in a room with panel windows behind which peasant maids paraded. The show was lit with imaginative atmospheric contrasts by Wolfgang Göbbel, and Nicky Gillibrand's costumes mixed the 1920s fascist formality of smart riding-breeches for Mazeppa himself with Russian peasant shirts and trews for Kochubei. Mazeppa's Cossacks were bald like their master, shirtless and in grey suits. The notorious public execution (which caused such grief for Steinberg) was performed not with chainsaws, as in David Alden's ENO staging, but with a tram that swayed downstage past a row of lamp-standards towards where Kochubei and Iskra had been stretched on the ground – their heads poking over the tram rails (the Quay Brothers, Bulgakov addicts, were referring to the opening of *The Master and Margarita*). Jones directed the emotionally devastating confrontations of the main characters ambitiously, considering he was handling an 'international' cast. The opening celebration was spectacular, with Cossacks dancing first among a V-shaped line-up of tables, then actually on the tables. Lloyd Newson's choreography gopak-ed fiercely. The central four characters had great dignity – especially Sergei Leiferkus as Mazeppa and Ljubov Sharnina as the nervous Maria. Tchaikovsky's melodies may be less memorable than in *Eugene Onegin*, but the ironies of the plot are arresting, especially in the love scene where Mazeppa fails to confess to Maria that he has just ordered her father's execution.

Jones's *Count Ory* for Kent Opera worked a limited repertoire of pantomime jokes too hard. The chorus-line of village boys and girls behaved ballet-style (Giselle, perhaps) in the first act, with the Count disguised as a hermit. Jones enjoys all references to classical dance. In the second act, when the Count and his men entered the convent in drag as a passing band of nuns, the jokes were very basic. Too much of the burden was left to the theatrical instincts of the performers. Richard Hudson's severely leftward-tilting design suggested a model of a castle ruin, with pinnacles and painted walls and a sort of drawbridge lowered on ropes to admit visitors. The second act had a Crusader tomb at the back and a stag's head on the wall jokily emitting steam (dried ice) at the height of the storm. Undeveloped ideas like the corpse of a Saracen and the shadow of a falling body on the right wall suggested unfinished work, compared with Jones and Hudson's staging of Judith Weir's *A Night at the Chinese Opera*, also for Kent Opera.

Jones's 1991 *Fledermaus* was one of the most ambitious ENO productions in a decade of producer's opera. It prided itself on going a long way too far. Like Jones's Feydeau *Flea in her Ear* at the Old Vic, it combined a hard-hearted view of human frailty and unfettered theatricality in exploring a banquet of *Gemütlichkeit*. The show's most brilliant icon was a little inset film to accompany the great alcoholic number *Brüderlein* (brotherhood). As swaying revellers crowded the front of the stage, a film projected on the backdrop showed various Persian cats parading in offcuts from advertising films, cats getting into tophats, cats with chocolates, cats stretching, cats thinking of No. 1 (*Just So* cats, walking alone). Everything about this staging was deeply, blithely, uproariously subversive. That would certainly be the word for Lowery, who has stated: 'Think about how it's usually done – and then do it differently.' Jones believes farce is cruel in order to be kind: ironical, rather than sentimental. Strauss's French-derived operetta benefited from a producer who took Feydeau as seriously as Shakespeare, which did not mean leaden irreverence in pantomime-style free comedy. The Saturnalian fantasy was explosive: chocolates in heart-shaped boxes, a cat pulling a gold and velvet coach in which a champagne bottle was enthroned – the opposite of tasteful propriety.

The flaw at ENO was the singing, though Anthony Mee's Alfred made a perfect tenor intruder, his oyster eyes pursuing the conductor's beat – seeking a stable centre in Jones's tottering world. Lesley Garrett's Adele stole the show – it is after all a role designed for the soubrette star. She stripped to the buff (back view only) at the end of her prison number for the benefit of the lanky Ida's Bacchanalian chorus of cockneys. ENO veteran Ann Howard, towering and mustachioed, was Orlofsky. Fenella Fielding (the famous British camp comedienne and revue artiste) did cooking lessons in the intervals – demonstrating first how to make strudel, then later how to use up party left-overs. She was to be seen at Orlofsky's, vainly trying to unload her product during a grand finale that included a chorus of cockney *coryphées* on roller skates. Such irreverences typified Jones's exhilarating excess. Lowery's funny 'deconstructionist' designs involved numerous set-changes. The hum-along overture, with the curtain raised a mere metre from the floor, was accompanied by a stream of fantasy sight-gags. A row of elegant long-gloved hands and champagne flutes danced with powder puffs, poured champagne into glasses, and selected chocolates from heart-shaped chocolate boxes. Ballerinas' legs on point (unattached, it was later revealed) jumped elegantly in an indulgent send-up. Up the proscenium on either side was a frame of Variety-style 1940s star photos, like the advertising outside comedy playhouses. When the curtain at last rose properly, to reveal a set like a Christmas card of a Vienna snowscape, Alfred was serenading Rosalinda from a crumbling, precarious ledge outside the apartment (as if he were Harold Lloyd).

Scarcely was one accustomed to the alarming perspective than the scene changed to two rooms inside with pregnant curvaceous cartoon-Biedermeier cabinets and a gothic kennel marked 'Herr poodle' for Rosalinda's lapdog. And, from then on in, Lowery's sequence of drop-in painted-cloth scene-changes never paused in its zany effervescence. Falke and Gabriel off to Orlofsky's were honoured with a pantomime pony-dray, a real coach pulled by a shire horse. The theme of the party in the central act was announced by jokey painted flats of giant bottles and hands poking out from the wings. Orlofsky's waiters in Lederhosen and feathered hats were as over the top as his pet gorilla (Deborah Pope in a monkey-suit, with tutu and tiara), which Eisenstein found quite disturbing. For the timepiece seduction duet a red-plush chaise longue that seemed as wide as the proscenium opening provided a suitably comic environment. For the Hungarian *csardas* torch-song, Rosalinda wore ropes of pearls, an Edna Everage-style mask, and a screamingly loud Hungarian peasant dress (garish, gathered and folksy – a *tour de force* by Lowery). The *csardas* was sung in front of a dropped-in painted back-cloth, the singer dwarfed by a giant curley Bösendorfer-style grand piano that was being 'played' by a lunatic caricature accompanist with legs 10 feet long and operated on sticks. The guests invited to witness Falke's plot stretched out on chairs at the front, their interest and boredom suitably choreographed. Jones provided a dizzy parade of puns, stage-effects and front-of-curtain confessions. Drinking has long been a great metaphysical excuse. He capped everything with a '*Traumbild*' strip-club fantasy parade of girls in Ziegfeld head-dresses, each representing a liqueur flavour, the spirit of Champagne in the most towering feather head-dress of all.

The concluding act in the prison had absurdly skewy, drunken cell doors; the Governor's desk and chair leant drunkenly, crazily. A 'silent film' Frosch (Matthew Scurfield, an actor who was a Jones veteran) was armed with awful Buster Keaton-style gags; Frank had a fetish drawer full of ballet pumps which popped jack-in-a-box-style out of his lop-sided desk. During the striptease for Adele's aria, Olga's ballerina gang were cheer-leaders. Even the plain white glittering front curtain dazzled the audience queasily. With this daring and minutely detailed *Fledermaus*, ENO set a new standard of excess. Some London critics said it was too clever by half – though Jones's staging of the eponymous Ostrovsky was unanimously welcomed at the Old Vic a few years before. The truth probably is that with stronger casting of the central roles, which really require virtuoso vocal performances, Jones's originality and manic inventiveness would have stood up. The intensely detailed acting Jones wanted and the Monty Python-style quick-changing montage of Lowery's sets and costumes were dangerously ambitious for an opera company which can almost never have preview performances to get a production polished up. All the hard-working outrageous vaudeville was meant to be an antidote to the sickly sentimentality of most *Fledermaus* stagings. Jones's black-hearted fun undermined the smugness and familiarity of the piece and moved Strauss's ambivalent drunken frolic on to uneasily shifting ground. In fact the social satire here was as combustible as in *The Marriage of Figaro*. The fierce humour acknowledged the libretto's French ancestry. What mattered most were Lowery's witty deconstructionist design gimmicks – and kaleidoscopic set-changes.

Jones staged *The Flying Dutchman* in January 1993 for the Netherlands Opera in Amsterdam – slightly 'coals to Newcastle'. The production was beautiful, logical, tautly directed, and theatrical, with designs by Lowery, and took as starting point Wagner's youthful politics and high artistic ideals. The conflict in Wagner's mind and life at the time of composition (1842) was between conformist domesticity and his art. In most stagings the shadowy occult figure of the Dutchman is central: a doomed out-cast eternally roaming the seas beneath blood-red sails, subject of the gripping romantic ballad that the heroine Senta sings in her first scene. This time, though the Dutchman was impressive and haunting, Lowery's woodcut-style designs and Jones's direction of acting and stage movement ensured that the whole cast was credibly vital – even Senta's dull fiancé Erik, one of the least engaging roles in the operatic repertoire. For Lowery the Dutchman and his galleon evoked the deep past; Senta's father Daland was a present-day ambitious adventurer, a sailor in contemporary Dutch merchant seaman's uniform with an eye for the profitable deal or the advantageous marriage alliance.

The music of *Dutchman*, Wagner's earliest success, is permeated with Bellini-like lyricism and passion. The tunes are potent, though Wagner was not yet at home with vast dramatic structures. The London and US premieres of the work were originally given in Italian. The irresistible tunes of the overture, suggesting the drugged and urging sweep of storm-tossed waves, are universally familiar, as is the calm sad statement of Senta's answering melody. Dramatically this is a naive work, even unsophisticated: arias do not link into a seamless process and there are recitatives and cavatinas. Jones achieved a cinematic dissolve for scene-changes using a gauze and bright lighting with masking blackout behind (Patricia Collins lit the production dramatically). The interior and seaboard set designs were emblematic, not naturalistic, arranging space for decisive encounters and telling exits. The doll-like spinning women in 1950s frocks mimed their work like automata, then were hurried off stage by the overseer to get them away from Senta's dangerous influence. With so much vibrant action, the audience quickly learnt how to read Jones's interpretation. When the Dutchman left his galleon and came magically to the front of the set (as if to a jetty) for his opening angst-filled aria, '*Die Frist ist um*', a cinematic square-blue framing light on the gauze defined the close-up. The look of the production was silvery monochrome, except for the royal blue of the Dutchman's antique seaman's smock, a blue adopted by Senta in place of her white frock and white socks immediately after she had literally dived through the picture of the Dutchman on the stage floor. On the wall during the famous spinning chorus, she had taken this picture down and carried it about as a sort of cult object. As she went through the picture, it was as if she were falling into another world. Lights in the auditorium flashed full on, a glaring shock for the audience but a warning of the coming encounter (breathtaking and extended) of the redeeming woman with her obsessive dream – Wagner's wish-fulfilment no doubt. At the close her jump into eternity was turned into a frozen image at the centre of the back-cloth.

Complex staging problems included the need to have on stage both the ghost ship and Daland's ship, when the Steersman had fallen asleep on deck. The music took up the evocative burden. Lowery's white-on-black drawing provided the modern square outline of the stern of Daland's vessel, where the sailors suggested the unsteadiness of the waves by their stylized movements, falling against each other as if driven by the storm – movements not unlike their drunken hornpipe carousing later. The galleon dominated the next scene-picture too.

Before the music started at the beginning of the opera, Jones showed a picture gallery on the stage with seven glowing colourful fish portraits, and a man dragging a black picture frame across the set. The overture began when the man placed the black frame on a space on the wall and stood back gesturing to it: the opera, perhaps, would be that black tale. Later, in the spinning scene, a similar wall-space was filled with a picture of the Dutchman pinned down on the ground while the other fish pictures turned into fishbones stripped clean of flesh (Daland's trade). Erik wooed Senta clutching a picture of a cottage, for domesticity. At the end the Dutchman's ghostly sailors were not on stage. Jones audaciously – lining up Daland's sailors at the front – implied that the auditorium and audience were the ghosts' world. An owl flapped past overhead; shoals of fish raced by. The Dutchman's crew sang their satanic text from the wings. Jones was ideally balancing the didactic and the theatrical.

Jones's *Giulio Cesare in Egitto*, created in March 1994 for the Bavarian State Opera in Munich, where Peter Jonas became Intendant after quitting ENO, shared the irreverent tone of his ENO *Fledermaus* but was simpler – with fewer of Lowery's wonderfully visual drop-cloths. It did have a towering Tyrannosaurus Rex on stage at the start, which gradually, after the initial scenes, subsided into a jagged crater at the centre of the stage. Ann Murray as Caesar wore a bald wig and camouflage kilt, khaki shirt, maroon beret and pair of Doc Martens; the head of Pompey was handed over in a Munich supermarket plastic bag. Ptolemy (countertenor Christopher Robson, for once not bald but in a Harpo

Marx wig) sported a puce uniform-suit with silver lamé stripes and played shocking jokes with Pompey's headless corpse, stuffing a large cocktail flag into its neck – the gory humour of 1990s Hollywood. Kathleen Kuhlmann as Pompey's wife Cornelia, wearing a dark blue velvet dress and an eye-patch like Wagner's 'warfather', stuck a Wotan-like spear into a huge dinosaur leg which Sesto (Trudeliese Schmidt) in yellow clown's jacket and check trews later extracted and applied in vengeance to Ptolemy.

The elements of Jones's staging of this, perhaps the greatest of Handel's operas, were even more unexpected than Willy Decker's Glasgow production in post-modern German style (see p. 402), or the famous videoed Peter Sellars version, set by the 'Cairo Hilton' with Caesar as a Kennedy clone. Yet Jones never forced the material unnaturally to his purpose. He simply substituted a living convention – the burlesque still loved on TV – for the dead decorum of *opera seria*. Handel's operas are tragi-comic melodic feasts of great psychological profundity, theatrically more than historically true. The characters and situations are painted by the composer in hit-tune messages. The Munich public quickly caught on that this was elevated fun. Caesar – having crept all the way from the wings to slip under an enormous sheet on a leopardskin settee next to the desirable Lydia (alias Cleopatra) – was called to battle and instantly snapped into a domestic macho routine, making his lady tie his Doc Marten bootlaces, foot proudly up on the arm of the settee. Caesar's famous aria for his diplomatic meeting with the treacherous Ptolemy (about the hunter tracking the spoor) was staged with a freeze-frame line-up of soldiers and bureaucrats and Ptolemy at the footlights, all with fixed false smiles. Caesar frisked Ptolemy's soldiers, and loaded them with weapons like Action Men in a comic daisy-chain of threatening poses.

Cleopatra (the formidable Pamela Coburn in red velvet dress and waitress apron) sang two early arias ravishingly as she was gradually suspended or 'flown' above the stage. A nuclear rocket climbed out of the crater during Cleopatra's closing plea to the gods at the start of act 2 – and exploded at the start of the naval battle after the interval at the opening of act 3, blowing a collection of (irradiated?) great white sharks out of the crater. Jones's ten-strong movement group switched from Egyptian to Roman, substituting berets for fezs, and – after committing suicide in despair, ahead of Cleopatra, jumping into the pit – quickly changed and came out of the pit, turned into Caesar's brave troops rescuing Cleopatra. Amir Hosseinpour's hand-jiving choreography and manic comic cameos were ever ready to fill in the narrative background with romp and riot. As Cleopatra, liberated by Caesar, sang her triumphing aria (*'Da tempeste il legno infranto,'*), a comic sequence of miniature opposites, cowboy and Indian, cop and swagman, Marie Antoinette and revolutionary guard, spaceman and space-monster, angel and devil, skirmished and then jumped into the pit together, in a gloriously euphoric cartoon-strip image of trouble resolved. Then, clearing the way further for the happy ending, Cornelia first forced Ptolemy back on to Sesto's spear till it projected from his midriff, then comically tortured him while singing her last aria, finally ripping the spear out as a blood bag burst in his mouth. Under the word Egypt a ringed map in the middle of the front-cloth showed modern suburban Munich – *Münchener Freiheit, Schwabing, Haidhausen* etc. In the final *tableau vivant* the cast, at last sporting 'authentic' classical garb, walked up the steps of an inner stage to meet their ultimate fates – the conspiring Brutus and Cassius, a little basket of asps, etc. etc., all taking their places in history, names neatly labelled on the steps. Yet none of this exuberant and strictly disciplined hyperactivity departed from Nicola Haym's text and drama.

The staging achieved cult status in Germany. Jones and Lowery's imaginations were organically as one, in total sympathy. The Spielberg elements (*Jaws* and *Jurassic Park* – though Jones had the idea of putting a life-size dinosaur on stage as a symbol of comic tyranny before the Spielberg film had emerged) registered that the keynote was entertainment, but also commented on the vocally competitive ethos of *opera seria* and of the characters of this story. The collage front-cloth showed a contemporary version of Apollo and Venus – male rational power versus female emotion. At the premiere a voice from the gallery in act 1 called *'Kinder, Kinder'* as the dinosaur collapsed, slowly, majestically, silently, during a break in the music, while the theatre rang with competing jeers and cheers: the phrase was suitably ambiguous. Who precisely were the kids? Lowery had a variety of inner stages for 'Lydia's' masque in act 2, including a frieze of baby-faces. His front-cloth was a bold caricature of Michelangelo in the Sistine (the creation of man). The few props included a large white stepladder and highly mobile settee on castors. The set was the full width and depth of the flat stage – into the wings and back to the doors and rear wall. A pseudo-romantic night-sky cyclorama was intentionally not big enough to fill the background. The details added up, because of how Jones explored and sustained the characterizations, using what he had learned from the music. Ann Murray was an amused, passionately sung, highly nuanced Caesar. The orchestral playing (under Ivor Bolton) was buoyant, hard-edged and fluent with powerful instrumental obbligati, the singing never masked. The British came to Munich, were seen, and conquered. Cheers (and a few boos) at curtain call went on for 15 minutes. Jones unpacked all the mixed motives in Handel's drama. Handel needs the irreverence and wit of surrealism or deconstructionist staging, with the wickedness and vulgarity of the burlesque (a tradition less dead than *opera seria*) to be viable in the theatre.

Jones's *Ring* designed by Lowery maintained both its strikingly unusual look and its special interpretative viewpoint all the way through: *Götterdämmerung* in October 1995 seemed the most assured conception of all, the climax of the Jones–Lowery approach. That should be the rule with the great tetralogy, but often is not. *Götterdämmerung* uncovered the intention behind this *Ring* production provocatively and inescapably. Jones's purpose was simply the latest stage in repossessing the Wagner heritage, as reflected in the philosophical and moral consequences of his work – the German fascism to which Wagner's ambivalent genius however regrettably contributed as godfather. Wagnerites want to shut their eyes to Wagner's posthumous role of court composer to the death camps, as if his artistic achievement exonerated him. But Jones's *Ring* faced the problem – by recognizing and representing the comic absurdity of the politics and philosophy alongside the tragedy. The Jones *Ring* happened in a domestic modern or post-modern suburban world, which was clearly and unfortunately our own world, one gone ecologically against nature and morally to seed. At the conclusion, after the collapse of the polystyrene walls of the set, Brünnhilde was led off upstage by the spirit of the waters of the Rhine. Parallel with that conception, Lowery's visualization drew on the world of surrealist 20th-century painting, evoking memories of de Chirico's associative brilliance. Jones and Lowery's tricksy approach to *Das Rheingold* and *Die Walküre* for Scottish Opera had visual qualities, but few coherent ideas about *The Ring*. At Covent Garden their apprenticeship in the north paid off.

Interpretation of *The Ring* has been through many stages in a short time. After the cleansed light-show of Wagner' grandson

Wieland, the romantically heroic political vision of Patrice Chéreau's leftist idealism, Ruth Berghaus's politically neutral, absurdist treatment, and Herbert Wernicke's cautionary reminder of how far *The Ring*'s wrongs remain embedded in continuing German culture (see p. 395), Jones at last and very subtly placed the Hitler issue on stage while also internationalizing the problem. For the moral crisis that took the form of the German mental breakdown of the 1930s and 1940s, with its utter perversion of politics and society, is not merely German but universal.

The moment in *Rheingold* when all the gods recognize that the solution to their liquidity problem is – plainly – theft was the crucial thematic starting-point for Jones, launching a theme that in the final phase of the tetralogy made complete sense. Commentators seeing the work as an epic from Wotan's point of view have described the cynical politics in which the god seems inescapably imprisoned as tragic. Jones's staging focused sharply on those choices which throw a devastating light on the moral realities. In this vision of the Wagner world, no issues were black or white, but Jones dug deeper by employing comic absurdity – even farce – to plumb the depths. Laughter is the only weapon powerful enough: seeing Wagner only in the black and white of tragedy was what led to Hitler. Epic theatre provides and needs the masks of both tragedy and comedy.

Jones could take such risks with decorum because he dealt with the text in such a musically responsive way – and Haitink's playing of the score was beautiful and sensitive, with the Covent Garden orchestra impeccable. The cast, too, acted with unwavering brilliance and commitment for Jones, showing total conviction and sympathy with his highly idiosyncratic approach. That says much for Jones's and Lowery's artistic integrity.

Their controversial *Das Rheingold* was strip-cartoon in approach – life with the Munsters (gods, giants and dwarves) marooned on the back of a whale. *Rheingold* could be said to be the prologue to a whale of an opera. The references in Lowery's design to a whale, like the cut-outs of bull, horse and ram suspended over the stage in *Die Walküre*, were obscure – but no more eccentric than dinosaurs in *Giulio Cesare*. The projection of the story was not radically changed: it was just the appearance of the mythology that Jones and Lowery recast. Both aimed for a new symbolism to engender a puzzled response rather than confident familiarity. The ecological references, the sense of nature,

the insecurity of theatrical invention, were the solution. The Rhinemaidens in their rubber nude-suits, looking like body-builders,
might genuinely have been able to protect the Rhinegold. Jones
exploited their sexuality brazenly, making them toy convincingly
with Alberich, an ordinary workman in typical modern Bavarian
soft hat. The game of sex and power was illustrated further by having the gold represented in the form of a glittering slipper – symbol
of a kind of feminine allure – which one of the Rhinemaidens
slipped on to her foot when she dipped it into the whale's blow-hole
(later to be the escape path or hatch to Nibelheim). Jones's visual
characterizations were both fascinating and amusing – the giants as
besuited Siamese twins, Freia as a single parent widow trailing a
ventriloquist's doll, Fricka tubby and vulgarly assertive in a wedding gown (her sole claim to status), Erda as a *Giselle*-like ballerina
(the actual singer unseen upstage). Wotan's sexual involvement with
Erda had never been expressed like that before: he embraced,
almost danced a little, with the dancer/Erda. But his proper role was
defined by the lab assistant's coat he wore: a moral sorcerer's prentice. Wotan instead of a 'spear' carried a long pole bearing a blue-
arrow road-sign pointing upwards (his one-way responsibility!).
This was real comic energy: the interpretative power of the ideas
lightly touched, never ponderous. Jones spotlit the meaning of the
dialogues with great clarity and an unerring sense of continuity.
This was gripping story-telling. At one moment the whole bizarre
crew of characters was lined out across the front of the stage, staring into the audience in naughty anticipation. The suggestion arose
that the gold, which could be stolen, would solve almost everybody's problem. Eyes rolled. You could see the cheating thoughts
going through the characters' minds. The production broadcast the
moral issue, comically and philosophically.

Lowery was less painterly than he can be in this opening section of the tetralogy. For *Die Walküre*, he reverted to a more pictorial style closer to his ENO *Fledermaus* and *Blond Eckbert*.
Compared with his earlier essay at designing *The Ring* for Scottish Opera, both of his two first *Ring* operas at Covent Garden
showed genuine dramaturgical engagement. The outward appearance of *Die Walküre* was more typical of his work, with different
white-on-black front-cloths before each act, and an abstract geo-
metrical design for the back-cloth in all three acts. Changes in the
look of the set were achieved with lighting. If *Das Rheingold* had
seemed inhabited by caricatures, and followed the narrative

tightly, there was more emphasis on poetry and expressiveness in *Walküre*. One of the most telling devices in *Rheingold* did extend to *Walküre*. In *Rheingold* the element of water (the Rhine itself) was suggested by a unisex movement group in blue trouser-suits with their faces covered: first one figure walked slowly up the whale-back slope, then a line of them (men and women), then later a flood of people (like bubbles in water) rhythmically almost running across the stage from left to right – the drift of the current, as it were. Now in *Walküre* the movement group changed from representing water to representing trees with bush-like branches sprouting from their shoulders masking their heads entirely. One 'tree', on cue, turned and revealed that 'it' was embracing Nothung (rather than the sword being stuck in a tree trunk). At the moment when Siegmund is supposed to pull out the sword, the sense of wounded nature could not have been more powerfully expressed – reluctant to surrender the weapon, the 'tree' as if wounded fell to its knees, shuddering when the sword was pulled away. As part of their tree portrayal, all the movement group's hands had twig-like extensions instead of nails. When Sieglinde awoke after the *Todesverkündigung* believing herself lost, and ran away from Siegmund, she ended up deep in a group of these 'trees': it was a beautiful evocation of her childish sense of loss. Jones staged the death announcement to Siegmund very precisely to demonstrate the vital moment of recognition and reversal (peripeteia and anagnorisis) when Brünnhilde suddenly saw what Siegmund's free-will rejection of Valhalla implied for her own responsibility. As at so many points in *The Ring*, neither music nor drama necessarily reveal whose reaction or attitude is most significant. Siegmund learns a tragic fate, against which he struggles vainly. Brünnhilde learns the meaning of human responsibility and the love which represents that humanity. The focus of the scene was radically different from any other account. Jones gave above all an extraordinary account of actors' intentions.

His liking for burlesque continued to be an important feature. Fricka stepped from a concertina-like armoured car, which earned much laughter from the audience. That release of tension gave her argument with Wotan a hard-edged coherence. Jones made *Walküre* as a whole consciously romantic in atmosphere but metaphysical in agenda. Lowery's outlandish ideas finally amounted to an autonomous and coherent vocabulary of symbols and colours. Neither Jones nor Lowery would regard the style of their approach as the last word on *The Ring*, visually or interpretatively. But Covent Garden's brave and experimental new *Ring* staging certainly belongs with Berghaus's, Wernicke's and Chéreau's in the gallery of modern classic interpretations. Jones was constantly attentive to the text. Haitink's subtle conducting allowed the singing to be never forced. John Tomlinson's Wotan was fresh and liberated (from the new Alfred Kirchner staging at Bayreuth). The casting of this *Ring* mixed familiarity and experience (Ekkehard Wlaschiha as a typically resolute Alberich) with novelty (Jane Henschel's sturdy Fricka, Robert Tear's fatalistic but depressed Loge, and Deborah Polaski's responsive Brünnhilde). Ulla Gustafsson's Sieglinde was like an early-music singer, direct, vibrato-free, edgy in tuning.

The brightest jewel in the staging of *Siegfried* was the sexually ambivalent Mime of Graham Clark, in a wig that evoked memories of Anthony Perkins in the persona of his dead mother in *Psycho*. Mime's house drawn by Lowery in silhouette emphasized this theme of perverted suburban domesticity, with John Tomlinson's Wanderer impressive yet irresponsible, acting crazy, certainly not the noble tragic figure of so many *Ring* productions. Fafner was a sort of tight-fisted housewife keeping the treasure in a utility-style bedroom cupboard – a mild monster with Hallowe'en pumpkin-head on a charlady's body. Having Fafner emerge from the wardrobe at the back of the set took away any sense of Siegfried's supposed heroism here. Lowery's picture-frame structure round the de Chirico-like set-design of the last two acts of *Siegfried* suggested the artificiality of young Siegfried's romantic discovery at that time and place: the improbable nature of the tale.

In *Götterdämmerung* Deborah Polaski's Brünnhilde became a powerless image of exploited suburban wifehood. The abuse of power remained constantly at the heart of Jones's production with Alan Held's vain Günther, Vivian Tierney's false-innocent Gutrune, and Kurt Rydl's cheerful, competent, not too intense yet quite insane Hagen. The image defining Jones's purpose most clearly was the Norns' prologue – played with the house-lights full up (a clear-eyed representation of a crucial scene that is often presented in an entirely somnolent fashion). Three middle-aged landladies in cardigans and 1940s frocks examined the front-cloth with its 'failed project' jumble of bold black-on-white images painted by Lowery. The Norn giving voice always addressed the audience perched on top of the prompt box. The cloth kept starting to rise and the Norns kept having to pull it down, like a roller blind running up out of control – as if what it was about to expose should not be seen. The subject of their presentations to the audience was precisely not what was shown going on. Jones comically and without labouring any overt references made the point of *Schindler's List*. What could not be discussed was being hidden. Brünnhilde in a red frock was enshrined in a doorway high up in the outline of another Lowery suburban house silhouette – a passive figure, powerless to act. Loge's fire blazed across the back of the stage. There was a red outline of Grane. Brünnhilde held Nothung. Siegfried in ochre trousers and canary shirt packed his briefcase, fitted on his Tarnhelm trilby – a husband off to the office. Brünnhilde gave him her shield adorned with a human face, and as he left contemplated the ring in the palm of her hand.

The Gibichungs' was a very clean, clinical place. Hagen was the sort of hard-working estate manager who would get rid of unwanted insects or any other problems in an instant: he consigned a large fly to a dustbin (symbol of the disposal of unwanted evidence and 'waste') which he carried away and dumped at the left of the stage. Gutrune had a beehive hairstyle, Günther wore red velvet trousers and an orange shirt. Hagen was in working shirt and trousers with braces. Hagen's manipulation of Gutrune was presented as overtly sexual – he continued the tradition of abuse represented in *Siegfried* by Mime. At Siegfried's call from the river he climbed up a ladder to check who was there. Siegfried rose at the back on a lift, seated on the silhouette of Grane, then rushed in to meet the weird Gibichung pair. Günther offered his hand to be shaken, but Siegfried pressed past him to shake hands with Hagen, who dumped the Brünnhilde shield in the dustbin as Siegfried downed the drugged cocktail provided. To prepare for 'Blood brotherhood', Hagen applied a hospital syringe to both candidates and deposited the blood in their glasses – which were also binned after use. Gutrune donned a new, salmon-pink diamante dress to say farewell to Siegfried and Günther, when they departed on the Brünnhilde mission, the latter in a huge grey fur coat. Hagen removed her cape and put it on himself, sat on the dustbin, held the (very British-looking) crown on his finger before finally putting it on his head. He went through Siegfried's briefcase, later making off with the dustbin.

The transition back to Brünnhilde's suburban house was a magical episode. A floodlight floated across the darkness at the rear of the stage. Back at the ranch, as it were, while Brünnhilde (framed in her doorway) examined her ring, Waltraute with an electric torch hunted all around the stage for her or, rather, for the ring. Then she knelt at the back to make her appeal, only her face visible above the floor. Brünnhilde was off stage, not attending. Waltraute tried to steal the ring; there was a struggle over Brünnhilde's cardigan, which Waltraute won. After Siegfried's return in the guise of Günther wearing a huge grey coat, and after his rape of the ring, he cruelly struck Brünnhilde and knocked her to the ground. Then he closed the door of the house, put a paperbag with eyeholes on her head, and led her off – ready for dreadful humiliations to come.

One of the ways *The Ring* embraces the epic tradition is with its digressions and recycling of significant memories: a process that has no place in normal theatrical narrative technique, but happens through Wagner's music. The theatre also hallows magic and myth – but Jones preferred to stage the paranormal diversions as drunken or drug-induced hallucinations. Thus Hagen's watch was a trance on heroin: which in no way distorted its psychological reality (like some of Hitler's most notorious henchmen, Hagen could please himself about drugs). He seemed to be sleepwalking with a rifle in hand, ever paranoid. Then he injected himself, squatting by the exit sign on the left, and saw Alberich as a figure literally swimming through the air, suspended and powerless. Alberich gave a clenched-fist salute to his heir as he talked of fighting heroes: Hagen, this gesture usefully recalled, was as much the underdog as Alberich.

The central act took place in a concrete bunker or blockhouse filled with beer-hall trestle tables running from side to side. Siegfried woke Hagen by kicking away the rifle on which he was resting. Hagen got on top of the tables to summon the vassals, who were a Dad's army in English tommies' metal helmets, dressed in pyjamas and shorts, a few in leather jackets. Jones scrupulously avoided identifying the vassals with 20th-century Germany. All of them were frightened of Hagen's rowdy bullying. There was much male bonding, and a charade of humiliation for one particular masculine victim. Waitresses with 1920s lace doilies on their heads paraded at the back. Günther arrived in a blue dinner jacket, a maid carrying his chair behind him. Another maid led on Brünnhilde with the paperbag over her head and wedding veils over her dress. Bowed down, she was forced terrifyingly and dangerously to walk blindfold along the tables to where Günther awaited her on the right. Never was the problem of Brünnhilde's situation depicted so painfully.

Brünnhilde was still kneeling on the tables in utter dejection after Siegfried had taken the paper bag off her head. The horrible, inescapable process of the rest of the opera, signalled by the reaction ('*Was ist?*') to Brünnhilde's shocked statement when she saw the ring on Siegfried's hand again, was focused and channelled by the layout of the tables – Hagen up on one at the back taking in everything. The tense accusations and denials were fiercer because of the enclosed environment, full of a menace to which the vassals, suddenly raising their weapons and fully armed, could easily contribute. Brünnhilde stripped off the wedding-veil coat for her betrayal of Siegfried in the trio of conspiracy. Hagen embraced Brünnhilde's shoulders exploratively. Günther, who had been hiding under a table, was forced to stand by Hagen, but crumpled to the floor again – the dream of false advantage shattered. Throughout this act, the hysteria engendered by often nearly comic business was palpably horrific – even when the humour threatened to collapse.

Siegfried's drunken (in Jones's version) reverie about the Rhinemaidens, at this stage no longer sporting nude body-builder rubber suits but shrunken and old in naked look body-stockings and high-heeled court shoes some sizes too big for them, took place around a sort of painted whale-like submarine. The image of a half-surfaced whale had been an element of Lowery's set for *Rheingold* – Loge and Wotan descended through its blow-hole to Nibelheim. Here again a paranormal diversion was 'explained' by Jones as drug-generated. The relationship between Siegfried and the maidens was comic, escapist and rather charming – relaxation before the coming tragic denouement. The spirit of the river (a masked man in blue) emerged from the whale-boat into which the Rhinemaidens eventually descended, and when the boat sank below stage Günther in Mafia-like coat, hat and dark glasses, Hagen in a leather jacket, and the troop of thug-like hunters in black balaclavas, entered slowly and lined up in a trench – ready for their schnapps-filled lunch-break during which Siegfried must precipitate his death. Hagen waited at the back taking swigs from his hip-flask. Space was made for him to approach Siegfried, whom he bayonetted in the back. The stage emptied. Siegfried regained consciousness, then died. Hagen turned to watch. The stage darkened totally for the death march, and then wall lights at the back conveyed that the scene had shifted. Siegfried was leaning against black steps at the back, in a similar position to that assumed by Brünnhilde for her long sleep. The lights came on and off. Then a large coffin moved on from the right: Hagen stood with one leg up on it – as if it were a hunting trophy. The row with Günther built violently. Then the walls collapsed in a massive and impressive movement, revealing themselves as not concrete but polystyrene: Hagen was unable to reach into the coffin, from which – after Brünnhilde had entered on the left with a pair of women assistants in black veils – blood started to stream, flowing over the front edge of the stage. All the ritual elements of the story were consigned to the cleansing fire. Finally the spirit of the river led Brünnhilde upstage. A warning light on top of a pillar at the back of the set gleamed ever more brightly.

People who are not opera enthusiasts must wonder why *The Ring* – which is only mythology after all – should generate such heat whenever it is (so expensively) staged. It is in the nature of epics, in these cinematic and propagandist modern times, that interpretation amounts to a political act. A director cannot now stage *The Ring*, even in a traditional way, without bumping into corpses. Jones's inventive and fresh Covent Garden *Ring* had two over-riding big ideas. First, it suggested that the problem of power, the fascist side of the work, was not just a German issue, but related to aspiring suburban politics everywhere. That was why the Norns (at the start of *Götterdämmerung*) were like a trio of old charladies gathered for a seance on a wet afternoon talking about doom, in front of a roller-blind front-drop covered in Lowery's reject graffiti representing the total 'artistic' failure of the 'Wotan' world project so far. The 'blind' threatened to roll up (like Pitt the Younger's maps of Europe), and finally ascended into the opera-house flies when the Norns' rope (in effect, the blind pulley) broke, exposing everything behind, everything that existed, the world as it was or is, to the Gibichungs' corrupt ambitions.

Secondly, parallel with the main narrative about the failure of Wotan and the gods (representing the *ancien régime* of old aristocrats) and Wotan's hand-over of responsibility to his selected humans (Siegfried and Brünnhilde), Jones and Lowery at crucial points disinterred an often neglected elemental aspect in Wagner's words and music – Nature, Erda (Mother Earth), the Rhine, desperately threatened by the unsavoury ambitions of Wotan,

Alberich, Mime, and Günther, indeed by the exploitative needs of human art and craft itself. Critics have often referred to the 'nature imagery' in Wagner's music: it should be seen as an ecological subtext. Lowery, the designer, symbolized that ecological current and crisis with a whale in *Rheingold*, and later notably at the start of act 3 of *Götterdämmerung*. But the whale image was submerged, not readily graspable. How many could tell that Wotan and Loge descended to Nibelheim through the blow-hole of a whale, or that the curved surface of the *Rheingold* set was meant to be a whale body? Commentators over the last 100 years have never made this issue an overt factor in Wagner's epic. Lowery wanted just to hint at it. These were poetic elements in his design concept: wonderfully suggestive in the movement group which at various points represented the spirit of the Rhine and, later, in October's initial *Götterdämmerung* performances, in the single man in blue make-up and suit, the spirit of the Rhine, who finally led Brünnhilde off upstage. For Lowery, like all fine designers, is right that the point of theatrical interpretation is not to reduce the work to a naively graspable thesis, or translate it into another, simpler language. The point is to ring significant bells, and direct the imaginative gaze occasionally to elements that may be part of the fabric Wagner built up. Any bells rung should not be over-loud. Jones's staging was important above all because it found a way – for the first time in the work's performance history – of asking the crucial question: is humanity reconcilable with nature? is there a possible future for our world? That moral undertow, rather than Gothic Revival aestheticism, is precisely why Wagner's *Ring* matters and has its central place in Western consciousness now.

Jones brought back *Götterdämmerung* for a few performances in February 1996 with an alternative cast. The result of his not entirely resolved revisions was that the third act seemed almost desecrated in the search for greater (too much?) clarity. The ecological blue male figure was cut, along with the Norns' cardigans: small points, no doubt. Instead the palpably feminine and constantly emoting figure of Anne Evans's vibrant Brünnhilde, in a Valkyrie-style trouser-suit, stood centre-stage on the prompt box, with, behind her, a smart-looking female extra standing on Siegfried's coffin, dropping the 'symbols' of Siegfried and Brünnhilde on to a sort of barbecue blazing from a large cardboard box. The back blockhouse wall surviving from the second act now tumbled much later on than previously, with a great gust of wind through the hall. There were no dignified female extras in blue dresses like Brünnhilde's to organize the funeral pyre. Instead Brünnhilde, having descended on a lift through the barbecue, reappeared far upstage as if taking part in a catwalk display of her smart suit, only to lean exhaustedly against the Valhalla tower – holding her shield with its tragedy mask in front of her: a repeat of the final image in *Die Walküre*. This neat tableau cleaned up the mystery and reduced the original imaginative stimulus of the staging as originally presented.

There were other changes which suggested a certain anxiety about the transparency of the ideas. The abusing of Brünnhilde by Siegfried when disguised by the Tarnhelm as Günther, putting a brown paper bag over her head at the end of act 1 and striking her to the ground when he seized the ring back from her, this time seemed to undermine the dramatic impact of her subsequent act 2 entrance into the fascist bunkhouse after Hagen's summoning of the Vassals (or tommies, as they were here). Polaski in October had made that ritual entry wearing a paper bag over her head painfully disturbing: her continuing humiliation intensely emphasized by her teetering procession across the tops of the bunkhouse tables – a purchased object in a paper bag staggering through that militaristic welcoming crowd to reach her 'husband' Günther. Jones's *Götterdämmerung* still boasted Kurt Rydl's superbly acted and sung Hagen, but the editing of the rich proliferating detail seemed in danger of clouding this *Ring* vision.

It remains an extraordinary achievement, however awkward to stabilize. With stage pictures and a theatrical narrative relating to that European and American suburban life which remains the glory and despair of our flawed civilization, Jones made *The Ring* into a paradigm of our current moral crisis. The detail of his and Lowery's work was certainly complex and quite hard to fathom. But producer and designer presented a serious viewpoint. That was surely beyond question: the staging exuded truth and wit. Its serious viewpoint needed the full theatrical range, tragedy *and* comedy. That is our political life today. There have been enough *Ring* productions that identify sentimentally with Wotan's tragedy, and somehow fail to recognize his extremely questionable moral status. Brünnhilde too, as a woman, is deeply flawed after she has lost her divinity. In the post-modern age which has learnt to doubt progress, Wagner's prophetic masterwork must seem profoundly pessimistic. Jones and Lowery's original and distinc-

tive Covent Garden *Ring* proved a milestone in the work's interpretative history. One day this production may stand beside
Covent Garden's fabled *Don Carlos* of Visconti.

Additional proof of Jones's originality and distinction, were it
needed, would lie in the way his highly talented disciple, Tim
Hopkins (born 1963), has emerged as a good director in his own
right with a succession of important productions. Hopkins staged
at the Almeida Theatre the most workable and musically distinguished of the late Stephen Oliver's many attempts to write serious opera: *Mario and the Magician*. His *Zampa* at the 1993
Wexford Festival was a brilliant piece of atmospheric comedy.
And his world premiere staging of Judith Weir's new opera, *Blond
Eckbert*, for ENO in 1994 was one of the most consistently stylish, well directed and visual productions of the first ENO season
under Dennis Marks's new management.

Oliver's *Mario and the Magician* (based on Thomas Mann, like
Death in Venice) was strongly autobiographical. Oliver was a control freak, and made the magician in his opera a sort of self-portrait, armed with his whip and intellectual detachment. Hopkins
focused this 80-minute long entertaining, vocally potent, post-
Verismo fable – laced with sexual innuendo and virtuoso demands
– on the 20th-century's most destructive delusion, the neo-fascist
myth of human omniscience. Oliver's melody has lacked the individuality of Britten's. But here his lines gripped, his characterizations were highly distinctive, the drama cleverly paced. Lowery
set the first half on a curling white vertiginous pathway in front of
a curtain with two doorways below a broken proscenium. For the
magic show of the second half the curtain was raised, and the pathway was revealed as shaped like a drawing of an eye. On the pathway potboys teetered or fell asleep at the hypnotist's will, Signora
Angiolieri almost vanished away, and finally (in a homosexual
frisson) Mario kissed the magician, the satanic hunchback who
was pulling all the strings. Mixing comedy, old-fashioned decorum and theatrical magic, Hopkins – with Richard Jackson as the
magician Cipolla – turned Cipolla's hypnotic conjuring session
into a tense, thrilling tour de force.

Ferdinand Hérold's *Zampa* was the missing link between
Rossini and Berlioz, as well as being a template for Offenbach,
Sullivan and Chabrier. At Wexford in 1993 Hopkins's daring,
complicated, extravagantly naughty staging was designed by
Charles Edwards. *Zampa* has a spaghetti-western plot, with *Don*

Giovanni-ish overtones, concerning a pirate on the make, who moves in on the Sicilian estate of Camille's father just as she is about to wed Alphonse. Camille's attendant, called Ritta (performed in the dotty style of Margaret Rutherford), was marrying Dandolo the castle steward, having lost her husband Daniel. But Daniel – one of many comic coincidences in the plot – had now become Zampa's first mate. The spoof gothic element was the fiancé of marble, the blessed Alice's statue, on whose hand Zampa jokingly placed his ring, as a result of which (in feminist consummation) she dragged him to hell like Mozart's Commendatore. Hérold's structurally ungainly comedy was tinged with hysteria. The pirate was a complex charmer. Hopkins provided theatrical panache to answer the musical grandeur of exciting vocal trapeze-work and witty Gallic absurdity. Ritta's marital complications and Camille's sentimentality registered in stylized vaudeville production numbers – with hula-hoops, leopardskin pants for the pirates, and furious Louis de Funes or Fernandel-style footwork. The opening scene had both the two virtuous tenors, the chorus girls and some chorus males in green uniforms hurdling over hedges – as well as pirates swinging on to the stage on ropes hung from the flies. At the denouement the silent statue, a black and yellow figure of fate, took Zampa through a stage trap with a puff of smoke that sent a shiver down the spine. Edwards's overcast, chiaroscuro, emotion-driven lighting threw clouds across the set when the tale turned tragic. Hopkins was ambitious, but his affectionate inventiveness never let the stylization become tiresome. The singing actors confidently rose to the challenges he set them.

His staging of *Blond Eckbert* at ENO also had acutely directed stylization of the acting. Ludwig Tieck's 1796 moral fairy-tale is about a couple whose robbery of a generous wealthy witch does not go unpunished, their secret misdeeds and murdering cover-ups incapable of being suppressed – like King Midas's ass's ears. (The story could be a parable about the human species' rape of the planet.) It required, in Judith Weir's simple atmospheric version, only four performers – though Hopkins included a real dog in the opening episode, led straight across the stage by a man who was (just) invisible behind the back-cloth, with the Bird suspended above – a singer in black feathery costume with headdress-cum-mask like an open beak, her fingernails extended like claws. The live dog was appreciated: animal obedience always wins sympathy. Lowery, to a greater extent even than in his *Flying Dutchman* or *Fledermaus* for Richard Jones, used a quickly changed sequence of drop-cloths and projections and silhouettes to tell the story and adjust the moral atmosphere. Nobody in Britain, perhaps in Europe, has Lowery's individual visual signature using primarily graphic rather than conceptual means.

The front-drop for the whole production was grey- and white-striped, like material for a shop blind. The curtain shimmered in a draught and then was drawn from the left across the stage, rather than raised. Using a curtain like that suggested the sense of hidden domestic guilt running through the story, the anxiety over what neighbours say. Lowery offered a blank landscape with five electricity pylons (Tieck's story was transposed to the present, more or less.) A cutaway on the left of the cloth revealed the figure of the black, magic bird, the witness of theft and generator of wealth, embodiment of the conscience. Eckbert entered from the right, his hands over his mouth, Berthe from the left, hands over her ears. They stretched their hands out, highly stylized, towards each other, backed out to opposite sides – the dog left too. The next front-drop was a spider's web of concentric circles, reminiscent of Wieland Wagner's 1951 *Parsifal* at Bayreuth: the bird launched into the narrative 'Far away, and long ago . . .' The set provided a sequence of atmospheric narrative pictures. Through clouds a little house appeared. The bird was flown off to the right, her hands gestured downwards. The light faded. An outline of a house interior took shape, drawn on a back-cloth, one huge gothic window on the left, a mound leading up to the door at the centre. Eckbert and Berthe were at home, she polishing up a shoe by the fire, he looking through the window on the left at the view of endless pines. A light in the distance moved closer. The pair reacted to the light, their gestures studiedly stylized and stilted. A major Hopkins achievement was to get Anne-Marie Owens as Berthe, Nicholas Folwell as Eckbert and Christopher Ventris as Walther, Hugo and the Old Woman to perform in such an acute style, using a rarefied, physically distinctive acting where the slightest look or gesture assumed significance. The pair watched the approaching possible visitor. The fire glowed red (Berthe's chair drawn by Lowery on the back-cloth). The visitor, preceded by a giant face at the 'window', turned out to be Walther, the ominous friend who asks the awkward question that suggests he knows more than he should, or that Eckbert and Berthe can tolerate. The appearance of the interior altered to accommodate him. He entered centre-stage just as his image was coming through the doorway on top of the mound drawn by Lowery. Wolfgang Göbbel's lighting revealed Walther's face and silhouetted him. Every reassuring ordinary gesture made by Walther, whether raising his cup or stretching out a hand, was turned by Hopkins into something threatening. The hunting horns in the score added to the ominous effect.

Berthe's ballad provided the opportunity for another series of descriptive scene changes. The gauzes suggesting the house windows, image upon image, remained for a time, then the tale led through the woods dominated by Berthe's memories – which eventually were made palpable on a back-cloth with silhouettes of the dog and bird as puppets on sticks. The golden eggs were laid – plopping into place. Berthe's story was a strange visual progress, up and down a mountainside, the whole stage becoming a kind of graphic screen of subtly changing colour.

Hopkins got remarkable playing from the performers, and the imagery of the staging was extraordinary. The actors became their graphic images. Simon Pummell had realized a film sequence as part of the production: the image of Berthe qualified Anne-Marie Owen's performance very tellingly. Another coup was the revelation that Walther knew the name of the dog, Strohmian, and therefore probably knew everything else. The letters of the dog's name were etched in fire in a little inner-stage cameo. Walther enjoyed the effect of his revelation on his victims. The decision-taking by the guilty couple was set against an equally extraordinary immobile environment, anticipating the leafy setting for Walther's murder. At the close of the act the three chief players looked through vertical slits in the front-drop.

Some of the most striking images came in the second act: against Lowery's magical drawing of forest trees, one saw the fatal crossbow bolt (a shaft of light behind the back-cloth), which eventually ended the detective-like leaf-gathering, make an endlessly slow passage across the back-cloth. Walther's odd behaviour was eerily and provocatively choreographed. The performers from time to time seemed to become physically part of the scenery, almost as if a graphic element on a back-cloth. The effect was like the use of live actors in some 1940s Walt Disney cartoon films. Berthe's sickbed was painted huge on a drop-cloth against rose-decorated 'wallpaper'; her top half looked as if she were lying there with her head on the pillow. Lowery managed the comic subtleties of perspective marvellously. Next to the bed was a slightly open door, a slit in the cloth through which Eckbert poked his bodily frame. When Berthe was about to disappear, her hand rested on the pillow for a moment before it too was drawn out of sight. The most extraordinary image of the whole production was the meeting with Hugo. Eckbert stood lost and abandoned in front of a massive road sweeping on arches from far in the distance on the right of the set to the left foreground. Contrary streams of traffic were suggested with lines of flashing red and white lights. After this encounter, Eckbert was raised high on a lift at the centre of the web front-drop which had figured earlier. The drained quality of the denouement – when he saw a peasant in a Spanish hat, trees in the distance, the old woman's house at the back drawn very small, a dog leaning beside it, the bird above commenting – enhanced the sense of fatalism and helplessness. Inescapable moral imperatives were resolutely outlined. Weir's finely judged, pure, accessible music was unpretentious, severe and simple. The studied coherence and highly specific flavour of Hopkins's staging and Lowery's designs were crucial. Hopkins's relation to Jones makes their work into a 'school': their output is the most unusual and imaginative of all British producers. Lowery is the most daring and distinctive of British designers because of his clear and profound dramaturgical analysis of both text and musical sub-text. He has all the instincts of a painter for mood and atmosphere, and translates the layers of a dramatic situation into images with a keen awareness of contemporary currents in art and architecture – as well as in music and the other performing arts. He also has a wonderfully anarchic sense of irony. The way Jones, Lowery and Hopkins upset some critics and audiences is deeply encouraging: they are well ahead of the game.

11 Graham Vick: neo-realism and emotion

Graham Vick's 1992 staging (for Glyndebourne Festival Opera) of *Pikovaya Dama* (The Queen of Spades) designed by Richard Hudson: the ghost of Felicity Palmer's Countess appears to Yuri Marusin's Herman. Photograph © Guy Gravett.

When Graham Vick directed *Lady Macbeth of Mtsensk* in 1995 at the Metropolitan Opera in New York, it was said that he transformed morale backstage. 'He made the chorus act, which is unheard of at the Met,' said Patrick Smith editor of *Opera News*. 'Maybe there was 40 per cent more happening on stage than ideal. But it was just the best, most theatrically serious production we have ever had.' Success like this did not take Vick away from the small-scale where he discovered his preferred style, simple, colourful, buoyant, humorous, the emphasis on acting and truthful emotions. He remained faithful to his visionary plans for the small City of Birmingham Touring Opera, and continued to direct work at the tiny private opera festival in Italy near Grosseto promoted by the English opera designer Adam Pollock, including his only play productions (in Italian in which he is fluent). His community performances of *West Side Story* at Saltaire Mills, Yorkshire, with an entirely amateur local company, showed what he believed about theatre, community and the moral and political debate. In 1965 Vick aged 12 had seen a television programme about make-up, acting and characterization with Tito Gobbi putting on false noses and turning himself into Gianni Schicchi or Scarpia or Rigoletto. He was 'struck, utterly and totally.' The first opera he saw was a local amateur *Il trovatore*. Later there were the Glyndebourne, Welsh National and Sadler's Wells tours. Mozart didn't appeal half as much as Peter Hall's magical production of Cavalli's *La Calisto*. Vick was a young singer, a bass lay clerk at Chester Cathedral, with singing lessons paid for by Birkenhead council. He went to music college to learn to be a conductor. The point and primary attraction of opera – as he saw and sees it – is the scale of intensity: 'That was what I've always responded to. Even with plays my strongest memory is of a virtually foreign passion and intensity.' The theatrical events of his Liverpool teens were Peggy Ashcroft in *Ghosts* with the RSC, and the National's *Dance of Death* with Laurence Olivier – which he found 'overwhelming for a boy sitting on his own in the gods at the Royal Court Theatre'. Their searing nature, which did not belong with the kind of life he was living, resonated with him. Theatrical excitement became an obsession, almost a drug. 'A bit of me woke up on those occasions which was not allowed out in the rest of my life.' He regards theatre work as an inescapable vocation and unquestionably a spiritual issue, though the word religion has the wrong connotations. 'Theatre and culture are part of a religious world. They all deal with the same thing.'

Vick's kind of work is emotionally honest and not surrealistic, the emphasis usually more on acting than design, physically vibrant but open to comic exuberance: his productions tend to feel a lot more conservative than David Alden's or Tim Albery's, but they are more poetic, less naturalistic than they look, in the way they explore psychology and ideas. Vick always tries to find an approach that can sit at ease with the natural world of the piece:

> The end of a director's work is to let a show alone. I'm there to make a production independent, so that life happens on the stage not controlled by me. What I'm doing must sit with the natural rhythm and inner world of the piece. The most depressing thing is to be in the rehearsal room trying to make the piece fit the set. But a certain extravagance is part of the operatic art. The physical action of singing generates an artificially high physical energy. Thank goodness, we have nearly passed the days of hands-in-your-pockets acting in opera, where a lot of effort was put into pretending you were not singing at all, but really doing a play. That has always seemed to me the phoniest of approaches.

Inasmuch as a conventional career pattern for the comparatively modern profession of opera producer has developed in Britain since the Second World War, Vick has followed it – unlike Tim Albery, Steven Pimlott, and David Freeman. In his early 20s he was working as a staff producer (assisting established producers in the business of creating new productions) at Glyndebourne and Scottish Opera. He was involved with Colin Graham in the brief existence of English Music Theatre (an attempt to run an ensemble company with a permanent membership in the late 1970s). But EMT, which was formed out of what was left of Benjamin Britten's English Opera Group, failed to achieve Arts Council support and disbanded in 1980. Vick became director of productions for Scottish Opera in 1984, a couple of years after Pountney had moved from Glasgow to ENO. His work has been marked by both a provocative streak and a readiness to operate on the most economical scale. The provocation was unwelcome in

Glasgow, particularly a Scottish Opera staging of *Don Giovanni* with graffiti scribbled on the back-cloth and a toilet in one corner. In fact his kind of freshness and modern style is seldom shocking or disturbing in what it shows. He distrusts pretension: he wants to speak clearly.

Vick has collaborated with a number of different designers, but has often preferred a simple visual aesthetic – even when not severely restricted (as in his small-scale touring productions) by budgetary considerations. His taste has a puritanical flavour. He has tended to resist the highly imaginative setting, though his much appreciated Covent Garden staging of Berio's *Un rè in ascolto* was full of diverting detail. He helped the ENO economy by providing a pair of cheap productions in 1983, using one basic set structure for both *Ariadne auf Naxos* and *The Rape of Lucretia*, designed by Russell Craig, a superimposed wood-strip stage floor jutting a little over the orchestra pit. The *Ariadne* prologue was directed by Vick with typical lively theatricality and despatch. Doors and windows in the *trompe-l'oeil* Advent calendar-style backdrop opened and closed as part of the manic manoeuvring of various little cameo situations on stage, and the sense of performance values thus established was skilfully blended into the more ambivalent aesthetic of the opera proper. Minimal furniture, a dining table in two segments, a pair of Baroque chairs, were soon crowded by theatrical trunks and business – hysterical goings-on, a bustle of bad jokes and brouhaha. The original Major-Domo in this often revived production was Donald Sinden in person, a tautology at full tilt, powdered, and perched on high-heels – all periwig, pursed lips, and flouncing ruffles. Vick directed his star and calculated the effects to make the games-playing in a very clever opera coherent. The concluding apotheosis – done with almost no physical grandeur – was necessarily economical. On the back of his reputation this *Ariadne* travelled – for instance to Amsterdam – but away from the Coliseum it never won many friends.

The first Vick staging to gain wide recognition and popularity with audiences was his *Madam Butterfly*, also for ENO, designed by Stefanos Lazaridis in 1984. Contrary to the Puccinian rule enunciated by Götz Friedrich – that these *Verismo* classics absolutely require naturalistic presentation – Vick and Lazaridis employed the metaphor that the black front-cloth was an old-fashioned camera lens, opening up like a camera diaphragm to reveal the set, and emphasized the biting political subtext of the opera: photography and tourist snaps made a convenient symbol of thoughtless and exploitative American intrusion. This conveyed just the right hint of Western imperialism. Butterfly dressed herself à l'Américaine once she had committed herself to Pinkerton. Instead of Pinkerton's last offstage words ('Butterfly! Butterfly!') leading into a stunned remorseful tableau, as if he were having sentimental second thoughts or at least gaining insight, his child Sorrow ran up the steps to his Yankee Dad, who carried him off to Kate and American comfort. Vick made *Butterfly* much more than a tragic sentimental love story. It became an effective parable of American interference in Japanese culture and of the casual exploitation of women. Probably Puccini, a philanderer rather on Pinkerton's side, was neither a feminist nor an anti-colonialist. ENO used Julian Smith's edition, first heard in Cardiff in 1978 for Joachim Herz's WNO staging, which restored 20 minutes of Puccini's cuts. The extra material strengthened the irony and forced the audience to regard Pinkerton's behaviour as intolerable. Puccini's cuts originated with a fear that he was serving too strong meat for 1904 stomachs.

Herz's classic staging in the Felsenstein manner had reminded its audience of the context with a cute Japanese model village at the front of the stage. But compared with the usual almond blossom prettiness, which it did not entirely neglect, Herz's staging was full of psychological realism and also extremely emotional. It started with a spotlight picking out the middle of the black front-drop, like an old movie, which expanded and then revealed the model Nagasaki. The house was quite Japanese and simple, rooms separated by sliding blank screens. As with Vick, Butterfly wore Western dress in the second act: her house had acquired flotsam from American culture – a gramophone, photos, a little toy lighthouse, a saddle-cum-rocking-horse for Sorrow. But the tradition was used too: the suicide as performed by the Komische Oper star Magdalena Falewicz was extremely distressing. She did the deed behind screens, then staggered out to where she had left Sorrow playing, then fell spread-eagled backwards towards the front of the stage, fluttering down in her white kimono with a delicacy and pathetic beauty somehow just like a butterfly. Herz was a true Felsenstein disciple in his neo-realist approach, and Vick's ENO staging, though mobilized quite differently, was geared the same way. Herz's *Butterfly* had been his passport to acceptability by the old Felsenstein hands when he inherited the company: 'They saw,' he said, 'that I was also able to make a kind of emotional theatre.' Felsenstein represented the opposite pole from Brecht. 'His theory and practice,' according to Herz, 'was a very emotional style of playing. As a teacher he never discussed technical questions; they were the premise. He only spoke about the human dimension. He wanted the spectator to be involved completely emotionally in the show. He said that the greatest moment in theatre would be for total strangers to be compelled by the shared emotional experience to greet each other like long-lost friends.' Felsenstein's aim for the performers was an emotional spontaneity that spectators could believe in, as if the singer were no longer a puppet of the composer's score. The stylization of Japanese traditional culture which is often represented to an extent in *Butterfly* stagings, of Kabuki theatre for instance, screens, cloths, white space, curtains, translucency, big shoes, strange hairstyles and costumes, wooden slats, ramps, planks, stilts, giant calligraphy even, provides a secure and truthful foundation for what must be a profoundly moving kind of musical theatre in effect close to Italian opera.

The first image Vick's ENO audience saw was a white wedding kimono spotlit at the back of the upper stage. The Lazaridis set was nothing – just black drapes, a black structure supporting the upper stage, which could contain an inner stage, and a deep space in front. As Puccini's opening fugue raced off, white panels from which one might imagine a Japanese house being constructed slid across the upper level, depositing magically, as they crossed, the servants whom Pinkerton was about to hire. There were steps down from the upper stage: beside them a black panel slid aside to let in Pinkerton and Goro the marriage broker, followed by the American consul Sharpless. The front of the stage became a kind of verandah, with wicker chairs brought out, bourbon flowing for the stars and stripes. An inner stage opened out, the set filled with wedding guests and soon Butterfly herself and her accompanying ladies, all kimono-clad. This was not naturalistic, but very lifelike in detail with devices borrowed from the Japanese theatre. At EMT Vick had assisted Colin Graham on Minoru Miki's *An Actor's Revenge*, and one of his most unusual CBTO commissions was Ravi Shankar's *Ghanashyam*. He turned the stage into the inside of a *camera oscura*, with sliding black side-flats and drops closing off the white back-cloth in the manner of a lens-aperture diaphragm. The adjusting white rectangle at the back, opening and closing, together with black drapes created a real sense of emotional perspective, of sharply lengthened shadows. Pinkerton's two-dimensional marriage to Cio-Cio-San was for souvenir snaps as well as sex. But the black and white contrasts in the structure of the stage were also used to lend a deepening, highly emotive perspective to Vick's closer focus on the exterior of the first act and the inside-outside quality of the second act locations. The play-acting element, familiarly in the servants' performance when Pinkerton is being shown round by Goro, had been emphasized in the neat tricks with sliding panels at the opening notes. Throughout, Vick's approach was objective and interpretative: one of the cleverest ENO stagings then. Yet the acting style was defined by the developed naturalism of Norman Bailey's well-observed Sharpless, and the emotionally aware Suzuki of Anne-Marie Owens (male and female 'chorus' figures whose faces mirror and lead the audience's response). Vick did not contradict tradition in the familiar stock of supporting roles, nor in the arrival of Butterfly and her clutch of kimono-clad lovelies strewing blossoms over the upper level of the split-level set, nor in her uncle the Bonze's condemnation and rejection. The 'local colour' avoided too radical a defamiliarization: this was and remained Japan through a Western lens. Prince Yamadori did his wooing in a white suit and spats. Butterfly's eventual suicide was transfiguring rather than depressing, because it was true to her Japanese culture and its sense of honour, the correct response to enslavement. Her wilful misunderstanding of the contract with Pinkerton was never dishonourable. She took the American at his word, which he would no doubt claim to have been as good as – were he not dealing with another race. Her adoption of American customs and culture was suggested with chairs and a Jesus picture. The production was finely lit by Matthew Richardson and maintained the new ENO aesthetic of Miller's *Rigoletto* and Hytner's *Rienzi*.

Vick did not return to ENO until 1989. He was busy in the intervening years at Scottish Opera, then with English Touring Opera which merged with Birmingham Music Theatre to become CBTO. He was also directing at Adam Pollock's Batignano. There were downs as well as ups – an execrable *Oberon* with new text by Anthony Burgess for instance. His Scottish Opera *Carmen* was a neat tour de force, with strong central idea and little superfluous decoration. The memory one retained was of the chorus seated at the start on a square of chairs arranged right round the stage. The minimal set was just a wall and a door that rose out of the floor at the centre of the stage. Vick concentrated on the coherence of the acting and the central confrontations. Inevitably, that was the mark of his stagings (with Jonathan Dove's cut-down orchestrations) for CBTO. *Falstaff* was a landmark in 1987, simply designed and lushly, colourfully costumed by Paul Brown in high-medieval Wars of the Roses period. As with the crafty tricks of his later *King Arthur* set for Vick, Brown's midnight-blue vertiginously raked stage fronted with a red curtain-cum-bedcover was a mass of 30 hinged trapdoors from which clipped bays like lolly-pops on sticks rose for Ford's garden in the second scene, or a single white balloon floated up as the waxing Windsor forest moon – whimsical but practical. A couple of doors in the backdrop allowed exits to backstage, while passages on either side of the stage ran to the rear of the set. The vast red curtain covering everything doubled as hanging or bedcover or all-purpose obstacle. For once Falstaff's complaints from the laundry basket were properly audible. While the damp Falstaff bemoaned his fate, the conspiratorial sextet in act 3 poked their heads through the stage traps at the front. Later Falstaff in Herne the Hunter antlers emerged in a cloud of dry ice, way upstage, from a cavernous trap. Vick's production used simple tricks perfectly in this essentially traditional approach, which managed both the forest atmosphere and a fragmentary naturalism indoors at Ford's despite the lack of details. The secret was in the enthusiasm of the acting.

Vick's *Magic Flute* for CBTO in 1988 also aimed at clarity and simplicity (good for audiences fresh to opera) with not a word of Schikaneder's text cut. There was no serpent or dragon: instead Tamino, in great panic, spun on to the stage unwinding from around his own body a long sheet (one end off stage) that he tangled all over the set, caught in the toils of a nightmare. Chris Dyer's set was the skeleton of a wooden pyramid with an upper platform, ladder steps in its legs. The stage was squared off and edged with curtain panels. Costumes had a tinge of Far East aesthetic, Sarastro's enlightenment more Buddhist than Masonic. But there was also the power of the dark side (Darth Vader from *Star Wars*) – the yin and yang of Tamino/Papageno against (and finally with) Pamina/Papagena. The magically calmed animals wore charming oriental theatre masks.

The combination of shifting romantic psychology and spectacular chorus scenes and dancing made Tchaikovsky's *Eugene Onegin* especially suitable for Vick's theatrical talents, as his 1989

ENO version made clear – and as his new production for the opening season of the new Glyndebourne opera-house reaffirmed. Instead of relationships ritualized by the voice classification of tenor, baritone, mezzo and soprano, Tchaikovsky's masterpiece presents a pair of souls out of phase, enduring the fatal necessity but impossibility of love and happiness. The primary need is the truth of the characters' feelings. 'Could all my dreams be self-delusion?' sang Marie McLaughlin's appealing and well acted Tatyana in the Letter Scene, words suitable for her text to Onegin. As the clouds (painted on flown stage flats) lifted and the room revolved, she went to her mirror, slowly opened her night-dress and looked shyly at her exposed breasts: a telling image for the powerful sexual needs of her frustrated character and also for the electricity of Russian romanticism. The self-questioning Letter Scene is key to the work, recognized as such by the public when they applaud the star soprano's aria. Vick's virtuoso staging recalled later the ironical little trumpet phrase that accompanies Lensky's second, Zaretsky, as he sings (in David Lloyd-Jones's translation), 'In my view duels are an art and must, as such, be fought correctly.' Zaretsky dismissed Lensky's corpse with a brief salute after it was all over, just raising his top hat once to register the death before striding off stage.

Placed decoratively in period, with pretty scenery and frocks, *Onegin* can be merely a touching anecdote of young folly. But Tchaikovsky's seven lyric scenes cover a large range of intimate revelation and social context, and invite something more fertile and challenging. Vick's ENO staging (the last Sadler's Wells version had been by George Devine in 1952) was scrupulously registered. Vick got exactly the right approach for the rush by the Larin women to remove their pinnies, rearrange the garden furniture and all be quietly seated for the cadence in the score when Lensky and his friend Onegin enter. He never worked against the grain of the musical or dramatic style, but concentrated on the epic scale of a full-blooded interpretation.

Sally Jacobs's designs avoided romantic anecdote, and provided a kind of dreamscape, a world of black, grey and red clouds painted on low flats that moved across the stage (itself defined by looming black flies and side-flats, rather like a 19th-century ballet set) to reveal the naturalistic location for each scene, such as a bed and writing table for the letter, or tables and lamps for the Larins' ball. During the country scenes a little wooden church dominated the view high up at the back. Costumes were mid-19th-century, colourful and handsome. The point of this denial of the expected – evoking Tatyana's bookish dreamy imagination – was to provide a historical and epic context. Avoiding standard naturalism also allowed for cinematic editing of the confrontations – at the Larins' ball, for the duel, and for Onegin's final desperate attempt to elope with Tatyana. In the opening scene the peasants flooded on to the stage and by weight of sheer numbers obscured the cloud-flats. The people became the setting, as indeed they did in a different way for the Larins' ball. Sean Walsh's choreography made far more of the peasants' song than usual, providing a little narrative ballet to fill out the chorus text. The dances at the Larins and Gremins were very accomplished. The waltzing was knitted into the narrative flow as it would be in a film. There was a panorama of different elements: the brawling soldiers on the right, the boy reading his book on the edge of the dance-floor, the guests carousing at tables behind, Tatyana with her back to the jollities (though it's her name-day ball) on a bench near the orchestra pit. She refused persistent invitations to dance. Then suddenly Onegin swept her off, up and over the platform. People kept bumping into each other on the floor. It was a country ball, full of the spirit that makes the parties and dances in John Ford's movies so infectious. Real life on stage. Walsh's mazurka and later his grand polonaise at the Gremins were more fully developed, more physically detailed and carried through than most opera-house dancing.

Vick's editing of the action at the Larins was extraordinary. Everything important happened in close-up at the front of the stage, yet never felt artificial. The crowd were an evocative, attentive backdrop until – enraged by Lensky's undecorous accusations – they pressed forward, pinning the principals even more cruelly at the front. Naturally Onegin remembered to kiss Madame Larina's hand before going. Lensky pushed through the mass in despair. At the Gremins, Vick seated the lovely Tatyana at the very front, beside one of the pompous columns that, with the 'love' arch and self-conscious polonaise, defined the aridity of her smart life. Her thoughts about Onegin before Gremin brought them together were crystal clear. For the final scene, Vick cleared the stage leaving the same white platform (of dance-floor and duel) as a level playing-field on which the two could meet as equals. The subtlety of Tatyana's feeling and the crudeness of Onegin's assumption that he could have a second chance were both exact.

The opera ended with the desperate Onegin questioning the audience, grimacing, hands tensed, asking as the Pushkin narrator repeatedly does in the poem what he should do. Jacobs's designs let Vick be both naturalistic and emotional, yet able to comment objectively.

Ravi Shankar's *Ghanashyam* for CBTO in 1989 was a danced-mimed tale of our times (nominally set in 1900) with Indian vocal and instrumental accompaniment created in experimental collaboration with Vick for CBTO. A fusion of Indian and European cultures, the narrative was simple and moving; dancing was complex, noble, strong and graceful. Just occasionally the dancers mimed to the singing or speaking. Paul Brown's boxed perspective design – off-white walls, a tap, a tree and three doorways revealing a statue or house interiors – was plain and telling. Vick's confident, supportive, and ungimmicky production was persuasive if naive. The story, which Shankar based on an episode in his own family in his childhood, concerned a North Indian dancer of genius, Ghanashyam, who – together with Raman and his wife Kanta, a pair of South Indian dancers – had formed a community of dancers in a small village. The work opened with an enjoyable Kathakali training session in their school, full of stampings, foot-stepping and slicing gestures with expansive stretching of legs and arms. Later Ghanashyam started to get hooked on drink, drugs and vice, coveted Raman's wife Kanta and eventually started to steal to feed his habit – first pawning his wife Lalita's bracelets, and later ripping off jewellery from a temple statue. He tempted Shiva the destroyer, of whom he dreamt in a drugged trance (a wonderfully poised dance episode for V. P. Dhananjayan in a blue cloth and startling head-dress, wearing the god's serene disinterested smile of destruction). When Ghanashyam's theft of a jewel from the temple was discovered he was chased to his death by the angry villagers. Then Kanta (finely danced and mimed by Shanta Dhananjayan) was possessed by Ghanashyam. The exorcist Ojah (also performed by Durga Lal in a flailing wig) could do nothing until Ghanashyam's widow Lalita (a touching performance by Renu Bassi) offered her own sad body as a home and mortal sacrifice for Ghanashyam's spirit which at last could go to its rest. A branch fell as the spell was broken, and Raman's virtuoso dancing lessons recommenced. The virtues of the performance were traditional, with the energy, imagination and star-quality of the two central couples, and above all of Durga Lal and V. P. Dhananjayan, both great stars in India. Their virtuoso use of the tradition that gave them their art was a daring venture for CBTO and Vick, who likes an unusual venture – especially when it incorporates such unfamiliar elements. As much as Peter Sellars, Vick draws on other traditions in the search for operatic renewal.

The Kurt Weill/Bertold Brecht *Rise and Fall of the City of Mahagonny* for the 1990 Maggio Musicale festival in Florence confirmed Vick's international reputation and the status which he had secured following the success of his Covent Garden production of Luciano Berio's *Un rè in ascolto* (also seen at the Bastille opera in Paris). Vick's approach to *Mahagonny* was Fellini-esque, right for Italian taste. The stage was full of style-conscious activity. The Florence cast – led by Catherine Malfitano's raunchy Jenny and the muscular, unspoilt Jimmy of Warren Ellsworth (who died a few years later far too young) – was starry and 'operatic' compared to the level of voices Vick usually used in Birmingham and Glasgow. The metaphor was 'Mahagonny Cinecittà'. Yvonne Minton as a Lauren Bacall look-alike provided a glamorous Widow Begbick, and Timothy Nolen was Peter Finch-like as Trinity Moses. The designs by Maria Bjørnson exploited the full naked height and depth of the Teatro Verdi – turning it into a kind of theme park evoking the world of cinematic illusion. The set reproduced the back wall of the theatre with, bursting through it, a tenement series of room-sets piled up like boxes from floor to ceiling, each peopled by Vick with life-like dramas: a porn cinema with a schoolboy and old men in dirty raincoats; a girl being raped; a crowd strap-hanging on the subway; a mother ironing; a schoolroom with victim in dunce's cap doing detention. Vick employed again an element that had helped flesh out effectively the amateur *West Side Story* which he staged under Opera North auspices at Saltaire Mill near Bradford. Saltaire's Bernstein was a 'promenade' performance. The main machine room of the mill where the action took place was filled with display stalls as in a market, each narrating a detailed subsidiary scenario about some aspect of American life in the 1950s. In Florence, interleaving with these illustrations meant exact blocking and manoeuvring of the actors, and complicated choreography by Sean Walsh. The ensemble work by the crowd of extras was top quality.

On the right in front of this simultaneous narrative wall was a revolving cactus made of neon-strips. Backstage on the left was a platform with a stuffed buffalo from which the Alaska quartet descended by ropes. Occasionally trap-doors opened in the stage floor to create a boxing-ring, or Hawaiian palm paradise, or prison-cell. Vick energetically filled out Brecht's quirky, satirical episodes. There was not much to enjoy in the revolting gluttony of Jack, eating his way through the innards of a dead horse, nor in the chorus-line tediously, mechanically parading through the brothel – though Malfitano's Jenny led a top-quality batch of Italian prostitutes. Vick physically staged what Brecht proposed should be done on film, and used a crackly voice-over in Italian (the performance was in the original German) in place of the scene titles Brecht wanted projected on cards. Revisualizing the stage directions achieved the effect Brecht sought by alternative means. In the third act trial of Jimmy, by Fatty, Begbick and Moses, all the main participants were seated in Dr Strangelove-like electric wheelchairs, terribly withered. Mahagonny was a sunset retirement home where 'standards' were being maintained in a travesty of justice – ending in corpses, coffins and total despair.

Also in 1990 Vick staged the Italian premiere of Tippett's *King Priam* (in Italian – *Il rè Priamo*), at Musica Nel Chiostro, Batignano, near Grosseto, the pioneering al-fresco opera festival in a renovated little monastery. It was ambitious to stage Tippett's opera, written for the 1962 Coventry Festival and Covent Garden, for Batignano, without conventional operatic facilities. Pollock was designer, and the stage was one end of a walled garden, audience seated on a ramp, orchestra on a platform high above a cypress hedge. In contrast to the theatrical exuberance and choreographic complexity of Vick's *Mahagonny* in Florence, *Priam* was simple and direct. Pollock used a real apple tree and its fruit for the 'judgment of Paris', adding a rock-like altar-cum-promontory on the left where the cot of the infant Paris was spectacularly consigned to flames. The stage area was marked out with gravel, carefully and almost continuously raked in expressively significant strokes by the Old Man, senior member of Tippett's Brechtian 'chorus' trio. The biggest dramaturgical problem was the switch from gnomic narrative to chorus commentary, and the sometimes banal tone of Tippett's own text. Vick was un-selfconscious about the structural fragmentation. Working almost without scenery, he moved the story along quickly. The singers were close to the audience and Priam's decision to reject the baby Paris, energetically precipitated by Hecuba rushing imperiously across the gravel, was gripping. The unprepossessing chorus provided a court for the

King, augmented with a few extras and maidservants. Mercury was initially 'discovered' up the apple tree. Evocation of Achilles's tent, or the Trojan camp, or Priam's palace, or the hunting fields where young Paris rediscovers his family, was left to the music and one's imagination. Vick concentrated on tautly articulating the relationships using the simple space of the gravel courtyard, entrances and exits exactly controlled. Even a small movement in a performer's expression or the direction of their attention was crucially important.

Vick's CBTO staging of *The Ring* in late 1990 was re-orchestrated by Jonathan Dove, but expurgated, in English, and in two parts – a fascinating critical experiment. Could the essence of *The Ring*, its story and the music that fleshes it out and evaluates it, survive compromises far more profound than are normal in imperfect performances? CBTO's almost ten hours of music-drama told the story very clearly and gave all the evocative endless melodics. It carried the message primarily through singing and acting. Vick and his conductor Simon Halsey cast a lot of bold voices, the women strongest but some of the men impressive. The performance was intimate but the singing style had Wagnerian scale, beauty and attack, often subtle consistency of line, and devotion in most quarters to getting the words across. Vick wanted to provide a vernacular performance, outlining the saga simply, clearly and traditionally – with appropriate voice-types and the characters given a look and feel that anybody familiar with children's versions of the Norse sagas would recognize. Chris Dyer's triple-decker set, lit perceptively by Nick Chelton, placed the intimate scenes under the audience's nose but could expand into the Gibichung's hall – where different levels and joining steps helped focus the various reactions to developing narrative. Dyer had an inner stage at the top of this pile, with sliding doors that could reveal Brynhilde (as CBTO spelt her name) in magic sleep, or Günther and Gutrune enthroned. The arch below turned into Fafner's cave or the Rhine, equally effectively. Vick's team achieved wonders with few props, a careful lighting rig on three sides and generous puffs of dry ice. As Strehler claimed and showed, there is no theatrical smoke without imaginative fire.

Dove's virtuoso reorchestration sent one back to Wagner's original with extra alertness. From the third Act of Siegfried on, with Wagner taking up the project again after twelve years, the task of converting floods of intricate orchestral colour was more severe.

The late Wagner orchestra is no longer just big battalions, but high technology. *The Ring Saga* (as Vick named it, like Peter Brook's *Tragedy of Carmen* and *Impressions of Pelleas* not claiming to be the real thing) may have seemed more in the spirit of the younger Wagner, but it reflected the musical atmosphere of the finished work. Even with cuts, some narrations remained too long and the singers had difficulty sustaining energy and clarity. A *Siegfried* that was only fifteen minutes longer than the shortened *Rhinegold* was drastic; length and ponderousness are part of Wagner's magic. Nevertheless, CBTO's successful experiment had implications. Performers can take liberties with a classic text while honouring their obligations to the work: in opera, what is essentially the work (is it the actual orchestration or the language?) may be in contention. Vick's CBTO stagings shared with David Freeman's Opera Factory work a back to basics strength of conviction, an inventiveness spawned by necessity: their unluxurious opera, exploiting conventions familiar in Grotowskian Poor Theatre and also used by Peter Brook, benefited from rejecting the trappings of established rich-man's opera. Economy of means demands greater intensity and conviction to support the audience's belief in what they are being shown, and is also practical for touring.

Vick's ENO *Figaro* in 1991 was his first collaboration with Richard Hudson (born 1954) as designer since their work together on *The Wreckers*, *La vie parisienne* and *The Dragon of Wantley* for Cambridge Touring Opera (Vick's almost student company). Vick and Hudson's starry, brightly coloured, sharp new *Figaro* was unflashy and simple, until the fourth and final act in the garden which is often considered a dramaturgical problem with its string of portrait arias, and disingenuous intrigue. John Graham Hall's leering vain stork of a Basilio lost his aria (but Marcellina kept hers). Basilio's aria would have been an ideal prelude to the painful shadowplay of masters and servants that followed. It was a strong young cast, Bryn Terfel and Anthony Michaels-Moore as servant and master, Cathryn Pope the Susanna and Joan Rodgers the arch, delicate, socially vulnerable Countess. The psychotherapy of act 4 should always be the heart of the matter – and Vick and Hudson's unpretentious approach was clear about that. The whole production was designed physically to progress towards the final act, with each consecutive set using a larger amount of stage space. Each of the first three acts was dominated by a wall across the stage angled against a garden-green flat stretching diagonally into the depths and plain night-blue stage wings. Each wall contained the necessary doors and windows for the farcical proceedings, yellow in Figaro and Susanna's room-to-be, white in the Countess's bedroom (which had no bed), and red and gold for the Count's formal salon of judgment and betrothal. At the start all three walls were visible, ready lined up right behind each other. Props and furniture were sparse. The emphasis was on gorgeous, glowing, 1780s costumes, and bold, larger than life characterizations (the Georgian theatre of Sheridan, big enough to command the stage irresistibly).

Vick's style as usual worked with rather than against the *Figaro* tradition. A white-wigged flunkey swept open the powder-blue front curtain bearing the unusual translation of the title, *Figaro's Wedding*. In each act, as yet another wall was lifted out there was a palpable sense of penetrating deeper both into the stage of the Coliseum and into understanding. Finally the magical garden was reached ('beneath the silken touch of evening' as Jeremy Sams's translation put it) where, instead of clipped bay trees and crumbling garden statuary, Hudson assembled all the furniture from the earlier acts now painted green. Naturalistic sound-effects – foxes mating, dogs barking, owls hooting – atmospherically filled the pools of nocturnal silence between numbers. This last act was Vick's most astonishing *coup de théâtre* of all, using the basic convention of Peter Shaffer's farce *Black Comedy* – where the joke is that the electricity has failed and everybody has to feel their way around the set, though in fact the stage lights are full up. The fourth act began in front of the curtain. Barbarina's search for the pin could not really be outside, as often pointed out. Marcellina deplored human infidelity and Figaro sounded off for suffering husbands before the scene moved to the 'pine woods' of amorous celebration. When finally the front curtain opened, it revealed the stage extended to the maximum in all directions. It was clear with the help of Nick Chelton's plain flat lighting that, actually, nobody on stage could see anything at all. They were always bumping into each other or into the green doorways. The Count even hung up his coat on Figaro's arm, mistaking it for a branch. The painful emotions combined with guffaws of laughter from the audience. And because it was possible to see how masters and servants were reacting to the uncertain charades, it was clear what was really going on – as no doubt was the case in Mozart's day, before modern gas or electric lighting tempted the theatre to mimic night-time. Being able to see the faces, the words of Sams's crisp, witty new translation with its fast pace, clever rhymes and lovely jokes could be heard, and precisely what was happening in all the intrigue, and what was understood or not understood by the victims on stage, could all be precisely followed by the audience.

Thus Susanna's '*Deh, vieni*' was more evidently a sex invitation to the absent Count (as it was also in Peter Sellars's *Figaro* in the Trump Tower, New York). Susanna stretched herself amorously on the Countess's footstool, with Figaro a few inches away wincing and miserable at the 'betrayal'. Later Vick's virtuoso command of stage dynamics enabled the Countess to be 'discovered' mid-stage, suddenly, at the final point of forgiveness, without being seen to enter. This was a perfect setting for the charismatic first London Figaro of the young Welsh singer Bryn Terfel, who promises to be the most compelling singer-actor to emerge in Britain in the 20th century.

Vick's *Queen of Spades* in 1992 was Glyndebourne's last new production in the old Sussex opera-house, robustly accompanied and conducted with three star Russian singers, all of whom acted vocally as well as physically, with imposing power and range. All totally identified with the poetry of the text, passionately enunciated. The Herman (Yuri Marusin) could utter with thrilling naked raw attack at the top of his voice. But when the dramatic idea required, he refined down to mezza-voce and a calculated whisper. Like Jon Vickers he had a controversial sound and a style that compelled attention, overwhelmingly emotional and heartfelt, hysteria and desperation never far away. The match between vocal and theatrical means also suited Sergei Leiferkus's charming, worldly wise Count Tomsky, telling his stories with spell-binding musical and dramatic imagination, and Dimitri Kharitonov's dignified Yeletsky. Tchaikovsky's opera is difficult to cast outside Russia. The central role, the crazily obsessive officer Herman, is almost too hyper-romantic and morbid. Vick provided comedy as well as fatalistic desperation. The opera seemed fiercely relevant for an age without dreams or certainties. Vick, making a triumphant Glyndebourne debut, responded beautifully and wittily both to the pretensions of the 1890s Russian fin de siècle when Tchaikovsky was writing (gently guyed by the composer) and to the period flavour of the Pushkin story set a century earlier. As so often he balanced challenging theatricality and historical decorum. Richard Hudson's costume designs were Pushkin period: for

the men, fine bright uniforms that imposed a stilted strutting pos-
ture, or 18th-century suits; for the women long, figure-hugging
Empire frocks. The Countess's Pompadour rig was just the right
gorgeously detailed ritual garb, echo of past splendours and key
to status. Hudson's period conception appealed to escapist Glyndebourne audiences and was well judged, the sets interpretative,
not pictorial or simply naturalistic. The main image was of ink
scratching out a blackness at the heart of the stage, of a suicide
note penned in fury with ink blobs turning into bare wintry trees.
In the Summer Garden at St Petersburg or by the Winter Palace
canal there were metal railings to divide and focus the stage space.
In Lisa's room there was, beside the square piano, a simple blank
wall against which the chorus of friends crowded, with a door to
the balcony, and a ladder down which Herman (preceded by his
shadow) climbed. The masked ball contained a scenic tour de
force when a huge golden operatic staircase was lowered from the
ceiling to provide the ideal entrance space both for Herman and,
eventually, for the Empress Catherine (who was never actually
shown). It also provided a stand for the audience watching 'The
Faithful Shepherdess', choreographed wittily and with tongue-
in-cheek authenticity by Ron Howell. The morbidity, signalled
before the curtain rose with a death-angel above the skewed front
curtain, climaxed with skulls and skeletons in the red-lit gam-
bling-house at the end. Even here Vick managed further ballad
and folksy cutaways. It was a story-telling production which, like
a Russian doll, uncovered layer after dramatic layer. Vick's
relaxed yet disciplined direction of the conversations and
encounters captured all pain, insecurity, passion and bruising that
accompanied every exchange in this devastatingly truthful opera
with its flavour of dark gold and incense and occasional shafts of
wintry sunlight beside claustrophobia and a stifling breathless-
ness. When Vick explored the desperate urgency that marks Herman's intrusion on Lisa, every tiny movement was a compelling
reflection of psychological reality. Staged as a neurotic quadrille
of wooing, full of physical magnetism and love, it was totally
credible when Lisa committed herself later to Herman. These
were real passions, however pathological. Vick's lightness of
touch with the Russian elements and crowd movement, for
instance in the gambling denouement, half hellish, half comic,
reflected his sense of rhythm and theatrical energy.

After the 1994 announcement of Vick's new post as director of productions at Glyndebourne, he also took charge of the first new production in the virgin opera-house, a marvellously refined Y*evgeny Onyegin* (as Glyndebourne called it – Vick likes special names) with Andrew Davis, the Glyndebourne music director, conducting. The new Glyndebourne scale proved exactly suited both to Vick's busy wide-screen intimacy at the Larins' ball, with wonderfully detailed crowds flooding in and out of a pair of double doors, and also for figures in a deep landscape, the isolated Tatyana awaiting her climactic confrontations with Onyegin (in scenes 3 and 7), with just a pair of chairs for company at remote ends of a diagonal, facing out and away, symbolizing the tragic misfit of Pushkin's great romance. Unlike his 1989 ENO production, which tried to evoke all levels of Russian culture, Vick's Glyndebourne version avoided being architecturally too specific especially in the grandeur of the Gremins, where a series of shining silky grey curtains (near the front, at mid-stage, and at the back) were pulled backwards and forwards across the stage, editing and isolating a series of ironical and frankly comic social groups and scenes. (This scene was not a success in Vick's ENO staging.) Richard Hudson's design concept for the whole production was simple and beautiful. Before her climactic encounter with Onegin in the third scene Tatyana could be seen reading alone at a cornfield edge. The period costumes, as in the *Queen of Spades*, were 'correct' Pushkin-era.

The opening was very bare – just a seat and table and baskets at the front of the set on the right where the family group sat. At the front of the stage an opaque drape like voile bed-curtains drew aside to expose the set: evoking the bedroom scene where the crucial confessional letter would have to be written. The girls' duet echoed from off stage. The set was box-shaped, its back open to the 'countryside' behind a rush fence with a grey-specked-yellow distant horizon backdrop, plain pine floor and simple panelling. Tatyana on her first appearance sat on the ground at the back, reading. The peasants swept in from the right in a growing diagonal for their corn pageant. The dancing was just enough managed – as if they knew they were on show, making an effort for the Larins. Tatyana confessed her dreams from the footlights. There was a sweet little game between Olga and Tatyana over the book she had been reading. Lensky and Onegin on first appearance were strikingly youthful and romantic. Tatyana was about to leave when Onegin literally swept her into conversation. The poise and atmosphere Vick achieved, using lighting to suggest the lengthening shadows of a romantic evening, were both simple and beautiful.

Tatyana's bedroom was arranged across the stage – just the minimum requirements, bed, table, chair, washstand, window – bare and large, like the potential of her unfulfilled life. After starting to write at the table she swept the pages on to the floor – got down to basics. Elena Prokina's secret smiles, the sense of her daring and discovery, were beautiful – also her sense of impending physicality, feeling the locks of her hair, rolling herself over on the floor, the carefully paced unbuttoning of her increasingly romantic passion. After Filippyevna had taken the letter, where Vick's ENO Tatyana bared and studied her bosom at the conclusion of the Letter Scene, at Glyndebourne he had the glowing Prokina, so subtle, pure and full of colour and imagination in her singing, end by pouring an entire bowl of water over herself: in tellingly physical release.

The meeting with Onegin had a terrifying isolation. The female chorus of fruit-pickers – a line-up across the stage on tiptoe, holding each other's hands in criss-cross pattern – moved in a slow dance along the front of the stage. The voile curtain at the front followed them over. On the stage were a pair of metal garden chairs, arranged diagonally, Tatyana on the one at the back on the right facing upstage, reading. At the agitated music, Tatyana rose, faced out to the right, then sat at the front on the left. Onegin entered, came towards her, passed her; she went upstage to the other chair as he delivered his terrible rejection without any real communication with her – almost as if he were as terrified and vulnerable as she. He sat at the front, back to back with her. She remained rooted to the chair in desperation as he, going past her upstage, just turned slightly.

At the Larins, with a wall across the stage containing two double doors, Tatyana hid behind the one on the left to avoid the party, but got swept up into the action as guests moved into the front stage through the doors. Then a bit more furniture was brought in, a table and samovar. A sofa held shoulder high was carried to the side of the stage: a child hidden under its coverings suddenly – in excitement and delight – peeped out. Vick worked at the relationships, the gestures, the movement (with Ron Howell's witty acute choreography). As at ENO the event had been imagined in exhaustive and lovely detail, a gallery of types. The dancing flowed back and forth between the back and front rooms. Children and young lads played, balancing on the bottom of upturned benches: real vitality and fun, however formalized the chorus-lines in the music. The fatal row between Lensky and Onegin blew up, unmistakably pointed, with Onegin's casual decision to wind up Lensky nicely explained. Lensky delivered the challenge with superb misery and rage – his body knotted with indignation. The delightful Olga was devastated, abandoned, at this falling-out. Vick was master of all the stage choral movement, painting in all the extraordinary detail. The Larins' ball is one of the two great contrasts with the essentially private processes of this emotional drama.

The privacy of the duel had an even more interior feeling than usual because it was observed from inside the barn where Lensky awaited Onegin, singing his farewell poem beside a pile of hay. This was Vick's most daring departure, though his staging was generally less simple and straightforward than it looked. The actual duel was outside the doors of a barn, the shots fired with the contestants out of sight, backed off to either side: the result was revealed by the return of Onegin, with Zaretsky's voice off stage. Onegin slowly, desperately moved down-stage as the curtain fell.

With a youthful cast, the ageing process for the final two grand scenes was carefully observed. Vick and Howell used the initial polonaise of the third act, with three ranks of opening and closing grey 'silk' curtains across the stage, to isolate a pas de deux, little cameos and dances, satirizing the upper-class St Petersburg scene with three frustrated females beating their fists on the floor and exquisite young men in elegant dances and poses. This gave a marvellous lift to the mood and released the tension before the closing tragic seriousness. There was a real Polonaise and Ecossaise with full chorus as well, in addition to the carefully staged satire. Gremin and Tatyana in grand choreographic sweeps reflected the restraint of Vick's staging as a whole. Each gesture was minutely observed. At the end of the scene Onegin pulled down the grey curtain at the back, revealing the original yellow-specked back-cloth. His circumstances had not changed. The final confrontation between Tatyana and Onegin mirrored in its restraint his third-scene rejection of her letter. Two Empire-style chairs were where the metal garden chairs had been. The way her arm collapsed from her breast had magic potency when, just before determining not to give way, she admitted in the final confrontation to still loving Onegin. Vick got Onegin's progress towards ever more desperate, more physical demonstration exactly right – but never let the basic restraint and delicacy be shattered. In some respects Vick's ENO staging of 1989 was more daring, but this later production was better judged and more precise in visual taste. Vick is the most consistently successful of all the new British producers, though he does not challenge the imaginative bravery and sheer theatrical genius of Richard Jones. His problem can be a certain insensitivity. Directing opera is a macho business, and the operas that have not suited Vick – Tippett's *Midsummer Marriage* at Covent Garden for instance – have been treated by him with a certain cavalier brusqueness and impatience. *The Midsummer Marriage* may seem clumsy and over-naive in its characterizations and philosophizing. But its affirmations and suggestive psychology can affect the audience profoundly if handled with delicacy and not allowed to seem too lumpen and awkward. Vick brought the story down to earth, made the mysterious Ancients tediously ridiculous, and failed to sort out a gently comic narrative that should prompt rather than satisfy imagination.

But *King Arthur or The British Worthy* in 1995 for the well-subsidized Châtelet in Paris, designed by Paul Brown, using a cast of 75, and with Vick's choreographer Ron Howell perfectly melding modern and Baroque movement, displayed Vick's robust organizational skill and perceptiveness at their most potent. Nobody before ever quite proved that semi-opera, the form into which Purcell poured such genius, could really work, be funny, moving and theatrically spell-binding. Brown had studied Dryden as a student, and Vick responded to the text's un-Shakespearian muscularity and directness, its affectionate English sense of irony. *King Arthur* was designed so that the music and visual elements of the play were as important as the words. Thus Vick resisted cleaning the material up, adjusting it to modern taste as most previous producers had done, or cutting any scene changes. Transformations were the name of the game in Purcell's Dorset Gardens theatre, and Vick did them proud: 'Our Britain really rises from the waves.' He and Brown rejected the authenticity of evoking the periwigged era of the Restoration and the Glorious Revolution, a time of low esteem for the English (rather like today), and a style that few now associate with the vigour of Purcell and Dryden. They were gently patriotic without tongue in cheek, but with humour: hence the final Masque's parade of plucky Brit heroes in the Second World War who stood up and were counted. It took a large budget, but *King Arthur* was vindicated by Vick, triumphantly and joyously. To hear the song 'Fairest Isle' in its original theatrical context was stirring (even in Veronique Gens's *communautaire* English): this was colourful dancing pantomime topped with ingenuous moral debate. The designs mostly combined heraldic bright colours, playing-card outlines, samurai attitudes, and unashamedly naive theatrical magic games with stage effects, which suited Vick's belief that going to the theatre is partly 'to become a child again', something 20th-century anguish about the future of opera can obscure. *King Arthur* was meant to be fun.

Dryden's touching and slightly absurd love story about Arthur and Blind Emmeline blends notions from Shakespeare's *Tempest*, *Dream* and *Henry IV*. The work is more than 50 per cent spoken text: only two characters sing as well as speak, the devil Grimbald and the spirit Philidel – in Vick's version nonchalantly acted and stylishly sung by Jonathan Best and Claron McFadden, often floating on wires above the set. For the spoken acting Vick avoided the cinema- or television-style that sits ill with classical English. Text, rather than psychology, was the starting point. The words dictated how the characters materialized, the opposite of Method. But that is Vick's directing technique in opera anyway. The performance was reminiscent of the 1960s Royal Shakespeare Company *Wars of the Roses* cycle: the rhetoric was projected with old-style RSC brio. The verse rang through the Châtelet, and the story sprang to life. The scenic tricks charmed, and looked ravishing. The emotions were touched. Brown's epic warrior costumes strutted and marched. Dancers and chorus singers were constantly switching masks – at one point becoming the bushes poking up through holes in the stage in the enchanted forest. A false Emmeline emerged from a giant tree, threatened with Arthur's axe. In bright royal blue the children's book pictorialism included a dragon-painted canvas screen and readily sprouting hedges and walls. A rising sun image on a screen at the back of the stage changed colour and, masking exits and entrances, speeded the scene changes. The impression was of a Pollock's toy theatre come to life. The ice masque with Cupid on a string blowing lust to melt the scene gave way to a final apotheosis of white cliffs of Dover, shepherds and sheep, Morris dancers in a barn, and the parade of heroes suspended like Christmas tree decorations around Britannia. There was a real atmosphere of release in the celebration of the end of war when suddenly the corn came up on the set and ordinary Kentish lads were singing about another way of looking at life. This sort of game required totally confident, secure judgment and taste. The disparate elements married perfectly. The biggest success perhaps was Howell's unaffected, exuberant dancing – in which, eventually, the whole chorus joined. To restore *King Arthur* was an important achievement at the tercentenary of Purcell's death.

Stephen Lawless's best work seems to fit quite closely in style and manner beside Vick's – though he was not a disciple in any sense. His thoughtful 1989 Glyndebourne Touring Opera staging of *Death in Venice* dug behind Britten's superficially respectable debate about truth and beauty to the tragic heart of the matter – that the paedophile infatuation in the Thomas Mann plot, unspoken, unexplained, may be a dead-end abyss as Aschenbach's line says: 'What if all were dead, and only we two left alive?' The sexuality contradicts the symbolism. With its guilt, tortuous ambivalence of feeling and barren love, *Death in Venice* presents the tragic dilemma in acknowledging homosexuality and recognizing its limitations. Lawless put this homosexual agonizing centre-stage in Robert Tear's imaginatively sung, truthful performance – for which Ian Spink's uncamp choreography (revised and improved at the production's 1992 revival) was a crucial context. As the last veils lift from Britten's life story, prurience is out of place. The terrible sadness of his music reveals all. However much he wanted to keep control and preserve privacy, the emotional deprivation was crying to be heard. Tear's Aschenbach presented that passion, vulnerable, unashamed, and desperate.

Britten was destined to deal over and over again with the unhappiness of unrequited homosexual love, and what the humbug about sex had done and was still doing to society – while the freedoms and maturity he campaigned for were not available to him personally. Yet he was proselytizing not for homosexuality, but for humanity. Tobias Hoheisel's romanticized classical designs provided a quick-changing, flexible, idealized environment, a cell with the promise of bliss always distant. There was almost no connection between Tear's ghost in Venice and the life he observed, except through the mediation of Alan Opie's superbly witty, ominous, gloriously sung chorus figure. The naturalistic hints were entirely viewed through Aschenbach's eyes. Daniel Squire's 17-year-old Tadzio, looking as lovely as Princess Di, remained unconscious and unsexual throughout.

Matthew Richardson is a protégé of Vick's, having often been lighting director for Vick's productions. But he is also a producer and in 1991 mounted one of the most remarkable stagings ever of Britten's *A Midsummer Night's Dream* – in Swedish for Norrlands Opera in a 270-seat variable space in the covered-over courtyard of what used to be the local fire-station of Umea. The interpretation was funny, honest and at times devastatingly moving. It showed that the Mechanicals need not be patronized and that Britten did give the young lovers enough red-blooded romantic energy in a work that is often staged as Baroque pantomime with cute exploitation of choirboys and a countertenor. As in *Rosenkavalier*, the feelings and comic perceptiveness are far profounder than the musical and dramatic material initially and superficially suggest.

The imaginative genius of Britten's fairy music is unquestionable. Richardson proved that, if you take the fairy king Oberon's motivation and character seriously, he is key to the opera's structure and can make it as subversive and intelligent a drama as the Shakespeare original, where the subject is both the reality of love and the nature of perception. The humour which focuses on the issue of truth and credibility in the theatre, and how the imagination operates – in speculation and experiment, on the personal and the scientific level – had usually been treated (especially in the case of the opera) as a mere childish game. Should one's point of view be Oberon's, or Puck's (the playful Robin Goodfellow), or Theseus's, or Bottom's, or one of the lovers'? A crucial issue with Britten is how to deal with the generous, slice-of-life cameos into which he breathed such recognizable but easily patronized lifelikeness. His operatic composition is superior to his songs precisely because his libretti are mostly not 'great literature' and his melody has to transform them. Richardson transposed this *Dream* to modern Sweden – though, in a world that played in the right perspective with pixies and Bottom's ass's head, the period was immaterial. The theatricality was unfettered. The adolescent Puck was flown about the stage mechanically on wires like Peter Pan: his ten pixies stuck their heads in vertical formation through the heavy earth-coloured curtains that cloaked the wide acting space at the start. But these theatrical fun and games were never an end in themselves, just the stuff of the poetic metaphor through which the humane wisdom of this wide-ranging drama was revealed. Magical theatre, and particularly magic opera in Handel's time, represents a special genre, which in the context of today's most adventurous operatic productions needs to be recognized. The transformations, visual metaphors, insecurity about what is inside or outside, contradictions of scale with disproportionately large furniture in tiny houses, can be potently effective in an *Alice in Wonderland* way as part of the armoury of a producer like Richard Jones. The management of reality in the theatre and opera-house is no new problem and opportunity – though some objectors to modern productions quickly declaring (like Victor Meldrew), 'I don't believe it', are blithely unconcerned about whether they *should* believe what they are offered, or *what* they should believe. If 'I don't believe it' is translated as 'I won't play with you', the truth about the criticisms becomes clearer.

The unconventionally shaped space (a 'shoebox' divided lengthways between seating and stage) put the audience in the same room as the performance. The stage, which flowed round the corners of the bench-seating for the spectators, was covered with tiny pebbles and surrounded by prefabricated concrete panels, one of which turned out to be rubber when Puck dived through it and disappeared – about to girdle the earth in no time. On the left the pebbled floor of Lars Ostbergh's set gave way to a little copse of delicate leafy trees opening on to another space, a world beyond, a room or courtyard out back. Above the stage there was an upper level catwalk below which Tytania's little bower, like a catacomb slab, was later revealed. She climbed to it up a loft-ladder that dropped down when she was ready for bed. The orchestra was placed in a pit even more submerged than usual, between stage and audience, which helped the excellent balance and acoustics. These physical arrangements helped the audience to observe and overhear, as Oberon would. Rather than fairy-tale pictures framed in a proscenium, this was Britten and Shakespeare's private world where characters exposed their true emotions – making themselves delightfully ridiculous into the bargain.

The Swedish countertenor Mikael Bellini as Oberon, who was neither camping it up nor playing games, wore a black velvet frock-coat and trousers, with a noble silver wig, and performed the part as a normal passionate operatic role. This masculine Oberon was as physically potent as Christina Falk's Tytania with her velvet gown, white slip and long Sutherland-as-Lucia wig (suggesting the coloratura Britten provided was not superficial, decorative and fairy-like, but neurotic and potentially bloody).

Richardson's *Dream* wasn't classless, just because it was Swedish. Britten's sense of class was as feeling and acute as Mozart's. Lysander and Hermia here wore yuppy mix-and-match casual clothes (he a waistcoat and denim blouson, she plainly braless). They were much more laid back and natural in feeling than Demetrius and Helena, who suggested a merchant banker and his doggedly devoted secretary (with properly supportive undergarment). At one delightful moment, Helena took off her high-heeled shoes to shake out some stones, and had to go chasing after Demetrius uncomfortably barefoot. As the experiments in Shakespeare's advertent (and Puck's inadvertent) love laboratory proceeded, the lovers became increasingly dishevelled, ragged and bloody, torn by brambles and cruelties. The crescendo of mutual violence reached a peak when Puck threw a firebucket full of water into poor, devastated Hermia's face. Some of the audience found that excessive and shocking, though Britten probably had it in him.

The Mechanicals were a typical Scandinavian work-team: Snout with a dirty face and welder's protective goggles was a modern tinker; Starveling was an old chap in a dapper two-piece without jacket, all set to measure inside legs. For their first entry the gang actually broke into the set, knocking a 'jagged' hole in the breezeblock wall on the right. Their theatrical adventure was dislocating and displaced. Equally the tale of Pyramus and Thisbe was a relevant parable, both for this tri-focal opera's thematic examination of human desire and for its wide comic range. Flute was a gungho young lout, much embarrassed initially by the demands of the Thisbe role, but transmuted finally into a lusciously liberated, funny drag act. Bottom's transformation achieved comic terror among his mates, so natural was the ass's head. The absurdity grew serious with the frank sexiness of Bottom's coupling with Tytania, vanishing from view only when the entwined pair lasciviously descended through a pantomime trapdoor into discreet privacy below. The coda with Theseus and Hippolyta, after the lovers had awoken from all the pain and grief of their midsummer nightmare, torn clothes mended, scratches healed, was like a modern Swedish wedding party. Theseus entered in black tie and tails, his Hippolyta in white frock and veil.

Richardson's coup was to show that Oberon, when observing the trauma which Puck's mischief had brought the lovers, was genuinely disturbed and challenged by what he saw, recognizing the mirror of his own tiff with Tytania. David Parry conducted more slowly and expressively than Britten on record, and the Swedish text was clearly comprehensible. The slow pace emphasized the intensity and passion of the music, and prepared for the moral transformation when Oberon, arrested in his course like Wotan by a sombre drum-roll, determined to set things right. Music and dramaturgy were organically linked. In opera it should be the case that everything meant by the dramatic process is figured both in music and in the theatrical interpretation.

The lighting, on which Richardson (well known as a lighting designer) collaborated with the set designer Ostbergh, carefully structured the narrative while sustaining the stormy intriguing atmosphere. The athletic, entranced and obsessive 15-year-old Puck (Kristian Widell), his nose pressed against the glass of a sweetshop window packed with sexuality and passion, was extraordinary. Richardson's *Dream* staging plumbed the depth and drama in Britten's opera, and this studied neo-realist approach really made the work seem newly minted.

12 Albery, Pimlott, Cairns: British expressionism

Tim Albery's 1986 staging (for Opera North, Leeds) of *The Capture of Troy*
first part of The Trojans) designed by Antony McDonald and Tom Cairns:
Ronald Hamilton's Aeneas reports back to John Hall's Priam and Pauline
Thulborn's Hecuba. Photograph © Andrew March.

The relationship between producer and designer, who takes the initiative or provides the leadership, is central to operatic interpretation and a highly personal issue. In opera, set and costume designs must usually be settled long before rehearsals start, so design decisions are the matrix or crucible for the process of staging to a greater extent than the power of the visual in theatre would anyway dictate. Tim Albery (born 1952) has explored this relationship more extensively than any other producer in this book because his early successes – in opera certainly – were achieved in collaboration with not just one but a pair of designers, with whom he formed a sort of troika: Tom Cairns (born 1952) and Antony McDonald (born 1950). It is not unusual for opera producers to work with different designers for the sets and the costumes. But in the case of Albery, Cairns and McDonald, in effect, the three collaborated equally on all aspects of production rather than specialising in separate departments. They were dramaturgs for each other, and their best work as a result had an extraordinary depth of focus – in the context of non-naturalistic and expressionist interpretations. This sharing differed, for example, from the relationship between David Alden and his frequent designer David Fielding. Alden's expressionism has represented a similar aesthetic, but stems overwhelmingly from the working out through particular performances of the producer's highly individual and powerful dramaturgical vision. Fielding set the environment in which Alden worked, with all its provocations and stimuli, but was less inclined to share in editing the process of production – as the Albery troika did.

The different attitudes and disciplines the three brought to bear on their collaboration stemmed from their very varied origins. Albery, academically speaking the brains of the operation, came from the famous London theatre-owning family and had been at Oxford before joining a post-graduate drama course at Manchester University – where he met McDonald, who had trained as an actor at the Central School of Speech and Drama. Together they worked with the Australian choreographer Ian Spink (a Merce Cunningham disciple) for the first time at the

Institute of Contemporary Arts in London on a theatre version of Peter Carey's *War Crimes* in the early 1980s, which used movement in a potent and non-naturalistic way. Spink, who also worked for Alden, was not an intimate part of the arrangement but represented a crucial aspect of their shared aesthetic: in fact what Spink had to say about their shared aims and objectives is highly relevant. When Albery and McDonald first encountered Cairns, who had been a teacher of art at school level, he was a student in Margaret Harris's design course at Riverside Studios. The three then joined forces on productions of *Venice Preserv'd* and *Hedda Gabler* at the Almeida Theatre, before launching into opera with Michael Tippett's *The Midsummer Marriage* for Opera North in Leeds in 1985, also later borrowed by Scottish Opera.

The mixture of their input – preparing their joint productions – was the vital point. Cairns was a real and talented painter with his own craft and style, and a strongly personal feeling for colour and abstract shapes. McDonald was more inclined to researching the right conceptual stimulus – closer in a sense to the method of Stefanos Lazaridis and his model box. Albery presided over the process and mobilized the acting, both of individual performers and of the chorus. In the context of their unusual settings, a variety of elements, similar in some ways to the work David Fielding provided for David Alden, though with more abstract and artistic details, required a great deal of scrupulous direction and much simple, subtle, psychological support for the performances. The mark of all the three's work was its rejection of boundaries and borderlines – just as Spink's response to the physical side of theatre allowed no real distinction to be made between acting and dancing. Spink, discussing his work on the Ritual Dances and other parts of *Midsummer Marriage*, said: 'Ideally when people see this they should get lots of ideas about what it is. I hope people don't get hung up on the fact that they can't connect it together, or it's not making logical sense.' He had provided the gopak for Alden's ENO *Mazeppa* – 'a series of disturbing images that were thrown in,' as he explained. Significantly, Spink (who created the Second Stride modern dance company with Richard Alston and Siobhan Davies) had also worked with McDonald and Christopher Fettes on a remarkable Scottish Opera production of Handel's *Orlando* in May 1985, a few months before the Tippett in Leeds, providing his movement group of ten with a striking pavane for lunatics and Victorian nurses, full of neurotic darting swoons and female strictness. Fettes was one of the founders in the early 1960s of the Drama Centre, a Method-based continental-orientated acting school formed by a group of refuseniks from the Central School of Speech and Drama. *Orlando* exploited Spink's and McDonald's affinity for magic and irrationalism which suited both the story (*Orlando furioso*) and Fettes's emphasis on going with emotional instincts. Fettes sadly did not continue in opera, but Albery pursued a very similar line of intensity and conviction in his work jointly with Cairns and McDonald. When Cairns went his own way as a producer/designer, he had as his essential associate the choreographer Aletta Collins.

To call the work of any or all of these talents expressionist is to stretch the word beyond its historical associations in the 1920s. But their common factor was a rejection of naturalism, a belief in an expressive and emotional visual discursiveness, and a conviction that the purpose of theatrical representation was not to define the nature of the work, to limit it to a particular narrative context, but to stimulate the audience's response to the material generally and its sub-textual associations. As Albery put it, 'A visual idea or an attitude can colour everything.' Movement and image are tools of free expression in this kind of theatre. The 20th century is the age of the moving image. Pop videos, performance art, television advertisements, and contemporary dance share methods and agendas. Movement, however unnatural it looks, however little it belongs within a normal social or narrative context, is expressive. The less natural the action on stage, the more audiences wonder why and what it portends. If the static image is telling enough, how much more moving can the moving image be? The shared theatrical taste of Albery, McDonald, Cairns and Spink was not drawn from Pina Bausch – but her target areas were similar. Spink through Bausch came to recognize the error of his previous assumption that 'performers shouldn't risk damaging themselves, or making a mess of themselves in front of an audience – as her performers did, destroying themselves on stage, exposing themselves quite ruthlessly. It was like gladiators, Roman games.' Instead he saw that 'one couldn't float around the stage and be very natural and organic all one's life. Certain areas of the subconscious I had never touched.' The collaboration between the three Ts (Tim Albery, Tom Cairns and Tony McDonald) and between Albery and either Cairns or McDonald was remarkably fertile and survived after Cairns had stopped working as a designer, though in the late 1980s Albery turned to other designers as well as McDonald – Hildegard Bechtler or Stewart Laing.

The primary model for Tippett's first opera, *The Midsummer Marriage* (1953), was *Die Zauberflöte*, parent of German-language opera. Albery's staging told the story simply and expressively, setting it in the 1950s when it was written in order to 'let it resonate without pinning it down too much'. Thus Albery found a simple answer for the slightly prudish, period sexuality of the lower-class couple Jack and Bella (Tippett's less substantial and more patronized version of Papageno and Papagena) with their naive innocence and uncorrupted view of the world: as if taken from Ealing Comedies and *The Man in the White Suit*. The somewhat embarrassing jokes of the piece are largely left to this pair. The chorus women and men hurrying into the 'clearing in the wood' where 'anything might happen', and where Mark was to get engaged to Jenifer, wore 1950s glad rags like the wedding guests in the film *Room at the Top*. The theme of Tippett's foot-tapping, throat-throbbing bundle of joyous music is the enlightenment of two parallel pairs of engaged couples – or in a way just the one more elevated pair, in this scenario, unlike *Die Zauberflöte*, via all sorts of semi-mystical developments. Mark, who in the first scene is bursting like a lark with ululating love-song, provides an essential ingredient of the brave new British operatic world that Britten and Tippett had conjured into existence after the Second World War. (Before that, opera in Britain was very largely a foreign art.) The Albery staging presented *Midsummer Marriage* as a sort of British *Bartered Bride*, its comedy as ethnic as its music, with Shavian quips and a thoroughly old-Left view of the world. Working man rebels against boss. Woman leads and decides. The people are bolshie. Tippett's score weaves together Elgar, Purcell, Thomas Morley and Vaughan Williams with a sense of dramatic order resembling *Meistersinger*. Behind the mysterious rituals to which Mark and Jenifer subject themselves there is a kind of neo-classical mythological tradition in which Fraser's *Golden Bough* is blended with the Jungian theory of dreams and a fatalistic pseudo-Hindu sense of worldly ebb and flow.

Their sloped post-modern set was equally a blend of places and notions. Cairns explained: 'We did not want to over-conceptualize. We wanted to abstract and generalize – not to be obscure, but so people could not say "Oh, it's like that" and stop thinking about it.' They did want the events to come alive, but not in a literal sense. A glass office block at the back on half-submerged classical foundations had, to one side, a lawn, to the other a road and then cinema seats (the world of the 1950s imagination) that merged into green branches. Albery relied on this surrealistic set, on the dancers choreographed by Ian Spink who dominated the second act, and on some of the chorus actions to suggest the fertile jungle or jumble of ideas and references in Tippett's more or less impervious text. His aim was to avoid being too indicative and straightforward, to avoid any sense of normality or actual happening, which was the failing of the Graham Vick production at Covent Garden, with its unbelievable and not very interesting characterizations that felt as if they were supposed to be realistic. The chorus procession in the third act with individuals held aloft in strange classical poses was extraordinary. Albery remembered King Fisher's limp (the tradition of the ritual murder of a lame fisher king was outlined in *The Golden Bough*), though he did not make heavy weather of it. Only the Hindu element of the giant lotus bloom containing the lovers (as proposed by Tippett's stage directions for the climax of the third act) was omitted. The symbols were not laboured – as they were in David Pountney's ENO staging (also 1985), to little effect. Few in Leeds would have known that Jenifer, after her ascent to heaven up a giant staircase on the left of stage, was thereafter as far-seeing as Athena, or that Mark, after his descent to hell through the roof of a 1950s apparently petrified car on a motorway on the right, had become a Bacchic figure. But then the composer himself said he did not want such things explicit.

The great aria of the clairvoyant Madame Sosostris (out of the first part of *The Waste Land* – T. S. Eliot had advised Tippett to be his own librettist) was delivered from a little chamber inside a giant inflatable gypsy. Dressed in cardigan and wedge shoes, she was sipping a cup of tea, reassuring and suburban, as she sang. She also stands for Tippett himself, the artist imagining life's true meaning, and therefore Albery had her contemplating earlier scenes as an anonymous, rather prosaic observer. At the end of the opera she watered the lawn on stage in front of a redbrick industrial-suburb view that was a final cloth dropped over the back of the set, while two children attempted to tidy the mess round a little model car on the right, just where Mark's gates to hell had been. This was a delicate hint at all the diverting asides and rich suggestions that might be prompted in an exploration of Tippett's work.

Ian Spink's balletic modern choreography for the Ritual Dances tautly projected the ecological narrative of the struggle in Nature for life and death, or perhaps its parallel in human domestic conflict. There was fine dancing from Spink's movement group led by Mark Ashman's Strephon, and generally the choreography closely matched Albery's response to the music and exploration of buried meaning in the acting performances. The interrupted first act Ritual Dance, done in Leeds in body-stockings, had been fitted with folksy white Greek costumes by the time Albery revived the production in Glasgow. The show was stolen by Patricia O'Neill's Bella, the perfect model of a comic secretary, able to do her hair and make-up while blithely singing.

One of the first projects dreamed up by Nicholas Payne when he moved from being controller of finance of WNO to become general director of Opera North was a joint production of *The Trojans*, to be directed by Albery and designed by Cairns and McDonald, and to be shared between Opera North, WNO and Scottish Opera. This *Trojans* proved to be a keynote production of the 1980s which established the new German-influenced or German-aware style more widely than ever before in Britain. The production, in English initially, emerged in two stages – with the Fall of Troy created in Leeds, and Carthage in Cardiff. Visually, Troy ravaged by war was indicated with an enclosed space backed by a smeared stormy abstract backdrop, and the suffering inhabitants in dirty ragged black togs careering down a curving slope at the back of the set. Albery caught the clangorous violence of this terrified doomed world, its horizon narrowing finally to the high-up chamber in which the women kill themselves. Earlier the walls had photos of victim heroes attached to them. The hysteria of the crowd movements at the start, rushing, crawling, contrasted very strikingly with the repose of the hierarchical leaders, Cassandra in red, Priam and Hecuba in purple, Chorebus in royal blue, Andromache (a danced role) in white. This made a telling contrast with the golden culture objects, almost like museum displays. Troy was shown desperate, hysterical, terminal, impelled in short order to the suicidal heroism of the Trojan women smothering their bairns and garrotting each other in a boxed-off room high up under the proscenium. It was a compelling evocation of the people's endless chain of sacrifice, the exhaustion of war. The entry of Andromache was choreographed (by Spink) in a swift line that contradicted the funereal music. Lucy Burge danced the role with painful emotion.

Andromache's reaction to the suffering, heroic male figure of Hector shown on the armour-plated wall at the back, and her relationship with Hector's son were equally poignant. McDonald and Cairns's designs were restrained and suggestive. The actual physical space of the Trojan scenes contracted as the war moved in on the falling city. Colour heightened the emotions. The changing shape and focus of the stage was also evocative. The set opened up at the back, with two narrow strips of red rising to the flies on either side of the proscenium ultimately to form a frame for the suicide room with wider metallic strips behind. The physical difficulty for the chorus of working on the slope at the back was potently expressive. The costumes, like the sets, were simple and stark, with some armour and shields in Troy, but no literal mimicking of 'historical' style. For Scottish Opera, Katherine Ciesinski's Cassandra (the role created by her sister Kristine in Leeds) turned herself into a convincing and terrifying image of the *'noir vautour'* (black vulture) mentioned in Berlioz's text, threatening the city with talons or fingers extended, crucified by apprehension, expressive gestures to match her vocal subtlety.

Carthage by contrast was ordered, vulnerable, civilized, with hammer, sickle, ship and cattle as prevailing images – though finally reduced to as parlous a state as Troy by the scale of Dido's frustrated commitment to Aeneas. To start with Albery emphasized the arts of peace, by contrast with Troy, expansive, warm domesticity – an almost Victorian family group around Dido. The stage was a white room, with four little statues of bulls on the back wall. In front was a three-part sloping walkway from which Dido addressed the assembly, with plain whitewashed planks for the floor: a neutral, almost informal setting. The development of Dido's passion for Aeneas, which happens more in the interstices of scenes, was fully described in dances that suggested nature and the hunt. Berlioz's opera invites a balletic dimension, which Spink's choreography for his Second Stride group (as in Opera North's *Midsummer Marriage*) innovatively provided both for the Royal Hunt and Storm and for the later interrupted celebrations. Suddenly in the Royal Hunt the forequarters of a vast jaguar jutted from the wings halfway across the stage – in the background was a suspended map of Africa in relief. Spink blended ballet and folk-dance, with contemporary and ethnic elements, in the staging of the purely orchestral parts of the opera. Dancers in classical ballet tutus reminded one of the cultural norms, the native French taste for the art of ballet, that formed the environment Berlioz worked in when he was creating his epic statement about violence and society. Carthage is ruled by a woman, and Albery emphasized the sense of ease and tolerance stemming from that. Iopas was a sort of Berlioz figure in black velvet jacket, taking the odd swig from a hip flask to boost his courage as he rather melancholically performed his court-poet duty, hymning Ceres. Narbal in dark suit and soft hat conveyed a similar sense of benevolent social concern. Dido of course wore widow's black: Coco Chanel demonstrated the power of the little black number, with or without sleeves. The separation between the ruling group and the ruled was indicated with a kind of affectionate informality. The dignified dances of builders, sailors and farmers (colour-coded yellow, blue and earth-red) had an entirely natural, gentle feeling, carnival-like rather than a demonstration of trade-union power. Their movements resembled Morris dancers, which fitted the ritual perfectly and reinforced the musical atmosphere. Albery showed both Dido's and Aeneas's people as refugees bent on creating a good life, if necessary with some cynical cheating. That sense of civilization was vital.

The tragedy of the final act was prefigured and precipitated with a theatrical coup. There was the chilling visitation of a blood-boltered Mercury, grinding his sword across the stage at the conclusion of act 4. There were also some rare shafts of social comedy in the sentries' dialogue just before Aeneas's great betrayal. Cairns and McDonald's setting here had an anticipatory and naturalistic high cliff on the right of the stage providing a sheltered look-out from which Hylas could sing his sweet, plaintive, homesick, poignant, long-arched song. At the close of the opera, instead of a funeral pyre, Cairns and McDonald gave Dido a red-covered metal Victorian bedstead, on which, assisted by Anna, she committed suicide. The bed was set in the seaside mud, silhouetted against a dark blue night-sky backdrop with a sort of *trompe-l'oeil* door where the adored Trojans made their definitive departure, escaping into dreamland – and history.

Britten's naval opera (*Billy Budd*) was Albery's first very finely crafted ENO staging in 1988. Albery identified Captain Vere obviously with the librettist E. M. Forster. Vere fails to come to the aid of the beautiful young sailor, who is falsely accused by Master-at-Arms Claggart and accidentally kills him. Officers, midshipmen and captain were smart blue-uniformed players in a Hollywood-style theme park ('the 18th-century naval experience'). Sailors, apart from a misty near-engagement with the French, were extras from Eisenstein's *Battleship Potemkin* – brutalized by posturing overseers in leather berets wielding staves and whips. The self-parodying sado-masochism made the opera's simplification of reality seem like monochrome weakness. Albery didn't get laughs, as he should have, from the comic racist trio ('Don't like the French'). Britten's second grand opera is even more naive and traditional in its structure than *Peter Grimes*. The lyrical music is far more ambiguous and subtle than the plot. Vere's guilty obsession with the sailors, signalled controversially when Albery's staging was new by Philip Langridge's action in getting down on his hands and knees and pressing his ear to his cabin floor to overhear their shanties, was omitted later when Albery revived his staging. Thomas Allen's emotional maturity and experience (as the original ENO *Budd*) lent power and weight to Albery's handling of the contemplative death-song as Billy awaited his dawn execution in shackles and was fed by the old salt Dansker. One of the most visually striking and memorable scenes showed the sailors stacked and cross-sectioned in cabins below deck – the sloping stage like a battleship in storm with its grey funnel and sombre back-cloth. *Budd* brought Albery's slightly disjunct intensity to reinforce the stylistic revolution of Peter Jonas's ENO.

Albery's *Peter Grimes* was less well calculated. It did not explain why Grimes was so hated by the Borough community, omitting any hints of the homosexual sub-text that Britten imposed on the original Crabbe poem. It also rigorously avoided the usual Borough cameos, at the expense of making the supporting cast seem colourless and the grim situations without humour. The village 'characters' became cyphers of intolerance, powerless against the lynch-mob mentality. Albery's direction was cool and mechanical, not exploring motivations. The presentation of the Borough as a single-minded monochrome monster, instead of an ambivalent web of conflicting opinions, deflated the tragedy. Britten, who understood both sides of the equation that Albery reduced to a mass ritual, showed in *Grimes* how intolerance and persecution arise from personal misapprehensions. (Mrs Sedley: 'It's more than suspicion now; it's fact.') Albery, working with Hildegard Bechtler (as he had in Bregenz for his staging of *La Wally*), turned the chorus scenes into stylized production numbers like some hard-working joke-free musical comedy. There were many freeze-frame moments, arms held hysterically akimbo.

Bechtler's severe and economical collaboration with Albery on the 1884 four-act Scala version of Verdi's *Don Carlos* for Opera North generated real theatrical excitement. Problem work *Carlos* may be, but Albery focused its intimate political drama challengingly at the front of the stage. In a small theatre there could not be the epic scale that Visconti achieved at Covent Garden, but Albery brilliantly exploited the emotional fervour of his male stars, John Tomlinson's passionately abrasive Philip and Anthony Michaels-Moore's beautifully sung, youthful, heartfelt Rodrigo. From time to time a scene such as Philip sleepless at his desk was framed by the lowering of a biscuit-coloured frontdrop with a square, room-sized opening cut out of it on the left to act as a sort of close-up. Bechtler's set used towering sombre walls, with back-cloths distressed and more mildly abstract than usual, the cracked floor arranged to channel stage movements dynamically. The production happened mostly at floor-level, apart from the striking *auto da fé* conclusion, with victims mounting a vertiginous ladder into the flies, struggling heavenwards, heading for a massive pyre off stage. The drama between characters was tight and meaningful, and Charles Edwards's lighting underlined the purity and simplicity of the stage pictures. Nicky Gillibrand's sombre period costumes (interestingly a mixture of 1860s and 1560s) suggested history without being fetishistic or merely decorative. The stylized choreography of the chorus had the atmosphere of Dutch or Spanish group portraits: dark blues, silvers, an angry red glow at the bottom of a back wall, a striking effigy set into the ground, a thicket of sticks for the rebelling masses, impressively stark elements.

Sometimes characters were 'discovered' already on stage when the frontdrop rose. The King suddenly appeared in the garden with Elizabeth and Rodrigo, Marquis of Posa. The Grand Inquisitor at first remained still despite his mobile wormlike music. The brusque Philip was stuck in vicelike regal impassiveness, his private thoughts uttered in whispery tones of a strange covered pensiveness. Spare, dark and gripping, Albery's production got close to the frustration and rage Schiller and Verdi put at the heart of the story – confronting the threat of liberalism, that continuing major issue of politics and religion.

Albery's use of a pair of designers – however well it worked for *Midsummer Marriage* and *The Trojans* – was extravagant, especially when the trio did not succeed. Later Berlioz ventures, *Beatrice and Benedict* at ENO and *Benvenuto Cellini* for Netherlands

Opera, fell flat. The humour was lame. Albery teamed up with Cairns for a brilliantly surrealistic, emotional and romantic *Finta giardiniera* for Opera North in 1989. This witty, eccentric staging of Mozart's first serious comedy was acutely acted, and the increasingly surrealistic distortion of normality in Cairns's sets brought out the complicated emotional twists and turns of the story, ending up with some pretty zonked-out behaviour by all the characters. The outcome of the story, prepared in the florid, neurotically complex arias, needed that kind of release. Cairns's strong colouristic sense was crucial – especially at the end of act 2, which in the WNO (1994) revival was beautifully lit by Charles Edwards. A red-streaked black curtain was drawn across the powder-blue drum of sky round the back of the set; the ill-matched pairs struggled over the collapsed green wall in search of the missing Sandrina and their own equilibrium. Librium, they all needed – Albery made the tale like an acid trip which at the Cardiff revival was even funnier, warmer, more humane. Matthew Epstein's WNO casting gave a special vocal edge too. Janice Watson's fiercely go-getting Arminda ripped into her blood-curdlingly delivered arias, a great battler in the war of the sexes – as the red plush velvet dress and Minnie Mouse wig provided for her by Cairns certainly led the audience to expect.

Albery's *Chérubin* at Covent Garden earlier in 1994 was a return to the sort of inventive form that had made the collaboration with Cairns and McDonald on *Trojans* so remarkable. It showed Albery's strong, previously hidden sense of humour – prompted by McDonald's irrepressibly irreverent design ideas. This was the British premiere of Massenet's sophisticated mood piece, an entertaining kind of post-Messager musical comedy written for the Prince of Monaco which the composer called a 'trifle'. McDonald's wickedly camp sense of absurdity avoided distorting too far the poignancy of this idealized hymn to youth. The staging was quite laid back about the tale it told, emphasizing timing and wit. Mildly daring in eccentricity Albery's approach worked perfectly for Covent Garden, partly because nobody complained about the producer undermining the beauty and power of a score of little musical repute that was mainly a shop-window for delicious voices, with a bit of dancing thrown in and a few gentle jokes about sex and passion. The operetta-ish good tunes could steal the show: in this Beaumarchais-derived, playful, *Merry Wives*-style plot a long way after *The Marriage of Figaro* (inspired by *La mère coupable*), ensemble values mattering most. The story was of rich young subaltern Chérubin in love with love wherever he could find it (kiss first, ask questions later). It needed and got a light touch – something Albery missed with the Berlioz comedies. Chérubin faced husbands on the prowl, switching his affections from childhood sweetheart Nina, ward of the Duke, to a Madrid ballet star, L'Ensoleillad. For the latter role Albery had both a dancer and a singer in razor-sharp substitution (the dancer: Lucy Burge, Andromache in Albery's *Fall of Troy*).

From her stunning first appearance, revealed behind vast chintz *trompe-l'oeil* double doors one step above the forestage, the fresh charismatic star Susan Graham as Chérubin was totally assured in this 'trousers' role, projecting truthful emotion without embarrassingly mimicking male quirks (though she thrashed the ground with her rapier very naturally). McDonald's designs used sliding panels and doors, with walls that moved aside magically, to focus and advantageously rearrange the stage. The opening in the kitchens, with mustachioed, red-faced and red-rubber-gloved chorus washing-up steamily below stairs – in zany dialogue with the Philosopher-cum-tutor in his wing armchair at the front of the stage, all beneath giant chintz red and pink camelias and peonies – defined the joky, kitschy (if not kitcheny) tone. The sets riotously blended rococo excess with modern French *nouveaux riches* taste. The hotel façade in the second act where Chérubin tried to engage in a sort of seduction marathon came direct from the Midi, glowing with pink shells: the metal front of L'Ensoleillad's romantic balcony loaded with neon bulbs suddenly flashed on for her moonlight duet with Chérubin balanced on top of a ladder. Husbands looked round walls and peered into the audience from halfway up the proscenium. The young lover fell from a high wall – but was not hurt, of course. There was a danced duel with quartet accompaniment, a set of chairs of descending sizes for the ballet star to cakewalk down – all below a starlit indigo romantic night-sky. Albery even created a big musical comedy show-stopper, with chorus of officers and girls flooding on to the set.

The final scene, after the night of adolescent love, was dominated by sombre peeling fleur de lys-patterned wallpaper in eau de nil – with a pink little romantic window at the bottom of a sweeping flight of stairs. The ballerina on her way to a tryst with the King declared, 'Who is this boy?' as she eyed Chérubin at the foot of the stairs. Cue for his Philosopher guardian, ever to hand as preserver, guide and *deus ex machina*, to draw a final lesson in growing-up from this morning-after moral. Suffering in love, Chérubin must settle for Nina. As the dancer and her troupe exited for the last time (Ashley Page's choreography was a frequent delight), they bore off as L'Ensoleillad's trophy the glass lightbowl at the foot of the bannisters. The final happy vision of the young pair, Nina and Chérubin, was ideally framed through the little pink window.

Albery worked with Stewart Laing as designer for the first time in 1994 on a Scottish Opera *Fidelio*. They decided that the structure of scenes in Beethoven's opera suited it to a strip-cartoon approach in the designs, and created a number of tiny rooms for various episodes, sometimes using as little as a ninth of the proscenium arch space for a box-like room-scene – rather like a medieval painting of a saint's life. Marzelline was ironing Rocco's and Fidelio's shirts while Jaquino wooed her, and then by the time she sang her aria about getting married she was upstairs putting the clothes away into drawers beside Rocco's bed. Pizarro rushed through a parade room, snatching his post, and went into an inner office to read the tip-off about the inspection by Don Fernando that precipitated his plan to dispose of Florestan immediately: the guards could be seen in the next room listening to his raging aria through the door. The well that was to be Florestan's grave and the room where he was chained were shown in a group of three little low cellars next to each other across the stage. Laing's confined spaces brilliantly underscored Beethoven's moral theme about liberty, and Albery's production related the staging and the dramaturgy to the often simple musical forms of Beethoven's composition.

It is a timeless story, and it was given in contemporary clothes, in an uncluttered 20th-century prison with a clean desks policy. Matthew Best's chilling Pizarro was not Napoleon but something even more deadly – a politically motivated, Nazi-ish bureaucrat in sober suit and polished black Oxfords, who became almost unhinged at the thought of Florestan ever being discovered alive, and who brilliantly pressurized Stafford Dean's Rocco to assist his dirty deed. Albery told the story unaffectedly. The naturalism of the acting in association with the comic-strip or doll's-house-like stage structure turned the sung and spoken words of the particular scenes almost into bubble captions. *Fidelio* is an opera where people seldom communicate their secrets to each other, as being too dangerous. When Beethoven switches with perhaps naive passion from his mock-*Zauberflöte* mode to his metaphysical vein –

as in Leonore's great scena, '*Abscheulicher*' where she finds the strength to defeat Pizarro, and later in her duet with the redeemed Florestan, '*O namenlose Freude*' – the characters unbuttoned themselves, spotlit at the front of the stage. Behind them another panel in the black front-cloth parted to reveal a coloured photographic montage of serene, happy nature: dawn through pine trees, or a flowery meadow above an alpine lake. The contrast with prison rooms all sharing one feature, a small barred window, could not have been greater.

The Prisoners' chorus was the first time the whole proscenium space and stage were used – with a wall at the back rising to release the captives, and a snowy mountainscape behind suggesting the hostile environment. The open space was almost paradoxically a pall over their temporary release. During the final chorus the mountain image grew smaller and smaller, more and more distant, on a rapid sequence of changing back-cloths, and finally was replaced by a cloudy sky and skyscrapers: a sombre question-mark over the freedom evoked by Beethoven's joyful conclusion. Elizabeth Whitehouse's Fidelio/Leonore wore a Mao suit that made her male disguise almost credible. Albery's cool, tactful but daring modern production, rivalling memories of the accomplishment of his *Trojans*, always affirmed the musical priorities.

Steven Pimlott (born 1953), like his near contemporary Albery, was closely associated with Cairns as a designer. He worked more frequently outside London or abroad or in the legitimate theatre – and had no ENO productions until after the Pountney–Elder regime had left (he had almost undertaken a co-production of *Cav* and *Pag*). Pimlott had a definite feel for the expressionist methods that Cairns and Albery used, though like Nicholas Hytner he was at ease with a straightforward narrative approach, as he showed with his populist *Carmen* at Earls Court. His modern-dress *Don Giovanni* for Opera 80 (1985), with the Don as a self-indulgent Sloane ranger and the Commendatore in regimental red dinner jacket, was designed by Cairns, with a single abstract square set whose walls offered as many escape routes to the languorous philanderer as a Spanish village. Leporello ended up in drag.

Pimlott's staging of *Samson and Dalila* at the 1988 Bregenz festival transferred well to the Amsterdam Musiktheater. Cairns's design for the opening act showed the Israelites as modern Jews in Israel pressing their hands in prayer against a kind of wailing wall. Samson threw down the boundary wire enclosing them. The

Philistines in pompeian red robes fell in a furious mêlée. Samson was won by Dalila with the help of a crowd of elegant dancing girls who invaded the synagogue meeting. He sat immobile as one girl danced with a Bible on her head while others stole prayer-shawls.

The second-act seduction happened beneath a vast night-blue cyclorama, with a desert mound, a stretching oasis pool, and some *deuxième empire* furniture. The fierce immediacy as Philistine hordes rushed through the pool on their way to capture Samson, kicking up a huge splash, made a spine-chilling image. In the third act Cairns preferred grandeur and artistic subtlety to the usual feebly pornographic orgy. The emphasis throughout was on the cultural antipathy between the deprived Israelites and the superior Philistines – rather than on spurious Philistine decadence. The temple of Dagon stretched into the distance beyond a massive wall on the right: high up on a walkway the Philistine chorus watched in stylish simple costumes (long red velvet dresses and gloves for the ladies; gloves, full-length black skirts and jackets for the gents). Aletta Collins's choreography for the final dance had a hypnotic expressiveness and beautiful rhythmic energy. There was no silly abuse of Samson – the High Priest just poured a glass of wine on his head insultingly. The interpretation relied on visual beauty, strong singing and an impressive sweep in the conducting.

Pimlott's Earls Court *Carmen*, for the impresarios Harvey Goldsmith and Mark McCormack, was designed on the largest scale by Stefanos Lazaridis. This was the most virtuosic arena opera production there has been in Britain, and toured the world to great profit. The production was in the round, exploiting brilliantly the idea of the bull-ring, and using a doughnut revolve to choreograph the action so that people on all sides of the stage were close to activity all the time. There were toreadors and imported flamenco dancers, with an interpolated dance episode at Lillas Pastia's (80 dancers choreographed by Aletta Collins – sometimes within the scene, sometimes as a sort of chorus commentary, Lorca-esque with the atmosphere of bloodlust). The main concept was to develop the idea of the ring as a gladiatorial space for Carmen's ultimate confrontation with José. Abandoning the physical appearance of cigarette factory or bar was liberating. Situation was defined by props, and some necessary furniture, but most importantly by the behaviour and action of the army of extras manoeuvred by Pimlott with a film-director's visual care. A performance like this in the round, with naturalistic, almost cinematic detail, with horses and crowds as in the Royal Tournament, had no frame of proscenium and darkness. Opera in the round challenges the usual naturalism of conventional opera. The audience must choose to accept the convention and ignore the people watching from the other side of the arena, which here was no difficulty.

The most dramatic entry was the line of smugglers descending a rope staircase from the roof a couple of hundred yards to the ring – slow and dramatic, naturalistic in fact. Absolutely Royal Tournament stuff. In the detailed confrontations on stage Pimlott emphasized melodramatic, intense intimacy – and achieved intoxicating performances from Maria Ewing and Jacque Trussel (among the various stars in alternating casts). A thrilling pageant, the production didn't take sides about the morality of the war – but it did achieve overwhelming tragic catharsis.

La bohème in September 1993 was Steven Pimlott's first ENO production at the Coliseum and the debut there also of Tobias Hoheisel, the German designer familiar in Britain from stylish Janáček stagings at Glyndebourne with Nikolaus Lehnhoff as producer. Pimlott and Hoheisel had collaborated on *A Masked Ball* in Antwerp: the aesthetic of their partnership matched Albery's operas designed by Hildegard Bechtler. *Bohème* was done without intervals, using a monumental London docklands loft setting, visually arresting, with a sweep of 'cast-iron' Corinthian columns from back to front separating an 'interior' two-thirds of the stage on the left from a vaguely exterior one-third on the right. The Bohemians seemed to be squatters in a rather grand industrial 'loft' space. On the left between a fine window and double doors a self-consciously basic, designerish, wood-burning stove kept up the naturalistic *Bohème* tradition.

Pimlott, who at the time had just followed Hytner in making a fortune from directing a musical (Lloyd Webber's *Joseph and the Amazing Technicolor Dreamcoat*), cleverly managed to satisfy the anecdotal narrative needs of Puccini's opera while relating it to the present age of radical right yuppies. *Bohème* is not 'about' real poverty, but – like those mawkish pictures of waifs that were so popular with Victorian captains of industry – satisfied the taste of well-to-do opera-goers for a misty view of those less materially fortunate. Few producers approaching a so familiar work, especially Puccini, have tried using a non-naturalistic environment. Cairns (who was very close to Pimlott before their traumatic collaboration on James Lapine and Stephen Sondheim's *Sunday in the Park with George* at the National Theatre) himself directed and designed *Bohème* in Stuttgart with abstract picture-frame sets and a Café Momus like a 1990s pop video. Pimlott at ENO combined the theatrical sweep of production numbers with various intimate echoes and suggestions. Musetta's song turned into a cake-walk and striptease on a long communal table with crowds of wealthy revellers. All the scene-changes between acts were managed in full view as if the location and waiters were available on hire. Hugh Vanstone's lighting defined the inner rhythms. The acting was intelligent, committed. The age disjunction between Roberta Alexander's mature, touching Mimi and John Hudson's fresh Rodolfo had logic for a relationship not made in heaven. Cheryl Barker's Musetta was a looker with a cutting, exciting voice. Pimlott's complex and detailed vision of *Bohème* swept the whole company along in enthusiastic support.

Cairns, like his fellow-designer, or ex-designer, David Fielding, developed the conviction that he should in future direct his own work in his own sets. In a medium where design is crucial and the main distinctive factor in most productions, it is commonplace for designers to take control of the entire process of theatrical interpretation. Franco Zeffirelli, Filippo Sanjust and Pier Luigi Pizzi were all designers before they took to directing. Designers are well aware that their ideas give a production its identity and a large part of its personality. Fielding, who collaborated most brilliantly with David Alden, and sometimes very well too with Nicholas Hytner and David Pountney, started by directing mostly in legitimate or fringe theatre, his own choice of apprenticeship. Manthey, who was Berghaus's designer, also later became his own producer. Stefanos Lazaridis too has had a crisis of ambition. After achieving fame, designers can easily lose the taste for collaboration.

Promoting designers into producers is a routine process. But the ability to perform both functions is rare, apart from Herbert Wernicke and the late Jean-Pierre Ponnelle. Mostly, opera benefits from varied input, which need not all be neatly sorted out pursuing one line of meaning as decided by the producer. It is a problem that stage directors like Trevor Nunn or Deborah Warner from the legitimate theatre, who spread their wings operatically, evidently dislike ambiguity. But designers often have an additional misconception, when they start to direct, of precisely what their new job entails. They may not have seen or experienced much of the business of direction, because it happens between the producer and the singers. Designers are problem solvers, producers are risk takers. Designers don't have to deal with the human angle, welcoming and sometimes melding with the particular insights of the performers, supporting them, boosting them, giving them faith, so that they can do the things they have to – which often they scarcely believe are appropriate or practical for communicating with an audience. Designers find it hard to turn into teachers and moral tutors and over-arching visionaries. They are not used to having control on a loose rein, to letting life breathe into the show. Opera is an arduous collaborative process, mining multifarious themes – which is why the idea of the dramaturg, a person whose primary purpose is to oil this process of research and imagination and self-criticism, can be effective for some producers, and useful for companies needing to know how, and in what direction, the interpretative process is moving.

Often designers working with a producer are in effect their own busy dramaturgs. But then what they proposed as designers was 'edited' by the producer – for the designer in that kind of team relationship is never the boss. Lazaridis, clearly, was a dominant designer to work with, a solver of problems who liked to know just how the production would be forced to run, thanks to the design-led decisions he had precipitated. Fielding and Cairns were less dictatorial about the working out of the production in terms of practical stage 'blocking' and acting. But each represented a specific kind of aesthetic. Cairns as a designer was one of the most painterly and colour-sensitive of British talents, and certainly the most abstract in the shapes and associations he used. Cairns and Nigel Lowery have the real individual signatures of all the wide and talented field of British designers born since the Second World War. Yet it is the producer who is responsible for much of the life of the production, and the designer is very little involved with all that. What producer/designers are least good at managing is generally the motivation of the performers, the manoeuvring of expressive movement and gesture, the confidence-enhancing liberation of the acting spirit inside the singers, and affection for them as autonomous elements in the production.

Cairns, though, in spite of all these problems, rapidly became a well-regarded producer. Working closely with his choreographer Aletta Collins as co-producer, he staged *King Priam* at Opera North, *La bohème* in Stuttgart, *A Masked Ball* in Munich, *Don Giovanni* for Scottish Opera, and Glyndebourne Touring Opera's new Harrison Birtwistle opera, *The Second Mrs Kong*. His *Bohème* showed considerable fluency in the intimate scenes, and went further than his feeling for *Priam* – though its abstract aesthetic was similar. The stage space was used simply and attractively. Cairns, being a painter, likes large flats, simple colour, a few telling brushstrokes, light and dark, and startling little details on a broad canvas. The scale of his looming *Bohème* sets suggested Adolphe Appia and Wieland Wagner. The recurring theme was a picture-frame: *Bohème* is about the romantic imagination, about how young people trying to make something of their lives are defeated by fate and hopelessness, dreams exploded, art crushed by life. Cairns freed the work from the hyper-realism to which it is habitually treated. His 'garret' featured the inevitable wood-burning stove at the front – its flue reaching into the flies. Across the back of the set a giant canvas was leaning, with a huge cracked and misty glass pane behind Rodolfo and Marcello that slid into the floor on Schaunard's arrival to reveal, inside a smaller frame, the students' 'real' room. A table and chairs, one of them painted royal blue with a silver crescent moon, suggested a disused loft colonized by the Bohemian quartet in their modish present-day garb. The café scene – a symphony of consumerist temptations – had bright yellow lights, spindly metal tables, a line of four dancing waiters, and a chorus in black wittily mobilized by Collins. The conflicts and bitter rows of the third act – outside a cellar bar suggested by a warmly lit trapdoor in the stage from which Rodolfo, Marcello and Musetta emerged – was played around two massive walls with doorways dividing up the space. The final death scene was in the first-act loft again, even emptier.

The wide spaces in place of quaint naturalism paradoxically emphasized the essential intimacy, emotionalism, isolation, and lost quality of the characters. One of the joys of Cairns's work on this familiar operatic workhorse was its naughty humour, enjoying the fabric of the piece. The staging was less unusual than its abstract look appeared. The young people came fully alive (Martin Thompson's ringing Rodolfo and Vladimir Chernov's robust Marcello especially) with Cairns successfully evoking the sadness of Rodolfo's hopes and memories with well observed musical flashbacks and reprised fragments. The problem of Cairns's work on *Giovanni* and *Masked Ball* was its lack of consistent coherence, its tendency to fall back on a decorative purely visual style – a lack, in fact, of defining expressive contextualization.

Tippett's second opera *King Priam*, whose theme was said to be 'the mysterious nature of human choice', actually shows choice as an illusion. The tragic story of Troy provides a Brechtian paradigm of human Fate, always interrupting the sentiment of its powerfully emotive musical gestures, cutting away shortwindedly and in a manner that does not elaborate on the concrete facts. At ENO, Opera North's 1991 team with a strong cast led by Andrew Shore gradually unfolded the passive tragic vision required, acting and singing with imposing intensity. Cairns's staging, with his own typically restrained and often abstract designs, found its security in the interior third act. His production was expanded for the Coliseum's cinerama proscenium and had brightly lit white surfaces where in Leeds it was a relentless shadowplay of glowing primary colours. The third act showed a broad opening in a white wall giving on to a white room with dirty charcoal wall-scribblings and a ledge where Priam placed the abused corpse of Hector. For Priam's visit to Achilles he rose from the floor, as in a dream, walked upstage naked, drew his toga after him. The back wall was flown out to reveal Achilles, black warpaint smeared under his enraged eyes, standing by the dancing flames of his camp-fire, with a few chairs for props. Mark Curtis's Hermes inspired and presided over rather than physically managed the transit of Priam between the warring camps. The final image of Neoptolemus, dagger raised behind him, leaving through the door by which he had come to kill Priam, was like a mythic painting on a Greek vase (the guiding inspiration of Cairns's designs). The fine downbeat conclusion showed a square boxlike column near Priam's corpse glowing blood red, in a sense carrying the tragedy back to the earth. Cairns's third act worked best because, like Nicholas Hytner's remarkable Kent Opera staging, it contained and projected the drama's rhetoric – as when the three servant-women become goddesses in the folds of a screen. The earlier, simpler, more cool scenes – often fronted with gauzes bearing the outlines of doorways (to perception) drawn in Cairns's highly personal line – looked as beautiful but less well conceived. The opening with an amphora on its side dominating the stage, a child figure near its mouth glowing white behind a front gauze, was too like a museum display case – not a fertile idea. The front gauze muffled the impact of early scenes.

The hunting narrative of Paris's restoration to his family, a picture on the broken shards of a vase, answered Tippett's fragmentary style in the opening acts neatly but undramatically. Grey curtains swept silkily across for set-changes. Red or yellow square columns lay on the floor. One was half raised, when Achilles's war cry interrupted. Translucent stones glowed with primary colours. These beautiful pictures were more artistic than theatrical. The passion of Paris and Helen lacked epic grandeur – with flailing movements on a prosaic stairway. Cairns and his associate director and choreographer Collins toyed half-heartedly with a few repetitive hand gestures. But the ENO direction was always more assured than in Leeds, and in the difficult concluding act the method was strikingly impressive.

For the whimsy of *The Second Mrs Kong*, very similar to what inspired the Sendak/Knussen *Where the Wild Things Are* and Prokofiev's *Love for Three Oranges*, Glyndebourne chose Cairns, some of whose visions have been the nearest thing to aesthetic beauty that the British opera scene offers, as designer/director, to take charge of the theatrical realization with his usual collaborator the choreographer Collins. Some of the pictures on the boat across Lethe – the sea to the world of the living (who turned out to be no different from the dead, or at least just as dramatically lifeless, lacklustre and unpacey) – were memorable, and intriguingly lit. The tunnel of the Styx at the opening of the second act with a boat flown from the flies moving downwards through the murk was visually compelling. The boat seemed to float across the proscenium. Much of the staging was deliberately obscure – and a lot less intriguing than Kubrick's *2001* which touched similar cultural areas. Philip Langridge was a charming Kong: bluff, amicable, grinning, schoolboyish – those dimples, as often, his most useful assets. There were some delightful jokes, like the golden sphynx that shook its tail in boredom and frustration (verbal humour, however, stemming from the conscious solecism). Nuala Willis was funny as the Sphynx, wagging her tail and making eyes at the audience – deeply scrutable (her stock in trade). There was little sign of directorial input from Cairns. Helen Field as Pearl was wide-eyed as ever, if slight in profile. Most of the other characters were whimsical in a deplorably Tippettian manner to little purpose. Cairns produced and designed the opera successfully. But the nature of the task did not require direction of real characters communicating with each other in psychologically truthful situations. The story of the opera, about the putative or potential after-life of fictional characters, was as fantastic as *Die Zauberflöte* if a lot less believable and involving. The context, a sort of Hadean wasteland of fantasy, was just a game. Cairns certainly gave the opera a delightful visual consistency, moving away from his usual brightly coloured abstraction. There was a lot of fun with video screens. He had put the show cleverly together. But it was still very organized and simple, lacking a proper range of acting or action, with little theatricality in its imagination. Collaboration between a producer and designer would have involved more questions being asked. Cairns's promise is amply confirmed in his originality and individuality as a designer. It is precisely the qualities that are not evident in his productions which are, at best, most characteristic of Tim Albery's – the witty blend of (sometimes ironic) comment and properly energized commitment from the performers.

However, Cairns's remarkable *Jenůfa* in Leeds for Opera North demonstrated that he had finally won his spurs as a producer, and was genuinely getting inside the individual acting performances of his cast – not just decorating them abstractly from the outside. The point of giving a designer the chance to direct is the possibility of realizing a consistent vision – through composed, as it were. *Jenůfa* was the first time that Cairns achieved a fully convincing balance between dramatic credibility and imagery. His production was more truthful emotionally and more natural in its energy than the heavily choreographed, expressionistic *Jenůfa* of Lyubimov at Covent Garden. A shadow of a millwheel dominated the first-act set, which was a yellow silhouette of a house against black, with a fallen tree trunk on a green raked floor, water in a tray running across the front of the stage, and water reflections playing across the whole space. (Tobias Hoheisel at Glyndebourne also used real water in a ditch.) The simplicity of the lay-out put the responsibility for the performance firmly on how the drama was enacted, and the cast had some very strong elements: Neill Archer was an ideal Steva, perfectly charming and feckless, with Stephanie Friede a most touching Jenůfa. Pauline Tinsley as the Grandmother was almost firmer in voice than Josephine Barstow's Kabanicha – though Barstow's final confessional scene was one of the best and most beautiful things she had done in ages. But what mattered with the first act was ensemble work, and the character of Laca – for which Julian Gavin was lightweight. With Collins as co-producer and choreographer, Cairns achieved a brilliant fluidity, an open unpretentious approach that explained everything about Steva and Jenůfa's personalities in great and painful detail. The last kiss Steva gave Jenůfa before rushing off was particularly devastating, defining the problems in an instant.

The second act brilliantly displayed Cairns's sophistication as a designer, differentiating very simply (using the house silhouette and gauzes) between the inside bedroom and the main room of the cottage so that the imagination travelled easily through all the situations – implicit, but not usually shown. Jenůfa sleeping, and her child, and the act of abduction were all brought into focus just by subtle changes of Wolfgang Göbbel's lighting. The third act was more experimental to look at, with the white-painted front room for the wedding reception (containing a few pieces of traditional painted Bohemian peasant furniture) altering physically – turning as one watched into a black pit of despair for the crisis of the discovery of the dead baby. The social detail was painted with scrupulous accuracy. The warmth in the lighting suddenly fled as the crisis flared (Jano's voice that of a boy treble here). Everybody abandoned Jenůfa in a stage that had become a sort of prison. It was left to Laca contemplating her from the very front of the set (at the 'footlights') to rescue her.

It is not true designers should stick to designing – though many of them should. But it is a very unusual designer who can learn how to direct. Cairns, having conquered the problem of building the production not on the imagery of the set but on the performances of the actors, seems to have learnt what made Albery such a potent collaborator. Both have demonstrated their imaginative power with singers, and continue to have enormous potential – using expressionist language on stage to convey emotional force.

13 A line of renewal: from Hall to Pountney

David Freeman's 1986 staging (for Opera Factory at the Queen Elizabeth Hall) of *Così fan tutte* designed by David Roger: Janis Kelly's Despina tries to wise up Christine Botes's Dorabella on Bondi beach. Photograph © Douglas Jeffery.

The formidable Lilian Baylis, who founded both the Old Vic and Sadler's Wells companies, was inspired by Victorian ideals of social improvement. She aimed to bring opera and theatre to the ordinary people of the grimy near-in London suburbs at Waterloo and Islington. Laying on culture would be as civilizing as modern plumbing and hygienic drains. Ticket prices had to be cheap and the language of opera performances the vernacular. The movement to mitigate the hitherto normal philistinism and commercialism of British cultural life pre-dated state subsidy or patronage of the theatre in Britain. But the real beneficiaries were not the working classes of Waterloo and Islington, many of whom were bombed out of their location in the Blitz and rehoused, so much as the ordinary middle classes. Thus did Britain become more European, and London more like a continental capital with established seasons of performing arts, sustained by local companies and orchestras. The most obvious mark of change was the creation of a national repertoire of operas, thanks mainly to Britten, and of local home-bred stars. In the early years of Baylis (the 1920s and 1930s) the Wells operated hand to mouth, and when Covent Garden opened up in opposition to the Wells in 1947 it was intended to show how opera should really be done. The adoption of an English-language policy at Covent Garden could scarcely have been more pointed and competitive: the takeover of the Sadler's Wells Ballet by Covent Garden sent a clear message. Even when the Arts Council was born after the Second World War and subsidy became available to the Wells, commitments to low seat prices and the English language were continuing constraints on experimenting with stagings or the hiring of vocal talents.

The quality of work at Sadler's Wells (in 1974 renamed English National Opera) has usually been regarded as second best to Covent Garden: a view only occasionally challenged over the last 60 years – for example, by the reputation and achievement of the Reginald Goodall English *Ring*, or by the adventurous design and production policy followed when Peter Jonas became ENO general director. The Covent Garden audience at a *Meistersinger* performance in the early 1970s had to be reassured by a patronizing speech from the management before curtain-up that Norman Bailey, standing in as Hans Sachs at short notice, was not unused to the German text, but had in fact sung the role at Bayreuth and elsewhere in Germany. The deathless English class system worked against Wells artists at that time. Singing in English was not always seen as a liberating obligation rather than a downmarket compromise, ensuring second-best standards. Real opera, for cognoscenti and wealthy patrons, has meant top international producers, singers, and conductors – usually foreign. As the Covent Garden opera company matured, and despite the middle European background of music directors before Colin Davis's appointment in 1971, all of whom were raised in operatic cultures where the vernacular was the norm, original language came to be regarded as part of the deal for the Royal Opera. Davis's arrival was even signalled by the Royal Opera board refusing to let him do a *Marriage of Figaro* in English in 1971, as he and his producer Peter Hall wanted. This precipitated Hall's resignation from the Royal Opera joint artistic directorship with Davis, and his subsequent departure for Glyndebourne, where, naturally, the possibility of *Figaro* in English never arose.

At Sadler's Wells during and after the war an English tradition of opera staging was successfully built up, consciously exploiting the distinction of various British theatre directors and designers such as Tyrone Guthrie, George Devine, Michel Saint Denis, Basil Coleman, Glen Byam Shaw, John Blatchley, Oliver Messel, Cecil Beaton, John Piper, Leslie Hurry, Motley, Ralph Koltai and Peter Rice. From 1959 to 1976 there were seventeen John Blatchley productions at Sadler's Wells/ENO, sixteen by Colin Graham, fourteen by Glen Byam Shaw, ten by Besch, seven by Copley, six by Coleman, five each by Wendy Toye and Geliot, three by John Cox, and Ralph Koltai designed twelve shows, Peter Rice seven.

Anthony Besch (born 1924) had assisted Carl Ebert and Günther Rennert at Glyndebourne, but in his own right only got to direct the Mozart squib *Der Schauspieldirektor* there, though he had much success at Scottish Opera. Colin Graham (born 1931) had taken over the English Opera Group in Britten's declining years and turned it into English Music Theatre Company. John Copley (born 1933) had been stage manager at the Wells and had directed competently at Covent Garden and Sadler's Wells in a fairly unadventurous and decorative style. Michael Geliot (also born 1933) served his apprenticeship at the Wells too, and Glyndebourne, and after being taken on to the WNO strength was responsible for many standard repertoire productions in Cardiff. All these producers grew up as opera specialists, as did some older modestly inspired hands: John Moody, Christopher West, Basil Coleman and Dennis Arundell. But this local tradition was not remarkable. In Germany, whether through Wieland Wagner or Walter Felsenstein, a more distinctive theatrical approach to opera was established by the 1960s, but insularity and a certain conceit about British theatre and design prevented much imitation. Imitation is how all performing arts advance, especially the ephemeral art of theatrical interpretation. The British tradition in the mid-1970s was glitzy, with pretty costuming, simple narrative and generalized, broad-brush direction of the characterizations.

Initially, the most successful innovators in British opera were not particularly revolutionary – Peter Hall, Elijah Moshinsky, and Jonathan Miller. Even a staging as unsatisfactory in many respects as the conductor Reginald Goodall's *Ring* (it was known by its conductor) at the Coliseum in 1973 played its part. In its visual style and casting this English *Ring* – designed in space-age, pick-à-stick style by Ralph Koltai and directed by Glen Byam Shaw and John Blatchley in an effective narrative manner – was wholly indigenous. Peter Hall was the great white hope of British opera after Georg Solti left Covent Garden in 1971. Hall, whose Shakespeare productions were not unaffected by the influence of the Berliner Ensemble's London visits, had made a striking impact at Covent Garden during the Solti years with *Moses and Aaron*, *Eugene Onegin*, *The Knot Garden* and *Tristan und Isolde*. His fine work at Glyndebourne started with *La Calisto*, *Il ritorno d'Ulisse* and *Le nozze di Figaro*. At Glyndebourne his designer for all of his early opera productions was John Bury. Together they later forged impressive if conservative interpretations of *Don Giovanni* (1977) and *A Midsummer Night's Dream* (1981). In 1975 at Covent Garden nobody would have expected such a remarkable achievement as Moshinsky's economical Brechtian *Peter Grimes*, excellent *Lohengrin*, and lucid theatrical *Rake's Progress*. Miller's work, too, whether for Kent Opera or ENO, confirmed a sense of rich promise, of theatrical achievement – especially his Coliseum *Rigoletto*. All three established an expectation of dramaturgical preparation, of thoughtful exploration of the themes and philosophy in an opera. Their kind of work was not just window-dressing, decoration, culinary opera. After Hall's abandonment of

Covent Garden, the Royal Opera tried to replace his projected role with a whole-hearted commitment to and from Götz Friedrich on a series of productions for Colin Davis. But Friedrich's *Ring*, designed by Josef Svoboda, lacked the imaginative distinction and individuality of Chéreau's at Bayreuth. His *Idomeneo* was a failure, his *Freischütz* was not much liked, and even his decent Covent Garden *Lulu* was overshadowed by the stylishness of Chéreau's in Paris. Friedrich at the Garden was proof that the management there in the 1970s wanted to be adventurous, and not just luxuriate in the hyper-realist tradition of Visconti and Zeffirelli.

It mattered that Hall was a native Englishman. Before him, British opera producers were second-best to foreigners like Ebert, Visconti, Zeffirelli, and Rennert, men from what was held in Britain to be the authentic operatic tradition (Munich, Berlin, Vienna, Milan). Sir Thomas Beecham had conducted and dominated the opera seasons at Covent Garden between the wars. But John Christie at Glyndebourne, and the post-war Covent Garden board, shopped abroad for serious talent as producers, conductors and singers. Ballet might be becoming home-grown; opera was foreign. Certainly the diaspora of genius from Nazi Germany transformed the terms of British enthusiasm for opera. The creation of Glyndebourne Festival Opera by Fritz Busch in the 1930s (sustained by Vittorio Gui from 1952 to 1964) was matched by the way Britten and Tippett reached back to Purcell in search of a lyrical musical language to project English words. A new performing tradition was created for Purcell's own operas. Then Glyndebourne's Monteverdi revival started with Rennert's staging of the lush Raymond Leppard adaptation of *L'incoronazione di Poppea* (1965), a phenomenon of British musicology. Janet Baker doubling as Diana and as Jove-disguised-as-Diana in Cavalli's *La Calisto* (1970), with Peter Hall as producer and John Bury as designer, was a greater landmark. Glyndebourne during the last 25 years of Sir George Christie's leadership has witnessed a process of naturalization, repatriation, and professionalisation – in place of a charmingly eccentric tradition in which extemporized picnic dinners defined the approach. The new Glyndebourne opera-house, a unique phenomenon in the world of opera, is a talisman of the operatic seriousness and commitment of modern Britain.

For a time Hall as a producer was more popular with the public, more interesting, more reliable than anything that Glyndebourne could conceivably have imported from abroad. Eventually the freshness of his work faded. It was a sign of the times that the arrival of Peter Sellars in Sussex eventually precipitated Hall's departure from Glyndebourne – and from serious work in opera staging. Hall's first opera production had been at Sadler's Wells, and was the premiere of a new work. That was the usual poisoned chalice for beginners. Nobody expected, or expects, new operas like John Gardner's *The Moon and Sixpence*, Hall's debut, to succeed in the longer term, or be memorable in the short term. In 1965 Solti and Sir David Webster engaged Hall for Schoenberg's *Moses and Aaron* (in English) at Covent Garden – and the newspapers were full of part-salacious, part-sceptical stories about orgies round the Golden Calf. Hall's love affair with opera took off. It almost saw him (in 1971) teamed up with Colin Davis at Covent Garden. Eventually from 1984 to 1990 he held a similar if less arduous position at Glyndebourne. In 1966, he did a *Zauberflöte* (in English) at the Garden; in 1970, the same year as *Calisto* at Glyndebourne, he and Colin Davis launched the world premiere of Tippett's *Knot Garden* (with designs by Timothy O'Brien and Tazeena Firth) at the Garden, and in 1971 Hall tackled both *Eugene Onegin* and *Tristan und Isolde* there, the former with beautiful designs by Julia Trevelyan Oman, the latter like *Calisto* designed by Bury (who was, at Stratford and elsewhere, Hall's most frequent and successful collaborator). All these productions by Hall were notable for the clarity and evocativeness of their designs, but perhaps Tippett's *Knot Garden* was the most remarkable of all in that respect. O'Brien's revolving set with a broken outer wall of steel bars managed to be at various times cage and garden and forest, rapidly moving between the different brief scenes of Tippett's scenario. Seldom has a new opera received so precise, well-judged and faithful a realization at its world premiere as this, with powerfully emotional and visually memorable performances of all the roles. Hall's staging defined the work superbly and answered many of its questions in a provocatively poetic fashion – very apt for the psychological obscurity of Tippett's text. In later attempts on the piece, only David Freeman's neurotic vision for Opera Factory worked as well.

In the 1960s Hall's Shakespeare productions such as *The Wars of the Roses* were visually plain and strongly orientated towards the text. With the exception of *Knot Garden*, however, Hall's opera productions, instead of sticking to the prevailing British theatre design tradition of 'poetic realism' – telling visual hints, but details not all filled in – attempted a kind of romantic natural-ism. During the 1970s theatre critics noticed (and deplored) in Hall's National Theatre production of *Volpone* that his style was increasingly 'infected' by the lavishness and period flavour of his operatic work. 'Poetic realism', notably represented in the stage design work of Jocelyn Herbert and developed from the reforms of Motley, was predominantly an abstracted, self-effacing mini-malist school. The principal virtue it sought was to be visually unwasteful. The greatest sin was to draw attention to the set for its own sake – or interpret the play through design. Poetic realism was influenced by East European theatre, and its prevalence in the 1960s and 1970s owed much to the London visit of Brecht's Berliner Ensemble whose aesthetic (suggested by Karl von Appen's designs as much as by the politics of relevance and com-mitment) suited a British puritanism that resisted extravagance of gesture, design or acting. Hall himself was never one of the Royal Court 'angry young men', though that tradition featured in the operatic work of John Dexter, William Gaskill, and – indirectly – Moshinsky and Miller. Hall's instinct was for warm and passion-ately verbal theatre, focused on the conviction of the actors. In opera he recognized audiences expected period atmosphere and narrative trappings. Such 'operatic' elements were already present in some of his Stratford Shakespeare work, such as the 1962 RSC *Midsummer Night's Dream* designed by Lila de Nobili, similar to the rococo extravagance of Oliver Messel – itself in turn stemming from the fanciful decors of Rex Whistler.

Hall's staging of *La Calisto* was above all a theatrical hit. Instead of Janet Baker's usual stiffness on the stage, Hall obtained fun and ease in her version of Jove disguised as Diana. But the freshness and invention of the acting was not the main cause of the success. John Bury's set design was a conscious homage to the Baroque theatre's aesthetic techniques in Handel's day at the Haymarket, London. The use of authentic-style slotted scenery allowed instant, visually beautiful changes. The colourful pictures did not use painted cloths, and the steeply raked stage platform was not at all historical. Its narrowing perspective stretched into the further recesses of Glyndebourne's stage space and penetrated areas far behind where most regular sets finished. Handel's castrati would have baulked at the difficulties, preferring to teeter and exude charisma on a flat stage. But the pseudo-baroque 'transformations' had a liberating impact at Glyndebourne. People were being invited to imagine something very different from their usual operatic diet, something which tallied with the unpretentiously charming and short-winded melodic music they were hearing. The rhythm of this work was like RSC productions. Though sung in Italian without surtitles, nobody had difficulty understanding what was going on.

Similar high-class burlesque provided the tricks and machinery adding to the profounder emotions of *Il ritorno d'Ulisse*, dubbed Monteverdi's Flying Circus because of all its suspended gods moving just beneath the flies and sometimes descending to engage more fully with the action on solid ground. In place of the steep ramp which in *Calisto* shot out to the back of the stage, Hall and Bury defined the effective acting area as a diamond jutting out over the edge of the orchestra-pit towards the conductor – marking a focus or point of command for the actor which remained a feature in other Bury set designs. In Britten's *Dream* there was a magical use of mirrors to evoke summer woodland night, with supernumeraries rigged up as logs and trees which could then shift and rustle magically and mysteriously – the lighting low and silvery enough to evoke the insecurities and fantasies of moonlit romance. An innocent childish reverie was the common denominator of the two early Baroque operas and the Britten. Recapturing a hyper-realist sense of period – another kind of fantasy – was the comic engine of Hall's *Albert Herring* at Glyndebourne too (with a different designer, John Gunter). But Hall's energies after the flop of his ill-prepared and unsuitable Bayreuth *Ring* began to flag. A certain surface polish and narrative facility became the point of the exercise. In his most efficient and long-lasting productions, *Eugene Onegin* at Covent Garden and *Don Giovanni* at Glyndebourne, the atmosphere of the setting and the behaviour of the chorus were less significant than the definition of the central dramatic situation, which Hall explored tellingly with Victor Braun and Ileana Cotrubas in *Onegin*, and Benjamin Luxon (later Thomas Allen) in and as *Don Giovanni*. Hall's *Eugene Onegin* created a separate period picture for each scene. But the secret of the staging was its intimacy, a sort of Chekhovian psychological delicacy defining the ambience. The duel in a snow-filled stark winter space was clearly the still emotional centre. As Don Giovanni, Luxon worked his charm in the revolutionary *fin de siècle* atmosphere as a sort of Regency beau. Hall found a way of carrying Mozart's difficult work right through to its metaphysical conclusion. The morality and Christian background were forcefully defined. Few stagings of *Giovanni* have succeeded as well. Hall's staging of *Tristan und Isolde* in 1971 at Covent Garden got less credit than it deserved: Bury arranged the bower of trees and mossy bank for the lovers' tryst in such a way that the branches could rise higher at the emotional peak of the scene. The production, successfully revived by Elijah Moshinsky with Jon Vickers as Tristan, managed to be both mythological and romantically historical at the same time. Hall's naturalism was far more sensitively judged than most subsequent attempts.

Elijah Moshinsky made his mark in opera around the same time as Jonathan Miller was moving in from a number of successes in the straight theatre, including working with Laurence Olivier at the National. But Miller concentrated for some years, while Moshinsky was making an impression at Covent Garden, on an unextravagant series of productions for Kent Opera with Roger Norrington conducting. Moshinsky won his reputation with his 1975 'cheap' (meaning economical) staging of *Peter Grimes* at Covent Garden with Jon Vickers in the title role. The idea for the production required poetic realism from designers Timothy O'Brien and Tazeena Firth. The budget was only what would have been available for refurbishment of the 1962 staging. Sir John Tooley's Royal Opera management was having to cut back on new productions, and it was an attractive calculated risk to allow Moshinsky his head. The set was extremely simple, firmly rejecting the pictorial olde worlde fishing village prettiness traditional for *Grimes*. Moshinsky took a Brechtian approach, focused on the individual characterizations. Vickers's version of the central role was indispensable, an anchor for a production effectively moulded around it. Moshinsky, and his movement assistant Eleanor Fazan, created a convincing, energized and passionate world to match and balance the epic Vickers performance. The quality of the crowdwork gave a sense of a society fraught with passions and conflicts: another solution to the 'cameo' problem in Britten – picturesque naturalism would have reduced the context to mere anecdote. The acting area (most of the stage space) was defined by three dull grey walls rising to the rear, rather like the playing area of a squash court. Two-thirds of the floor space formed a sandy strand with planks laid at the front. The whole set sloped up towards the rear. Movable sections of floor at the sides served as jetties. Naturalistic details included a few chairs and tables and a couple of fishing boats at the back, with sails stowed for the coming storm. A section of floor could be raised to form a wall at the front for the inquest court of the Prologue. Auntie's tavern was indicated with curtains on a wire stretching from side to side of the stage. Only Grimes's hut got a fuller realization. Fazan's dances performed by extras at the rear of the stage for the evening festivities and celebration at the start of the third act, with warm sundown lighting by David Hersey, were memorably atmospheric, flowing effortlessly in and out of the main action. The period suggested by the costumes was half a century later than Crabbe's poem. Moshinsky visualized some striking moments: Vickers emerged in a romantic and traditional fashion through stage mist to sing his valedictory mad-scene; the lynch-mob forcefully called out Grimes's name shouting straight into the auditorium from the footlights. Emotion, the crucial balance in Grimes himself between poetry and materialism, was well caught.

Moshinsky made his reputation on work at Covent Garden – a prestigious and dangerously exposed path to fame, involving quality rather than quantity of output: very different from a company man like David Pountney at Scottish Opera and ENO. Moshinsky's 1980 *Masked Ball* with Pavarotti at the Met was disliked by the conservative New York public. Years later, when he returned to the Met, his approach had changed from Brechtian effects to conservative decorativeness. He has been a reactive producer, thriving on challenges and difficulties – especially the problem of international stars (Vickers again in *Samson and Dalila*, Cappuccilli and Bruson in his *Macbeth*, Domingo in *Otello*). Moshinsky, exploiting his jejune and youthful intelligence, had transformed Vickers's performance as Tristan in a revival of the Hall staging at the Garden by getting him to remove his built-up platform shoes just before the curtain rose on Kareol. This made Vickers shorter, but, more important, stopped him walking ponderously, like an astronaut on the moon. The effect was to free up the fire and extremism in Vickers's approach to Tristan's final decline. Moshinsky's second Royal Opera production, *Lohengrin* in 1977, was a challenge in a different way. As with his successful revival of Hall's *Tristan*, Moshinsky had to find a suitable metaphor for the magic – the arrival of the hero-knight to redeem the reputation of that pre-Freudian case, Elsa. Underlying the story of pagan gods, 12th-century low-countries tribes and imperial Christianity, there lurked Wagner's festering religious scepticism. That suited the philosopher in Moshinsky, working for the first time with RSC designer John Napier (of *Cats*), with whom he also later did a Royal Opera *Macbeth*. The set was a simple white scrim box, a raked stage floor, and an assembly of tribal and religious totems mounted on sleds. The chorus of nuns, monks, knights and towns-people in authentic 'dark ages' period costumes were marshalled by the Byzantine monarch Henry the Fowler breaking off from a crusade against the heathen Hungarians to deal with a little local difficulty. The miraculous arrival of Lohengrin had dazzling aplomb: René Kollo in white with flowing blond wig rose through a trap near the footlights facing upstage. His golden shield with swan emblem was slung on his back like a cowl; it shimmered brightly, later, as he sang his farewell to the *'liebe Schwann'*. A gauze separated him from the crowds awaiting on stage, singing their welcome. As he moved towards them the gauze lifted, and he literally stepped into their world. At the end, after Lohengrin had restored Gottfried, the people's true prince, the gauze dropped down again between the mysterious hero and the world which he had so fleetingly and strangely touched, and Elsa died heartbro-ken struggling against the gauze, punished for ignoring Lohen-grin's taboo on questioning his name and origins. *Lohengrin* was another 'economical' staging, marvellously clear and clean. The central characters felt real and emotionally truthful and passion-ate. The intimate love scene of Elsa and Lohengrin at the start of the final act was believable.

The lessons of *Lohengrin* were applied to Moshinsky's intelli-gent, attractive, Cardiff staging for WNO of *Ernani*, with Maria Bjørnson's simple galleried set and double doors at the centre of the back wall. But the wittiest, most intelligently realized of all his London opera productions was *The Rake's Progress*, product like *Grimes* of a stimulating collaboration with Timothy O'Brien, that most dramaturgically thoughtful of designers. It was a pity this Covent Garden *Rake* came so soon after the famous (and in its own different way brilliant) David Hockney *Rake* at Glynde-bourne. The critics – thrilled by the visual coherence of Hock-ney's Hogarthian mimickry – were less receptive to the colourful varied O'Brien approach, with all the intellectual baggage of Moshinsky's concept, though Hockney's jokey Hogarthian cross-hatching was irrelevant both to the opera's moral conun-drum, its critique of experience and reason, and to Stravinsky's

sense of musical and operatic history, his citations of earlier operatic music. Moshinsky's *Rake* was a typically brainy neo-classical
affair. He visually defined the link between Tom Rakewell and the
young Wystan Auden, equally open to experiments in life. Robert
Tear's Tom was ideal for this. Moshinsky also played a Brechtian
game with the implied naturalism in the designs – as in Georgian
theatre, characters stepped in and out of role, or moved aside to
point out the implication of their action, enjoying the alienation.
This followed hints in the witty text, like Nick Shadow's asides to
the audience. Moshinsky and O'Brien made the lyrical-cum-
moral underpinning credible. Ann Trulove, as Rakewell's conscience and neglected inspiration, loomed large without
sentimentality. O'Brien's sets used cut-outs of trees, pastel skies,
naive brick walls and façades within a Georgian false proscenium
that was completed with candelabra attached to the walls of the
apron stage. There were gentle design games with perspective in
the opening and closing scenes. Bedlam was linked to Tom's first
rave in London: whores and roaring boys in Mother Goose's
brothel became a chorus of lunatics to be quelled by the emotional
repose of the Venus and Adonis 'masque' of Tom's death. Quick
switches of setting or changes within scenes were facilitated by
bringing down a painted front-cloth (reproducing Poussin's *The
Realm of Flora*) – giving instant cinematic dissolve from one
tautly drawn situation to another. The graveyard denouement was
stark and striking, its metaphysical overtones plainer than in
Hockney's design. The collector's mania of Baba the Turk made
for a glorious auction scene. The Faustian compact between Donald Gramm's lively Shadow and Tear's intelligent Rakewell had
vaudeville flair with humourous song-and-dance routines, a bit of
Maurice Chevalier tap devised by Eleanor Fazan. (Gramm's premature death was very bad luck for the production.) Moshinsky's
wicked humour, evident in his ENO *Meistersinger* and *Bartered
Bride*, has been less in evidence since, though it surfaced again in
his beautifully directed *Beatrice and Benedict* for WNO in 1994.
The Rake's Progress showed rare comic flair. Moshinsky needs
more prompting than the cautious, decorous American designer
Michael Yeargan provides. His former natural irreverence could
be delicious.

Jonathan Miller had a reputation in the world of opera before
he had really achieved anything. He was a well-known phenomenon in the theatre, a polymath media figure. That was part of the

reason for his Glyndebourne staging of *Cunning Little Vixen* going to the Frankfurt Opera in the first year of the Gielen regime – though it was an effective and carefully unsentimental interpretation. His Kent Opera productions were thin, though he often latched on to a specific and inspired realistic idea, such as the terminal incapacity of Violetta in the last act of Kent Opera's *Traviata*, and the medically correct last-minute recovery that brought her to her feet for a moment before dying in Alfredo's arms. Miller's productions in the early 1980s concentrated on essentials. Set designs were neutral. The focus was on the acting of the principals, which was where Miller lavished (and still lavishes) most of his interest. He found simple distinctive ideas to motivate the performers and give a frame to his staging. His *Traviata* had a sense of Victorian photographs about it: most confrontations in its early acts were between people who were seated. But his decent puritanical *Falstaff* and *Eugene Onegin* were unfinished.

Rigoletto at the Coliseum in 1982 with John Rawnsley in the title role was very different in scale and in ambition. It was a complete transplanting of the work to a period (the 1950s) and a place (New York's Little Italy) that were distant from Verdi, despite supposed and cliché-ed cultural links. Miller had invented before – giving the Countess in his *Marriage of Figaro* at the Coliseum a whole nursery brood. His direction of the ENO *Otello*, with Charles Craig and Rosalind Plowright as the Moor and Desdemona, was workmanlike – from the same drawer as his diplomatic management of Laurence Olivier at the National Theatre in the late 1960s. *Rigoletto* set a startling new direction. Transplantation made the opera more vital, relevant, effective and certainly fun – trading on *The Godfather*. The designs by Patrick Robertson and Rosemary Vercoe evoked the New York painter Edward Hopper, with fine results in the second and last scenes, Rigoletto's brownstone tenement and the bar by the water (the Hudson or East river) where Gilda sacrificed herself. Rawnsley's Rigoletto was still hunchback and joker – but his work was as head-waiter in a bar patronized (owned?) by 'Dook', a gangleader. The naughtiest moment of the production, enough to wipe away memories of all Miller's pomposities and pretensions as a media star, showed 'Dook' singing along with the jukebox *'Donna è mobile'* in Sparafucile's café. Miller's *Rigoletto* hit the jackpot. The work seemed genuinely renovated by this new context. Updating a classic was unoriginal – tuxedos in *The Ring* were familiar at Bayreuth, and

Peter Sellars in 1981/2 was setting Handel's *Orlando* at Cape Canaveral as a space fantasy. Tyrone Guthrie's modern-dress *Hamlet* with Alec Guinness before the Second World War could be seen as a reversion to the Garrick 'modern dress' performances of the mid-18th century. If the story of *Rigoletto* were not historical and about a specific period, if realism were immaterial, why not time-travel many operas to where they fitted best? ENO's singing in English suited transposition.

Miller's ENO *Mikado*, done in twee 1920s or 1930s nursery style, updated to the era of Agatha Christie and teacakes and bellboys with a post-modern set by Stefanos Lazaridis, used an approach pioneered by *The Black Mikado*, which made Gilbert and Sullivan into a jazz/rock opera. Miller's *Tosca*, for the Florence Maggio Musicale with Eva Marton in the title role, took as inspiration Rossellini's neo-realist *Roma, Città Aperta*, and moved Puccini's opera to the last days of Italian fascism in the Second World War. In London for ENO that transposition was less effective, where the Mussolini experience had no resonance. Also Lazaridis's symbolically tilted and distorted classical set had to be curtailed for the shallower Coliseum stage. Nor was there a buzz from Miller as a foreigner working his magic on international stars.

In all three cases, the change of clothes – however effective as a refresher or defamiliarizer – was not organic to the dramaturgy. Miller's skill in *Tosca* was the manipulation and motivation of the central characters. His crowd-work meant little and the design did not distil the meaning. As interpreters, Miller, Hall and Moshinsky were essentially conservative and reactive. Miller takes few significant imaginative risks, and applies his theatrical skill in a conventional way. Moshinsky has taken up the banner of operatic conservatism, fighting back against 'deconstructionism' which he calls ironical, distancing and therefore implicitly false to the emotional character of opera. Hall's unhappy experience in Bayreuth with *The Ring* in 1983, the self-conscious pictorialism of his stagings since, and the ending of his role at Glyndebourne, have led him back to legitimate theatre. In *Grove Opera* Max Loppert wrote that Moshinsky – it will do for Miller and Hall – aimed to 'shed fresh illumination on a score without going violently against its grain'.

One of the first operatic outsiders in Britain to make an impression at ENO after Chéreau's centenary *Ring* at Bayreuth was the

Australian David Freeman (born 1952), who created his own company, Opera Factory, in Sydney in 1973 while still a student. In a number of ways Freeman was different from other British newcomers. His acknowledged influences were not European, so much as Peter Brook's 'empty space' idea of theatre and an Artaudesque emotional release against the background of an unostentatious design aesthetic quite like the poetic realism of George Devine's Royal Court. Significantly Freeman had Jocelyn Herbert as designer for the ENO world premiere production of Harrison Birtwistle's *Mask of Orpheus* and staged the premiere of Nigel Osborne's *Hell's Angels* (a failure, as it turned out) at the Royal Court. Freeman's instinctive taste in sets and costumes was economical, if not minimalist. He did not use design as a means of interpretative statement. Yet, even though his collaboration with the designer David Roger after many productions seemed to run out of steam, even though Freeman himself in the early 1990s looked as if he needed to recharge his batteries, his best work was liberating, influential and formative in building Britain's operatic new world. He shared a similar career trajectory with the American Peter Sellars: both played the title role in *King Lear* during student days. Both liked to work with an ensemble of their own choice, actors and singers as a family. This new theatrical tribalism related to the intensely effective Poor Theatre approach appealing more to Freeman than to Sellars. The company itself in this kind of theatrical tradition amounts to a political statement. Freeman's style, like Sellars's, could seem stuck in a studentish timewarp. Like Sellars he was genuinely committed to tackling new operas, though he was not lucky in his choices. Freeman himself took the title role when his Sydney Opera Factory did Monteverdi's *Orfeo* as its launch production. Later, after he had re-formed his company both in Zurich in 1976 and in London in 1981, it was his *Orfeo* – staged under the ENO umbrella, first on tour at the newly restored Theatre Royal Nottingham and then at the Coliseum with Anthony Rolfe Johnson in the title role – that launched him on the British scene.

Freeman's *Orfeo* was in a class of its own in 1981. The revival of interest in early operas had been more musical than theatrical – apart from Peter Hall's stagings of Cavalli and Monteverdi at Glyndebourne a decade earlier. Since these 17th-century operas dealt with mythical figures (nymphs, gods, satyrs) their atmosphere and costumes were usually classical in flavour and fairy-tale in remoteness. Freeman, by contrast, for *Orfeo* used more or less contemporary Balkan peasant costumes, with many rugs and carpets from Asia minor hanging in the centre of the stage. The opera became a Macedonian village drama. He had no special dancers, instead requiring the entire 20-strong ensemble of peasant-costumed performers, conducted by John Eliot Gardiner, to take part with equal facility in singing narrative madrigals, in communal dancing and in other dramatic tasks. This was a ritual involving all, not a museum-piece staggering effortfully on to the stage. The audience did not need to make allowances: with Freeman the material seemed completely present-day. By relating the tale to such a specific context, the theme became more powerfully universal. Monteverdi's opera is always painful, emotional and truthful, but when it appeared so natural an expression of a human group the effect was devastating. Where had Freeman got his concept? The theatre of Peter Brook offered many of the elements, but Freeman's formula was original. Hayden Griffin and Peter Hartwell's designs for this ENO staging were minimal. There was no set – just a stage floor, largely unadorned. Tension was sustained entirely by characters and groups working in relation with each other. The production was the performers.

Freeman's Opera Factory, mostly with David Roger as designer, obviously was based on Brook, Grotowski and Artaud. His rehearsal methods always involved a great deal of extemporized workshop action, getting to know other members of the company (often with no clothes on). That sort of thing may generate backstage jokes in the profession, but Freeman's companies were different. He wanted to treat his singers exactly like actors. The performers were the show, which chimed well with Freeman's liking for a 'found space' as his basic theatre. Freeman's earlier Opera Factory productions often showed the benefit of his undoubted flair for casting. He was never reluctant to tackle new or difficult modern operas. For him the opera in hand was always modern. His staging of Tippett's *Knot Garden* for Opera Factory used a theatrical metaphor that helped tensions build with quicksilver switches of intent. To get into the Garden, the singers had to climb over a wall with a stepladder. A clutter of chairs on stage obstructed the performers, who writhed and tumbled about the set – evoking in body language the fragmentary social relationships that were the composer's theme. Freeman provided a rush of semi-lunatic imagery and uncompromising expressionist acting, articulating Tippett's fragmentary scenes in a continuous sweep, making us follow its characteristically disparate jumble of American slang and Shavian and Shakespearian references, telling the story as a kind of Jungian notebook.

The intensity of Freeman's staging of Birtwistle's *Punch and Judy* at the Drill Hall (a cellar off the Tottenham Court Road, London) was not unlike the Lindsay Kemp *Salome* and *Midsummer Night's Dream*. The child's playground, with swing, seasaw and ladders contradicting the world of adult violence, remained a Freeman theme. Grimaces, distorted physical postures, a would-be decadent and perverted sexiness were Freeman trademarks and helped disturb any lingering audience complacency. His performers had to work so hard, they would glisten with sweat.

Cavalli's *Calisto* in 1984 looked and felt very different from the charming period gloss Hall gave it at Glyndebourne in 1970. Freeman turned the prologue into a Victoria Wood backstage farce. Three beauty queens, Miss Nature, Miss Eternity and Miss Destiny, sat at their dressing-room mirrors discussing the latest rising star, Calisto. Jove was a cigar-smoking tycoon out of the television soap-opera *Dynasty*, with Mercury as his PA on roller skates. Diana's nymphs pranced around in virginal white Victorian shifts. The thirst-quenching spring was a bottle of Coke. Pan and his satyrs were rowdies in baseball caps inscribed with their team name 'Goats', which was also printed on the ball. Juno was an Evita-like harridan who summoned up two equally formidable Furies clad in two-piece suits and 1940s fox-furs. When Jove revived the desert, instead of the leafy slotted scenery of Hall and Bury at Glyndebourne, Freeman had grey plastic cloths pulled off shapeless mounds around the stage. Helium-filled balloons shot up from patches of butcher's grass. Calisto was not turned by Jove into a cuddly bear, but instead pelted with mud which the smart Furies extracted from their handbags wearing red rubber kitchen gloves. This flurry of comic detail was combined with sharp-edged individual characterizations. The ensemble, doubling many roles, was wickedly frank. Marie Angel (later Freeman's wife) was the severe frowning Juno and also the gum-chewing cheerful Eternity. Freeman balanced downmarket fun with a lot of inventive and truthful glosses on what was happening.

He was also eager for operatic experiments – for instance, running Reimann's opera based on the Strindberg *Ghost Sonata* in repertoire with the play itself. He staged a conflation of both

Gluck *Iphigenia* operas. Gluck's Enlightenment response to the classical theme naturally softened the stone-age savagery of the original crimes of the House of Atreus, which Freeman chose to emphasize. Human sacrifices – the duty and pain around them – are the theme of both operas, so he staged the works in a context where sacrifice might seem believable, not just theoretical. But his break with the decorum of *opera seria* and Augustan French classical theatre offended purists deeply. And his usual Peter Brook-style rehearsal process did not manage to make the cast into credible sacrificing savages. Here was another problem layer of authenticity and convention, growing ever more complex with the tension between the civilized language of Gluck's music and the appearance of the characters: drugged victims smeared with ritual face-paint, carrying aboriginal shields and spears in a mud kraal beside a totem, some wearing orange head cloths and leg bracelets. During the struggles of Orestes against the furies, a group of crazed tribesmen, he was literally gnawed at. This was a very long way aesthetically from both Gluck and the Hollywood neo-classicism which was then the prevailing aesthetic of Gluck performances. At least in this distant primitive world musical utterance became a natural emotional manifestation. Freeman's taste for rough opera seemed appropriate for mining the myth in its original state.

The Opera Factory cycle of the Mozart/Da Ponte operas was a calculated bid to strengthen the company financially – tackling surefire, popular, commercially safe repertoire. Freeman's continued survival as an 'independent' was remarkable, considering how rash were risks like *Iphigenias*. Freeman staged *Così fan tutte* first in 1986, as the other half of a South Bank summer season by Opera Factory which presented the world premiere of his well-judged staging of Harrison Birtwistle's *Yan Tan Tethera*, a folksy rural idyll with the devil intervening. *Così*'s success (the best of his Mozarts) enabled Freeman to go on to *Figaro* and *Giovanni* with the added help, after the *Così* was well revived at the South Bank in 1988, of television recordings of the whole cycle.

Freeman found his model for *Così* in the painful farces of Alan Ayckbourn. He placed the opera near a sandy beach house in present-day Bondi in his native Australia, or perhaps Viareggio, and used a new translation by Anne Ridler, which included turning the Italian title into 'All can be faithless'. The secret at the heart of *Così*, which is also the soul of farce generally, is the brutal and dangerous emotional vulnerability of people revealing themselves to be in love. Freeman made the situation seem entirely natural and believable. The Arab lovers from Bahrain (?perhaps) were really recognizable: the men took their parts with proper gamesmanship, no winking or cheating on the deal with Alfonso. What was most engaging about Freeman's funny, touching production was the way it enacted physically the descriptive psychotherapy and confessional lyricism of Mozart's music; especially at the end of act 1, the climax of the farcical events, when the worm turns, and the start of act 2 when the women decide to respond to their new lovers' attentions by admitting their naughty, subconsciously chosen swap of the 'fair' and 'dark' ones. Despina's Japanese mesmerist wove a physical tangle with a folding deck-chair and the two pairs of lovers that really reduced the audience to hysterical laughter and applause. As always at his best, Freeman had an acute eye for demonstrative physical theatre. The motives of each member of the sextet were exactly explored. Big numbers carried all the emotional weight Mozart intended, staged intimately but with striking focus. Despina responded to the lengthy orchestral introduction to Fiordiligi's 'Come scoglio' by handing round a tray of cocktails, topping them up and providing olives on sticks too – even accepting a Sobranie cigarette from one of the 'Arabs' as all settled in comfortably for the 'scene'. Marie Angel's sincerity as she 'protested too much' made her ready for Ferrando to pluck, after the despair with which she voiced 'Di tornar'. Her dressing-up in army fatigues, pushing her locks under a maroon beret, looking almost masculine, was very convincing. The scenes of wooing all had a physical vitality and sexiness that would formerly have been inconceivable in opera. The artless simplicity with which the basic story was told included Despina's switching disguises (into yet another outrageously comic costume) just upstage behind a pair of well-stacked clothes horses. The Arabs threw themselves at their targets. Every glance between the characters had to be watched. However far Freeman has left behind such accuracy and electricity, his achievement with this Così will never be forgotten – the concept perfectly supported in David Roger's designs, matching and never overstating the farcical developments.

The progress of ENO's reputation which culminated in the handover to Dennis Marks in July 1993 started with Stephen Arlen's appointment to succeed Norman Tucker in charge of Sadler's Wells in 1966. Arlen made the momentous decision to move the company to the Coliseum in 1968, but all too soon afterwards died unexpectedly in January 1972. Lord Harewood in the resulting emergency was the obvious candidate to take over – importing the sense of national importance and cultural destiny which he had witnessed, and which had inspired his commitment, at Covent Garden in the post-war decade when stars like Flagstad were prepared to learn Wagner in English. If the Wells were to be taken seriously, it would have to allow itself grander expectations, nourish aristocratic ambitions. ENO in the 1980s followed a policy like Covent Garden's after the war, when Peter Brook was shocking the patrons with his stagings. Harewood, who was not a Brook supporter in the 1940s, was crucial to ENO's raised status since 1979. The chemistry involved adopting the new name of English National Opera in 1974. Could that have been achieved without the royal advocacy of Harewood as first cousin to the Queen? Would the appointment of Mark Elder as music director have been risked, after the difficult brief episode with Sir Charles Groves, without such a distinguished, established, experienced anchor? Without Harewood's active presidency as general director (then chairman of the Board) would the installation of a trio of young Turks at the top of the company have been sustainable? Especially considering that David Pountney, as director of productions, displaced Colin Graham, Britten acolyte and creator of the old-style Wells and ENO stagings. Harewood's continuing as chairman in 1993 provided continuity after the handover to Marks, with Sian Edwards as a very inexperienced and (it turned out) short-term music director.

The primary aim of artistic policy at ENO under Mark Elder's regime in the 1980s (Elder–Pountney–Jonas as it became) was to establish ENO at the Coliseum as a recognized centre of excellence, comparable at least in theatrical impact to the best at Covent Garden and the top international opera-houses abroad. Part of that task was to make an advantage of the apparent disadvantages of ENO's constraints – limited funding, English language and the classlessness of the company's audience. The move from Islington to St Martin's Lane obscured the Baylis vision. Frank Matcham's huge Edwardian palace of entertainment was in the heart of the West End – not on the doorstep of the working-class. ENO's agenda was also affected by the television age. If ENO were to continue the Baylis commitment to the deprived urban poor as its primary task, the ENO opera-house would need to be in the outer suburbs – Tottenham or Catford, Croydon or Edgware. Peter Jonas's bequest to the company was the purchase of the Coliseum freehold, with Government help. Owning its own theatre gives ENO a firmer sense of establishment. That purchase would not have been seen as justifying public money, if ENO itself had not during the 1970s and 1980s become a popular artistic pace-setter.

Lord Harewood, Peter Jonas, Mark Elder and David Pountney helped to ensure that opera could play a full part in British theatrical life. But ENO's new reputation for modern productions did not set its artistic policy apart from Glyndebourne, Scottish Opera, or Opera North. There was clearly no longer just one way of adding up serious operatic equations. Glyndebourne had done its own pioneering with Peter Hall since the late 1960s, seeking a distinctive freshness and originality. The baton of novelty and imagination was passed between various operatic institutions. For instance, the small touring company Opera 80 (now English Touring Opera) did important pioneering work during the 1980s when the conductor, David Parry, himself closely associated with Colin Graham's English Music Theatre Ensemble in the previous decade, was its music director. Its controversial but memorable *Don Giovanni* directed by Steven Pimlott upset audiences, though Parry was ousted from his leadership. The examples of Patrice Chéreau and the Frankfurt producers associated with Ruth Berghaus were noticed. What were embryonic tendencies for opera designers in the previous decade now formed a coherent body of work.

The 1991–3 seasons at ENO, the last under Jonas, were difficult. Sentiment turned against his regime. Audience figures in the recession dropped. A decision to cut back on new stagings and exploit the existing stock was mistaken, though these seasons included Jones's *Fledermaus* and Alden's *Ariodante*. In opera, public sentiment is as changeable as weather. ENO's public proved sensitive to the price of tickets which had been pushed up as high as the market would bear in the circumstances of the late 1980s. Despite its Baylis principles, ENO had to test the market to see how expensive ticket prices could be, the only way to enhance the budget and pay for creative risks. In principle, though, ENO prices should be as cheap as possible, and part of the budget should be spent on making opera accessible to those for whom price is a barrier. Two blockbuster Verdi stagings in 1992, *Don Carlos* by Pountney and *La forza del destino* by Nicholas

Hytner, were failures. Some critics suggested that ENO's modern and style-conscious interpretative approach was mistaken, or had been a passing phase. A sign of the times (and of *The Times*) was the scorn heaped by some influential critics on an adventurous and well directed staging of *Julius Caesar* for Scottish Opera in Glasgow by Willy Decker. The public in Glasgow and elsewhere adored the show, had no difficulty understanding its supposedly obscure 'deconstructionist' method. At the National Theatre and Royal Court, non-naturalistic or partly surreal and highly visual stagings by Stephen Daldry of *An Inspector Calls*, *Machinal* and *The Kitchen* were exceedingly successful with audiences.

Ever since Elder became music director in 1979, the ENO record of success was mixed – as is normal for opera companies the world over. Elder assembled and sustained a top-class opera orchestra, and kept open house for talented foreign conductors. His fourteen years at the helm had no vocal results to compare with Goodall's *Mastersingers* and *Ring*. But his commitment to a distinctively theatrical vision of how ENO should work, a vision endorsed by Lord Harewood, led to the establishment of the triumvirate with Pountney and Peter Jonas. In a real sense, those were the Elder years. Jonas on joining the company declared his admiration for Colin Graham's production of *War and Peace*, but that was not to be the model for ENO in the coming years. Despite a couple of invitations, Graham took himself off to Saint Louis. The truth is, he was increasingly out of touch with the new ENO aesthetic. In practice, the producers supported most fervently by Jonas were Richard Jones and David Alden – the first requirement of a serious impresario being a taste for experiment and adaptation.

The presiding genius of the Elder years was David Pountney, not because his productions were all marvellous. Like Elder, Pountney was a highly skilled leader of taste who enabled many other talents to thrive. With the best of his work he set a real example of innovation and adventure: producers were *in* at ENO. There were famous fallings-out and exclusions of established producers. Jonathan Miller, for example, after some big successes declared that he was quitting the British opera scene. But he was an institution himself, not a person who fitted into institutions. Along with Colin Graham, John Copley (another long-time regular) disappeared from the lists of the invited, and Anthony Besch (whose old productions of *Count Ory* and *Die Zauberflöte* went on being revived) was never asked. But the opportunities for new design and production talents were vital. There was also a big commitment to composers and new operas and workshop activities with school-students, such as the Contemporary Opera Studio and the Baylis Project.

The distinctive productions of the early Elder years were Freeman's Balkan village *Orfeo* and Miller's *Rigoletto* updated to mafioso New York. There were other enjoyable shows, earlier and later, such as Graham's downmarket user-friendly *Merry Widow* (so much more entertaining than Andrei Serban's arty version for WNO), Miller's *Otello* (indelible for Charles Craig's last great performance in the title role) and *Arabella*. Later there was John Cox's Quality Street *Così*. After Pountney arrived as director of productions, the notable stagings each season were many. All Moshinsky's ENO work, Ligeti's *Le grand macabre*, *Mastersingers of Nuremberg* and *Bartered Bride*, was excellent. Sadly he decided the ENO management was not giving him the casts he needed and took himself off to West End commercial theatre. Pountney's own best stagings were his exuberant *Valkyrie*, *Doktor Faust*, *Lady Macbeth of Mtsensk*, *Hansel and Gretel*, *Falstaff*, *Macbeth*, and *The Adventures of Mr Brouček*. In later revivals his *Queen of Spades*, *Cunning Little Vixen* and *Rusalka* were impressive. Graham Vick's shows at ENO were almost all superb, apart from his too prosaic *Timon of Athens*. He succeeded with *Ariadne on Naxos*, *Madam Butterfly*, *Eugene Onegin*, *Rape of Lucretia*, and *Figaro's Wedding*. David Alden was a constant winner, from *Mazeppa*, to *Simon Boccanegra*, to *Masked Ball*, to *Oedipus* and *Bluebeard*, to *Ariodante*. Miller's *Mikado*, as rehearsed by David Ritch, earned unflagging popularity. Nicholas Hytner's *Rienzi* and *Xerxes* were striking, the latter revived over and over again. Tim Albery's *Billy Budd* was a revelation. Keith Warner's *Werther* was decent. Richard Jones's *Love for Three Oranges* (borrowed from Leeds) was enormous fun, and prepared the ground for the madly extravagant theatricality of his de luxe Christmas Pudding *Fledermaus*. Designers who were given their heads included Stefanos Lazaridis, Maria Bjørnson, David Fielding, Richard Hudson, Nigel Lowery, Antony McDonald and Tom Cairns. It was a golden era. These interpretations were state of the art, and the careers of Hytner, Freeman, Vick, Albery, Jones, Warner, Steven Pimlott and Tim Hopkins were not limited to the Coliseum.

Nicholas Hytner (born 1956) had his big successes early, and, after making a mark with his witty, joyous ENO staging of Handel's *Xerxes*, he turned away from operatic collaboration, which had worked so well for him with David Fielding as designer, complaining of the low standard of the acting abilities of his operatic casts. There was always a slightly self-regarding element in Hytner's operatic productions: he got almost too much pleasure from his own bright ideas. His Royal Opera production of Tippett's *Knot Garden* opened a mere month after his new ENO *Magic Flute* (both designed by Bob Crowley). That was a risky work schedule; neither production achieved the truthfulness, wit, invention, or clear acting, that distinguished his best productions.

Hytner made his mark initially with an economical Kent Opera production of Britten's *Turn of the Screw* – notable for simplicity, directness, lack of pretension. Douglas Heap, the designer, used a white gauze box to define the acting space within which were naturalistic but minimal props. The fact that this staging unusually had children in the roles of both Flora and Miles, the girl as well as the boy, may have owed as much to Kent Opera's finances as to Hytner's vision, but the result was strong. For his Kent Opera *Marriage of Figaro* in 1981, with Fielding as designer, the set was dominated by huge country house windows in grand rooms (Figaro's bridal chamber was no broom cupboard). There was a fine atmospheric outlook on distant classical ruins and pine trees which, in the last act, was reversed – the action being in the ruins with a fine view of the house. The work became a Mansfield Park farcical house-party entertainment adapted by Laurel and Hardy. The Count was a children's comic-strip cad. The crowd work was lively, but there was little affection mixed with Hytner's impressive flair.

Rienzi (1983) for ENO was a trend-setter in its uncompromising 'modern' and updated approach. It was the first of three experimentally cheap stagings not intended to enter the revivable repertoire. Large-scale rarely produced works were chosen and the chorus did not have to learn their lines by heart, but carried scores. However, it was Hytner's *King Priam* (1984) for Kent Opera that was his real breakthrough, followed by the famously enjoyable *Xerxes* (1985) for ENO. So popular was this hit that the team, Hytner and Fielding, were specifically engaged to repeat their magic on *Giulio Cesare* in Paris (achieving less happy results). With *Priam*, as with Freeman's Opera Factory *Knot Garden*, the production confronted certain structural quirks or weaknesses characteristic of Tippett operas, and by means of that Fielding achieved a coherent style and powerful stage imagery for the classical story, with its Brechtian qualifications. Tippett's opera had not often been staged then. New works need a number of interpretations to reveal their secrets. Hytner was the first properly to explore the raging emotion in this epic story, the nagging conundrum of how morally to reconcile heroism and pacifism. His theatrical flair was just what the text needed. The opera became a taut, exciting statement about violence and passion. There was still something unresolved about the cerebral, mysterious final act, with its dialogue between Hecuba, Helen and Andromache, its reconciliation of Priam and Achilles, its sense of fatalism leading to the King's death. The tension between violence and Brechtian debate registered strikingly both in the staging and in Roger Norrington's conducting. Tippett's attitude to war turned out to have a strange ambivalence.

Fielding's designs exploited the blend of ancient and modern, classical and contemporary in the piece. The column on the left of the inner proscenium resembled reinforced concrete and metal; on the right the column was classical. The inner stage was enclosed with corrugated plastic panels that slid aside to show a smoking landscape of war. When things grew clearer, the stage turned out to be a sort of ruined room in an old mansion with (in act 1) most of the back wall missing, doors hidden in neo-classical plasterwork panels on either side of the stage, and another door in the surviving bit of wall at the back – behind which rose a rag-rolled, blue-washed sky-cloth. As the war progressed through the later acts, the back wall showed the marks of destruction; finally sandbags were piled almost to the top of the set. Using skilful lighting this essentially simple structure could also suggest a feeling of open countryside beyond Troy for the scene where Paris rejoined his family. At Paris's judgment, the central plastic panel was open: the masked gods stepped forward from behind a red drape with Hermes suspended from the flies. Paris the playboy wore a Lurex suit like a 1970s pop star; for war he adopted leather trousers and fetishistic armour. The Trojans were almost more homo-erotic than Achilles and Patroclus. Priam and Hecuba wore fairy-tale robes, the King at the end in sacrificial white. Dialogues had naturalistic liveliness. The Brechtian chorus figures – nurse, young soldier, old seer, the god Hermes, the servant girls commenting, as it were, from outside – were presented in a dramatically secure way. Hytner edited and controlled the performances immaculately. It was a visual feast, combining the smoke and brightness of war with the sense of an enclosed room, a prison, from which there could historically be no escape, a room with plaster walls and panels already ruined, which as the opera went on assumed the aspect of a war-torn city.

Hytner's *Xerxes* was a key event at the Coliseum during the early years of the Elder–Pountney–Jonas regime – and one of the most brilliant, entertaining and thoughtful of all the ENO modernist stagings of the 1980s, well deserving the ovation it got at its premiere. Hytner took the drama seriously, valuing Handel's obsession with the game of love – his conviction that the heart is the Achilles heel of any human power structure. The original casting of 'high voice' castrati and women suggested an equality in love, and Hytner responded to the profundities in Handel's ideally paced lyrical outpourings. Fielding's sets switched between a Baroque interior, a sort of museum or health spa hotel, with a view of Vauxhall Gardens painted on the walls and also on the central doors, and an open perspective of the very distant and therefore miniature ruins of Persepolis in the desert (at the back of the stage) below a ravishing and varying sky, sometimes sunny, sometimes stormy. Fielding's design was key to the production's success – in a sense it was Fielding's rather than Hytner's production. The design principle shared the quotation mentality of Robin Holloway's neo-romantic music or Mauricio Kagel's ironical jokes – seeing the 20th century as the place where history came to rest. Fielding's interpretative collages made the context meaningful and recycled the ideological issue disguised by the love interest. Fielding's museum imagery was no accident. His surreal dislocations were acutely expressive, and answered the hysteria in the melodic style of the arias – a typically Handelian phenomenon. Fielding made Auden's link with Handel tangible, that gamesmanship so crucial in the plot and entertaining to the audience.

The chorus in the framework established the social situation of many scenes – such as the unveiling of a potted tree at the opening, which accompanied Xerxes's larghetto aria '*Ombra mai fù*'. They seemed to be on a perpetual grand tour dressed as Handel clones in statuary grey silk like the famous Roubilliac sculpture of the composer in the Victoria and Albert Museum. In 18th-century indoor hats, they were attended by bald, white-headed and gloved

valets, who moved the props needed for the unending series of ceremonial 'Persian court life' occasions. Like any respectable audience they kept their heads buried in programmes and newspapers
(*The Inquirer*) for most of the time – especially if too much overt
passion became embarrassing, as it tended to. Following Handelian stage technique Hytner enjoyed his visual jokes and placed
his principals in front of them. One of the most memorably
prickly encounters was in a cactus court, with Persepolis behind.
The humans dwarfed the Persepolis landscape. Some of the comic
effects dwarfed them. The front of the stage was closed off with a
curtain of butcher's grass which for one scene was lowered till the
audience could see over it, then raised to become a high hedge
being clipped by a valet. Topiary statues of Assyrian beasts slid on
stage to amaze the company. A cornucopia of good laughs spurred
ever stormier and more impassioned expositions of love. The
greenery everywhere recalled Addison's 'sudden greens and
herbage'. The famous bridge over the Hellespont, a substantial
model in a glass case, collapsed like a Heath Robinson contraption. There were rain effects as well as lightning. Hytner provided
his own witty translation for the singers – as felicitous as his
scrupulously detailed direction. The Audenesque felicity of Hytner's English suggested he was injecting Auden's ideal (from *The
Dyers' Hand*) into the show – that Xerxes's country was Auden's
monarchy elected by lot for life (with statues of defunct chefs on
every corner). The mixture of reasonableness and ardent high sen-
tience was one of the exquisite pleasures of the staging.

For *The Cunning Little Vixen* at the Châtelet in 1995 Hytner,
fresh from Hollywood and *The Madness of King George*, recognized that in this case the purpose of staging was fantasy and childish folk-memory of a semi-anthropomorphic rustic ideal. The
strip cartoon that gave Janáček the character of his Vixen also suggested an unusual economy of structure. The music paints scenes
with all the detail needed, in a narrative process more akin to a
sequence of cartoons than to the laborious and fulsome scene-setting and conversation of most operas. The audience's imagination
fills in, of course.

Bob Crowley's designs, happy and perfectly judged, had a cinematic fluency where dreamlike suggestions of insect and animal
life under foot flowed from each other uninterrupted. The floor
was flat because the chosen language of the non-human life was
balletic – choreographed with charm and energy by Jean-Claude

Gallotta in a rich jumble of partnerships and demonstrations. Busy dancers, as imaginatively clothed as Andrew Lloyd-Webber's (or Trevor Nunn's) Cats, blithely relished their hyperactive dimension, using a language drawn from the classical tradition. The scene-setting was blissfully innocent and simple too. A series of pale green arches, giving a perspective of distance, filled variously with an ever-mobile forest of Sendak-like nobbly, pointy tree trunks. Leaves were left to the lighting. Sometimes trunks descended horizontally, narrowing the perspective down to the undergrowth, better for Janáček's insect characters. The scenes in the village had more threatening, barren trees. The pub was a giant structure like a squat Bohemian or Frankenwein bottle towering into the flies. Its label was a window on to a live picture of boozing and maudling.

The rhythm of the myriad scene-changes was fertile and acute. The audience were invited to dream beautiful sad dreams with which the dancing readily belonged. The effect was sealed by the unrestrained playing of the Orchestre de Paris conducted with magisterial light-footed delight by Sir Charles Mackerras. The authentically 'Bohemian' members of the cast were good actors. The cock and hens scored their usual hit, ending up strangled rather than bitten by the young vixen. The dream ballet with a Montgolfier balloon bringing down a mate for the dream Vixen was fun. The Fox and Vixen were delicious, especially, in their domestic scene of wooing on a huge, steeply raked double-bed, coloured like a floor of autumn leaves. The upside-down fence for the teacher's drunken meander was typical of Crowley's witty designs.

Thanks to the extrovert imaginative calibre of his operatic work, Hytner became one of the most admired directors of his generation in the legitimate theatre. A Cambridge varsity wit from Manchester, he directed Schiller at the Royal Exchange Theatre there. Perhaps his intellectual fascination with text made him too impatient with opera, a design-led medium. The promise of his early successes with Fielding as designer was never really explored. Perhaps his facility made him too efficient at sorting out the meaning and dramaturgical challenge. Technical fluency can limit imaginative range.

David Pountney (born in 1947 and thus 20 months younger than Moshinsky) was the pivotal figure of the revolution in British operatic production – not least because of his staff position as

ENO director of productions. But, considering this historic role, his output as a producer at ENO was uneven, the style of his work eclectic and inconsistent. The acting in his productions did not always achieve a special coherence, though he more than anyone could secure performers known for their acting. Until he left ENO in 1993 Pountney always had an insider career – with Scottish Opera, then with ENO. As an insider he was accustomed to working with existing material, available casts – to some extent he was slave to practicalities. But whatever the quality of his ensembles he was a highly successful pioneer of conceptual design and staging in Britain. His best productions were design-led, based on effectively fertile imaginative collaborations.

His 1972 debut at Wexford with *Katya Kabanová* demonstrated a genuine eye for acting performances: Sona Cervena was the Kabanicha, and the great sweeping bows with which she, after Katya's suicide, thanked the townspeople for their help were a chilling climax to her superb performance. Sue Blane and Maria Bjørnson were the straightforward designers, uncluttered realism – Moscow Arts style – the inspiration. Wexford was small-scale and had to be cheap. The outdoor scenes had a wooden built-up embankment in front of a neutral backdrop. Indoors were curtained screens with a carved chair, stools, an icon. The storm effect, dominating the whole work, was achieved through Robert Bryan's exceptionally sensitive lighting, changing as responsively as the emotional climate. Underlying everything, almost as if under the stage, the Volga flowed, archetypal, symbolic. Pountney, knitting the threads together, implied a world of busy activity just off stage. But the intensity and sharp focus, including the impressive debut of Elizabeth Connell as Varvara, were not for a long time repeated in Pountney's work, though he was prolific in Britain and abroad.

Pountney was a company man, the solid professional working at Scottish Opera for ten years, and at ENO for nine, squeezing overseas work into his schedule. At ENO Pountney started in 1977 with the world premiere of David Blake's *Toussaint*, conforming broadly to the Colin Graham ENO house style of the time. Once he had joined the ENO establishment, he sought a radical transformation of the company aesthetic. His taste for dramaturgically based design led to opportunities for many other less experienced producers. He responded at once to continental aesthetic developments, such as the Chéreau *Ring*. His Scottish

Opera *Don Giovanni* and *Bartered Bride* were effective, not remarkable. His ENO *Carmen* (1986) revisited in a more populist vein territory mapped out by Lucian Pintilie at WNO. His ENO *Macbeth* (1990) affectionately cloned a David Alden staging. His were eclectic enthusiasms.

Pountney's most frequent and successful designers were Sue Blane, Maria Bjørnson (for the *Valkyrie* of his abandoned ENO *Ring*, his famous Janáček series, and many earlier productions in Glasgow), Stefanos Lazaridis and David Fielding. The latter two – who were later to strike out as producers or director/designers in their own right – were problem solvers, closing off possibilities for the producer rather than opening them up. Pountney set a good example in his collaborations with designers. He established a feel for ENO productions that was a complete break with what had gone before. He ensured guest production teams were welcomed, supported and assisted, acknowledging their serious creative status. His ENO *Rusalka* created some memorable images. It transposed, with Freudian hints, an improbable and tiresome late romantic fairy-tale to a Lutyensesque Edwardian nursery, with the witch Jezibaba like Mrs Danvers in *Rebecca*. *Rusalka* was justly famed, though its dreamy bleached Edwardian costumes and its puppet-like rag-doll kitchen-boy and maids plucking headless stuffed ducks became stylistic clichés. Transformations of the stage were sudden and romantically theatrical, done with powerfully atmospheric lighting. Some mechanical tricks were unconvincing as imagery – like the perspex box in which the nymph Rusalka was imprisoned at court. It was an early instance of what became a tired Pountney theme. Regardless of dramaturgical aptness or the actual circumstances of the plot, mechanical behaviourism was the great inner truth that Pountney always seemed to be proclaiming. Design that was so literally assertive rather than suggestive might be convenient but was less imaginatively stimulating. Lazaridis as designer tied up too exactly the lines of movement suggested by his fully conceived spaces and hindered the freedom and discovery of the acting. Automatically his tragic operatic figures were victims of circumstance. Both *Lady Macbeth of Mtsensk* and *Doktor Faust* depended on a striking singular mechanical set concept by Lazaridis. The notion of updating *Lady Macbeth* to Russia in the Stalinist Thirties, when the opera, newly composed, was subject to political censorship, obscured the universality of its theme. Lazaridis's set decked with butcher's meat became an ironical backdrop for production numbers, though the opera was not staged to ritualize regrets for the sad history of its composer's creative life.

The danger for Pountney was always the kind of obviousness and imaginative coarseness typified by his *Orpheus in the Underworld* (1985) with Gerald Scarfe designs. The trouble with using stage-effects so boisterously and enthusiastically, when a designer like Lazaridis offered them, was that the toys diverted Pountney from fleshing out the central characters. The cuddly aspects of his *Cunning Little Vixen* staging, a well-travelled popular hit everywhere but created for Scottish Opera and WNO in Glasgow, and premiered at the Edinburgh Festival in 1980 (and still in ENO's repertoire fifteen years later), led some audiences to the perverse conclusion that it was a happy opera. It might be truthful, unblinking, accepting – but happy? The nature that is thrown into relief is human nature, and the challenge is to balance enjoyment with discomfort.

Pountney's populist instinct worked well in *Falstaff* (1989), repatriated to the world of British sit-coms and *Carry On* films, energetically acted and carried off with tremendous vulgar vitality and distinctive downmarket designs by Marie-Jeanne Lecca. If Pountney's and Lazaridis's *Macbeth* (1990) adopted the style of David Alden and David Fielding, with Banquo riding a horse on top of a wall, and an epic-scale curtain, and Lady Macbeth's bedroom vertiginously perched up a wall, and green Swarfega blood, and a hillside peopled with naked mannequins, it managed to present effectively the conflict in the work between Macbeth's immorality and virtuous Nature. The ecological theme in the original play, not only because of Birnam Wood moving, looms less evident in Verdi. Ian Spink made memorable choreography and mime for the witches' coven.

One great disappointment Pountney and Elder faced was the collapse of their *Ring* project. Regardless of the problems of casting, a flaw could be detected in Pountney's approach to the one *Ring* opera which they did manage to stage in 1983: *The Valkyrie*. The first act presented a cavernous Edwardian country-house landing from whose great 'upstairs-downstairs' stairwell sprouted the giant tree in which Wotan implanted the sword, Nothung. As in his *Rusalka* Pountney indulged his taste for massive Lutyens-like fireplaces – suggesting the alienation of Sieglinde from the sturdy sombre Hunding (Willard White) by providing separate hearths and chairs on opposite sides of the stage. Spring was tellingly sprung – answering Alberto Remedios's ringing tones as Siegmund with sunshine on leafy boughs behind the stairwell and trees at the back of the set. But the discovery of the sword in the tree, signalled with lit-up branches like a Trafalgar Square Christmas tree, was less satisfactory. Fricka was a Queen Mary lookalike in toque and pale lilac lace dress. Wotan sported a claret brocade waistcoat, cravat, frilly cuffs, and lavish fur housecoat. Nothing very original in that. The Todesverkündigung (Brünnhilde's death announcement to Siegmund) was in a monumental library, enclosing part of the revolve for the Valkyries' Ride.

Superficially Pountney and his designer Bjørnson came up with a brilliant solution for that paean to bloodlust, the Ride of the Valkyries, whose music was used to accompany the napalming of Vietnamese villagers in *Apocalypse Now*. Elder and Pountney were uncomfortable with the heroism and violence, as many producers have been. The issue of heroic death is difficult for modern liberal producers: Chéreau, Hall, Berghaus and Friedrich all had bodies or dummies lumped round the set. Berghaus's naked young men were an image of passivity not linked to the music. For Pountney and Bjørnson at the Coliseum the curtain rose for the third act on a kind of mobile war memorial, with winged victories and tall columns of pompously inscribed battle names marking the outer limits beyond which, on the cyclorama, clouds fled past. The floor of the stage was filled with an astrolabe-like assembly of concentric circles moving in contrary motion through a steep rake – so that when the stage was not aligned on one plane the two circles formed constantly changing, roller-coaster perspectives. On the outside edge were written more dates and names (Gilling, Nidhogg, Suttung, Vafthrudmir – mythical confrontations). At the revolving centre was a polished black rock, summit or tombstone. Valkyries in shining winged headdresses, prancing dangerously with the agility of circus ponies from one moving surface to another under the dramatically glaring floodlights, seemed almost to be flying. Later, bursts of flame erupted through the flooring grilles of the outer circle. Bjørnson and Pountney evoked traditional Wagnerian images with modern glosses.

The risk with such a self-consciously spoofed, effectively critical, presentation of the razzmatazz of the Valkyrie chorus was to convert the scene almost into a circus stunt – the revolve imposing its own challenging choreography while a platoon of buxom sopranos jumped around the edges like performing seals or ponies. The problem was to know what kind of world was intended by the third act after Wotan's tragic intervention in the battle of Hunding and Siegmund at the close of the second. Maria Bjørnson's theatricality related this to the privileged references of the opening acts. But the new ritual ethos was undermined by Pountney's studentish enthusiasm and taste. *The Ring* needs more than bright ideas.

Various Pountney productions have had an unfinished air – for example the mobile surrealistic tower-room in Robin Holloway's *Clarissa* never properly belonged with the rest of the stage space. The conceptual value of Fielding's set petered out as it reached the wings. Perhaps Pountney, so long at the decision-making heart of companies, was too secure, too uninterested in real risks. He relied too easily on what might be clichés. His fondness for particular performers and for nostalgic Edwardian grandeur, the white costumes of old monochrome photos, rag-doll-like kitchen choruses (*Rusalka* and *Königskinder*), mobs of automatons (*Wozzeck*) was debilitating. But sometimes he obtained strong performances from his stars.

The recipe worked best in Pountney's staging of *Hansel and Gretel* with Lazaridis as designer. The dramaturgical discovery of the production included having the singer who played the Mother also take the role of the Witch. The set included typically wonderful machinery – a full witch's kitchen was buried below the quiescent grassy suburban hillside of the opening scene, with its municipal bench, picket fences and five model doll's-house-like desirable residences, their chimneys smoking comfortably against a winter backdrop of starry sky and crescent moon or sometimes full moon. A plaster of Paris garden gnome was all one saw of the usual fairy-tale fauna. It later got knocked to pieces by the Mother as she set out, horridly transformed, on the Witch's ride. Then the steeply raked stage opened up like a lid to reveal a lovingly assembled 1950s design nightmare – pink and white square-patterned curtains and pelmets, china sink, geyser, fridge, gas cooker, comfy put-u-up, table and chairs, shelves, cupboard. And of course a broomstick.

Lazaridis's neat mechanical tricks reinforced the inspired dramaturgical concept, paralleled by Felicity Palmer's doubling of the roles of Witch and Mother. Equally appropriate was the parade of 1950s icons, in blazing heavenly white, guarding the sleeping waifs

like angels – symbols of suburban security such as milkman, postman, corner-shop granny, National Serviceman and his sweetheart, Mr Pastry with a birthday cake, Salvation Army matron
with flag and tambourine, house decorators with ladders, a perky
cinema usherette with tray and Kia-Ora, PC Dixon of Dock
Green, and a pair of lovable tramps (a.k.a. Sandman and Dew
Fairy) – a 'back to basics' nostalgic line-up of how things ought
still to be ordered. The obvious target was suburbanism and routine child abuse beneath the cosy surface. But there was healthy
ambivalence in the sentiments. The whole show looked memorable, worked on all levels. This world of childhood was still
romanticized – but recognisably local in that Hansel wore a Fair
Isle short-sleeve pullover and knee-length shorts, with Gretel in
flowery frock, grey cardigan and plaits. The Mother's hair was
buried away below a scarf turned into a char's turban. The everyday elements had the nice mix of playfulness and purpose. The
gingerbread house that rose through the turf after the children's
lost night-out was a perfect image of suburban reassurance, covered in frosty icing, deliciously yummy. The denouement was
even more dramatic than usual. The Witch's pink kitchen collapsed and split in two like Mime's forge struck by Nothung.
Eventually as the stage picture settled back to a friendly verdant
slope, numerous traps opened up in the ground to release all the
gingerbread kids in 1950s clothes. Norman Bailey's Father and
Felicity Palmer's now purified mum also emerged from the hillside, all smiles. Pountney and Lazaridis managed a textbook gentle deconstruction, full of wit and genuine perceptiveness.

Pountney and Lazaridis had developed their collaboration with
continuing success at the Bregenz Festival in a number of epic-
scale productions on the floating lake stage for audiences of almost
7000 per night that did not compromise their interventionist dramaturgical approach. The 50th Bregenz Festival in 1995 marked
also the 50th anniversary of what the Bregenz artistic director
Alfred Wopmann, who has supported enthusiastically the new
British producers, called 'the liberation of Austria'. The opera,
Fidelio, had rarely been given such massively grand treatment.
Lazaridis's scientific miracle of a staging involved 43 hidden loud-
speakers and a programmed 52 millisecond delay between the furthest and the nearest, as well as a hydraulically rising and falling
suburban street on which normal everyday German life carried on
regardless of the prison tower looming into the sky behind and

equally ignoring an endless weary procession of widows in black with black boxes in their arms wending their way along the street. Pountney's striking concept, which was never in danger of being overpowered by Lazaridis's sets, touched raw nerves in Vienna. The complaint went that people did not want to see themselves mirrored on stage.

Pountney's *Fidelio* provided a painfully relevant context for a question posed by Beethoven, which Wopmann crystallized in a programme note as 'Freedom: Utopia or hope?' How should Beethoven's low-life framework be matched with the high moral aspirations of the burdened central couple? Where had the rejoicing crowds in the final scene been all along? Why only at the last moment did they emerge to welcome Don Ferdinand? Liberation was done with yankee razzmatazz as Ferdinand arrived American-style on a motor-boat election tour, complete with a skyful of exploding fireworks, a lit-up sign reading Liberté, Egalité, Fraternité, picture opportunities with young soon-to-be voters, and a boatload of bouncing Majorette cheerleaders decked with French revolutionary colours. The finale became less affirmation than admonition which suited Beethoven's prophetic vision (defined in the characters of Rocco and Marzelline) of the unquestioning, culpable ignorance that was to undermine the Nazi dawn of European democracy when it finally arrived 100 years after his death. The peasant comedy about money and minding your own business should be articulated as something like an audience's experience. Beethoven made everybody except Fidelio an accomplice in Don Pizarro's abuse of power.

Lazaridis's huge picture included a black boxlike television set of a room for Pizarro, also a Big Brother television presence in Rocco's life. Behind the music we heard the echoing boom of deep prison doors. As the prisoners got their glimpse of freedom singing their hopeful chorus, the shutters grindingly wound up to reveal their tiny clean modern cells like bureaucratic pigeonholes. Florestan's cell, with its bread and chalice in a museum exhibition case (a little touch of Jesus), was also like a giant TV set at the heart of the prison tower, moving forward into close focus for Leonore's crucial challenge to Pizarro.

ENO in the 1990s is something like the Vienna Volksoper, or Opéra Comique in Paris, or City Opera in New York. It cannot afford international top stars, who would not often be prepared to sing in English (and might be incomprehensible if they did). But

ENO has shown that it can be more serious artistically than the 'people's operas' in those cities. When David Alden staged *A Masked Ball* at the Coliseum nobody dismissed it as a less worthwhile effort than the Covent Garden diet.

A large number of new British producers and designers became names to reckon with during the decade after 1982 when David Pountney took up the post of ENO director of productions. The new Jones/Lowery *Ring* at Covent Garden is a healthy sign of the recognition gained by imaginative and unconventional work. In 1986, when Mike Ashman's Royal Opera production of *Der Fliegende Holländer* designed by David Fielding was unveiled there, it was heckled and booed: a style that would have sat comfortably at the Coliseum was too modern for the other London opera-house. Though the Jones *Ring* earned plenty of jeers when *Das Rheingold* and *Die Walküre* opened, the management stood by the chosen design and production team – even when that meant losing Waltraud Meier as Sieglinde.

Some of the newcomers were inevitably not going to be universally welcomed, their work even less well understood by critics than by the public. Yet the brightest and most innovative producers and designers of the new operatic generation had for the time being become first choice at the Garden, or so it seemed when Nicholas Payne, the incoming opera producer in Jeremy Isaacs's team, engaged Tim Albery and Antony McDonald to make their Royal Opera debuts with Massenet's *Chérubin* in early 1994. In those other new 1994 productions, *Katya Kabanová* and *Traviata*, the choice of Trevor Nunn and Richard Eyre respectively as producers was conservative – wasted opportunities.

Equally, Graham Vick's arrival as Glyndebourne's director of productions in 1994 suggested a considered commitment to modern theatricality by the Sussex festival with its newly built opera-house. This was surprising in view of the mostly conservative tradition there over 60 years, though it was Glyndebourne that introduced Peter Sellars to Britain and had co-produced his controversial Brussels creation, *The Death of Klinghoffer* by John Adams. Vick, after successes in Bologna, Florence, New York and Berlin, was an international name – along with Elijah Moshinsky and Jonathan Miller, directing at the Met. The Young Turks had become the Establishment.

Some of the new directors, like their operatic counterparts in Germany, Italy and France, worked in legitimate theatre as well.

353

By the 1990s there was no more talk of opera needing an injection of skilled talent from the legitimate theatre. Simon Callow might direct *Fledermaus* (for Scottish Opera) or *Carmen Jones* (for Ed Mirvish's Old Vic), just as Sir John Gielgud had been in charge of *A Midsummer Night's Dream* at Covent Garden in 1961 (where he offended the Aldeburgh establishment by preferring the theatrically experienced American countertenor Russell Oberlin to Alfred Deller as Oberon). The fact that Trevor Nunn and Richard Eyre had huge popular successes directing American or British musicals might make them likely candidates for opera, though Eyre's opera debut with *Traviata* at the Garden looked as if it were intended to be conventional. Nunn's *Idomeneo, Porgy and Bess* and *Così fan tutte* at Glyndebourne, his *Porgy* and *Kata Kabanová* at Covent Garden, were well observed, but undemanding narrative productions. Both Terry Hands's *Parsifal* and Bill Bryden's *Parsifal* a few years later at the Garden were inadequate, prosaic, and unsuccessfully conceived. Bryden's uncomplicated and playful *Cunning Little Vixen*, though stronger and atmospheric, was still soft-grained and unenquiring. Theatre directors new to opera are often overwhelmed by the sheer inventive and emotional power of the music. They also want to sort things out and explain them clearly, resolving ambiguities natural to opera as an art-form with music, words and stage context repeatedly qualifying and complicating apparent simplicities.

The traffic nowadays is two-way between opera and straight theatre. The view has been canvassed that, in Britain, opera is where the most adventurous kind of theatre is to be found. Thus Nicholas Hytner succeeded with various opera productions (*King Priam* and *The Turn of the Screw* for Kent Opera, *Xerxes* at ENO) before getting the chance to do *Miss Saigon* or *Carousel* and make his fortune. Opera, though not commercial, is a testing ground where results are watched by impresarios with commercial flair. A comparative newcomer like Stephen Daldry has many invitations to direct opera, all regularly rejected.

14 Brian McMaster's eclectic imports

Lucian Pintilie's 1985 Welsh National Opera staging (at the New Theatre, Cardiff) of *Rigoletto* designed by Radu and Miruna Borozescu: Donald Maxwell's Rigoletto and Anne Dawson's Gilda prepare to observe Sean Rea's laid back Sparafucile in his hellish boiler room by the Mincio. Photograph © Catherine Ashmore.

When Brian McMaster became general administrator of WNO in 1976 he decided that, as soon as practical and if it could be afforded, foreign producers should get serious, considered and important opportunities to do new productions with the company. Lord Harewood at ENO in the 1970s had made a point of opening up to foreign talent. McMaster had been his director of planning, having already acquired a taste for and knowledge of adventurous European opera stagings during a recording industry apprenticeship in A & R (artists and repertoire). In 1974 at ENO the composer Hans Werner Henze was producer of the British premiere of his own opera *The Bassarids*; in 1975 Joachim Herz directed *Salome* at ENO, and in 1977 there was Jean-Claude Auvray's production of *La bohème*. But Harewood could not make foreigners the central issue, because the English-language tradition at ENO, a crucial cultural asset for Britain, was a constraint over which singers and producers from abroad could be engaged – and in Harewood's days both law and trade union attitudes restricted the management's ability to engage non-nationals or non-Commonwealth artists.

In Cardiff, however, it was possible to have an eclectic policy regarding original language or English translation. And McMaster balanced the opening to Europe with a commitment, often with dubious results, to bring in untested British 'drama producers' to WNO. It is true that Michael Geliot had helped 'to shape the company into a world-class ensemble', as *Opera Grove* says, since WNO's repertoire was significantly expanded by Geliot with *Lulu* in 1971, *Billy Budd* in 1972, and another Welsh world premiere, Alun Hoddinott's *Beach of Falesa*, in 1974. But after 1976 Geliot tended to oppose McMaster's policy until he resigned as artistic director in 1978, taking legal action to obtain a severance contract which gave him five new productions (of which only Martinů's *Greek Passion* was a real success). The reputation of WNO improved in spite of disasters like Geliot's infamous *Don Giovanni* in which the Don, descending to Hell, awkwardly inserted himself into a drawer in his dinner-table while it billowed smoke like a short-circuiting hostess trolley. In McMaster's opinion,

Geliot and other established British opera specialists had had a good run of opportunity over many years at WNO and Sadler's Wells – and the results compared feebly with the productions he had admired in Europe.

Design, McMaster said in 1976, was 'the *only* exciting thing about British theatre at the moment'. But in his early years Cardiff was not famous for production values. William Gaskill's *Barber of Seville* was a harbinger of good intent, slipped into the first McMaster season when his hands were untied by a production store conflagration (that most traditional engine of theatrical renewal). William Dudley's set was a model of theatrical economy, clearing space for vitality and action: on one side of the stage a vignette of Seville streets, attractively painted on a series of flown boards, arranged a telling perspective and provided a frame from which Almaviva's band of serenaders seemed to jump like a pop-up story book; on the other side of the stage were the necessarily solid window, balcony and door for Bartolo and Rosina. Linking these sketchy elements was a Spanish-style inlaid floor, slotted to allow scenery to slide on stage from the wings, and in the background horizontal white louvred canvas strips against a pale idealized blue sky-cloth. Gaskill, though unpretentious and cautious in this operatic debut, achieved masterly ensemble timing. But this *Barber* was a lively touring show that caused no traditionalists any heartburn. McMaster in 1976 knew his agenda of revolutionizing opera production would be unpopular with some. Sadly Gaskill's subsequent productions (*Bohème* in 1977 and *Lucia* much later in 1986) were not an advance. His *Bohème* aimed at '*realistisch Musiktheater*' but with the typically short British rehearsal schedule (compared to what Felsenstein allowed himself) was just dull with sub-fusc designs by Hayden Griffin. Though relaxed and truthful in its acting, in vocal terms it was feebly cast. McMaster gave him another chance, but Gaskill's *Lucia* proved desperately mediocre and misguided.

McMaster next invited David William, a well known theatre director in Wales, to open the new season in September 1977. The assignment was *Queen of Spades*, and McMaster arranged for him to collaborate with the German designer Wilfried Werz, to back up his lack of operatic exerience with a Komische Oper-style commitment to the dramaturgical exploration. The opening night was a memorable operatic disaster. The contrast with Chéreau's Bayreuth *Ring* and its surrounding controversies, which had just provided me with some of the most stimulating and exciting times I had ever spent in or around a theatre, could not have been sharper. Sitting at the front of the stalls of the New Theatre, Cardiff with a friend beside me who was an Australian actor, our reactions degenerated along with the performance into helpless hysteria. *Queen of Spades*, with its surrealistic blend of naturalism and poetry, its creaky formal structure, is not a beginner's work. Chorus entries and exits in the opening scene (nannies and soldiers in the park) immediately undermined the attempts at naturalism. But then the ugly old Countess's false nose fell off her face just when she dropped off to sleep – before Hermann's entry demanding the three-card secret. Her head flopped forward on to the arm of her chair, and the nose took up a commanding position on the floor beside her where it stole the rest of the scene – Gogol intruding grotesquely into Pushkin. Allen Cathcart's Hermann was transfixed by the absence in the middle of the Countess's face – his discomfort being the main sign of life in a catatonic performance. Later the dancer Svetlana Beriosova, who had made a 'guest appearance' as the Empress Catherine after the Baroque play-within-a-play, snagged her ermine on each of her overdemonstrative curtain-calls.

WNO's Janáček series (*Jenůfa*, *The Makropoulos Case*, *The Cunning Little Vixen*, *Katya Kabanová* and *From the House of the Dead*) with David Pountney productions and Maria Bjørnson as designer, had launched with *Jenůfa* before McMaster arrived. His first crisis was to engage a producer for the opening production of the season, *Orpheus in the Underworld*; at the last minute he was able to borrow a French but undistinguished staging by Louis Ducreux, recently opened. Then there was Ian Watt-Smith's staging of Tippett's *Midsummer Marriage* designed by Koltai with Annena Stubbs costumes, an abstract, symbolic and effectively neat sub-Bayreuth staging. McMaster broadened the repertoire, but many of his choices inevitably did not relate to his main theatrical vision. The early McMaster years saw all sorts of unremarkable productions, including John Copley's *Peter Grimes* and *Tosca*, Adrian Slack's *Turn of the Screw*, Geliot's *Coronation of Poppea* and *Andrea Chénier*. One of the better of these economical shows was Stewart Trotter's *Traviata*. Later McMaster invited Giles Havergal of the Glasgow Citizens Theatre to direct *Barber* and *Figaro*, resulting in shows livelier than Gaskill's *Bohème* and *Lucia*, but nothing special. A good Havergal *Entführung* at

Gelsenkirchen had encouraged McMaster, but that early promise was never realized in Cardiff. None of Havergal's work was as worthwhile as Philip Prowse's staging of Handel's *Tamerlano*, though Prowse made more impact at Opera North, for example, with Ponchielli's *Gioconda*.

The definitive break with theatrical mediocrity in Cardiff, the real start of the McMaster revolution, was Harry Kupfer's staging of *Elektra* in March 1978 followed by Joachim Herz's *Madam Butterfly* in September. Kupfer's staging presented a surrealistic world startlingly different from anything Cardiff had seen before, far more energetic and involving. WNO was suddenly the home of work as serious as anything British opera-houses had seen that decade. Wilfried Werz's set suggested the world behind the proscenium was of epic dimensions dominated (and from some seats almost obscured) by a headless shattered statue of Agamemnon standing in a Dali-like melting courtyard of shiny, plastic-looking stones. The courtyard was on a raised platform, set well back, from which yellow-lit wooden fencing surrounded the stage with a ceremonial flight of steps at the back, shiny polythene wrapping, and odd relics of old sacrifices (such as a naked girl) hanging from the flies. The maids in the opening scene raced around the stage with Liliputian ferocity, making insanely hurried gestures like bloody warders in an asylum. The slaves were scantily, oddly dressed. Klytemnestra made a stunningly horrid entrance from the palace: the fence behind the steps glided upwards and she staggered forward as overdressed and encrusted as the Great Orlando in Lindsay Kemp's version of *Salome*, surrounded by a court wrapped together in cellophane, costumed and painted like a riot of Beardsleyesque homunculi. Compared to this bizarre array, faces picked out (notably in the case of the Young Servant) like Picasso cubist portraits, Elektra herself was a sober figure, her visage expressionistically pallid like a Pabst heroine. Kupfer and Werz gave *Elektra* an extreme but consistent style in acting and design, resonant and right for the modernism of Strauss and Hofmannsthal. Anne Evans as Chrysothemis bared her breasts, and hinted at a lesbian infatuation for her sister. Kupfer wanted to recapture the theatrical shock caused by the original performances. McMaster's WNO agenda was clearly to make the public sit up.

Herz's *Butterfly* by comparison was sober, beautiful to look at, and continuously naturalistic – while making something unusual out of the familiar cherry blossom and Japanoiserie. Rodney Milnes called it a 'despicable forgery' because it reverted to the earlier version of the score subsequently rejected by Puccini, which was less indulgent to Pinkerton's suspect morality and American imperialism. As a result the Herz version was assumed to be Marxist. It started with Pinkerton at the left of the stage taking a snapshot: a spotlight picked out the middle of the black front curtain, then the light expanded like the first shot in a 1930s film to reveal, below, a model-village Nagasaki at the front of the stage, and behind it a simple Japanese house with sliding screens between rooms, nestling under blossom-filled boughs. Herz confirmed standard visual and anecdotal expectations of the narrative, then cut across the conventions. Cio-Cio-San and Suzuki scattered white blossoms, little Japanese (called Nips by Pinkerton in the new WNO translation) minced about obsequiously, spoofing a stage-Japanese manner. But Herz's approach turned what can be seen as merely a domestic tragedy into a burning icon of self-deception. He presented the culture clash strikingly yet without overstatement, through the Americanisation of his Butterfly herself. Waiting for Pinkerton's return, she wore an American dress, surrounded herself with the flotsam of American culture, photos, a gramophone, a toy lighthouse, a sort of rocking-horse. Goro waved choice geisha snaps for the sexploitative young naval officer to choose from. The events of the opera were pared to spontaneous essentials. Tradition was not neglected. Butterfly committed suicide behind screens, then staggered to where her little son had been playing.

McMaster's foreign guests tended to come in two varieties: realistic and surrealistic. Both were intended to fulfil the WNO commitment to theatricality, and most succeeded. One of the first of the neo-realists was Peter Brenner who staged Reginald Goodall's *Tristan und Isolde*. Not much of a theatrical experience, this was Goodall's event above all, with the bonus of young Linda Esther Gray's remarkably promising Isolde (promise alas not fulfilled) and a decent Tristan from John Mitchinson. Kupfer's *Fidelio* (designed like *Queen of Spades* and *Elektra* by Wilfried Werz) was out of the Felsenstein stable, set in a featureless Nazi prison-camp compound, the corners of the set enclosed by four floodlight pylons, but with 18th-century pigtails and costumes blending Napoleonic and modern. Its keynote was dignified simplicity, though its closing tableau of dead bodies was a different sort of qualification, throwing up that Amnesty International agenda, the suffering of prisoners. Once again conservatives went on about Marxism. Such references do not necessarily earn the expected credit. Other examples of more or less realistic music-theatre, East Berlin-style, were André Engel's *Salome*, Elijah Moshinsky's *Ernani*, and work by the young Swedish producer (and Royal Theatre actor) Göran Järvefelt, a particular McMaster favourite, starting with *The Magic Flute*, continuing with *Ballo in maschera*, *La bohème*, *The Ring*, and *Traviata*. Järvefelt was not a Felsenstein disciple but partook of much the same aesthetic, not least because of his German designer Carl Friedrich Oberle. He was more influenced by Ingmar Bergman's sense of truth and delicacy, the gentle humour and relaxed naturalism that mark Bergman's Drottningholm *Magic Flute* for instance. In a special class were Rudolf Noelte's miraculously sensitive and well-observed *Bartered Bride*, one of the most refined and touching achievements of the McMaster years, and Peter Stein's *Otello*, *Falstaff*, and *Pelléas et Mélisande* – the greatest international coups of McMaster's whole regime.

The Romanians introduced by McMaster – Andrei Serban, Lucian Pintilie, Liviu Ciulei and Petrika Ionesco – were not always theatrical surrealists. Serban got too many chances to parade his eclecticism, considering the variable achievement of his *Eugene Onegin*, *Rodelinda*, *Merry Widow*, *I Puritani*, and *Norma*. Mike Ashman's *Parsifal*, Tim Albery's *Trojans*, and Helmut Polixa's *Fledermaus* came from much the same drawer as Ciulei's *Così* and *Wozzeck*, with naturalistic acting, coherent graspable narrative format, and comprehensible but distinctive designs. The most outlandish and brilliantly individual work of McMaster's entire regime were Pintilie's two stagings – *Carmen* and *Rigoletto* – and Ruth Berghaus's extraordinary *Don Giovanni* (see p. 129). It was these controversial blockbusters that defined WNO's notoriety as pioneer of the new and criticized 'opera production' ethic.

Järvefelt's *Ring*, a remarkable company achievement, was not visually or theatrically memorable. Its modest straightforward story-telling worked best in *Die Walküre* where the imagery of Oberle, Järvefelt's usual designer, did not seem too prosaic. Impressively, its casting was almost entirely local to WNO, many singers tackling roles for the first time. A more significant aesthetic statement (for the future of WNO) was Järvefelt's *Magic Flute*, which introduced him to British audiences in 1979, a breath of fresh air for the company. Opera audiences laugh indulgently at end-of-the-pier routines. Self-consciously comic *Magic Flute* stagings often degenerate into quaint farce and mumbo-jumbo, while sententious *Magic Flutes* can be as po-faced as a philosophical text. Folklore elements like the old crone who becomes a busty young Papagena, once Papageno has given his word to marry her, invite burlesque. Järvefelt and Oberle balanced the human comedy simultaneously with deep seriousness. The Three Ladies, the Boys, the Queen of the Night, Monostatos, were cool, sober, flesh-and-blood people, with comprehensible and involving motivations. In performance the force of the text varies, but in Mold, north Wales, at the premiere the words were followed in great detail. The theme of testing and questing (just like *Star Wars*) was not a pretext for smug jokes and a cosy happy ending, but a necessary ritual revealing the true quality of human life. It was a penetrating reading of the text, a view of the *Magic Flute*'s enigma that combined affectionate laughter and spiritual joy. The frequent 'moral' conclusions were delivered out front, house-lights up. As in Hockney's Glyndebourne *Magic Flute* – as in most productions – Järvefelt exploited pantomime and fable with the dragon and the menagerie of wild animals tamed as if by Orpheus. Oberle's single set, with a centre-stage platform steeply sloping away from the front against a white back-cloth, allowed more dramatic fluency than Hockney's witty game with drop-cloths. Stairs borne on little arches on either side of the stage, rising in perspective towards black-masked exits and a jumble of bare tree trunks, logs and rocks, were gradually removed as the performance went on and briefly replaced with little flowers. There was none of the Masonic paraphernalia and mock-Egyptian-cum-Californian references of Hockney's witty perspective games, which held the seriousness at a safe distance. Oberle's animals – elephant, gorilla, chimpanzee, crocodile, lion, goat, polar bear – acted out their involvement in Tamino's quest for Pamina. The spoken (English) dialogue sounded completely natural, untheatrical and free of operatic diction. The charming Papageno made his suicide attempt seem quite serious; there was a resolute Tamino and a responsive Pamina. The key was the way Järvefelt made the priests' debate over Tamino's trials more than just ritual.

Järvefelt's stagings of *La bohème* and *La traviata* were frankly conventional and run-of-the-mill, though the Me-generation designer aesthetic of the latter was typical of 1988. In both cases

Järvefelt took up assignments abandoned by, respectively, Pintilie and Noelte. *Ballo in maschera* was Järvefelt's finest hour, exploiting Dennis O'Neill's star central performance and references to Gustav III's familiar Drottningholm theatre. As a Swede Järvefelt naturally restored the opera to Verdi's original location, the Stockholm court of the stage-struck monarch, which the censors had switched, improbably, to New England.

A masked ball is a truth game. Nothing in *Ballo* may safely be taken at face value. Feelings are ambivalent, and there are ironical, black humoured switches and changes in the plot. When Amelia and Gustav reveal their mutual infatuation for the first time, Verdi suggests how fragile and temporary their passion must be with the great love duet's whizzing, slippery accompaniment. The timing and restraint at this storm centre involved a sharp build-up of tension in the staging. *Ballo* is full of rumours, intrigues, suppositions, play-acting. Which of the confessions are meant to be sincere? Gustav and Amelia may be toying with a delusion. Järvefelt balanced history and romance. Gustav spent the prelude and many later bars brooding over a model of his Royal Theatre on the right at the front of the stage with a little puppet stage beside it, authentic 1790s scenic drops, and dolls modelled on the opera's characters – including an unlikely miniature of Donald Maxwell's Anckarstroem. The action took place on a rising stepped ramp of plain floor-boards, moved around the centre of the stage for different scenes. Ulrica, the fortune-teller, was interpreted straightforwardly. The courtiers got into their sailor disguises at the end of the first court scene; when they unmasked after the fortune-telling, they were welcomed and encouraged by the populace, and launched into a theatrical reprise of Gustav's coronation, complete with crown and robes. The great love-duet with Amelia below the picturesque snow-swept gallows (ideal conditions for a passion-killing flower) was the musical triumph of the show – as Verdi meant. The morning-after confrontation between the minister and his erring wife, when she picks out the conspirators' lots, was less good. When Gustav was pierced by Anckarstroem's bullet, his death shortened by Verdi to a few bars of heart-rending music, he sprawled headlong across his toy theatre. The harping on Gustav's thespian mania and on the ambivalence was echoed in Oberle's period sets and costumes and in the front-cloths rung down between scenes, never masking the scene-changes behind or making the illusion solid. This was not slavish naturalism: the acting was stylized to communicate meaning rather than mimic life. Characters who play-act, rather than just fulfil their roles, are always the most vivid. To share the secret of theatrical illusion with the audience, to step through the looking-glass and employ what Brecht called alienation (as old a device as theatre itself), is to intensify the meaning and range of the whole event. Järvefelt's *Ballo* was an opera about opera, meshing illusion and reality, truth and intrigue, comic conspirators and tragic guilt. As a former actor, Järvefelt firmly resisted the routine that opera can be.

Though WNO's singing standards under McMaster were not ideal, casting showed theatrical sense and a desire to furnish the producer with worthwhile material. This was certainly true of the discovery of the late Warren Ellsworth, subsequently memorable as WNO's Mowgli-like Parsifal and Siegmund. Ellsworth was cast as Jenik in Noelte's touching and truthful *Bartered Bride*. His performance encapsulated what Noelte sought. On the surface this seemed a usual *Bride*, with Jan Schlubach's barn-like single set, and colourful peasant costumes designed by Elisabeth Urbancic. The stage presented the interior of a Bohemian lath-and-plaster walled building, with beams and thatched roof, barn doors at the back opening on to corn stacked on a featureless, flat field under a sunny sky. But the eternal verities that concerned Smetana were less about spring festivals and circus carnivals, more to do with love and marriage – as in Smetana's acknowledged model, Mozart's *Figaro*. Noelte's scrupulous naturalism underlined the epic emotional core of the work, while never denying a place to the dancing peasants and stuttering tenor and last-act tightrope walk and bear-suit. There was no 'operatic' behaviour. Realism ruled – as it then almost never did in the time-warp stagings at the Prague National Theatre. With each tiny detail closely observed, every gesture had to come from truthful expression. The comedy was serious.

In the opening scene the chorus decorated the barn for harvest festival. On either side were rows of tables and benches; lighting was natural and expressive. The open space at the centre of the barn acted as a forum where fraught feelings could be released. After selling out his love for Helen Field's strongly emotional Marenka, Jenik sang his aria pacing pensively up and down. Their earlier duet had brought them eventually to a table downstage right where they joined hands with beautiful sincerity. The quintet of parents and marriage broker, twisting Marenka's arm in the last act, was very believable. The vibrant beer-swilling of the second act was rhythmic and convincing. The youthfulness of Jenik and Vasek was poignant, the latter a sympathetic naive child, funny but not an object of farce.

A beneficiary of McMaster's ill-fated determination to combine the talents of Reginald Goodall and Rudolf Noelte for WNO's first ever *Parsifal* in 1983 was Mike Ashman (born 1950), then a promising staff producer with the company. When Noelte backed out of the assignment, having fallen out with Goodall over the casting, McMaster gave Ashman the chance to take over and tackle the Wagner on his own: an auspicious start to his career. Ashman's *Parsifal* was not flawless, but it had remarkable freshness and originality. With a better designer he might have succeeded in doing what Moshinsky did at Covent Garden with Jon Vickers and *Peter Grimes* eight years earlier. Time for preparation was short and the second act flower maidens were done as Victorian-era pornography, with Klingsor as a frock-coated capitalist gent. None of this belonged conceptually with Ashman's pictorial and convinced approach to the Grail hall and its sacred spring nearby in the outer acts. What defined the production was Ellsworth in the title role – a natural performer of fine spiritual quality, a child of nature who could not have suited better Wagner's *'reine Tor'* (pure fool). Ellsworth erupted on to the stage, brandishing bow and arrows, splashing through the sacred waters where Amfortas was about to undergo his ritual ablution, hunting and holding his quarry of a noble swan. The breach in decorum registered wonderfully, as if a wolf child had broken into a formal dinner party. Ashman's concept contrasted Wordsworthian nature with theoretical, conventional civilization. The designer Peter Mumford strikingly transformed this Eden-like garden into the Grail hall: a grid of lights and platforms descended from the flies, a bit like a Spielbergian spaceship landing in clouds of dry ice. The handling of rituals was relaxed, making both the people and the events believable. Ashman found the right ingredients for the central theme – Wagner's surprising (and questionable) regression to a simple moral world of sexual purity, honour and honesty. With such an epic endeavour, even getting only part of the work right was remarkable. WNO's production (thanks to Goodall's preparation and Donald McIntyre's experienced Gurnemanz) outshone both of Covent Garden's two bites at the task. Ashman moved on, eventually, to direct *The Ring* in 1997 for Norwegian Opera, Oslo.

McMaster's belief in opera as truthful theatre, rather than mannered costume charades, was fully borne out. The reformed WNO standard of music-theatre, the company commitment to serious and sometimes highly idiosyncratic work, eventually won over Peter Stein. McMaster pursued Stein for years, before engaging him. After his unhappy experience with the *Ring* in Paris, Stein had written off opera as a fruitless experiment for him. The new spirit in Cardiff changed his mind. But the Verdi masterworks, *Otello* and *Falstaff*, which he first tackled for the company, were not easy to cast with idiomatic singers of sufficient style and distinction really to serve Verdi's music. With *Otello*, it was hard to find a top calibre cast that would suit Stein and be eager to work the way he wanted. It almost proved Stein's genius that without real Verdian singing his interpretation carried such conviction. This was, unquestionably, theatre plus.

Lucio Fanti, Stein's set designer for his Verdi operas, proclaimed an aesthetic of 'period narrative painting' in *Otello*. He defined the proscenium with a large, plain, golden, chamfered picture-frame in front of which two steps led down to a narrow forestage at the bottom of the frame, where one would expect a brass plate with the artist's details. Richard Armstrong, the conductor, launched into that wonderfully direct, stormy, thrilling opening – and at once the red plush panel inside the frame slid up, and the bare boards of the square stage space filled suddenly with purposeful, hurried, milling crowds, urgent, anxious, acting as if with one mind, a storm embodied in human form. Moidele Bickel's costumes and the buildings painted on the hinged flats that formed the sides of the set immediately defined the context. This was the renaissance: Verdi's renaissance, the ultimate application of the old master's reawakened genius; Shakespeare's renaissance as revived by Boito; and Stein's too after a ten-year break from the opera-house. The imagery was of the Florentine early Renaissance, with architecturally framed groups of people. The sides of the set were hinged, able to swing open and admit the pressing chorus. There was a sense of speed. The action raced almost faster than the eye could follow. Stein's direction made the focus flash unpredictably from point to point. The presence and vitality were overpowering. The chorus stopped, started, reformed, broke, in a constant impression of nervous alarm and surprise. Then they would assemble in a knot, like a whirlpool or an animal at bay, singing with the unbridled physical exhilaration Verdi invited and the Welsh National chorus generously provided.

At the back and behind the side-flats, steps led away and down. The rear of the stage like an art gallery had a large canvas with a stormy sky in front of which a jagged metallic fork, shaped like lightning, pointed downwards – reflecting flashes of blinding, laserlike intensity. At the end of the first act, when Otello and Desdemona hymned their love, the stormy canvas was replaced with a moonscape, which later gave way to a blue sky and fluffy clouds, and later still in the Council Chamber to angry waves. Imagery and pictures were a theme.

Stein and Fanti's picture-frame was not a game. It suggested the sharp subtle perspectives in the work, reminding audiences where the pictorial language came from. Stein's production wore the tradition of operatic *Otellos* lightly. When the Moor was supposed to approach Desdemona's bed with scimitar held high, he did just that. Even the curtain of Victorian melodramatic narrative paintings was drawn into play: jealous red, with flame tongues of indiscretion, a pair of flimsy red drapes in act 2 symbolized Iago's intrigue, isolating him to sing his Credo on the forestage. In the handkerchief scene the curtain within whose toils Otello strove to overhear Cassio was thick plush red. One of the most astounding of the production's visual images had Otello fall into his epilepsy centre-stage, dragging the drape in consequence almost halfway across the proscenium. With a touch of theatrical daring, Stein placed Otello, Cassio, and Iago in line at the front of stage, Otello of course unseen by Cassio, the large lace kerchief dancing like a poison cloud between all three.

The production's major accomplishment was Stein's ability to use expressive tricks without being slave to them. The lighting subtly distinguished outside and inside and time of day, while also suggesting a broader emotional agenda. There was a threatening jealous red zone, left of stage, into which Otello immediately passed after his very first heroic entry, contrasting with the colour yellow on the right and blue at the back: hints not laboured. The purity of Desdemona's final scene was devastating. Helen Field in gloriously sensitive voice (though no Verdian) sang most of the Willow Song upstage, facing her mirror, a fat candle burning beside her, then gave her '*Ave Maria*' straight out to the audience. The interior door on the right, the cold moonlit window high above it, were as Verdi and Boito's stage directions indicate. The

Moor shut the cupboard door on the mirror and candle for his final desperate deed. The strangling was naturalistic, shocking. Desdemona's mouth gasped, upside down – he raised her arm and let it fall to check she was dead. There was perfect tact too in that final image, the last kiss that Otello did not achieve, as his arm tried to cradle the memory of their plighted troth, slowly falling away to Verdi's cadence and closing punctuation. The poised fatalism of the last act, even with Iago's flurry to escape, exactly answered the unsettling chaos earlier in the council chamber, with Otello pacing through the crowds distraught, physically attacking them, laying them flat like victims of plague in a biblical painting, furious to clear the stage after publicly cursing his bride.

Stein accepted the challenge of pictorial theatre, and, with apt reference to the method of early Renaissance narrative painting, went beyond it into a kind of expressiveness that pursued every level in this terror-struck work. Specially well-marshalled was the great council chamber sextet. The acting was determined and economical, each movement or gesture weighed. The narrative line stretched but never tore. The scene where Desdemona raised her arm in a firm gesture pronouncing her honour, and then was later almost thrown off stage, had a forceful conviction. The stage space gradually narrowed down, as Otello's obsession grew all-consuming, a telling expressive frame for the drama, almost like cinematic montage. This is what *Gesamtkunstwerk* should be about. *Otello*, not a political work, speaks of humanity not society. Its moral burden is the nature of truth – with jealousy secondary. Stein arrestingly faced the vacuum of egotism. The staging's truthfulness may have been conventional outwardly, but Stein responded to the musical opportunities with stimulating ease.

Stein's *Falstaff* and *Pelléas* both lacked quite that special revelatory energy. His *Falstaff* was teutonic in flavour, opening in a clean little *Weinstübe*. Moulding the production round Donald Maxwell, a comparatively young star who was also Stein's Iago, initially risked some of the resonance of Falstaff's physicality. The true Stein genius came out in the scene just before the Herne Oak frolics, with Verdi's conspiratorial part-writing outside the Garter inn and Falstaff half-drowned. Stein impeccably caught the gossiping conspiracy of the wives, the obscured egotism and jealousy of Ford, the eager youthful innocence of Fenton and Nannetta. Fanti's solid Elizabethan sets provided different physical levels and visual perspectives, but mainly defined the social ambience.

Movement and gesture became a stylish liberating rhetoric, especially for the eupeptic Alice of Suzanne Murphy. The interpretation escaped from English preconceptions to the Italian passion and warmth of Boito and Verdi. Stein's teutonic humour acquired a relaxed glow in later revivals, though Ford and his men's hunt for the fat knight was manically boisterous and over the top, the elastic of comic hysteria almost too loose.

Maxwell's account of the great title role, voice ample enough, personality generous, randiness and good humour compelling, really developed. His entry with antlers matching the oak in Windsor Park, anxious and fearful of getting in too deep again, was a lovely coup. The staging of the fugal finale ('*Tutto nel mondo è burla*': the whole world's folly) allowed full rein to Stein's managerial genius, the polyphonic entries of each singer made round the back of Maxwell's rubicund Falstaff, the crowd gathering and ebbing with delight, Sir John finally rising on wires into the dark sky in burlesque apotheosis.

Stein's *Pelléas et Mélisande* was a spectacular British debut for Karl-Ernst Herrmann as designer, a frequent Stein collaborator. The atmospheric sets had the sharp-etched enchanted tone of Yellow Book woodcuts. Each scene got a different picture: all the stage dimensions were exploited. Diagonal steps across the proscenium described the castle terrace, perched high above the misty ocean over which a ship set out on a mysterious voyage (climbing up a taut wire, in a trick of naive theatrical perspective). Mélisande's tower window, from which her golden tresses poured and through which Yniold spied for his father, was at the top of the proscenium on the extreme left with the ground falling away to a distant lake or seaside and twinkling lights or stars in the blackness opposite. One registered the headiness of innocent discovery and two souls isolated in mutual feeling. The setting was perfect, as was Jean Kalman's lighting on the trees in the first lost-in-the-forest scene-change from spring green to silver-pink. The lighting was equally subtle on the marching columns of flat dark tree trunks that marked off the well-court outside the gates where the fatal kiss occurred: Golaud's sword glinted dazzlingly from the trees. Other striking scenes included the grotto with its sleepers and sparkling water (on a lid that opened up from the floor); the dangerous shelf and vertiginous stairs where Golaud saved his brother Pelléas from falling; and the battlement with its blinding disc of sunrise. Herrmann is a visual wizard. These sets typified his acute, black-dominated, shiny aesthetic much seen at the Monnaie, Brussels, during the Gerard Mortier years. With neurotically obsessive, finely observed acting and unerring atmosphere, Stein's staging was brilliantly controlled.

But the work of Stein, and of Ruth Berghaus whose remarkable WNO *Don Giovanni* was described in Chapter 7, was already known at least in Germany. McMaster's Romanian guest producers were far more of an adventure, and therefore greater credit to his daring as an impresario. In many ways the greatest risk he took, leading to the most remarkable outcome, was the hiring of Lucian Pintilie whose highly unusual *Carmen* and *Rigoletto* shared spectacular and unexpected magnetism, astoundingly open emotions and an almost vaudeville sense of fun. Like Berghaus, Pintilie generated many complaining letters to the WNO management. But McMaster – unlike the little touring Opera 80, which met similar outrage over Steven Pimlott's *Don Giovanni* in 1985/6 and got cold feet about innovative productions – continued to explore new talents.

For Pintilie *Carmen* was above all the liberator's opera, the first work to be mounted after every revolution, the most popular opera in the world. So he put it in contemporary dress and imagined it being performed as a kind of communal celebration in a newly liberated central American or south-east Asian town: a kind of *MASH Carmen* defamiliarized and freshened with all sorts of theatrical tricks and outrageous jokes. When Micaela sang of José's village and his mother thinking of him, a ghastly little model village was pushed on stage on tracks at the front (later used for a ciné-camera). When Escamillo launched into the Toreador song, he was stopped in full stream by cheers of happy recognition from the entire company and had to start all over again – twice. To make humour like that function took courage, energy and total commitment from the performers. Pintilie, who was by profession a film-director not an opera producer, attributed his style to the fact that he came from Bessarabia, part of Romania absorbed into Russia: 'They often say back home that I've many Russian characteristics – such as my inclining to the grotesque and the metaphysical both at once. That's very Russian; think of Dostoievsky.' His aim had been to break with Soviet-style naturalism, as Romanian theatre had liberated itself after 1962 on the wings of Giorgio Strehler's Goldoni and Shakespeare productions and Peter Brook's famous *King Lear* with Paul Scofield. 'You must know the naturalistic school,' Pintilie pontificated, 'but not be limited by it.' His *Carmen* entirely depended on energy, and in a poor performance (such as one might see a few times) there was nothing there. 'Every evening it's a gamble. If the performers haven't the vitality it's lost. If I don't tell the story, I have to replace the narrative with something else – with the joy of playing *at* a story. And to play with a work, you must have that sexuality of the words' – in the natural language of the performers. In *Rigoletto*, working in Italian, chorus and even stars tended to play just the music.

For *Carmen* Pintilie used the broad, crude devices of poor theatre or street theatre, not bothering to sustain any sense of naturalism – though the staging was too extravagant of gesture to be really classifiable as Grotowskian. It sent up the operatic conventions that it endorsed: like Escamillo's hit-song, Carmen's was interrupted with enthusiastic applause by crowds of urchins and extras on stage, when the first familiar notes were barely through her lips. Pintilie's genius lay in articulating criticism of the work in the performance, and staging (in a way) the performance history simultaneously. To interpret is to criticize. Pintilie made his audience observe how it was looking at the opera. The truck on rails with the model village for Micaela's 'And there's the village I remember' was not just decorative fun – though Pintilie's production was infectiously entertaining. The outlandishly burlesqued details reinforced Bizet's poetry. Pintilie's *Carmen* for the 1980s, with Morales, José and Zuniga in American Vietnam war jungle fatigues, with the face of Samoza irrelevantly decorating a tent at the heart of the rubbish tip into which designers Radu and Miruna Boruzescu converted the stage, did not lecture the audience, or add up prosaically, or squeeze Bizet into a preconceived concept. This was the most liberated, vital, enjoyable *Carmen* that we in Britain had seen in years. It exploited the fact that an audience habituated to television – and to variety acts on television – need not be led through narrative. So Pintilie had a single set, a centre-stage revolving cage from which seats could be suspended on which Carmen could swing free, or Zuniga be debagged, blindfolded and executed at the end of the Lillas Pastia scene – like the accused in front of a terrorist kangaroo court. On the revolving fair-ground floor below, as the text put it, 'People wander, people come, people go' – as puppet figures. Beyond this central activity, and lining the edge of the stage, were plastic rubbish bags piled up like the edge of the ring at a circus. Here the master of ceremonies was a black Ringmaster. And in the final, bullfight act the Mayor turned out to be an Uncle Sam on stilts. With one of the rapid mood-switches that characterized Pintilie's staging, pomposity was exuberantly pricked as the Mayor's trousers were pulled down to reveal the stunt-man's suspender straps. The stage was littered with oranges, or drenched in confetti, or awash with mad gestures – such as the men keeling over in Carmen's path, 'slain' by her wiles. Escamillo, a sequinned pop-star, signed autograph-hunters' books, mugged to a hand-cranked movie-camera (reminiscent of Louis Malle's film *Viva Maria*) and stood on a box to seem taller than Carmen for their final joint entrance.

The vulgar fireworks of this *Carmen* were pure theatre magic. The power of the show was the continuing reminder of what made *Carmen* immortal. The sexual conflict was set indelibly against a credible and everyday backdrop, fierce and epic. Felsenstein would have allowed it as '*realistisch Musiktheater*'. With the power of Bizet's miraculous melodies, the violence of lust and will were thrown up against equally registered pastoral domesticity, church, showbiz: Carmen as woman unbound.

Pintilie's vision of the Duke in *Rigoletto* was essentially a figure of ridicule and selfish pride, undercutting the image of charming adventurer that every tenor imagines for himself. That was why the second act presented him at a work-out in his private gym, an original touch immediately understood by audiences, to judge from their laughing and cheering. But it led to a famous and depressing row with the conductor Richard Armstrong over a sight-gag in that scene, when the Duke was supposed to thump a punchball so hard that it came back and hit him in the face. Armstrong refused to conduct if that happened, the change in the production was made against Pintilie's wishes, and the producer remained in his hotel room on the first night. 'Why do they ask me to work for them, if they do not have confidence in my solutions?' Pintilie asked. The elements of parody and usually self-conscious performing were essential to the production. Pintilie felt obliged to push his mockery, as he called it, as far as he could go. His open criticism of the famous Jonathan Miller staging in 1950s Little Italy, New York, was, 'How does that Mafia angle nourish the real centre of the work? It is not enough to change from the expected costumes and period. That is only the start of exploration.' Pintilie could not read music, but he had an instinct for what the music was doing. He responded to the revolutionary

373

musical style of the *Rigoletto* fourth act. His staging put the focus entirely on Gilda's metaphysical gesture of self-sacrifice, with the surrounding narrative elements done almost abstract. His method was startling. The door at which she knocked, guarded by Sparafucile, was a hellish metal gate like an oven door. Gilda ascended a spiral staircase to heaven, as it were, after Rigoletto had found her body. The staging said something new and important about the power and responsibility of the jester as professional entertainer, about the risks and dangers of the calculated blasphemy which is art. Rigoletto's endorsement of the vice of the Court might have been just work – not his Credo, but only a game. Yet the fatal consequence was as inescapable as in *Don Giovanni*, the opera which Verdi's *Rigoletto* counterpoints and echoes both in its ominous brass writing and in the character of the wronged father Monterone.

Pintilie presented the Duke, devil with all the best tunes, as moral crux of the opera. A *simpatico* Duke reduces Rigoletto's misfortune to a merely private tragedy. In this idea he was influenced by a Roland Barthes essay on James Bond, defining Fleming's hero as one of those mediocre people outside the world of tragedy, someone immune from real feeling. So the staging offset the Duke's musical charms with a grotesque court stocked with drag queens and vampires, the Duke himself a pill-popping, oyster-swilling, Presleyesque absurdity, untouched by violence, not a hair out of place. The final scene became the effective metaphysical statement it should be. Gilda's ascension up the spiral staircase was an emotional and sublimely definitive evocation of the themes of forgiveness, revenge and justice. The staging moved from camp orgy to coal hole. The courtiers who had overheard Gilda confess to Rigoletto that she had been sexually abused by the Duke suddenly poured a streaming avalanche of soot and 'coal' through the lunette windows of richly vulgar, mother-of-pearl set high up in the walls. The same windows emitted the terrifying storm chorus of humming. The pace quickened in act 2 after the abduction of Gilda, when the Duke, continuing his gym work-out, first lamented and later revelled in the prospect of seducing her. After the sick feverish first act, the clarity yet comic absurdity here was crucial. The work-out tied in with the musical forms when an exercise bike fitted well against a fast quaver accompaniment figure.

Pintilie compared the positive benefit of theatre and filmdirectors turning to opera against the 'vicious problems'. Opera was an ancient form that had rejuvenated itself, he said, 'like when a 50-year-old woman who has started ageing has a facelift. That's a cheat, and there are producers in opera who wish to be nothing more than plastic surgeons and cover the lines in the face. All they do is use the decor so that it resembles more closely the concepts of contemporary visual art. There are formulas. It's easy. One stops the singers being too ham. There are lighting effects. It's all superficial. I believe in being more radical, suicidal even. At the risk of getting things wrong I wish to rethink an opera in a more profound manner.'

Pintilie regarded *The Magic Flute*, which he staged at the Aix-en-Provence Festival in 1984, as the 'best ever' opera. He had read a Mozart letter with a sentence that he thought should be the key to staging it: 'All life is only a series of tests, of preparations for death,' an idea that profoundly touched him. The episodes of *The Magic Flute*, he said, should be just a metaphor for existence, as in his production:

> Life is a spiritual exercise to prepare for death. At the end of my production, Tamino and Pamina were old, and I made the Trials very hard for them. Pamina's hand was really burned in the trial by fire, and the water was almost a torture. The emotional effect was formidable. It is true that Judith Blegen walked out on the production. She said what I wanted her to do was not Mozart. But the girl who took over had a huge success, because the public was touched by this radical vision – even though I didn't achieve all my intentions. Part of the cast believed in what we were doing. I tried to go as far as you could go. For me it is a deep thing to be involved in opera. I tremble. I'm so much touched. I want to affect the audience's thinking – not to change the opera, but to be faithful to what I think was never discovered. To uncover the interior joy of the piece really rejuvenates it.

That in retrospect should be the liberating motto of McMaster's revolutionary and internationally famed WNO, and also of the young team (later joined by the brilliant conductor Paul Daniel) that Lord Harewood promoted to run ENO and Opera North from the early 1980s. In Cardiff foreign and new producers showed what could be done for opera. A standard was set, a challenge issued. Miraculously, fresh talents appeared in the British opera world capable of fulfilling the new demands for sense, poetry, and no-holds-barred theatricality.

The British, with Shakespeare at the source of their theatre, must be sympathetic to the empirical character of live performance. The

British opera scene since the Chéreau *Ring* has seen the best talents freed from the prison of old operatic ways and conventions about staging. Thanks initially to McMaster's importation of European talents in Cardiff – like Pintilie, Berghaus, Ciulei, Noelte, and even the questionable Serban – it was plain that things did not have to be done as they had been. In Britain there is now a remarkable renaissance of stage directors and designers who are finding their way to Germany – where their resourcefulness and good sense, their humour and fluency, their lack of preconceptions (sometimes lack of rigid concepts at all), are found refreshing and vital. In opera a calculated empiricism is the only abiding rule.

15 Frankfurt and after: from Neuenfels to Decker

Herbert Wernicke's 1991 Brussels Opera staging (at the Monnaie) of
Götterdämmerung in his own designs: William Cochran's Siegfried arrives at
the sparsely furnished court (with grand piano under dustcover but breathtaking views) of Victor Braun's Günther and Margaret Jane Wray's Gutrune –
Artur Korn's Hagen watching from the side. Photograph © Klaus Lefebvre.

Museums are by no means a 20th-century invention, but even such *bona fide* contemporary arts as film, architecture, modern painting and pop music – to judge from the recycling that is characteristic of all of them – are now really museum arts. Opera certainly has become a museum art in the course of the century. The Western world is into ancestor worship. Modernism is art for the few, arcane, recherché. Post-modernism is a nostalgic rearrangement of history, using more accessible and popular objects, methods and details from the past, but certainly betraying the artist's responsibility to make the world new.

Any artistic director of an opera company, pondering what repertoire should be tackled, knows that both popular demand and operatic history prescribe a certain body of works – *Carmen*, *The Marriage of Figaro*, *The Barber of Seville*. Prejudices and personal taste, the privilege of the modern impresario, may exclude some of that inner core of necessary operas. Gerard Mortier, head of the Salzburg Festival, avoided programming any Puccini during his ten years in charge of the Monnaie in Brussels. But no opera repertoire can exclude Mozart or Wagner or Verdi or Offenbach or Richard Strauss or Beethoven or Johann Strauss or Mussorgsky or Rossini or Tchaikovsky or Donizetti altogether. It is hard to imagine a company that does not attempt Janáček, Gluck, Handel, Britten, Monteverdi, Bellini, Purcell, Smetana, Weber, Massenet, Lully, Prokofiev, Lehár, Giordano. Few companies tackle more than ten operas a year, no more than half being new productions. In a decade, an artistic director might achieve 50 new productions but more likely fewer than 30. During Michael Gielen's remarkable ten years in charge of the Frankfurt Opera there was an impressive total of 49 new productions in the main house, with 35 revivals of productions which the company had in store, five concert performances of operatic rarities, and four experimental shows in the Kammerspiel. Sadly, though strongly identified with contemporary music, and a composer himself, Gielen in the same period managed just two newly commissioned operas. Performance is like conservation. Opera companies are museums in that they conserve acknowledged masterpieces by performing them, and since contemporary audiences are alienated from new works, the main operatic diet is anyway well-worn old works. Distinction does not depend on international status or a budget for top stars. In the world of opera, money and fame often substitute for imagination. Companies without privileges must use imagination instead of cash. Frankfurt, WNO and ENO have all had serious problems, though Frankfurt's financial security is envied by every British company. Frankfurt also has a famous and marvellous stage to work with, technically equipped with the latest machinery and including the largest stage revolve in Europe. Frankfurt can do the transformations in the outer acts of *Parsifal* as Wagner wanted them – in full view. Yet Frankfurt has a lower rating in the hierarchy of German houses than Hamburg or Munich or even Stuttgart, and pays its singers accordingly.

The most important project of Michael Gielen's launching season at Frankfurt in 1977/8, the breakthrough for his regime, was Luigi Nono's *Al gran sole carico d'amore* in June 1978. Two years earlier one of Gielen's first moves on his arrival was to engage Klaus Zehelein as chief dramaturg in the new regime. Zehelein (born 1940) studied philosophy, German literature and music with Adorno and Horkheimer at Frankfurt University. He went to the Darmstadt modern music summer school each year from 1959 to 1963, the triumph of serialism when Stockhausen and Boulez were in attendance too. He started as dramaturg in Kiel (1967–71) for both opera and straight theatre where the composer/conductor Hans Zender was *Generalmusikdirektor*, and at Frankfurt in 1986 Zender's *Stephen Climax* was one of the few new operas premiered during the Gielen years – without much success. All Gielen's planning was done jointly with Zehelein, who was more actively involved in artistic policy and production work than most German dramaturgs who concentrate mainly on programme note research. The motto of the new regime might have been the word '*Durchbrüche*' (breakthroughs) which became the title of the regime's souvenir book in 1987: *Durchbrüche – 10 Jahre Musiktheater mit Michael Gielen*, by Hans-Klaus Jungheinrich and Mara Eggert (Quadriga Verlag, Weinheim & Berlin). '*Durchbrüche*' was a favourite Adorno term which he applied to Mahler, referring to the composer's ability to define his musical invention so that revealing unadulterated emotional truth took precedence over any display of technical musical prowess. Gielen had a particular musical and political sympathy for Nono's work, but

Zehelein was thinking how enormously impressed he had been by Ruth Berghaus's direction of *Elektra* in East Berlin in the 1960s. He proposed to Gielen and Dr Christoph Bitter (Gielen's co-director for his first two and a half years) that she should stage the Nono. Berghaus was then director of the Berliner Ensemble and the East German government would not let her travel. So Jürgen Flimm did the job, with Karl-Ernst Herrmann as designer. This was the first of many Frankfurt productions on which Zehelein worked his superior imaginative and disciplined magic as part of the creative team. Though nominally chief dramaturg he was often effectively codirector. Nono's work was harbinger for the distinctive reputation of the new Frankfurt regime, defining its adventurous and controversial interpretative policy.

Gielen's taste expanded. The Frankfurt company acquired a pretty revolutionary reputation. The audience began to complain and absent itself. Ticket-sales fell dangerously. Gielen's repertoire was unusual. The approach to staging and design was unpopular. Only after some years did a different public arrive to replace the more conservative ticket-holders. Fortunately the city fathers and Hilmar Hoffmann, their cultural advisor, were ready to wait. First nights were often riotous. The conservative element turned out armed with whistles and football rackets to disrupt the applause. But when Gielen left in 1987, a new audience had by and large become enthusiastic devotees. As with Chéreau's *Ring* at Bayreuth, the pendulum of taste had swung.

Gielen engaged Harnoncourt and Kupfer in the early phase of his Frankfurt regime. In the early 1970s, the operatic agenda in Germany was being set by Felsenstein's disciples at the Berlin Komische Oper (Götz Friedrich, Joachim Herz and Harry Kupfer). It soon turned out that Harnoncourt, for example, had conflicting artistic objectives – devoted to 'what Handel wanted'. Gielen started from a different aesthetic. As a composer closely involved with the travails of contemporary music, both its creation and its interpretation, Gielen took a utilitarian view and treated the music of the past as contemporary and available. The question for him was not 'what Handel wanted' but 'what Handel might want now'. And even that, in the absence of Handel, was less important than 'what interests *us* . . . what *we* want'. After the experiments of his first years, Gielen's choice of interpreters was unapologetic, and he put his reputation solidly behind the most controversial work.

Gielen and Zehelein attracted a distinct stable of designers and producers, building on to their existing company with sympathetic and accomplished singers. For example, Günter Reich and William Cochran were to be found in leading roles in the 1978/9 season. The designers in the Frankfurt stable were Erich Wonder, Marco Arturo Marelli, Karl Kneidl, Axel Manthey, Andreas Braito, Raimund Bauer; the producers who created the Frankfurt style were Alfred Kirchner, Hans Neuenfels, Ruth Berghaus, Karl Kneidl, Christof Nel, Jürgen Tamchina, Renate Ackermann, and much later Herbert Wernicke – who also (as always) designed his own *Hoffmann*.

In 1976 when Gielen started he had immediately to confront questions of taste, interest and performance aesthetic vital to performance. Having conducted a Messiaen premiere for the BBC in 1962, he was from 1978 to 1981 to be chief guest conductor in succession to Boulez of the BBC Symphony Orchestra, with its consistent modern music policy. Zehelein had an equally uncompromising post-Darmstadt belief in the avant garde. This shared musical and historical vision explains why Frankfurt, without a 'resident producer' or theatre-orientated *Intendant*, was responsible for its controversial pioneering of new approaches to operatic staging. Zehelein's musical training and commitment were crucial in Frankfurt, where there was no conflict between the musical and the theatrical aspects of interpretation. For Gielen the theatrical realization of opera was essential for the vitality of performance, and what was being called 'deconstruction' offered a genuine way forward. The reputation of the company for innovation made casting harder. Gielen explained, 'We don't find it very easy to get people with good voices to come and rehearse for seven weeks. But voice is not everything. The Amneris in our *Aida* second cast flatly refused to cooperate in our production. So I had to throw her out. But we still had to pay her.' Gielen also had a composer's commitment to the notes in the score, insisting on accuracy. The Frankfurt emphasis on theatricality was absolutely in line with the old Bayreuth tradition. Cosima Wagner put it eloquently: 'The tendency of our art proceeds from the drama. The Bayreuth stage gives us the drama transfigured by the music . . . I can't help it: a good orchestra and good choruses are all very well, but if the action on stage does not make one forget everything else, then the performance is a failure, even if they sing and play like the angels in heaven!'

Gielen was drawn to areas of repertoire neglected in other German opera-houses at the time: the Baroque of Rameau, for example. *Castor et Pollux*, conducted by Nikolaus Harnoncourt and designed by Erich Wonder, opened his fourth season in October 1980. Zehelein's Darmstadt influences made him unsympathetic to the neo-romantic or minimalist 1980s trends in new opera. Gielen's taste was broader, but Britten was effectively banned in Frankfurt, as were Tippett, Henze and Rihm. Apart from Schreker's *Die Gezeichneten* (The Branded Ones) and Zimmermann's *Die Soldaten*, Gielen and Zehelein's repertoire was mainstream, which perhaps made the theatrical experimentation even more noticeable.

Gielen was not a typical career music director in the German opera-house tradition. He was already 50 when he came to Frankfurt, whereas Clemens Kraus, at the start of his notable time there in 1924, had been 31, and Georg Solti was 40 when he arrived in Frankfurt in 1952. Gielen was not making a career move but was interested in a specific roster of operas which he had not performed on stage before – to explore what they could mean both for him, and for an intelligent audience. Boulez in 1976 had demonstrated with the Bayreuth centenary *Ring* an uncompromising commitment to new theatrical interpretation. Gielen's Frankfurt could regard the Chéreau *Ring* as having started something new which needed to be sustained and extended.

His first season at Frankfurt brought Jonathan Miller's *Cunning Little Vixen* (from Glyndebourne) and Harnoncourt for Handel's *Giulio Cesare in Egitto*. There were six new productions in Frankfurt in 1977/8. Only fourteen operas newly staged during Gielen's time were 20th-century. Erich Wonder, a crucial and innovative collaborator, designed the Handel. Gielen's opening production, *Don Giovanni*, had period-flavour sets and costumes by Andreas Reinhardt characteristic of the East Berlin school. *Tannhäuser* (designed by Carlo Tommasi) and *Il trovatore* (an Andras Fricsay staging) were solidly conventional off-the-peg grand opera. But then the artistic scandals started, with *Aida* in January 1981, a collaboration between Zehelein and Hans Neuenfels as joint producers and dramaturgs, the sets by Erich Wonder, costumes by Nina Ritter. What really infuriated the critics and the public was the staging of the triumphal march, where they could reasonably suspect they were themselves being guyed. Dominating the back of the set were tiers of opera-house boxes providing a mirror, as it were, of a traditional opera-house auditorium. The Frankfurt audience watched assorted ranks of Victorian-style ladies in tiaras and ballgowns and gents in white ties and tails looking back at them from red plush Scala-style opera boxes. The march itself was a comic Nazi militarist ballet, with salutes and goose-steps. The production put traditionalists in the dock and made fun of them. Elsewhere Neuenfels evoked a governmental establishment world of bureaucracy, privilege and religious secrecy with hints of a more Italian 1930s fascism. This was not like Jonathan Miller's ENO *Rigoletto*, successfully forcing its references into a coherent narrative. Radames was a grey-suited young bourgeois, dreaming of archaeology and poetic adventure, unearthing an Egyptian bust beneath the linoleum. Aida was a *Gastarbeiter*, scrubbing floors and picking up clothes like a Philippine maid. Amneris was a fashionable heiress from a film by Bertolucci. The King of Egypt was already half wrapped-up like a mummy. Amonasro was a black man, his defeated people covered in black body make-up, behaving like apes. Ramphis was a sort of malevolent Buddha.

Aida was not Zehelein and Neuenfels's first collaboration. They started with Schreker's *Gezeichneten* in January 1979, and in March 1980 tackled Busoni's *Doktor Faust* – a more effective and credible achievement than *Aida* which is not a philosophical work in Busoni's sense. The theme of private emotion and public responsibility suited the changing constitutional perspectives of Verdi's Italy, but *Aida* is naive and emotional, not cerebral.

Busoni's adaptation of a medieval puppet play about Faust was very modern and overtly metaphysical. Its subject was the power of man as lord of the universe, the 20th-century delusion of human progress. *Aida* is a workable opera, whether done seriously or superficially. *Doktor Faust* needed extremely careful handling. It was never finished by Busoni and its music is often undramatic. The producer of *Aida* could react against a tradition. The producer of *Doktor Faust* had to establish a specific convention of performance for a rarity. The Verdi needed defamiliarisation: the Busoni's fragmentary elements had to add up to something coherent. Two roles in Neuenfels's *Doktor Faust* have to be mentioned. The late and much lamented Günter Reich made Faust himself into a shambling professorial bear of a man, the embodiment, with his woolly grey pullover, of intellectually remote academe. William Cochran's fleshy, thickset Mefistofeles in a gor blimey cap and loose-fitting working-man's coat was this Faust's perfect alter ego. Pictures of this principal pair show how the style of the interpretation was set by their characterization.

Neuenfels and Zehelein used the massive Frankfurt revolve to suggest both the excursions in Faust's mind, and the 'theatre' of diversions provided by Mefistofeles which Faust's compact had brought him in return. A Baudelaire quote projected on to the front-cloth read: 'Every man who wants to know the secret of life must sell his soul.' At the same time the house-lights suddenly flashed on, spotlights wandered around the auditorium, and floodlights shone on the orchestra – as if the opera-house were challenging new candidates to enter another devilish pact. Faust's traditional drawing-room/study at the start was a little box inset at the front of the stage: comfortable living in Busoni's era complete with a tray for coffee on an antique table, and Wagner as a slightly comical white-jacketed gentleman's gentleman. The production used powerfully evocative, nostalgic images from Faust's family background – at the mention of Cracow a little domestic cutaway was conjured up on the stage right beside him. The production played constantly with memory and the imagination, Faust's reveries inviting a cinematic fluency. After the devilish students in military cloaks had provided him with the magic tome, Faust staggered back to the desk in his own room. For Busoni's 'Second Prologue' he was discovered reading the *Clavis astartis magica* beside an ominous postchaise with a towering stepladder draped in a white dustcover: an extraordinarily striking image. To summon Lucifer he put on motorist's goggles, took off the dustcover and started to climb the steps. The offstage chorus summoned him down again, and after pausing beside the door to the postchaise he began a memorable procession through a series of almost identical offices in what seemed like a secret police headquarters: the revolve being divided into a sequence of small triangular sectioned rooms. In each office there was a spiv in a dark suit and trilby, or alternatively a vamp (Levis, Asmodus, Beelzebub) at a desk, opening a briefcase. Each office was lit with a bright anglepoise lamp in the corner; each had a second mysterious door (often with a number flashing over it) inviting Faust to his next 'temptation'. Sometimes a girl or a man pulled him towards the desk. After rejecting each of them Faust, with his last hope, came to the front of the stage – and stepped back to the desk in his own room again. The impression was cinematic and haunting – technically demanding to stage, but brilliantly apt. It was a good curtain raiser for Mefistofeles, whose first move was to put a cloth cap on Faust's head and hand him a walking-stick.

Faust picked up a bust of Goethe, put it on the table. The journey began. Before the fatal contract was signed Faust and Mefistofeles were already walking through a crowd on the revolve. The scene changed to a Victorian restaurant full of waxworks, and then to a cathedral with Romanesque chapels and organ music (for the Intermezzo), where Gretchen's brother was praying, the episode very romantically staged. Faust had a front seat in a box that suddenly appeared in time for him to watch Mefistofeles's friar act, with jugglers and acrobats. Undertakers carried off Gretchen's coffin. Distant instruments sounded from the remote back of the stage as the revolve swung round on its epic shadowy journey, arriving at a bizarre art deco hotel lobby with a reception desk, palm fronds, bell boys, luggage (a ballet sequence during one of Busoni's interludes). Then the scene switched again to the ducal park at Parma, where the Duke and Duchess were Fauntleroy-like children dwarfed by their furniture. The novelty provided by the famous doctor for the Duchess was the screening of a film of Faust's marriage to a great gathering. The Wittenberg tavern scene, next, was a university lecture hall, its most striking coup the Duchess's baby sent to Faust from his death bed. One of Mara Eggert's more memorable production photographs shows Cochran's Mefistofeles and the baby (a doll). Faust had a flashback to one of the secret triangular rooms of his initial encounter with the diabolicals. The baby was an augury of Faust's resurrection in the closing moments. After his death, a nude young man rose out of the stage beside him and walked off to the corner, putting on some trousers. The nightwatchman, a journalist, asked, 'Did this man have an accident?' and slapped Mefistofeles before dragging off the body. The traditional *Faust* was a time-travelling love story. For Busoni it became a Candide-like progress which Neuenfels realized theatrically as touching on the dangerous knowledge of the modern age. The Faustian compact was not just made by one man, but by the race. Neuenfels's theatrical virtuosity provoked all sorts of visions and dreams without attempting to resolve all the questions raised. But Busoni's *Faust*, like Goethe's, is more about the human soul and its aspirations than about damnation – part of a moral maze that includes *Paradise Lost* as well as *Brave New World*.

Alfred Kirchner's not unconventional productions of *Jenůfa* and *Die Soldaten* were two of the most successful and effective of the whole regime. Marco Arturo Marelli's sets for the Janáček drew on the peasant location, the sense of a small-town rural community, but had aspirations to something beyond. He exploited the full stage depth available in Frankfurt. On the right was a wall of wooden boards with hidden doors and windows stretching far upstage. On the left there seemed to be a mill without a wheel. Water was reflected under the duckboards that rose towards a grass sward far upstage on which a few skeletal fruit trees were silhouetted against a pale grey-blue sky. The boards of the stage floor were separated into different groups, like a patchwork of small-holdings for subsistence farming. The set was brightly lit at the back. In the second act the foster-mother's house was suggested just with a bed at centre-stage, a long muttoncloth hanging behind it from the flies, a chair, a figure of the Virgin and child on a bracket, a wall of planks on the left too, candles and an icon, gauze covering the trees at the back. To the right, through a window and door the winter blew snow flurries after the baby had been disposed of. The front curtain was like a patchwork of lace-edged table cloths sewn together, the rule of respectability. The third act, like the first, had a table covered in a cloth set at the centre of the stage, waiting for the wedding. The production realized both the dreaming of Jenůfa herself – her gaze penetrating deep into the wings – and the barely submerged violence and frustration. There was sudden, shocking malevolence in the third-act stoning of the Kabanicha's wooden house wall (to the right of the set) by the men of the village. The agenda of Janáček's first great opera, woman as victim, woman not empowered to act, was brilliantly established. William Cochran was vulnerable, bitter and ambivalent as Laca, playing the jealous rival for Jenůfa who finally shares male power with her – accepting her in marriage – with much subtlety, moving hints of brute unconsciousness or immature male awkwardness. The marking of Jenůfa's cheek by Laca, his knife inside a posy, caught perfectly the mix of devotion and resentment in the raw wounding. At the end Laca's setting up of the furniture knocked down by the villagers, spreading wide a bearlike embrace for Jenůfa, caressing her scarred cheek as she sat calmly at the table facing the future, was deeply moving.

This was natural unpretentious work. The design for *Jenůfa*, though not strictly naturalistic, provided a context for fluid transpositions between an emotional naturalism in individual performances and telling choric movements. The aesthetic was not radically different from Nikolaus Lehnhoff's approach to the opera at Glyndebourne except that Marelli's sets were interpretative, and less consciously picturesque than Tobias Hoheisel's. The acting for Kirchner was fresh, believable, and unselfconscious, and the production survived the vagaries of the German repertoire system (repeat performances with months between them) for eight years with its impact undiminished.

Bernd Alois Zimmermann, many of whose works were premiered by Gielen, expected a full range of extravagant multimedia effects to put the message of his operatic version of *Die Soldaten* across, with television screens and simultaneously performed scenes on different levels transforming Lenz's moving but straightforward 1776 drama into a showy phenomenon. In the Stuttgart staging Kupfer had famously and colourfully done what the composer asked, but Kirchner's Frankfurt staging notably did without multimedia. (The opera was in Opera North and Covent Garden plans, but was not staged in Britain until 1996 – by David Freeman for ENO.) Kirchner achieved memorable focus and concentration with an almost abstract setting by Karl Kneidl, a sort of wartime rubbish tip, its walls lined with German uniforms, which contrasted powerfully with Nan Christie's isolated figure as Marie in pure white – opera as documentary. The sombre echoes were all of German militarism, with women as necessary victims. The excitement was not Kirchner's unusual method, but the dramatist's and composer's passionate vision. The production credit in the programme book mentioned a six-man team: Gielen, Kneidl, Zehelein, Kresnik and Walsh, as well as Kirchner. The unity of their approach made what could have seemed dauntingly complex (both in musical language and in theatrical demands) absorbable and coherent – even in some ways romantic, however bleak the conclusion. As in *Jenůfa*, the role of the male chorus was vital.

Though Frankfurt producers represented different aesthetic styles, they shared a similar motivation. They certainly did not need to conform to an image of deconstructionism. There was genuinely no house style. Christof Nel's *Falstaff* in January 1985 was midway between Neuenfels and Kirchner in approach. Nel had previously, with Zehelein as dramaturg, produced Frankfurt's new *Freischütz*. Subsequently he tackled *The Bartered Bride*, translating the folksy sentimentality to modern suburbs, with motorway drives through the countryside shown on video screens. This responded less interestingly to the spirit of Smetana's masterpiece than Kupfer's Komische Oper staging, with its pantomime pig roaming the stage and its precise view of human motivation. The designer of Nel's *Falstaff*, Andreas Braito, was an architect who had never worked in the theatre before – a situation typical of the experiment and adventure Gielen encouraged. Frankfurt took a far-sighted and rare positive interest in designers from outside the closed world of opera. The sets had nothing to do with the tavern interior, Tudor panelling, hangings and period atmosphere usually assumed appropriate. Nel's Falstaff was almost nude in the opening scene, inhabiting a featureless round black void to which there was access only through a hole high up in the back wall, where Bardolph was sitting silhouetted against the light (or a moon in the night sky). At the centre of the set was a mound of excrement, or something like it. The veteran Canadian Louis Quilico was a Falstaff without padding, wobbling his own hairy paunch at the audience. The featureless void where Falstaff lived represented his insatiable appetite, and symbolized a totally consumerist approach to the world. In this privacy, Falstaff's stomach was the centre of the universe. His appetite *was* his universe. The idea did not cramp the Falstaffian fun Quilico provided.

This was a more exuberant experience than Peter Stein's beautifully poised but humourless interpretation for WNO in 1988. Nel turned Pistol and Bardolph into Beckettian disreputables in their master's solipsist universe. Nel's *Falstaff* was a Verdian *Endgame*. The black set showed a rounded Falstaff world without doors and corners. Everything and everybody coming into it had to slip down a treat. With Falstaff nearly naked, a sort of superannuated Silenus, the link between sex and food was easy to believe. In the third scene, for the visit of Quickly (the veteran Anny Schlemm), the round tube to Falstaff's stomach was at floor level, and characters entered through it. For the penultimate scene, after the laundry basket episode, Falstaff was discovered collapsed at the bottom of a red throat-like column stretching to the flies, a monumentally sore deep throat.

Ford's world was totally different – a mechanically laid-out space of doors and corners and stairs: all sections, and order and technology. For the 'garden' scene two stairs descended from either wing on left and right symmetrically to a platform against a blank, silvery, steel-like flat: a brutalist version of a formal opera staircase. Verdi's lunatic gabble choruses and structural neatness, focusing the world into which this lord of misrule with his wanton appetites wished to intrude, could scarcely have been better illustrated. Each character was crisply defined in physical appearance: Nannetta like Lewis Carroll's Alice, Ford whey-faced with smarmy hair. The steps were an aid to good delivery of the complex fugal polyphony in the rhubarb choruses for the contrasting little choirs around Ford and Alice, husband and wife. With so much humour and charm in individual performances, like Ellen Shade's lovely Alice, there was no need to paint a period slice of life. Caius for once was not a parody schoolmaster. The last act, with costumes that evoked the well-upholstered era of Verdi's composing of *Falstaff*, was a musical medley full of intimations of mortality and echoes from other famous midnights, other inquisitions in earlier Verdi scores. Nel used the widest, deepest stage to summon up a rich carnival of references, with long-lasting visual echoes, not sombre but strangely blissful. This colourful coda was artificial, but the spirit of comedy thrived.

The group of interpreters Gielen gathered around him proved that the renewal of the tradition of theatrical interpretation was a viable agenda in opera. Gielen's success was based on a taste for fresh thoughts and new designers, and a resolute determination to back up the interpretative team in their explorations. There was enormous excitement about all this theatrical work. Like the Jonas regime at ENO, Gielen's regime was much missed in succeeding years. The challenge for a management is to get a consistent standard. The spread of achievement in Frankfurt between 1977 and 1987 was even more important for the health of opera in Europe than, for instance, the fabled Klemperer era at the Kroll Opera in Berlin from 1927 to 1931. It was typical of the German system that Bertini, once in charge, took against the achievements of the Gielen era. New regimes are often opposed to what they replace. Dennis Marks's main agenda at ENO, after taking over from Peter Jonas, seemed very similar. Even if the Frankfurt Opera stage had not been burnt down the November after Gielen left, would Bertini ever have revived Berghaus's *Ring*? Five years in the fragile world of theatrical fashion is a long time. Gerard Mortier, leaving Brussels for Salzburg, sold to Frankfurt Herbert Wernicke's Brussels *Ring*, lock, stock and barrel. Sylvain Cambreling, Bertini's successor, presented Wernicke's *Ring* (made for Brussels in 1991) at Frankfurt in 1995. Berghaus's *Ring* became history in the 1990s, despite the excellent private videotapes of it in the Frankfurt archives.

Gielen acknowledged his regime had 'an easy life compared to the political atmosphere into which the Kroll was born'. When Frankfurt voted a Christian democrat majority on to the city council, the year after Gielen was appointed, 'nobody of that party, not even the mayor, ever tried to interfere or question our subsidy'. Gielen in 1987 said that his team tried 'to be interesting every time, which is not always successful. I think in the time we've been working, we've done more interesting new productions than any other theatre in the world. Anyway, it's a record I'm proud to claim.' When he left Gielen was awarded a state prize for his work at the Opera. His acceptance speech declared, 'only operas that dare a lot should be subsidized'.

One of the newest talents to be engaged by Gielen and Zehelein in Frankfurt was Herbert Wernicke, who designed and directed *Les contes d'Hoffmann* for them in April 1985. Wernicke was that rarity: a designer who understood perfectly the business of being a producer, developing ideas and images as well as the acting in rehearsal. He had originally trained as a conductor and composer. He worked closely with a dramaturg of his choice – for his Frankfurt *Hoffmann*, Hans-Jürgen Drescher. This production was one of the few from the Gielen era to be successfully revived under the successor regime, in November 1992. Among the best Wernicke productions were a *Meistersinger* in Hamburg (borrowed for the Palais Garnier in Paris during the final opera season there before the opening of the Bastille in 1989), *Duke Bluebeard's Castle* in Amsterdam in 1988, a fascinating *Ring* in Brussels in 1991, a brilliantly economical *Moses and Aaron* for the Alte Oper, Frankfurt, and the Paris Châtelet, and a pocket *Fledermaus* in 1992 in Basel – his home and professional base.

The striking and memorable set for Wernicke's *Hoffmann* was based on the famous 19th-century Spitzweg painting *The Poor Poet* – a room with a bed and table and silhouette of Mozart on the wall, and an open umbrella floating up in the corner of the ceiling. The first scene used this room as a kind of box inset, on the scale of a tiny hotel bedroom. The Muse arrived armed with bottles. For each further stage of Offenbach's magical episodes the room was expanded, in a sort of *Alice in Wonderland* or drugged experience where the dimension of space distorted. First there was the meeting with fellow students drinking round a table. Then the Dr Coppelius show with Olympia on top of an improbable machine and the whole audience standing round with

391

Pavarotti-sized hankies at the ready. Only very briefly did Olympia appear as a human singer; for most of the scene she was just a doll. Then the Antonia episode with grand piano had a huge door at the back on the left with an equestrian Commendatore-style statue outside. Then Giulietta's brothel in Venice had a whole gondola stretching across the stage: frock-coated top-hatted gents squinted through holes in the walls to observe the strange things going on off-stage – which was not frustrating for the audience, as Wernicke had such intriguing performances on it. Finally the whole generous depth of the stage behind the proscenium was used for the return to Hoffmann's meeting with his fellow students after the drunken dreaming. In each new scene the umbrella in the corner became larger. Never were changes in scale so tellingly and poetically advertised, a wonderful context for William Cochran's musical, passionately frustrated, sharply acted performance as the poet himself.

Duke Bluebeard's Castle for the Netherlands Opera, with Tim Coleman as Wernicke's dramaturg, opened with a terrific flourish. There was a silky swishing as the black dust covers that had been masking the stage ran away like water through a giant doorway at the centre of the triangular set. The stage picture uncovered by this process was simple and stark. A white floor raked steeply upstage to a corner at the centre, with two white walls tilted vertiginously forward, towering into the flies. Through the open doorway in the left wall, next to a 30-foot-high panelled door in the right wall, stars and a thin crescent moon shone in an aquamarine sky. The set looked beautifully simple, though not at all the 'vast circular gothic hall with steps and seven doors' of Bartók's libretto. Then a voice started whispering the ominous prologue over the PA – with its key phrase 'Where is the stage: within? without?' – and a little stream of red blood crept under the huge door, gradually streaking along the white blotting-paper-like floor towards the front. This proclaimed the subsconscious world of Bartók's psychodrama with its suffocating determinism, its cruelties and murders, its contrast between lavish orchestral images of nature and the dark, unnatural and inhumane Id. Bluebeard always had the sweet voice of reason and affection, yet the overwhelming impression was of his deep mourning for the involuntary horror within the human soul – the original premiere in 1918 was six months before the Armistice.

When the speaking voice stopped and music started, the red

plush curtains closed and the lights came on again in the auditorium at the back of which Bluebeard and Judith entered, reluctantly working their way on to the stage. When the curtains opened again the blood was gone. Each time Judith or Bluebeard dragged open the monumental door pivoted at the corner of the set, their action closed the doorway in the other wall. Each time the door opened it revealed a wall of grey breeze-blocks, growing ever higher. At the seventh door both doorways were totally sealed. What Wernicke did not show, though, was anything behind the seven doors as Judith gradually stripped away pretence and illusion from her relationship with Bluebeard. There were no keys to turn in the lock, and few physical equivalents of the narrative images so voluptuously described in the music. Instead of finding Bluebeard's other wives behind the seventh door, Judith mimed their roles herself. Bluebeard throughout wore a grey suit, like a minister in some East European government. At one point he took off his shoes and socks. At another he mimed the action of striking with an axe. Judith was in a graceful white 1950s ballgown and traced the threshold of the open doorway and the front of the stage, balancing nervously. Wernicke seemed to be wanting the audience to fill in for themselves ideas evoked by Judith's descriptions of her psychological, imaginative journey to Bluebeard's heart. Wernicke also had the work performed twice for the same audience each evening, with the palindromic effect of ideas spiralling back from the second time round, so that Judith and Bluebeard ended where they started, leaving through the back of the theatre. The only visual difference between the two versions, apart from the actual movements of the singers, were the seven television sets on stage showing video clips from the first time through: conceptual theatre at its most rarefied, defining the inescapable *Huis clos*. The opera was sung in its original Hungarian (without surtitles), so the public had to apply imagination: Wernicke concentrated on the objective and conceptual rather than matching the opulent suggestiveness of the score.

Wernicke's spirited and witty *Meistersinger*, orginally created for Hamburg in 1984, was staged in a giant shoebox. French Wagner enthusiasts (as hysterical French campaigns against Chéreau at Bayreuth showed) find Wagner no laughing matter and were not amused. But, sung in German, perhaps little of the text was understood and Wernicke's intelligent transparent staging was geared for a German audience – self-critical, rather than self-congratulatory.

Meistersinger having been Hitler's favourite opera lends a frisson to its xenophobic pan-German sentiment, and Wernicke faced head on residual sentimentality about that. The sober tableau of the set without front curtain at the start was a chair with a gown slung over it, a lute, a book. These disappeared behind red plush curtains when the overture started, and when the curtains parted for the chorale in church the congregation was facing straight into the auditorium, men on the left of the aisle, women on the right – in more or less modern dress, with many of the ladies in black hats. The men all had dubiously rouged complexions, suggesting irascibility or inebriation. For Wernicke the eternal verities of *Meistersinger* were very teutonic: tradition reigned, but *Meistersinger* was not just a lesson about modern Germany. The men left the church before the women. Eva, with blond plaits and blue frock buttoned up the front, was the typical Fräulein. Walter, in a light summer suit, rather like John Wayne at the end of his career, was a suitable candidate for the prize rather than an enthusiastic youngster. Wagnerian heroines seem to like paunch. David had the eager air of a junior bureaucrat or a house-captain at a private school. The other apprentices wore unisex black shorts and boots, with white shirts and socks: like the Hitler *Jugend*. David used a blackboard to explain things to Walter, who was busy taking notes. The humour got very lumpen, with the prentices de-bagging David. Beckmesser arrived wearing a Homburg hat and dirty mack, carrying a suitcase with his Master's robe. It was freemasonry. The comedy with the marker was broadly played, but with much detailed observation from Richard Salter's Beckmesser, including comic business with a coathanger and red socks. The audition ended with paper darts flying in all directions.

Good jokes are worth repeating. Having modelled his Beckmesser on Zero Mostel in *The Producers*, though Salter wasn't allowed to consider himself funny, of course, the second act conflict with Victor Braun's disenchanted Sachs was played to the hilt. Wernicke adopted the popular anti-Semitic view of Beckmesser so rigorously that at the end of the opera, after rushing away from the hearty Nuremberg Rally-style revels, the character was not even permitted a curtain-call until everybody else had drunk their fill of applause. Wernicke made Beckmesser (a sort of Malvolio) into the focus of feeling, not whitewashing his unattractive priggishness and clever folly, but exploring the dangerous conformism into which Wagner traps his audience with the virtuous simplicities of the Beckmesser/Sachs juxtaposition.

A leafy Lindenbaum sprouted at the centre of the box set for act 2, with its house windows, doors and cupboards all round. The sense of a claustrophobic neighbourhood was perfectly caught. For the final scene, after the great musical set-pieces of Sachs's house at the start of act 3, the stage became a kind of Oktoberfest beerhall, as local as the summer fête in Britten's *Albert Herring*. All the Mastersingers and their wives were cheered when they entered. Only Beckmesser, wifeless, got no applause. His need to win was painfully obvious. Wernicke's eyes and ears as re-interpreter of Wagner were clear and sharp. This was a Volkswagen (or people's vehicle) which examined what Volk (demos) really meant for good and ill in Germany.

Gerard Mortier, when he took over the Salzburg Festival in 1992, closed his era at the Brussels Monnaie in style with four *Ring* cycles staged by Wernicke, a co-production with Barcelona (whose opera-house shortly afterwards burnt down) and Frankfurt – where Mortier's music director Cambreling (who was also successor to Gielen and Bertini) conducted the staging again in 1995. Few opera companies, as opposed to summer festivals, would contemplate or be able to afford launching a *Ring* in one week. Berghaus's in Frankfurt in the mid-1980s took fifteen months to assemble; Richard Jones at Covent Garden in 1994/5 took about thirteen. Some opera-houses can barely manage four new productions in a year. Hence the popularity of *Ring* designers who use a single design concept for all four parts, with a set that can tour the world, earning royalties, and be easy to rehearse. Wernicke's single-set *Ring*, though, was varied and rich in imagery and symbolism compared with Götz Friedrich's Berlin time-tunnel or Harry Kupfer's Bayreuth Festival airbase runway after nuclear meltdown.

Wernicke employed an original and novel theatrical symbolism. He for the first time introduced into the credits such unexpected figures as Grane (Brünnhilde's horse played by a dancer Thomas Stache in a Bottom-style horse's head), Fricka's rams and Wotan's ravens, also in anthropomorphic heads, and a Papagena-style Woodbird flying across the back of the stage like Peter Pan. The basic set resembled the floor of a disused factory that might have been converted into a film studio, with metal lamps hanging from the ceiling and derelict electric fittings by the firedoors at each corner. There were trapdoors in the floor and ceiling. The back wall, like a huge stage proscenium, disclosed a scene of mountaintops and pine trees in graphic relief where the Giants removed two rocky summits and planted a Parthenon-like Valhalla which at the end burst into flames. The golden ball of Rhinegold hove into view like sunrise on the mountaintops – and was stolen by Alberich (or to be accurate his double) scaling the mountainside in a trice. The sparse furniture of the set included a tatty grand piano with a player's chair on which, almost throughout, Erda was seated in widow's weeds. This piano did service also as a podium to be used for the delivery of interpretatively important statements by Wotan or whoever, and later was Brünnhilde's bed when she was put to sleep. Music, it suggested, was the engine of Wagner's philosophical system. There were film floodlights, a vast old black leather settee with its stuffing falling out that was plainly intended as the seat of power, an armchair in similar decline, a thick maroon girdle symbolizing fate for the Norns, various rocks and an anvil.

Costumes encapsulated the characterizations and how their roles were to be understood. Alberich was a black-toned craftsman, a union leader perhaps. Günther, marvellously witty and wimpish, was a vain figure in Ludwig II-type uniform (Victor Braun doubled this role and a moving, dangerously committed Wanderer, whose trick spear 'broke' prematurely while he was consulting Erda, the black widow on the piano seat). Loge was a laconic compère in carrot-coloured toupée, Mime a bald roly-poly. Fricka looked every inch a queen in ballgown and tiara. There was a romantic-looking Siegmund in Lederhosen, and a subtle well-developed character for Siegfried also in Lederhosen, with a sock round his ankle until he smartened up and put on court uniform for the wedding to Gutrune (Cochran's musical acting and singing owing much to the Jon Vickers-type instinctive, suffering hero). Props included a massive shining sword, and sundry spears and winged helmets from the established tradition.

When the Wanderer's spear was shattered by Siegfried it landed in that armchair, thanks to mechanical theatrical magic, and was later, in *Götterdämmerung*, rescued from the chair to become the weapon with which Hagen murdered Siegfried. The tarnhelm was a theatrical mask – recalling Wagner's desire to revive the ancient Greek religious drama with his new *Gesamtkunstwerk*: Siegfried and Günther took possession of Brünnhilde's rock moving back to back like Siamese twins. Grane's unicorn-horn, broken off by Wotan to symbolize Brünnhilde's loss of immortality, lay around the set till Brünnhilde took it up as a talisman to counter Waltraute's desperate plea. Eventually it burst into flame and became the torch with which she lit Siegfried's pyre. (Waste not, want not.) Evoking thoughts of Wagner the cineast manqué, Wernicke flashed up extracts from Wagner's stage directions like silent-film titles on a grey front-cloth during interludes between scenes – for example at Siegfried's death march.

Wernicke developed the symbolic ecology of *The Ring* so that one followed a narrative which, rather than convert fabricated antiquarian mythology into naive fable, explained the highly contemporary death of God – and the process whereby humanity without divine arbiter or assistance must take control of fate and morality. Alberich, the maker, the craftsman, finally exited below stage dragging the rope of destiny. As designer and stage director Wernicke came up with a provocative, fascinating, often witty and entertaining response to the physical elements and intellectual import of Wagner's extraordinary epic. When Wernicke's staging moved to its highly theatrical denouement, huge chunks of the factory walls on stage literally collapsed.

Wernicke's *Fledermaus* in Basle was extremely economical, done with a cast of mostly actors with just three proper singers for the roles of Adele, Rosalinde and Eisenstein. There was no stage chorus because this was a small-scale version re-orchestrated by Wernicke himself and the conductor/pianist, Franz Wittenbrink, in a manner similar to Jonathan Dove's cut-down versions of *Falstaff* and *Magic Flute* for City of Birmingham Touring Opera. Some chorus material was sung from the orchestra-pit, though the cut-down orchestra of nine instruments including conductor-cum-pianist was placed on a small platform below a giant fob-watch at the centre of the set, which was an unfurnished curving red plush circular staircase that climbed round this orchestral platform. The stairs went all the way from below stage up into the flies – symbol of the social climbing which is such an important theme of the comedy. Cast and instrumentalists wore present-day clothes, the orchestra in tails and ghostly white make-up. Wernicke's approach mixed subtleties and deliberate coarsenesses. The funniest, wickedest idea (very Teutonic) was that Eisenstein arrived at Orlofsky's party desperate to go to the lavatory, but was then unable to escape from his aristocratic host or evade the sequence of encounters and events. By the time the mysterious Countess arrived he was cross-legged with desperation. The dreadful denouement (of the joke) came with maximum embarrassment after Eisenstein went into hysterics explaining the origin of Falke's Fledermaus nickname, collapsing with laughter at his own cleverness and wit. Wernicke had it all acted very convincingly – Eisenstein's legs crushed together and then, when he lost control, bandily splayed to avoid clinging wet trousers.

The big benefit of casting *Fledermaus* with actors was that roles with not much to sing, especially Falke and Frank, came fully to life and gave a theatrical depth and balance to what can be a vocal-star show. Josef Ostendorf's Falke really pulled the strings, a brooding, saturnine heavy. Jürg Löw's Frank (a popular local star in Basle) got more outrageously drunk than any other *Fledermaus* prison governor ever, crawling upstairs in the third act in Adele's over-large dress. Wernicke's plain staircase set, symbolizing ideally the insecurity of social aspirations and personal relationships, was a new and original approach to an operatic cliché, the grand entry. Being drunk and having fierce rows on such a staircase was physically dangerous, as the audience's gasps showed when Frank raced downstairs almost tripping over himself. But through all this farce, Wernicke drew totally truthful emotions from his performers. Timing and characterization of this naughty pocket *Fledermaus* were deliciously nuanced. Wernicke's talent for truthful acting confirmed him as the most able director-designer working in European opera since the death of Jean-Pierre Ponnelle. Unlike Ponnelle, whose stagings came from a production-line, Wernicke's work was too individually geared to clone. *Fledermaus*, which transferred to the Stuttgart Opera, benefited wonderfully from such detail and subtlety.

The contrast between a naturalistic, effectively non-interventionist operatic style and a conceptual evaluative approach could scarcely have been better demonstrated than in two productions of Schoenberg's *Moses and Aaron* in 1995 – by Peter Stein at the Amsterdam Musiektheater in October and by Wernicke at the Châtelet Theatre in Paris a month later. Stein had Pierre Boulez conducting, frigid and unaesthetic in approach despite Schoenberg's request for expressiveness (though for Boulez clarity is expressive by itself). Wernicke collaborated with the conductor Christoph von Dohnanyi who obtained a heavenly beauty from the Philharmonia Orchestra. Schoenberg's debate about how the people of Israel could be made to believe in and appreciate the One God, a god they could not see or know, without traducing his remote otherness by attaching to him the attributes and limitations of a humanly created deity, was a surrogate debate about the nature of artistic responsibility: how to realize the artist's vision, which was never fully or properly expressed. Form versus content. What really was it to give life to the notion of an 'ineffable deity', to use good biblical words? Schoenberg the artist was in sympathy with Aaron the interpreter, the priest, the presenter, but recognized that in the process of creating – in that potentially blasphemous act of divine imitation – the original remote concept became a free agent, uncontrollable, misrepresentable.

There must be the right tension between the unattainable perfection of knowing and the unsatisfactory but assistant means to the knowledge. Both Moses and Aaron must play their roles, and Moses is always frustrated by Aaron's mediation of the vision in his mind. In an ideal sense, the theme of Schoenberg's opera is analogous to the current controversies about operatic interpretation: didactic versus narrative, loaded qualification versus simple representation, Wernicke versus Stein. The question for interpreters of the whole corpus of operatic literature is how to make the audience believe in the substance of the work, and what to make them believe – during the process of performance when the work is anchored (or earthed) in the experience of the present day by a living interpretation, a process religious missionaries call 'inculturation'. *Moses and Aaron* is not the only opera *about* interpretation. Bartók articulated a similar problem of knowledge in *Duke Bluebeard's Castle*, where each 'room', so meticulously portrayed in musical terms, was another facet of the central conundrum – how to penetrate the secrets of another person's ego or 'heart'. Both are problem operas for staging, with music that seems more effectively evocative of their themes than any staging could be. The sub-text of *Bluebeard* was the battle of the sexes. Judith was woman as victim, who never got the understanding or experience of her spouse/master that would free her from thraldom – though the most impressive operas from the 18th century on have furthered the cause of sexual equality and the empowerment of the weaker sex by presenting woman as an heroic and effective agent of change whose cry at its highest pitch dramatizes all the most important questions of life.

But *Moses and Aaron* places the issue of interpretation centre-stage. Moses's concept of God is turned by Aaron into a language that the people of Israel can grasp – but as they adopt the imagery, they distort it. The purity of Moses's vision is, literally, inexpressible. The fabric of expression, an ornate and alluring musical fabric, inevitably transmutes what is being expressed – for it has a life of its own. Similarly, there is no such thing in the theatre as an interpretation without complexity, responsibility, consequence: the term *inconsequential*, critically applied, is itself loaded. To emphasize one drift of meaning may be to dam up and obscure others. Thought and expression are never inert.

There were no blinding flashes of painful light from the stage into the auditorium in Wernicke's *Moses and Aaron* as there had been in Stein's staging, where fierce, aggressive banks of floodlights offered a simple but striking physical suggestion of the unseeable and unknowable, an experience for the audience of the frustration of Moses. Wernicke ensured that the issue remained firmly conceptual – inside the audience's mind. In Stein's staging the stylization of crowd movements, the people of Israel in the desert, resembled the epic theatre of his Shakespeare productions, where background and incidentals were always less important than the management and dynamics of debate within a large space, often listened to and involving large numbers of supporters. But there was also in *Moses* an evocation by Stein's designer, Karl-Ernst Herrmann, of divine light, blazing directly into the eyes of the audience: a blinding revelation. There was a sort of burning bush. Across a backdrop ran a neon zigzag line. Herrmann made no attempt to disguise the mechanical nature of this stage environment – like a laboratory, like graph paper. Yet costumes were more modern than biblical, until the arrival of the Ephraimite and his supporters on horseback in Arab rig to join in the worship of the Golden Calf evoked a blend of Hollywood and modern Islam.

Nothing Stein put on stage distilled the essence of Schoenberg's remarkable music-drama: the definition of a concept originally verbal but needing realization in theatrical terms. Indeed many of Stein's details were unconsciously comic and feeble. The orgy was tasteful. The arrival on each side of the stage of two lorries involved in the fabrication of the Golden Calf suggested we would shortly meet Widow Begbick (from the Brecht/Weill *Rise and Fall of the City of Mahagonny*).

Wernicke (as always his own designer) brought to the Châtelet a version of a production orginally devised for the Alte Oper, Frankfurt, with no backstage or theatre machinery for complicated scene-changes. He focused the performance with fierce clarity on the central issue. Instead of crowds of wandering Jews, and later the fake sexuality of mimed excesses, the set presented a tower of Babel leaning backwards in teetering perspective pierced by a regular series of windows through which the chorus and occasional soloists could poke their heads and bodies (usually armed with scores to sing from). At the front were mountainous piles of books and stretching towards the front from the central opening of the tower a yellow pathway ran to the right and eventually over the orchestra-pit into the auditorium. Moses's staff was a useful shovel with a long handle, held either way up, digging, cultivating, investigating. The Golden Calf was a golden-calf mask (suggesting shared delusion) adopted by practically all on stage including Moses himself, who was never during the performance physically absent from the stage – just as, even when he is up Mount Sinai, one never feels he is absent from Schoenberg's mind or from the work. The action was focused almost exclusively at the front of the stage on the principal characters: such events as the brutal shooting (by the Ephraimite) of the protester against Aaron's new rite, who – despite Aaron's warning hand and attempt to stop him – had dropped and broken a golden-calf mask on the floor, were far more shocking than in Stein's more conventional action at this point. Wernicke constantly suggested implications and references, the rich, politically dangerous background of the debate.

Charles Rosen maintained in his monograph on Schoenberg that this opera was best treated as oratorio, performed unstaged. Wernicke supported the strength of the musical performance by not attempting naturalistic manoeuvres. All the choruses were clearly audible, all the subsidiary vocal lines – and Dohnanyi's realization of the music's romantic aspirations recalled that Schoenberg wanted to emphasize the allure of Aaron's case, in contrast to the *Sprechstimme* of Moses, depending on the word to persuade. Schoenberg wanted the dice to be loaded, as art (human creativity) loads them. In a sense the Châtelet *Moses* was semi-staged, but it was powerfully acted by Philip Langridge's passionately concerned Aaron, at every point making the argument of the work more immediate. The audience became part of the debate, especially when the front row of the stalls proved to be occupied by a chorus of objectors who harangued Aaron, standing up indignantly – later moving on stage to each take a glass of wine from a flunkey's tray – comically encapsulating the alcoholic abandon of the Dance. The sexual orgy was a violent mating ritual between the Ephraimite and one woman. The four suicides were balletic almost, or mimed. The performance evoked reality when appropriate, but fluently moved into the conceptual and interpretative. All the men wore dinner jackets, the women sober black dresses. The emotion of Moses's failed attempt (as depicted in Aage Haugland's compelling performance) was far more disturbing than in the Stein staging. However finely Chris Merritt sang Aaron's part for Stein and Boulez, however dignified his movements, David Pittman-Jennings's Moses played the prophet rather than shared the problem. Wernicke brought out the tragic frailty of the whole notion, where Stein presented a stylish but mundane account of the events.

The adventurous Frankfurt regime did not discover the other genuinely original and distinctive German opera producer of the mid-1990s, Willy Decker, who was working at Cologne, a competing house, and whose more famous successes were not until after Gielen's departure from Frankfurt. Decker's unusual and virtuosic staging of Handel's *Julius Caesar* for Scottish Opera in Glasgow was the most unusual the company had originated in years. It was funny, entertaining, and crystal clear in its intention, yet did not neglect the opera's cruelty and ambivalent seriousness. It was hated by conservative critics, but the quality of the ensemble playing showed the cast's enthusiasm for Decker's daring and strikingly calculated approach. Born in 1950, trained as an assistant of Hans Neugebauer in Cologne, by the mid-1980s Decker had acquired a reputation both in Germany and abroad – with some work in the US and South America as well as Europe. He achieved recognition with productions of *Faust* (Cologne, 1988), Bibalo's *Macbeth* (Oslo, 1990), and *Doktor Faust* (Leipzig, 1991). He concentrated exclusively on opera, and this staging in Glasgow was one of his most adventurous outside the circuit of smaller German operahouses. Decker like Alden was not frightened of mixing naturalism and expressionism in the same sequence or scene. He had no preconceptions about decorum on stage, and so was liberated to do what needed doing, to touch on hidden elements and then immediately switch to something on the narrative surface. His *Wozzeck* in Amsterdam and *Peter Grimes* in Brussels further established his reputation. His style in origin was firmly post-expressionist and typically modern German, but it was not just that.

It was not easy for modern taste to accept the outrageous irony and satire of Baroque opera's castrato vehicles, for whose original audiences there was something fascinatingly improper yet intriguing and impressive about the great castrato opera stars, deprived of their manhood for the sake of art. The castrati were musically profound, yet with a frisson of the dubious shocking vulgarity of a variety act like Barry Humphries's Dame Edna Everage. Everything Decker did in *Julius Caesar* made dramatic sense, was witty, and visually striking. The complex storyline was easily followed. Handel, man of theatre, would have had a good time, even if he missed the castrati's inimitable vocalise.

There is no simple right way of staging Handel's masterpiece. The problem with Handel – and with most *opera seria* – is that Baroque feathered headdresses, a neutral neo-classical set and ritual courtly manoeuvres do not register the subtle ironies and hidden motivations that would have been plain to Handel's contemporaries. Any puffed up heroism was qualified in the original 1724 staging by the unnaturalness of the voices and physical state of at least three of the cast, played by '*musici*', megastar castrati. That was why Peter Sellars repatriated the opera to familiar American territory, a sort of Gore Vidal East Coast Ivy League world where politics blended imperceptibly with soap opera.

But John Macfarlane's teetering stepped pyramid set in the colour of yellow desert-sand crowned with a giant paper crown, which all on stage at various times struggled to possess (both at the start and in a final reprise that included some musical grafting at the end), was a marvellous metaphor for the social and political agenda. Sometimes the crown bumped precipitately to the bottom of the steps. This slippery political stairway on which the protagonists had to perform was no nursery slope. Macfarlane's inventions included, from time to time, a towering metal throne that was sometimes securely set up on the steps, sometimes laid across them, a negotiating round table fixed vertiginously across the pyramid, a black tomblike monument for Pompey's memorial procession, a bedlike platform for Cleopatra, and a little theatrical backdrop and curtains dropped in for the alluring coup with which 'Lydia' (Cleopatra's alias) got Caesar infatuated. Macfarlane made his name as a designer of ballet: here he was relishing the chance to make a set that would have been certain disaster for any classical dancer.

The Romans (Caesar, Sextus, Curio) had formality – dinner

suits and black bowties. Ptolemy, Cleopatra and Nirenus were bald and tended to wear white. Achillas had a leonine mane and desert army gear. But it was the absolutely serious presentation of the plot developments and manoeuvres between characters that made the production. Caesar's great aria with four horns about the huntsman silently tracking the spoor became a formally danced encounter with Ptolemy which demonstrated conclusively the superior political sophistication of the Romans. Over and over again, the staging wittily indicated the political state of affairs. The unusual arrangement of the music (using Brian Trowell's English translation) brought the sung text and the drama closer together, and Samuel Bächli's somewhat romanticized conducting set a firm lead. The three countertenors, Michael Chance's playful consider- able Caesar, Timothy Wilson's elegantly avuncular, almost blind Nirenus, and above all Christopher Robson's irrepressible and uncompromising Ptolemy, were fascinatingly differentiated – even if as countertenors they lacked ideal or castrato-like vocal fire. Decker played up the dynastic incest and perverse sexuality traditional to Egyptian royalty with a delightful scene where Ptolemy in red lips and wearing his sister Cleopatra's red dress comically admired himself, cowering among large protective mir- ror walls.

It is always a nice question how emotional Berg's *Wozzeck* should be – with so many shadows of sentiment in its complex subtle score, quite apart from the deterministic corners into which Berg and Büchner (author of the original play) paint its characters. Chéreau in Paris in 1991 polished up the mannered theatricality of meetings between the Hauptmann and Doktor. Deborah Warner in Leeds in 1993 focused on the suffering Marie. Both resorted to a sort of subjective poetic realism, potently emotional, to arouse sympathy – as if the audience ought to identify with the low-life townscape of the narrative. Decker's *Wozzeck* in Amsterdam was by contrast rigorously objective, its theatrical language simple and plain – with a clownlike physical exuberance and breadth of ges- ture universally allowed which expressed the situations dry-eyed, without artiness. The material was as detached and autonomous as cartoons by Steve Bell. Wolfgang Gussman's designs were varia- tions on a simple theme: the gabled peasant house (not unlike Peduzzi's mobile Brio blocks in the Chéreau *Wozzeck*) inside a rectangular yellow ochre stage space that varied in scale from scene to scene. German cottages had a conveniently recognizable shape. When Wozzeck said the moon was bloody, in the second scene and later when he killed Marie – lashing out almost feebly, mechanically, with none of the usual expressionist relish for violence – the ochre glowed orange-red. The houses had black daub surfaces, sometimes with windows or doors. A tiny black gabled model hinted at distant habitation, as Andres and Wozzeck collected sticks in the second scene. Each taut cameo opened and closed with a black frontdrop – sometimes expanding like a camera oscura.

As with Decker's *Julius Caesar*, the stage action was never for a moment naturalistic. It was a series of cartoons, powerfully coherent, suggestive, stripped like clowning to expressive essentials. There was no waste, no blinking from the robustness of the ideas. The images had an iconic quality – most memorably when Marie read the Bible inside a tiny gabled house like a kennel, with the child at the back. As she raised her head into the apex, her arms formed a crucifixion shape and the child clung round her knees. Another time she cradled the child like a Pietà. Decker simultaneously evoked the art-world of 1923 and the ancient severities of gothic sculpture, firm bas-relief or linocut. But these were momentary flashes, never laboured.

David Pountney at ENO had also tackled the mechanistic quality, but fatally allowed his Wozzeck and Marie too much self-conscious sensitivity. Decker's characters were all unconscious, alive on stage only in their actions. They wore costumes that presented them as semi-comic cyphers. The Hauptmann had Hitler hair and a bright blue uniform. The Doktor was a spidery cricket-like caricature in green tails and top hat. Both inhabited worlds remotely inaccessible for Wozzeck. The Hauptmann as if in a puppetshow leered from a hatch in his house, throwing his legs over the window sill like Mr Punch, almost impossible for Wozzeck to shave or serve, an awful incubus whom the 'Mensch' literally had to lug about on his back. The Doktor examined Wozzeck from the top of his roof scrabbling about on metal footholds like a stick insect. The soldiers wore off-white fatigues. The dormitory was one of the gabled houses on its side, piled with sleepers. The Drum-major was a red devil with feathered helmet. The dancers at the pub were commedia del'arte figures with pointed paper noses. The girls were whores in white shifts and red wigs.

The appearance of the idiot (Alexander Oliver) was a theatrical coup, showing a leg from a mound of drunken humanity as if it belonged to one of the whores. Then, rising to his feet, the idiot turned to the audience, removed the flowing wig he was wearing, revealed who he was – strangely touching. Wozzeck's death after the murder turned the drowning into a stage trapdoor disappearance. The closing image reversed the invariable black on yellow theme from negative to positive, with Marie's child (a miniature Wozzeck) walking upstage towards a gabled house-shape in bright yellow silhouette. Decker held to the conventions of this stage language with unwavering conviction. The hard focus and sheer discipline of the direction were enormously impressive. The performers worked well for him, though only Marilyn Schmiege as Marie had a voice of real quality, the ability to register the *Sprechstimme* without rasping and barking.

Decker's *Peter Grimes* at the Monnaie in Brussels in April 1994 confronted in a unique way the problem of homosexuality and sexual abuse implicit in the opera – though not implicit in Crabbe's poem, *The Borough*. The reality of Britten's life provided the motivation for his tackling the story, and therefore homosexuality needs to be registered somehow without being laboured. Decker did not exaggerate, and with such a masculine actor as Cochran in the title role pederasty would not have been spotlit. But both in the relationship with Ellen, and in the intimacy of the scene at Grimes's hut – where Grimes cuddled up round the Prentice on the same bed, while singing of his dreams – the complicated and displaced emotions, ambitions and commitments of the story were provocatively suggested. It is a nice question how homosexuality should figure in the staging of Britten's operas. Can the submerged sexual identities of his characters somehow resonate in performance? Should the agenda of Britten's own homosexuality be seen just as an advantageous surrogate for social exclusion or isolation? Britten's sexuality explains many things about his theatrical works, and was the motive for his choice of operatic material. His operas commonly present not just a love 'that dare not speak its name', but a love that dare not speak nor even sing. Apart from *Albert Herring* and *A Midsummer Night's Dream* the idea of men wooing women pleasurably does not occur. The serenading of Nancy by Sid serves mainly to emphasize Albert's total lack of female interest. Herring may not be homosexual, but the fact that his breaking out involves getting drunk and disappearing – or that's his story – suggests Britten identified strongly with him, for incipient alcoholism was one of the composer's ways of answering his own frustrations. In the Britten canon there is plenty of passion, tortured, suppressed, regretted, feared: but rarely the security and blind abandon of love. That stubborn refusal to sentimentalize has given his best works their stature – as forceful in their way as the feminist operas of Janáček.

Decker showed graphically how Grimes could not bear to be touched by Ellen Orford, the woman of his plans and dreams. Yet he was not a misogynist – Ellen was the nearest thing to his best friend in the community. He struck her as he would strike his prentices, though he had no qualms about relating to them or physically dominating them. Her obvious love for him, considering his reputation, was inexplicable – though he told her 'If you – take your hand away – what's left?' Decker did not insist on a one-track view of the 'truth' of what happened.

It is not and need not be clear whether Grimes sexually abused his prentices, or merely beat them or roughed them up because they were too slow on the uptake ('an idiot's drooling gaze'). But in the parallel instance of *Billy Budd*, Vere's moral failure to intervene must stem from the fact that the Captain shares (in his inner soul) the Master-at-arms's dark sexual obsession. Budd's felling of Claggart was felt as a rejection by Vere too. As for poor Miles in *The Turn of the Screw*, racked in a tug-of-love between the Governess and Quint, non-parents who like competing lovers both want to possess him, who are his 'kind'? What is the 'queer life' he has been leading?

It is wrong to purify Britten's operas of sex, and pretend that homosexuality is incidental to them when it is so central (except in *Midsummer Night's Dream* and *The Rape of Lucretia*). The hatred of the Borough folk for Grimes, though invested by the composer with a certain rollicking provincial theatricality more reassuring than terrifying (a mildly nightmarish version of Warlock's *Cricketers of Hambledon*), never explicitly touches on sexual abuse. But early versions of the libretto prove that for Britten Grimes's outsider status was both social and sexual: when the Borough's charged hatred burgeons it needs to register something more fundamental than common brutality.

Jon Vickers's revolutionary interpretation of the title role masked almost all the internal feelings of the character beneath epic, monumental charisma with no hint of homosexuality – and little evidence of real violence. But all the cruelty Crabbe described pulsed through his performance, though the apparent nobility and suffering of Vickers's Grimes turned the dark side into a kind of dangerous schizophrenia. Vickers reacted against the intelligent, poetic, sensitive Peter Pears version of the relationship betwen the Prentice and Grimes. Few great operas present such central ambivalence to the interpreter. Philip Langridge for Tim Albery at ENO was closer to Pears, a haughty, intelligent figure – not somebody in the grip of a fundamental force, like sex, beyond his control. Anthony Rolfe Johnson in Joachim Herz's conservative staging for Scottish Opera was roughly sensitive, and more reserved than Vickers. But in all these versions the Prentice was a passive cypher.

The Decker staging, with its simple set by John Macfarlane beneath a lowering sky-backdrop full of angry clouds, alone confronted the homosexual issue. In the prologue Grimes spotlit carried a coffin symbolizing the guilt for the Prentice's death up the raked stage. The Borough, a crowd, assembled around Swallow – sometimes on a formal seat, held above them, sometimes moving towards Grimes in interrogation – bodies pressed about Swallow like the eddying of a tide. The crowd for a time took over the coffin deposited by Grimes. The stage was edged in dark. Decker and Macfarlane were not interested in anecdotal fishing-village imagery, boats, nets, or pots. Decker painted his meaning with the movement of chorus and individual characters, focused always in grim physicality. Though Albery at ENO tried to achieve a social focus he suppressed the individuality of the leading personalities. Decker, with his non-naturalistic style of gesture and movement, could emphasize the individuality of Britten's provincial cameos simply by peeling them away physically from the coherent chorus mass. His direction of the chorus, person by person, was subtle and potent in its detailed ensemble work.

At the close of the prologue he suggested the parameters of Grimes and Ellen's relationship poignantly and tellingly – leaving no doubt they were physically incompatible. They sang: 'Your [my] voice is like a hand that I [you] can feel and know here is a friend.' Grimes was not facing her. Their hands on the floor touched, she in a sort of suffering Magdalen position, her whole frame yearning to serve him. As the music moved into the spare lyrical sea interlude, the staging pursued the theme. The looming, huge, dark, claustrophobic walls of Macfarlane's set at the back parted to show a monochrome skyscrape of smoky clouds threatening storm. Ellen and Grimes almost came together in embrace.

He turned to kiss her, but could not. Then he went back to where he had left the coffin and carried it upstage as the musical interlude continued. She stopped him, leant against his back. He moved on out at the back over a floor which was rising like sand-dunes on a beach. Her whole being expressed her love. As the dark, tragic front-cloth closed the scene, she was isolated in front, moving off stage, while backstage the chorus began to sing 'Oh, hang at open doors the net, the cork'.

When the first act opened, instead of fishery work the Borough was presented as a church congregation at choir practice, men to the right, women to the left, in two blocks on either side of a central aisle – rehearsing their music, totally conformist. Ellen took the seat awaiting her – but did not raise her music to cover her face as the ordinary people of the Borough usually, conventionally did. Auntie and Bob Boles, the methodist preacher, broke decorum on their entrance. She sat on the men's side. Balstrode, at his mention of storm and sea horses, sat by Auntie. Parson Adams turned to conduct. The first bit of colour – though sombre too – was the nieces' costumes. (The period of the staging and its costumes looked like the 1840s, when Crabbe wrote his poem.) Grimes just pulled on ropes, after he asked for 'a hand'. Ellen intervened, held on to Grimes's shoulder, while he kept his hand on top of hers. Old Methody Boles was the focus of the anti-Grimes feeling, always needing to be restrained: Cochran as Grimes sat at the front of the stage, the choir chairs were overturned in disorder. As the storm rose, Balstrode shook his head at Grimes's self-deluding talk of marrying Ellen: there might be 'grandeur in a gale of wind to free confession, set a conscience free', but for Balstrode clearly Grimes's situation was incapable of such a solution.

During the storm the ground at the back of the stage physically rose. When the front-cloth opened on the Bear tavern, the stage floor had become vertiginous and drunken. Auntie's walls were red, with a massive door at the top right hand corner of the set. It was closing time, two long tables stacked centre-stage. Gradually during the scene the storm blew in more and more of the inhabitants of the Borough as if gathering for the confrontation with Grimes over the boy. The pub was re-opened. The various little inner scenes were marked with an increasingly ferocious atmosphere. The nieces paraded on the tables, now lined up as a sort of cakewalk. Balstrode looked up their skirts. But when he made his point about tolerance ('We live and let live, and look we keep our hands to ourselves') he extended his arms to embrace the whole community – turning it into a political statement, almost as if he were standing for office. Once again Decker focused on what is usually presented casually as an opportunistic momentary response. Here was the central social principle that stirred the composer. When the news came that the cliff was down by Grimes's hut, the whole assembly raised their hands in glee.

'Mind that door', signalling Grimes's arrival, announced his entry with a massive silhouette on the back wall. His mad visionary aria about the Great Bear and Pleiades was delivered from the doorway, facing the crowd gathered downstage left. Later the Prentice entered – a small figure utterly alone, also by this ominously enlarged door. Slowly, almost like an automaton, he moved down the sloping stage to his new master. The whole scene was on the edge of a psychological precipice.

Because John Macfarlane's sets for Decker embodied qualities of feeling, claustrophobia, blinkered vision, tempestuous circumstances rather than anecdotal details, the sweep of events and musical pace pressed forward through the first and second acts. This Brussels production emphasized how much of Britten's drama was completed in those first two acts. The beauty and terror of the third act denouement lay in its static, arrested, insoluble character for which the composer provided a kind of emotional agony that never, however, sentimentalized. Sunday morning of the second act picked up again the central image of the Borough as a conformist religious community: two flats, angled to make a kind of enclosure in front of the ominous cloudscape at the back of the set, revealed a scene dominated by a processional cross. Clothes (Sunday bonnets) defined the day. At the front Ellen's scene with the Prentice had a desperate inevitability: the boy leant with his head against the wall at the side of the stage. 'A bruise' – the words gave a signal to the boy to fall to the floor, as if re-enacting Grimes's brutality. Later the boy was knocked flying by his master. Again with Ellen's hand offered, touching Grimes, his reaction was furious, repelling: 'Take your hand away.' He struck her, pushed her to the floor. The Prentice went to her, to share her victim-lover status. Britten like Grimes mixed paternal and other longings in his view of the young whom he wanted close to him.

The decision of the Borough to investigate Grimes's 'exercise' was taken at a hurriedly convened meeting seated at tables, a communal mobilization not a lynching party, with Parson Adams sufficiently in charge. The crowd swept around with the violence of a storm. Hands pointed. Bowles took the initiative, standing on one of the tables. Ellen, accused, almost seemed to be in a confessional with Adams at the central table. The back of the stage was erupting, rising physically, like the rage of the community or waves in a stormy sea. The procession passed upstage over this hillside leaving the quartet of fallen women on the slope, Ellen, Auntie and the nieces. When they had finished singing their haunting ensemble the rest of the Borough women, a threatening alienated force, returned over the horizon at the rear of the set.

Grimes's hut literally jutted over the cliff at the back: one bed, a pair of seaboots, a red jersey knitted by Ellen for the boy on the bed. Grimes lifted the boy up exuberantly when announcing they were going to sea, later stroked his head. The boy tried to escape, crawled away from Grimes, was caught again. After the boy's fatal fall down the cliff and the visitation of the Borough leaders, Grimes re-entered the scene – climbing back up from the cliff edge at the rear of the set, rolling the Prentice's body on to the stage. He laid it on the bed, bent over it in despair, before covering it with a sheet.

The last act brought the mad nightmare to a desperate end. The Borough inhabitants were gallivanting in fancy dress at Auntie's, wearing farm animal masks – men as pigs, Auntie as a hen, parson Adams as a sheep, Mrs Sedley as a crow. At the back two fiery red flats, arranged as they had been for Sunday morning church, enclosed a dance space. Ellen's aria about embroidery 'brooding on the fantasies of children' was ravishingly sung by Susan Chilcott making a profound effect. The misery of Grimes's mad scene against a drained black and grey background soon blended into the final vision of the Borough as religious conformists occupying blocks of church pews, their choir music raised in front of their faces – their vision in blinkers. Ellen left Grimes's coat at the front of the stage after he had gone off to his suicide – Swallow remarked on the boat sinking too far out to sea for them to do anything about it. Ellen took her proper place on the women's side of the seated chorus.

Brussels used a fine largely British cast, and the music, conducted with passion, pace and dramatic flexibility by Antonio Pappano, a New York Italian though born in London, threw its painful spell. Decker achieved scrupulous clarity, mobilizing the sub-text. By lighting up Grimes's conflicting incoherent feelings for his boy Prentice, whatever their balance of sexual emotion and adult paternal concern, by making so clear Grimes's physical and sexual alienation from Ellen, Decker effected a radical departure in *Grimes* interpretation. The honest presentation of the submerged sexuality authenticated the opera's violence. Decker unlocked the closet agenda of the piece.

The final moment in Decker's staging had first Balstrode and then Ellen raise their music to cover their faces, powerless to change. But opera can change us and our preconceptions, if we let it – for music gives it that power. That is why we must allow full creative freedom to those trying to bring this most demanding and challenging of the performing arts fully to life on the theatrical stage in the opera-house. Opera is theatre, which means very different rules, and a different kind of order, from those that prevail in music alone.

16 21st-century opera
– going for a song

Richard Jones's 1991 English National Opera staging (at the London Coliseum) of *Die Fledermaus* designed by Nigel Lowery: Vivian Tierney as Rosalinde in extravagant disguise as a folksy Hungarian countess lets fly with memories of 'her homeland'. Photograph © Robbie Jack.

The 20th century has been good for opera in many ways. Opera has become a familiar household product on television and on compact disc. It is used and appreciated by – or, rather, its best, most memorable musical moments are familiar to – a wider public around the world than ever before. It has been well funded – both by generous rich patrons and out of state subsidy. It may be an exclusive, demanding and elitist art-form – as its enemies frequently say – but it continues to mobilize a public that has grown more passionate about its virtues and attractions as the century wears on. It is controversial and often in the news. People care when opera-houses burn down, which unlike churches and cathedrals they are very prone to do. Opera-houses have been built and old stages have been refurbished. The opera-house in Sydney is an icon of modern architecture, an acknowledged thing of great beauty, though as a practical opera-house it is very far from ideal. The opera-house in Zurich caused violent riots, when plans for its costly reconstruction were announced. Despite being commercially exploited on record and on television or film, opera has not been tamed or reduced by or made the servant of those media. It has stubbornly remained what it always was: words and music in dramatic context, assembled with all sorts of elusive intriguing ideas that matter enormously.

The musical language preferred by serious modern composers, artists who are expected to survive the eventual judgment of history, without doubt became increasingly unvocal after 1945. There are now very few song-writers of originality or lyrical facility who can marry their skill to good present-day dramatic poetry. Are there any serious composers at all who are really worthwhile and distinctive song-writers now? The heart of the operatic convention is the necessity of song, the acceptance that what is being said needs to be sung. But sequences of notes which together do not amount to a musical statement that people want to hear (uttered by a voice they like) can scarcely claim necessity. That is the central fallacy of many attempts at modern opera.

Song may come in many different shapes. The order of notes offered may never before have been considered lyrical or telling, but the authenticity of operatic or lyrical utterance lies in the fact that an audience will hang on this sung music. Their concentration and responsiveness are willing and therefore pleasurable and affectionate. They can listen to the words, and the relationship of pitches carrying those words, being simultaneously qualified in a coherent syntactical sense – just as they hear them. Song is not only words attached to a musical shape of notes – it is an organic relationship between different notes and words. There can be an infinite variety of musical languages and images, but they have to be apprehendable.

Many musical traditions seem to have vanished over the last five decades which formerly provided useful tools for opera composers: symphonic argument, choral coherence, for example. Some of these elements have migrated to pop music and jazz, from where they might well in theory be borrowed back. But it is of great significance that the pleasure principle no longer seems to apply in opera. What worthwhile serious music being written today offers anything to listeners in the way of simple pleasures? Pleasure has given place to effort and duty for those still taking the art of music and opera seriously. Modernism is not a phenomenon that can be disregarded, or that any serious enthusiasts can turn their back on and ignore. It remains unavoidable. The operatic future cannot lie in writing down to the taste of the public, or compromising. In any case, the breaking-up of the 19th-century musical conventions – including the logic and decorum of the diatonic system – has in effect expanded the possibilities of expressiveness. Sounds that would have seemed meaningless a century ago are now potent with significance and dramatic consequence. But composers have to reacquire the confidence to be simple as well, especially in dramatic music and opera. Timing and a sense of dialogue or rhetoric are absent almost entirely from most of the more distinctive and memorable serious composers of the last 30 years. Harrison Birtwistle's operas, since the extraordinary achievement of his *Punch and Judy*, evoke various impressive musical landscapes during their sometimes over-extended courses. But the music that he gives to the voices has little light and shade, small rhythmic interest, scarcely any of the rhetoric that marks his orchestral writing.

To regard opera as a museum art, or even a dead art, is to ignore the changing circumstances of operatic life. Musical invention has not stopped. What has become problematical is song. It is true that opera cannot remain for ever on a treadmill of historic revaluations. But the fascination with new and altered theatrical styles in the opera-house over the last twenty years has proved how worthwhile and resilient the art-form remains as a resource worth performing and interpreting. And there has been plenty of basic material to concentrate on – quite apart from the established pantheon. Works that are being dug up from the distant past, or from the forgotten and neglected 1950s or 1930s, may not be in unlimited supply. Yet fresh ears and eyes are exploring what may have seemed less than successful when first exposed to public view. And repetition does not dull the masterpieces in the repertoire that go on attracting audiences reliably, almost however they are staged. In an age when people read the same books and see on videotape the same films over and over again, the opera audience is evidently in no danger of crossing a boredom threshold, of becoming too familiar. Musical taste which used to be ephemeral, and therefore prone to boredom, is now infinitely various. Taste which rejects much that is new, or suspects it will not even be worth considering, is truly catholic as, nowadays, it ventures into the past.

The breach between the composers and the public which has got wider in the course of the century is a fact of life, and it is probably an advantage that the growth of the repertoire has as a result slowed down. It amounts to a pause for breath, a long slow backwards survey, made easier by the availability of recording – which increasingly encourages the modern mind to think of and look to the past. Composers who should have the skills and inclination to write operas for today's audiences seldom provide what audiences want to hear. The dreams they have are too challenging. The sounds they want do not support an exchange of words between singer and audience. The harmonies and melodies they give singers are neither emotionally true nor reward their performers' wish for coherence and accomplishment.

The operatic past is still not properly in focus. The aesthetic character of 17th- and 18th-century opera has proved far more elusive than its mere notes and words suggested. In the relationship of dramatic poetry and melody, the balance of interest and energy associated with either words or tunes has varied radically over the few centuries since opera started. The view from the 21st century will be distorted even further by the gradual acceptance of the complexity of Berg and Schoenberg – and perhaps eventually Stockhausen – into the popular arena. We look back at history

417

from the vantage point of the present, a present where Puccini still reigns supreme and where melody is the key to attention and emotion. The challenge of difficult operas in the 20th century has been musical, not dramatic or verbal. But one should think of these new works as software with which audiences must become familiar if they are to operate them. The same goes for performers. Can new music be properly tuned, even, before its singers know where the lines are going and how they relate harmonically? Every note in an opera depends for its sense on context. Its value relates to the attitude and direction of the line of which it is part, and where that line is taking the music as a whole. Listening leads to hearing and making sense, but so much modern art of any sort seems to need decoding before it can be used.

The emphasis in this book on making different kinds of sense through re-interpretation will be taken by some as proof of the degeneration of opera. Theatre and opera-house have indeed been more than just a discipline and filter. They have levelled out the high aspirations of the modern artist and composer. It is extraordinary and should give us pause – that, after all, Puccini remains the sure-fire product of which opera audiences never tire: the centenary of *La bohème* finds it still one of the most popular works of all. Its longevity and the permanence of the musical language it uses are unprecedented in musical history. The operatic past is becoming increasingly distant but its masterworks seem impervious to fashion. Or rather the natural ebb and flow of aesthetic taste has been arrested by the mechanization of memory. Performers no longer require new material to arouse the interest of their public.

Chéreau's *Ring* at Bayreuth in 1976, a landmark production in the history of opera staging, was launched in the year Benjamin Britten died – the last composer of musical distinction to gain entry to the operatic pantheon, and Britten was criticized (and almost silenced) by the censorious modernists for writing in a too conservative manner as the 1950s wore into the 1960s. The many 20th-century operas amount to few classic masterpieces. Richard Strauss, Puccini, Janáček, Britten, and Berg will count as the professional opera composers of the century, though *Wozzeck* and *Lulu* are atypical. It is a line that has temporarily come to an end. The well-made standard good opera for audiences to enjoy, without being a masterpiece, has vanished. Attempts in the media to greet efforts by distinguished serious composers as the towering masterpieces of the age convince nobody.

Instead, the 20th century offers a catalogue of special cases: Ravel's *L'heure espagnol* and *L'enfant et les sortilèges*, Pfitzner's *Palestrina*, Bartók's *Duke Bluebeard's Castle*, Prokofiev's *Love for Three Oranges* and *Betrothal in a Monastery*, Schoenberg's *Moses and Aaron*, Shostakovich's *Lady Macbeth of Mtsensk* and *The Nose*, Gershwin's *Porgy and Bess*, Poulenc's *Dialogues des carmélites* and *Les mamelles de Tirésias*, Tippett's *Midsummer Marriage* and *King Priam*, Birtwistle's *Punch and Judy* and *Yan Tan Tethera*. Few are genuine popular hits in the Puccini mould. But that is unsurprising, for most would-be 20th-century opera composers have had to re-invent the ground rules of composition, and sought untried tales for each new work, devising a personal language specially for the job. Can theatrical opera survive for ever on revivals that only ring superficial stylistic changes? Can a fresh musical voice immediately fit into a vernacular framework as *Peter Grimes* did in 1945?

Audiences in America and Holland can be primed to welcome the works of Philip Glass and John Adams, though their arias (such as they are) cannot survive lifted out on their own. Corigliano's *Ghosts of Versailles* found an audience at the New York Met in 1991. But these have been cases of tolerable music, not compulsive. Operatic music may be popular, and may attract listeners on radio and television. But if there is to be a future for opera, the tradition of music for singing has to be respected by composers and served. The trouble with television, film, and modern methods of recording and reproduction is that they have homogenized standards and tastes. However, there are signs that opera is not doomed to a museum existence or obsolescence. There are composers like Oliver Knussen, Gerald Barry, Judith Weir and Param Vir (in the British Isles) who have found recipes that work or who have musical (lyrical even) voices of individuality and genuine distinction. Neo-classicism in the manner of Stravinsky and Prokofiev cannot be expected to work again. The burden on composers is to find a new kind of song, a new way of expressing lyrical energy. There has to be a new form of colouring, or coloratura, that is worth the effort of singing.

Live performance of classic opera is also being served by an encouraging new interest in adaptation and performance on the intimate scale, either with piano accompaniment or re-scored for just a few instruments – which also happens to be more economical, even perhaps commercially viable. Britten's experiments with chamber-scale operas at Glyndebourne and in Aldeburgh gave him the control over how they were first performed which he felt essential. He was a man of the theatre, and it is unlikely that a composer who does not write for specific circumstances and the artists he knows and has chosen to work with (as Verdi did) will ever become operatically fluent. Britten disliked the backstage politics that afflicted the launch of *Peter Grimes* at Sadler's Wells, *Billy Budd* and *Gloriana* at Covent Garden, and *The Rape of Lucretia* and *Albert Herring* at Glyndebourne. But these five operas all emerged within a span of eight miraculous years. That required an interested audience and managements eager to furnish productions. Until a similar kind of support is given to talented composers who want to serve both drama and singers, and who have something real to say in their music, new operas will not happen. A new aesthetic, a new expressive language in the musical theatre, will require confidence and patience. In order to go forward it may be valuable to go backwards, to mix music and words as they were in the distant past of Purcell or of the earliest *opera seria* when the music served the text and found its function in a secondary, more discreet role. The audience may have to be weaned with a different mixture, a different kind of novelty.

Nobody can say that there is a lack of interest in musical shows in the West End or on Broadway – where the theatres are full of the popular equivalent of opera. The appetite for musical theatre at the end of the 20th century seems to be more insatiable than ever before. Meanwhile, ironically, spoken theatre in London and New York is as comparatively specialized as modern opera. Something is wrong somewhere. The wider public in the age of Andrew Lloyd-Webber is deeply interested in the musical and theatrical elements from which opera also can be built. The taste for unpretentious musicals is well attested. The phenomenal interest in music theatre scarcely looks like circumstances amounting to a crisis for opera. The taste for music generally should represent an opportunity. But serious composers still refuse to adapt to the new realities. Fashion continues, but opera temporarily has removed itself from that world. Might not a composer with some sense of Baroque shape and the melodic and rhythmic imaginativeness to be able to stop and start in the inner structures of his music-drama one day resuscitate the *Singspiel*? Comedy and spoken text could move abruptly but without strain into song and back again. The lack of likable new operas might be solved by recourse to the difficult Purcellian field of semi-opera. Less music, more text – perhaps more satisfaction on the part of the audience and tolerance of awkward kinds of experimental musical expressiveness. An understandable reason for the operatic public's old-fashioned taste is the unstoppable, oppressive volume and density of so many modern attempts to write opera by serious (often serial, or post-serial) composers. If audiences were given a break and offered inviting, witty and truthful dramatic material, they might more rapidly familiarize themselves with the structural dynamics of new operas.

Theatrical conviction cannot be compromised. The versions of *Carmen* and *Pelléas* done by Peter Brook, David Freeman's best productions of chamber operas, or chamber adaptations of originally more grand operas with Opera Factory, and Graham Vick's adaptations with English Touring Opera and City of Birmingham Touring Opera have proved over and over again the effectiveness of a whole-hearted concern with theatrical values. There are alternatives to the tyranny of big stages, inflexible stars, and the established tradition of undying masterworks at the New York Met, La Scala, the Bastille, or Covent Garden. Arena opera too has given a hint to thousands at Earls Court or Verona of the continuing allure and genius of Verdi in *Aida*, Bizet in *Carmen*, and Puccini in *Tosca*. But consumerism only keeps the taste ticking over, reminds the public where those favourite bits belong. It cannot be the answer to the theatrical future. Opera on the epic scale with electronic amplification is too coarse to involve minds in the complex passions and politico-philosophical agendas embedded in these musical classics. Opera is essentially about acting and singing, making narrative and music speak in particular context. It is about prompting the imagination of the audience not swamping and directing it.

There is a large television audience for opera. Could the future of opera be on television? The economy of scale that television allows makes the grandest artists affordable – and a few broadcast performances do amount to something artistically. Television is building opera audiences; it is a popularizing force. Videos are an important utility and learning tool. Productions of opera for video such as Ingmar Bergman's *Magic Flute* have been very engaging – suggesting there might somehow be a bridge between opera and film. But opera on television is not the same art. Bergman devised a context for his Drottningholm *Magic Flute* of an audience shown reacting. He framed a live performance on film. The truth is that opera, live, means singers delivering physically – almost like athletes. If sport were edited, it would be a cheat. On television the audience has to watch close-up from camera positions that focus and interpret the sequence of actions for them in a version of tunnel-vision. The emphasis is invariably too visual for an art that must command the ears, and in the hierarchy of seeing and hearing seeing almost unavoidably takes precedence. Only in the live opera-house can there be the right balance between the visual context and the aural events.

Of course, the serious effort to create bespoke operatic work expressly for the box has been helpful to and profitable for the creators. Actors appreciate making a living from television drama, but know that the real place for acting is the live theatre. Yet television commissioning editors and programme makers are tantalized by opera. It must mean something that the general producers of both London opera companies in the mid-1990s were former television executives. The fact that opera in the flesh can draw vast crowds, and combine glamour and serious artistic quality, indicates to those who control television that it is a natural art for what has become the most powerful and profitable medium of the day. Television can even appear to preserve what in the theatre is ephemeral – though that in fact is an illusion, since what is preserved is not the real thing. Hence the speed with which Peter Sellars's Mozart productions or Handel's *Giulio Cesare in Egitto*, based on actual theatrical performances, were consigned to tape. Hence the bizarre experiment of the 'real place' (if not 'real time') *Tosca* and the friendly spectacle of the three competing tenor-gladiators serving their popularity. But most television opera continues to be live relays – performances overlooked by the cameras, but missing the magic of live performance.

In 1951 Gian-Carlo Menotti wrote *Amahl and the Night Visitors* for NBC. In 1971 Britten wrote *Owen Wingrave* for the BBC. More recently the BBC did Mark-Antony Turnage's *Greek*, a version of *Oedipus* by Steven Berkoff. In the cinema *Les parapluies de Cherbourg* with its sentimental romantic singing of everyday inconsequential dialogue seemed musically thin and dramatically bizarre. The history of cinema includes important musicals written expressly for film. But the issue always must be why the characters sing rather than speak – in so naturalistic a medium, even more than within the conventions of live theatre. In the theatre and opera-house that game with convention and realism is never so artificial. The BBC in 1992 showed a version of Marschner's *The Vampire* turned by Nigel Finch into a 'soap-opera' series updated to the present: but the style of the music and the aria form did not suit such self-conscious treatment. Channel 4 in 1993 invested £3 million in six newly commissioned 50-minute television operas, declaring that the visual approach rather than the music had been the starting-point in choosing the six composers. Only *The Triumph of Beauty and Deceit* by Gerald Barry had the originality to survive. A former pupil of Kagel, with a flair for coloratura excess, dramatic dialogue, situation and character, Barry's step-dancing robustness amd harmonic coherence were dramatically potent. In none of the 160 or so necessary operas that form an intelligent operatic repertoire for responsible opera companies (not all masterpieces) does music have second place. Opera, on the brink of the 21st century, is certainly music-led.

Royal Opera and ENO workshops for operatic experiment were thoroughly tried out, and not the answer to the creation of new British works either – to judge from the Royal Opera's Garden Venture, and ENO's Contemporary Opera Studio, though the latter under the control of David Pountney engendered Param Vir's *Snatched by the Gods* and *Broken Strings*, which made a remarkable impression at Hans Werner Henze's month-long music-theatre festival in Munich in 1992, staged by Pierre Audi in restrained, carefully focused productions. Almeida Opera in Islington presented a few works of promise: including Wolfgang Rihm's *Lenz*, John Casken's *The Golem*, and Gerald Barry's *The Intelligence Park* staged by David Fielding, about a castrato eloping with an heiress in Handelian Dublin with good roles for countertenors. Stephen Oliver's *Mario and the Magician*, based on the Thomas Mann story, and the joyfully unpretentious, musically accessible and effective adaptation of Ostrovsky's bubbling *A Family Affair* by Julian Grant were among the successes there.

London has tasted a great deal of brand new opera. With the exception of a few individual items, such as Tippett's first three operas (*The Midsummer Marriage*, *King Priam*, and *The Knot Garden*), some of Harrison Birtwistle's, and the work of Judith Weir, it is true that most – like the suitors of *Turandot* – have been found wanting. Both Covent Garden and ENO have done Weir's work proud. Her first opera – *A Night at the Chinese Opera* – was a real draw for the public in 1987 staged by the now disbanded

Kent Opera. *The Vanishing Bridegroom*, written by Weir for her native Scottish Opera in Glasgow in 1990, toured to Covent Garden. ENO's spring repertoire in 1994 included Weir's new full-length opera, *Blond Eckbert*, staged by Tim Hopkins with designs by Nigel Lowery (see pp. 256–59). Weir, whose works have also been heard in the United States, could well become the first woman composer to enter the operatic pantheon. She combines theatrical vision with firm musical control and economy, though the language of her music is not assertive or enormously striking.

The issue in 21st-century opera will be the musical discourse, not the manner of staging the material. The existence of the cinema would seem to preclude a return to simple narrative form. Editing disparate elements together, overlaying narrative with discursion, a conscious playing with sub-text: all these methods are so much part of the subtlety of film and of video treatments of song material for rock musicians that the theatre and opera are unlikely to be straitjacketed, simplified and purified. What is there after post-modernism? Will there be a rejection of complexity? Will popular taste become alienated from history, from an awareness of previous models? Will there be a renewed confidence about the present and distaste for the past? Will the whirligig of fashion slow down, or even stop?

Musical language is bound to change. It will only take a few successes in a particular style for a different language to become really popular. If audiences can once again enjoy voices in new melodies and a different musical language, one perhaps capable of embracing both dramatic crises and comic revelations, there will be no problem renewing the repertoire – adding to it, even. Yet it is hard to imagine, after the building of the classic operatic pantheon over the last 200 years, that there will ever be a real reversal of taste – unless there is a radical change in the nature of Western culture.

Singers in the 20th century, despite the conservatism of their profession in musical taste, have shown themselves very adaptable – highly sophisticated and adept at learning to manage and make elegant the widest variety of musical languages. Music that sounded awkward if not impossible to sing, when it was first composed by Schoenberg or Boulez, after a few decades has appeared completely within the normal capacity of a considerable range of different performers. Familiarity has made music approachable that at first seemed meaningless.

But song is the real issue. The through-composed opera has

been far harder to write and to listen to – because the kind of musical language found among respected and worthwhile serious modern composers has provided no structural assistance to listeners or to the composer struggling to honour some kind of graspable shape in the narrative. Song remains what draws the public to an interest in operatic material. Song is what is memorable. Song is the means whereby the themes and ideas of past operas are brought to life. Song is the essence of the drama that producers and designers are reacting to as they prepare to mobilize the work on stage. Poetry must sing. Poetic drama must sing. When it can once again, opera will have found a voice for the new millennium. It was not modernism itself, or serial composition, that silenced song in contemporary music: it was a kind of rhetorical exhaustion. The language of the songs to come, and of the operas that such language will make possible, will not need to reject modernism in its various guises – but will go beyond it, no doubt exploiting the hints of a fragmented linguistic structure in the writing of Janáček and Britten as well as in the angular paeans of Berg. The subjects of those operas to come will also be different. Perhaps for a time it will even be better if the poetry of the new operas seems more important than the music – or as important. Drama in music does not mean the music must always be predominant, especially if the shaping of the discourse allows the words to tell more effectively. But music, wherever it is applied in opera, will have to be authentic and fresh, good enough to stand alone sometimes, good enough to be wanted and popular. Such music is certainly kicking in the womb of the 20th century.

Appendix

Bühnenreform (Theatre Reform) by Alfred Roller

from *Der Merker*, i (1909–10), pp. 193–7.
Translated by Meredith Oakes

Daily life has become much more exciting than it was, while the theatre in general is correspondingly more boring. At least so it seems. Perhaps just by contrast. Because of this, people concerned with the theatre now give more attention than they should to its secondary aspects. To design, for example, about which much more has been said and written than is helpful for its development.

And everyone has his say!

It has often struck me that when someone who does not deserve a hearing starts to talk about art, he always excuses himself by saying: 'I know nothing about music (or painting, or poetry), but I think that . . .' before giving of his wisdom. Only when people talk about the theatre do they omit the introductory excuse: in this area everyone considers his opinion to be valuable and justified. It would be very interesting if someone were clever enough to explain why this is so.

For myself I am convinced that the problems of theatre reform will be solved not through theoretical discussions but through a great many experiments, and that in particular, anything that visual artists have to say about the essentials of this matter will be either self-evident or totally incomprehensible. If you wish to hear me out, you will have to be content with the following peripheral and incidental observations.

Would it not be better to reflect on what theatre was at the start, and on what we have made of it in the course of time? And to ask, above all, whether in its present form it is still viable and healthy? Could it not be that the travelling theatre was healthy and right, and that all permanently established theatre is merely decadent? To be in a different place every three weeks, startling the philistine, giving him the excitement he longs for, preserving the sense of the exceptional! A thespis-van, what fun!

But a permanent theatre! Serving up the exceptional, 300 times a year! For every good performance of a work of art must be in some way exceptional. By that I mean that it should stand out from ordinary daily life and project beyond it. – This is what has always drawn people to the theatre, this view into another world that excites, stirs, uplifts, un-nerves, diverts, in any case engages! If the theatre becomes merely a part of ordinary life it gradually loses this attraction.

I know that the theatre also functions as a social manifestation and as a business. But these aspects are of secondary interest, if we are to consider the possibility of investing it with new life.

So: a sacred and festal art, or a permanent institution for edification and entertainment?

Certainly I would not like to hear *Tristan* or *Figaro* or *Fidelio* every day of the week; and probably every great work of art is someone's *Tristan* or *Figaro* or *Fidelio*.

Repertory theatre seems to me to be simply a mistake. Admittedly Gustav Mahler was able to show that sacred festival performances [*Weihefestspiele*] of works in repertory are possible. But he imposed this through his own inordinate strength, quite against the tendency of his organization.

It would be rash to suppose, for example, that there could ever exist the thousands upon thousands of strong personalities that our current abundance of permanent theatres requires. And what is to interest us on stage, if not strong personalities? Occasionally perhaps just the beautiful sound of a voice or the agility of a virtuoso. But in the long run? And what, if not boredom, can be dispensed by all those countless others who have chosen the stage as their calling? Chosen! There it is. – If, in earlier times, many people were driven to the theatre by the narrowness of bourgeois life – nowadays, most have chosen the stage deliberately. In earlier times they were wild [*durchgängerisch*] spirits, marked creatures whose perpetually precarious lives lent them a feckless charm. But these numerous honest persons on the stage today, learned owner-occupiers, professionals and businessmen: can they bring us the extraordinary, which is what we expect from the theatre? Good citizens and hardworking people just like them are sitting in the stalls: the public is familiar with them through its own daily experience. Why should it bestow special attention on them as soon as they put on make-up and bright clothes, and why should it believe them when they speak great or terrifying or sweet words? Or when they sing their parts more or less correctly?

So why do we stick to a kind of theatrical activity which seems no longer to be viable? Granted, new and contemporary forms are continually arising, but in their lack of tradition they are naturally not exalted enough to meet with serious encouragement or to win favour with the cultivated! Isn't a good film to be preferred to a bad performance of Schiller?

Our theatre fails to satisfy the more serious part of its public, so in order to re-structure it we first set to work on design. But is this not the wrong way round? Production is, after all, the art of presentation, never an end in itself: an altogether secondary thing, ineluctably taking its principles and rules from the work itself, and having no guiding principle other than that of fulfilling the quite particular, often unique requirements of that work. So what can it mean to be seeking a new production method? 'Do you favour stylization or illusion?' one is continually asked, 'three-dimensional sets or backdrops?' – just as at table one is asked, 'Would you like white wine or red?' No choice is actually possible in these questions; they are answered within the work that is to be produced. But one must know how to read and listen one's way to this answer! Each work of art carries within itself the principles of its production. – Rules and methods established today can be stood on their head by a poet who comes along and creates a work tomorrow. Should he be prevented? In Shakespeare they speak the scenery. Genius can look after itself. Admittedly we are vulgar enough to throw in naturalistic sets along with his abundant imagery.

The truth is that production today is at the same point as it was 100 years ago. In fact it has regressed from there; for in those days writers and musicians were well aware that theatre is performance, and they knew exactly what kind of stage these performances that they were writing and composing would take place on, whether they were sacred festivals or slapstick comedies. Today the one writes for an arena, the other for a tiny auditorium, a third would prefer his works performed in the open, or with a cyclorama that suggests the open, while most, when they write or compose, barely think about a stage at all. Only about our bad theatrical habits. Let us also not forget that three quarters of the repertoire in our theatres consists of works from the past. And all these works, which came into being in such varied circumstances, are performed in the self-same theatrical space. Is it any wonder that full justice is done to none of them, and that their impact is weak?

What is more: if anyone took the trouble to draw up plans of the spaces called for by our writers in their stage directions, some very remarkable architecture would result! In very few writers have I found a clear notion of the spatial structures in which their plots are to unfold.

Gordon Craig looks foward to a time when painters and designers will write their own plays; I would be satisfied if the writers of today's works would simply think in terms of a particular stage and its requirements. Some do. But how few they are! And how rarely does a newish work find its effectiveness increased through performance! For a strong theatrical effect, in the best sense of the words, depends entirely on the combined action of all elements on the stage.

The strange play put on last summer by young Kokoschka in the open air theatre of the Kunstschau was probably not a great literary achievement; I am no judge of that. But the complete originality of the visual and poetic intention it showed, the forethought as to the given physical circumstances under which it was to be played, produced a theatricality, in the best sense, whose power was irresistible, and of which even a small portion would have been enough to save many of the new works put on in recent years, some perhaps of high literary quality, from failure.

Singers and actors, too, generally see things in terms of the old proscenium arch stage [*Kulissenbühne*]. Whether the set represents the primeval forest, or a drawing room, or the North Pole, they stand either 'right' or 'left' (on exactly the same spot each time) or 'take the centre' – obviously because on our stages, whether decorated according to this principle or that, nothing else is possible, and because what the writer has commanded them to sing or say can probably best be sung or said from these particular favourite places. And people imagine that a theatrical renaissance can proceed from a renaissance in theatre design!

The indifference shown by our writers towards the physical and practical requirements of the stage, the disparity of the assumptions about staging that emerge from their works, the lack of connection between the average actor or singer and the design of his surroundings: all this simply indicates that we do not really possess a living theatrical form of our own, that we are still using our scoffed-at inheritance, the proscenium arch stage, which is just variously dressed up and titivated, not genuinely transformed.

The panoramic horizon, three-dimensional sets, adjustable horizons, rotating stages, swivelling stages, pneumatic bellows, pneumatic fire, electric light, diffused lighting, chemical fog, painted flats, travelators and all our other extravagantly praised 'modern achievements in theatre technique' that continually excite the press and public, are in fact simply masks and disguises for the old proscenium arch stage. The disease started with 'closed sets'; after that there was nothing for it but to drain the cup to the dregs and to exploit and exhaust all the possibilities offered.

So Reinhardt was quite right, in his *Midsummer Night's Dream* and subsequent productions, to take all these attempts at elaboration of the proscenium arch theatre to their logical conclusion, thus leaving the way open for genuinely new forms in the future.

In any case, why does the public not resolve whole-heartedly to support experiments being made in many places by individual artists in the direction of a new theatrical form? Because of weakness and sentimentality. Many people would like a new, more satisfying form of performance, but without relinquishing their old familiar stage picture. They declare themselves unable to do without theatrical illusion. Then, armed with binoculars and glasses, they do everything they can to break down that illusion. And when they succeed they are shocked, like children reaching after soap bubbles who cry when the suds get in their eyes.

It is not a matter of some artist or other discovering a new way of using our traditional stage which can then be followed by every hack: it is a matter of writers, public and designers together becoming aware of the basic sense of all theatre as performance, and, discarding outworn forms, trusting in our own ability to create new ones.

Not 'stage reform', then, but 'theatre reform'!

It is a matter of resolutely turning our backs on frivolity and our accustomed vulgarity (known as 'tradition') in order to achieve a theatre that will live once more, where what happens on stage frankly signifies, rather than being, or pretending to be.

And when we have our own living literary and musical theatre, then at last we shall know how the great works of the past should be performed today.

Theoretical discussions will not bring us nearer this goal: only a prodigal outlay of work and countless serious experiments.

Visual artists can only say: 'Let us try!'

Postscript

My first opera was *Carmen*. I don't remember much about it. I was 4. We lived in Southsea, near the King's Theatre. It was 1947. I was taken by my father's mother (I think). We sat in the gallery, and left before the end 'to avoid the rush'. It must have been the Carl Rosa tour. I was a keen balletomane already.

My next *Carmen* was 22 years later, in 1969, in Cluj, Romania, done in Romanian with a substitute Don José singing in Bielorussian. I was not an opera fan. My music had followed a different course after I gave up ballet-dancing at 7. I had been a choirboy at Chichester Cathedral – plainchant, polyphony, Widor – and then a choral scholar at Oxford.

I had seen *The Barber of Seville* in a Southsea cinema when I was about 7, and a few years later I remember listening to *Don Giovanni* on the Third Programme. When I was 14 a cousin organized for the whole family to squeeze into a Covent Garden box for free and catch Jon Vickers as Handel's *Samson*: Joan Sutherland was the Israelitish Woman. 'Let the Bright Seraphim' was a number we Chichester choristers had sung. Opera For All, or some similar set-up, gave me my first *Don Pasquale* – visiting my school, Hurstpierpoint, in the Downs north of Brighton. But my real operatic education started when I was invited to Germany at 18 by a middle-aged cousin, a judge on the International Restitution Court in Herford, R. C. Swayne, always known as Tim. He was a confessed New Bayreuth supporter (since 1951) and a good friend of Ellen and Wolfgang Wagner, though his enthusiasm for the new abstraction was moderate. Wolfgang's *Ring* in 1961 was my operatic and Wagnerian baptism of fire. I napped during the first act and often sat in the Wagners' private box. Afterwards Tim and I, another cousin Eve Hollis, and Sarah Turnbull all went on to Salzburg for *Idomeneo*, *Simon Boccanegra*, *Così fan tutte* and *Der Rosenkavalier* – the Mozart and Strauss with Schwarzkopf and Ludwig, the Verdi with Tito Gobbi rolling his eyes round the Felsenreitschule.

I was back at Bayreuth in 1962 with Tim and an Oxford mate, Charles Rankin, for *Parsifal, Tannhäuser, Lohengrin* and *Tristan*: all staged by Wieland Wagner, the *Tannhäuser* with the 'shocking' (to some traditionalists) black Venus of Grace Bumbry, the *Tristan* with Birgit Nilsson whom I had thrilled to as Brünnhilde in *Siegfried* the previous year. Then again on to Salzburg for *Figaro, Iphigènie en Aulide*, and *Il trovatore* with Franco Corelli and Leontyne Price. And Karajan. In Venice I saw *Otello* al-fresco on the steps of the Doge's Palace. During my Oxford years, I got *Peter Grimes* twice: Covent Garden and Sadler's Wells were both touring almost identical 'vernacular' productions, with Ronald Dowd in the title role. I went to Covent Garden again in 1962 for the London premiere of Tippett's *King Priam*.

In the 1960s I went quite often to Covent Garden, to *Billy Budd, Don Carlos, Masked Ball, Benvenuto Cellini, Traviata, Otello, The Trojans, Wozzeck, Moses and Aaron*. I began to take opera more seriously working for the magazine *Music and Musicians*, which I was to edit for 30 issues. In 1968 I got to Glyndebourne (for *Die Entführung aus dem Serail* with Margaret Price). Having auditioned as a countertenor for Nikolaus Harnoncourt in 1968, I was singing Purcell in Stockholm, Bach in Bremen and at the Konzerthaus in Vienna. My operatic debut, directed by Harro Dicks, was as Monteverdi's Ottone in Harnoncourt's arrangement of *The Coronation of Poppea* in Darmstadt at the Orangerie, the extemporized opera-house which had been the Landestheater's little home since the ducal opera was bombed. During rehearsals I lapped up Winton Dean's Berkeley lectures, *Handel and the Opera Seria*, and at once wanted to put into practice all his ideas about performance at the King's Theatre in the Haymarket in the 1720s and 1730s. I had just seen Peter Hall's staging of Cavalli's *La Calisto* at Glyndebourne, which owed much to Dean.

Becoming editor of *Music and Musicians* soon afterwards, I was initially more into theatre and cinema than opera. But I had been bowled over by Jon Vickers's overwhelming *Peter Grimes*, performed with what was surely the impact of Callas. His 1966 *Parsifal* at Covent Garden was unforgettable too. I began to see how a performance creates its own theatrical conventions, and makes the improbabilities of the form insignificant. So when I reviewed John Copley's feckless revival of his Gluck *Orfeo* staging at Covent Garden, I began to develop my ideas about how it ought not to be done. I persuaded the *Guardian* to let me review the Rudolf Bing farewell gala at the Met in New York, and that same 1972 summer was allowed about £4 expenses to cover Götz Friedrich's *Tannhäuser* at Bayreuth, also for the *Guardian*. I began to recognize what excited me in opera production, what I felt was needed to match the power of the music. Opera was not a bizarre theatrical backwater – or did not need to be.

Five years later, when I reviewed the first revival of the Chéreau *Ring* for the *Guardian* in 1977, I was ready to welcome a far more alert and challenging approach to the dramatic ideas. By then I was a regular opera reviewer for the paper, and writing an opera column for *Vogue*. From Peter Hall my taste was progressing to Elijah Moshinsky. I liked the ideas he and Tim O'Brien touched on in their Covent Garden *Peter Grimes*. The possibilities seemed endless. If there were bounds to decorum, they were certainly very wide. I was eager for change by the time I saw Berghaus's *Parsifal* in Frankfurt in 1985 – thanks to the *Guardian*'s features editor, Richard Gott, who had been thrilled by her Welsh *Don Giovanni*, which I had had doubts about. As the 1980s wore on, and the Elder–Pountney–Jonas regime established itself firmly and famously at the Coliseum, opera plainly was becoming a vital and leading part of British theatrical life.

I interviewed Brian McMaster for the *Guardian* in December 1976, soon after he arrived in Cardiff. He said, 'I have this rather unpopular idea at the moment that this is the age of the opera producer. It's not the age of the great singer.' (With hindsight, the question has not been about the greatness of singers, during a time when there have been some wonderful voices and very fine artists, but about the different role singers have been performing in the art – acting, in both senses, for directors.) The producers McMaster said he had his eye on to import to Cardiff if money were no object were Lavelli, Kupfer, Ronconi, Strehler, Chéreau, and Hall. In fact he only managed to attract Kupfer of that list. But it was an extraordinary declaration of intent at that time, and McMaster's regime in Wales became justly famed. I was as severe about many of David Pountney's Janáček stagings for WNO, as I was about Andrei Serban's efforts. But many WNO first nights were eye-openers. The same was true as Mark Elder settled in at the Coliseum. Exciting, inspirational singing and conducting are wonderful and irreplaceable. But a production of originality and imaginative energy, where the fire of theatrical interpretation burns dangerously bright, can feed one's soul and be passionately important for weeks. The work commissioned by Peter Jonas at ENO could be as daring as that risked by McMaster in Cardiff, and was the necessary and appropriate follow-through on McMaster's revolution – in that Jonas and Pountney and Elder were more often than not working with youngish British talents as designers and directors. Pountney in a sense was the guru of novelty at ENO, presiding over the production department as a welcoming influence for new, different, unusual and distinctive approaches. The value of the artistic commitment represented by this quite small group of people who had power in UK operatic institutions at a crucial time (all of them in various ways protected by the umbrella of Lord Harewood) simply cannot be overstated. We, critics and audience, were witnessing an artistic campaign and a transformation. Eventually, thanks to McMaster's lieutenant in Wales, Nicholas Payne, that campaign produced a domino effect in Leeds with Opera North and ultimately at Covent Garden. Glyndebourne was a parallel process, sometimes compromised, sometimes extraordinarily daring. These decades of my adult life as an opera enthusiast have been wonderful ones to be alive in. It has been a time of birth and rebirth – as the live theatre should always be, but inevitably sometimes is not. The public's taste naturally continues to change. Today's vastly extended opera audience, so much more accustomed to daring than it used to be, includes many who expect to find the familiar operatic masterpieces explored and challenged when they are performed. There is no crisis of too much intervention or imagination by opera directors or producers: there is only good work and poor work, some of it traditional and narrative, some of it innovative and fascinatingly imaged and edited. If performance is not an experiment of sorts, it is unlikely to be an experience.

Index

Figures in italics refer to captions.

Ackermann, Renate, 382
Actor's Revenge, An (Miki), 267
Adams, John, 58, 63, 73, 168, 202–5,
    207, 221, 353, 419
Adelaide, 74
Adorno, Theodor, 105, 106, 139, 142,
    157, 380
Adventures of Mr Brouček, The
    (Janáček), 340
Aeneid (Virgil), 145
Aeschylus, 63
Ahnsjö, Claes H., *166*
Aida (Verdi), 138, 382, 383–4, 421
Aix-en-Provence Festival, 375
Ajax (Sophocles), 199
Albani, Emma, 77
Albert Herring (Britten), 19, 75, 325,
    395, 406, 420
Albery, Tim, xiii, 92, 264, 314, 315
    and Bechtler, 296
    and Laing, 296
    and Payne, 14
    'troika' with Cairns and
        McDonald, 293, 294, 295
    productions
        Beatrice and Benedict, 302–3
        Benvenuto Cellini, 302–3
        Billy Budd, 300, 301, 340
        Capture of Troy, The, 292, 304
        Chérubin, 229, 303–5, 353
        Don Carlos, 302
        Fidelio, 305, 306
        finta giardiniera, La, 303
        Hedda Gabler, 294
        Midsummer Marriage, The, 75,
            294, 296, 297, 298, 300, 302
        Peter Grimes, 301, 408
        Trojans, The, 145, 298, 299, 300,
            302, 306, 362
        Venice Preserv'd, 294
Alcina (Handel), 185, 186
Aldeburgh, 31, 75, 420
Alden, Christopher, 169, 170
Alden, David, 83, 169, 264, 293, 294,
    339, 402
    and British operatic thinking, 13
    brought to the Coliseum, 171
    criticism of, 20
    recognition of his stature, 171
    and Sellars, 13, 170–71, 194, 197
    productions
        Ariodante, 185–7, 338, 340
        Bluebeard's Castle, 181, 182
            340
        Elektra, 183–4, 189
        Macbeth, 347, 348
        Masked Ball, A, 171, 178–81,
            340, 353
        Mazeppa, 171, 172–6, 236, 340
        Oedipus Rex, 38, 181–2, 340
        Simon Boccanegra, 176–8, 185,
            340
        Tannhäuser, *166*, 187–9
        Tristan and Isolde, 189–94
        Wozzeck, 184–5
Alexander, Roberta, 309
Alice in Wonderland (Carroll), 155,
    287, 391
Allen, Thomas, 301, 325
'allographic' art-works, 45
Almeida Opera/Theatre, Islington,
    255, 294, 423
Alston, Richard, 294
Alte Oper, Frankfurt, 400
Amahl and the Night Visitors
    (Menotti), 422
American National Theater, Kennedy
    Center, Washington, 199

Amis, John, 3
Amsterdam, 201, 203, 217, 235, 239,
    265, 402, 404
Amsterdam Musiektheater, 2, 80, 219,
    306, 398
Andersen, Stig, 221
Andrea Chénier (Giordano), 359
Angas, Richard, 235
Angel, Marie, 334, 336
Antigone (Orff), 168
Antwerp, 169, 308
Apocalypse Now (film), 349
Appen, Karl von, 324
Appia, Adolphe, 66, 81, 85, 91, 95,
    101, 102–3, 311
Arabella (Strauss), 340
Archer, Neill, 314
arena opera, 421
Argento, Dominick, 168
aria/s, 119, 120, 121, 122, 123, 133–4,
    137, 138, 185, 187, 202, 205, 208,
    214, 223, 239, 240, 242, 243, 276,
    297, 303, 305, 343, 365, 404, 411,
    419, 423
Ariadne auf Naxos (Strauss), 8, 159,
    265, 340
Ariane et Barbe Bleu (Dukas), 158,
    159–60
Ariodante (Handel), 185–7, 338, 340
arioso, 205
Ariosto, Lodovico, 185, 186
Aristophanes, 48
Aristotle, 64, 97, 176, 181
Arlen, Stephen, 336
Armida abbandonata (Jommelli), 40
Armstrong, Richard, 83, 367, 373
aroma-cards, 235
Artaud, Antonin, 332, 333
Arts Council, 32, 264, 319
Arundell, Dennis, 29, 31, 321
Ashcroft, Dame Peggy, 263
Ashman, Mike, 353, 362, 366–7
atonal music, 122
Auber, Daniel, 69
Auden, W.H., 39, 72, 90, 329, 344
Audi, Pierre, 423
Audran, Edmond, 69
Australia, 74, 169
auteurism, 202
authenticity, 41, 42, 44, 45, 46, 50, 56,
    68, 73, 85, 93, 102, 117, 243, 279,
    283, 322
'autographic' art-works, 45, 46
Auvray, Jean-Claude, 357
Ayckbourn, Alan, 335

Bach, Johann Sebastian, 158, 160, 434
Bächl, Samuel, 404
back-cloth/drop, 81, 86, 87, 127, 180,
    192, 199, 203, 216, 237, 238, 241,
    246, 256, 258, 265, 267, 271, 282,
    298, 301, 302, 306, 346, 350, 429
Bailey, Norman, 268, 320, 351
Baker, Dame Janet, 322, 324
Balazs, Bela, 181
bald wigs, 105, 241
Balfe, Michael, 69
ballad operas, 69
ballet, 3–4, 22, 26, 30, 81, 86, 87, 88,
    96, 110, 186, 203, 230–31,
    299–300, 322, 384, 403, 433
Ballet (Haskell), 26
Ballo in maschera see A Masked Ball
'Ball's Pond Road school', 183
Barber, Samuel, 73
Barber of Seville, The (Rossini), 31,
    76, 127, 358, 359, 379, 433
Barbier, Jules, 230
Barcelona, 71, 395
Barenboim, Daniel, 71, 116, 123, 147
Barker, Cheryl, 309
Baroque opera, 81, 85, 185, 208,
    383, 403
Baroque theatre, 324
Barry, Gerald, 73, 419, 423
Barstow, Dame Josephine, 33, 314
Bartered Bride, The (Smetána), 25–6,
    296, 329, 340, 347, 362,
    365–6, 388–9
Barthes, Roland, 374
Bartók, Béla, 73, 181, 392, 419
Basel, 96, 391, 397, 398
Bassarids, The (Henze), 357
Bastille *see* Opéra Bastille, Paris
Baudelaire, Charles, 385
Bauer, Raimund, 382
Bauhaus, 86
Bausch, Pina, 200, 295
Bavarian State Opera, Munich, 166,
    187, 228, 241

Baylis, Lilian, 31, 74–5, 319, 337, 338
Baylis Project, 340
Bayreuth, 10, 19, 20, 41, 42, 49, 62, 77,
   95, 97, 100, 101, 103–8, 110, 111,
   112, 115, 116, 122, 127, 138, 146,
   173, 194, 248, 257, 322, 325, 330,
   331, 381, 382, 383, 393, 418, 433,
   434, 435
BBC Symphony Orchestra, 382
Beach of Falesa (Hoddinott), 357
Beaton, Cecil, 320
Beatrice and Benedict (Berlioz),
   302–3, 329
Beaumarchais, Pierre-Augustin Caron
   de, 212, 303
Bechtler, Hildegard, 296, 301, 302,
   308
Beckett, Samuel, 44, 109, 148, 155,
   156, 161, 193
Beecham, Sir Thomas, 26, 134, 322
Beethoven, Ludwig van, 65, 66, 67,
   198, 305, 306, 352, 379
Beggar's Opera, The
   by Gay and Pepusch, 19
   music arr. Britten, 31, 32
behaviourism, 130, 131, 347
bel canto, 66, 104, 208
Bell, Steve, 404
belle Hélène, La (Offenbach), 32, 87
belle Vivette, La (Frayn reworking of
   La belle Hélène), 87
Bellini, Mikael, 287
Bellini, Vincenzo, 65, 73, 76, 169,
   240, 379
Bennett, Richard Rodney, 73
Benvenuto Cellini (Berlioz), 170,
   302–3, 434
Berg, Alban, 8, 34, 35, 62, 64–7, 73,
   116, 117, 122, 171, 184, 404, 417,
   418, 425
Bergé, Pierre, 71
Berghaus, Ruth, xiv, 76, 90, 92, 103,
   221, 309, 338, 376, 382
   choreographs the battles in
      Coriolanus, 127
   and jokes, 229
   as 'post-modern', 9
   productions
      Ariane et Barbe Bleu, 158
      Barber of Seville, The, 127

Don Giovanni, 49, 127, 129–33,
   215, 371, 435
Elektra, 381
Entführung aus dem Serail, Die,
   128, 133–8, 163, 186
Makropoulos Affair The,
   128, 129
Parsifal, 13, 127, 128,
   138–43, 435
Patmos, 158–9
Ring, 13, 110, 126, 127, 138, 143,
   145, 146–58, 163, 245, 248,
   349, 390–91, 395
Rise and Fall of the City of
   Mahagonny, The, 158,
   160–62
Rosenkavalier, Der, 158,
   162–3
Trojans, The, 13, 86, 128, 129,
   138, 143–6, 158, 163
Zauberflöte, Die, 128, 133
Bergman, Ingmar, 27, 33, 230, 362,
   421–2
Berio, Luciano, 73, 265, 273
Beriosova, Svetlana, 359
Berkeley, Busby, 161
Berkeley, Lennox, 32
Berkeley lectures, 434
Berkoff, Steven, 422
Berlin, 322, 353
Berlin Schaubühne, 76, 179
Berliner Ensemble, 34, 105, 127, 321,
   324, 381
Berlioz, Hector, 143, 144, 145, 163,
   255, 299, 300, 302, 304
Bernstein, Leonard, 39, 73, 273
Bertini, Gary, 127, 143, 390, 395
Besch, Anthony, 320, 339–40
Best, Jonathan, 284
Best, Matthew, 305
Betrothal in a Monastery (Prokofiev),
   419
Biblical scholarship, 42
Bickel, Moidele, 54, 123, 367
Bilby's Doll (Floyd), 171
Billy Budd (Britten), 31, 75, 107, 170,
   300–301, 340, 357, 407, 420, 434
Bing, Rudolf, 435
Birmingham, 273
Birmingham Music Theatre, 268

Birtwistle, Harrison, 73, 86, 311, 332, 334, 335, 416, 419, 423
Bitter, Dr Christoph, 381
Bizet, Georges, 70, 77, 372, 373, 421
Bjørling, Jussi, 74
Bjørnson, Maria, 273, 328, 340, 346, 347, 349, 350, 359
Black Comedy (Shaffer), 277
Black Mikado, The, 331
Blake, David, 346
Blane, Sue, 346, 347
Blatchley, John, 320, 321
Blegen, Judith, 375
Bliss, Arthur, 23
blocking, 94, 128, 310
Blond Eckbert (Weir), 246, 255–9, 424
Bluebeard's Castle (Bartók), 181, 182, 340, 419
Boder, Michael, 138
Boecklin, Arnold, 114
bohème, La, (Puccini), 23, 31, 92, 96, 308–11, 357, 358, 359, 362, 363–4, 418
Bohemia, 68
Bohemian Girl (Balfe), 69
Boito, Arrigo, 169, 367, 368, 370
Bologna, 353
Bolton, Ivor, 244
Bond, Edward, 172
Bond, Paul *see* Fielding, David
Bondy, Luc, xiii, 109, 121, 179
Bononcini, Giovanni, 40
booing, 49, 107, 108, 173, 187, 244, 353
Boris Godunov (Mussorgsky), 19, 20, 21, 23, 173, 222
Borough, The (Crabbe), 406
Borozescu, Miruna, *356*, 372
Borozescu, Radu, *356*, 372
Bosnia, 173
Botes, Christine, *318*
Bouffes du Nord, 27, 28
Boulez, Pierre, 62, 103, 116, 146, 158, 380, 382, 383, 398, 402, 424
Bournonville, August, 129
Braito, Andreas, 382, 389
Braun, Victor, 325, *378*, 394, 396
Brecht, Berthold, 19, 34, 41, 44, 50, 64, 104, 105, 127, 128, 153, 160–61, 162, 267, 273, 274, 324, 365, 400

'Brechtian', 75, 90, 154, 200, 274, 312, 321, 326, 327, 329, 342
Bregenz Festival, 82, 235, 301, 306, 351
Bremen, 434
Brenner, Peter, 361
Britain, 74
   critical response to the Chéreau *Ring*, 107
   the most adventurous recent British designing, 93
   vernacular design tradition, 92
   writing on *The Ring*, 106
   see also England
British Broadcasting Corporation (BBC), 98, 382, 422, 423
Britten, Benjamin, 14, 19, 31, 32, 35, 68, 73, 75, 107, 170, 205, 255, 264, 285–9, 296, 300, 301, 322, 325, 326, 337, 341, 379, 383, 395, 406–7, 410, 418, 419–20, 422, 425
Broken Strings (Vir), 423
Brook, Peter, xiii, 12–13, 31, 103, 110, 128, 332, 333, 335, 337
   aftermath of his work at Covent Garden, 14
   attempt to convert Covent Garden to 'good theatre', 23, 24
   and Dali, 22, 23–4
   and David Webster, 19, 21, 22
   end of association with Covent Garden, 27
   on Felsenstein's *Bartered Bride*, 25–6
   opposition to, 20, 21, 22, 23, 26, 76
   Paris experiments (1992), 27, 28
   and *Peter Grimes*, 22
   as premature in what he wanted to do with opera, 13
   productions at the Met, 27
   productions
      Boris Godunov, 19, 20, 21, 23
      Impressions of Pelléas, 27, 28–9, 276, 421
      King Lear, 45, 371
      Marriage of Figaro, The, 23
      Midsummer Night's Dream, A, 45

Salome, *18*, 19, 20, 21, 23–4,
    26–7
Tragedy of Carmen, The, 27, 28,
    93, 276, 421
Brothers Quay, 91, 92, 230, 236
Brotherston, Lez, 92
Brown, Paul, 269, 272, 283, 284
Bruguière, Dominique, 123
Bruson, Renato, 327
Brussels, 353, 390, 402, 410, 411
Brussels Opera, 205, *378*
Bryan, Robert, 346
Bryars, Gavin, 58
Bryden, Bill, 354
Büchner, Georg, 10, 64, 123, 404
Bühnenreform (Roller), 20, 427–31
Bulgakov, Mikhail, 236
Bumbry, Grace, 434
Burge, Lucy, 298, 304
Burgess, Anthony, 268
Burgess, Sally, 181
burlesque, 242, 244, 247, 325
Burney, Charles, 85
Bury, John, 92, 321, 322, 324, 325, 334
Busch, Fritz, 322
Busoni, Ferruccio, 73, 384, 385, 386

Caccini, Giulio, 63
Caesar and Cleopatra (Shaw), 208
Cairns, Janice, 175, 176, 179, 180
Cairns, Tom, 187, 293, 294, 306, 340
    and Nicholas Payne, 14
    as a talented painter, 294, 310, 311
    'troika' with Albery and
        McDonald, 293
    productions
        bohème, La, 92, 308–9, 310, 311
        Capture of Troy, The, 292
        Don Giovanni, 310, 311
        finta giardiniera, La, 303
        Hedda Gabler, 294
        Jenůfa, 314–15
        King Priam, 310, 311, 312, 313
        Masked Ball, A, 310, 311
        Midsummer Marriage, The,
           294, 296
        Samson and Dalila, 80, 306, 307
        Second Mrs Kong, The,
           311, 313, 314
        Trojans, The, 298, 299, 300, 303

Venice Preserv'd, 294
Calisto, La (Cavalli), 106–7, 171, 263,
    321–5, 334, 434
Callas, Maria, 32, 49, 103, 110, 434
Callow, Simon, 354
Calzabigi, Raniero de', 66
Cambreling, Sylvain, 390, 391, 395
Cambridge Touring Opera, 276
Camden Festival, London, 40
Canada, 74
Cape Canaveral, 199, 331
capitalism, 106, 160
Caplat, Moran, xiv
Cappuccilli, Piero, 327
Capture of Troy, The (Berlioz),
    292, 304
Card, June, *126*
Cardiff, 83, 183, 298, 303, 321,
    435, 436
    see also New Theatre, Cardiff;
        Welsh National Opera
Carey, Peter, 294
Carl Rosa opera company, 433
Carlyle, Joan, xiii
Carmen (Bizet), 4, 27, 28, 31, 49, 50,
    70, 77, 92, 93, 268–9, 306, 307–8,
    347, 371, 372–3, 379, 421, 433
Carmen Jones (musical), 354
Carré, Michel, 230
Carsen, Robert, 169, 170
Caruso, Enrico, 74
Casken, John, 423
casting, 82, 83–4, 93–7, 162, 197, 216,
    239, 333, 343, 398
Castor et Pollux (Rameau), 383
castrati, 25, 49, 66, 122, 134, 210, 324,
    343, 403, 404, 423
Cathcart, Allen, 359
Cavalieri, Emilio de', 65
Cavalleria Rusticana (Mascagni), 306
Cavalli, Pietro Francesco, 40, 68, 106,
    205, 263, 322, 332, 334, 434
cavatinas, 240
CBTO *see* City of Birmingham
    Touring Opera
Cendrillon (Massenet), 169
Central School of Speech and Drama,
    293, 295
Cerha, Friedrich, 34, 116
Cervena, Sona, 346

Chabrier, Emmanuel, 255
chainsaws, 83, 171, 173, 175, 182, 236
Chaliapin, Feodor, 23, 26
Chance, Michael, 404
Channel 4, 423
Châtelet Theatre, Paris, 116, 122, 158, 185, 283, 284, 398, 400, 401
chauvinism, 108, 134
chef-dramaturg, 41, 76, 105, 127, 381
Chekhov, Anton, 64, 102, 198, 325
Chelton, Nick, 275, 277
Chéreau, Patrice, xiv, 13, 76, 82, 92, 93, 144, 146, 163, 194, 338, 393, 435
    artistic vision, 119
    and choice of Peduzzi as his designer, 109
    and Liebermann's Paris Opéra term, 34
    and movement, 109
    seen as 'post-modern', 9
    and the spoken theatre, 109
    and style of acting, 109
    productions
        contes d'Hoffmann, Les, 118–19, 198
        Lucio Silla, 120–22
        Lulu, 116–17, 122, 162, 322
        Ring, 10, 19, 42, 49, 50, 77, 85, 97, 100, 103, 104–5, 107–8, 110–16, 119, 122, 123, 124, 127, 132, 147, 172, 173, 245, 248, 322, 331, 346, 349, 358–9, 376, 381, 383, 418, 435
        Wozzeck, 122–4, 184–5, 404
Chernov, Vladimir, 311
Cherry Orchard, The (Chekhov), 34
Chérubin (Massenet), 229, 303–5, 353
Cherubini, Luigi, 66
Chicago, 74, 218
Chichester Cathedral, 433
Chirico, Giorgio de, 86, 244, 248
Chitty, Alison, 86
choreography, 77, 121, 123, 127, 128, 136, 145, 162, 173, 175, 186, 188, 193, 200, 202, 203, 205, 220, 224, 236, 239, 243, 271, 274, 279, 281, 282, 283, 285, 298, 299, 302, 305, 307, 314, 344, 349
Christianity, 42, 43, 135, 139, 153, 159, 175, 183, 224, 231, 326, 327
Christie, Sir George, 322
Christie, John, 31, 32, 322
Christie, Nan, 388
Christie, William, 225
Ciesinski, Kristine, 299
Ciesinski, Katherine, 299
Cimarosa, Domenico, 68
cinéma vérité, 203
cinema/cinematic, 4, 8–9, 12, 25, 28, 30, 51, 57, 59, 62, 71, 72, 81, 101, 109, 114, 174, 273, 422, 424
City of Birmingham Touring Opera (CBTO), 96, 263, 267, 268, 269, 272, 273, 275, 276, 397, 421
City Opera, New York see New York City Opera
Ciulei, Liviu, 200, 362, 376
Clarissa (Holloway), 350
Clark, Graham, 248
Clemenza di Tito, La (Mozart), 121
Cleopatra e Cesare (Graun), 40
clothes, 5, 31, 59, 110, 111, 116, 119, 122, 136, 139, 180, 212, 331, 397
    see also costumes
Cluj, Romania, 433
Cobb, Cheryl, 211
Coburn, Pamela, 242
Cochran, William, 80, 378, 382, 384–7, 392, 396, 406, 409
Cocteau, Jean, 87, 182
Coleman, Basil, 31, 32, 320, 321
Coleman, Tim, 392
collage, 8, 102, 230, 243
Collins, Aletta, 295, 307, 310, 313, 314
Collins, Patricia, 188, 240
Cologne, 83, 402
coloratura, 137, 167, 202, 287, 419, 423
commedia del'arte, 162, 405
composers (creation of new works), 35, 55, 65
condenado por desconfiado, El (Tirso de Molina), 130
conductors
    and 'producer's opera', 49
    and stage direction, 82–3
    task of, 55
conformism, 174, 394, 409
Conklin, John, 98

Connell, Elizabeth, 191, 346
conservative/conservatism, 9, 20, 21,
    103, 104, 108, 232, 327, 331, 362,
    381, 408, 424
Constant, Marius, 27, 28
constructivism, 145, 221
consumerism, 61, 72, 106, 162, 311,
    389, 421
Contemporary Opera Studio, 340, 423
contes d'Hoffmann, Les (Offenbach),
    104, 118–19, 382, 391–2
contextualization, 11, 42, 57, 58, 311
Copland, Aaron, 73
Copley, John, xiii, 169, 320, 339,
    359, 434
Corelli, Franco, 434
Corigliano, John, 63, 98, 168, 419
Coriolanus (Shakespeare), 127
Coronation of Poppea, The (Mon-
    teverdi), 64, 155, 203, 211, 322,
    359, 434
Corsaro, Frank, 169
Così fan tutte (Mozart), 60, 64, 130,
    135, 137, 214, 215, 318, 335–6,
    340, 354, 433
costumes, 3, 24, 26, 30, 31, 81, 85, 102,
    105, 108, 114, 117, 121, 123, 128,
    129, 133, 145, 156, 158, 159, 160,
    173, 186, 189, 193, 234, 236, 239,
    256, 267, 269, 271, 277–80, 284,
    293, 299, 302, 307, 328, 332, 350,
    359, 364, 367, 373, 383, 390, 396,
    405, 409
    see also clothes
Cotrubas, Ileana, 325
Count Ory (Rossini), 236, 339–40
Court Jester, The (film), 233
Coventry Festival, 274
Cox, John, xiii, 88, 89, 320, 340
Crabbe, George, 301, 327, 406,
    407, 409
Craig, Charles, 330, 340
Craig, Edward Gordon, 66, 81, 85, 91,
    101–2, 103, 120, 124, 265, 430
Cricketers of Hambledon, The
    (Warlock), 407
Croce, Arlene, 168
Croft, Richard, 225
Crowley, Bob, 341, 344, 345
csardas, 238

culinary opera/theatre, 20, 122, 321
culture
    internationalism of, 68
    language culture, 58–9
    and Modernism, 102
    re-creating, 198
    and the religious world, 264
Cunning Little Vixen, The (Janáček),
    330, 340, 344–5, 348, 354,
    359, 383
Cunningham, Merce, 169, 293
cyclorama, 243–4, 307, 349, 429
Czechoslovakia, 75, 86, 91

da capo form, 208
Da Ponte, Lorenzo, 60, 131, 198, 212,
    213, 215, 335
Daldry, Stephen, 130, 185, 339, 354
Dali, Salvador, 18, 20, 22, 23–4
Dallapiccola, Luigi, 73
Damned, The (film), 116
Dance of Death (Strindberg), 263
Daniel, Paul, 375
Daniels, David, 226
Dante Alighieri, 64
Darmstadt, 434
Darmstadt modern music summer
    school, 380, 383
Davies, Arthur, 178, 180
Davies, Siobhan, 294
Davis, Sir Colin, xiv, 33, 181, 320,
    322, 323
Dawson, Anne, 356
de Niro, Robert, 172
de Waart, Edo, 203
Dean, Stafford, 305
Dean, Winton, 434
Death of Klinghoffer (Adams), 168,
    202, 204–6, 221, 353
Death in Venice (Britten), 255, 285
Debussy, Claude, 27, 28, 29, 73, 201,
    211, 218, 220
Decker, Willy, xiv, 14, 229, 242, 339,
    402–12
deconstructionism, 9, 10, 23, 47–8, 56,
    62, 92, 103, 104, 162, 238, 239,
    244, 331, 339, 382, 388
decorum, 3, 10, 15, 43, 48, 64, 65, 121,
    129, 174, 177, 207, 210, 229, 235,
    242, 245, 366, 402, 409, 416, 435

definitive performance, 50–52
Delius, Frederick, 75
Deller, Alfred, 354
Dent, Edward, 22, 27, 31, 130
Derrida, Jacques, 47
design, 81–98
    decor, 98, 375
    decorative, 87, 92, 103
designers, 309–10
Dessau, Paul, 127, 160
Destinn, Emmy, 77
determinism, 392, 404
deus ex machina, 188, 211, 305
Deutsche Grammophon, 106
Deutsches Museum, 158
Devine, George, 29, 31–2, 270,
    320, 332
Devlin, Michael, 171
Dexter, John, 33, 88, 168, 324
Dhananjayan, V.P., 272–3
dialectical theatre, 128
dialogue, 110, 121, 122, 131, 161, 183,
    199, 216–17, 246, 304, 363, 416,
    422, 423
Dialogues des carmélites (Poulenc),
    419
Dickie, Brian, xiv
Dicks, Harro, 434
Dido and Aeneas (Purcell), 19
dinosaurs, 241, 242, 243, 245
dispute, La (Marivaux), 109
'dissolve', 240, 329
Divino afflante spiritu encyclical, 42
Dix, Otto, 161
dodecaphony, 67
Doghan, Philip, 230
Dohnanyi, Christoph von, 398, 401
Doktor Faust (Busoni), 340, 347,
    384–6, 402
Dolin, Anton, 4
Dollarprinzessin (Fall), 71
Dolton, Geoffrey, 234
domesticity, 75, 90, 239, 248, 299
Domingo, Placido, 49, 74, 327
Don Carlos (Verdi), 32, 33, 255, 302,
    338–9, 434
Don Giovanni (Mozart), 7, 49, 76, 77,
    116, 127–33, 153, 171, 214–15,
    255–6, 265, 306, 310, 311, 321,
    325–6, 335, 338, 347, 357, 371,

    374, 383, 433, 435
Don Pasquale (Donizetti), 32, 76, 433
Donizetti, Gaetano, 73, 76, 379
Donnellan, Declan, 161
Donnelly, Malcolm, 175
Donnington, Robert, 106
Dorset Gardens theatre, London, 283
Dove, Jonathan, 96, 269, 275, 397
Dowd, Ronald, 434
Downes, Edward, xiii
Dragon of Wantley, The (Lampe), 276
Drama Centre, 295
drama producers, 29
dramaturg/dramaturgy, 13, 19, 40–41,
    59, 61, 82, 84, 85, 86, 93, 94, 98,
    133, 138, 160, 189, 246, 259, 274,
    276, 289, 293, 305, 310, 321, 328,
    331, 345, 346, 350, 358, 380, 383,
    388, 391, 392
dramma giocosa, 130
Drescher, Hans-Jürgen, 391
Drill Hall, London, 334
Drottningholm, 421
Dryden, John, 283, 284
Ducreux, Louis, 359
Dudley, William, 358
duels, 282, 325
duets, 185, 190, 224, 225, 238, 304, 306
Dukas, Paul, 159, 160
Duke Bluebeard's Castle (Bartók),
    391, 392–3, 399
*Durchbrüche – 10 Jahre Musik-
    theater mit Michael Gielen*
    (Jungheinrich and Eggert), 380
Dyer, Chris, 269, 275
Dyer's Hand, The (Auden), 344

Earls Court, London, 306, 307, 421
East Berlin, 19, 29, 381, 383
East Germany, 33, 34
Ebert, Carl, xiii, 33, 320, 322
Ebrahim, Omar, 201
Eco, Umberto, 63–4
Edinburgh Festival, 348
Edwards, Charles, 92, 189, 255, 256,
    302, 303
Edwards, Sian, 337
Eggert, Mara, 143, 147, 380, 386
Einstein on the Beach (Glass), 168
Eisler, Hanns, 127

Elder, Mark, xiv, 31, 171, 191, 306,
  337–40, 343, 348, 349, 435, 436
Electrification of the Soviet Union,
  The (Osborne), 199, 200–202
Elektra (Strauss), 105, 183–4, 189,
  360, 381
Elgar, Sir Edward, 296
Eliot, T.S., 297
Ellsworth, Warren, 273, 365, 366
EMT *see* English Music Theatre
enfant et les sortilèges, L' (Ravel), 88,
  91, 419
enfants du Paradis, Les, 10
Engel, André, 362
England, 63, 68, 69, 75
  see also Britain
English Music Theatre (EMT), 264,
  267, 320, 338
English National Opera (ENO), xiv,
  14, 20, 31, 38, 62, 76, 83, 87, 98,
  122, 161, 169–72, 174, 175, 176,
  185, 190, 198, 201, 234–7, 239,
  241, 246, 255, 256, 264–8, 270,
  276, 280, 281, 283, 294, 297, 300,
  301, 302, 306, 308, 309, 312, 313,
  319, 321, 327, 329–33, 336–41,
  346, 347, 348, 352–3, 354, 357,
  375, 380, 384, 390, 405, 408, 411,
  423, 436
English Opera Group, 31, 75,
  264, 320
English theatre, 108
English Touring Opera, 268, 338, 421
Enlightenment, 121, 134, 188, 335
ensemble theatre, 30, 31
Entführung aus dem Serail, Die
  (Mozart), 32, 128, 133–8, 163,
  186, 359–60, 434
Epstein, Matthew, 303
Ernani (Verdi), 328, 362
erzählerische Arrangement, 128
Eugene Onegin (Tchaikovsky), 7, 27,
  29, 32, 33, 56, 236, 269–72,
  280–83, 321, 325, 330, 340, 362
Euripides, 63
Evans, Anne, 253, 360
Everding, August, 187
Ewing, Maria, 308
expressionism, 66, 122, 181, 200, 222,
  232, 293, 306, 333, 402

extras, 114–15, 122, 222
Eyre, Richard, 353, 354

Falewicz, Magdalena, 266
Falk, Christina, 287
Fall, Leo, 71
Fall of Troy, The see Capture of Troy,
  The
Falla, Manuel de, 73, 91
Falstaff (Verdi), 31, 90, 96, 269, 330,
  340, 348, 362, 367, 369–70, 388,
  389, 397
Family Affair, A (Ostrovsky), 423
fanciulla del West, La (Puccini), 75
Fanti, Lucio, 54, 367, 368, 369
farce, 209, 229, 237, 245, 334, 335
fashion, 9, 13, 39, 44, 59, 65, 85, 98,
  112, 168, 178, 390, 420, 424
Faust (Gounod), 27, 70, 77, 402
Fazan, Eleanor, 326, 327, 329
Fedorovich, Sophie, xiii
Felsenreitschule, Salzburg, 433
Felsenstein, Anneliese, 138, 373
Felsenstein, Walter, 14, 19, 25, 29, 33,
  34, 49, 50, 76, 92, 104, 105, 127,
  173–4, 266, 267, 361, 362, 381
feminism, 29, 67, 134, 139, 159, 162,
  256, 407
Fernandel, 256
Fettes, Christopher, 294, 295
Feydeau, Georges, 237
Fidelio (Beethoven), 33, 67, 305–6,
  351–2, 361–2
Field, Helen, 234, 313, 365, 368
Fielding, David, 92, 174–9, 183, 189,
  293, 294, 309, 310, 340–43, 345,
  347, 348, 350, 353, 423
Fielding, Fenella, 237–8
Figaro's Wedding, 276–8, 340
Financial Times, 185
Finch, Nigel, 423
Finnie, Linda, 179
finta giardiniera, La (Mozart), 303
Firth, Tazeena, 326
Flagstad, Kirsten, 337
flats, 88, 92, 180, 233, 267, 270, 311,
  389, 431
Flea in her Ear, A (Feydeau), 229,
  235–6, 237
Fledermaus, Die (Strauss), 31, 96–7,

219, 237–9, 241, 246, 257, 338,
  340, 354, 362, 391, 397–8, *414*
*Fliegende Holländer, Der see Flying
  Dutchman, The*
flies, 96, 97, 118, 124, 144, 151, 180,
  233, 270, 302, 313, 325, 366, 387,
  392, 397
Flimm, Jürgen, 381
Florence, 63, 65, 89, 353
Florence Teatro Communale, 50
Floyd, Carlisle, 73, 168, 171
Flying Dutchman, The (Wagner),
  2, 239–41, 256, 353
folk dance, 299
folk-singing, 73
Follies (Sondheim), 161
Folwell, Nicholas, 257
Footfalls (Beckett), 44
Ford, John, 176, 271
Forster, E.M., 300
forza del destino, La (Verdi), 338–9
'found space', 333
France, 63, 66, 69, 70–71, 74, 105,
  108, 167
Frankfurt Opera, 13, 20, 41, 49, 76,
  86, 105, 110, 116, *126*, 127, 128,
  129, 131, 135, 138, 140, 143, 144,
  145, 147, 157, 158, 162, 330, 338,
  379–85, 387–91, 395, 402, 435
Frankfurt school, 105
Fraser, Sir James, 296
Frau ohne Schatten, Die (Strauss), 20
Frayn, Michael, 87
Freeman, David, 14, 84, 86, 215, 264,
  276, *318*, 323, 332–6, 340,
  341, 421
Freischütz, Der (Weber), 76, 322, 388
French classical theatre, 120, 174, 335
French opera, native, 7, 34, 68
Freni, Mirella, 56
Freud, Sigmund, 27
Fricsay, Andras, 383
Friede, Stephanie, 314
Friedrich, Götz, xiii, 25, 33, 50, 76, 91,
  103, 105, 173, 183, 265, 322, 349,
  381, 435
Frigerio, Ezio, 92, 104
From the House of the Dead
  (Janáček), 359
front-cloth/drop, 114, 118, 119, 139,

182, 209, 230, 236, 243, 246,
  248–9, 257, 259, 265, 302, 306,
  329, 364, 385, 409
Funes, Louis de, 256
Furlanetto, Ferrucio, 116
Fürstner (publisher), 75

Gall, Hugues, 71
Gall, Jeffrey, 209, 211
Gallotta, Jean-Claude, 344–5
Garbo, Greta, 117
Gardiner, John Eliot, 333
Gardner, John, 323
Garnier, Charles, 70
Garrett, Lesley, 178, 237
Garrick, David, 44, 66, 331
Gaskill, William, 324, 358, 359
Gate Theatre, London, 130
Gavin, Julian, 314
Gay, John, 19, 69
Geliot, Michael, 32, 320–21, 357,
  358, 359
Gelsenkirchen, 34
Genet, Jean, 117, 187
Geneva, 95, 169, 170
Gens, Veronique, 284
Georgian theatre, 89, 277, 329
Georgiadis, Nicholas (designer), 86
Gerhard, Roberto, 73
Germany, 63, 69, 71, 74, 108, 167,
  220, 321
  designers' theatre language, 105
  Jones's *Giulio Cesare* achieves cult
    status, 243
  opera companies, 14
  opera houses, 22, 26
  politics in opera, 67
  repertoire system, 388
  voice types, 96
Gershwin, George, 73, 419
Gesamtkunstwerk, 59, 77, 103,
  369, 396
geschiedene Frau, Die (Fall), 71
Gezeichneten, Die (The Branded
  Ones) (Schreker), 383, 384
Ghanashyam (Shankar), 267, 272–3
Ghost Sonata, The (Strindberg), 334
Ghosts (Ibsen), 263
Ghosts of Versailles, The (Corigliano),
  98, 168, 419

Gielen, Michael, 13, 41, 49, 76, 105, 127, 128, 133, 138, 143, 144, 147, 155, 158, 160, 330, 379–84, 388–91, 395, 402
Gielgud, Sir John, 30, 354
Gigli, Beniamino, 74
Gilbert, Sir William Schwenck, 69, 331
Gillibrand, Nicky, 236, 302
Gilmore, Gail, *126*, 145–6
Gioconda (Ponchielli), 360
Giordano, Umberto, 379
Girl of the Golden West, The see *fanciulla del West, La*
Giulio Cesare in Egitto (Handel), 199, 202, 207–11, 223, *228*, 241–4, 245, 339, 341, 383, 402, 403, 403–4, 405, 422
Glasgow, 273, 298, 339, 348
Glasgow Citizens Theatre, 359
Glass, Philip, 14, 58, 63, 168, 419
Glatt-Behr, Dorothea, 133
Gloriana (Britten), 75, 420
Gluck, Christoph Willibald, 8, 19, 64–8, 76, 335, 379, 434
Glyndebourne Festival Opera, xiii–xiv, 14, 31, 32, 33, 35, 85, 88, 90, 91, 130, 169, *196*, 199, 201, 205, 215, 216, 222, 225, 226, *262*, 263, 264, 270, 278–81, 308, 313, 314, 320–25, 328, 330, 331, 332, 334, 338, 353, 354, 363, 383, 420, 434, 436
Glyndebourne Touring Opera, 200, 285, 310–11
Göbbel, Wolfgang, 179, 183, 191, 236, 258, 315
Gobbi, Tito, xiii, 263, 433
Godard, Jean-Luc, 203
Goehr, Alexander, 73
Goethe, Johann Wolfgang von, 64, 230, 384
Golden Bough, The (Fraser), 296, 297
Goldoni, Carlo, 64, 371
Goldsmith, Harvey, 307
Golem, The (Casken), 423
Goodall, Sir Reginald, 319, 321, 339, 361, 366
Goodman, Alice, 203, 204, 205, 216
Goodman, Nelson, 45

Gothic revival, 3, 90, 101
Gott, Richard, ix, 435
Götterdämmerung (Wagner), *100*, 108, 113, 115, 128, 147, 156–7, 211, 244, 248–54, *378*, 396
Gounod, Charles, 70, 77
Graham, Colin, 169, 264, 267, 337–40, 346
Graham, Susan, 304
Gramm, Donald, 329
gran sole carico d'amore, Al (Nono), 380
grand macabre, Le (Ligeti), 340
Grant, Julian, 423
Granville Barker, Frank, 34, 95, 109
Graun, Carl Heinrich, 40
Gray, George, 191
Gray, Linda Esther, 361
Greek festivals, 48, 102
Greek Passion (Martinů), 357
Greek theatre, 21, 63, 65, 101, 396
Greek (Turnage), 422
Greenfield, Edward, 107
Griffin, Hayden, 333
Griffiths, James, 181
Grosses Festspielhaus, Salzburg, 111
Grotowski, Jerzy, 276, 333, 372
Grove Opera (Loppert), 331
Groves, Sir Charles, 337
Grünewald, Matthias, *220*, 221, 222
Guardian, the, 107, 111, 435
Gui, Vittorio, 322
Guinness, Sir Alec, 31, 331
Gunter, John, 325
Gussman, Wolfgang, 404
Gustafsson, Ulla, 248
Guthrie, Tyrone, xiii, 22–3, 27, 29, 30, 31, 32, 320, 331
Gypsy (Sondheim), 220

Hagenau, Heinz, *126*
Haitinck, Sir Bernard, xiv, 245, 248
Hall, John, *292*
Hall, John Graham, 276
Hall, Sir Peter, xiii, 14, 32, 33, 173, 320–27, 330, 331, 332, 334, 349, 434, 435
    productions
        Calisto, La, 263, 321
        Don Giovanni, 130, 321

Eugene Onegin, 56, 321
Knot Garden, The, 321
Marriage of Figaro, The, 321
Moses and Aaron, 321
ritorno d'Ulisse, Il, 321
Ring, 107, 108, 146
Tristan und Isolde, 193, 321
Halsey, Simon, 275
Hamburg, 83, 380, 391, 393
Hamburg Contemporary Music
    Theatre, 34
Hamilton, Ronald, 292
Hamlet (Shakespeare), 31, 331
hand-jiving, 169, 198, 206, 220, 243
Handel, George Frederick, 7, 8, 19,
    39, 40, 49, 63, 65, 68, 185, 186,
    207–11, 222, 224, 225, 242, 244,
    286, 294–5, 324, 341, 343, 344,
    379, 381, 383, 402, 403, 422, 433
Handel and the Opera Seria
    (Berkeley lectures), 434
Hands, Terry, 354
Hansel and Gretel (Humperdinck),
    340, 350–51
Happy Days (Beckett), 148, 156
Hardy, Janet, 184
Harewood, Lord, xiv, 33, 171, 337,
    338, 339, 357, 375, 436
Harnoncourt, Nikolaus, 381, 383, 434
Harries, Kathryn, 2
Harris, Margaret (known as Percy),
    294
    see also Motley
Hart, Lorenz, 198
Hartwell, Peter, 333
Haskell, Arnold, 26
Haskin, Howard, 218
Hasse, Johann, 40, 68
Haugland, Aage, 402
Hauk, Minnie, 77
Haussmann, Georges, 70
Havergal, Giles, 359–60
Haydn, Joseph, 68
Hayek, Friedrich August von, 130
Haym, Nicola, 210, 211, 243
Heap, Douglas, 341
Hebert, Bliss, 170
Hector, Denise, 196
Hedda Gabler (Ibsen), 294
Heinrich, Rudolf, 33, 92

Held, Alan, 248
Hell's Angels (Osborne), 332
Henry IV (Shakespeare), 284
Henschel, Jane, 248
Henze, Hans Werner, 73, 158, 357,
    383, 423
Herbert, Jocelyn, 86, 324, 332
Herkomer, Sir Hubert von, 101
Hérold, Ferdinand, 255, 256
Herrmann, Karl-Ernst, 370, 381, 400
Hersey, David, 327
Herz, Joachim, 33, 76, 266–7, 357,
    360–61, 381, 408
heure espagnole, L' (Falla), 91, 419
Heyworth, Peter, 21
Higglety Pigglety Pop! (Knussen), 91
Hiller, Johann Adam, 71
Hindemith, Paul, 73, 220, 221, 222
Hirsch, Peter, 138
histoire du soldat, L' (Stravinsky), 198
Hitler, Adolf, 106, 173, 245, 394
Hockney, David, 85, 87–90, 91, 328,
    329, 363
Hockney Paints the Stage
    exhibition, 88
Hoddinott, Alun, 357
Hoffmann, Hilmar, 381
Hofmannsthal, Hugo von, 8, 162, 163,
    183, 360
Hogarth, William, 85, 90, 328
Hoheisel, Tobias, 285, 308, 314, 388
Holland, 419
Holland Festival, 203, 218
Holloway, Robin, 3, 343, 350
homosexuality, 285, 301, 406, 407, 408
Hope-Wallace, Philip, 26–7
Hopkins, Tim, 13, 235, 255–9,
    340, 424
Hopper, Edward, 98, 330
Horkheimer (at Frankfurt
    University), 380
Horváth, Ö. von, 64
Hosseinpour, Amir, 242–3
Houston, 74, 203
Houston Grand Opera, 171
Howard, Ann, 237
Howell, Gwynne, 193
Howell, Ron, 279, 281, 282, 283, 285
Hudson, Richard, 91, 92, 230, 233,
    234, 237, 262, 276–80, 309, 340

Hugh the Drover (Vaughan
    Williams), 74–5
Hugo, Victor, 231
humanism, 162
Hunt, Lorraine, 209, 226
Hurry, Leslie, 320
Hytner, Nicholas, 14, 75, 171, 174,
    176, 268, 306, 308, 309, 312,
    338–9, 340, 341–5, 354

*I was looking at the ceiling and then I
    saw the sky* (Adams/Sellars), 221
Ibsen, Henrik, 64
idealism, 64, 145, 245
ideology, 66, 162, 205, 222
Idomeneo (Mozart), 64, 322, 354, 433
impresarios, 55, 57, 62–3, 69, 70, 71,
    84, 307, 379
Impressions of Pelléas, 27, 28–9,
    276, 421
In Search of Wagner (Adorno), 105
incoronazione di Poppea, L' see
    Coronation of Poppea, The
Indian theatre, 216
Indonesian theatre, 169, 216
Inspector Calls, An (Priestley),
    185, 339
Institute of Contemporary Arts,
    London, 294
Intelligence Park, The (Barry), 423
Intermedii (Cavalieri), 65
internationalization, 58, 59, 69, 245
interpretation, 3, 5, 11, 12, 13, 15, 20,
    30, 39–52, 55, 56, 57, 59, 61, 62,
    73–4, 77, 85, 93, 94, 96, 103, 104,
    112, 114, 115, 120, 124, 130, 133,
    138, 151, 158, 174, 189, 198, 202,
    208, 210, 223, 225, 230, 234, 240,
    244–5, 270, 286, 289, 293, 307,
    309, 370, 382, 385, 389, 390, 399,
    400, 407, 435–6
Into the Woods (Sondheim), 91, 230
Ionesco, Petrika, 362
Iphigenia in Aulis (Gluck), 335, 434
Iphigenia in Tauris (Gluck), 335
Isaacs, Sir Jeremy, 353
Isabella of Lorraine, 65
Isis, 21
Israel, 171
Italian Girl in Algiers, The (Rossini),

90, 104
Italy, 69–70, 71, 74, 104
    politics in opera, 67
    resurrection of opera in, 32, 63

Jackson, Barrie, 21
Jackson, Richard, 255
Jacobs, René, 40
Jacobs, Sally, 270
Janáček, Leoš, 14, 35, 65, 68, 73, 160,
    308, 344, 345, 347, 359, 379, 387,
    407, 418, 425, 435
Jarry, Alfred, 89, 102
Järvefelt, Göran, 34, 362–5
Jaws (film), 243
Jenůfa (Janáček), 314–15, 386–8
Johnson, Anthony Rolfe, 332, 408
Johnson, Dr Samuel, 74
jokes, 133, 135, 155, 160, 205, 209, 229,
    236–7, 242, 265, 277, 278, 296,
    303, 313, 343, 344, 394, 397–8
Jommelli, Nicolò, 40
Jonas, Peter, xiv, 20, 171, 187, 241,
    301, 319, 337, 338, 339, 343, 390,
    435, 436
Jones, Gwyneth, 106
Jones, Richard, 187, 221, 283, 287, 339
    and the Brothers Quay, 91
    and burlesque, 242, 244, 247
    and Hopkins, 13, 235, 255–9
    productions
        bête, La, 229
        Count Ory, 236–7
        Flea in her Ear, A, 229, 235–6,
            237
        Fledermaus, Die, 237–9, 241,
            246, 257, 340, 414
        Flying Dutchman, The, 2,
            239–41, 256–7
        Giulio Cesare in Egitto, 228,
            241–4, 245
        Into the Woods, 230
        Love for Three Oranges, The,
            234–5, 340
        Macbeth, 232–3
        Manon, 233–4
        Mazeppa, 82, 83, 235–6
        Mignon, 230
        Night at the Chinese Opera, A,
            237

Rake's Progress, The, 230
Rigoletto, 231–2
Ring, xiii, 20, 110, 232, 244–55, 353, 395
Too Clever By Half, 229
Joseph and the Amazing Technicolor Dreamcoat (Lloyd Webber), 308
Jungheinrich, Hans-Klaus, 380
Jungian psychology, 296, 334
Jurassic Park (film), 243

Kabuki theatre, 81, 216, 267
Kagel, Mauricio, 343, 423
Kallman, Chester, 90
Kalman, Jean, 370
Karajan, Herbert von, 434
Kašlík, Václav, 33
Kathakali dance, 272
Katya Kabanová (Janáček), 346, 353, 354, 359
Kaye, Danny, 233
Kelley, Frank, 215
Kelly, Janis, *318*
Kemp, Lindsay, 334, 360
Kempe, Rudolf, xiv
Kenny, Sean, 32
Kent Opera, 75, 236, 312, 321, 326, 330, 341, 354, 423–4
Kerman, Professor Joseph, 72
Khovanshchina (Mussorgsky), 170
Kiel, 380
Kierkegaard, Sören, 188
Kimm, Fiona, *196*
kimono, 28, 266, 267, 268
King Arthur or The British Worthy (Purcell), 269, 283–5
King Lear (Shakespeare), 45, 198, 332
King Priam (Tippett), 75, 274–5, 310–13, 341–3, 354, 419, 423, 434
King's Theatre, Haymarket, London, 324, 434
King's Theatre, Southsea, 433
Kirchner, Alfred, 13, 49, 76, 147, 248, 382, 384–6, 388
Kitchen, The (Wesker), 339
Klee, Paul, 123
Klein, Allen Charles, 170
Klemperer, Otto, 25, 390
Kneidl, Karl, 382, 388
Knot Garden, The (Tippett), 33, 321,

323, 333–4, 341, 423
Knussen, Oliver, 73, 91, 169, 313, 419
Kokoschka, Oskar, 430
Kollo, René, *166*, 189, 328
Koltai, Ralph, 86, 320, 321, 359
Koltès, Bernard-Marie, 109, 119
Komisarjevsky, Fedor ('Komis'), 30, 108
Komische Oper, East Berlin, 25, 29, 34, 49, 76, 105, 127–8, 174, 266, 358, 381, 389
Komlosi, Ildiko, 162
Königskinder (Humperdinck), 350
Konzerthaus, Vienna, 434
Korn, Artur, *378*
Kott, Jan, 61
Kraus, Clemens, 383
Kresnik, Hans 388
Kroll Theatre, Berlin, 25, 390, 391
Kubelik, Rafael, xiv
Kubrick, Stanley, 313
Kuhlmann, Kathleen, 242
Kunstschau, 430
Kupfer, Harry, xiii, 76, 146, 160, 360, 361, 381, 388, 389, 435
Kuzma, Sue Ellen, 215

Lady Macbeth of Mtsensk (Shostakovich), 263, 340, 347–8, 419
Laing, Stewart, 92, 296, 305
Lal, Durga, 272–3
Lancaster, Osbert, 87, 90, 91
Landestheater, Darmstadt, 434
Langridge, Philip, *38*, 182, 219, 301, 313, 408
language
  body, 212
  dance, 203, 205
  design, 174
  English, 74–6
  expressionist, 315
  gestural, 81, 108, 128, 145, 169, 207, 216, 224
  musical, 64, 67, 68, 77, 168, 205, 322, 415, 416, 418, 424
  avant-garde, 65
  Berg's, 35
  Messiaen's, 206, 207
  modern, 73

Schoenberg's reform of, 72
shared language of music and
    drama, 56–7
Wagnerian, 35
sexual, 212
theatrical, 94, 97, 105, 131,
    160–61, 225
verbal
    craze for Italian-language
        opera, 68
    original, 167, 198, 320
    of poems, 45
    shared with the audience,
        5, 6, 95
    and surtitles, 6–7
visual, 81, 207
language culture, 58–9, 63
Languages of Art (Goodman), 45
Lapine, James, 308
Large, Brian, 108, 111
Larson, Susan, 202, 209, 211, 213, 215
Last Summer, The (Pasternak), 201
Lavelli, Jorg, 34, 219, 435
Lawless, Stephen, 13, 285
Lawton, Jeffrey, 54, 184
Lazaridis, Stefanos, 86, 92, 93, 265,
    267, 294, 307, 309, 310, 331, 340,
    347–8, 350, 351, 352
Lecca, Marie-Jeanne, 348
Lecocq, Charles, 69
Leeds, 75, 297, 298, 299, 312, 313, 315,
    340, 404, 436
Lefebvre, Archbishop Marcel, 42
Lehár, Franz, 379
Lehmann, Lilli, 77
Lehnhoff, Nikolaus, 308, 388
Leiferkus, Sergei, 7, 236, 278
Leipzig, 402
Lenz, Jakob, 10, 388, 423
Leppard, Raymond, 322
Levine, James, 106, 147
liberalism, 302
Liebermann, Rolf, 34, 69, 70
Ligendza, Catarina, 143, 156
Ligeti, György, 340
lighting, 5, 8, 28, 29, 49, 59, 66, 77, 82,
    86, 88, 89, 97, 103, 106, 111,
    113–14, 120, 123, 124, 136, 156,
    159, 175, 179, 181, 182, 183, 188,
    191, 193, 201, 205, 206, 216, 225,

234, 236, 240–41, 246, 248, 249,
    257, 258, 266, 277–8, 289, 309,
    312, 315, 342, 346, 347, 368, 370,
    385, 396, 431
Linbury Prize for Stage Design, 93
Lippi, Marcello, *228*
Lisbon, 71
literalism, 12, 42, 95, 193
live performance, 94, 96, 419
Lloyd Webber, Andrew, 308, 345,
    420
Lloyd-Jones, David, 270
Lobel, Adrienne, *196*, 213
Lohengrin (Wagner), 77, 101, 321,
    327–8, 434
London, 7, 30, 60, 83, 171, 240, 332,
    420, 423
London Coliseum, 20, 33, *38*, 62,
    169–72, 177, 182, 189, 265, 277,
    308, 321, 330, 331, 332, 337, 338,
    340, 349, 353, *414*, 435
London International Festival of
    Opera, 143
Long Beach Opera, 169
Loppert, Max, 185, 331
Los Angeles, 74, 89, 171, 220
Love for Three Oranges, The
    (Prokofiev), 91, 234–5, 313,
    340, 419
Löw, Jürg, 398
Lowery, Nigel, xiii, *2*, *38*, 92, 181,
    228, 232, 233, 237–41, 243–9,
    252–9, 310, 340, *414*, 424
Lucia di Lammermoor (Donizetti),
    358, 359
Lucio Silla (Mozart), 109, 116,
    120–22, 123
Ludwig, Christa, 433
Ludwig II, King of Bavaria, 71
Luig, Michael, 138
Luisa Miller (Verdi), 32
Lully, Jean-Baptiste, 68, 70, 379
Lulu (Berg), 34–5, 116–19, 122, 162,
    322, 357, 418
Luxon, Benjamin, 325
Lyric Opera of Chicago, 184–5, 211
lyricism, 35, 240, 336, 419
Lyttelton stage, Royal National
    Theatre, London, 109
Lyubimov, Yuri, 200, 314

MacArthur Foundation, 170
Macbeth (Verdi), 103, 232–3, 327, 328,
 340, 347, 348
McCormack, Mark, 307
McCracken, James, xiii
McDonald, Antony, 294, 295, 340
 and Cairns, 92
 and The Capture of Troy, 292
 and Chérubin, 229, 303, 304, 353
 and Hedda Gabler, 294
 and The Midsummer Marriage,
 294, 299, 300
 and Orlando, 294, 295
 and researching the right conceptual stimulus, 294
 'troika' with Albery and Cairns, 293
 and The Trojans, 298, 299, 300, 303
 and Venice Preserv'd, 294
McFadden, Claron, 284
Macfarlane, John, 403, 408, 410
McGegan, Nicholas, 187
Machinal (Sophie Treadwell), 339
McIntyre, Donald, 366
Mackerras, Sir Charles, 345
McLaughlin, Marie, 270
McMaster, Brian, xiv, 14, 32, 33, 34,
 357–62, 365, 366, 367, 371, 375,
 376, 435, 436
MacNeil, Ian, 92, 185, 186, 189,
 190, 193
Madam Butterfly (Puccini), xiii,
 265–8, 340, 360–61
Maddalena, James, 196, 204, 209, 215
Madrid, 71
madrigals, 65, 333
Maeterlinck, Count Maurice,
 27, 160, 220
Maggio Musicale, Florence (1990),
 161, 273, 331
Magic Flute, The (Mozart) see
 Zauberflöte, Die
Mahler, Gustav, 12, 20, 24, 49, 77, 91,
 101, 380, 428
Makropoulos Affair, The (Janáček),
 128, 359
Malfitano, Catherine, 273, 274
Malle, Louis, 373
mammelles de Tiresias, Les (Poulenc),
 88, 419
Man and His Music (Mellers), 40

Man who Mistook his Wife for a Hat,
 The (Nyman), 168
Mann, Thomas, 255, 285, 423
Mann, William, 108
Manon (Massenet), 233–4
Manthey, Axel, 13, 90, 92, 126, 127,
 129, 138, 139, 142, 143, 145, 146,
 148, 152, 153, 155, 156, 309, 382
Mantua, 63
Marelli, Marco Arturo, 382, 387
Marenzio, Luca, 65
Mario and the Magician (Oliver),
 255, 423
Marivaux, Pierre de, 109, 135
Markova, Alicia, 4
Marks, Dennis, 255, 336, 390
Marriage of Figaro, The (Mozart), 23,
 31, 34, 68, 76, 92, 109, 173, 198,
 212, 213–14, 239, 276–8, 303,
 320, 321, 330, 335, 341, 359, 365,
 379, 434
Marschner, Heinrich, 71, 423
Martin, Bruce, 126
Martinů, Bohuslav, 357
Marton, Eva, 331
Marusin, Yuri, 262, 278
Marxism, 33, 104, 105, 131, 132, 153,
 173, 361, 362
Mascagni, Pietro, 25
Mask of Orpheus (Birtwistle), 86, 332
Masked Ball, A (Verdi), 171, 178–81,
 308, 310, 311, 327, 340, 353, 362,
 364–5, 434
Massenet, Jules, 77, 234, 353, 379
Master and Margarita, The
 (Bulgakov), 236
Mastersingers of Nuremberg, The
 see Meistersinger von
 Nürnberg, Die
Matcham, Frank, 337
Mathis der Maler (Hindemith),
 220–22
Maurel, Victor, 77
Maw, Nicholas, 73, 90
Maxwell, Donald, 54, 235, 356, 364,
 369, 370
Maxwell Davies, Peter, 73
Mazeppa (Tchaikovsky), 82–3, 171,
 172–6, 179, 235–6, 294, 340
media stars, 197, 330

Medici, Ferdinando de', 65
Mee, Anthony, 237
Mefistofele (Boito), 169
Mehta, Zubin, 187
Meier, Waltraud, 124, 189, 353
Meistersinger von Nürnberg, Die
    (Wagner), 49, 188, 296, 319–20,
    329, 339, 340, 391, 393–5
Melba, Nellie, 77
Melbourne, 74
Meldrew, Victor, 287
Mellers, Wilfrid, 40
Menotti, Gian Carlo, 73, 422
mère coupable, La (Beaumarchais),
    303–4
Merker, Der (Roller), 427
Merritt, Chris, 402
Merry Widow, The (Lehár), 340, 362
Messager, André, 69, 303
Messel, Oliver, 85, 320, 324
Messiaen, Olivier, 198, 206, 207,
    219, 382
metaphysics, 27, 129, 139, 144, 149,
    189, 194, 215, 231, 239, 247, 305,
    326, 371, 374, 384
Metastasio, Pietro, 39, 40, 65, 66,
    67, 120
Method acting, 49, 66, 295
Metropolitan Opera House, New
    York, 27, 29, 31, 49, 50, 74, 75,
    88, 90, 91, 106, 167, 168, 263,
    327, 353, 419, 421, 435
Meyerhold, Vsevolod, 199–200
Michaels-Moore, Anthony, 276, 302
Midsummer Marriage, The (Tippett),
    75, 179, 283, 294, 296–8, 302,
    359, 419, 423
Midsummer Night's Dream, A
    as opera (Britten), 169, 286–9, 321,
    325, 354, 406, 407
    as play (Shakespeare), 44, 45, 56,
    230–31, 284, 324, 334, 431
Mignon (Thomas), 230
Mikado, The (Gilbert and Sullivan),
    234, 331, 340
Miki, Minoru, 267
Milan, 19, 120, 322
Miles, Alastair, 218
Miller, Jonathan, 14, 45, 98, 171–2,
    197, 234, 268, 321, 324, 326,

329–31, 339, 340, 353, 373,
    383, 384
Milnes, Rodney, 361
minimalism, 58, 168, 169, 203, 205,
    324, 332, 383
Minter, Drew, 209, 211
Minton, Yvonne, 273
Mirvish, Ed, 354
Mishima, Yukio, 187
Mitchell, Clare, 231
Mitchell, Donald, 130
Mitchinson, John, 361
Mitropoulos, Dmitri, 22
Mitterrand, François, 70, 71
model box, 89, 93, 294
modernist/ism, 15, 35, 49, 56, 58, 59,
    68, 77, 101, 102, 183, 201, 205,
    207, 379, 416, 425
Molière, 64
monologues, 183, 203
montage, 239, 306
Monteverdi, Claudio, 19, 21, 40, 58,
    60, 63, 64, 65, 68, 71, 106, 155,
    203, 211, 322, 332, 333, 379, 434
Moody, John, 321
Moon and Sixpence, The (Gardner),
    32, 323
Morell, Thomas, 223
Morley, Thomas, 296
Morris, Mark, 203, 205, 224
Mortier, Gerard, 205, 371, 379, 390,
    391, 395
Moscow Arts Theatre, 29, 102, 346
Moses and Aaron (Schoenberg), 33,
    321, 398–402, 419, 434
Moshinsky, Elijah, xiii, 14, 75, 90, 98,
    321, 324, 326–9, 331, 340, 345,
    353, 362, 366, 435
Mostel, Zero, 394
Mother Courage (Brecht), 128
Motley, 86, 320, 324
movement groups, 242, 247, 253, 298
Mozart Companion (Robbins Landon
    and Mitchell), 130
Mozart, Wolfgang Amadeus, 19, 60,
    62–8, 71, 72, 76, 89, 101, 109,
    116, 120, 121, 133–8, 160, 163,
    187, 198, 211, 212, 213, 215, 217,
    256, 263, 288, 303, 320, 326, 335,
    336, 365, 375, 379, 422, 433

Mozart's Operas (Dent), 130
Mumford, Peter, 366
Munich, 20, 22, 83, 127, 241–4, 310,
    322, 380, 423
Munich Biennale, 156, 158
Murder in the Cathedral (Pizzetti), 32
Murger, Henri, 92
Murphy, Suzanne, 370
Murray, Ann, 187, *228*, 241, 244
Music and Musicians, 434
Musica Nel Chiostro, Batignano, near
    Grosseto, 263, 268, 274
musicals, 69, 205, 308, 420
Mussorgsky, Modest, 201, 379
mythical figures, 332

Nabucco (Verdi), 33
Napier, John, 328
Napoleon III, Emperor of France, 70
National Theatre, London, 30, 109,
    185, 263, 309, 324, 330, 339
nationalism, 68, 69, 158, 172
Nel, Christof, 13, 49, 382, 388,
    389, 390
Nelson (Berkeley), 32
neo-classicism, 19, 48, 63, 64, 66, 68,
    90, 114, 120, 178, 329, 335, 342,
    403, 419
neo-realism, 13, 215, 266, 289, 361
neo-romanticism, 383
neon, 139, 141, 150, 206, 217, 219, 304
Netherlands Opera, *2*, *80*, 218, 239,
    302–3, 392
Neuenfels, Hans, xiv, 13, 49, 76, 138,
    194, 382, 383, 384, 385, 388
Neugebauer, Hans, 402
New Bayreuth, 9, 19, 57, 62, 102, 433
New Menoza, The (Lenz), 10
New Statesman, 20
New Theatre, Cardiff, *54*, *356*, 359
New York, 31, 34, 71, 74, 75, 89, 95,
    171, 353, 420
New York City Opera, 74, 167,
    169, 352
New Yorker, 108, 168, 199
Newman, Ernest, 21
Newport, Vivienne, 188
Newson, Lloyd, 236
Nicholas Nickleby (Dickens), 230
Nicolai, Otto, 71

Nietzsche, Friedrich Wilhelm, 106,
    153, 188
'Nietzschean', 140, 153
Night at the Chinese Opera, A (Judith
    Weir), 237, 423–4
Nikolais, Alwyn, 169
Nilsson, Birgit, 434
Nilsson, Pia-Marie, 162
Nixon in China (Adams), 168, 202–4,
    205, 216
Nobili, Lila de, 324
Nöcker, Günter, *166*
Noelte, Rudolf, 14, 116, 362, 364, 365,
    366, 376
Noh theatre, 81, 146, 216
Nolen, Timothy, 273
Nono, Luigi, 380, 381
Nordic, 102, 106
Norrlands Opera, 286
Norma (Bellini), 76, 362
Norrington, Roger, 326, 342
Norwegian Opera, Oslo, 367
NorWest Holst scheme, 171, 174
nostalgia, 92, 108, 116, 144
notation, 41, 45, 46, 47, 60, 63
note rows, 67
Novello, Ivor, 4
Nunn, Trevor, 230, 309, 345, 353, 354
Nyman, Michael, 58, 168

Oberle, Carl Friedrich, 362, 363, 364
Oberlin, Russell, 354
Oberon (Weber), 69, 75, 268
Obolensky, Chloe, 28
O'Brien, Timothy, 86, 90, 92, 323,
    326, 328, 329, 435
obscurantism, 128
Observer, 23
Oedipus Rex (Stravinsky), 32, *38*,
    181–2, 340
Oedipus (Sophocles), 422
Offenbach, Jacques, 69, 87–8, 119,
    255, 379, 391
Old Vic, London, 31, 32, 74, 237, 239,
    319, 354
Oliver, Alexander, 405
Oliver, Stephen, 255, 423
Olivier, Sir Laurence (Lord Olivier),
    30, 263, 326, 330
Olsen, Frode, 225

Olympians, The (Bliss), 23
Olympic Revels, 69
O'Neill, Dennis, 364
O'Neill, Patricia, 298
Opera 66 (Osborne), 34
Opera 80, 49, 230, 231, 306, 338, 371
Opera America, 74
Opéra Bastille, Paris, 70–71, 116, 206,
    273, 391, 421
Opéra Comique, Paris, 352
Opera Factory, 84, 215, 276, 318, 323,
    332, 333, 335, 341, 421
Opera For All, 433
Opera Grove, 357
Opera Industry in Italy from
    Cimarosa to Verdi, The
    (Rosselli), 55
Opera News, 263
Opera North, xiv, 14, 91, 145, 233,
    234, 292, 294, 298, 299, 302, 303,
    310, 312, 314, 338, 360, 375,
    388, 436
opera seria, 14, 39, 59, 67, 68, 83, 109,
    120, 121, 210, 243, 244, 335,
    403, 420
opera-houses, 415
operetta, 69, 71, 96, 97, 237
Opie, Alan, 201, 285
Oporto, 71
Orangerie, Darmstadt, 434
oratorios, 65, 68, 120, 182, 186, 205,
    222, 223–4, 225, 401
Orchestre de Paris, 345
Orfeo ed Euridice (Gluck), 64, 66,
    76, 434
Orfeo, L' (Monteverdi), 64, 106,
    332–3, 340
Orff, Carl, 168
Orlando (Handel), 185, 199,
    294–5, 331
Orpheus in the Underworld (Offen-
    bach), 87, 88, 348, 359
Osborne, Charles, 34
Osborne, Nigel, 73, 200, 201, 202,
    207, 332
Ostbergh, Lars, 287
Ostendorf, Josef, 398
Ostrovsky, Alexander, 423
Oswald, Heinz, 162
Otello (Verdi), xiii, 32, 76, 327, 330,

340, 362, 367–9, 434
Owen Wingrave (Britten), 422
Owens, Anne-Marie, 257, 258, 268

Page, Ashley, 305
Page, Steven, 230
Pagliacci (Leoncavallo), 306
painters, 85–8, 93
Palais Garnier see Paris Opéra
Palestrina (Pfitzner), 419
Pallavicino, Carlo, 40
Palmer, Felicity, 176, 184, 219, 262,
    350, 351
Palucca, Gret, 128
pantomime, 87, 89, 91, 112, 236, 237,
    238, 284, 286, 363, 389
Pappano, Antonio, 411
Parade (Satie), 88
parapluies de Cherbourg, Les
    (film), 422
Paris, 7, 27, 34, 83, 404
Paris Opéra (from 1875 the Palace
    Garnier), 34, 69, 70, 104, 116,
    118, 119, 207, 219, 391
Parry, David, 289, 338
Parry, Susan, 190
Parsifal (Wagner), 13, 19, 35, 44, 62,
    67, 107, 127, 128, 138–43, 153,
    188, 354, 362, 366, 380, 434, 435
Pasternak, Leonid, 201
Patmos (Schweinitz), 158–9
Patti, Adelina, 11, 12, 77
Pavarotti, Luciano, 5, 49, 74, 167, 327
Payne, Nicholas, xiii, xiv, 14, 32, 298,
    353, 436
Pearl Fishers, The (Bizet), 32
Pears, Peter, 31, 408
Peduzzi, Richard, 85, 92, 93, 100, 104,
    105, 109–12, 114, 116, 117,
    120–24, 138, 162, 404
Pelléas et Mélisande (Debussy), 27,
    33, 201, 217, 218–20, 362, 369,
    370–71, 421
Pepsico SummerFare festival, 198, 212
Pepusch, Johann Christoph, 19
Perchance to Dream (Novello), 4
Perfect Wagnerite, The (Shaw), 77,
    105, 109
Peri, Jacopo, 63
period performance, 5, 10, 28, 46, 47,

73, 92, 112, 180, 234, 269, 278–9, 280, 302, 324, 328, 330, 331, 364, 383, 389, 409

Perkins, Anthony, 248

Perry, brothers Eugene and Herbert, 214, 215

Peter Grimes (Britten), 19, 22, 31, 32, 75, 301, 321, 326–7, 359, 366, 402, 406–12, 419, 420, 434, 435

Petipa, Marius, 129

Pfitzner, Hans, 73, 419

Philharmonia Orchestra, 398

philistinism, 427–8

philosophy, 20, 39, 44, 47, 48, 51, 57, 59, 75, 85, 105, 110, 129, 143, 163, 168, 181, 210, 244, 246, 283, 321, 328, 363, 396, 421

Picasso, Pablo, 86, 87

Piccola Scala, Milan, 103, 104, 116

pictorialism, 331

Pikovaya Dama see Queen of Spades

Pimlott, Steven, 14, 49, 80, 264, 306–9, 338, 340, 371

Pinter, Harold, 109

Pintilie, Lucian, 14, 34, 49, 50, 83, 200, 231, 347, 356, 362, 364, 371–6

Piper, John, 320

Pittman-Jennings, David, 402

Pius, XII, Pope, 42

Pizzi, Pier Luigi, 309

Planché, James Robinson, 69

plasterwork, 185, 342

Plato, 47

Plowright, Rosalind, 330

Poel, William, 109

poetic realism, 324, 332

Poetics (Aristotle), 97, 176

Poisoned Kiss, The (Vaughan Williams), 75

Poland, 86

Polaski, Deborah, 162, 248, 254

Polixa, Helmut, 362

Pollock, Adam, 263, 268, 274

Pollock's toy theatre, 284

Poltava (Pushkin), 172

polyphony, 65, 67, 158, 390, 433

Pompidou, Georges, 70

Ponchielli, Amilcare, 360

Ponnelle, Jean-Pierre, 116, 169, 309, 398

Poor Theatre, 276, 332, 372

Pope, Cathryn, 276

Pope, Deborah, 238

Porgy and Bess (Gershwin), 354, 419

Porter, Andrew, 108, 199, 233

post-expressionism, 402

Post-modernism, 9, 75, 98, 109, 114, 158, 181, 230, 242, 296, 379, 424

Poulenc, Francis, 73, 88, 419

Poulton, Robert, 234

Pountney, David, xiv, 14, 31, 171, 199, 264, 306, 309, 327, 337, 339, 343, 359, 405, 423, 435, 436

productions

   Adventures of Mr Brouček, The, 340

   Bartered Bride, The, 347

   Carmen, 347

   Cunning Little Vixen, The, 340, 348, 359

   Doktor Faust, 340, 347

   Don Carlos, 338

   Don Giovanni, 347

   Falstaff, 340, 348

   Fidelio, 351–2

   From the House of the Dead, 359

   Hansel and Gretel, 340, 350–51

   Jenůfa, 359

   Katya Kabanová, 346, 359

   Königskinder, 350

   Lady Macbeth of Mtsensk, 340, 347–8

   Macbeth, 340, 347, 348

   Makropoulos Case, The, 359

   Midsummer Marriage, The, 297

   Orpheus in the Underworld, 87, 348

   Queen of Spades, 340

   Rusalka, 340, 347, 348, 350

   Toussaint, 346

   Valkyrie, The, 340, 347, 348–50

   Wozzeck, 122, 350, 405

Poussin, Nicolas, 329

Power, Patrick, 234

Prabhavalkar, Nigel, 230

Prague, 68

Prague Biennale, 91

Prague National Theatre, 365

Pre-Raphaelites, 90

Prévost, Abbé, 233

Price, Leontyne, 434
Price, Margaret, 434
prima-donnas, 34, 49
principal-boy, 162
problem-solving, 90
produceritis, 14, 20, 30, 82
Producers, The (film), 394
'producer's licence', 43
producers' opera, 49
producers, role of, 57
Prokina, Elena, 281
Prokofiev, Sergei, 35, 73, 91, 235, 313,
    379, 419
Proust, Marcel, 27
Prowse, Philip, 360
Psycho (film), 248
psychology, 27, 31, 57, 72, 94, 106,
    110, 121, 128, 137, 185, 189, 209,
    242, 250, 264, 269, 279, 283, 323,
    325, 393, 410
psychotherapy, 60, 276, 336
Puccini, Giacomo, 25, 35, 62, 65, 66,
    69, 72, 73, 75, 92, 162, 169, 265,
    266, 267, 308, 331, 379, 418,
    419, 421
Punch and Judy (Birtwistle), 334,
    416, 419
puppets, 169, 197, 198, 216, 231,
    258, 384
Purcell, Henry, 19, 75, 283, 285, 296,
    322, 379, 420, 421, 434
Puritani, I (Bellini), 362
Pushkin, Alexander, 172, 278,
    280, 359

Queen Elizabeth Hall, London,
    143, *318*
Queen of Spades (Tchaikovsky), 262,
    278–9, 280, 340, 358–9
Quilico, Louis, 389

Racine, Jean, 64, 120
Raffeiner, Walter, 143
Raine, Craig, 200, 202
Rake's Progress, The (Stravinsky),
    85, 88, 89, 90, 230, 321, 328–9
Rameau, Jean-Philippe, 68, 70, 383
Ramey, Samuel, 169
Ramicova, Dunya, *196*, 204, 223
Rankl, Karl, xiv, 21, 22, 26

Rape of Lucretia, The (Britten),
    19, 265, 340, 407, 420
Rapunzel, 198
Rattle, Simon, 218
Ravel, Maurice, 73, 88, 91, 201, 419
Rawnsley, John, 330
rè in ascolto, Un (Berio), 265, 273
Rea, Sean, *356*
realism, 25, 66, 85–6, 101, 102, 103,
    110, 128, 199, 200, 202, 207, 331,
    346, 361, 365, 423
reality, 4, 81, 95, 111, 122, 124, 130,
    173, 279, 286, 287, 365, 402
recitative, 58, 120, 121, 122, 205, 240
recordings, 46, 47, 51, 52, 57–8, 61, 63,
    72, 73, 83, 335, 415, 417, 419
    video *see* video recordings
reform opera, 64–7
Reformation, 221, 222
rehearsals, 93–4
Reich, Günter, 382, 384
Reimann, Aribert, 334
Reinhardt, Andreas, 383
Reinhardt, Max, 75, 95, 108, 109, 110,
    158, 431
religion, 20, 42–3, 44, 63, 64, 102, 131,
    132, 142, 204, 207, 210, 264, 302,
    328, 384
Remedios, Alberto, 349
Renaissance, 63, 64, 367, 369
Rennert, Günther, 33, 320, 322
reorchestration, 96, 275
repertoire, 35, 39, 40, 55–77, 96, 104,
    116, 127, 147, 171, 212, 215, 233,
    240, 348, 359, 379, 381, 388, 417,
    423, 424, 429
Resistible Theatres (Stokes), 101
Reszke, Edouard de, 77
Reszke, Jean de, 77
revolve/revolving stage, 129, 141,
    143–6, 150, 152, 153, 156, 157,
    162, 323, 349, 380, 385, 386, 431
Rheingold, Das (Wagner), 76, 112,
    113, 114, *126*, 128, 148–9, 151,
    153, 154, 234, 244, 245–7, 251,
    253, 276, 353
Ricciarelli, Katia, 49
Rice, Peter, 320
Richardson, Matthew, 13, 268, 286,
    288, 289

Richardson, Sir Ralph, 30
Ricordi, Giulio, 11, 12, 50, 69
Riddell, Richard, 181
Ridderbusch, Karl, 100, 113
Ridler, Anne, 335
Rienzi (Wagner), 174, 268, 340, 341
Rigoletto (Verdi), 83, 98, 171–2,
    231–2, 268, 321, 330, 331, 340,
    371, 372, 373–4, 384
Rihm, Wolfgang, 73, 383, 423
Rimsky-Korsakov, Nikolai, 73
Ring (Wagner), xiii, 3, 10, 13, 19, 20,
    33, 42, 49, 50, 67, 77, 85, 91–2,
    95, 97, 103–8, 110–19, 122, 123,
    124, 127, 128, 132, 138, 143,
    145–58, 163, 172, 173, 199, 232,
    244–55, 319, 321, 322, 325, 330,
    331, 339, 346–50, 353, 358–9,
    362, 367, 376, 381, 383, 390, 391,
    395–7, 433, 435
Ring Saga, The, 275–6
Rise and Fall of the City of
    Mahagonny, The, 158, 160–62,
    273–4, 400
Rising of the Moon, The (Maw), 90
Ritch, David, 340
ritorno d'Ulisse in patria, Il (Mon-
    teverdi), 64, 106, 321, 325
Ritter, Nina, 129, 146, 383
Riverside Studios, 294
Robbins Landon, H. C., 130
Robertson, Patrick, 330
Robinson, Douglas, 22
Robinson, Faye, 136
Robson, Christopher, 186, 228,
    241, 404
Rodelinda (Handel), 362
Rodgers, Joan, 276
Roger, David, 318, 332, 333, 336
Roller, Alfred, 12, 20, 24, 49, 75, 77,
    91, 101, 162, 427–31
Roma, Città Aperta (film), 331
Roman theatre, 21
romanticism, 67, 68, 96, 218, 270,
    285, 404
Romeo and Juliet (Shakespeare), 23
Romeo and Juliet (Sutermeister), 32
Ronconi, Luca, 435
Roocroft, Amanda, 187
Rootering, Jan-Hendrik, 166

Rosell, Ingrid, 105
Rosen, Charles, 401
Rosenberg, Pamela, 160
Rosenkavalier, Der (Strauss), 20, 75,
    158, 162–3, 163, 286, 433
Ross, Elise, 218
Rosselli, John, 55
Rossellini, Roberto, 331
rossignol, Le (Stravinsky), 88
Rossini, Gioacchino, 72, 76, 255, 379
Rotterdam Philharmonic Orchestra,
    218
Rousset, Christoph, 40
Royal Court Theatre, London, 30, 32,
    86, 89, 172, 263, 324, 332, 339
Royal Exchange Theatre, Manchester,
    345
Royal Northern College of Music,
    233
Royal Opera House, London, xiii,
    xiv, 12, 14, 19, 20, 21, 22, 23, 24,
    25, 26, 29, 31, 32, 33, 56, 65, 70,
    75, 76, 88, 90, 91, 105, 167, 169,
    170, 183, 186, 193, 220, 229, 232,
    244, 246, 252, 254–5, 265, 273,
    274, 283, 297, 302, 303, 314,
    319–22, 325–8, 337, 341, 353,
    354, 366, 388, 420, 421, 423, 424,
    433–6
Royal Shakespeare Company (RSC),
    263, 284, 324, 325, 328
Royal Shakespeare Theatre, Stratford-
    upon-Avon (previously
    Shakespeare Memorial Theatre),
    21, 23, 30
Rudner, Sara, 206
Rusalka (Dvořák), 340, 347,
    348, 350
Rushdie, Salman, 44
Rydl, Kurt, 248, 254

Sabado, Keith, 205
Sadler's Wells Ballet, 319
Sadler's Wells Opera, xiii, 32
Sadler's Wells Theatre, London, 27,
    29, 31, 32, 33, 74, 263, 270, 319,
    320, 323, 336–7, 358, 420, 434
Saint François d'Assise (Messiaen),
    198, 206–7
Saint-Denis, Michel, 30, 32, 108, 320

Sallé, Marie, 186
Salminen, Matti, 115
Salome (Strauss), *18*, 19–24, 26–7, 33,
   334, 357, 360, 362
Saltaire Mills, Yorkshire, 263, 273
Salter, Richard, 394
Salzburg, 109, 116, 390, 433, 434
Salzburg Felsenreitschule, 206
Salzburg Festival, 206, 379, 395
Sams, Jeremy, 277
Samson and Dalila (Saint-Saëns), 32,
   80, 306–7, 327
Samson (Handel), 433
San Francisco, 71, 74
Sanjust, Filippo, 309
Santa Fe, 171
Satanic Verses (Rushdie), 44
Satie, Eric, 107
Saved (Bond), 172
Savoy operettas, 69
Sawallisch, Wolfgang, 187
Scala, La *see* Teatro alla Scala, Milan
Scarfe, Gerald, 87, 91, 348
Scarlatti, Alessandro, 40
Scènes de la vie de Bohème
   (Murger), 92
Schaaf, Johannes, 219
Schaal, Hans Dieter, 86, 129, 143, 144,
   145, 158, 159
Schauspieldirektor, Der (Mozart), 320
Schenk, Manfred, *126*
Schenk, Otto, 106
Schikaneder, Emanuel, 216, 269
Schiller, Friedrich von, 64, 302, 345
Schindler's List (film), 249
Schlemm, Anny, 389
Schlieker, Hans-Joachim, 160, 161
Schlubach, Jan, 365
Schmidt, Jacques, *100*, 104, 105, 110,
   117, 121
Schmidt, Trudeliese, 242
Schmiege, Marilyn, 406
Schoenberg, Arnold, 35, 67, 72, 73,
   205, 323, 398–401, 417, 419, 424
Schreker, Franz, 73, 383, 384
Schütz, Heinrich, 71
Schwarzkopf, Dame Elisabeth, 433
Schweinitz, Wolfgang von, 158, 159
Scofield, Paul, 371
Scottish Opera, 145, 171, 244, 246,

264, 265, 268, 294, 298, 299, 305,
   310, 320, 327, 338, 339, 346–7,
   348, 354, 402, 408, 424
Scottish Opera-Go-Round, 232
Scotto, Renata, 49
Scurfield, Matthew, 239
Seagull, The (Chekhov), 30
Searchers, The (film), 176
Seattle, 74
Second Mrs Kong, The (Birtwistle),
   311, 313–14
Second Stride dance company,
   294, 299
Second Vatican Council, 42
Secunde, Nadine, 189
Sellars, Peter, xiii, 34, 82, 422
   and Alden, 13, 170–71, 194, 197,
     273, 332
   and British operatic thinking, 13
   and casting, 84, 197, 216
   and Hall's departure from
     Glyndebourne, 323
   hand-jiving gesture language, 169,
     198, 206, 216, 220, 224
   and Indonesian theatre, 169, 198
   and jokes, 229
   as a master of theatrical language,
     225
   and puppet theatre, 169, 197, 198,
     199, 216
   stages the *Ring* for puppets, 199
   and translated opera, 197, 198
   use of publicity, 197
   productions
     Ajax, 199
     Così fan tutte, 212, 214, 215
     Death of Klinghoffer, 168, 202,
       204–6, 353
     Don Giovanni, 212, 214–15
     *Electrification of the Soviet
       Union, The*, 199
     Giulio Cesare in Egitto, 199,
       202, 207–11, 223, 242, 403
     histoire du soldat, L', 198
     *I was looking at the ceiling and
       then I saw the sky*, 221
     King Lear, 198–9
     Marriage of Figaro, The, 212,
       213–14, 278
     Mathis der Maler, 220–22

Nixon in China, 168, 202–4
Orlando, 199, 331
Pelléas et Mélisande, 201, 217, 218–20
Rapunzel, 198
Saint François d'Assise, 198–7
Tannhäuser, 211, 218
Theodora, 222–6
Zauberflöte, Die, 196, 199, 201, 215–18
semiotics, 119, 202
Sendak, Maurice, 87, 91, 169, 313, 345
Senso (film), 69
Seraglio see Entführung aus dem Serail, Die
Serban, Andrei, 34, 340, 362, 376, 435
serialism, 380, 425
sex, 113, 123, 129, 130, 131, 139, 174, 175, 186, 187, 190, 201, 212, 218, 220, 246, 248, 249, 268, 278, 285, 289, 296, 303, 372, 401, 402, 404, 407
sexual equality, 399
Sezession, 91
Shade, Ellen, 390
Shaffer, Peter, 277
Shakespeare, William, 10, 21, 22, 51, 55–6, 60, 64, 67, 74, 95, 98, 101, 102, 232, 233, 237, 286, 287, 288, 321, 323, 334, 367, 371, 375, 400, 429
Shakespeare Memorial Theatre *see* Royal Shakespeare Theatre
Shankar, Ravi, 267, 272
Sharnina, Ljubov, 236
Shaw, George Bernard, 77, 95, 105–6, 109, 132, 208, 334
Shaw, Glen Byam, 32, 320, 321
Shawe-Taylor, Desmond, 20
Sheridan, Richard Brinsley, 64, 277
Sherlock, Ceri, 131
Shiff, Buki, *166*, 187
Shimell, William, 131
Shore, Andrew, 312
Shostakovich, Dmitri, 73, 419
Siegfried (Wagner), 108, 111, 128, 153–6, 248, 249, 276, 434
Sills, Beverley, 167
Simon Boccanegra (Verdi), 50, 103, 176, 179, 185, 340, 433

Sinden, Donald, 265
Singers of Italian Opera (Rosselli), 55
Singspiel, 71, 420
Slack, Adrian, 359
Smetana, Bedřich, 65, 365, 379, 389
Smiles of a Summer Night (film), 230
Smith, Colin, 234
Smith, Craig, 202, 211, 214
Smith, Julian, 266
Smith, Patrick, 263
Snatched from the Gods (Vir), 423
soap opera, 153, 160, 210, 215, 220, 334, 403, 423
socialist realism, 25
Socrates, 47
Soldaten, Die (Zimmermann), 383, 387, 388
Solti, Sir Georg, xiii, xiv, 32, 33, 107, 146, 321, 323, 383
Sondheim, Stephen, 91, 161, 220, 230, 308
song, 415–16, 425
Song of Norway (adapted from Grieg), 4
Sophocles, 63, 183, 199
Soviet Union, break-up of, 173
Spain, 63
Spatz-Rabinowitz, Elaine, 208
Spiegel, Der, 62
Spielberg, Steven, 167, 243
Spink, Ian, 92, 175, 285, 293, 294, 295, 297, 298, 348
Spitzweg, Carl, 391
Spoleto Festival
  Charleston, 171
  Italy, 104
Squarciapino, Franca, 104
Squire, Daniel, 285
Stache, Thomas, 395
stage
  designs, 5, 90
  directions, 21, 50, 57, 84, 101, 112, 144, 274, 397
  directors, 57
  managers, 57, 81
  space, 23, 28, 81, 85, 86, 94, 98, 110, 111, 113, 115, 118, 124, 127, 143, 311, 324
Stainer, Sir John, 31
Stalin, Joseph, 173, 199, 200

Stalinism, 174
Stanislavsky (Konstantin Alexeyev),
    29, 30, 102, 110, 199–200
Steiger, Anna, 201
Stein, Peter, 14, 34, 54, 94, 103, 110,
    116, 179
  productions
    Falstaff, 362, 369–70, 389
    Moses and Aaron, 398–402
    Otello, 54, 362, 367–9
    Pelléas et Mélisande, 362, 369,
      370–71
    Ring, 76, 367
Steinberg, Pinchas, 82–3, 235, 236
Stephen Climax (Zender), 380
Stockhausen, Karlheinz, 62, 73,
    380, 417
Stockholm, 434
Stokes, John, 101
Stone, Oliver, 167
stories, 3, 4, 5, 42, 43, 88, 95, 101, 120,
    128, 129
  fairy-, 89, 91
Strandt, Marie-Luise, 128, 133,
    158, 160
straniera, La (Bellini), 169
Strasberg, Lee, 49
Strauss, Johann, 96, 237, 239, 379
Strauss, Richard, 20, 23, 24, 65, 73,
    162, 184, 187, 360, 379, 418, 433
Stravinsky, Igor, 73, 85, 90, 158, 181,
    182, 198, 201, 328–9, 419
Strehler, Giorgio, 19, 76, 92, 103–4,
    105, 109, 123, 128, 144, 177, 275,
    371, 435
  productions
    Marriage of Figaro, The, 34, 198
    Simon Boccanegra, 103
Streit, Kurt, 196, 218
Strindberg, August, 64, 334
strip cartoon, 181, 219, 243, 245, 305,
    341
structuralism, 119
Stubbs, Annena, 359
Stumphius, Annegeer, 196
Stuttgart Opera, 22, 83, 92, 158, 160,
    162, 309, 310, 380, 388, 398
sub-text, 66, 129, 147, 214, 219, 233,
    253, 265–6, 295, 301, 399, 424
Subsequent Performances (Miller), 45

subsidy, 167
suburban/suburbanism/suburbs, 243,
    248, 249, 254, 351, 388
Sullivan, Sir Arthur, 69, 255, 331
Summers, Jonathan, 190
Sunday in the Park with George
    (Sondheim), 308–9
Sunday Times, 87
Sunset Boulevard (film), 189
surrealism, 15, 45, 48, 102, 103, 110,
    128, 159, 160, 179, 180, 185, 244,
    297, 303, 339, 359, 360, 361
surtitles/supertitles, 6–7, 58, 95, 167,
    198, 217, 222
Susa, Conrad, 171
Sutermeister, Heinrich, 32
Sutherland, Joan, 433
Svoboda, Josef, 33, 91, 105, 322
swivelling platform, 91–2, 105
Sydney, 74
Sydney Opera House, 74, 415
Sylvan, Sanford, 204, 205, 215
symbolism, 49, 85, 102, 112, 117, 137,
    142, 159, 181, 206, 236, 245, 247,
    253, 285, 297, 395

Tablet, the, 3
Tales of Hoffmann, The see contes
    d'Hoffmann, Les
Tamchina, Jürgen, 382
Tannhäuser (Wagner), 103, 166, 173,
    187–9, 211, 218, 257, 383,
    434, 435
Tauber, Richard, 74
Tchaikovsky, Pyotr Ilyich, 7, 82, 171,
    172, 173, 176, 205, 269, 270,
    278, 379
Tear, Robert, 248, 285, 329
television, 8, 98, 147, 167, 174, 199,
    206, 207, 215, 242, 295, 372
television opera, 415, 421, 422, 423
Terfel, Bryn, 276, 278
Ternina, Milka, 77
Tetrazzini, Luisa, 77
textual understanding, 6
Tharp, Twyla, 169, 205
Thatcher, Margaret (later Baroness),
    87
Théâtre des Amandiers, Nanterre,
    109, 121

theatre of the mind, 95
Théâtre Nationale Populaire (TNP), 104, 105, 109
Théâtre Royal de la Monnaie, Brussels, 116, 371, *378*, 379, 391, 395, 406
Theatre Royal Nottingham, 332
Theodora (Handel), 222–6
Thielemann, Christian, 188
Third Programme (BBC), 433
Thomas, Ambroise, 230
Thompson, Margaret, 311
Three Tenors, 167
Thulborn, Pauline, *292*
Tieck, Ludwig, 256
Tierney, Vivian, 148, *414*
Times, The, 108, 339
timing, 111, 117, 144, 207, 235, 398, 416
Timon of Athens (Stephen Oliver), 340
Tinsley, Pauline, 314
Tippett, Sir Michael, 33, 73, 75, 179, 205, 274, 283, 294, 296, 297, 312–13, 322, 323, 333, 334, 341, 342, 359, 383, 419, 423, 434
Tirso de Molina (Gabriel Tellez), 64, 130
TNP *see* Théâtre Nationale Populaire
Todesverkündigung, 113, 247, 349
Tomlinson, John, 248, 302
Tommasi, Carlo, 383
tonal equality, 67
Too Clever By Half, 229, 234
Tooley, Sir John, 33, 34, 326
Toren, Roni, *166*, 187, 188
Toronto, 74
Tosca (Puccini), 62, 110, 331, 359, 421, 422
Touchstone, The (Rossini), 90
Toussaint (Blake), 346
tragedy, 97, 153, 193, 209, 232, 245, 254, 300
Tragedy of Carmen, The, 27, 28, 93, 276, 421
tragi-comedy, 130, 137, 242
Transformations (Susa), 171
traviata, La (Verdi), 22, 31, 330, 353, 354, 359, 362, 363–4, 434
tribalism, 175, 176, 332

trilbies, 31, 98, 133, 145, 152, 154, 157, 158, 160, 175, 249, 385
triple-decker set, 275
Tristan und Isolde (Wagner), 33, 77, 89, 116, 189–94, 321, 326, 327, 361, 434
trittico, Il (Puccini), 75
Triumph of Beauty and Deceit, The (Barry), 423
Trojans, The (Berlioz), 13, 86, 128, 129, 138, 143–6, 158, 163, *292*, 298–300, 302, 303, 362, 434
Trotter, Stewart, 359
trovatore, Il (Verdi), 263, 383, 434
Trowell, Brian, 404
Trussel, Jacque, 308
truth, 3, 6, 12, 15, 25, 28, 60, 61, 82, 94, 97, 102, 174, 182, 200, 203, 210, 242, 254, 333, 398, 407, 421
Tsypin, George, 200, 205, 214, 219, 221
Tucker, Norman, 32, 336
Turn of the Screw, The (Britten), 171, 341, 354, 359, 407
Turnage, Mark-Anthony, 422
2001: A Space Odyssey (film), 313
Tynan, Kenneth, 31

Ubu Roi (Jarry), 89, 102
Umea, Sweden, 286
United States of America, 30, 66, 71, 74, 167, 168, 169, 171, 197, 199, 204–5, 222, 223, 240, 419, 424
Untouchables, The (film), 172
Upshaw, Dawn, 206, 226
Urban, Joseph, 91
Urbancic, Elisabeth, 365
Utzon, Jörn, 74

Valhalla, 51, 113, 114, 149, 151, 247, 254, 396
Vampire, The (Marschner), 423
Van Allan, Richard, 182
Van Dam, José, 207
Vancouver, 74
Vanishing Bridegroom, The (Weir), 424
Vanstone, Hugh, 309
vaudeville, 137, 239, 256
Vaughan Williams, Ralph, 74, 296

Venice, 434
Venice Preserv'd (Otway), 294
Ventris, Christopher, 257
Vequel-Westernach, Max von, 128–9
Vercoe, Rosemary, 330
Verdi, Giuseppe, 8, 11–12, 65, 67, 69,
73, 82, 172, 176, 178–81, 190,
231, 233, 302, 330, 338, 348, 364,
367–70, 374, 379, 384, 389–90,
420, 421, 433
verismo, 25, 66, 69, 255, 265
vernacular, 68, 71, 74, 75, 92, 112, 205,
211, 275, 320, 419
Verona, 421
Vestris, Lucia Elizabeth, 69
Vick, Graham, 13, 161, 421
and Lawless, 13, 285
and Richardson, 13, 286
productions
Ariadne auf Naxos, 265, 340
bohême, La, 96
Carmen, 268–9
Don Giovanni, 265
Dragon of Wantley, The, 276
Eugene Onegin, 269–72,
280–82, 340
Falstaff, 96, 269
Figaro's Wedding, 276–8, 340
Ghanashyam, 267, 272–3
*King Arthur or The British
Worthy*, 269, 283–5
King Priam, 274–5
Lady Macbeth of Mtsensk, 263
Madam Butterfly, 265–8, 340
Magic Flute, The, 96, 269
Midsummer Marriage, The,
283, 297
Oberon, 268
Queen of Spades, The, 262,
278–9, 280
Rape of Lucretia, The, 265, 340
rè in ascolto, Un, 265, 273
Ring Saga, The, 275–6
*Rise and Fall of the City of
Mahagonny, The*, 161, 273–4
Timon of Athens, 340
vie parisienne, La, 276
West Side Story, 263, 273
Wreckers, The, 276
Vickers, Jon, 31, 278, 326, 327, 366,
396, 407, 408, 433, 434
video close-up, 205
video recordings, 59, 85, 96, 110, 113,
147, 212, 213, 214, 242, 390–91,
421, 424
vie parisienne, La (Offenbach), 276
Vienna, 24, 49, 70, 212, 322, 352
Vienna Hofoper, 77, 91
Vienna Opera, 12, 20
Vienna Volksoper, 352
Village Romeo and Juliet, A (Delius),
32, 75
violence, 111, 113, 118, 171, 172–4,
175, 183, 187, 201, 288, 300,
334, 387
Vir, Param, 419, 423
Virgil, 145
Visconti, Luchino, xiii, 32–3, 69, 103,
104, 116, 255, 302, 322
Viva Maria (film), 373
Vogue, 197, 435
voice types, 96
voice-overs, 274
Volpone (Jonson), 324
Voss, Manfred, 110

Wagner, Cosima, 49, 382
Wagner, Ellen, 433
Wagner, Richard, 3, 8, 9, 13, 19, 20, 50,
51, 55, 57, 62, 65, 66, 67, 71, 77,
91, 92, 95, 101–6, 110, 111, 112,
114, 121, 129, 139, 141, 142–3,
148, 149, 153, 155, 160, 163, 172,
187–90, 205, 239–42, 244, 245,
250, 252, 253, 254, 275, 276, 328,
337, 366, 379, 380, 385, 393–7
Wagner, Wieland, 9, 19, 49–50, 57, 62,
102, 107, 138–9, 194, 244–5, 257,
311, 434
Wagner, Winifred, 173
Wagner, Wolfgang, 9, 19, 103, 104,
107, 433
Wagner's Ring and its Symbols
(Donnington), 106
Waiting for Godot (Beckett), 148
Wakhevitch, Georges, xiii, 20, 21, 23
Walküre, Die (Wagner), 107, 113, 114,
115, 128, 149, 151–3, 156, 157,
244–7, 254, 340, 347, 348, 353
Wally, La (Catalani), 301

Walsh, David, 388
Walsh, Sean, 271, 273, 388
War Crimes (Carey), 294
War and Peace (Prokofiev), 339
Warhol, Andy, 73
Warlock, Peter, 407
Warner, Deborah, 44, 309, 404
Warner, Keith, 340
Wars of the Roses cycle, 284, 323
Waste Land, The (Eliot), 297
Watson, Janice, 303
Watt-Smith, Ian, 359
Weber, Carl Maria von, 65, 66, 69, 71,
    75, 76, 379
Webern, Anton von, 71, 158
Webster, Sir David, 19, 21, 22, 27, 323
Wedekind, Frank, 35, 64, 116, 153
Weikl, Bernd, *166*
Weill, Kurt, 66, 73, 127, 160, 162,
    273, 400
Weimar era, 20, 113, 115, 128, 221
Weir, Judith, 73, 255, 256, 419, 423–4
Welitsch, Ljuba, *18*
Welsh National Opera (WNO),
    Cardiff, xiv, 14, 32, 33, 49, 50,
    54, 76, 127, 128, 129, 131, 145,
    169, 172, 183, 184, 189, 200, 231,
    263, 266, 298, 303, 321, 328, 329,
    340, 347, 348, *356*, 357–62, 365,
    366, 367, 371, 375, 380, 389, 435
Wernicke, Herbert, xiv, 14, 76, 92, 96,
    110, 194, 229, 245, 248, 309, *378*,
    382, 390, 391–402
Werther (Massenet), 77, 340
Werz, Wilfried, 358, 360, 361
West, Christopher, 321
West Side Story (Bernstein), 263, 273
Westbrook-Geha, Mary, 211
Wexford Festival, 40, 169, 230,
    255, 346
Where the Wild Things Are
    (Knussen), 91, 313
Whistler, Rex, 85, 324
White, Willard, 219, 220, 348
Whitehouse, Elizabeth, 306
Whitworth-Jones, Anthony, xiv
Widdell, Kristian, 289
Widor, Charles, 433
Wild Duck, The (Ibsen), 34

Wilde, Oscar, 23, 24, 85
Wilhelm Meister (Goethe), 230
William, David, 258
Williams, Daniel Lewis, 162
Willis, Nuala, 313
Wilson, Robert, 168–9, 199, 202
Wilson, Timothy, 404
wings, 28, 122, 144, 230, 242, 243, 277,
    350, 389
Winiewicz, Lida, 138
Winter's Tale, A (Shakespeare), 121
Wittenbrink, Franz, 397
Wlaschiha, Ekkehard, 248
Wonder, Erich, 129, 162, 382, 383
Wopmann, Alfred, 351, 352
World Cup Football, 72
Wozzeck (Berg), 62, 116, 122–4, 171,
    184–5, 350, 402, 404–6, 418, 434
Wray, Margaret Jane, *378*
Wreckers, The (Smyth), 276

Xerxes (Handel), 176, 340, 341,
    343–4, 354

Yan Tan Tethera (Birtwistle),
    335, 419
Yeargan, Michael, 98, 329
Yellow Book, 370
Yevgeny Onyegin see Eugene Onegin

Zagrosek, Lothar, 216
Zambello, Francesca, 169, 170
Zampa (Hérold), 255–6
zarzuela, 71
Zauberflöte, Die (Mozart), 32, 34, 88,
    89, 96, 128, 133, 191, *196*, 199,
    201, 215–18, 269, 296, 305,
    313–14, 323, 339–40, 341, 362–3,
    375, 397, 421–2
Zeffirelli, Franco, xiii, 32, 104, 309, 322
Zehelein, Klaus, 13, 41, 76, 105, 127,
    128, 138, 139, 155, 160, 380–85,
    388, 391
Zender, Hans, 380
Zhu, Ai-Lan, 218
Ziegfeld Follies, 91, 239
Zimmerman, Bernd Alois, 73, 383, 388
Zurich, 332, 415